T0287945

ROBERT MORRIS

INSIDE THE REVOLUTION

Robert M. Morris

Robert Morris: Inside the Revolution

Published by:
Trine Day LLC
PO Box 577
Walterville, OR 97489
1-800-556-2012
www.TrineDay.com
trineday@icloud.com

Library of Congress Control Number: 2022931458

Morris, Robert M.
Robert Morris: Inside the Revolution—1st ed.
p. cm.

Epub (ISBN-13) 978-1-63424-388-9
Print (ISBN-13) 978-1-63424-387-2
1. Morris, Robert, -- 1734-1806 -- Finance, Personal. 2. Morris, Robert, -- 1734-1806 -- Homes and haunts -- Pennsylvania -- Philadelphia. 3. Founding Fathers of the United States -- Finance, Personal. 4. Biography and Autobiography -- Historical. 5. Merchants -- United States -- Eighteenth century. 6. Capitalists and financiers -- United States -- Eighteenth century. 7. Revolutionaries -- United States -- Eighteenth century. I. Morris, Robert M. II. Title

First Edition
10 9 8 7 6 5 4 3 2 1

Distribution to the Trade by:
Independent Publishers Group (IPG)
814 North Franklin Street
Chicago, Illinois 60610
312.337.0747
www.ipgbook.com

Publisher's Foreword

Yankee Doodle went to town
A-riding on a pony,
Stuck a feather in his cap
And called it macaroni.

Yankee Doodle keep it up,
Yankee Doodle dandy,
Mind the music and the step,
And with the girls be handy.

It seems ages ago. I was a young kid visiting Mount Vernon. I had been there many times. My folks were from out West and when family friends came, we took them to see George and Martha Washington's home. On one trip I became acutely aware of the "slave quarters" out back, I truly didn't understand, I was only about six or seven-years old, but something didn't seem right.

There was the big house with columns, an expansive lawn, big porch, huge rooms lavishly decorated, and then behind the house a bunch of small sparse shacks where the slaves lived.

Growing up in northern Virginia in the 1950s was quite the introduction to mid-20th century American life. African-American folk were there, but weren't allowed to participate fully in daily life.

This was all very confusing to a little white boy, who had been steeped in WWII and America's declarations of freedom, liberty and independence. It didn't compute. But then what could I do? I was just a child.

Reading *Robert Morris: Inside the Revolution,* brought back those feelings. Will we ever perfect our Union? I hadn't learned much about Mr. Morris growing up – at least that I remember. Washington, Jefferson, Madison, Adams, Paul Revere, Patrick Henry, Betsy Ross and others were the pantheon of American heroes, but no Morris.

And that is not all that I wasn't taught. I remember the day in the 1980s at a public library when I came across a book about the 1933 "Business

Plot" against Franklin D. Roosevelt. I was absolutely gobsmacked. Why had I never heard of General Smedley Darlington Butler? I knew about Eisenhower, MacArthur, Patton, Pershing, and of course, Robert E. Lee, but not Smedley. I loved history, took every class that was offered, talked my way into upper-level courses in college, but no Smedley. And very little Morris. Why?

Was it because they were uninteresting or unimportant? Not really ... for without General Butler's actions putting the kibosh on the fascist Business Plot we might not be able to read this book today, and without Morris' actions there would *not* have been an United States of America.

Robert Morris was a signer of the Declaration of Independence, the Articles of Confederation and the United States Constitution. He was the first executive of our fledgling republic, because someone had to figure out how to pay for the rebellion and figure out how to become a new nation – something revolutionary: freedom for all, not just the high-born. They were men of their Age, but were striving towards a better future.

Benjamin Franklin and Robert Morris worked well together. General Washington visited often and asked Morris to be the first Treasury Secretary, Robert suggested his friend Alexander Hamilton. Morris established the Bank of North America and was the "U.S. Agent of Marine" overseeing the Continental Navy during most of the Revolutionary War.

Morris, Franklin, Jefferson and others tried to end the "peculiar institution" as slavery later became known as, but were stopped by similar currents that still cycle today, creating divisions and strife. The Slave Trade Act 1807 put an end to the slave trade in the British Empire, and slavery was abolished England in1833, but it took another generation and a "Civil War" to resolve it here. And, sadly, the remnants and dregs of that conflict are still being used by factions – to create divisions and strife

I commend, Robert M. Morris for this fine history book. TrineDay is honored to publish *Robert Morris: Inside the Revolution*, a deep-dive into how "We the People" became the United States of America. Long may our republic live. Onward to a more perfect Union!

Onward to the Utmost of Futures!
Peace,
RA "Kris" Millegan
Publisher
TrineDay
March 7, 2022

This book is dedicated to Julianne, the buddies, and freedom loving people everywhere who can't help but think for themselves, particularly those rare individuals who seek new insights even when the process is uncomfortable.

Robert Morris

Engraving after a painting by Alonzo Chappel

"Americans owe, and still owe, as much acknowledgement to the financial operations of Robert Morris, as to the negotiations of Benjamin Franklin, or even to the arms of Washington."

Table Of Contents

PREFACE

When Americans think about the American War for Independence their minds fill with episodes of bravery, hardship, and valor that won the freedom of a nation. The names Lexington Common, Bunker Hill, Ticonderoga, Trenton, Valley Forge, Kings Mountain, the Cow Pens, and Yorktown sound like the muster role of victory. Surprisingly however, besides guerrilla style sniping, there were only about thirty days of major land combat during the seven years of Revolutionary War. That is an average of four and a quarter days per year. It is also a revelation to learn Washington did not win many of these fights, and in the south, General Nathanael Greene lost almost all of them. Considering, fewer American foot soldiers died fighting during the whole Revolutionary War than died during the three-day Battle of Gettysburg, one starts to wonder how a group of loosely joined colonies won their independence from the world's greatest superpower.

More than anything, the American Revolutionary War was a political act, and it started in the colonies with a disagreement over taxes. For the British government, the tax question escalated into a question over their authority, and the king's pride was at stake. The Americans saw unchecked and unjustly used power as a threat to their freedom, which, they feared, would ultimately lead to their enslavement. The mandated influx of enslaved Africans only served to reinforce that idea. For one side to win, the other had to undergo a change of will. Ultimately, there was a shift in political leadership within the British Parliament and the war ended in favor of the Americans. The pressure to bring that change about came on land, at sea, and in the council houses of both sides.

With this in mind, I left the visions of battlefield combat to others and looked behind the scenes to discover the ways and means of victory. I focused on Robert Morris, who during his lifetime was seen as the equal to Washington and Franklin; but now he is barely remembered, if at all. Morris' political struggle during the Revolutionary Period extended from 1764, well before the first box of tea was dumped in Boston Harbor, and continued to 1795, the end of his term as the senior senator from Pennsylvania. Morris' weapon of choice was his pen. It was the practical and familiar instrument of a businessman, a correspondent, an investor, an administrator, and a visionary. He used his quill to sign the Declaration of Independence, the Articles of Confederation, and the U.S. Constitution. With each successive document, his shared dream of creating a new nation came closer to reality.

An examination of Morris' career helps to explain many aspects of this period that would otherwise remain a mystery. When Morris is omitted from history, as he is so often today, the account necessarily becomes clouded within a myth of inevitability. This myth creates a mist from which a new nation, powered by the engines of free enterprise, emerges almost magically from the farms and fields of colonial America. This foggy fairy tale is used to describe the coordination of French and American forces at Yorktown as some kind of "miracle." It is used to gloss over the effort to maintain the Continental Army between the battle of Yorktown, in 1781, and the establishment of peace in 1783, two years later. The myth of inevitability covers the omission of the facts that explain the actual driving forces behind the forging of a nation from thirteen cantankerous mini countries. When considering this popular myth, it is useful to remember that these events did not just happen, people made them happen.

As I worked to uncover the record of Robert Morris, I engaged in a process of discovery that was akin to putting together a piece of pottery that had been shattered and scattered in a twenty-acre field. That diffusion was due to an unfortunate series of events; first of which was the 1789 work *History of the American Revolution* by Dr. David Ramsey. It mentions Morris just once, as a member of the Pennsylvania delegation. Unfortunately, this set the tone for future historians. This is interesting because Dr. Ramsey was a contemporary of Morris, and the Doctor was in the Congress while Morris was there. So, why the obvious omission? It is possibly because two years before he published this work, he married the daughter of one of Morris' most inveterate political opposites, Henry Laurens. Additionally, Ramsey's brother married the sister of the artist Charles Wilson Peale, who was also politically opposite Morris. While a reader may think it would be too much to believe that omitting Morris from such a seminal work of American history was an act of partisanship, I'll point out that as I'm writing this book the US Congress is mulling a bill that would forbid the federal government from acting to commemorate the presidency of Donald Trump in any way, reminding us that nothing is impossible in politics.

Many later authors followed the same pattern; even as recently as a popular book on John Adams, one finds fewer than five references to Morris, even though Morris and Adams worked together for years. Why would this continue? Because after years of bold successes, the very end of Morris' career was disastrous, thanks largely to the Financial Panic of 1797. That economic calamity became grist for the partisan mills of his rivals. Next, in 1800, his political party suffered a major defeat, and for decades thereafter, his political adversaries were able to control the official interpretation and popular view of Morris' story. To make matters even more difficult, around the time of the Civil War, many of Morris' papers were dispersed, destroyed, or lost, so the documentary record was fragmentary, at best. Finally, during the post-civil war era, some politicians sought to redeem the faction that lost the war by rebranding their Party of Slavery as the Party of Jefferson, that is to say the party of "all men are created equal." To that end some historians set about reinterpreting Jefferson, to whom the party's roots were traced. Over 80% of the professors in large universities in the United States are members of the modern Party of Jefferson, so it should come as no surprise that the history taught in many universities today is descended from the aforementioned period, when so much effort went into the reconstruction of Thomas Jefferson's legacy. As can be expected with such historiography, much has been overlooked. However, this predisposition has resulted in the publication of over 400 books featuring Thomas Jefferson in the ten years between 2000 and 2010.

In the early 20th century, the intellectual movement known as Progressivism supplied an additional force that worked against the full understanding of Morris' career. As it gained favor in the salons of academia, and in the halls of government, the idea of individual progress became secondary to the ideal of social progress. Dismissal of the so-called "Great Man Theory" was used to reinforce this. The Progressive transformation was followed by the growing influences of Socialist philosophers, and the resulting new thought stream further joined with post-modernist ideas. Even though it is obvious that groups consist of individuals, the leaders of the Progressive movement favored the idea of community, generally one they wish to manage, over the rights and prerogatives of individuals with different ideas.

Robert Morris did not have to contend with these exact "isms," but he had to contend with organized groups whose economic understanding was similar, and in many ways prototypical, of the later movements.

His cure for the economic ills of his day was the establishment of free markets, and opening economic opportunity to everyone, not just a select few. Morris' demonstrated ability to overcome the fanciful economic theories of his time, with successful results has, until now, been largely ignored. The result is a growing approval of socialism, and the shrinking appreciation for the free enterprise system that Morris embodied. There have been fewer than ten books on Morris published in the last 100 years.

In developing this book, I encountered a wide variety of historians, few of whom were either helpful or encouraging. As a result, the book does not necessarily conform to some consensus formed from the layers of interpretation that have been put down for over 200 years. It is truly a new look at an old subject. Consensus historians may object to such an effort, but I hope they consider the work as one that provides insights they overlooked.

In keeping with my decision to open this new inquiry, I have chosen to include quotes from original documents. I have done this for a number of reasons. Primarily, I think the best way to learn about the events, and the people involved, is to read about them in the words of the participants. Finally, I have used these quotes because I think they are interesting as language. Modern English has been badly treated in recent years, to the impoverishment of all. English is an exact and subtle language, and its use can be seen in these old letters and documents. Reading these quotes puts us into the minds of the writers, and if we forget how to read what the Founders wrote, we may soon forget the meaning of their words as well.

Introduction

In 1781, the American Revolution was teetering on the cliff of failure. The Continental currency was worthless. America was surrounded by enemies, and suffering from internal political divisions. Washington's army was stalled in rural New York, where it was confronted with poverty and mutiny. America's southern army was in rags, and on the verge of starvation. Partisan insurgents on both sides waged ruthless campaigns in the back country. There were just two useful ships left in the Continental Navy and not enough sailors to get them to sea. At the same time, the British held two of the largest American cities. Their armies roamed the countryside at will. They held military outposts in the western territories, and they blockaded seaports from the Gulf of Maine to South Carolina. To complicate matters, America's allies expected the revolution to fail. They worked in the background to carve up the continent for themselves as Spain blockaded the Mississippi and France sought a separate peace with England.

The condition of weakness was largely the result of the idealistic philosophical and rhetorical underpinnings of the revolution itself. The revolution was personified as a revolt of the virtuous citizen patriot against wicked greedy King George III, so it was anti-monarchical in nature. The American leaders designed their system as a republic, similar to the structure of ancient Rome in the days before it became an empire. At the start, this worked to America's advantage. For example, ambassador Franklin, with his plain Quaker garb and habits, was admired in France for his republican simplicity, particularly when compared to the luxury of the court of Louis XVI. (The term, republican, as it is used here, does not refer to the name of a modern political party.)

While monarchies are ordered in a top down hierarchy, republics are distinguished by citizens electing volunteers to take on the role of representative. However without the heavy hand of a king to enforce order, a republic relies on these public servants to be virtuous and informed when they gather to make decisions for the good of all. The ideal of Republican Virtue relies on fearlessness, education, modesty, and self sacrifice.

In practice, these civic virtues can run thin, resulting in less success than initially anticipated.

In the face of these external and internal difficulties, Congress set aside its long-held ideas about "Republican Virtue" and governing by consensus, and unanimously selected Robert Morris to be the Superintendent of Finance. He became the first civilian executive with continental responsibilities. This unique office has been described as being similar to the office of Prime Minister, but Prime Ministers are first members of Parliament. Morris was brought into government from the outside. From this new position, he ran the finances. This connected him with much of the war effort, because nearly everything government does requires money. Additionally, as head of the "Marine" he commanded the Navy. He had business partnerships with foreign representatives, and discussions with diplomats residing in Philadelphia, many of whom viewed his appointment as a critical step toward victory. After the war, Morris was a delegate to the Constitutional Convention. Washington was Morris' house-guest while he marked up the draft of Article Two. There is no transcript of those private chats, but Morris' experience as Superintendent is reflected in those edits made in the design of the Executive Branch. As the national executive in charge of treasury, the navy, and with a role in diplomacy, Morris blazed the administrative path that ended with the formation of the American Presidency.

Before Morris was appointed, he smuggled guns and powder for the war, his ships became Naval warships, he supplied Washington's troops using his own materials and credit, he was attacked in the press by people who encouraged justice to be served up by street mobs, and he had been investigated by proslavery forces in Congress. He explained his commitment to the American cause in a letter to Joseph Reed, "…it is the duty of every individual to act his part in whatever station his country may call him to in hours of difficulty, danger, and distress.." His political adversaries maintained that he had darker motives.

How had the "Spirit of '76" devolved into this condition in just five short years? The former colonies chafed against one another because they were as culturally different as separate nations were in Europe. In effect, the localists worked against the nationalists instead of working solely towards victory. To protect their power as state leaders, the localists from various states made common cause under the banner of protecting their Republican Virtue, as they defunded the army, the navy, and refused to allow a tariff to repay the loans used to fund the war. The way out of this situation is the story of how America managed to overcome the odds and succeed, in spite of the best efforts of many of its leading citizens. The situation in which America found itself during 1781 developed along lines that stretched eastward across the Atlantic, and back hundreds of years.

-|-

During medieval times the Britons and Anglo Saxons had, with varying degrees of success, fended off invaders of their island. That is, until 1066, when the Norman descendants of the Vikings arrived, brutally subdued them, and forced them into virtual slavery for over a hundred years. Tens of thousands died fighting Norman control, and the survivors never really gave up their traditional ways. As part of the conquest, the Norman barons took control of the existing feudal structure in England and began operating the properties as their own independent fiefdoms. Unlike the rulers they replaced, they did this without any sympathy a common heritage might engender. Their Baronies and Dukedoms were like small states within the kingdom, in a way that was somewhat analogous to the political autonomy the early American states had before the Constitution was ratified. As the generations passed, the wealth of the aristocracy increased, and they finally rebelled against the king. The conflict was resolved at Runnymede when, in 1215, a workable arrangement was made. After a rocky start, Norman England operated under the Magna Carta, which codified the relationship between the people and the King. It required the King to respect the rule of law, which meant he had to work with the large landholders, i.e., Lords and Barons, who were dealing with locals, most of whom were not Norman. The locals were considered to be like property of the nearby potentate, and as such were generally forbidden from traveling outside the realm, or from choosing their own path in life. A butcher's son became a butcher, a farmer's son became a farmer, and going out to seek one's fortune was the stuff of fairy tales.

As the medieval period went on in England, the King had increasing difficulty counterbalancing the power of the Lords, and so he encouraged the incorporation of towns. The towns gave rise to markets and civil governments that were not based on land and inherited titles. Those governments acted as a check on the power of the Lords and Barons. This autonomy annoyed the Lords and Barons who expressed the feeling that towns and cities were sores on the body politic. It was during this time that, as Adam Smith observed, "merchants, like all the inhabitants of the burghs, were considered as little better than emancipated bondsmen, whose persons were despised, and whose gains were envied." Over time, towns in medieval England grew into cities, and the civil administration counted on merchants to sustain the towns with trade.

The wealth of the English towns increased, and control of finances moved from the Lord's counting house, to the merchants, and then to financial markets. The development of banking, credit lines, and private financial networks eventually made the king just another supplicant at the teller's window as monarchs ran up larger and larger bills in their endless wars of conquest and geographic expansion. The expression, "Money is the root of all evil," was revived during this period when fealty to the king and allegiance to country was no longer the motivation for armies. Instead of being able to rely on the ancient bonds (which really amounted to forced labor), a monarch had to pay his army with money. The resulting need for funds served to increase the value of trade, and the importance of the merchant class. This did not please the Lords and Barons, who were more interested in controlling their land holdings than in learning new skills.

Christian European monarchs sought to maximize the return on their kingdom's trade, and they had long since tired of paying tribute to the Muslims in the Middle East for the right to send goods along the Silk Road to Asia. In the 15th century, Spain and Portugal broke free of the Caliphate and took to the seas in pursuit of riches. Safety was not found in the Mediterranean, as Moorish pirates, based in North Africa, were a constant threat. To avoid them, the Catholic Iberians sailed south around Africa to Asian markets in the east, and later they sailed west and stumbled upon America. Spain, and Portugal dominated these roads to wealth for a while, but with the help of superior naval technology, a few fire ships and fortuitous storms, Anglican England won her place on the ocean by defeating the Catholic Spanish Armada in 1588. This opened up the world of sea-borne commerce to them.

The growth of merchant fleets and the importance of seagoing trade quickly became central to the success of the British Isles. However, unlike their continental counterparts, the British Constitution ruled, and commerce was not the possession of the king. One observer noted that in France the king could crush commerce, but in England the opposite was true. Ironically, that condition existed because an earlier king wanted to increase his power in relation to the power and autonomy of the Lords and Barons.

By the 17th century, European ocean-going vessels connected the world through trade. These networks gave rise to the development of colonial empires. These colonial empires gave growth to mercantile fortunes, as traders moved goods between the colonies and the homeland. Merchants operated under royal charters, or parliamentary ones, all with military protection. Monarchs tried to manage this new power. However, as the wealth of merchants increased, so did their influence. In England, that resulted in the legislature passing laws to control the markets in ways that favored certain merchants and businesses, in a system that became known as mercantilism. These laws deranged the economies, in a way, and made some well-placed individuals rich at the expense of many citizens. The citizens noticed, but they were unable to coordinate any way to stop the trend. Even the large landholders were unable to rein this in, because only the merchants had the knowledge and experience to operate the indispensable system. This added to the distrust felt by the citizens and landlords, who suspected that merchants were looking out more for themselves than society. Naturally, landlords were also looking after their own interests, but since they controlled vast tracts of land, which held sizable portions of the population, they saw themselves as parts of the kingdom. Merchants just had less real estate, and a smaller constituency, even as they wielded financial might.

-|-

Unfortunately, during the first half of the 18th century, European colonial trade practices did not engender peace, and the state of human affairs was trending towards despotism, militarism, and slavery. The European monarchs, whose kingdoms operated somewhat like vertically integrated monopolies, wanted to expand their geographic holdings, because the economic basis for their nations was the control of productive lands, and the trading rights that went along with them. As a result, the Western European states were often at war with each other over that limited commodity, land.

The century started off with a conflict over the control of Northern Europe that brought fighting to Sweden, Denmark, Norway, Germany and Poland. The remnant that was the Holy Roman Empire was aligned with the Hapsburgs. They worked to maintain their dominance over Christendom as they fought the Muslim Turks in the East and disavowed the Protestants in the West. Then there was the war over the succession of the Spanish Throne, which caused the mobilization of armies across Western and Southern Europe. This was followed by the War of Austrian Succession in central Europe, the War of Jenkins' Ear between Spain and

England, and finally the Seven Years' War between France and England which spread to the New World. There, England contested with Spain for Florida, and with France for parts of Canada and various West Indian islands. For their part, Catholic Spain and France were not about to let the Protestant English control the West Indies or the vast expanse of North America without a fight. Spain and France were proud European states with Catholic rulers connected through the Bourbon family to the Ancient Regime, which traced its roots through sixteen generations of kings back to the 700's and the family of Charlemagne.

Behind all of this activity, the political and military power rested in the hands of a few interlocking families. Prominent among these families were the Bourbons of France and Spain, the Hapsburgs of Austria, the Stuarts of England, the Hanovers of Germany (of which King George III was one), the Wittelsbachs of Bavaria, and the Romanoffs of Russia. These kings and their courts operated standing armies and paid them with the tax money the army collected. The army, in turn, maintained the borders and stood ready to increase the holdings of the king. Monarchs went into debt when taxes alone were not sufficient to fund new wars. As war debts increased, so did the taxes that were collected to pay those debts. Amidst all this, the commoners' rights diminished to a degree unimaginable a hundred years earlier.

The trend to build empires extended well beyond Europe. In Asia, the Manchu dynasty expanded its control of China to encompass modern day Manchuria, Mongolia, and Tibet. In India, the British fought the French and Marathas kingdoms for control over the subcontinent. The Russian Empire was expanding south to the Black Sea and into Eurasia, where they fought with the Ottoman Turks. The Ottoman Empire stretched from southeastern Europe, near Vienna, through the Middle East. It also encompassed North Africa from the Suez west to Morocco, south from Egypt to the Sudan. The Ottomans connected with existing Muslim trading networks that reached south to the horn of Africa and west across the sub-Saharan Sahel region through Timbuktu to the Atlantic.

The world's empires required manpower, and as might be expected, many of the monarchs had little concern for the powerless. Throughout history, victors enslaved the conquered, but these arrangements were somewhat ad hoc, varied, often short lived, and usually not inherited. It was a known economic system of neighbor exploiting neighbor as the price of warfare. By the 18th century the Ottoman had been working with local sub-Saharan African kings who, for over 700 years, had developed and operated the African slave trade along established routes. Arab traders used these routes to encourage the spread of Islam, converting Mali in the 8th century and Nigeria in the 9th century BCE, for example. Millions of enslaved Africans went through Zanzibar, and across desert trails to the Sudan before being shipped further north and east into captivity. Unfortunately for the boys, many of them suffered castration because that increased their price on the market. The Ottoman in Northern Africa were not content with enslaving animist Africans, and they made a concerted effort to enslave Christian Europeans as well. For example, women held in those harems pictured in the modern mind as gauzy sensual pleasure zones, were, in actuality, Christian women who spent their stolen lives as sex slaves for the enjoyment of some Muslim potentate. According to Professor Robert Davis, the practitioners of Islam captured between one and one and a half million Europeans, both men and women, between 1530 and 1780.[1] Among this hoard was one John Smith, who freed himself, through trickery, and went as far west as he could. There, in Virginia, he met Pocahontas, the Powhatan Princess; and the rest, as they say, is history.

During the 17th and 18th centuries, the Catholic Iberian kingdoms sent ships to the existing slave markets in coastal western Africa. Their ships stopped at special ports called castles or forts, where the trade was conducted with the local Muslim authorities. This system was somewhat similar to the one used by China, later, when they operated special trading ports called "hongs." Catholic Iberian princes and kings encouraged traders to carry animist black Africans to the New World to work the extensive slave powered colonial empires. The use of slavery to clear land and work plantations devastated the local indigenous populations and moved almost nine million unwilling Africans to South America and West Indian island plantations.

None of this would have been possible without the eager cooperation of local sub-Saharan kings and princes who sold millions of their neighbors into slavery. In the year 2000 Senegal's president Abdoulaye Wade said his family had been involved. Benin's ambassador Cyrille Oguin agreed, he shared in the responsibility for this terrible human tragedy.[2,3] In the distant past, West African royal converts to Islam told themselves that their animist neighbors, from other tribes, were unworthy of respect as people. Consequently, these slave-mongers not only justified their actions this way for the local market, they made this point to foreigners who came to buy slaves, leading Christian colonists in the Americas to adopt this convenient lie as an excuse for their own behavior. This position was later taken up by Richard Colefax in the run-up to the Civil War.[4]

One report from the 18th century reveals that the vast majority of "slaves are bred in the inland parts of Africa, and sent for sale, according to the want those people are in for European manufactures; the same as an ox or horse is taken to market when a farmer in England wants money to pay his rent or for other purposes."[5] This is one explanation of how it came to pass that about ten million people could have been removed from the continent of Africa by a few Europeans. It's a matter of perspective to decide if slaves were bred in villages for export, or captured in battle, because raiding a village and taking the inhabitants into slavery would seem like an act of war to the victims. The perpetrators may just tell their customers otherwise. To see similar behavior in the modern world, look to Sudan, Nigeria, Mauritania, Algeria and Libya where lively slave markets thrive into the 21st century, and at least one half of a million black Africans are enslaved by Muslim traders. Similarly, the 18th century trans-Atlantic slave trade would not have existed without willing buyers and sellers. Without a supply, however, the would-be buyers would have done something else to meet their needs. One of the solutions was the free market for labor, as it developed in the western world.

-|-

The loss of civil rights in Europe, and all of this killing, selling, and stealing of people around the world made the 18th century a time during which there was widespread reexamination of the intellectual, spiritual and social structures that held societies together. Such re-evaluations had occurred at other times of great change as well with the adoption of Christianity by the Roman Empire, with the spread of Buddhism in central Asia, with the growth of Taoism in China, the acceptance of Hinduism in India, and later the spread of Marxism in Europe. The intellectual movement known as the Enlightenment emerged in the eighteenth century. It can also be seen as an effort to create order from the endless chaos brought on by the conflicts that had washed over the European continent for generations. Great thinkers tried mightily to define the relationship between the ruler and the ruled, between God and man, and between reason and emotion.

Men turned their thoughts to finding natural laws that would reveal universal truths. The idea of objective fact was given a boost with the development of the scientific method. The pursuit of order and harmony was extended to music and architecture. This was no underground movement, but rather leading universities sponsored it, as did the ruling houses of Europe and England. It seemed the whole Western World sought greater understanding of the universe around them. They attempted to rationalize everything. They categorized living things into groups. They took measurements of the earth and sky. They devised methods of economic efficiencies. They undertook to create machines to do useful work. They parsed political systems. They attempted to understand human nature.

Key among the considerations was an exploration into the role of luxury in the creation of the turmoil in Europe. By the 17th and 18th centuries, it had been forgotten that during the Middle Ages the pursuit of luxury by the clergy was the real corrosive social force. As it happened, during that long ago time, the congregants began to distrust the Church, and to think of it as being corrupt, because the clergy used the tithes they received to please themselves; instead of helping the poor, as intended. The idea of luxury as a corrupting influence can be traced to this trend, because everyone expected the Church to be charitable and the churchmen to be virtuous, while few expected the same from a monarch. Nevertheless, over time the original idea was popularized and enlarged to include others.[6]

This broader interpretation evolved to the point that some considered luxury itself to be a corrupting influence, and the source of conflict. They thought living closer to nature would purge the soul of vices. Tales of the noble savages filtered in from America and seemed to confirm this notion. However, these tales were edited to hide the reality of conditions in which these "noble savages" lived. There was little mention of living in smoky windowless huts with dirt floors, or sleeping on grass mats in winter, or of drudgery due to lack of wheels or horses, or their practice of slavery, or of the plagues of insects in their homes, or of their polygamy and its role in their wars. These things were conveniently omitted, and the "noble savage" became a romantic ideal in the mind of many intellectuals and the supposed solution to the corruption of man. Most European Americans were not about to sleep on dirt floors or otherwise live like the Native Americans, so they offered the idea of "Republican Simplicity" as the cure for the corrupting influences of luxury. The southern planters often extolled the virtues of such simplicity as they walked the wide porches of their graceful mansions and superintended their slave-powered properties.

However, blaming a single human foible for all the ills of mankind required one to ignore the cultural and economic realities of the time. They can be forgiven; just as a fish cannot imagine life outside the water, most men cannot imagine a world outside their own experience. In 18th century Europe, the prevailing economic system had descended, organically, from medieval times. As such, it was tightly managed by an elite, which, in turn was protected by its military. In that scheme, real estate was held by monarchs, lords and barons in huge land monopolies, and business enterprise was limited to government sanctioned mercantilism, which consisted of a set of interlocking monopolies that controlled the markets and products of those domains. This meant growth by one country would require a loss by another country, because growth was synonymous with geographic expansion, and land was a limited commodity. Often such modifications in ownership were accompanied by warfare. Some may say the desire for growth is caused by the lust for luxuries, but this thinking overlooks such things as increases in population, changes in weather, and disagreements among the rulers of the day over power, religion, and the division of spoils.

Nevertheless, this "zero-sum" condition was the basis for most of the economic thinking that prevailed before Adam Smith and like-minded men had their say. It was easier for many intellectuals to tinker mentally around the edges and hope that by fine-tuning a human trait all will be well, than it was to overhaul an entire culture or preach revolution. Such a revolution was only possible in America, where the history was shorter, the opportunities were greater, and the control was weaker.

When most Europeans arrived in North America, the majority of North American coastal Natives had already died from epidemics. The diseases were brought by the small number of early explorers who whose personal microbiomes brought devastation to a continent full of a wide variety of people who already lived there. As a result of these plagues, the scarce and precious resource, land, was available to new settlers who arrived in droves. The distribution of it was uneven according to the practices found in the various colonies, but people could get it. Individual ownership of property, individual rights under the law, and a Protestant belief in an individual responsibility based on a personal connection with God, all combined in the American psyche. However, this new way of being did not necessarily lead to a revolution against the king, and many colonists were against the very idea of it. After all, there had not been a successful republic on Earth since Rome became an empire in 44 BCE; and supporting such an idea seemed ill-advised to many. Nevertheless, the Revolution did occur, and a central element to the American Revolution was the shifting of the prevailing old-world economic model based on centralized control of property and trade, into a system based on widespread individual property ownership, individual responsibility, minimal taxation, the rule of law, and after a good deal of struggle, opening the economic system to everyone.

-|-

From the time of their arrival in North America, the colonists operated under elected assemblies, which were populated by prosperous land holders who were not interested in taxing themselves. Some might call them plutocrats. When the King's representative arrived in each colony, as the appointed governor, he was supposed to be supported by that colony. This is similar to the idea that the head of a company should be supported by revenue from that company. However, in the case of the colonies, it was up to the assembly to decide how much money the governor would get, and mostly they decided he should get very little. This put the governor in the disadvantaged position of being an executive without means and beholden to the locals for his sustenance. It was usual for an assemblyman to get elected by appearing to be for the people, and against the governor. By the time of the Revolution, the Assemblies in the various states were well rehearsed in the art of making the executive beg for his supper.

Back in England, the leadership secretly worried they would lose control when the Americans got too numerous and wealthy. It was commonly understood that population was power, so while the home country could not stop the birth rate, they did their best to keep their colonies poor. They devised an economic system, operated by their merchants, that took almost all of the money back to England. Consequently, the colonials were not immune to feelings of distrust towards merchants, and the landed elites in America felt themselves to be at the mercy of these far away people upon whom they depended to sell their farm products in a controlled market. This was particularly true among the Virginians, known as the Tidewater elite, whose tastes and pretensions outstripped their income.

In addition, duties were put on various items shipped to the colonies. These duties were easily evaded because the colonial merchants were able to convince the powers-that-be in England that the Americans would spend more on British goods with the profits from smuggling than their government would gather in tax. The duties remained on the books, but they were not collected, practically speaking, because the colonists controlled the courts where the trials were held. The thinking of Sir Robert Walpole won the day and was exemplified by the saying "leave well enough alone."[7] This typified the period of benign neglect which allowed self-government in the colonies to develop. Walpole's economic lesson would later give weight to the idea of free trade. Merchants in America, who did not pay the tax, amassed fortunes, and when the tax collectors eventually came, these merchants were willing to risk those fortunes in the name of even greater economic and political freedom.

-|-

Regardless of the overarching similarities in the way the colonies related to their mother country, Britain's North American colonies were populated by settlers who came in groups from separate parts of England at different times for identifiable reasons. Each group brought a distinct cultural identity along, which acted as the center of their new lives in America. The timing for these waves of colonists, and most of the differences between the colonies, can be traced to the period shortly after the reign of Queen Elizabeth I. She left no heir and successor, and after her death, the Scottish Stuart kings were installed on the throne.

In a bold move, suitable to a recently installed monarch, the new Stuart king, James I, granted a charter to a group of businessmen calling themselves The Virginia Company. This group created the first American colony, Jamestown. It was 1607, just four years into the new king's reign. The founders of Jamestown were conservative Englishmen, whose loyalty was to the king, but whose Anglican traditions were formed during the Elizabethan era. They operated under a royal board of trade. England had no other practical way to have colonies. There was no administrative system in place, and no money to develop one. After all, at the start, there was little to administer other than a few adventurers in the woods on a remote and unexplored landmass.

The Puritans were the next set of adventurers to colonize America. They thought the Anglican Church in England was corrupt and too worldly, and they were not happy about being forced by the state to pay for its support. Originally, King James I collaborated with the Puritans who wanted him to make the Anglican Church into a Puritan church. After failing to convince James to change the Church of England, a zealous few left the country and moved to Holland. They stayed there for a while, but when their children started to lose their English ways and become Dutch in habit, the parents decided to set off for the New World. They ended up in Massachusetts. The Puritans were not royalist in nature, but they were not poor; instead, they were more of a middle-class group. Though they failed to get the king to change the Church of England, they were not suffering from religious persecution. Perhaps disappointment is a better word. Some who remained even held seats in Parliament.

Over the course of the next twenty years, many of the English, who favored rule by an elected Parliament, became more and more annoyed with the monarchy. One can understand that the royal style of the Scottish Stuarts, which was based on the divine rights of kings, would be unpopular among people who held their individual rights to be dear. This dissatisfaction resulted in The English Civil Wars, and the Parliamentarians defeated the monarchy in 1649. Shortly thereafter, Oliver Cromwell rose to power as their leader. He distinguished himself by selling the King's art collection, which was the best in the world at the time. The ensuing puritanical period was marked by laws of restriction that banned dancing, theatre, hats with feathers, clothes with bright colors, and other frivolities considered luxuries by the Roundheads. Oh, those wicked luxuries.

The conservative Anglican Virginians were in favor of King Charles I, the son of their royal sponsor, James I. When Charles I lost the throne, and his head, in 1649, some of his supporters, known as the distressed cavaliers, left England. They went to Virginia and the south to join their like-minded ex-patriots and brought their aristocratic perspective with them. Later in England however, in a reversal, Cromwell and his Parliamentarians lost power, and this led to the Restoration of King Charles II in 1660. Many of the English, including Samuel Pepys, were pleased to see a King return to put the "Jolly" back in "Jolly old England." After that, many Puritans, who favored the disgraced Cromwell, went to Massachusetts and New England. By 1700, there were over 100,000 in that region. They brought their puritanical ways, so there was no card playing, theatre, dancing, or bright colors in the colony. While the modern idea of puritan mores centers on sexual behavior, the larger view shows that Puritans believed in regulating the kinds of luxurious activities they thought were antisocial. In today's society they would be perfectly comfortable banning trans fats, SUV's, candy bars, and tanning beds, in other words, doing other things viewed by more free-wheeling individuals as nanny state intrusions. The Puritans also instituted theirs as the state religion of Massachusetts, and that remained in effect well into the 19th century. Some of their dark homes still stand in the early 21st century, reminding us of how they lived, and the unsmiling portraits of these men and women dressed in black look down from the walls in the Museum of Fine Arts in Boston, reminding us who they were.

The Quakers in England originally supported Cromwell. Over time, they grew disenchanted with his excesses, and they finally helped a new king, Charles II, to gain the crown. They were rewarded with a central colony, Pennsylvania. This colony was not a joint stock company, but a proprietorship, and as such was owned by William Penn, personally. Penn sold large parcels of land in his colony to other Quakers who operated farms and mills and grew wealthy with land rents and fees. Penn initially made money, but the administration of the colony got the best of him. He went bankrupt and spent time in debtor's prison. However, Penn's Quaker idealism put an imprint on the state that lasted for centuries.

A fourth group, largely Presbyterian, generally supported Cromwellian anti-royalist thinking and was encouraged to go to the back country of the colonies. This group, referred to as the Scots-Irish, came from areas in the British Isles that bordered larger conflicting monarchical states. As such, they adopted a disdain for authority, and a penchant for living simple lives. Their descendants provided America with pioneers, and cowboys, as well as several Presidents, war heroes, and a large percentage of the population in rural America. Nevertheless, during the 18th century many of them stayed in the populated areas and added much-needed talent and manpower to the early colonial economy. They were tradesmen, sailors, and were known at the time as "the meaner sort" because many had not acquired wealth.

This rambling collection of pioneers and tradesmen shows another unique element of the American experience: The freedom to travel. In Europe and England at that time, individuals were not free to migrate from town to town. The rulers saw populations as part of the countryside, and the guilds were not generous in providing openings to strangers. In England, documents similar to visas were required for relocation from one Barony to another. Mostly people stayed where they were born, unless uprooted by war or famine. This was not true in the North American colonies. While many stayed within their colony and thought of themselves as citizens of Virginia, for example, others did not, and they moved in search of opportunities. One such person was Ben Franklin who moved from Boston to the larger city of Philadelphia to ply his trade as a printer.

The challenge for revolutionaries, like George Washington, Alexander Hamilton, and Robert Morris, who wished to build a unified nation in America, was to overcome the cultural differences that had developed over the generations. It turned out that the first place the various groups were forced to work together directly was the Continental Army. That institution's power as a unifying force was one of the reasons its continued existence became such a bone of contention in the Continental Congress. In any case, before the 1760's the English thought it would be impossible for the American colonies to cooperate with one another. If it had not been for a series of English policies that played into the hands of America's radicals, the colonies would not have been pushed together and the story of North America would have been very different.

Endnotes

1. Robert C. Davis, *Christian Slaves, Muslim Masters*, pg. 8
2. Benin Apologizes for Role in Slave Trade, *Boston Globe*, 19 April 2000
3. *Richmond Times-Dispatch*, 29 June 2003
4. https://lccn.loc.gov/11006103
5. *Documents Illustrative of the Slave Trade to America*, 2:518-519
6. Adam Smith, *Wealth of Nations*, pg.918-919
7. *Struggle for Power*, pg 91

I

Last Days Of Colonial Life

Enter Robert, actually Bobby

Robert Morris was born in Liverpool on January 31st, 1734. He was soon baptized in the first Anglican church built after the Restoration. The cold gray stones must have echoed with his cries as his young mother and twenty-seven-year old father looked on. So it was that winter, a baby boy arrived in Britain's second largest city and joined its population of about 20,000. In a few years Robert, Jr. became a toddler, and his family called him Bobby. No one could have imagined he would later risk everything to cleave the colonies from England.

The city's seagoing tradition set Bobby's hometown apart from the inland agrarian parts of the country. It was more open to the world, and so had a greater diversity among its citizens. For example, there was a growing Jewish presence, and also a small community of free Blacks. That openness came at a price, however. Liverpool started to see the growth of smuggling, and the beginnings of the British slave trade at about fifteen ships a year. By the end of the 1700's Liverpool became England's major slave trading port.

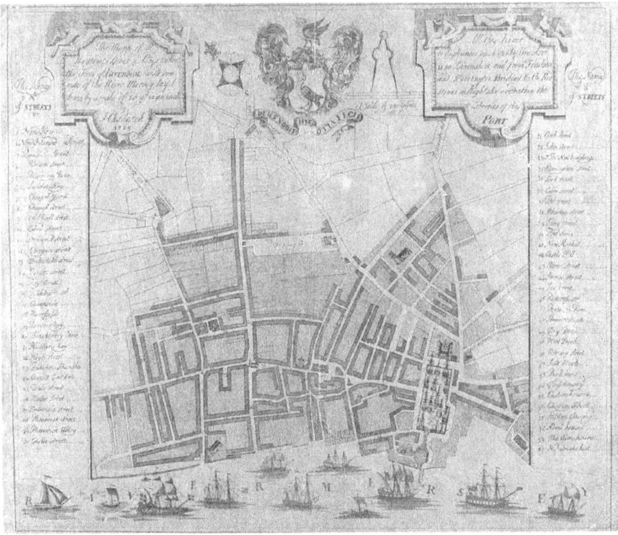

Liverpool 1725, Muir's Bygone Liverpool.

The Morrises had lived for generations in this seafaring city. Robert's grandfather, Andrew, was a mariner of modest means when local ships were going to Hamburg, Norway, Holland, Flanders and the Baltic. Robert's father, also named Robert, was on his own early in life because both of his parents had died by the time he was nineteen. As a youth, he was employed as a nail maker and iron monger, a trade open to people without an extensive education.

As time went on, Liverpudlian ships went to Virginia, Maryland, and Africa. Growing trade meant greater opportunities. Bobby's father was offered a position by a local politician and merchant, who was also a prominent member of the church the family attended. Bobby's father accepted and left his loved ones behind, to build a new life for them in the colony of Maryland. There he worked in Oxford, starting as a tobacco factor for Foster Cunliffe & Sons, most likely under contract as an apprentice. Unfortunately, while Mr. Morris was away, Bobby's mother, Elizabeth Murphet, died in Liverpool, and according to family members, Bobby's grandmother raised him until he was in his early teens. By then, he was old enough to join his father in America. During this time, Liverpool was the main entry port for American colonial cotton which went to Manchester and fueled the growth of that first industrial city. So, as a youth, Bobby was an eyewitness to the start of the Industrial Revolution.

Bobby's father stayed in Maryland, and worked for the trading firm, Foster Cunliffe & Sons. He bought tobacco from farmers and readied it for shipment to Europe. He also received ships from Europe for his employer. These ships carried supplies, housewares, luxury goods, and sometimes indentured servants and slaves. He became an honorary member of the area's most prestigious social club, The Tuesday Club, where he would occasionally play his violin as a part of the festivities. Another honorary member was the Reverend Thomas Bacon, a friend of Bobby's father, who looked after the well-being of slaves in the area and built a school for their education.[1]

Bobby's famous prowess in business came to him naturally. His father was a sagacious fellow, and as such, he formed the first independent board of standards for tobacco quality.[2] The rating system developed by that board assured buyers in the Old World that the products they bought from Maryland met the quality levels they expected. This was popular with buyers, and Oxford, Maryland, became an important center for the tobacco trade. In a second innovation, Bobby's father was the first to keep his accounts in terms of money instead of tobacco. At the time, tobacco acted as a kind of currency, but was really an item of barter. By using currency, instead of a perishable and variable commodity, he was able to provide his employers with the kind of regularity in his accounts that is vital to success in business.[3*] There were also stories that he followed conventional behavior for the time, particularly for a man who had so recently risen from the ranks himself. It is said he could be haughty and overbearing, and occasionally harsh with those who worked for him.[4] There is some reason to believe this may have ultimately been to his detriment.

When Bobby reached the age of thirteen, he left his childhood home to join his father on the eastern shore of Maryland. Once there, he discovered a woman named Sarah Wise was in his father's life. A little over a year later, Bobby had a new baby half-brother, Thomas.

Bobby's father hired a tutor to teach the teen, but the relationship was not very productive. He asked his son what was wrong; and Bobby replied, "I have learned, sir, all that he could teach me."[5] Soon after that Bobby ended his formal schooling and started his career in earnest. His father contacted Robert Greenway.[6] Greenway was a Philadelphia merchant and librarian for the Library Company.[7] That was a Ben Franklin civic enterprise consisting, mostly, of 3000 books from the private library of James Logan, the Penns' leading state administrator, and mentor to Franklin himself. Greenway arranged for an apprenticeship, and Bobby went to Philadelphia to work for Willing and Company. The head of that company, Charles Willing, was a respected Philadelphia merchant and local political leader, who also did some charitable work with Benjamin Franklin. During this period, Bobby was a teenager and too young to be on his own, so he lived with his father's old friend, Mr. Greenway. Greenway's access to the Library Company's collection would provide a perfect quiet playground for a youngster to educate himself, when he wasn't out on the town that is. Life in Philadelphia must have seemed somewhat familiar to Morris since it was a busy seaport like his native Liverpool.

Bobby's progress from adolescence to adulthood was abruptly accelerated in 1750 when his father died from a freak accident; about which it is said, his father had a premonition. According to the legend written down by his granddaughter, Maria Nixon, Mr. Morris had a dream that he would die from a wayward shot fired from a departing vessel. People with a less supernatural outlook consider that he knew of a disagreement between the crew and the owners of the ship, and what some assign to premonition was actually awareness of a practical management issue. Nevertheless, it was the custom of the day for ships near port to fire a cannon to announce their arrival and departure. It was Bobby's father's job to oversee the ship, and so he was on it when the ship was about to leave. However, because of his concern for his physical well-being, he asked that the traditional shot not be fired. This supposedly caused worry among the superstitious crew, so the shot was to be delayed until Bobby's father was on shore and out of range. It had been arranged for the captain to put his finger on the side of his nose to signal the gunshot. Mr. Morris and his land bound associates left the ship and started rowing to the shore. It is said, that an untimely fly bothered the captain and it landed on his nose. When the captain shooed the fly, he touched his finger to his nose and this signaled the gunshot.[8] A shot was fired while Mr. Morris was still in the rowboat as it approached the shore. A wad from the cannon hit him in the arm. He died three days later from the wound.

The myth started by Maria Nixon has been embellished by succeeding family members to endow some of the Morris family with "second sight." Such claims are best left to family lore. However, it was noted by several of his friends, including Colonel Jeremiah Banning, that Mr. Morris' favorite dog, Trey, an English spaniel, stayed with him all during his illness. When he died, Trey lay down the under the bed and died on the spot. The elder Morris left Bobby an inheritance of about £2,500, which he later used to his advantage as a merchant.[9]

Bobby, now young Robert, grew into his position as clerk. The first indication of his abilities as a merchant became clear before he was nineteen. He was still working for Charles Willing & Co., when he managed to establish complete control over the flour trade in Philadelphia. Philadelphia was much smaller then, and the merchants were collected in one part of the city. One day, when Charles Willing was out of town, a message arrived in the office that the price of flour was due to rise. The sandy haired youth with piercing blue eyes visited each flour merchant's office. Once inside he offered to buy all their flour at an agreeable price, and on terms he could manage. He repeated this until he had visited all the offices in the port city. One can only imagine the surprise of the other merchants when they discovered he owned all the flour, and they had to go to this boy to buy their flour at the price and terms he could dictate. Charles Willing returned and discovered what Robert had done. In response to the complaints of other merchants, Mr. Willing asked them if they might have done the same if a similar opportunity presented itself again. They had to admit they would, and their anger dissipated.[10]

Robert continued to work in Charles Willing's office, where he and Charles' son, Thomas, would later become good friends. Charles Willing took a paternal interest in Robert and wrote to him fondly, as a father might.

The surviving letters from this period show that Morris was popular, known to enjoy himself at a party or two, and that he was likely to have a girl on his arm on these occasions.[11] In the early part of the 1760's Robert met a woman about whom little is known, probably because she and Robert never married. Together they had a baby girl who was born in 1763. The girl was known as Polly Morris. Robert supported her and provided for her education.

Life in the City

Philadelphia was a lively port city with paved streets lined by wooden and brick buildings. It was a colonial capital on the western edge of a great Empire, and it attracted opportunity seekers from England and Europe. Many came. Some did well, while others failed. More followed, found suitable homes, and the city grew. The city's grid of streets stretched along the banks of the Delaware River for about two miles, or over twenty blocks from Penn Treaty Tree in the north, down to Southwark. At the time, if one traveled west from the Delaware River, he would find that Philadelphia was just about four city blocks deep. The other twenty or so streets that made up the rest of William Penn's grid were not yet paved or populated.

A progression of wooden docks protruded eastward into the Delaware River along the whole length of the waterfront. There one could see every kind of ship afloat: sloops, ketches, brigs, brigantines, barquentines, barques, ships, schooners, punts, rowboats, skiffs, cutters, and occasional-

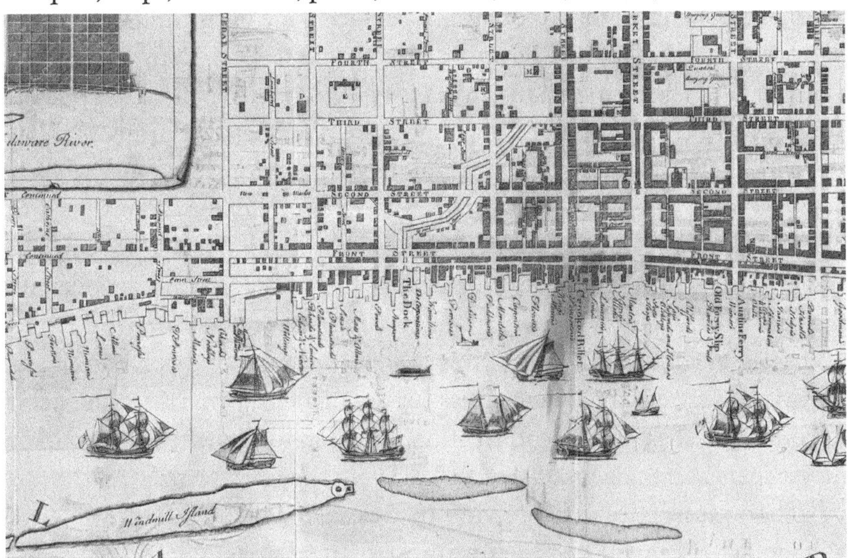

By 1762, the improved portion of Philadelphia extended as far west as Sixth Street. The port connected the city to the world, and ferries from the opposite side of the Delaware River carried travelers and trade from rural New Jersey. (Philadelphia, 1762 Library of Congress).

ly even a polacre. These vessels varied in length from sixteen feet to over two hundred. The air over the wharves was filled with flags, spars, and rigging, and the rigging was often full of men preparing for a voyage.

Philadelphia was the hub of a dynamic market that was diversely populated. There were solid Quakers making their cautious way in business. There were farmers of German descent who passed through on their way to buy and sell. There were some enslaved Blacks, as well as free Black artisans and laborers with services to offer. There were travelers like the Scots-Irish on their way to carve a home in the wilderness. There were also merchants of all descriptions. The merchant community was a heterogeneous lot of risk takers who tried their skill and luck moving cargo across the ocean. There were small-scale dry goods merchants, shopkeepers really, who tried to sell their imported British manufactured goods before their credit was called. These minor vendors lived the same kind of lives as contemporary tradesmen. There were also middling merchants who rented space on other people's ships for short trips. Others owned ships that carried larger bulk cargo, like flaxseed to Ireland, flour to Bermuda or maybe a little smuggled rice to Spain. The fortunes of these merchants often rode on the arrival of one or two fully laden ships. They all developed a well-defined system for getting the most utility from their assets, well before there were banks. They had letters of credit, bills of exchange, and currencies to transfer value from one holder to another.

The merchants in this colonial city pursued a life of risk and enterprise, balancing on the slim line between success and failure. Many an anxious week would pass as a merchant waited for the moment when his ship would come in. A merchant might be trading from a rented warehouse one day, but with a few good deals, and doubling up his position, he might own two ships the next year. The following year his house might be up for sale, but he would keep plying his trade in the hopes of walking away with enough to acquire an income that would come at less personal cost. This encouraged the successful to diversify their holdings into real estate, ironworks, and eventually manufacturing. The stress and uncertainty of this life of physical risks at sea, and the financial risks in the markets, gave rise to the habit of constantly seeking new information, which in turn created a market for newspapers and trade broadsheets, filled with the latest pricing data.

Economic life was unforgiving in this colonial town; even Charles Willing, who was one of the most prominent businessmen, said that his days were full of cares and anxiety.[12] During this period, the wealthy merchants in Philadelphia did not live as well as the middle-class Englishmen who stayed in England. In the 1750's, a successful Philadelphia merchant might have an estate worth £5,000 to £8,000. Each had most of his assets tied up in his stock for trade, so from that £5,000 one has to count in ships, warehouse space, cargo, etc. The vast majority of smaller traders valued their estates at or below £500.[13] In 1760's Philadelphia, only about 10% of the people with taxable assets over £300 were merchants.[14] The most prosperous were the Quaker proprietors, who had gotten their land from William Penn. They were landholders with flour mills, and tenant farmers who paid them land rent. They also controlled the Assembly.

Merchants tended to live in the most bustling part of the city, and they kept their homes near the docks. Even after they had made enough money to move west, away from the noise and smells of the most crowded areas, they kept their primary residence in the center of the commercial action. Those who could, bought a secondary residence, a country seat, but that was the exception. Most lived in brick dwellings similar to those owned by artisans and professionals. These were different from the kind of wooden buildings found on the narrow alley streets where the servants and laborers lived.[15] These alleys were sometimes paved in wood block, or not paved at all. The more prosperous people usually lived in two- and three-story brick structures with a small fireplace in almost every room. There was no central heat, and the city was experiencing a series of very cold winters. This period was at the tail end of the "Little Ice Age," and the Delaware River froze over each winter, which stopped commerce. One can easily imagine the bitter wind blowing off the nearby frozen river, singing through the icy rigging of the ships, and buffeting the wooden casement windows on a long winter's night.

The brick houses had cellars where people would store apples and roots like potatoes and turnips. Sometimes there would be a turtle tank down in the floor. It was round, about ten feet in diameter, and three or four bricks high. This tank would contain a few snapping turtles that would live in the cellar and eat the rats that came up from the river into the house. On occasion, the turtles would be cooked to provide a special meal for the guests. Even today, members of Philadelphia's old families recognize "real" snapper soup by the kind of bones found in it.

Cooking was conducted in a large fireplace in the kitchen using pots on swinging metal arms, and instead of using burners, cooking pans were put on metal stands with feet resting in the coals. A wood fired oven would be used to bake bread and the bottoms of the loaves would always come out burned, and this was called cake. Beds were wooden frames with a rope mesh that would hold up a straw or horsehair mattress. Lighting was provided by tallow candles or whale oil lamps, but this was expensive, so most people went to bed shortly after the sun set. People had few changes of clothing, so the general lack of closets was not seen as a hardship. Life, however, was not easy. French visitors commented on the beauty of the young women, and the deleterious effect the harsh conditions had upon them as they brought up their large families.

During the summers, the narrow streets and even more narrow sidewalks would cluster people together as they went about their business. The opening of a window allowed a breeze to move the heavy, hot, and humid air through the house. This would bring in insects along with the smells and noise of the animals and citizens going by outside. The sidewalks were curbed with long vertical slabs of slate and paved in brick, like the buildings. The streets were kept as clean as possible considering the amount of animal traffic in the city. Some streets were paved with Belgian block style cobblestones that had been brought to Philadelphia.

In those days there were just a few tall buildings in Philadelphia; and these were easily identified by their spires. The State House was the tallest building in the colonies at the time. The other spires were churches and acted as landmarks for people coming up the river into the port, and as spiritual landmarks for their congregations.

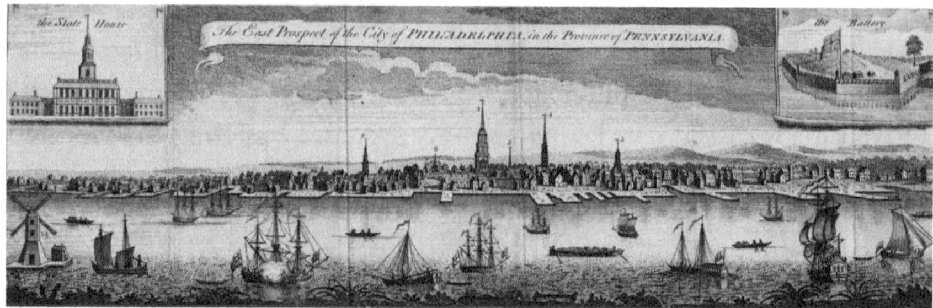

After a view made by George Heap, by direction of Nicholas Scull. "The East Prospect of the City of Philadelphia, in the Province of Pennsylvania." From *London Magazine*, 1761

Living the Life

> They breakfasted at eight or half-past; and by nine were in their counting houses, laying out the business of the day; at ten they were on their wharves, with their aprons around their waists, rolling hogsheads of rum and molasses; at twelve, at market, flying about as dirty and diligent as porters; at two back again to the roll-

> ing, heaving, hallooing, and scribbling. At four they went home to dress for dinner; at seven, to the play; at eleven, to supper, with a crew of lusty Bacchanals who would smoke cigars, gulp down brandy, and sing, roar, and shout in the thickening clouds they created like so many merry devils, till three in the morning.[16]

Morris swam happily in this swift river of enterprise. If he was not risking his lot in the market, he was making friends and business contacts in town. He was also an avid joiner and founder of civic groups like the Sons of St. George.

At the age of 20, Morris and a few friends, notably Thomas Willing, Archibald McCall, and Tench Francis, were among the 500 subscribers to the initial funding for the Old London Coffee House. It sat right in the middle of the commercial action, on the southwest corner of Market & Front streets. The term "Coffee House" was somewhat of a misnomer since they served meals and alcohol as well. Over time, it became an informal center for the merchant community's commercial activity and social gatherings, sometimes holding auctions out front. Men of business, or the law, usually had an office for their professional use, but they would regularly gather in public houses, or taverns. Often a business or civic association would have a particular room in their chosen public house where they would meet, conduct business, and discuss the news of the day.

In those days, associations for business and society were mostly formed along religious or ethnic lines with Anglicans joining with Anglicans, Quak-

Old London Coffee House in Philadelphia. Credit: Library Company of Philadelphia.

ers with Quakers, Jews with Jews, Catholics with Catholics, etc.[17] These cultural groupings were based on familiarity and common expectations, and they provided a context where one got to know one's peers. On occasion, there were animosities between the various cultural groups. Charles Willing, for example, was heard mumbling derisively about "those broad brims" when he talked about a disagreement he had with a Quaker in town.

Morris was an orphan and an immigrant who was free to choose and to adopt the cultural attributes that he liked. Without paternal constraints, he often crossed social boundaries and worked with diverse groups. This came in handy, years later, when Morris was able to borrow money for Washington's army from a Quaker, and Quakers were famously pacifist and tight with a dollar. This was not a small accomplishment for an Anglican like Morris.

Ordinarily, to reduce unnecessary risk, merchants evaluated one another before engaging in commerce. Generally, men would be judged for moral hazard by their selection of friends, their personal and professional habits, their neatness, and their punctuality. Nevertheless, a man's ability to conduct business was ultimately based on his history of making timely payments. This regularity assured one's partners that a payment made on a preliminary venture would arrive on schedule, so they could take a second risk and keep business moving. This was particularly important because it often took over eighteen months to close the books on one ocean going shipment. All of these attributes combined to form that all-important quality, the reputation. Without a good reputation, a merchant's fortunes were severely compromised. With a good name, a merchant could raise funds, conduct business, and stand among his peers with his head held high. Morris wrote, "I declare that the character of a real merchant, a generous, open and honest merchant, is a character I am proud of."[18]

The constant level of uncertainty and the associated stress kept these businessmen alert for new markets, trends, and advances in technology. This honed their minds to seek opportunities, or to create them if none existed. In some ways, the distance was not far between the risky business of merchants and real gambling; for example, on the other side of the Atlantic, Lloyds of London started as a gambling club, with regular meetings in an English coffee house. Maritime insurance was based on several people wagering that a ship would complete its trip, and others betting it would not. A Philadelphia merchant placed his bet that the value of a commodity would be higher in the West Indies than in South Carolina. The trade in shares of companies is an act of the same sort, a purchase is a bet for success, and a sale of shares is a hedge on failure. The modern Philadelphia Stock Exchange traces its roots to The London Coffee House, claiming it was the first stock exchange in the nation. The relationship between risk, reward, and finance was well established in the merchant society of Philadelphia, a small city on the edge of a large empire.

-|-

Philadelphia was not only a trading center; it was the capital of the colony of Pennsylvania, so political discussions focused on English politics and their effects on colonial life. There were two main political factions. One was the faction of the king. It was known as the Court Party but was also called the Tories. At the time, the current king, George III, was busy expanding his influence by placing political appointees into towns and villages around England. He did this for much the same reason that earlier kings created towns to counterbalance the power of the lords and barons. This way, George III populated those places with people friendly to his aims and extended his monarchial power over Parliament while enriching his friends with concessions. This political technique was called "corruption" by critics, because it corrupted the original intent of the Parliament as being representative of the indigenous population. Consequently, when people talked about the king using new funds to support "placemen and pensioners," they really meant that the king would use the power of patronage to grow his influence in Parliament by "corrupting" it through this insincere seeding of fraudulent representatives. The king used the votes he gained by this technique to increase taxes. These funds were used to finance wars and colonization, and to protect trade that most often benefited the king's allies.

The other political faction was called the Whigs. It has also been known as the Country Party and was originally the party of the lords and barons. This faction was mostly concerned with maintaining the English Constitution, which was not a single document, but the weight of hundreds of years of legal decisions. This tradition protected the rights and liberties of citizens like themselves and limited the influence of the king. The Whigs were not happy to pay taxes that were used to enrich the king's friends. People who populated the Country Party mostly lived outside of London, and were prosperous villagers, farmers, owners of the country estates, and others who were not part of the king's circle and didn't want their political power to diminish.

The king was very competent in implementing his plan and growing his power; consequently, the Country Party became more anxious with each successful step the king took. The more apprehensive they became, the more heated their rhetoric grew. One of their chief concerns was the growth of the militaristic state, which they feared would be turned against them. In England, this fear eventually diminished in favor of viewing the military as a means of protecting the people from foreign enemies. That transformation in thought was not completed in America.

Colonial interest in English politics grew, as the colonies increased in importance to England. During the previous hundred years or so, the colonial assemblies in America had operated with minimal direction from the Parliament, the King, his Board of Trade, or the various appointed governors. The royal charters of the colonies harkened back to the earliest days when each colony was a privately owned money-making affair with a governor sent by the king. This meant that Parliament could regulate them, as they would any private company, which they did very little, but the states were only willing to accept the right of parliament to regulate their trade through the Board of Trade.

In this way, the colonies were insulated from most of the political difficulties in both England and Europe. Naturally, the Atlantic Ocean provided a competent barrier to daily interference, and the other European powers had plenty to occupy themselves within their own colonies. This condition did not last forever, and the European powers pursued their interests in North America. France, for example, thought it would be clever to confine the British colonies to the east of the Allegheny Mountains by creating a ring of forts to make a connection between French Quebec and French New Orleans. The British had a different idea and formed land development companies that had designs on that same territory. The Native American groups sided with France because the French had established trading relations with them, and mostly left them alone.

These conflicting approaches led to a 1749 property dispute in the Ohio Territory, which involved George Washington. That developed into "The Seven Years War," also known as the French and Indian War. It was fought between England and France from 1756 to 1763, and it set into motion a series of events that, years later, resulted in the American Revolution. In the process, there was an early attempt at coordinating the defensive activities of all the colonies, known as the Albany Plan, which was somewhat similar to the structure adopted later under the Articles of Confederation. In addition, Americans experienced the mobilization of the citizens into militias, the depredation of the merchant fleet by privateers, the introduction of a standing army to the colonies, and the growth of slavery. Most significantly however, this conflict alerted the colonials to the true nature of Parliament. At the same time, it focused Parliament's attention on a set of colonies that they had largely ignored for about 150 years, and found them to be flexing their muscles, growing in population and wealth, and, they feared, possibly heading toward independence.

The Seven Years War also brought two friends closer together. At the time, Thomas Willing, was completing his education in London, when he was called back to Philadelphia to look after his ill father and his business, where Morris was working.

Conflict always raises insurance rates, and when, in 1756, it became too dear, or impossible to get, two daring proto-Americans, Willing and Morris, put together their own insurance operation with five other merchants to raise eighty thousand pounds to insure their ships and offer coverage to other merchants as well.[19] Around the same time, Willing was also on the Indian Affairs Board, which was a government sanctioned organization put together to manage that volatile trade. It was lucrative, however, and they raised funds for the business by selling bonds at 6%. This was the beginning in their mix of private and public work, funded by pooling the capital of others. Willing did the paperwork, and Morris was there to support and learn. Their competitors, who just traded with their own funds, worried the Willings would be able to control whole markets with these pools of money. This was just the first stirrings of a new force in America now called Capitalism.

At the same time, Robert Morris was promoted from his job as a clerk. At the age of twenty-two, he became the supercargo on Charles Willing's ships, which were trading in the West Indies. It was Morris' job to conduct the transactions for the company while the ship was in foreign ports, and to manage the finances for the voyage.[20] This meant risking life and limb sailing the contested Caribbean Sea. While at sea, Willing's vessels were targets for French Privateers because they were British merchant ships sailing from the colonial port of Philadelphia. One ship was caught, and Morris was captured along with the rest of the crew. Privateers were mostly interested

Thomas Willing, by H.B. Hall, 1877

in the price they could get for the ship and its contents, but sometimes the crew would be impressed, and other times they would be put ashore. Occasionally the ship's managers were held for ransom. It is said, in this case, Robert was put into a Cuban jail for two months. After his release, it is rumored, he befriended an influential Frenchman, and by fixing this man's watch Robert earned a small bit of money. Others have speculated that Morris was seeking alternative employment opportunities in the islands. In either case, he was able to make his way from the Caribbean back to Philadelphia, but without the original ship or cargo.[21, 22] His friends were glad to see him in any case.

On May 1st, 1757, shortly after Morris' return from his adventures with the French privateers, Thomas Willing asked him to become a minority partner with a twenty-five percent interest in a new company. Morris was twenty-three years old when he invested his inheritance to become a business partner with his friend.[23] They bought three ships from the fleet that had belonged to Charles Willing's old company, and so it was that these two young men started their company in the midst of a war.

The new partnership was known as Willing, Morris & Co. They handled a wide variety of shipments: flour, tobacco, salt, rum, wheat, molasses, indigo, and sometimes the transport of immigrants who came from Europe to Philadelphia as indentured servants. Rarely, an acquaintance would request that they transport a slave from the West Indies to Philadelphia. Usually, indentured servants from Europe worked for their sponsor for four or five years, before they were free to pursue their own lives. Other times there would be an apprenticeship contract of five to seven years. Robert Morris Sr. would have come to America under one such contract to Foster Cunliffe & Sons, just as Bob came to Philadelphia as an apprentice to Charles Willing. People came to the colonies under these conditions because North America was a place where people could escape from the domination of others, and eventually get their own property. The indenture was worth their time. A measure of this trend can be understood by seeing that in 1789, the year of the Constitution, 90% of the free male citizens of Pennsylvania owned enough property to qualify as voters. People wanted to work for themselves after their indenture was up, and when they moved on, this added to the persistent labor shortage. People were constantly brought in to fill new and existing positions.

Philadelphians preferred European laborers, but the Seven Years War made them scarce because workers stopped crossing the Atlantic.[24] Simultaneously, the British Crown needed warriors. As potential free workers went to war in Europe, the English slave trade was promoted as an alternative source of labor for the colonies. Not coincidentally, it was largely controlled and operated by the king's political allies.[25] The Court Party took hold of this opportunity and made it an official policy to increase the slave trade to America.[26,27] Most colonies were under the jurisdiction of the Royal Board of Trade, and Cromwell's Navigation Acts, and particularly, Pennsylvania's charter put the merchants at the mercy of the Crown. The demand for workers continued, and so, according to royal policy, the ancient practice of slavery grew in the colonies. It was under the conditions of this captive market that these British subjects, Willing, Morris & Co., acted as agents, selling slaves imported by others from the West Indies. Between 1757 and 1761, they advertised twenty-three slaves for sale in these agency arrangements, using the *Pennsylvania Gazette.*[28] Mostly they advertised one or two at a time. However, on one occasion they offered a "parcel," which meant ten.

The ensuing years of war harmed the local economy by depriving the area of labor, which was already in short supply. In 1762, Willing, Morris & Co. joined with twenty-five individuals and petitioned the Governor of Pennsylvania for wartime relief on the import duty on slaves. They hoped the labor pool might increase, which would stabilize the prices of necessary items like flour.[29] This particular document was written when Thomas Willing was seeking public office as Mayor of Philadelphia, and Robert was a junior partner in the firm. Curiously, the men did not sign it as individuals the way all the others did, rather it was signed, "Willing, Morris & Co."

This ambiguity in the record about Morris' thinking on the subject of slavery is a consistent thread that runs the length of his life story. It opens the door to people who wish to project their own ideas onto Morris and makes their interpretation of him into a reflection of what people want to find, instead of what is actually there. This is just one reason many historians find interpreting Morris to be complicated.

Shortly after the petition, Willing, Morris & Co. sent their brig, *Nancy,* out on two voyages to Africa. Contrary to popular thought, slave trading was not a sure road to riches. In fact, even the Royal Africa Company operated at a loss,[30] which, in itself, explains why the king's allies used the government's power to force the slave trade on their American colonies. According to existing estimates,[31] Willing, Morris & Co. would have lost about $1,770 Spanish milled dollars on the first trip because they carried only 1.3 slaves per shipping ton,[32] unlike more successful traders who packed them in at five per ton. Another difficulty they encountered during the first trip was illness among the Africans on board.[33] Once the vessel arrived in Philadelphia the company provided medical assistance to the sick, but they were unable to sell even half. To increase their trials in this business, it seems that many of their customers were slow to pay, if they paid at all. Of the one hundred seventy-five they brought to America on the *Nancy*, Willing, Morris & Co. sold less than sixty-five slaves into the greater Philadelphia, New Jersey, Delaware area. They ended up moving more than half of the Africans to Virginia.[34]

During the second trip they carried even fewer per ton, but they traveled a shorter distance and took them to the West Indies. After that second trip, French privateers took their ship as it was outbound on a third voyage. That event ended the business for these Philadelphians.[35] They lost their trading capital, and one third of their small fleet in the form of one vessel, which cost over $17,000. In sum, the business was not good for them, and they never re-entered that trade.

In their last agency deal, in 1765, they advertised seventy who were brought in from Africa on the ship *Marquis de Granby*.[36] The records indicate that the slaves were not sold in Philadelphia by Willing & Morris, but instead the owner took the ship and cargo to a new agent in Jamaica.[37] As soon as they could, Willing, Morris & Co. refocused their efforts on bringing indentured workers from Europe to meet the demand for labor.[38] Pennsylvanians preferred European workers anyway.

Shortly after the Seven Years War, Willing and Morris tried to diversify their holdings. They purchased Orange Grove, a 3,000-acre property near Baton Rouge, Louisiana, through their agent, Oliver Pollock. It was a passive investment for these British subjects, and the land was supposed to be operated as a plantation by Willing's brother, who frequently worked with Pollock. They wrote, We "submit our estate to your direction without reserve assuring ourselves that it will under your auspices be conducted to the best advantage."[39] They intended to grow indigo, but only got as far as building a few structures. Much later Morris wrote, "But being obliged to abandon this settlement during that [Revolutionary] War, and upon the peace, it having fallen within the Spanish Dominions. We have never claimed the Land or Buildings." They lost the property when Spain gained Louisiana as part of the Treaty of Paris, signed in 1784. Morris continued, "Upon apprehending danger at Orange Grove, we purchased a tract of land on the Spanish side of the River, to which the Overseer took the Negroes and movables, which were afterwards sold. I think it cost us only

250 dollars"[40] They never recovered their investment. That half-hearted attempt at being an absentee landlord, which resulted in a loss of $250, was as close as Morris came to being a slaveholder of the kind so often found on southern plantations.

Morris never wrote down his thoughts about slavery, except to refer to slaves as those "unfortunate people." He was not an ideologue on the subject, and he seemed to accept slavery as a fact of life, which would persist until the duly elected legislature changed the laws. He lived in a transitional time, and in such times remnants of the past persist. Like many men who could afford to before the Revolution, Morris owned a few slaves who worked in his house. When one, named Hero, ran away during the family's flight from Philadelphia, Morris placed advertisements in the *Pennsylvania Evening Post* to find him. Otherwise, he let him go. Years later, a friend of Morris' encountered Hero, and found him in uncomfortably reduced circumstances. Through the intermediary, Morris offered him his old position back. Hero refused, and that was the end of their connection. By the time Morris lived on High Street he owned no slaves. Morris held no animosity towards the people of African descent. According to the records of the Pennsylvania Executive Council, Morris had been robbed of 400 gallons of rum, but instead of insisting on jail or the possible fine of £2,000, Morris allowed that the thief, who was a free black man, might serve his country better in the Pennsylvania militia.[41]

However, he was a practical man of his time, and during the Revolution, Robert's daughter Polly married a veteran of that war, Mr. Charles Croxall. Mr. Croxall had difficulty managing his business, and in the 1780's Robert provided them with an estate in Belvedere, New Jersey, which he helped populate with eight slaves to work the farm. Robert also set up a trust so Polly might, "have money and leisure to procure good Education for your children, and instead of being constantly in a fret as it seems to me you are, you might have an easy mind, give comfort and pleasure to your family, and be at peace and friendship with your neighbors."[42*]

In the years after independence was declared, both Willing and Morris quietly sided with abolitionists, including Benjamin Franklin, Anthony Wayne, John Hancock, John Jay, James Wilson, William White, Gouverneur Morris, and Alexander Hamilton. Lines are not always neatly drawn, and Morris' friend George Washington was a slave holder, but at the end of his life he freed the slaves he owned. Many of his political opposites were slave traders, like the Browns, of Rhode Island, and Henry

Laurens of South Carolina; and slave holders like the Lee family. However, during the war, Morris owned a privateer vessel that attacked the slave trade on the high seas. His business partner in that venture, William Bingham, became a staunch abolitionist upon his return to Philadelphia. In the 1780's, Morris led the political group in the Pennsylvania Assembly that defended the Abolition law from those who sought to weaken it. Later, his son Robert married the daughter of the former president of the Pennsylvania Abolition society. His brother-in-law was involved in an early version of a Back-to-Africa movement, which was seen at the time to be part of the solution to the slavery question. Morris' economic program, as presented in 1781, was designed to weaken the institution of slavery with tax measures that made it economically unattractive. Later, Morris employed a freed slave as an indentured servant in his house. In 1783, while the British were leaving New York, at the end of the war, and Americans were clamoring to get "their slaves" back, Morris aided the effort to get some three thousand black individuals out of New York, and safely to Canada.

In 1784, he started a shipping firm in Virginia, and did not use it to import slaves into that slave state. It appears that over the decades that passed from the time Morris owned a few slaves, he changed his thinking on the subject. During his time of influence on national affairs the institution of slavery was on the decline, even with renewed calls of abolition coming from Virginia.

Slowing the Slave Trade

Much has been written about the importance of the colonies as a market for British products. The British used the Navigation Acts of 1651 to control this trade, treating the American colonies as a source of raw materials, and a market for the merchandise turned out of British factories. Americans understood they were enriching England, and they developed some manufacturing of their own, on the sly. One economic element they could not, as yet, produce quickly enough was laborers, regardless of the prodigious efforts of the women in Pennsylvania, many of whom had over ten children apiece. Laborers were imported, both as indentured servants and slaves, and there was a population of slaves in every colony during the 18th century.

It is difficult for modern people to comprehend the reason for slavery. In most basic terms, slavery is an ancient economic system, and it took some time to replace it with the new free enterprise system Morris championed. The slave trade was promoted to enrich the politically connected traders in England, but it existed because people needed workers, and at that time there were three kinds: slaves, indentured servants, and hired help. The vast majority of immigrants wanted to be independent, so there were many more trades-people than people looking to be hired as employees.

During the whole eighteenth century, the combined total of slaves that entered the Philadelphia, New Jersey, and Delaware ports was just over 1,300. Ninety percent of them entered during and shortly after the Seven Years War. In contrast, tiny Rhode Island imported 3,000, during the same seven-year period. About 25% of the slaves brought into Philadelphia came on ships owned by Rhode Islanders Messers D'Wolf, Aaron Lopez, and Jacob Rivera.[43] These merchants also carried slaves up and down the whole coast, even as far as South America. Mr. Lopez was so successful as a merchant that in 1759 he had the honor of laying the cornerstone of Touro Synagogue in Newport Rhode Island, which is the oldest standing synagogue in America today.

Among the Philadelphians in the business there was one company that brought in 264;[44,45,46] another carried 130;[47,48] a third group brought in 50,[49,50,51] some traded but brought in even less,[52,53] and there were others who brought in a few upon request. According to a study published by the Historical Society of Pennsylvania, one hundred forty-one people sold slaves in Pennsylvania between 1682 and 1766.[54] The Quaker temperament and local tax laws made this trade unattractive, so the "Quaker City" never played a large role. Philadelphia merchants were minor operators when compared with those who supplied the whole hemisphere. During the 18th century, The Royal Africa Company carried over 198,978.[55] The Dutch West Indian Company carried over 158,647 slaves.[56] Middelburgsche Commercie Companigne carried over 41,194.[57] It would take a political and economic revolution in the market to stop the buying, selling, and owning of people. Those changes were under way in America, and Morris was at the forefront of the effort.

After the Seven Years War, the influx of slaves, England's new tax policies, and the breach between the colonies and the Crown, all combined to create the requisite set of conditions. Responding to English tax policies in the mid-1760's, Morris and Willing promoted and signed the first Non-Importation Agreement. The voluntary non-importation pact was aimed at showing Britain the importance of the American market, and it marked the end of the importation of slaves into the Philadelphia region. After that expired, the Quaker leaders of Pennsylvania passed a significant increase to the import duty on slaves to discourage the trade from restarting.[58] In 1773, this import tax was increased again as a way to stop the trade completely. As one might expect, the British were not pleased. Richard Jackson spoke in Parliament on the subject, "The increase of the duty on negroes ... is manifestly inconsistent with the policy adopted by your lordships and your predecessors for the sake of encouraging the African Trade."[59] Pennsylvania was not alone in its effort to stem the tide of slaves into America during the decade before the Revolution, but it was successful. Pennsylvania's efforts to stop the slave trade were not overruled by the British Government; but only because events elsewhere attracted the Crown's attention.

The colony of Massachusetts also dealt with the growth of slavery within its borders. In 1767, merchant John Hancock led the Sons of Liberty to sign their voluntary Non-Importation Agreement. In March of the same year, the elected representatives of the colony of Massachusetts attempted to ban the importation of slaves, but the Colonial Governor would not sign the bill.[60] At the same time, slave trading played an increasing role in the economy of Rhode Island, from the production of rum by slaves to the shipping of people as slaves. This can also be seen by the fact that the same Rhode Islanders who brought slaves to Philadelphia collectively carried over 20,000 to North and South American markets. The far-ranging Rhode Island slave traders did not adhere closely to the early voluntary Non-Importation Agreements.[61] However, slave shipments into Rhode Island stopped when Congress passed the second Non-Importation Agreement in the 1770's.[62]

In England, the opposition Whig party saw the slave trade in terms of royal excess, and as a member of that group a Virginian, Arthur Lee, wrote blistering essays in favor of abolition.[63, 64*] In 1770, the Virginia Association passed a bill barring the importation of slaves.[65] This early effort to end the slave trade in Virginia was overruled by the British Crown. It was this move by the Crown that caused the Virginia Assembly to complain to the king in 1772, and later it brought Jefferson to condemn the slave trade in his original draft of the Declaration of Independence. That condemnation was removed from the final version by those who benefited from the system, or so Jefferson said.

People in Georgia generally conformed to the voluntary Non-Importation Agreement of 1767, but then slaves were being brought in overland from South Carolina. During the 18th century the greatest importation into South Carolina occurred between 1750 and 1770.[66] South Carolina attempted to end the importation of slaves in 1765[67] and again in 1769.[68] These efforts were defeated by politically powerful traders, like Henry Laurens,[69] whose company had brought in 928 slaves in 1762.[70] Not surprisingly, the first non-importation effort was circumvented by a few of the more active traders who contracted with a number of complicit merchants, including Mr. Lopez from Rhode Island.[71] Laurens operated his slave trading company, called Austin & Laurens, from 1751 to 1762, after which Laurens traded on his own and was active until 1774, the year of the Non-Importation Agreement.[72] It is worth noting that one of Lauren's business partners in the trade, Richard Oswald, was the principal owner of Bunce Island, a slave trading fort off Africa, and a member of The Royal African Company trading firm.[73] Laurens and Oswald kept up communications on their mutual interest in the slave trade even while Laurens was incarcerated in the Tower of London in 1783.[74] Later Mr. Oswald sat across the table from Laurens during the Paris peace negotiations in 1784. It is a small surprise that Laurens inserted language into that document requiring payment to Americans for slaves lost during the Revolution.

The growth of slavery may have benefited large landholders and some traders, but it was a cause for alarm among the freeholders in South and North Carolina. In Rowan County, North Carolina, they passed a resolution in 1774 which said, "That the African Trade is injurious to this Colony, obstructs the Population of it by freemen, prevents manufacturers, and other Useful Emigrants from Europe from settling among us, and occasions an annual increase of the Balance of Trade against the Colonies."[75] In other words, slavery was holding back the economic prospects of the free citizens, while it helped the plutocrats who owned hundreds, and ran the state. The citizens in these states would have to wait until 1864 to see the end of slavery.

Into the Public Eye

A critical point in the negotiations that ended the Seven Years War was determining which asset the French would surrender to the English – Canada or Guadalupe, the sugar island. It was a close call because the income from each area was roughly equal. The final decision for England to take Canada meant that France would no longer be a threat to the existing thirteen British coastal colonies. That allowed the Americans to focus on themselves, and not have to worry about relying on their mother country for protection. Unfortunately, after the war was over, the French didn't actually leave the western lands, so the British decided to move some troops into North America to occupy the western forts and provide support to the colonial governors in some eastern cities. These troops were inflated in the minds of the more radical members of the Whigs in Massachusetts to signify the creation of a repressive "standing army" under the control of the royally appointed Governor. They saw this as the first step towards greater taxation enforced by the mother country, the eventual subjugation of the population, and the resulting loss of Liberty.

Parliament inflamed these fears in 1765 by passing the Stamp Act, which was an effort to get the Colonies to help pay for the recent war, and new troops at the border. Once this step was taken, these Englishmen in America looked to the law for protection. They argued the British constitution stated that taxes could only be levied with the consent of the governed, and only a representative in Parliament could grant that consent. The cry over this injustice became, *"No taxation without representation."* Americans offered the compromise that they would accept the right of Parliament to regulate trade, under the 17th century Navigation Acts, but they would reserve the right to tax themselves. The British found this line of reasoning very odd and wondered why these colonials saw themselves to be outside the laws that all other Englishmen must obey. The tax seemed so reasonable from the British perspective, that Benjamin Franklin, who was in London at the time, proposed John Hughes to be the tax collector in Philadelphia. Richard Henry Lee, of the famous Virginia Lee family, put himself forward as a candidate to become the stamp tax agent. He was not selected.[76] He then turned his energies against it.

To Americans, the willingness of the Parliament to ignore their protests and to pass a tax they saw as "unconstitutional," created a concern beyond the tax itself. The colonists argued that once they were firmly placed outside the protection of the law, then all their rights were in jeopardy. The progression of growing arbitrary power leading to high taxes, the growth of the military state, and loss of personal freedoms, had been taking place in other states in Europe for decades, so it was reasonable for the colonists to conclude that England was moving in a similar direction. They noticed that Parliament's policies had already brought on the rise of slavery in the colonies, and many people in America concluded that a government who promoted the enslavement of one group would soon turn to others.

During the period many observed this trend, and in an effort to encourage the spirit of the Revolution, Thomas Burke wrote, "No alternative was left to the Citizen but to rouse into a Soldier or Sink into a Slave and entail Servitude Irrevocably on his posterity."[77]

John Reynall, a Quaker gentleman, wrote, "the point in dispute is a very Important one, if the Americans are to be taxed by a Parliament where they are not nor can be Represented, they are no longer Englishmen but Slaves."[78]

Years later, an American commissioner exploring a peaceful settlement of the conflict wrote, in 1778, "I believe that to be bound by laws, to which he does not consent by himself or by his representative, is the direct definition of a slave. I do therefore believe, that a dependence on Great Britain, however the same may be limited or qualified, is utterly inconsistent with every idea of liberty…."[79]

William Hooper wrote to Joseph Hewes on the topics of funding the Army, when he stated, "Disband your Army & you are Slaves to a British Tyrant."[80]

The fact of slavery was present and vital to the people of America. It was not just rhetorical flourish to write about the topic, it was a real concern. With the freedom of every English citizen in the colonies apparently at risk, a group of prominent Philadelphia lawyers met at Mullin's Beef-Steak House on Water Street, and the conversation turned to the Stamp Act. A vote was taken on the subject, and only three lawyers voted to stand up against the tax. The rest, being members of the bar and by oath "officers of the court," voted to uphold the laws of England,[81] after all they could just pass the tax onto their customers. Additionally, the lawyers had knowledge of other taxes that had been passed by Parliament, but never collected, because the judges and juries were colonial and indisposed to rule against fellow colonists.

On the other hand, the merchants organized the local resistance to the Stamp Act. It occurred to the American merchants that the new funds would go to creating courts that would enforce the existing import tax laws, and they were far from happy about that. The end of the Seven Years War had resulted in reduced trade. With the local economy weakened, and their profit margins dwindling, they could not afford to see their livelihoods disappear with a tax that could make them lose money on every transaction. They formed a forty-member committee called the Merchants and Traders of Philadelphia. Thomas Willing and Morris both joined this group, and Willing became chairman. The Merchants communicated with the Massachusetts merchant-backed group, the Sons of Liberty,[82] and other concerned businessmen in the British Colonies, even as far as Bermuda. The techniques and relationships developed in this inter-colony association proved to be so successful that they were maintained, and eventually resulted in the creation of each colony's Committees of Correspondence, which over time developed into the Continental Congress. Many of the same people played active roles in all of these groups, but, as usual, after the merchants took a stand, the lawyers joined and eventually dominated the effort.

Taking cues from local merchants, there were violent protests in New England, which resulted in various Stamp Tax collectors' houses being destroyed and their possessions obliterated. Each event followed a pattern, wherein the likeness of the tax collector was hung in effigy, and then the next day his quarters were attacked. While the merchants were active behind the scenes, it was the laborers, and other lower middling types, who conducted the business of destruction.

In Philadelphia, public attention focused on John Hughes, the man who would be in control of the tax stamps. On the day the stamp ship arrived, muffled bells rang in towers around town. Bell ringers, sponsored by the Merchants and Traders Association, roamed the city streets of Philadelphia. Some of these bell ringers were people who worked as clerks in the merchant firms; others were the slaves of a few prominent merchants. This quiet noise brought a large crowd into the park behind the State House. A group of seven men emerged. This delegation went to John Hughes' home. Robert Morris acted as the spokesman for that small group, and he negotiated with Hughes.[83] Morris convinced Hughes not to distribute the abhorred stamps. Morris' arguments were compelling and supported by the crowd outside the State House, not far away. Later, Hughes wrote, "That if I did not immediately resign my office my house should be pulled down and my substance destroyed."[84] After a series of meetings with Hughes, the committee convinced him to send the hated, unused stamps, back to England.

The relationship between Thomas Willing's role as the chairman of the merchants' association, and Morris' role as street activist, reflects their respective positions within the company. Willing was the senior partner; and had been educated in London. He was elected Mayor of Philadelphia in 1763, and in the same year he married Anne McCall, a young lady from a prominent family. Willing served in the Pennsylvania Assembly from 1764 to 1767 and was making his way in society. Morris was a junior partner who never graduated from secondary school. He was a detail-oriented manager of the shipping concern, but apart from his affable nature and many friends, he had no family connections to bolster his fortunes. He did, however, have little Polly to support, and it was around this time that he took on the added burden of looking after his teen-aged half-brother, Thomas.

Thomas had been living with his mother in Maryland before Robert brought him to Philadelphia and paid for his schooling. Later, Robert tried to interest his half-brother in business. One can see Robert's own personal history, as a young teenager without parents, working within him as he tried to build a family and keep his loved ones close and cared for. With these personal arrangements, and his work in the rough and ready world of shipping, Robert was closer to the crowd in the street than to the political elite of the day. Unlike the elites, he could be seen, at times, in a leather apron, rolling barrels down his company's dock as he unloaded a newly arrived cargo. That was all about to change. In 1766, Governor Penn appointed Robert to be one of the wardens of the Port of Philadelphia. A port warden had the job of seeing that arriving ships went to the customs house, that departing ships also complied with the laws, and that the pilots were able to guide the ships to port. This position would soon put Robert into the middle of the action again, particularly considering the role Custom's House played in the tax system.

Basing their thinking purely on economic grounds, Parliament repealed the Stamp Act in 1766. American merchants owed over £4,400,000 to English suppliers,[85] and they refused to pay as long as the Stamp Act was in effect. The British sellers complained to their government. Parliament soon saw the nation was losing more in payments than they would make in the tax and canceled it. Americans were ready to go back to the way things were. However, the British felt they had to respond to the American rhetoric about Parliament's right to tax the colonies and passed the Declaratory Act, asserting the authority of Parliament over America. Americans saw that as a face saving move – and shrugged. John Townsend did not. He was the head of the British Board of Trade, and in 1767, he encouraged Parliament to pass a series of duties laid upon American ports known as the Townsend Acts, to which the Americans quickly objected.

Morris, as a Warden of the Port, supported Willing's effort to resist the Townsend Acts. Morris was in constant contact with ship owners, captains, and pilots, and so was in the perfect position to spread the word about a proposed, self-imposed embargo. Over fifty merchants signed the resulting Non-Importation Agreement of 1767, and it meant the cessation of all imports from the British Empire into Philadelphia and other American ports. As an organizer supporting this agreement, Morris became known as a local political leader from the business community. The public could see that by helping the resistance Morris was hurting his own economic interest, and this gave him credibility that could otherwise not be bought.

In Pennsylvania, the more radical citizens proposed forming a Committee of Inspection and Observation to enforce this ban. Ballots were drawn up and voted on. Morris was elected to this committee. He was a natural choice because he was already a warden of the port. The Non-Importation Agreements buffeted the fortunes of Willing, Morris & Co. In response, they became involved in a number of different lines of business. They acted as real estate agents, and then buyers and sellers of land.

Robert's star was rising in other ways as well. On March 2nd, 1769 he married Mary White, the daughter of a prominent Maryland family. Mary's brother, William White, would become the leader of the Episcopal Church in Pennsylvania. Mary was twenty at the time of their marriage. Robert was thirty-five, and an established merchant who was being accepted by more and more people in polite society. They lived in the thick of Philadelphia's merchant life, as they shared a row house on Front Street below Dock Street. It was less than two blocks from the Delaware River.

Mary Morris, etching by Hart after a miniature portrait by Trumbull

From their home they could see the masts and spars of the ships towering over the nearby roofs and hear the slapping of rigging in the wind. The rumble of heavily loaded wagons rolling over cobblestones was a familiar sound in the streets nearby. The damp smells of the river and passing horses added their unique contributions to the quality of life near the docks. Their first son, Robert, was born that year on December 19th, and he must have been seen as a fine Christmas present. Before the next year was over, Robert bought a farm along the Schuylkill River as a place for escape from the city, and a haven for his family. He called it "The Hills," and as time went on it was to be the scene of domestic bliss, careful cultivation, rare plants and animals, splendid dinner parties with famous guests, and ultimately, great trial.

Robert kept looking for opportunities to grow his business, and his family was growing as well. His second son, born in February 1771, was named Thomas after his maternal grandfather, Thomas White. In August of 1772, a third son, William, was born. William was named after Mary's brother, whom she called "Billy." During this period, Robert invested more into The Hills. There were barns, granaries, and even a house for a gardener. Robert bought the farm next door, and the estate grew to be over three hundred acres.

"The Hills," the favorite Residence of Robert Morris, on Lemon Hill.

Morris' property stretched from what is today Girard Avenue to the Art Museum, and from The Schuylkill River to Ridge Avenue. Modern Philadelphians would be amazed to see the bow front farmhouse and greenhouses overlooking the Schuylkill River, instead of the familiar sights of Henry Pratt's party house called Lemon Hill, and Boat House Row. They would also be surprised to learn that the earthwork ditch for the now abandoned train track running through the Spring Garden section of that city, was originally dug by the Canal Company of Delaware and Schuylkill,[86] in which he owned shares, as they attempted to connect the two rivers.

Tending to War

In 1770, the economic harm brought on by the Non-Importation Agreements was in everyone's mind. It became a badge of honor, and the mark of a patriot from the high born to the low, to use homespun clothing, instead of imports. At the same time, the presence of English soldiers in Massachusetts added insult to injury and resentment grew. On March 5th, a group of rowdy citizens left a local bar, and harassed a lone soldier who was stationed at the Boston Customs House. The sentry felt that he required assistance. He called for more troops and they arrived. This caused more citizens to gather around. Events spiraled out of control as the crowd threw snowballs and sticks at the soldiers. Then the soldiers fired on the crowd. They killed five people including Crispus Attucks, an escaped slave who was part of the violent mêlée. Paul Revere's illustration of the event was published, and the news about British soldiers shooting citizens spread far and wide. The British officer in charge was put on trial and found innocent. This outraged the citizenry who had their own opinions on the matter, opinions that were based on newspaper accounts, and not evidence presented at the trial. The radicals used the verdict to support their claims about British injustices.

Much has been made of the fact that John Adams was the lawyer who defended the unpopular soldier during the trial, mostly because of how uncomfortable he was made to feel. A certain variety of modern lawyer uses this effort of his as an example of an American heritage that requires the robust defense of even the lowest, most depraved and obviously guilty repeat offender. In fact, the right to council was put into the U.S. Constitution. What is routinely overlooked in such arguments is the fact that defending the soldier was like defending a policeman in today's America, because Massachusetts was still a colony and the soldiers were not across the battle lines, at the time.

Across the ocean, Parliament responded in 1770 to the Non-Importation Agreements by repealing all the Townsend Acts, except the tea tax. Ordinary trade started again with some tea smuggling now in the mix, but the slave trade did not restart in Philadelphia. Willing Morris & Co. remained active in the tea trade, however, and took on new consignments and shipments during this period.

Self-styled free trading colonial merchants, identified by some as smugglers, were not pleased that the tea tax survived. Sixty percent of the tea drunk in Massachusetts, and ninety percent coming to Philadelphia was brought in extra-legally,[87] so there was a strong incentive for the colonial merchants to resist a tea tax that was designed to rid the coast of tea smuggling. It was noted at the time, "Not until Parliament finally provided for stricter enforcement of the laws did the smugglers claim their activities to be patriotic. Then they succeeded in convincing the American public that their search for illegal profit was somehow part of the common fight for freedom."[88] This was possible because the merchants pointed out that the colonies would lose control of the local government as tea tax money was meant to pay the salaries of the royally appointed Governors and judges.[89] Radicals in Boston called this tyranny, and with the backing of merchants, they rejected the idea that Parliament had the authority to tax anything, and they were eager to make a dramatic point over the remaining tea tax. On December 16th, 1773 they dressed as Indians and boarded East India Tea Company

Boston Tea Party

ships. Then, they dumped three hundred forty-two chests of tea into the harbor. Hundreds of other Bostonians watched in silence.

The same point of protest was made differently in the Quaker City. Beginning in October, the Philadelphia citizens Committee for Tar and Feathering informed Delaware River pilots that if they helped the notorious tea ship *Polly* into the port, these pilots could expect a new coat of "pitch and feathers."[90, 91] On December 27th, 1773 the captain of the *Polly*, one Mr. Ayers, ignored the dangers and followed a second ship up the Delaware River without using a pilot. Ayers anchored the *Polly* away from port and rowed in from the ship. A crowd of 8,000, representing about thirty percent of the city's total population, met Captain Ayers when he came ashore. They were highly disciplined, including members of the "Committee for Tar and Feathering." The crowd parted to form a lane so the captain could attend a meeting at the State House.[92]

A committee of the Wardens of the Port, including Robert Morris, discussed the issue with Captain Ayers. He was informed that his ship was not to be received, but he could buy supplies for his return trip. This was enough to convince the good captain not to land his tea ship in Philadelphia. He turned the *Polly* from that port and returned to London, thus avoiding an incident similar to the Boston "Tea Party."[93] The participants must have recognized this as an episode where one tea merchant, Ayers' company, was being expelled from Philadelphia by at least one other tea merchant, Morris.

Primarily, the British thought it strange that the colonists refused to be taxed. Additionally, they were displeased and offended with the Philadelphians' disrespect for Captain Ayers, but they were openly hostile to the treatment meted out by the Bostonians, and their destruction of East India Company property. In an effort to isolate and selectively punish Massachusetts, they passed a set of legislation that effectively created an embargo on the port of Boston. Colonists throughout America were outraged by the Crown's behavior and dubbed the laws the "Intolerable Acts." Outrage has a way of creating more outrage. Much to the Crown's surprise, these Intolerable Acts caused the colonies to work more closely together; and resulted in the convening of the first Continental Congress in Philadelphia. In a show of support for Massachusetts, the Continental Congress agreed to protect that colony if it were attacked. This was the cauldron within which the violence in New England was brewed.

It was during this period that Achard de Bonvouloir visited Philadelphia. He was a minor noble Frenchman traveling from the French West Indies, through Philadelphia, to learn what was going on in the American Colonies. He was acting as a confidential informant (spy) for the King of France, who was interested in American intentions towards Canada. He met with members of the Congress before going to London to meet with the French Ambassador there. Congressmen thought they might be able to get some weaponry from France, using him as a channel. It seems he was transparent about the true nature of his work.

In response to the Intolerable Acts, the Continental Congress passed the second Non-Importation Agreement on Oct. 20, 1774. This time, the slave trade was explicitly mentioned. "We will neither import nor purchase any slave imported after the first day of December next; after which time, we will wholly discontinue the slave trade and will neither be concerned in it ourselves, nor will we hire our vessels, nor sell our commodities or manufactures to those who are concerned in it." The arrival of new slaves into Pennsylvania had been stopped, but there was an existing population of slaves in that state. The existence of the slave population had to be considered in light of the subsequent Declaration of Independence in 1776. Many in Pennsylvania thought it high hypocrisy to allow slavery under such a Declaration. It would take another four years before the Pennsylvania Act for the Gradual Abolition of Slavery was passed in 1780.

The second non-importation agreement had greater force than the earlier voluntary one, and farmers and merchants, up and down the Atlantic seaboard, felt its effect. For his part, Morris sought to bring this tax dispute to an acceptable, reasonable resolution. He wrote to his agent in Cadiz, "I recommend constantly a steady, manly, but decent and peaceful opposition is most likely to ensure success."[94] After all, peace brings prosperity, and he had a thriving business, property, as well as an extended family, which included three boys of his own, and in July of 1774 he saw the birth of his daughter, Hester, whom they called Hetty. In an effort to avoid war, Morris created a political connection to the pro-American Whigs in Parliament through one of his commercial contacts in England, Richard Champion of Bristol.

Like Morris, Richard Champion was a Whig and a merchant. He held the patent on a variety of porcelain and was a leader in that industry, competing successfully with German Meissen pottery, and the Wedgwood Company. Champion was also a Quaker, and active in politics. In 1774, Richard Champion revived the political fortunes of Edmund Burke when he supported Burke's re-election to a seat in the House of Commons. Burke had been Lord Rockingham's secretary in 1766. At that time, both he and Lord Rockingham sought the repeal of the Stamp Act and renewed peaceful commerce with America. Burke had held his seat in Parliament for eight years. However, in 1774, his sponsor, Lord Verney, decided not to back him, and until Champion stepped in, Burke expected to leave elected office that year. The election was close, and the loser protested Burke's victory but Burke won the seat in November 1774. Champion and Burke kept up a close personal relationship for years.

Richard Champion

These men, Burke, Champion, Willing and Morris, wanted to demonstrate that it was in the economic interest of both sides to reach a peaceful resolution to the grievances expressed by the colonies. On Jan 17th, 1775, Champion wrote to Morris, "I am glad that this first service of Mr. Burke to his friends here, should be of the first advantage to your house" [Willing, Morris and Co.][95] So, it was with Richard Champi-

Edmund Burke

on that Morris encouraged Edmund Burke to use his position and powers of persuasion in Parliament to reverse the king's course and make peace with the colonies.[96] Little encouragement was needed to convince Burke to take a course he believed to be correct. Unfortunately for England, this effort was rebuffed.

In February 1775, Champion wrote, "Burke's defense of America against the violent measures now carrying on and in support of the commercial interests of both countries, but in vain ... all our petitions have been treated with contempt."[97] One month later, in March, Edmund Burke delivered his famous speech, *"Conciliation with America."*

On March 6th, 1775, Richard Champion wrote to Morris: "Our representative Mr. Burke has exerted himself in the cause of the Colonies with a warmth, which becomes the dignity his publick, and the honesty of his private character and however wanting any of the Americans may have been in support of their own cause, every man who appeared in their defense here, was supporting in their persons the Liberties of the Whole Empire which cannot be constitutionally taxed without the consent of the people or their representatives. If a revenue is found in America it will only be used to strengthen the enormous power of the crown by adding to the list of Placemen and Pensioners."[98]

Morris' association with Champion yielded more than speeches in Parliament. Both men considered the king's actions to be illegal under English law, and believed it was important to defend the law for the benefit of all of the citizens of the British Empire. To that end, Champion acted as Morris' eyes and ears in 1775 and 1776, that is to say, up until the Declaration of Independence made it treasonous for Mr. Champion to provide intelligence to Americans.[99] Champion considered this when he wrote, "It will soon be very difficult to keep up correspondence, and if these violent measures encrease (sic), rather dangerous, as the letters in the post office are now opened."[100]

While Morris worked through intermediaries to avoid conflict, events were tending towards violence in Massachusetts. The Governor noticed the citizens were becoming agitated, so he sent a contingent of soldiers from Boston, through Lexington to Concord, to gather up the militia's stores of weapons and powder. Alarmed locals decided this step was meant to deprive them of their rights as free citizens. They confronted the soldiers, and on April 19th the "Shot heard around the world" was fired in Concord, Massachusetts. The British regulars felt the sting of the militia as the troops returned from Concord and Lexington, back to Boston.

The Battle of Lexington, Amos Doolittle engravings of the Battle of Lexington and Concord, December 1775, reprint by Charles E. Goodspeed, Boston, 1903

Three days later, April 23rd, was the day dedicated to the patron saint of England, St. George, and members of the Society of the Sons of St. George were meeting in the old City Tavern in Philadelphia. Robert Morris was a founding member of that philanthropic society which had been formed to help indigent Englishmen in America. He was the presiding officer that day, and just as Morris raised his glass to propose a toast, a messenger burst into the room with news of the fighting in Concord and Lexington. The festivities stopped abruptly. The hall emptied almost immediately. People rushed out, and in their hurry to leave, they knocked over the chairs and tables that stood in their way. A few close friends remained, including Morris and his good friend, Judge Richard Peters, who recalled the event to biographer Robert Waln, Jr. It was in that nearly vacant hall, among the disarray caused by the shocking news of the shootings in New England, this small band of men remained and pledged their energies to the Revolutionary cause.[101] Morris was forty-two years old. He was a married man with young children, and assets that could be seized by the British. It took his wife, Mary, some time to become happy with Robert's decision. Over the years, others wavered, but he never turned his back on that commitment. In June Morris wrote, "Poor America. This is the beginning of troubles, but it is better to die bravely, than to be starved by pickpockets."[102]

Across the Ocean

By 1775, Benjamin Franklin had been living in London for over fifteen years. There, he acted as Agent for the Colony of Massachusetts, wrote several influential broadsides, consulted with members of Parliament, and among other things, he represented a real estate company with interests in the lands west of the Appalachian Mountains. Shortly after news of the fighting reached him, he put his business interests aside and returned home. He arrived in Philadelphia on May 6th. Four days later, he joined Thomas Willing, John Hancock and the fifty-six others as members of the Second Continental Congress.

Among that fifty-six was Richard Henry Lee, a former candidate for stamp tax agent, and then current congressman from Virginia. Two of Richard's brothers stayed in London after Ben Franklin left. One, William Lee, was an aspiring merchant and alderman in the City of London. The other, Dr. Arthur Lee, was, like Franklin, a business agent for Massachusetts, but he also represented a land development company that competed with Franklin's. Arthur Lee had no fondness for Benjamin Franklin, and at one point, he expressed his frustration by saying that the only way he might advance in life would be if Franklin died.

Dr. Arthur Lee

The three Lee brothers were from the famous family of Virginia that owned over 30,000 acres of land. The fourth and eldest Lee brother, Philip, had the vast majority of the place because he inherited it through the laws of primogeniture. He stayed there, and he operated the plantation with the help of two hundred slaves. Arthur, however, was not included in that, and instead was educated in England at Eton. He gained his medical education at the University of Edinburgh in Scotland, and his law degree in London, after reading the law in London's Inns of Court. He was active in English politics and a follower of the "Real Whigs." The Real Whigs were the radical branch of the opposition party in England and were well known for their lively style of communications. Lee distinguished himself as a practitioner of this style with a series of political articles published in America and England under various pseudonyms. These pieces were well read in New England, and that work endeared him to the Whigs in that region. Arthur Lee was a regular correspondent with admiring friends, John and Samuel Adams.[103] In addition, he maintained his relationship with his brother, Richard Henry Lee, back in America. Unfortunately, Arthur's personality was difficult, and that made him unpopular with many of those with whom he worked in Europe.

While in London, he and his brother, William, gravitated towards the company of "Real Whig," John Wilkes. Wilkes was a notorious dissolute, a vulgar and popular demagogue who had supported the American stamp protests. At one point, his inflammatory rhetoric landed him in prison, which caused him not to be seated in Parliament, even though he had been elected. There was a citizen's movement to release him that gave strength to the idea of protecting the freedom of speech and the press. After he left prison, the Lee brothers did not abandon him, but many of his more influential backers did. They considered that he was more interested in himself than the Whiggish cause which he represented.[104] Wilkes, however, was still well regarded by "the common people in London." He was eventually seated and was also elected to be Lord Mayor of London. Wilkes also had the dubious, posthumous distinction of being the namesake for John Wilkes Booth, even though he was no relation.

Arthur Lee attended many gatherings at the home of John Wilkes, and there, he was introduced to Pierre Augustin Caron de Beaumarchais. Beaumarchais started his working life as a watchmaker, but he rose to prominence as a famous litigant, an arms merchant during the Seven Years War, confidant to the princesses of France, and as a playwright. He wrote, *The Barber of Seville*, and *The Marriage of Figaro*. He made enough money to purchase a position as a judge, and that entitled him as a French aristocrat, but he was not a noble by birth. During this period in London, Beaumarchais was acting as a secret agent for Louis XIV in the case of the mysterious Charles Geneviève d'Eon de Beaumont. D'Eon had been the head of the French Royal Dragoons and was one of the finest swordsmen in the realm, but seemed so feminine his masculinity was questionable. D'Eon had previously used this attribute in the service of King Louis when, in the guise of a woman, he befriended Catherine the Great, to the benefit of France. That was before he fell from royal favor.[105] Afterwards, D'Eon fled to England as the result of a failed blackmail scheme, and Beaumarchais followed, under cover. While there, Beaumarchais made an effort to take the pulse of the body politic in England and to learn more about the conflict with America. He became attracted to the mixed crowd around the Lord Mayor of London, John Wilkes. It was there he first met Arthur Lee.[106]

Beaumarchais became fascinated by the idea that the Americans were willing to stand up against an obviously superior foe. This seemed very brave to him in light of France's defeat during the Seven Years War, and it served as an example of the power of their righteousness. Contemporary French philosophers had written about the natural savage and the power of nature to instill virtue in man. Beaumarchais saw the Americans in a light of noble virtue, unsullied by Europe's overly sophisticated aristocratic past, filled with wars and the endless pursuit of luxury. He requested help for them from the king, but the king would not.[107] After all, Louis had signed a peace deal with England, not too long ago, and thought it bad form to go back on his word.

Rumblings of War

Across the ocean, war fever was spreading in the American colonies as militia style military actions were taken against the hated, so-called, standing army. The Green Mountain Boys, led by Benedict Arnold and Ethan Allen, used money supplied by Connecticut merchant, and Congressman, Silas Deane, in a successful campaign to capture Fort Ticonderoga on May 10th, 1775. The next day, in a related move in the New York's Champlain Valley, Allen and Seth Warner led the militia to victory in the Battle of Crown Point. Such successes by the militia gave life to the idea that a Revolution could be won quickly by the, more or less, spontaneous expression of popular resistance. This was before the British truly organized to confront the Americans.

The actual fighting was far away from Morris in Philadelphia. However, Morris was doing his part, via Champion, as he pursued life and business. By this time, Willing, Morris & Co. had become a leading shipping company, with over twenty ships,[108] and a network of agents in far flung ports. While Morris' influence on its operations increased, the firm grew. He moved from being a minority partner to the most active partner in the firm.[109] Before the Revolution broke out, Morris provided an overview of their situation, "It is known that besides our capital in trade we posses (sic) valuable landed estates, [and] that we are totally free from encumbrances."[110]

Willing, Morris & Co. also conducted financial transactions with a variety of people at this time, including women who participated in their business ventures. On June 2nd, 1775, they made a promissory note to a Mrs. Meredith.[111] This practice amounted to a method of providing women with an income derived from their assets, taken as a loan to the merchant concern. In other words, a bond. In this way, women could earn money on their capital and protect the principal through the note. The idea that women had property rights was not found everywhere in the colonies at this time.

During this period, Willing, Morris & Co. also started a bank, using their experience in the details of accounting associated with the shipping business.[112] This was before the Declaration of Independence, and both Willing and Morris were still British subjects. When the Crown learned that Willing, Morris & Co. was operating a bank, the bankers were forced to stop. Morris' wish for things to go back to normal, after the Seven Years War, and the tax protests, was unfulfilled. Instead, a pattern emerged that England was interfering more and more in the affairs of the citizens of the colonies, first in trade, and then in commercial relations. This added to the general concern that freedoms were eroding, and that trend was moving closer and closer to Morris' life.

With military activities underway in the northern colonies, the Continental Congress decided to choose a person to take control of the northern militias and lead them as a true army. They considered George Washington's experience in the French and Indian War, and his personal suitability for this important leadership job. Others wanted to lead the army themselves. Washington did not actively campaign for the job because doing that would seem ungentlemanly, pushy, and even ambitious. However, he did happen to appear in Congress dressed in his best military uniform, and by doing so he made it plain that he was ready for the job, if called. Congress appointed George Washington to be Commander in Chief of the Army on June 15th. Just two days later, the situation in Massachusetts tended to war with the militia under the influence of the radical leaders. Ten thousand Americans took on six thousand five hundred Brit-

The Death of General Warren at the Battle of Bunker Hill by Turnbull – 1786

ish Troops in the bloody Battle of Bunker Hill in Charlestown, Massachusetts. News of this violence spread throughout the colonies and resulted in states preparing themselves for British retaliation. As the states created their "Committees of Safety," Washington headed north to take command of the mixed militias in Cambridge, and to create a continental army.

Shortly after Washington headed north, and nearly a month after the action taken by the Green Mountain Boys, Morris was appointed to the Pennsylvania Committee of Safety. Benjamin Franklin was the senior member of that committee, and as such was the President of the group. Morris became Vice President. At first, his duty was to import arms and ammunition for the safety of the colony. During the next month, they built up a small gunboat navy by getting eighty rifles for boats to defend the Delaware River. Morris engaged Colonel Anthony Wayne and Captain Francis to be Minute Men on these riverboats.[113, 114*] The Committee of Safety went about the business of constructing the defenses for the city and state. They built up forts, organized the militia, and gathered together weapons. They devised a method of managing the river traffic with a chain and submerged obstacles to compel ships into a channel they controlled. These barriers were used to good effect and deterred the British Navy from attacking Philadelphia from the Delaware River.

Morris prepared for war, but he had also continued his efforts to make war unnecessary by supporting John Dickinson's "Olive Branch Petition." This petition was signed in July by members of Congress and taken to England by William Penn's grandson, on behalf of the colonies, one year before the Declaration of Independence. Penn stayed in England during the war and left behind his fine house at 190 High Street, which was generally understood to be the best house in town.

Endnotes

1. *The Archives of Maryland* V75, new preface 1
2. *Narrative of the Principal Incidents in the life of Jeremiah Banning, Written by Himself*, 1793
3. His ledger survives today in the Maryland Archives because, due to the scarcity of paper, the unused portion of the book was used as a fee book by the Clerk of the Court from 1762 to 1763 *Eleventh Annual Report of the Archivist of the Hall of Records*, FY 1946 V 448, pg. 26.
4. Colonel Jeremiah Banning's Journal
5. John Sanderson and Robert Waln, *Biography of the Signers*, 5:189-190
6. Ellis Paxson Oberholtzer, *Robert Morris: Patriot and Financier*, pg.3-4
7. Charles Rappleye, Robert Morris, *Financier of the American Revolution*, pg.8
8. Colonel Jeremiah Banning's Journal
9. Harlow Giles Unger, *Robert Morris - The patriot who paid for Washington's war*, pg18
10. *Biography of the Signers*, 5:191
11. Robert Morris Papers, Levis Collection, Historical Society of Pennsylvania, call #1957
12. Thomas M. Doerflinger, *A Vigorous Spirit of Enterprise*, pg.140
13. Ibid, 130-131
14. Ibid, pg. 65
15. Ibid, pg. 40
16. Jeremiah Wadsworth, *Federalist Entrepreneur* p.73 n1, ref Rappleye pg. 15
17. *A Vigorous Spirit of Enterprise*, pg. 59
18. Rappleye, pg. 26 ref. *Deane Papers*, 4:34
19. Rappleye, pg. 15
20. Charles Willing & Son Letterbook 1754-1761, pg. 171 Historical Society of Pennsylvania, Call # AM.9320
21. Clarence L. Ver Steeg, *Robert Morris, Revolutionary Financier: With an Analysis of His Earlier Career*, pg. 3
22. Oberholtzer, pg. 9
23. Ver Steeg, pg.4
24. *Documents Illustrative of the Slave Trade*, 3:454
25. *Documents Illustrative of the Slave Trade*, 2:474-485
26. *Thomas Jefferson, June 1776, Rough Draft of the Declaration of Independence, Library of Congress*, Microfilm Reel: 001, Series 1: General Correspondence. 1651-1827
27. Pennsylvania Magazine of History and Biography (PMHB), Historical Society of Pennsylvania (HSP), 97:43
28. *Pennsylvania Gazette*, items # 25284, 26076, 26206, 26565, 28558, 28712, 36325
29. *Documents Illustrative of the Slave Trade*, 3:454
30. Adam Smith, *Wealth of Nations*, pg. 851
31. *Documents Illustrative of the Slave Trade to America*, 2:579-580
32. *The Trans-Atlantic Slave Trade* CD-ROM
33. *Pennsylvania Gazette*, June 3, 1762
34. *The Trans-Atlantic Slave Trade* CD-ROM
35. The Trans-Atlantic Slave Trade CD-ROM
36. *Pennsylvania Gazette*, July 25, 1765
37. *The Trans-Atlantic Slave Trade* CD-ROM
38. *Pennsylvania Gazette* of January 23, 1772
39. *Naval Documents of the American Revolution*, 3:1336
40. Account of the Property of Robert Morris—By Himself, pg. 19-20
41. *Records of the Supreme Executive Council*, reel 37, frames 160-161
42. Polly was no stranger to Robert's second family. His son was named a trustee of the estate.
43. The Trans-Atlantic Slave Trade CD-ROM
44. *The Trans-Atlantic Slave Trade* CD-ROM
45. *Documents Illustrative of the Slave Trade* 3:455-6
46. *Pennsylvania Gaze* item #27079
47. *The Trans-Atlantic Slave Trade* CD-ROM
48. *Pennsylvania Gazette* item #27406
49. *The Trans-Atlantic Slave Trade* CD-ROM
50. *Pennsylvania Gazette* item #16642
51. *Documents Illustrative of the Slave Trade*, 3:455
52. *The Trans-Atlantic Slave Trade* CD-ROM
53. *Documents Illustrative of the Slave Trade*, 3:209
54. PMHB 88:52
55. *The Trans-Atlantic Slave Trade* CD-ROM
56. *The Trans-Atlantic Slave Trade* CD-ROM
57. *The Trans-Atlantic Slave Trade* CD-ROM
58. *Documents Illustrative of the Slave Trade to America*, 3:409
59. PMHB 97:43
60. *Documents Illustrative of the Slave Trade to America*, 3:73
61. *Documents Illustrative of the Slave Trade to America*, 3:217-245

62. http://www.earlyamerica.com/earlyamerica/milestones/nonimport/text.html
63. Louis W. Potts. *American National Biography Online*
64. Nearly twenty-five years later however, when the Quakers petitioned Congress to abolish slavery throughout America, it was the same Arthur Lee who led the committee that refused the petition.
65. *Documents Illustrative of the Slave Trade to America*, 4: 157
66. *Documents Illustrative of the Slave Trade to America*, 4:244
67. Ibid 4:415
68. Ibid, 4:433
69. Ibid, 3:168-170; 4:241, 386, 387
70. Edward Ball, *Slaves in the family*, pg.428
71. *Documents Illustrative of the Slave Trade to America,* 4:415
72. Ibid, 4:468
73. Ibid, 4:440
74. Ibid, 4:471
75. Documents Illustrative of the Slave Trade to America, 4:237
76. Rappleye, pg. 156
77. *Letters of the Delegates to Congress*, 7:147
78. *A Vigorous Spirit of Enterprise*, pg. 181
79. *Letters of the Delegates to Congress*, 10:162
80. *Letters of the Delegates to Congress*, 5:521
81. *Biography of the Signers*, 5:193-194
82. American Philosophical Society (APS) 973.2 M31 V1
83. Charles Henry Hart PHMB V1 ref. Hughes' Letters in "2 Hazard's Register, 247"
84. American Philosophical Society (APS) 973.2 M31 V1, Folio 13
85. Theodore Draper, *A Struggle for Power: The American Revolution*, pg. 341
86. Morris' Account, pg. 72
87. *Struggle for Power* pg. 390
88. Ibid, pg. 393
89. Ibid, pg. 379
90. Pennsylvania Gazette, Nov. 27, 1773
91. Pennsylvania Magazine of History and Biography, XV:390-391
92. History of Delaware County, Pennsylvania, pg. 39
93. Eleanor May Young, Forgotten Patriot: Robert Morris, pg. 27-28
94. Rappleye pg. 28.
95. Richard Champion, pg. 39-40
96. Richard Champion, pg. 55
97. Richard Champion, p. 43
98. *Naval Documents of the American Revolution*, 1:422-424
99. *Naval Documents of the American Revolution*, 1:382, 385
100. Richard Champion, pg. 62
101. *Biography of the Signers,* 5:196-197
102. Rappleye, pg. 26
103. *American National Biography Online* http://www.anb.org/articles/01/01-00505.html
104. *Richard Champion*, pg. 49-50
105. Georges Lemaitre, *Beaumarchais*, pg. 161-163
106. *Revolutionary Diplomatic Correspondence*, 1:520
107. *Beaumarchais*, 175-179
108. *Morris Papers* Levis collection Historical Society of Pennsylvania (HSP), call #1957
109. Ver Steeg, pg. 4
110. C. Ver Steeg pg. 5 , ref. *Morris Papers* NYPL
111. HSP Lewis Collection, Willing and Morris Business Papers, 1756-1777
112. Robert E. Wright, *The First Wall St*, pg. 27
113. Minutes of the Pennsylvania Committee of Safety
114. * Shortly before this, Anthony Wayne had been a leading member of the Chester County Committee of Safety when he signed a letter questioning the basis for slavery in light of the state's pursuit of liberty. Private Collection.

II

Into the Continental Congress

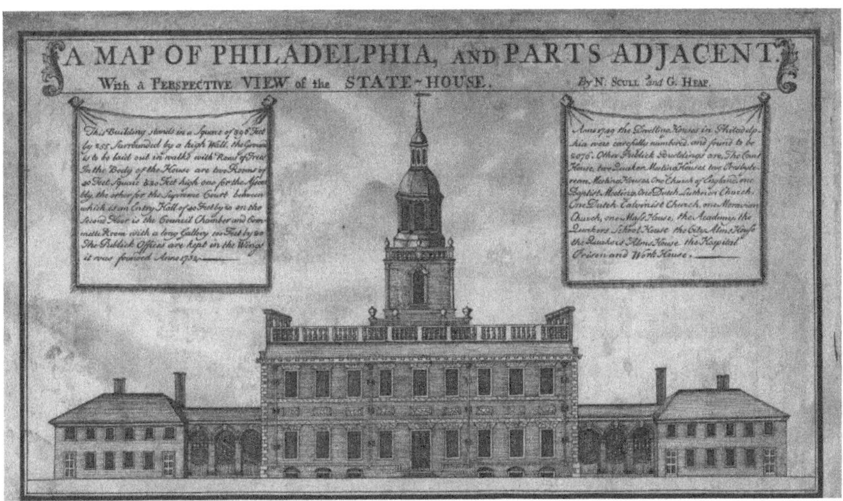

The elected leaders of the separate colonies sent their representatives to Philadelphia. However, those colonial assemblies saw the Continental Congress as an organizing committee created to coordinate state efforts to confront the British, not as a governing body. Often, the congressmen in Philadelphia operated under instructions from their home legislatures and had little latitude in their actions. The questions for Continental Congress quickly became: can such a committee have an army? A navy? Does it have the power to incorporate businesses? Can it have the power to tax? Taking a cue from Franklin's 1754 Albany Plan, the question of an army was quickly settled in the affirmative, but there were members who disagreed and worked during the war to undermine it. The other questions, such as the existence of executive administrators, dogged the Continental Congress for years, and the lack of resolution hampered the war effort.

In 1775, the Continental Congress delegated tasks to subcommittees; each was made up of elected members. Some were formed for special purposes, like drafting a document. Others were formed to conduct long-standing business, like the Board of War. Sub-committees always reported their group decision and were directed to action by Congress. For this reason, it is often difficult to attribute the actions taken by a committee to one individual. Democratic impulses of the day caused people to stay away from individualism in government. It can also be said that such anonymity shielded the members in the event the rebellion failed.

General Washington was not one to hide within the committee structure, and on July 2nd, 1775, he arrived in Cambridge to take command of the mixed militias that had gathered there. He marked the beginning of the Continental Army when he informed the soldiers that they "are now Troops of the United Provinces of North America."[1] Horatio Gates was at his side as adjutant general.

Back in Philadelphia, the Continental Congress anticipated more military action, and resolved on the 15th to encourage citizens to procure gunpowder.[2] Morris and Franklin responded by organizing the first covert action in the history of the United States. They put their plan into motion when they arranged to trade flour for gunpowder with Colonel Henry Tucker of Bermuda. Bermuda was an English colony at the time, and on equal footing with the fractious colonies on the east coast of the American mainland. Ezekiel Hopkins, a Rhode Islander, and former slave ship captain, was chosen to command the lead ship because of his success as a privateer captain during the Seven Years War.

A month after the resolution, Morris loaded two ships with his flour. Captain Hopkins, and a second American vessel, sailed to a rendezvous off the coast of Bermuda. There they met with Colonel Tucker's men. At night the party went ashore and raided the arsenal. A sailor was lowered by rope through a skylight in the roof, and after the sailor opened the doors, the waiting crew rolled barrels of gunpowder down to the dock and onto the rowboats. 1800 pounds of powder were quickly and quietly transported to the American ships.[3] In return for Tucker's assistance, Congress created exemptions in the Non-Importation Agreements that allowed Bermuda to continue receiving necessary food supplies from America. Twelve days later, the powder was ready to use in Charleston, South Carolina. The rest was shipped to Philadelphia, but little went to Washington's army in New England.

Once the materials had been delivered, it came time for Congress to pay, but they objected to the price. It may be noted, however, none of them had taken the risk. After the job was done it was easy to complain about the details and judge with the benefit of hindsight. For those in Congress who had been unfamiliar with Morris, this small controversy served as the basis of a first impression of him. Understandably, their conclusions matched their existing prejudices. To some he was seen as an upstart merchant who was motivated principally by profit, instead of appearing as a bold and enterprising patriot who did what they could not.

Congress eventually put aside the pricing squabble, and in an effort to control future costs, they entered into their first official government contract with Willing, Morris and Co. The merchants agreed to supply twelve six-pound brass guns, a thousand barrels of gunpowder, and "muskets & bayonets & five thousand gunlocks double bridled."[4]

With a few war supplies in hand, Congress moved ahead with plans to enlist Canadian support for the revolt, by military means if necessary. In late summer 1775, Generals Philip Schuyler and Richard Montgomery went from Crown Point in New York's Champlain Valley to Canada. Later, General Arnold and his contingent met up with them to reinforce that campaign.

A Deepening Commitment

Under the volunteer leadership of Franklin and Morris, the Pennsylvania Committee of Safety continued with its local military preparations. In August, they outfitted the armed galley *Franklin* to defend the Delaware River, and put Captain Nicholas Biddle in command. This was the first of Biddle's naval assignments.[5] Morris' commitment to the cause expanded in October 1775, when he was elected to the Pennsylvania Assembly, and became the President of the Pennsylvania Committee of Safety.[6] Morris' friends advised him against a political career. They felt he did not have a predisposition to politics, since he was a man who preferred action to debate. They also thought his open and direct nature put him at a disadvantage in his dealings with others who favored political infighting, called "intrigues" in those days. While his conduct was never mean, Morris often grew impatient with the endless debates that led nowhere, and with protocols that delayed necessary steps instead of facilitating them.

Morris was a member of the Pennsylvania Assembly when the Continental Congress formed the first Marine Committee to outfit ships of war. There were three members for that committee, all were New Englanders chosen from the ranks of Congress: John Adams, John Langdon, and Silas Deane, who acted as chairman.

Morris was no stranger to the uses of ships to advance the effort. The previous spring, before the approaching war made trade impossible, Morris combined commerce and patriotism when he sent his best ship, *The*

Black Prince, to England on one last trading mission. Captain John Barry had sailed her to England, for Willing, Morris & Co, on May 7th. The *Black Prince* arrived in Bristol in June. Morris had rushed the ship from the port of Philadelphia, but then the ship sat in Bristol for over a month before it was time to ship out, on August 10th. Barry arrived back in Philadelphia on the 13th of October 1775. He carried critical intelligence that two unarmed brigantines were coming from England with war supplies. This news confirmed earlier reports about the same shipment.[7] The circumstances indicate that the source of this intelligence was Richard Champion, who had pledged to keep Morris informed of political and military developments as he became aware of them.[8]

On the day The *Black Prince* brought the news to the Continental Congress, it was learned that Washington had already built up a small fleet of three schooners in New England. With the urgings of the Marine Committee, Congress resolved to configure, or "fit out" two ships of war, and seize the unarmed British brigantines. One of the American ships was the *Lexington.*[9] Congress did not, at this point, vote to build a Continental Navy, but rather to control state vessels by virtue of paying for their conversion to warships.

Two weeks later, Congress decided it needed more ships and they did not have to look far because Willing, Morris & Co. had the use of over twenty. On November 3rd, the Pennsylvania Assembly elected Morris to the Continental Congress. Within a fortnight, the Continental Congress appointed Morris, Benjamin Franklin and Thomas Lynch to the Marine Committee to provide vessels for the cause, to get one ready to sail as soon as possible, and to devise ways and means for employing them.[10] The next day, Morris sold his finest ship, *The Black Prince,* to Congress. It was renamed the *Alfred* and became the first ship in the newly created Continental Navy,[11] and the first ship used by the U.S. Marines.

Later that same month, Morris sold another of his ships, *Sally,* to Congress. The ship, *Sally,* was renamed *Columbus,* and it joined the core of the new Navy.[12] The other two ships in the first four, which were renamed the *Cabot* and the *Andrew Doria,* had been owned by the Browns of Providence.[13,14*,15**]

In November, as the *Alfred* lay attached to the Willing & Morris wharf, John Barry was put in charge of converting the merchant vessels *The Lexington, Alfred,* and *Columbus,* into warships. Barry's efforts won him wide acclaim, and in some circles earned him the title, "Father of the Navy."

Continental Ship *Alfred* (1775-1778) Painting in oils by W. Nowland Van Powell. Courtesy of the U.S. Navy Art Collection, Washington, D.C.

On November 28th, one member of Washington's makeshift New England fleet used a clever subterfuge to capture the British ordinance brig, *Nancy*, without firing a shot. Captain Manley approached this ship and pretended to be a pilot who would guide that ship into the port of Boston. Once aboard, the Americans commandeered the ship,[16] and took possession of a vast array of weapons, but no gunpowder. The other two ships in Washington's small fleet did not fare as well, and caused the General much vexation, particularly the one commanded by Captain Broughton who found American merchant ships easier prey than Royal Navy ships.[17]

Morris continued to look for a peaceful resolution to the disagreement with Britain. On December 9th, 1775, he sent a letter and two newspaper articles to Josiah Hardy, the British Consul at Cadiz, Spain. He tried to explain that the citizens of America were being forced to fight for their rights but would be pleased to be at peace with England if the crown would only treat them like English citizens. Morris wrote,

> They do not act against Great Britain until drove to it by some apparent necessity.... We love the people of England. We wanted no other Friends, no other Allys, but alas if they cannot be content to Consider Us as Brothers entitled to the same freedom, the same privileges themselves enjoy, they cannot expect a people descended from their own flesh & blood, long Used to & well acquainted with the blessings of freedom, to sit down tamely & see themselves stripd of all they hold dear. For my part I abhor the Name & Idea of a Rebel, I neither

> want or wish a Change of King or Constitution, & do not conceive myself to act against either when I join America in defense of Constitutional Liberty. I am now a Member of the Continental Congress & if I have any influence or should hereafter gain any it shall be exerted in favour of every measure that has a tendency to procure Accommodation on terms consistent with our just Claims & if I thought there was any thing ask'd on this side not founded in the Constitution in Reason & Justice I wou'd oppose it..[18]

Morris kept appealing for a peaceful resolution, based on the recognition by the Crown that Americans have the same rights as other Englishmen. In the interim, he prepared for a conflict he hoped would never come.

Peace overtures notwithstanding, on December 9th, 1775, Richard Champion provided Morris with key pieces of new information that had been shipped over to America, stuffed in the bottom of a bread barrel. First was the Prohibitory Act. This act was passed in response to the formation of the Continental Congress and their resolve to act as one in defense of Massachusetts. By creating that unity, they became as liable as the one state had been. It embargoed all the colonies, so it prohibited commerce between the colonies and the rest of the British Empire, and to enforce this, it allowed the British to attack American ships, and to close their ports by force.[19] This looked a lot like a promise of war, but there was a sweetener. There was the mention of a peace commission that would arrive to discuss ways to end the conflict. Morris put his hopes into that idea.

Champion also wrote to Morris about large armed British contingents being sent to America to enforce the new Act, "The whole force is to 26,000 men including those now in America ..." He went on to say the new troops would be deployed to New York, Virginia, and South Carolina, "perhaps 8, 6, & 4,000 men to these places, but the numbers are not ascertained though they will be strong bodies."[20] This information proved to be very useful in organizing defenses for American cities. It was because of this letter that Fort Moultrie was made ready for the British attack that came six months later, in June 1776.

Also in December 1775, Congress' Committee of Secret Correspondence made Arthur Lee a secret agent in London.[21] Unfortunately, Lee was unable to confirm Morris' information. Lee maintained the British were sending soldiers to Quebec and Albany.[22] A British spy, who was in Lee's employ as a secretary, had apparently duped him. Little has been made of the fact that Morris was correct and Lee was not, yet it would be reasonable to conclude the distinction was not forgotten by Arthur Lee, who esteemed his own reputation very highly.

Congress continued to add work to Morris' plate. On December 11th, he was chosen to be a member of a committee "to devise ways and means for furnishing these colonies with a naval armament, and report with all convenient speed."[23] On the same day, the Pennsylvania Committee of Safety directed "Messrs. Willing and Morris & Co, to load the ship Neptune, Robert Collins, master, with the produce of these Colonies, for the purpose of procuring said articles [Powder, Arms, &c,] from foreign parts."[24] These two resolutions were aimed at the same goal, and they reflect the relationship between Congress making its wishes known on the one hand, and the states taking action on the other. Morris was also commissioned to negotiate bills of exchange for Congress, and to borrow money for the Marine Committee.[25] In negotiating bills of exchange for Congress, Morris was attempting to withdraw American funds from British banks before such transfers became impossible.

Onto the Secret Committee

The Secret Committee, sometimes called the Committee of Secret Commerce, was created to procure war supplies; pay for them; and to distribute them. It started operation in September 1775, under the leadership of Samuel Ward of Rhode Island, a colony with a storied past as a smugglers' haven. On December 18th of that year, Morris joined the committee.[26] Samuel Ward died of smallpox three months later, in March 1776, and Morris was made chairman.[27] Other members included Thomas McKean, Josiah Bartlett, Benjamin Franklin, and Richard Henry Lee, none of whom had ships or other means to conduct the secret war trade.[28] Joseph Hewes, a merchant from South Carolina, joined the Secret Committee in January 1776. After working there for a while he wrote, "There are but few merchants in that Assembly, which makes that kind of business fall heavy on Mr. Morris & myself."[29]

To do its work, the committee contracted with a variety of merchants in different states. Those agreements were among the few acceptable ways that merchants could conduct trade under the existing non-importation acts. Alternatively, merchants might be granted a special charter to trade on their own accounts.[30] Naturally, this system favored patriot merchants, and those within political circles, while it punished the Tories. Included in the list of contractors were Nicholas and John Brown[31] and Ezekiel Hopkins, of Rhode Island.[32] Alexander Gillon, member of the South Carolina Provincial Congress,[33] Nathaniel Shaw, Jr., member of the New London Committee of Correspondence,[34] Thomas Mumford, of New London, Connecticut,[35] Johann Philip Merkle, of New York,[36] Button Gwinnett, of Georgia,[37] Silas and Barnabas Deane, of Connecticut[38], John Langdon, of New Hampshire,[39] Philip Livingston, of New York,[40] Samuel Mifflin and George Clymer,[41] the brothers Chevalier,[42] Thomas York,[43] John Brown,[44] John Ross,[45] and Blair McClenachan,[46] and Willing Morris & Co.,[47] all from Philadelphia. Among those who were not included was Tory merchant, David Franks of Philadelphia.

The operating agreements provided the ship owners with a payment for each month the boat was in Continental service. In one such contract, James King and Joseph Harper of Philadelphia received £120 Pennsylvania pounds (or $329) per month for the use of their *"one hundred tonne"* brigantine. There was no mention of payments for the crew. In some other arrangements, merchants got a fee per hogshead, or by the barrel.[48] The Congress also agreed to insure the voyages and reimburse the owner if the ship was sunk or captured. Ships were rated differently; one at £650,[49] another at £5,000 and another at £3,000.[50] Sometimes Congress would insure only half the value of the ship.[51] All operating costs were to come from the monthly amount as set out in the deal, but any money paid was deducted from the value of a ship that was lost. Commissions of 2.5%, and sometimes 5% were due to the merchants for successful transactions, as Congress utilized the credit and trading networks of private individuals in the effort to acquire war materials.[52] Clearly, the road to riches was not paved in 2.5% commissions, but merchants were happy to undertake the public work as a means of staying in business because it allowed them to operate under the existing self-imposed embargo. The merchants mixed public and private cargoes in the same shipment because the volume of public goods was often not sufficient to underwrite the voyage. They still had to face the British embargo on the open sea.

Other links in the supply chain also operated with commission agents. They were employed in the commissary and quartermaster corps to purchase goods from local farmers and distribute them to the army. There was no money for any other course of action. Congress had no way of hiring merchants who could make more money elsewhere, and most Congressmen did not have the skills themselves to conduct the business. These conditions forced all the leaders, including the more radical ones: McKean, the Lees, and the Adams', to rely on merchants, even if they did not fully trust them to put the public good ahead of personal gain. Patriotic Congressmen naturally thought they should be treated with special favor, and because they were generally ignorant of the merchant's ways, they suspected that every merchant was cheating them. Adams wrote, "When almost every public department among you is filled, as I am informed, with men of rapacious principles, who sacrifice the common weal to their private emolument...what good can be expected from the wisest institution."[53]

In some cases, this suspicion was well founded, but not always. During the years Henry Laurens headed the Congress, 1778 and 1779, Congress spent millions. It was feared that half of that was lost to fraud and pricing irregularities. As time progressed there were investigations, but, somehow, they always focused on those who favored nationalism over parochial control. The Dean brothers, Thomas Mifflin, Benedict Arnold, Nathaniel Greene, Jonathan Trumbull, Jeremiah Wadsworth, William Shippen, and later Robert Morris were all made suspect, while Virginia merchant William Lee, for example, was never questioned. Oddly, Congress never investigated a single farmer for overcharging. This was not for lack of opportunity. In the minds of some congressmen, the only way for a merchant to prove his virtue was to die in poverty. On the death of one merchant a congressman observed that, "the deceased ... is represented to be of fair Reputation, and that he died in low Circumstances; which are presumptions that there has been no embezzlement of the stores purchased or received by him."[54]

In actuality, merchants lived and died based on their personal credibility in trade. They used their ordinary modes of business in their efforts to provide war supplies. They treated Congress like any other customer when they loaded goods and financed voyages. This was their version of fairness. It was also common for these private men of business to finance a government cargo, in anticipation of repayment if the goods were needed and cash was in short supply.[55] The landed gentry in Congress relied on the merchants for the ships, credit, and contacts that provided the only lifeline for the Revolution, but they were still not satisfied with them. Reacting to Congressional complaints one merchant grumbled, "Such is the cursed disingenuity and ingratitude of mankind, that after a man has sacrificed his time and fortune in serving them they'll declare they have been cheated, though it's impossible to tell how."[56]

Morris put these prejudices aside and worked to drum up support for the Revolution. As a leading merchant he had much to lose by working with the rebels, however he had given his word, so he used his most persuasive techniques to convince other people to aid the effort. He addressed each individual according to the motivations of the recipient. Morris wrote to some merchants to encourage them to risk their ships and sailors as part of the war against British commerce. When he discussed this, he often did so in terms of the potential profit that would come from success. Neither Morris nor other merchants saw a conflict of interest in this kind of appeal; rather they believed that individuals should be encouraged to help and be rewarded for that.

These appeals were not always about money. In a letter dated January 30th, 1776, six months before independence was declared, Morris attempted to convince Samuel Inglis to take up the rebel cause by appealing to him on the basis of shared values. Morris stated that his choice to back the rebels was made on the principle that the Colonies were in the right. He encouraged Inglis to make the same decision on the same basis and take the same risks. "For my part I considered this Subject early & fixed on principle the part I should take in the unhappy Contest. I sided with this Country because their claims are founded in Justice and I wish every Friend to the American Cause may act on the same principle that every Tory wou'd consider it well before they act against it, but I doubt [think] your Friends have only thought the Power of Great Britain insurmountable & founded their Conduct on that belief. This I believe to be the case with most of the Tories in America."[57] Years later, Samuel Inglis became a partner in a firm called Willing, Morris and Inglis.

To Build a Navy

"Preparation for WAR to defend Commerce." Etching by William Birch.

The late fall weather of 1775 had not been kind to the Continentals in the field, and neither had the British. Generals Schuyler's, Montgomery's, and Arnold's bold northern campaign had been under way for months, but it failed in December when their joint colonial forces were repelled in Québec City. Arnold's bitter cold trudge up the Kennebec River Valley and through northern Maine, was for naught. They retreated through New York State. British troops, under General Guy Carleton, followed the American forces south, and harassed them as the Americans returned to their stronghold in Crown Point.

In mid-December, Congress authorized the construction of thirteen frigates for the Continental Navy, and Morris was put in charge of building four of them in Philadelphia. It was Morris' habit to ask for bids from contractors before the work was to begin, and Joshua Humphreys' firm won the job on all four.[58] Humphreys' association with Morris lasted many years and continued up to the time, almost twenty years later, when he supplied Morris with the designs for the first six ships in the United States Navy, including the designs for the *USS Constitution*, after and forever known as "Old Ironsides."

In the wisdom of the Marine Committee the construction of the thirteen frigates was dispersed among the colonies of New York, Connecticut, Massachusetts, Maryland, the Carolinas, and Pennsylvania. As it turned out, this was a very good move for several reasons. The economic benefits were spread among the colonies. The work could be accomplished more quickly because it was set out to different locations. Finally, the British would not be able to stop the project completely by seizing one city. Unfortunately, it turned out that many of these ships, particularly those to northeast of the Hudson, languished in an unfinished state so long that they were lost to the cause without ever firing a shot. Several of those shipyards were so busy churning out privateering ships for owners who had ready cash, they were slow to do work for a far away, and nearly broke Congress. One New England foundry preferred to make cannons for its owners, who ran privateers, instead of filling Continental orders.[59] From the start, however, the Continental Navy was expected to enlarge itself through taking prizes at sea, to protect the merchant ships conducting the war trade, and to project American authority into European waters.

December 12th The Marine Committee moved ahead to get the existing ships to sea, and John Barry was commissioned to be the captain of the *Lexington*. Congress cleared Morris to: "fit out armed vessels,[and] be authorized to give able-bodied seaman that may be willing enter on board the ships of war of the United Colonies, eight dollar per calendar month."[60] At this time, when the Americans were hiring seamen to serve at their own free will, the British were impressing sailors, which meant the English sailors were actually being kidnapped and forced to work on warships.

A week later Esek Hopkins was made Commander in Chief of the Navy, but generally, finding the good captains was difficult. Morris described the characteristics he sought, "You will please to employ a Sprightly, Active, Sensible Man that is faithfully attached to the Interest of America to go Master of this Vessell, a Man of Spirit he should be because we shall direct her to be armed..."[61] Soon, a man fitting that description showed up on the scene, John Paul Jones.

The frigate construction project took much longer to complete than expected. In addition to the funding problems, there was a severe manpower shortage caused by the need for troops in the militia, and for troops to fill the state commitments to the Continental Army. The Philadelphia frigates were not finished by March, so when Congress needed a fast ship Morris sold them another one of his own, the *Molly,* which had been named after Morris' wife, Mary. That ship, a one hundred foot brig, was renamed *The Reprisal,* and put under the command of Captain Lambert Wickes. Wickes had formerly sailed this same ship for Willing, Morris & Co. so he knew her well. *The Reprisal* sailed from Philadelphia in June 1776 to take Mr. William Bingham to Martinique, and return with weapons of war. She met up with *Lexington,* under the command of John Barry. During that voyage they assisted the Continental brig, *Nancy,* which was being pursued by six British men-of-war, to deliver 200 barrels of gunpowder to the Americans. The *Nancy* was beached, unloaded to the *Lexington,* and blown up on shore as a booby trap to foil the British sailors who tried to seize the landed hulk. Captain Wickes lost his brother in the episode.

The Continental Congress worked to build a national naval force, but the states that were supposed to supply the funds were content with their own locally controlled and deployed fleets. Eleven of the states had their own navies; in fact, the *Lexington* was a Maryland ship, even though the Congress took command of her by virtue of their role in funding her acquisition. These state navies were independent from Congressional influences and jealously guarded by their local governments. It was not unusual for the ships of these navies to stay within their own waters, even when they may have been useful elsewhere.

One of the main challenges that faced the Continental Navy was Congress itself. Some members of Congress thought that a standing army was against their Republican Principles, and they saw the Continental Navy in

The Lexington, Drawn by F. Muller, National Archives, ARC ID 513013

the same light. Taking on the political perspective of the lords and barons of medieval England they revived the old Country Party arguments and contended that their local militias would spontaneously arise as needed and this was adequate to fight the British Army. Similarly, they thought that a series of state controlled "gunboat navies" would be sufficient to defend the American Coast against the British Navy, because these navies would be run by the states for their own protection. The more nationalist position was advanced to the contrary. The nationalists argued that military activity on land or sea, without coordination, would waste their efforts and would lead, at best, to uneven results. These philosophical discussions stood in the way of the practical business of supplying the army, building the navy, winning the war, and unifying the nation. The people who were wary of creating a national power structure in North America thought that would interfere with their intention of being rulers of their own states.[62] However, they admitted that collaboration between states was a necessity in a time of trial.

Congress may well have been advised to take a lesson from the Continental Army and work together for better results. In one such teaching moment, on March 17, 1776, Washington and his army positioned forty-seven cannons on Dorchester Heights. These heavy field pieces had been dragged hundreds of miles through the wilderness, with little more than grit and dreams of liberty to fuel the men. One can only imagine the surprise of the British in Boston, when they faced the guns that had been captured at Ticonderoga, almost a year earlier. This show of strength was so convincing that the British evacuated Boston Harbor. Lucky thing too, Washington had the cannons, but did not have the gunpowder to fire them. General Washington had taken to filling barrels with sawdust to fool his own troops into thinking they had the gunpowder they needed. Unfortunately, no matter how heroic that effort was, forty-seven cannons would not be enough to fight the British Empire in an eight-year war.

On April 6th Morris wrote to Washington's adjutant, Horatio Gates, to congratulate him on the removal of General William Howe from Boston. "I do most sincerely congratulate you on that important Event, and altho my Scenes of Action are in another line, I almost envy every one of you that share the Glory of driving them from their den.[63] Morris went on to express his desire for a peaceful resolution as he hung his hopes on a promised peace commission, "Where the plague are these Commissioners, if they are to come what is it that detains them; it is time we should be on a Certainty & know positively whether the Liberties of America can be established & Secured by reconciliation, or whether we must totally renounce Connection with Great Britain & fight our way to a total Independence. Whilst we Continue thus firmly United amongst ourselves there's no doubt but either of these points may be carried, but it seems to me, We shall quarrel about which of these roads is best to pursue unless the Commissioners appear soon and lead us into the first path. Therefore I wish them to Come, dreading nothing so much as even an appearance of division amongst ourselves."[64] Morris expressed his praise for Gates' work, and his hopes for peace in his typical open-hearted fashion.

General Horatio Gates was a former military officer who had fought in the French and Indian wars. He had left the British army after failing to receive a commission that he felt he deserved. Then in, 1772, he moved to what is now West Virginia, where he rekindled his acquaintance with another former English military man, Charles Lee. Gates was a cagey politician, so naturally he wanted to know more about this Congressman from Pennsylvania, Robert Morris. He turned to the Congressman from Massachusetts, John Adams for information about Morris. On April 27th, 1776 John Adams responded:

John Adams

"You ask me what you are to think of Robt. Morris? I will tell you what I think of him. I think he has a masterly Understanding, an open Temper and an honest Heart: and if he does not always vote for what You and I should think proper, it is because he thinks that a large Body of People remains, who are not yet of his Mind. He has vast designs in the mercantile Way. And no doubt pursues mercantile Ends, which are always gain; but he is an excellent Member of our Body."[65]

It appears that Adams' impression of Morris was affected by the earlier pricing disagreement. In any case, Morris wanted peace; Adams was on the path to war. This was just one of many dissimilarities between them. Adams' characterization of Morris was a result of the cultural differences between his well-established Calvinist thinking and Morris' background. Morris was an Anglican, and a self-taught merchant who never went to college, or even finished grade school. Morris' manners were not polished. He spoke with the directness fitting a man who dealt with ships and sailors, and who was at home buying and selling in the free marketplace. Unlike Adams, who was a lawyer, Morris was a not a man of letters.

Many men, who found their way into business, society, and politics through inherited wealth and family connections, viewed Morris with suspicion. He was a merchant in a time when merchants were viewed by some as being below a yeoman farmer in social rank, and when the term, ambitious, was used as a pejorative. He was also the object of envy from those with little property who were less able to improve their economic condition. At this time in history, America was still a colony of England and despite the democratic rhetoric; the social divisions in England were well established in America.

Even so, Morris' experience in business led Congress to choose him to look after their finances, and it also led individual leaders to seek his assistance with their financial affairs; for example, General Charles Lee asked for Morris' help as late as April 1776. Morris tried to transfer funds to America from Lee's bank account in England,[66] before Independence was declared. However, this kind of aid was no guard against the prevailing attitudes. If Morris seemed to Adams to be "interested in gain,"[67] this view was even stronger in the South, where old families were brought up to see merchants as a necessary evil. To them, a merchant did not produce anything of value and they were nothing more than a means to buy imports, and to sell the items grown on their plantations. Many southern planters, like most farmers, were risk-averse. While they worked to run their plantations well, most did not often seek new opportunities outside their field, during the colonial period. Morris represented something foreign, destabilizing and even threatening to these conservative Southerners – an economically mobile middle class.

Morris, the clerk, merchant and activist was in his early forties. He was about six feet tall, somewhat overweight; he walked with a cane; and he suffered terribly from allergies. His allergies were so pronounced that he was often unable to see for days at a time. His sandy hair was starting to thin a bit, but his expression revealed the intensity that was required to accomplish his goals. He was openhearted, cheerful, honest, inclusive, and could be direct to the point of being blunt. He was passionate on subjects that were important to him and was not afraid to speak his mind. He expected the best of others, and to his detriment he often placed trust in people he should not have. He would get angry at times, and people could tell when he was. He was verbally skilled and agile in debates, and he earned a reputation of being able to get the best of almost any adversary in a debate on the floor of the Assembly. During a debate over the future of the bank a Mr. Finlay remarked, "that wealth has a tendency to counteract our manners and the principles of our government..." Morris responded, "If wealth is so obnoxious, I ask this gentleman, why is he so eager in the pursuit of it?"[68] For all his forcefulness, he had a subtle way of thinking. In a way that accords with Quaker habit, he often made the effort to see conditions from the perspective of others. He used this ability, along with some wit, to make his points. This ability to place himself in the shoes of others would help him to move across the religious borders of society and keep cordial relations with Quakers, Anglicans, Catholics and Jews, while others tended to stay within their groups.

Morris was respected and well received, but he was never really accepted as an equal by the society of the day, even among his fellow Anglicans. For example, his long-time friend and business partner, Thomas Willing, was a manager of the socially important Philadelphia Dancing Assemblies. Morris never was. He and his wife attended for a while but only as members. For all his success and influence, he was not from the landed gentry during a very class-conscious time. He was without family backing, in a day when family pedigree was the basis for social standing. His detractors made a point of noticing his humble origins and orphan status with sly references to him being a "natural child." (A phrase of the day used to indicate a child born to an unmarried couple.) Morris knew who he was and he did not hide it. On occasion, he would entertain his guests with stories of his experiences on board ships and his dealings with some of the rougher elements of society. Once these stories started, the women and children would leave the room. A respected Quaker, Dr. Benjamin Rush, wrote about Morris saying, "Robert Morris is bold sensible and agreeable. His peculiar manners deprive him of much of that popularity usually following great exploits of public and private virtue. He is proud and passionate and has always had virulent enemies as well as affectionate friends."[69]

Secret Agencies

The European kingdoms saw the growing conflict in America as a state of unrest tending to a civil war. Their monarchs were reluctant to become involved in another sovereign country's internal political turmoil. At the same time, these kingdoms were pleased to see their chief rival embroiled in a conflict that had the potential to weaken it, and perhaps provide the other Great Powers of Europe with opportunities for geographic expansion. These European Kingdoms were not interested in helping the fledgling revolution openly with loans or grants; certainly not until they were sure of some success. However, they were happy to get American goods at prices below what had been paid when Britain controlled the market. Of course, this had to be done quietly.

Under these circumstances, Morris operated a clandestine network to get war supplies from Europe in return for American products. He enlisted his existing business associates in North America, the Caribbean Islands, and Europe for this work. He then conducted it under the auspices of the Secret Committee. These arrangements allowed friendly countries to assist with little risk to themselves. This commerce helped to establish America's credibility. That, along with military victories, and some very clever diplomacy, was vital to attracting allies and making treaties as time went on.

One of Morris' key contacts was the twenty-four year old William Bingham, who had formerly worked with Willing, Morris & Co.,[70] and who, while he was in Philadelphia, had held the position of secretary to the Secret Committee.[71] Bingham had once been the British Consul at St. Pierre, but upon his return to Martinique, aboard the *Reprisal,* he became the Willing, Morris & Co. agent in the West Indies.[72] After he was installed, he promoted American interests with propaganda, smuggling, and privateering. Stephen Ceronio in Hispaniola, Estienne Cathalan in France,[73] John Dorsius in Charleston, South Carolina,[74] John Dupuy at Mole, St. Nicholas, Cornelius Stephenson and Hericus Godet on St. Eustatius,[75] and Oliver Pollock in New Orleans were all commercial agents who worked with Morris before they worked for the nation. In fact, Pollock and Morris had sailed together for Willing and Company many years earlier. Morris also had commercial connections in Cadiz, Spain. In the same vein, Morris set up Thomas Morris with a Willing Morris, & Co. office in Nantes, France to create a supply line for goods and correspondence that were to be smuggled past the British Navy.

Thomas Morris was Robert's twenty-four year-old half-brother. As a youth, Robert had taken good advantage of the opportunities presented to him when he was thrust into the counting house of Charles Willing, so it was reasonable for him to expect Thomas to do the same. Robert hoped Thomas would leave his wild friends and ways behind once the yoke of responsibility was placed upon him. Unfortunately, Robert underestimated Thomas' appetite for excess in France. Robert's failure to understand the character weaknesses of some people, and to give them the benefit of the doubt when others might not, was a curious long-term failing on his part. Some may say this was his ultimate undoing. His affection for Thomas, and the family bond he felt, blinded him to the nature of the younger man. He thought that Thomas was just merry and fun loving; and did not see the tragic flaws of the person in whom he placed much hope, faith, and expectation.

By engaging his family and his business network Morris was risking all he had, and his very life, but he did not do so out of 100% altruism. Sailors must be paid. Captains worked on commission. Ships cost money, and Congress had little or none of it. Morris labored long and hard for the cause without a salary. He did not have a family fortune or a slave-powered plantation to provide financial backing for this. He had to make money to survive. He used his own ships, and contracted the ships of others, including merchant firms like John Brown of Rhode Island; Johnathon Hudson of Baltimore; Norton, Thurston, and Beale of Virginia; Carter Braxton also of Virginia; Benjamin Harrison of Virginia; and Hewes & Smith of North Carolina.[76] Some of these men also supplied the raw materials of tobacco and indigo that were shipped out to France. All of the private firms that conducted the business did so on a commission basis.[77] At the same time, in the American and British

Navies, the captain and the sailors were awarded a percentage of each prize their ship took in battle, which is why British officers bought their commissions in that Navy. This was the prevailing system of the day, and Morris saw no ethical conflict in any of this because he was paid only if the shipment was a success.

Morris was acting on his belief that if one were to create a free country, there must be encouragements for people to participate, voluntarily, in the success of the new country. Morris was of the opinion that self-interest was a good motivator in a free society, and this thinking was in line with the philosophy of David Hume. (The basic argument is that society is made up of individuals, so if each individual is free to pursue his goals then everyone in society is free to pursue their goals, and that makes for a free society.) People like Morris, who had to make their own way in life, said that government service should be attractive to all men, especially those with executive ability. He acted on his belief that public work and self-interest were compatible.

Morris' approach can be traced to two practical origins. His experience as a merchant demonstrated that in the ordinary course of business, both sides of a transaction achieve their aims in the same deal, and they do this on a voluntary basis. Secondly, Morris came of age in Philadelphia, which was a city steeped in the Quaker tradition of reciprocal morality. The Quaker idea was to treat others according to the golden rule, and this was an underlying social construct in their dealings with each other and non-Quakers; for example, they believed in religious liberty for themselves, so it was natural that they allowed it for others. In another example, their knowledge of the importance of freedom for themselves led them to support freedom for slaves. The idea of reciprocal morality was a basic tenet of life in Philadelphia, even if it was not perfectly practiced.

On the opposite end of the political spectrum, there were people who promoted the view that government service was a high calling to be performed without pay or regard to self-interest. Of course, this much-heralded view, if followed, would have precluded anyone but the wealthiest from holding a leadership position. The strongest voices for this perspective often belonged to those who masked their self-interest by directing public attention to the supposed low motives of their political opposites. This tactic was generally effective when the presumption of virtue was with the accuser, as it was with the landowning elite. When put into practice, such systems have historically favored the theoretically "disinterested" leaders and alienated others by removing their motivation and ability to participate. One such example was ancient Athens, where an aristocracy managed a society of artisans and slaves.

There were those who stood against the very idea of engaging people on the basis of self-interest. They based their objections on the calculation that if one person was getting his way then another has to lose. This theory of relationships has its roots in the medieval habit of seeing wealth in terms of controlling the scarce resource, land, and the exploitation of others. Not surprisingly, this view was a common perspective among members of the agricultural interests who controlled vast tracts of land, and whose system of chattel slavery was among the most exploitative on earth. Their cultural habit of seeing the world in terms of winners who take advantage of life's losers, gave them a psychological model that they successfully applied when dealing with others not like themselves; others including their own slaves, and the backcountry malcontents with whom these southerners made common cause.

The idea of enlightened self-interest in Government was in operation during Morris' tenure in the early war effort. This was done out of habit, belief, and necessity. Robert was a merchant trader, and it was up to him to make money every day in order to provide for his somewhat sprawling family. This required time, and he was dedicating an increasing amount of his energies to the Revolution. If he could not combine the two, he would have to abandon one or the other. He was not going to forsake his family, and he had given his word to support the Revolution, so he was bound to do both, because, when he made his pledge, he did not make an idle promise. His word was the basis of his livelihood. If he said he would pay for a shipment, then he was bound to do so. It often took up to eighteen months to close the books on one shipment, so one's credibility was the basis of one's credit rating. If he did not make good on his promise, he would never be trusted again and he would be out of business. By vowing to support the Revolution, Morris put himself in the position of supporting the war, or proving himself a liar, which would have ruined him both personally and professionally. The stakes for breaking one's word were high indeed. The only higher risk was in the possibility that the Revolution might fail.

It takes discipline to implement a government program based on the idea of enlightened self-interest. Some people are more disciplined than others, so it might be expected that in the early days before checks were put into the system, the self-interest was not always enlightened. Between 1776, and 1780, the commissary, the hospital, and the quartermaster's department all fell under suspicion. The effort was ripe with temptation. Congress eventually decided that it was a bad idea for the same person to be in charge of both purchasing items from vendors and issuing the same supplies to the army.[78] The commissary department was taken off commission and put on salary, and as a result, many of the experienced individuals left because they could make more money elsewhere. Shortly thereafter, the commissary department stopped functioning. The timing for this administrative change was unfortunate, because it caused the Revolution's greatest unifying force, the Continental Army, to suffer in Valley Forge.

Morris' ships were put to work in another way as well. On January 30th, 1776, he was appointed to the Committee of Secret Correspondence,[79] which was convened to communicate with those abroad who could assist the revolt.[80*] Morris understood he was not expected to be a correspondent, but rather to use his ships and commercial connections as part of this diplomatic effort.

Deane goes to France

Silas Deane was the son of a blacksmith who married well, became a merchant, and later a member of the Continental Congress from Connecticut. He had financed the capture of Fort Ticonderoga and had been a leading member of the Secret and Marine Committees. Early in 1776, during his tenure Julien Alexandre Achard de Bonvouloir, the somewhat secret agent from France, returned to Philadelphia and met again with the members of the Committee of Secret Correspondence. They deduced that Bonvouloir's offers to supply arms must be coming from the French crown, and to sort the whole thing out they determined to send Deane to France. At the same time two somewhat dubious characters arrived on the scene offering munitions from France, intimating they were connected with the French Crown, which they were not. These were French merchants, Pierre Penet and Emmanuel de Pliarne. They would eventually do business with Congress, and the Browns in Rhode Island, among others. Bonvouloir was recalled to France, and the Crown then assigned fulfillment to Beaumarchais.[81]

The Connecticut merchant, Deane, prepared to leave Philadelphia for Nantes, France, to join the American agents as an official, if secret, representative. At this point, getting Deane to Europe was not as simple as one might have hoped because the British were enforcing their blockade by patrolling the seas and looking for troublesome Americans. He left Philadelphia in March 1776, but difficulties with head winds and British warships slowed the trip and put both Morris and Deane in a tight spot. Morris wrote, "I was sorry to find by your Note of the 8th that you determined to wait at Chester for the Pilot Boat because certain Gentn seem exceedingly anxious that you sho'd be gone & you know well how tedious & troublesome it is to obtain decisive orders on any point wherein Public Expense is to be incurred. I cou'd not send a Boat without orders unless at my own Expence and altho I obtained such orders yesterday yet I was so harassed between the assembly & Congress that it was not in my power to dispatch her. I am attempting it this Morning & hope she will depart in time to put this onboard the Brigt and then run down before you."[82]

Deane's ship slipped out, and after a brief stopover in Bermuda, for a little Secret Committee business, he arrived in Nantes, France, in June. There he adopted the cover story of being a commercial agent for Willing, Morris & Co. This was before Independence was declared, so he needed an overt reason for his presence in France to mask the covert purpose. Once Deane joined the team, they commenced to procure war supplies from France. In addition, Deane promoted the business he had with his brother, Simon. Deane was also working for various private firms on the Eastern Seaboard, and he represented a land development company with properties west of the Appalachian Mountains.

As part of the operational mode, it was common for a private ship crossing the sea with Continental goods to carry cargo on other accounts as well. Just as a truck or ship today may have several palettes, each belonging to a different client, these ships carried materials for a number of customers. The Continental Government was just one of many. This mixing also helped to hide the purpose of the shipments if the ship were stopped at sea by the British Navy.[83]

Willing, Morris, & Co. was not the only private firm involved, but it was a significant one. The risks of treason were great, and the financial rewards were modest. During the time between September 27th, 1775 and August 26th, 1776 the Secret Committee spent $841,633[84], to gain war supplies from Europe. Morris' businesses operated under five supply contracts, and a total of $429,000 passed through their offices. This situation should not be surprising, given the fact that Morris had one of the largest private merchant fleets not in Tory hands, that the work had to remain secret to succeed, and that by August 12th, 1776 only Robert Morris and Ben Franklin remained on the Secret Committee.[85] At the rate of 2.5% per transaction, the combined total commission paid to Willing, Morris, & Co. for this business would have been about $21,450.

Considering that a sailor made $8 per month and estimating that there were on average fifty sailors per ship, and each voyage took about two months, then total crew salaries would be $1,600 per round trip. Multiply that by five because there were five contracts in that period, for a total cost of about $8,000 to Willing, Morris, & Co. Allowing that the government shipment payment of $329 per month, ($1,316 for the round trip, or payment of $6,580 for five trips) would actually cover food for the crew, wear and tear to the ship, the sails, and rigging, and contribute to the crew's salary, although this is not stated in the documents, then the Willing, Morris, & Co. were $1,500 in the red before the commission was paid.

After meeting costs, the remainder of the total commission would be divided among all the partners of Willing, Morris & Co., and the captains. There were at least three partners. If one forgets the captains (which would not be popular) and gives just the partners equal shares, then the most Morris would have gotten in his pocket for the year of financial, political and personal risk, would have been about $7,000. That was eleven times the annual wage for a newly hired sailor, or about enough to buy a new ship. This sounds like a lot, but several years later, Thomas Jefferson was offered the job of being a diplomat in Paris. This assignment was far away from any actual risk or fighting and there was plenty of time to spend on other pursuits. Congress set this Virginia gentleman's salary at $11,000 per year.[86 87*]

The challenge to America in 1776 was to supply the army without generating oversized debts, or falling prey to other nations through excessive entanglements, or deals made from a weak position. Morris used his roles as the Chairman of the Secret Committee, and a leading member of Committee of Secret Correspondence, and the Marine Committee to operate a system of getting supplies without compromising the future of the nation. He followed three tracks. Continental privateers and the Continental Navy were given the task of interdicting British ships at sea. These ships were brought to a port. The goods were used or sold, and the ship was sold or converted to a Continental ship. The Continental Navy effort was directed from the Marine Committee. The second track was to use trade with foreign governments to procure needed goods for the war. This effort was directed from the Secret Committee. On the third track, Morris and Franklin sought to acquire loans from the French – loans that would be repaid with future trade.

There were difficulties. One source of money for supplies came from British ships that Americans took as prizes in European waters and sold in Europe. The act of seizing ships at sea is dangerous, and many good vessels and men were lost in the process. Also, as a matter of course, the English patrolled French, Dutch, and Baltic ports looking for their property. Often the ships were recognized and returned to England, so little was gained. It was necessary for Morris' team to "repaper" these prizes so they could be sold in Europe as non-British vessels. Robert's half-brother, Thomas, performed these conversions and got the money that was used to buy war supplies.

The use of trade was tricky since France was technically at peace with England, so they were obliged not to trade with the Rebel Americans. This problem was solved with good old smuggling techniques. Goods were shipped in and out of France on French ships, or ships with false registration. The cargo was transferred to or from American vessels in the French or Dutch West Indies, and then brought onward. This bit of legerdemain was used to distance the French from the Rebels, and keep the real relationship hidden so the trade could continue. Morris explained this system to Silas Deane.[88] In one instance, for example, he instructed Deane how to transfer cargo in Bermuda away from port, and how to gain false papers for Willing, Morris & Co. ships before sending those ships on to France.[89, 90] This activity by the Secret Committee not only supplied the Americans with arms during the earliest days of the struggle; it also was a means of building credibility with the French Crown. An international relationship was formed based on mutual benefit and provided a foundation of trust for the more formal alliance that would follow some years later.

St Eustachia By K.F. Bendorf, 1780 Courtesy of the Vereeniging Nederlands Scheepvaart Museum, Amsterdam.

Bermuda, Martinique and Santa Domingo were not the only islands Morris used for this kind of smuggling. St. Eustatius also served as a transshipment point for war supplies from Europe to the former colonies.[91] Mr. Samuel Curson and Mr. Isaac Gouverneur both became agents on that island.[92] Later they were captured by the English and treated badly. St. Eustatius recognized the American flag when the *Andrew Doria* came flying the Stars and Stripes into port on Nov. 16, 1776. This did not please the British. St. Eustatius, also known as the Golden Rock, was also a key port in the slave trade as run to South and Central America by the Dutch.

Back in Philadelphia, the Continental Congress decided that because so much Continental business was being conducted at the Willing, Morris & Co. wharves, it would be wise to consider their wharves as a Naval Base. In 1776, Congress ordered that soldiers move from their barracks in the Northern Liberties section of town, and for the first time stand guard at this new base.[93] Willing, Morris & Co. warehouses were adjacent to the docks, and were used to store the materials that came in from Europe, but they stayed in private hands.

To provide an idea of Morris' influence and involvement, it is interesting to see the associations between the events and the man behind them. On the 10th of June, Morris, as chairman of the Committee of Secret Correspondence, arranged with the Marine Committee, of which he was a leading member, to issue orders to Captain Wickes, who had sailed for Willing, Morris, & Co. before the war, to take Mr. William Bingham, who had been associated with Willing, Morris, & Co., to Martinique aboard *The Reprisal*, a former Willing, Morris, & Co. ship. Bingham went to act as the newly appointed agent from the American colonies. By putting a trusted representative into Martinique, Morris was able to implement his plan for transferring goods between France and the Colonies. Historian E. James Ferguson noted that in general, the large merchant's "affairs were therefore complicated and obscure, projected through a network of hidden personal connections and fostered at every turn by mutual patronage."[94] Morris' reliance on close associates was typical behavior for a merchant of the day, and it was prudent to use trusted allies, in light of the secret nature of the work.

Robert used every technique he knew to move his mission forward. He took on more and more of the work of the committees created by the Continental Congress. He dug into the details of finance for the Congress, he managed the building of the ships, and he put his fortune and the future of his children at risk, yet little is known of how this affected his life at home. The best physical indication of that lies in the relatively long period between his third child, Hester, and his fourth, Charles. Charles was born in July 1777, three years after his sister, Hester, and after the critical step of announcing independence. Robert's wife, Mary, was from a respected family in Maryland. When she married a rising figure in colonial society, she could hardly have expected a revolution to come along and sweep away old alliances and put her life at risk. She also had to cope with Robert's support for his first daughter Polly, and his attachment to his irresponsible half-brother Thomas. In addition, she had a husband who was spending much of this time away from her, toiling with reduced pay on a cause she had not chosen. It is not hard to imagine that there was some friction in their relationship at this time. This would have dug deeply into Robert's heart, but it appears he put that aside. He focused on the goal, because if that were not reached, then everything he held dear would be destroyed.

Morris' roles on the Secret Committee, the Committee of Correspondence, and the Marine Committee put him in the unique position of coordinating the naval efforts in terms of obtaining supplies, intelligence, and engagements with the British at sea. Fortunately, he had experience as the owner of a fleet of ships to draw upon, as he worked through the committees to utilize the small Continental Navy. He frequently instructed captains at sea as to the best course of action. For example, in response to one message, Ezek Hopkins, Commander of the Continental Navy, wrote to Morris on March 28th, 1776, "I received your orders on the 5th..."[95]

In May, the Secret Committee chartered the brigantine *Polly* for a trade mission. On the 14th, Morris wrote to the captain to tell him that, because the Continental Fleet was protecting him, he was under the command of that fleet, and so must obey their orders and signals. Morris warned the captain that his pilot must not be captured by the British. Pilots guide ships into port after they come within sight of land. They have special knowledge of the local hazards in the rivers and bays, so the capture of an

American pilot would be of great help to the British.[96] Unfortunately, the *Polly* didn't succeed in the mission and was captured by *HMS Orpheus* on July 3rd.

> Sir
> Philada. May 14th. 1776.
>
> You are to put yourself under the Command of the Continental Fleet now going down the Bay and proceed down in Company with them Agreeable to such orders and Signals as they may think proper to give you. You must most carefully avoid the Enemy's Ships, Tenders, Boats &c. and be particularly careful to send your Pilot or put him on board one of the Continental Armed Vessels for he must not get into the hands of our Enemy's on any Account. You will take the first fair Opportunity of getting out to Sea, and then make the best of your way in the due prosecution of your Voyage Agreeable to the orders already given you.
>
> I am, Sir, Your hble Servt. By order of the Secret Committee,
>
> Robt Morris, Chair Man[97]

There were those who disparage the conduct of the Continental Navy because the Navy was not always used aggressively against British war ships. Others recently have taken to doubting the need for a Continental Navy,[98] and they argue for a more guerrilla style force of gunboats that would attack British ships when they were near shore would have been as effective and less expensive and not so pretentious. This is basically a rehash of the old arguments of those members of Congress who wished to weaken the Nationalists. It goes unobserved, by such critics, that many state navies were so configured, and that getting the various states to support or duplicate the effort in other states would be difficult and would not necessarily have improved the results. It completely overlooks the role of ships going to and from Europe, and the effort to take the war to England with raids from the sea. One might also consider that the British had over 400 ships in their navy, and the loss of one ship would most likely have led to the arrival of two more. Angering the British Navy had already resulted in the razing of Falmouth, and the commander of that mission had been instructed to inflict harm on towns from Cape Anne to Machais.[99] Morris' view from the Marine Committee was less about a naval war of attrition, and more about using the navy to support the war effort by protecting commerce, which would result in getting supplies for the Army, as well as funding the war, and cementing alliances.

Morris worked within the existing committee structure of the day and used his board positions to argue for better support for the Navy. Running a Navy by committee was difficult, particularly when some committee members viewed the Commander in Chief of the Navy as being insufficiently aggressive. Hopkins kept the tiny navy at sea, and he was careful in his use of the ships. He often avoided engagements he judged he could not win, and on occasion conducted the ships under his command without close regard for the direction of the Marine Committee.

Many naval officers thought the Marine Committee was less effective than a single executive would have been. For his part, Morris and his allies in Congress supported the idea of hiring executive officers to run government departments. They had difficulties uniting Congress behind this idea because many members wanted direct Congressional control over all operations, and those people thought that elected representatives should do this work instead of paid executives. Unfortunately, the resulting subcommittees and boards suffered from a number of problems. Some Congressmen took on too much work to do all of it well. Membership in the committees changed as people won and lost their elected positions, which resulted in a lack of continuity that hurt the effectiveness of the departments. Also, long distances and slow transportation caused many members to be absent from Congress for extended periods.

A significant roadblock to the creation of executive offices was the political tendency to keep power away from any form of centralized government. Instead, most members of Congress used their positions to benefit their home state and to improve their own popularity. In addition to state pride, there was always the rhetoric of maintaining their Republican Virtue which was a code for their dreams of local control, all of this was a symptom of the underlying cultural forces at work in the former colonies that kept the states apart.

These local American concerns would eventually affect America's allies in Europe, but for the time being, America put forth a united front to the Ancient Regime. Previously, Beaumarchais had been observing the progress of the American efforts from his position in London as a spy for Louis XVI. He evaluated the weaknesses of the American militias and again tried to convince the king to send gunpowder and engineers to help them. The time was not quite right, yet. However, Beaumarchais foresaw doom for America coming in the form of an army of Hessian soldiers hired to help England crush the uprising in the unruly colonies. As a result of their earlier contact with Bonvouloir, the secret committee sent a message to

Pierre-Augustin Caron de Beaumarchais (1732-1799)

the French Crown. It went first to Arthur Lee, then to Beaumarchais, and on to the Court. The proposal that Arthur Lee forwarded contained an offer from Congress to establish a formal trading relationship with France. Later, Lee would interpret his role in delivering this message as an entitlement to run the business.

The French people were sympathetic to the Americans, but the French Crown balked. The king of France was not ready to move against a fellow monarch. However, when a British warship seized one of the American trading vessels heading to Nantes, the scales were tipped. The French king was offended by English pretensions that they owned the whole ocean, and he decided to help the restive colonies.[100]

The French Crown invested 1,000,000 livres and helped Beaumarchais set up a merchant firm to provide secret aid to the American cause.[101*] The Spanish crown invested a similar amount, and Beaumarchais raised another million from private investors. Thusly, he was empowered by the French and Spanish Crowns to act as a secret agent and intermediary between the American Rebels and European suppliers. This provided the French Crown with sufficient distance to deny they were assisting the Rebels, and also to deny Beaumarchais' claims when the trades went bad. At the same time, Louis' cousin, the King of Spain, could take advantage of the new arrangements. All of this was in motion in the background before Deane arrived, so he was pleasantly surprised to see how easy it was to make arrangements soon after his arrival.

These developments also set the scene for the first important schism in American political history, the Lee/Deane Affair. It is a bitter irony that Beaumarchais was so convinced of "American Virtue" by Arthur Lee, that in 1777 he sent over a million livres in war supplies to America without a contract or even a letter from Congress, only to learn much later that Arthur Lee actively stood in the way of the very payments that could save Beaumarchais from ruin.

Over the course of the next few years, Beaumarchais found himself to be a victim of a political intrigue that would ultimately result in the formation of America's two-party system. First it was Silas Deane, a New England merchant and son of a blacksmith, against Arthur Lee, a proud Virginian, and scion of the Tidewater elite. Support groups for each individual developed into "factions" which were seen at the time as the Merchants against the Farmers. Later the body politic divided into the "monocrat" Federalists against the "agrarian" Anti-Federalists. Later still it would be the Republicans against the Democrats. Political historians argue against drawing direct connections between the Federalists and any modern party because so many of the transitory positions taken by the original groups were adopted by the opposite groups in subsequent years. The alert reader will notice however, that some themes keep resurfacing, even until the early 21st century. These similarities are based on the underlying cultural forces that have always woven in and out of the political fabric in America.

Impending Independency

In December 1775 Parliament passed the Prohibitory Act. This was in response to the establishment of the Continental Congress, and in effect, put the same measures that existed in Massachusetts onto the rest of the colonies. If they wanted to act together, they would suffer together, or so the thinking went. It established an embargo against the colonials and legalized the seizure of their shipping. In effect it was a declaration of economic war on the Colonies. These acts also offered the hope of conciliation with the promise of peace commissioners, who were a long time in coming.

In early 1776 the conflict could still be called a tax protest, even though blood had been spilled on both sides. Following the traditional Quaker path with Benjamin Franklin and John Dickinson, Morris hoped to avoid war as he worked for reconciliation with England. All that was required was for England to agree to back down on the most important issues of principle. Other men, like Adams and the Lee brothers, were adamant about independence from England because they subscribed to the Radical Whig, or Real Whig, school of thought. They attracted the more extreme elements of the backcountry Scots-Irish with highly righteous rhetoric common to the English Country party. In their campaign to become leaders in their own sovereign states they rode the radicalized popular sentiment towards independence without a clear idea of how it would be won. The brutal techniques that the British used to suppress the colonies, gave currency to the more radical pronouncements of the pro-independence groups in America.

On February 15th, 1776, Morris wrote a letter to Mr. John Herries, a Member of Parliament, wherein Morris cautioned that the Crown's efforts to suppress the colonies were actually making the situation worse:

> America has long been charged by her Enemies in England with aiming at Independency. The charge was unjust, but we now plainly see, that the burning of Towns, seizing our Ships, with numerous acts of wanton barbarity & Cruelty perpetrated by the British Forces has prepared Men's minds for an Independency, that were shock'd at the idea a few weeks ago. This you may depend on, and should this Campaign open with furious Acts of Parliament, you may bid adieu to the American Colonies. They will then assuredly declare for Independency...[102]

By the beginning of April the *Wasp* had made her way back from New England to Philadelphia for repairs and to patrol the Delaware. Mid-month, the British sent two ships up the Delaware to enforce the Prohibitory Act and threaten Philadelphia: the forty-two gun ship, *HMS Roebuck* and the twenty-eight gun frigate, *HMS Liverpool.* The *Wasp* was on patrol, and upon seeing she was outgunned, she went up the Christiana Creek. The *HMS Roebuck* ran aground and the *Wasp*, along with thirteen armed river galleys, came out of the creek and attacked. After a two-day engagement the *Roebuck* and *Liverpool* left the Delaware Bay. This opened up an opportunity for a spate of renewed trade.

In May, Captain Wickes sailed *The Reprisal* from L'Orient, France. He left in the company of the *Lexington* and the *Dolphin* to bring the war to the enemy's shores. They harassed British shipping, cruising around Ireland and through the Irish Sea. This small squadron took eighteen prizes, even sinking two within sight of port.[103] The British, so-called Lords of the Sea, were horrified.

Morris wrote Deane in France, and detailed the results of the recent battle, involving the *HMS Roebuck* and *HMS Liverpool,* that temporarily broke the blockade. He also clarified the connection between coastal defense and commerce in a letter he wrote to Silas Deane on June 6th, 1776. After that, he counseled, "All this you'll think has little to do with Commerce but that's a mistake for in Consequence of this Action all the Fleet of Merchantmen have got safe out to sea, several vessels have got safe in and we have some trade revived & Consequently a better prospect of making remittances to you than at the time you Sailed. Our Cruizers are also got out and I expect will be very serviceable and continue increasing their number & shall Constantly go on making additions to our Navy but we want our Seamen home again."[104] Morris summed up the role of trade in the war effort and showed how the Continental Navy was used to support commercial activity that paid for war supplies, i.e. "making remittances to you." Also, there was a hint of Morris' expectation that the small navy would grow by seizing British ships, as well as a note of caution there. He realized this is a dangerous way to make a Navy when he wrote, "but we want our Seamen home again."[105] Morris' idea of naval success was not focused on destroying ships and killing sailors, but rather in growing the Navy and commerce, thereby sustaining the nation.

Later, the American captains, who had defended Philadelphia from their armed galleys, were faulted for not sinking the British ships, and they in turn blamed their lack of supplies and pointed to the Committee of Safety, meaning Morris who was in charge. It was very much like Morris to let the ships leave, alive, with their tails between their legs, instead of sinking them. There was, as yet, no war, but the "meaner sort" was disappointed and wanted a more decisive victory. Their complaints set off an investigation by the Assembly, which ultimately concluded that the Committee of Safety was not at fault. This was seen, by some, as a somewhat self-serving conclusion because Morris was prominent on the Committee and the Assembly, and so the report did not satisfy the more radical members of the population. Their distrust grew for the managers of the city's defenses and that reinforced their idea of a novel grassroots form of military organization where the soldiers would vote for their leaders, and the tasks they would perform. This was not supported by other military leaders, but the Pennsylvanians would have their Associators, none the less.

Within the Congress, Adams had long been agitating for separation from England. He seized on the political opportunity for change presented by the nearby river battle and proposed that each state should rid itself of the old governments, loyal to the crown, and create new American governments. This resolution was adopted after much controversy in the Congress. It was in this atmosphere that the old Pennsylvania Assembly started to dissolve.

Clearly, the British were being inflexible. Morris knew that Britain's intention to demolish American commerce would compel the colonies to declare their independence. Conditions in Congress had gotten to the point that any further appeal for moderation would be seen as favoring the King's position. On June 5th, 1776 Morris wrote to Silas Deane in France to inform him of the state of affairs. Morris' hopes for reconciliation and peace were dashed. "I never lost hopes of reconciliation until I saw this answer which in my opinion breaths nothing but Death & Destruction. Every body sees it in the same light and it will bring us all to one way of thinking, so that you may soon expect to hear of New Governments in every colony, and in Conclusion a declaration of Independancy by Congress. I see this step is inevitable and you may depend it will soon take place."[106]

Morris sent this information to Deane as a leader of the American secret agents in France, so Deane could prepare for the approaching war. Among the conditions all Americans faced was the lack of silver coins for trade, and the lack of dry goods in the colonies due to the Non-Importation Agreement. The opportunity to make money by shipping goods to the colonies, and of course getting some silver to the American side of the Atlantic, would be helpful during the expected war. Morris wrote, "if you can send us in this way £20 to £50,000 sterling it will yield Fortunes to us all, and you may depend on my utmost exertions to get the Goods safe in, to sell them well and to make speedy remittances."[107] This was almost a full month before the Declaration was signed.

Deane's status as a merchant was enough to open him to suspicion of profiting from manipulations in the insurance and stock markets. The idea that he was "playing" in the markets did not endear him to the Americans who stayed at home, particularly those who considered themselves Farmers.[108] Later, it was suspected in Congress, particularly among Arthur Lee's allies, that Silas Deane made a quick side trip to a London gambling house and used his inside knowledge to place a bet that an alliance between America and France would come to pass.[109] However, besides the Lee brothers, the only member of the American team who was actually in England at the time was Dr. Edward Bancroft. Bancroft was a former student and trusted friend of Deane's, whom, at the urging of Franklin,[110] Deane contacted. Later Deane asked Bancroft to act as his secretary and interpreter in France, and for help with the Indian Goods trade. Bancroft had met with Deane in France, but it was during Bancroft's trip back to England in the June/July time-frame that he enlisted himself as a spy for the British before he returned to work with Deane in Nance. While there is no other explanation for the source of the rumors about Deane's supposed perfidy, it is only speculation based on circumstances that leads one to conclude Bancroft was involved in promoting the gossip. After all, sowing doubt about Deane in Lee's mind would have been good counter-intelligence tradecraft.

While hidden dangers proliferated in Europe, Pennsylvania was at a political crossroads. The Pennsylvania Assembly had adjourned without authorizing the call up of the six thousand troops Congress had requested.[111] They failed to act because the pacifist Quaker Assembly wanted to avoid war with Britain. Their inaction led to the demise of that Assembly a few weeks later. It was replaced with a more radical group who disliked the proprietary government. In fact, they disliked almost everything Quaker and Anglican, and built their politics to reflect that. One went so far as to admit, "We despise you."[112] This group dedicated much of their energy to promoting their local political agenda, most particularly getting their hands on the property of the Quakers, even when their time would have been better spent fighting the British.

Although the Assembly had changed, Morris kept his positions within the Continental Congress and continued to prepare for war. Still, he remained vocal as a moderate in his opposition to declaring independence. There were a number of reasons for this stance. Such a declaration meant starting a war, and wars are easier to start than to win. He thought the colonies had no real idea how tenacious King George III was, and that any war would be long and hard fought. Morris had been trying to acquire supplies for the military, and he knew they didn't have the money, materials or alliances in place for a long war. He observed the behavior of Congress and considered his experience as a street activist. He doubted such political structures were good long term governmental modalities, as had been expressed in Pennsylvania under their new Constitution. He concluded that the colonies were not really ready for self-rule, and without a centralized governmental structure, the states would eventually fight against each other. Morris understood that Britain's inflexibility had made a peaceful settlement impossible, and that all the colonies would soon be united. Privately, he hoped that his opposition to independence would result in his release from public service, which would allow him to go back to a non-public life.

Two days after Morris' letter to Deane, a fellow Secret Committee member, Richard Henry Lee, proposed a resolution in Congress to separate from England. Five days later, Congress resolved to create three committees, one for drafting a Declaration of Independence, one for drafting the Articles of Confederation, and one for drafting a Model Treaty to guide foreign relations. These three committees were given equal weight because each performed a necessary task.

Independence may be declared, but it must be won, otherwise the declaration would have a hollow ring. In order to win independence, Congress determined that the states should have an over-arching governing structure to see themselves through the war. That was the reason to create the Articles of Confederation. It was obvious to all that winning the war would take money. What was not so obvious was where that money would come from. The Model Treaty was drafted to act as a basis for trade relations with foreign nations. Trade would not only provide immediate arms and war supplies, but long-term benefits as well, including the development of alliances. John Dickinson, Benjamin Franklin, John Adams, Benjamin Harrison, and Robert Morris were the members of the Model Treaty committee.[113]

While Congress debated independency and the states prepared their civil defenses, the British were busy sending thousands of troops to suppress the revolutionary spirit in America. On June 28th, 1776 the British arrived at the major southern trading center: Charleston, South Carolina. The town of Charleston was less than a mile wide, and about one-and-one-half miles long. It rested in a harbor just off the Atlantic Ocean and was an important port for the exportation of the products of southern plantations. It was also main entree port for the slave trade. A fort sat on Sullivan Island across the harbor from the city of Charleston. This fort guarded the mouth of the harbor, and it was on that spot the American militia members took their position. The militia was ready for the arrival of the British forces because Morris had shared the contents of the secret letter he had received, from Richard Champion, warning America of such an attack.[114] This foreknowledge allowed militia from Pennsylvania and Virginia to travel south and join forces with the local militia in South Carolina to hold that fort, now called Fort Moultrie. They were armed with the gunpowder Morris' ship brought in from Bermuda back in 1775. General John Armstrong of Carlisle, Pennsylvania, had gone south with five hundred frontier riflemen and the Pennsylvania Associators. They fought alongside Virginia's General Charles Lee and his frontiersmen, and the South Carolina militia with their long rifles and cannon. The British sailed into the harbor, with the *HMS Roebuck* as their flagship. They ringed the city with their ships. At 11:00 AM the British opened fire on the fort. They sent eight war ships in for closer attack, but the attack was blunted when three of the ships ran aground. The others anchored nearby.

Battle of Ft Moultrie by John Blake White
US Senate Collection

The British attempted to deliver a six-thousand-man invasion force, many from the grounded vessels. The British Navy bombarded Ft. Moultrie with over one hundred cannon firing on the fort. The southern sharpshooters earned their reputations on this day by picking off British soldiers aboard the ships as these troops tried to disembark and invade America. The colonial resistance from Ft. Moultrie was so stiff that the British invasion fleet finally retreated and headed for New York City. The three grounded ships had to wait for the tide to rise before they were able to limp out to sea.

Endnotes

1. *George Washington Papers at the Library of Congress*, 1741-1799: Series 3g Varick Transcripts, 1:4
2. *Naval Documents of the American Revolution*, 1:892
3. Letters of Delegates to Congress, 1:475-476
4. Letters of Delegates to Congress, 2:74
5. *Naval Documents of the American Revolution*, 1:1032
6. *Pennsylvania Gazette*, Item # 21133
7. Letters of Delegates to Congress, 2:114
8. *Naval Documents of the American Revolution*, 1:393; 3:371-373
9. Ibid, 2:442
10. *Naval Documents of the American Revolution*, 2:1050
11. John Nixon deposition Re: The Black Prince HSP - *Naval Documents of the American Revolution*, 2:1093
12. Minutes Pennsylvania Committee of Safety Nov 21, 1777 Naval Documents of the American Revolution, 2:1093
13. *Naval Documents of the American Revolution*, 3:1775-1776
14. The *Alfred* and the *Columbus* served under such captains as John Barry and John Paul Jones until 1778. That year, The *Alfred* was captured and was then used by the British. The *Columbus* was lost in combat.
15. The ability to raise a naval force from private ships was one of the reasons Morris would later champion the creation, maintenance, and protection of a large merchant fleet.
16. George C. Daughan, *If by Sea*, pg. 42-43
17. Robert H. Patton, *Patriot Pirates: The Privateer War for Freedom and Fortune in the American Revolution*, pg. 30-31
18. Letters of Delegates to Congress, 2:471
19. Ibid, 3:307-308
20. *Naval Documents of the American Revolution*, 3:416
21. Revolutionary Diplomatic Correspondence, 1:517
22. Revolutionary Diplomatic Correspondence 1:540
23. *Journals of the Continental Congress*, 3:420
24. December 11, 1775 Minutes of the Pennsylvania Committee of Safety
25. Dr Mease Biographical sketch of Mr. Morris, for, The American edition of the new *Edingurgh encyclopaedia.* Philadelphia: Parker, 1816
26. *Journals of the Continental Congress*, 6:1067
27. Letters of Delegates to Congress, 3:377
28. Ibid, 4:132
29. Ibid, 6:510
30. Letters of Delegates to Congress, 3:309
31. Ibid, 2:522
32. Ibid, 2:475
33. Ibid, 2:253
34. Ibid, 2:319
35. Ibid, 2:402
36. Ibid, 4:331
37. Ibid, 4:445
38. Ibid, 3:82
39. Ibid, 3:291
40. Ibid, 3:59
41. Ibid, 2:417
42. Ibid, 2:447
43. Ibid, 2:487
44. Ibid, 3:306
45. Ibid, 3:329
46. Ibid, 2:512
47. Ibid, 2:485
48. Ibid, 6:606
49. Letters of Delegates to Congress, 3:184
50. Ibid, 5:206-207
51. Ibid, 6:606
52. Ibid, 25:564
53. The Revolutionary Diplomatic Correspondence of the United States, 4:194
54. Elizabeth Nuxoll and E. James Ferguson, *Investigation of Government Corruption During the American Revolution*, pg.16-17
55. E. James Ferguson, *Power of the Purse*, pg.72-74
56. Elizabeth Nuxoll and E. James Ferguson, *Investigation of Government Corruption During the American Revolution*, pg.17-18
57. Letters of Delegates to Congress, 3:170
58. *Naval Documents of the American Revolution*, 2:719
59. *Patriot Pirates*, pg. 88-90
60. Journals of the Continental Congress, 3:428
61. Letters of Delegates to Congress, 3:643
62. *A Revolution in Favor of Government*, pg. 204
63. Letters of Delegates to Congress, 3:494
64. Letters of Delegates to Congress, 3:494-5
65. Ibid, 3:587

66. Letters of Delegates to Congress, 3:576-7
67. Ibid, 3:587
68. Proceedings of the General Assembly of Pennsylvania 3/3/1786
69. Howard Swiggett, *The Extraordinary Mr. Morris*, pg. 88
70. Letters of Delegates to Congress, 4:134; 4:129n
71. Deane Papers, 1:137
72. Letters of Delegates to Congress, 5:169
73. Robert Morris Papers - Letters from Stephen Ceronio; Letters from Estienne Cathalan - Levis collection HSP #1957
74. Letters of Delegates to Congress, 6:623
75. Rappely, pg.75
76. Ver Steeg pg. 20-22
77. Letters of Delegates to Congress, 3:314
78. Elizabeth Nuxoll and E. James Ferguson, *Investigation of Government Corruption During the American Revolution*, pg. 22-25
79. *Journals of the Continental Congress,* 4:104
80.* After July 4th, the Committee of Secret Correspondence became the Committee of Correspondence. Later still, it became the Office of Foreign Affairs, and ultimately became today's Department of State
81. https://www.encyclopedia.com/history/encyclopedias-almanacs-transcripts-and-maps/achard-de-bonvouloir-et-loyaute-julien-alexandre
82. Letters of Delegates to Congress, 3:366
83. Ver Steeg, pg. 10
84. Letters of Delegates to Congress, 2:72-73
85. Ibid, 4:658
86. Nuxoll, Elizabeth M. & Gallagher, Mary A. Y., *Papers of Robert Morris*, 9:362
87.* While there was great uproar in the Press about "profiteering" merchants, there was no complaint about Jefferson's salary. (All $ values are stated in Spanish Milled Dollars, which were not subject to inflation.)
88. Deane Papers, 1:172-177, 1:232-237
89. *Naval Documents of the American Revolution*, 4:578
90. Letters of Delegates of Congress, 3:466
91. Robert Morris Papers - HSP Levis Collection and Pennsylvania State Archives
92. Revolutionary Diplomatic Correspondence, 4:405
93. *Naval Documents of the American Revolution*, 2:613
94. *Power of the Purse*, pg.71
95. *Naval Documents of the American Revolution, 1777*, 7:1318
96. Letters of Delegates to Congress, 3:676
97. Letters of Delegates to Congress, 3:676
98. *If by Sea*
99. *If by Sea*, pg. 44
100. Revolutionary Diplomatic Correspondence, 2:85
101.* A livre was originally the equivalent the English pound, but the coin had devalued, and during the Revolution was equal to about 25% of a Spanish milled dollar.
102. Letters of Delegates to Congress, 3:258
103. *Dictionary of American Naval Fighting Ships* - Naval Historical Center http://www.history.navy.mil/danfs/r5/reprisal-i.htm
104. Letters of Delegates to Congress, 4:154
105. Ibid, 4:154
106. Letters of Delegates to Congress, 4:146
107. Letters of Delegates to Congress, 4:155
108. American National Biography, https://www.anb.org/view/10.1093/anb/9780198606697.001.0001/anb-9780198606697-e-0100213?rskey=uRYP-3v&result=1
109. *Power of the Purse*, pg. 90
110. Deane Papers, 1:127
111. Letters of Delegates to Congress, 4:276-7
112. Rappeleye, pg. 86
113. *Journals of the Continental Congress,* 5:432
114. Letters of Delegates to Congress, 3:307-308

III

The War Begins

Adam Smith wrote, "*The leading men of America, like those of all other countries, desire to preserve their own importance. ... They have rejected, therefore, the proposal of being taxed by parliamentary requisition, and like other ambitious and high-spirited men, have rather chosen to draw the sword in defense of their own importance.*"[1]

Declaration of Independence

The Continental Congress decided that in response to the ongoing abuse from England they would become independent. Their next step was to issue a declaration. Often such expressions were printed as broadsides in the newspapers or issued in pamphlets. Various states had already issued declarations of their own. Virginia had issued a Declaration of Rights, for example.

Years later, it became Jefferson's dying wish that he be remembered as the author of the Declaration of Independence, and it should be so. Also, it should not be forgotten that Jefferson labored in the Graff House in Philadelphia during those days in June and early July 1776 while he wrote the immortal words, "all men are created equal." One wonders how his attending slave, who shared his quarters in Philadelphia, would have considered those words. According to one source, Jefferson was asked about the apparent contradiction of a slaveholder making such a claim. The source says Jefferson, "For a moment was dumb with astonishment, then: *'By God! I never thought of that before.'*"[2] While it is difficult to substantiate that anecdote, it is believable because it is an indication of his cultural norms, and shows that through years of conditioning, he and his like-minded slaveholders had developed the mental habit of dehumanizing the slaves. Such was the kind of thinking that prompted Samuel Johnson, the famous Tory writer, to ask, "How is it that we hear the loudest yelps for liberty among the drivers of negroes?"[3]

While Jefferson worked on the declaration he did not work in a vacuum. Apart from the committee's input, Jefferson reworked portions of George Mason's earlier "Declaration of Rights" into the preamble of the

Declaration of Independence. One finds this phrase in Mason's Virginia Declaration of Rights, "That all men are by nature equally free and independent, and have certain inherent rights, of which, when they enter into a state of society, they cannot, by any compact, deprive or divest their posterity; namely, the enjoyment of life and liberty, with the means of acquiring and possessing property, and pursuing and obtaining happiness and safety." Jefferson modified this to read, "that all men are created equal, that they are endowed by their creator with certain inalienable rights, that among these are life, liberty, and the pursuit of happiness."

Where Mason wrote, "That all power is vested in, and consequently derived from, the people; that magistrates are their trustees and servants, and at all times amenable to them." Jefferson rewrote, "Governments are instituted among Men, deriving their just powers from the consent of the governed..."

Where Mason wrote, "That government is, or ought to be, instituted for the common benefit, protection, and security of the people, nation or community; of all the various modes and forms of government that is best, which is capable of producing the greatest degree of happiness and safety." Jefferson rewrote, "to institute new Government, laying its foundation on such principles and organizing its powers in such form, as to them shall seem most likely to effect their Safety and Happiness."

The Declaration of Independence was not just a philosophical statement, after the preamble they added a list of specific grievances for pre-

The Congress Voting Independence, Robert Edge Pine.
Morris, seated left in white stockings, expressing his reservations.

sentation to England and the world. These are enumerated in the Declaration and were viewed at the time as the most important part of the document. On July 2nd, the Declaration of Independence came from the drafting committee. It was time to make a stand.

There were two critical votes. The first was held on July 2nd. That was the vote to separate from England. Robert Morris and John Dickinson did not attend that vote. Morris could not, in good conscience, reverse his earlier stance that independency was misguided. On the other hand, Morris knew the separation resolution would pass, and that if it were to succeed it would have to be unanimous. Morris abstained from voting. By removing himself from the room he allowed the vote to separate to become unanimous, and therefore to be as powerful as possible. On July 2nd, Georgia and South Carolina demanded the removal from the Declaration Jefferson's condemnation of slavery; by leaving on that day, Morris also avoided an opportunity to comment on removing that condemnation, the slave trade, and King George for encouraging those things.[4]

The second critical vote was on the wording of the Declaration document itself. Conventional wisdom holds that Morris was absent from the famous vote on July 4th, 1776. This is based on the recollection of one of Morris' political opposites, Thomas McKean, made over forty years after the fact. Also, according to McKean, it was raining the day Morris was absent. The meteorological record shows that it was sunny on the 4th, but it did rain on the 2nd. This leads scholars to conclude that over the forty-year gap in time McKean may have confused Morris' absence on the 2nd with what happened on the 4th.

Thomas Jefferson's contemporaneous notes state that the whole Pennsylvania delegation voted for the wording of the Declaration. Morris was part of that delegation, but was he there? A clue can be found in the record of other activities undertaken on the 4th of July 1776. Morris was assigned duties that day on some matters relating to naval affairs, and he was working on the business of organizing state militias. It was standard practice for Congress to assign duties only to people present in the chamber, so this assignment indicates Morris was present on that day.[5]

Morris was well aware of Congress' actions on the 4th and took practical steps toward getting ready for the upcoming war. In addition to accepting assignments from Congress, Morris was concerned that Pennsylvania's militia would not be available for the looming conflict.[6] He must have been considering the pacifist direction of the Quaker Assembly when, on that day, he sent a message to several state committees, calling an organizational meeting to prepare the middle states to support each other in the event of war. He called on them "...to devise the most expeditious mode of raising and marching the Militia of the Province to the Assistance of the Neighboring Colonies."[7]

Morris was sure the Declaration would pass, and it is clear that he was in the Hall during part of the day. However, Morris later expressed his thoughts on the matter by saying that he had hoped his opposition to the whole affair would make him so unpopular that he would be released from government service. This was not an ill-founded assumption. All the delegates from Pennsylvania who opposed the Declaration were soon removed from office; all except Morris, who was returned to the Continental Congress on July 20th. In the final analysis, his actions supported the measure by allowing it to pass without a dissenting vote, but his effort to remove himself from public service by speaking out against the Declaration failed. Morris was worried about sunshine patriots, and the false impression given by radical leaders that the war would be a short one.

Morris and Franklin sent the Declaration of Independence to Europe to inform the countries there that the "United Colonies" had broken from England. This was done through the Committee of Secret Correspondence and on July 8th it went out to Silas Deane in France.

> Sir, With this you will receive the Declaration of the Congress for a final separation from Great Britain. It was the universal demand of the people, justly exasperated by the obstinate perseverance of the Crown in its tyrannical and destructive measures, and the Congress were very unanimous in complying with that demand. You will immediately communicate this piece to the Court of France, and send copies of it to the other courts of Europe.
>
> B Franklin
> Robert Morris[8]

He followed up with a letter in support of armed action against the crown. On July 10th Morris wrote to the American agents in France, "Capt Parker has orders to arm & fit out the *Dispatch* in a Warlike manner and we hope you will advise & assist him in doing it. You'll please to procure him the assistance of the most skillful Persons, Tradesmen &c for doing that business & supply him with money to purchase Cannon, Swivels, Howitzers, Musquets, Powder, Balls &c."[9]

On July 21st, Morris wrote to the head of the Pennsylvania Assembly, Joseph Reed, on the importance of arming for war. Shortly thereafter, that

Quaker-dominated government was dismissed. The new group that took political control eventually chased from Pennsylvania many people from the old Quaker government and their co-religionists. This left conditions of uncertainty, and a power vacuum resulted in the state. During the next fourteen years there was a struggle over what political system would fill that vacuum.

When Morris realized that he could not hold back the pro-independence movement he did not go home and nurse a grudge, instead he joined his countrymen and supported their decision. His willingness to act with the will of the majority is testimony to his dedication to democratic principles. As he put it, "I think an individual that declines the Service of his Country because its Councils are not conformable to his Ideas, makes but a bad Subject; a good one will follow if he cannot lead."[10]

[Complete quote below.]

> I am sorry to say there are some amongst us that cannot bear the thought of reconciliation on any terms. To these men all propositions of the kind sound like high Treason against the States and I really believe they would sooner punish a Man for this Crime than for bearing arms against us…
>
> I am not for making any Sacrifice of Dignity, but still I would hear them [the British] if possible, because if they can offer Peace on admissible terms I believe the great majority of America would still be for accepting it. If they can only offer Pardons & that is fully ascertained it will firmly Unite all America in their exertions to support the Independency they have declared and it must be obvious to every body that our United Efforts will be absolutely necessary. This being the case why should we fear to Treat of Peace or to hear the Commissioners on that Subject. If they can offer terms that are advantageous & honorable for this Country, let us meet them. If they cannot We are not in a situation or temper to ask or receive pardons & all who don't mean to stoop to this Ignominious submission will consequently take up their Arms with a determination to Conquer or die. If they offer or desire a Conference & we reject it, those who are already dissatisfyed will become more so and others will follow their example & we may expect daily greater disunion & defection in every part of these States. At least such are my apprehensions on this Subject. I have uniformly Voted against & opposed the declaration of Independence because in my poor opinion it was an improper time and will neither promote the interest or redound to the honor of America, for it has caused

division when we wanted Union, and will be ascribed to very different principles than those which ought to give rise to such an Important measure. I did expect my Conduct in this great Question would have procured my dismission from the great Council but find myself disappointed for the Convention have thought proper to return me in the New Delegation, and altho my interest & inclination prompt me to decline the Service yet I cannot depart from one point that first induced me to enter in the Public Line. I mean an opinion that it is the duty of every Individual to Act his part in whatever Station his Country may Call him to, in times of difficulty, danger & distress. Whilst I think this a duty I must submit, altho the Councils of America have taken a different course from my Judgments Sc wishes. I think an individual that declines the Service of his Country because its Councils are not conformable to his Ideas, makes but a bad Subject; a good one will follow if he cannot lead.[11]

John Nixon reading the Declaration to American Citizens, drawn by E.A. Abbey

Into the Details

The great and small details of government were the business of the Continental Congress. As a member, Morris kept his eyes on getting guns and money for the war; for example, three weeks after independence was declared, he wrote to Washington about the imminent arrival of five tons of musket powder and the continuing effort to create more in three powder mills in New York.[12] In addition, he looked after Congress' money, and he helped individual Congressmen with their personal finances. His efforts to withdraw Charles Lee's funds from Lee's bank in England stalled after the British learned about the Declaration. It was assumed that they had seized Lee's assets. Morris was holding Lee's mortgage and Congress worked to establish a fund to get Lee out of debt. This was out of a feeling of obligation for General Lee's service at the Battle of Fort Moultrie. Morris was also handling funds for some of General Gates' private affairs, and on the 25th of July wrote to him about his family's stay with the Morrises and commiserated about the unfortunate death of a horse.[13]

On August 2nd Morris put his misgivings aside and signed the Declaration of Independence along with the other members of Congress. Years later Dr. Benjamin Rush, of Pennsylvania, recalled the "the pensive and awful silence which pervaded the house when we were called up, one after another, to the table of the President of Congress, to subscribe what was believed by many at that time to be our own death warrants."[14]

On August 11th Morris focused his attention on France. Simultaneously, six thousand English soldiers arrived in New York harbor from their drubbing in Charlestown, South Carolina. He wrote to Silas Deane about Continental business with his half-brother, Thomas, and asked Deane to look after him. Morris thought his brother would be an asset to the cause, "I flatter myself he will prove a valuable & useful acquisition to you, as you'll find him Master of the Language, tractable, Capable & quick of apprehension.... He possesses a good deal of Mercantile knowledge & is acquainted personally and by Fame with many of the first Houses in Europe. Therefore it seems to me the present opportunity of Improving our Fortunes ought not to be lost especially as the very means of doing it will Contribute to the Service of our Country at the same time"[15] Morris' idea of being able to do well by doing good, as he expressed here, was typical of his ability to operate on several levels at once.

Morris continued to import Continental war supplies along with commercial products on ships traveling on both Willing, Morris & Co's. and Deane's accounts. His plan was to reinvest the money made from private trade, immediately, in goods for export. "Now if the goods arrive safe we can sell them instantly for ready Money at very high prices and would immediately invest the money in the purchase of tobacco, indigo, flour, wheat & such other produce as may suit the French Market."[16] This kind of doubling up was the spirit of risk in those days. It was the general operating procedure of the mid-Atlantic merchant society: to make hay while the sun shone. He left the details to Deane in France and his agents in the South. At the same time, he continued to be busy with disbursements of continental monies for troops in the field,[17] and to make offers to purchase ships that had been damaged in service.[18] Morris arranged to buy a ship for the Continental fleet from John Hancock, and to load it with salt to gain funds for the war. He allowed Willing, Morris & Co to act as a means of financing the purchase.[19] There were no banks in America at that time and merchant firms were often called on to provide financial assistance to Congress.

That summer, Robert Morris and Thomas Jefferson were on the same committee to create the first postal service.[20] They also shared an interest in new technologies. Morris marveled at the new invention called "disappearing ink" and he promoted its use for secret communications, the likes of which he often found himself writing. At the same time, he was busy with the business of war, but even as he prepared, Morris was clearly not interested in spreading the conflict. He worried that his instinct for peace and prosperity might be at odds with the means of winning. He wrote in confidence to his friend John Jay, "It appears clear to me that we may very soon involve all Europe in a war by managing properly the apparent forwardness of the Court of France. It's a horrid consideration that our own safety should call on us to involve other nations in the calamities of war. Can this be morally right or have morality & policy nothing to do with each other? Perhaps it may not be good policy to investigate the question at this time."[21]

New Arrangements

A new class of politicians moved forward to create a replacement government in Pennsylvania. They were motivated by the Declaration and the failure of the anti-war Quaker Proprietors to raise an army. Publisher Benjamin Franklin was busy on Continental matters during these early days, but he took time to act as a figurehead for the effort to write a new constitution for Pennsylvania. Others did much of the work. Brewer Timothy Matlack, mathematician James Cannon, Dr Benjamin Rush, Dr. Thomas Young, of Boston Tea Party fame, and writer Thomas Paine worked mightily to draw up a new state constitution. None had much, if any, practical governing experience. A few were Presbyterians. The only reason to mention that these were Presbyterians is to provide context for their democratic ways. During this period, the Presbyterians would elect the member of their congregations whom they wanted to lead the services, so they were well familiar with direct democracy.

The tendency in Pennsylvania toward a unique kind of direct democracy was so strong that the state even had a brand of militia group that elected its own leaders and voted on the military actions they would take. They called themselves, Associators. One such leader was John Armstrong who had fought at Ft. Moultrie, and who became famous for his exploits in the Wyoming Valley some years later. Washington discovered early on that the Associators in his army were somewhat difficult to manage. At one point he even requested that Morris deprive them of weapons because he was not sure how the arms would be used. These militiamen were so disinterested in the chain of command that later on in the conflict, the Pennsylvania line in the Southern Division was often involved in mutinous rumblings.

The war effort moved ahead in Congress and in the field. The momentous events of July and the commencement of the declared war made Morris' work even more urgent. The effort to enlarge the number of allies to the Revolutionary cause had failed in Canada. However, as a member of the Committee of Secret Correspondence, and the Secret Committee, Morris kept working to establish positive relations through trade with Native Americans in New York and west of the Allegheny Mountains.[22] Morris wrote to Deane, "We have a number of the six nation Indians now in the city upon the most favorable terms and I hope shall be able to continue them in our friendship."[23] Members of the Secret Committee from Virginia, were in favor of courting the Indians in the Ohio region. Virginia's claim on that area was an important motivation in that decision.

Before the conflict, the British had provided the Six Nations with a variety of European goods as a way to keep the peace and to encourage good relations. The Americans attempted to take on this role with goods brought to the Indians from Europe. Unfortunately, this trade was the most difficult to conduct. The British controlled the St. Lawrence, which had been the route for much of this trade, so Americans needed to transport the bulky goods past British warships, and then overland to suspicious partners via dirt footpaths in horse-drawn wagons. Guns for the troops had a priority over a risky effort into this business. The existing alliance between the British and the Six Nations also presented a problem, especially considering that when the British were in pursuit of Americans in northern New York State everyone went through a lot of Indian Territory. Americans discovered that shooting at prospective allies was a bad form of diplomacy.

All of the Six Nations turned against the former Colonies except the Oneida. Thomas Jefferson wrote to John Page from Philadelphia in August, "I am sorry to hear that the Indians have commenced war, but greatly pleased you have been so decisive on that head. Nothing will reduce those wretches so soon as pushing the war into the heart of their country.

But I would not stop there. I would never cease pursuing them while one of them remained on this side the Mississippi."[24]

For his part, Morris worked to find a way to build a positive relationship with the Six Nations. His old friend, Willing, had experience in the Indian trade because he had been a commissioner in this line of business, since 1758.[25] On September 12th, 1776 Morris wrote again to Silas Deane, "I hope your Credit has been sufficient to procure the Indian Goods and that they are on the way out, for they will be much wanted and we shall not give over remitting until you are fully enabled to pay for them."[26] Unfortunately, Deane relied on Bancroft's help in this business, and Bancroft was secretly working for the other side.

It is interesting to note the differences in tone and approach to relations with the Native Americans. Morris wished to create friends through trade and reduce conflict while Jefferson's bellicose approach and thirst for revenge pushed him to recommend a policy of ethnic cleansing. Morris' approach is more in line with the Quaker culture of Pennsylvania; a culture that values peaceful relations, and multiculturalism. Jefferson's response is more in keeping with his background as a member of a leading Tidewater family. Their culture valued total victory and used revenge to regain lost honor. History reveals which approach was eventually followed.

In the same letter to Deane, Morris mentioned the lack of ships to conduct trade, and that this condition provided opportunities for those with ships who took the risks. He used such observations to encourage others to engage in the trade of supplying America during the war. This observation on the law of supply and demand, and others like it, were often used against Morris by his political enemies who either did not take the risks themselves or wished to control the business. Morris also expressed the thought that his half-brother Thomas might be best suited for private business, and not political business. He had no way of knowing at the time that one of the readers of this letter would be a British spy, or that the very subjects about which he was so worried would come around to him again and again in his career.

While English spies in France got the inside story from reading the commissioners' mail, the British army headed south through New York State to advance their strategy of cutting the colonies in two. On August 7th General Arnold took command of a collection of ships to patrol Lake Champlain and to halt the advance of the British. This flotilla was similar to the "gunboat navies" found on the coast in each state at that time. More ships were added to Arnold's command and eventually there were sixteen in all.

While Arnold was busy defending New York from the advancing British, Jefferson resigned from Congress and returned to Virginia and his ailing wife. Morris wrote to him and wished him well. He thought Jefferson had made the right decision because in his view Jefferson's philosophical nature was better suited to pastoral pursuits like farming, than the nitty-gritty of government.[27]

Meanwhile, Lord Richard Howe, and the much-anticipated delegation of British commissioners, approached the Congress to open negotiations and seek reconciliation. Congress dispatched a delegation consisting of men from various parts of the continent as a demonstration of American unity. The members were: Benjamin Franklin from Philadelphia, John Adams from Boston, and Edward Rutledge from Virginia. The September 11th meeting was held on Staten Island, New York. The Continental representatives were unable to back away from the Declaration of Independence, so they attempted to define independence in a way calculated to satisfy American goals and English tradition. Lord Howe was unable or unwilling to agree, and the negotiations failed to produce any result. The British continued their pursuit of Washington's army.

Rough Trade, Free Trade

The Secret Committee tried to supply the Virginia Committee of Safety with war materials, but a series of events including ships being sunk and captured, brought this to an unsatisfactory conclusion. One ship was forced onto a beach in Maryland. The black powder aboard blew the ship apart, and the local militia had to be dispatched to pick up the stores that littered the nearby beaches and woodland.[28]

The Continental Navy was obviously out-gunned, and the merchant fleet was under constant attack from British warships and privateers. The Americans tried in vain to get the French to provide naval assistance, but it was more than a simple matter of asking for help. An alliance was needed and the effort to draft a model treaty was still underway. Morris and John Adams worked on the draft of that treaty, long after Jefferson went back to Virginia. Congress accepted the Model Treaty in September. The treaty announced American dedication to free trade between the U.S. and other nations on a non-political reciprocal basis.[29] It was also a recognition by Congress of existing American non-political trade arrangements with France, that had been under way for over a year, under the cover of being a Willing and Morris agency. In addition, the model treaty opened the door to Spain, and later even England.

Whereas the Declaration of Independence defined the relationship between man and government, the Model Treaty defined the way the government would relate to other governments in the world. Unlike existing treaties of the day that relied on mutual defense, blood ties, or political allegiance, the Model Treaty was a unique and groundbreaking document. It was based on peacefully binding nations through reciprocal commercial arrangements. When Congress looked back on this period, they assessed this work: "The year 1776 includes some of the most important acts and papers of the Continental Congress. The Declaration of Independence, the first forms of the Articles of Confederation, and the plan of treaties with foreign Powers were of high moment; and any one of these papers, when measured by results or consequences would be sufficient to distinguish the legislation of this year."[30]

It is difficult to tell who authored the Model Treaty because the nature of the committee system masked the roles of the participants. It is, however, instructive to look at the participants and see whose ideas most closely resemble the final product of the committee. Six months earlier Morris had written to Charles Lee on the topic of foreign relations where he cautioned against a political alliance and said,

> ... it is only protection to our Trade that we can want from any Country in Europe, the benefit of that trade will always most readily be admitted as a full compensation for the Protection of it hereafter, although the Ministers of Great Britain were not satisfied with it; If we by resistance obtain proper terms, reconciliation and connection with Great Britain, we want no other protection than hers. If by our own Force of Conduct, we establish an Independent Empire, notwithstanding the utmost exertions of Britain, there is not a Nation in Europe, but will be glad to treat and trade with us on our own terms: therefore I think it best to persevere in our own measures, and depend on our strength, which I believe is quite sufficient; and if so, we shall ever after hold respectable consequence in the World"[31]

This statement to Charles Lee was the basis for the Model Treaty. Morris, the merchant, was a proponent of free trade and he dedicated much of his energy, while in office, to maintain this ideal. In addition, Morris was an Anglican, but he was a product of the greater Philadelphia Quaker culture that esteemed reciprocal relationships, and this was exactly what the Model treaty proposed. Adams was not dedicated to that ideal and would speak against free trade on more than one occasion.[32] It appears that the Model Treaty was drafted by Adams because he was a lawyer by trade, but the intent of the treaty matched the substance of the system Morris believed in, and had been operating for over two years.

The finished Model Treaty was the document that the Commissioners took to France and used as the basis for America's first international agreement. It was also the document that John Jay later brought to Spain in search of support from that kingdom. Ultimately, it acted as the basis for American foreign policy for generations.[33] When it came time to send a delegation to France, three men were chosen as Commissioners. To symbolize the unity of the former colonies, each man came from a different section of the United States. Silas Deane was from New England. Franklin was from the middle states, and Jefferson was from the Old Dominion. Jefferson declined the honor and stayed in Virginia where he worked on that state's laws. On October 22, 1776 Arthur Lee, another Virginian, was appointed in his place. Deane was already in France, working on trade arrangements.

Slow Progress in the Statehouse

The Pennsylvanian doctors, artisans, authors and radicals had been working over the summer to create the new constitution for the state. Their goal was to make a most democratic and responsive system of government, and they enshrined it in the first Pennsylvania Constitution. The new constitution was adopted September 28th, 1776. From that point on those who favored it called themselves "Constitutionalists." They vested all power in the Pennsylvania Assembly. There were elections every year, and the members were limited to four consecutive years of service. There was no Governor, no Senate, no Supreme Court; in short no real checks and balances. There was a "Supreme Executive Council" with a President for regular administration, and a "Council of Censors" which was elected once every seven years to oversee the implementation of the Pennsylvania Constitution. It was as if the House of Representatives were able to create laws without any worry of contradiction. This unicameral system was the most "democratic" they could imagine. However, their version of democracy was not inclusive. Instead, it was largely designed to limit participation to those who agreed with the drafters. To accomplish that goal, their new "test laws" resulted in the disenfranchisement of nearly 40% of the voting public.

The new Pennsylvania Assembly got off to a slow start. The people who disagreed with the "Constitutionalists" were reluctant to support the efforts and waged a kind of political boycott. Many of the experienced candidates refused to run under the new constitution. New delegates had to be elected, but the election did not happen until November.

Other states were also writing new constitutions, many of which, like Massachusetts, Virginia and New York, kept their familiar systems intact. When those old governments were dismissed, the people who took over moved ahead with familiar ideas and political structures, but different allegiances. True to their parliamentarian roots, the people of Massachusetts retained their town meeting style of government.

Virginia adopted its new state constitution on June 29th, 1776. As descendants of the distressed cavaliers, the large landholders in Virginia were very conservative in their outlook. The Virginia Constitution was not as radical or "democratic" as the Pennsylvanian. Instead, it maintained a government with three branches, a bicameral legislature, an executive, and a judicial arm. They kept the same system of voting rights as before, the militia officers stayed the same, and tax payments were directed to the Assembly. A quick glance at the Virginia Constitution provides a reference point for those who seek antecedence for Madison's proposal of the Virginia Plan, years later at the Constitutional Convention in 1789. Upon examination, one finds that experience was also the guide for the creation of a Bill of Rights under the United States Constitution. The plantation owners held the Assembly in Virginia, and the Assembly appointed local tax collectors and law enforcement officers who were most assiduous in their duties when they were not dealing with members of the elite. The middle class in Virginia and other southern states was almost non-existent in terms of political power, and they were often the focus of official actions. Of course, the slaves were under the purview of their legal owners, so the state of their affairs was administered at home. With this in mind one can see why the call for a Bill of Rights to be added to the US Constitution came from Virginians who were familiar with abuses of power.

Scarcity and the War Trade

The Revolution was well underway while the lawyers in their respective state houses worked on state constitutions. Morris, however, was deeply involved in the finances of the war effort and was using his line of credit in London banks to purchase military supplies. He was not pleased to learn that the British government was interfering with his personal finances, as they had with Charles Lee's. They caused his notes to be protested, meaning the checks he wrote were falsely made to "bounce." He wrote, "The Amot hitherto is not above £2000 Stg & We have not £4000 depending but it now seems a matter of doubt whether any bills will be paid or whether they will Seize on the property of Individuals. If they do that we must make Reprizals here and in the mean time we shall use our utmost endeavours to lodge sufficient Effects in Europe to make good yours & all other engagements on Account of the Publick."[34] Morris changed course and looked more to his European contacts; fortunately he had a banker in France named Mr. Grand. However, as noted earlier, there was a dearth of silver money in America, which meant that payments had to be made in commodities. Morris cautioned Deane that during the conflict future remittances, in the form of farm products, would be difficult to send to Europe because the bulky nature of American goods made the shipments of them slow and easy targets at sea.

War supplies did arrive in America, in any case. To the delight of many, six hundred units of canvas were unloaded in Maryland. No sooner had they been unpacked than the marine, the army and the Maryland Committee of Safety all wanted them. General Washington's troops took possession because they needed tents. Morris was disappointed because he wanted sails for the ships. He wrote to the state Committee of Safety, "The Marine Committee remonstrated against this measure alleging that none of the Continental Vessels cou'd be sent out if this Canvass was taken from them. No matter they were told the Soldiers shou'd have Tents if they stripped the Yards of those Continental Frigates & Cruizers that had sails made up, & in Consequence of this measure which nothing but the extreme necessity of our Army could justify, We have now a passel of fine Vessels lying here useless at a time they might have been most advantageously employed."[35] There were no textile mills in America at the time.

Competition for scarce resources reinforced the idea that a strong alliance was needed to secure future shipments. While this effort was under way, unofficial help was made available. On October 1, 1776 Morris and Franklin received a verbal report from Mr. Thomas Story, who had been sent to France by the Committee of Secret Correspondence the previous December. Mr. Story related that Arthur Lee requested Story to tell the Committee that he, Arthur, had been communicating with the French ambassador, the Duke de Vergennes. The Duke told Arthur, "The French Court could not think of entering into a War with England, but that they would assist America by sending from Holland this Fall £200,000 Sterling worth of Arms and Ammunition to St. Eustatius, Martinico, or Cape Francois; that application was to be made to the Governors or Commandants of those Places by inquiring for Mons. Hortalez and that on Persons properly authorized applying, the above Articles would be delivered to them."[36] Hortalez was the fictitious name under which Beaumarchais operated his arms business. The time was still not right for official help, but the French were willing to provide aid, secretly, under those strict conditions.

Morris and Franklin concluded,

> We are also of opinion that it is unnecessary to inform Congress of this Intelligence at present because Mr. Morris belongs to all the Committees that can properly be employed in receiving & importing the expected Supplies from Martinico, St. Eustatia or Cape Francois and will immediately influence the necessary measures for that purpose. Indeed we have already authorized Wm Bingham Esqr. to supply at Martinico & St Eustatia for what comes there & remit part by the Armed Sloop Independence Capt Young promising to send others for the rest. Mr. Morris will apply to the Marine Committee to send other armed Vessels after her & also to Cape Francois (without Communicating this advice) in Consequence private Intelligence lately recd that Arms, ammunition & Clothing can now be procured at those places.
>
> But shou'd any unexpected misfortune befall the States of America so as to depress the Spirits of the Congress, it is our opinion that on any event of that kind, Mr. Morris (if Dr. Franklin should be absent) should communicate this Important matter to Congress, otherwise keep it until part of or the whole Supplies arrive, unless other events happen to render the Communication of it more proper than it appears to be at this time.
>
> B Franklin
> Robt Morris[37]

Richard Henry Lee and William Hooper both agreed with that conclusion.[38] As members of the Secret Committee, they had learned through experience that sharing secrets with the whole Continental Congress was a certain way to broadcast the information to the whole world. John Jay concurred with this view in a contemporaneous letter that he sent from Fishkill, New York. He wrote, "I wish the Secret Committee would communicate no other Intelligence to Congress at large, then what may be necessary to promote the Common Weal, not to gratify the curiosity of individuals. I hint this, because a copy of a Letter from A.L. [Arthur Lee] to that committee has lately been sent by a Member of Congress to a gentleman of his acquaintance who is not a Member of Congress... For as to binding certain Members of the House to Secrecy by oaths or otherwise, would be as absurd as to swear

Lee (no matter which of them) to look or feel like Ned Rutledge, &c."[39] In other words it would be useless.

Congress approved the Model Treaty on September 24th. They soon needed a fast ship to take it and the American emissaries to Europe. In his role as a member of the Committee of Secret Correspondence Morris wrote to the Commissioners in Paris on October 24th, 1776, to inform them that Dr. Franklin was on his way on *The Reprisal,* which was commanded by Captain Wickes. Morris expressed his pleasure at the success of the small Navy when he said, "*The Reprisal* is a fast sailing Ship and Capt. Wickes has already done honor in Action to the American Flag."[40] Captain Wickes was expected to bring some indigo to Nantes, drop off Dr. Franklin, then, as a privateer, take to sea again in search of prizes. After delivering his passenger, Captain Wickes captured six ships as prizes on the first cruise, which ended in February 1777. The prizes were taken to Port Louis, and then the ship went to L'Orient for refitting. The Nantes office of Willing, Morris, & Co. converted the trade goods into the supplies of war for the mission. The plan worked and Captain Wickes became the first American to sail European waters and take British ships.[41, 42, 43, 44]

The months passed; the war plans were well underway, but Pennsylvania was still without a viable government. That state had not even held an election. Nevertheless, the Continental Congress moved ahead as danger neared.

Franklin's fellow commissioner, Silas Deane, continued to play many roles from his position in Paris, even before his official papers arrived. He was a commercial agent in France for Connecticut, and had for some time been an undercover commercial agent with Willing, Morris & Co. He worked in Nantes with John Ross and Thomas Morris to supply the tools of war to the Revolutionaries. However, Deane's work to promote the business interest of his own brother Simeon became the source of some friction between Silas Deane and Robert Morris.[45]

Silas Deane

One of the key roles played by Silas Deane was to recruit talented military specialists to help the Revolutionary cause. Among the officers he was able to attract were the Marquis de Lafayette, Casimir Pulaski, Baron von Steuben, and Johann De Kalb.[46] These people provided great aid to the new nation in spite of the language barriers that existed between them and the English speaking Americans. Deane also sent to America a variety of French soldier adventurers whose participation was less well appreciated.[47]

During the fall of 1776, Beaumarchais was back in France where he was beginning to operate the trading house Roderigue Hortalez & Co. He attempted to contact Arthur Lee to start the process of conducting business with the Americans. Unfortunately, it was impossible for him to reach Lee consistently. Beaumarchais wrote Silas Deane, "I have received no answer to my last communications [with A. Lee], in which I endeavored to definitely arrange the terms of this important affair… I ask nothing better than to recommence in a surer and more connected manner the negotiations which I must regard as having failed with other persons."[48]

As an agent for the Secret Committee, Deane stepped up and fulfilled the trade relationship with Beaumarchais. Deane was a merchant in his own right, and Willing, Morris & Co. was already operating its secret agency in France. Deane was assisted by William Carmichael, whom Deane had made his secretary.[49, 50] After that, the Hortalez business in France was conducted mostly by Deane with help from Willing, Morris & Co. agents.[51]

Back in June, Arthur Lee had written to Charles W. F. Dumas in Holland, about the Hortalez arrangements,[52] but Lee did not follow up. Dumas was a native of Switzerland who lived in The Hague, and who had been recruited by Franklin to act as a secret agent for America.[53] Deane dispatched his secretary, William Carmichael, to meet with Dumas. On that trip Carmichael met with Mr. Grand,[54] a brother to Morris' French banker, and the man who became the agent for the loan from France.[55]

The popular vision of John Adams is that he arranged loans from the Dutch. While that is true, those loans were made in 1782 and 1783, nearly six years later. The 1776 support for the American cause from the French via Holland was the result of the groundwork laid by the people working in London, the Willing, Morris & Co. secret agency in France, and the efforts of Charles W. F. Dumas. These secret agents created a trusted relationship with the French and a system for the delivery of the needed supplies long before Independence was declared, before Franklin arrived in Passay, or the Treaty of Alliance was signed over a year later in 1778.

As outlined by Vergennes, Hortalez & Co. acted as a conduit for the first supplies sent from France, and funding for that passed through Grand in Holland. It just so happened that during this period the French Army was upgrading its weapon systems, and that made many old-style weapons available for the Americans. Beaumarchais wrote to Deane, "One of the considerations the most important to our success, will be to have ships ready to embark the men, arms, munitions, and goods on their arrival at the ports.... If you will answer for the American ships, I will answer for the aid from Europe..."[56] Ships were found, and the trade began.

In one deal Deane arranged with Beaumarchais for the purchase of "cloathing for Twenty thousand Men, thirty thousand Fusils [muzzle loaders], one hundred Tons of Powder, Two hundred Brass Canon, Twenty four Brass mortars with shell, shot, Lead &c in proportion."[57] These materials were sent to the Revolutionaries and American tobacco was expected in return. The supplies went via French ships and transferred to U.S. ships in Martinique, Hispaniola, and St. Eustatius under the watchful eyes of Stephen Ceronio, William Bingham, and Richard Harrison. Some ships and their supplies arrived but others were lost at sea.[58] [59]

As time went on, Beaumarchais' company operated from Bordeaux, Nantes, La Hâvre, and Marseilles.[60] He acquired the use of fifteen ships through a contract with John Joseph de Monthieu.[61] The ships in Beaumarchais' network most often went to Martinique or Santa Domingo where American agents were stationed. From there they usually went north to Portsmouth, New Hampshire to avoid the British blockade. This northern unloading point was closest to the Northern Division of the Continental Army. So, they received more supplies than Washington's army, and those supplies helped Gates and Arnold in the battle of Saratoga, nearly a year later.[62]

In the fall of 1776, Beaumarchais wrote Morris to say, "Your Friend, Mr. Deane, is the most useful man in all your French affairs, & whom the Republic ought the most to rely on."[63] This decision by Beaumarchais caused much vexation in the heart of Arthur Lee, who wrote Congress, "It is in consequence of this that I find the promises that were made me by the French agent in London, and which I stated to you by Mr. Storey and others, have not been entirely fulfilled. The changing of the mode of conveying what was promised was settled with Mr. Deane, whom Mr. Hortalez found here on his return, and with whom all the arrangements were afterwards made"[64]

It is only reasonable that Beaumarchais would work with Deane and Willing, Morris & Co. They were present at the critical time when Lee was absent, which spoke well for their reliability. They were established merchants with good credit, ships, offices, dock space, and commercial agents in France, Spain, Italy and the New World. While Arthur Lee was a learned man he had little or no experience in trade. Arthur's brother, William, presented himself as a merchant, but he was an alderman in London, which made him suspect; he had no official role at the time, and was not included. Ultimately, Beaumarchais and Deane did not fare well in the deal. Later, Arthur Lee made it his mission to deny Beaumarchais payment, and then have Deane removed at the very moment of his triumph. Arthur falsely maintained the supplies were a gift. The French crown would not comment at the time because by doing so they would admit they had taken sides in a civil conflict, while their participation was still a secret. To further complicate matters the English pressured France into passing various ordinances against shipping war supplies to America. France complied as part of their program of official denial. These ordinances were poorly enforced, but local French officials did harass Beaumarchais' agents as he worked in his secret capacity for the King.

Thomas Morris' role increased when, in October, he was made Superintending Agent over all European Concerns.[65] Thomas was in a position to sell tobacco sent in payment from America, and to sell ships taken as prizes by American privateers.[66] He also became more involved with Deane in the effort to win allies among the Six Nations with the Indian goods trade. Naturally this would put Thomas in close contact with Dr. Bancroft, whom Deane had enlisted in the same line of business. Robert wrote to Deane about his brother, "he is instructed amongst other things to make up to you what you have other ways received short of the forty thousand pounds Sterling for the purchase of Indian Goods."[67] Robert knew Thomas' tendency to play harder than he worked, so he again asked Silas Deane to look after Tom, and to help guide his decisions.

The business of getting supplies from Europe continued and credit was growing tight. There was a lot of writing back and forth on the topic of the Indian Goods, but the effort was not going well (possibly due to the influences of Dr. Bancroft, British spy), and it was eventually abandoned. In total \$80,000 was allocated by Congress for goods that did not arrive.[68] Morris claimed the funds were shifted to the general account when the business became untenable, but Arthur Lee and some modern consensus historians attribute this gap completely to Morris as the personification of

Willing, Morris & Co., a perception that Morris objected to at the time. While many modern historians have taken their cues from Lee and focused exclusively on Morris, who was in Philadelphia at the time, they generally overlook the role of others in the French agency.

The war trade was never simple. When secret supplies were sent across the ocean the documentation was kept in a weighted sack that could be thrown overboard if the British attacked, or they were placed on the bottom of a barrel that would sink if needed. With this in mind it is understandable that there might be some lapses in documentation. In one such occasion there was a shipment of twenty casks of black powder consigned to one Nathaniel Shaw, Jr. who was the Continental Agent for Connecticut. It arrived without sufficient documentation, so Morris wrote: "In the Brig at Maryland is also arrived 133 bbs. & 20 Casks of Powder for you which we suppose to be on Continental Account, and shall give the Board of War an Order to receive the same, but if we are mistaken & this should be private property you will set us right and we will either pay you powder or Money for it."[69] One can hardly imagine what Mr. Shaw meant to do with 20 casks of black powder, but this was Morris' way of resolving the question.

The Battle of Trenton

As 1776 slipped into fall, Benedict Arnold and his gunboat navy patrolled Lake Champlain. Under General Sir Guy Carleton's direction, the British ordered prefabricated ships brought overland from Canada and assembled in New York. Carleton built his own squadron of 20

Defeat of the American Fleet under Benedict Arnold off Crown Point in Lake Champlain. (National Archives of Canada, Battle of Valcour Island by V. Zveg)

ships to take control of the lake from Arnold's fleet. Starting on October 11th the brave flotilla of small American ships fought well against the British in a series of lake battles, one of which was the Battle of Valcore Island. The Americans ultimately lost the fighting, but they slowed the British advance towards New York City; and by October 20th General Carleton decided to return to Canada for winter quarters. This stopped him from joining General Howe in the south as Howe pursued Washington.

Washington's career as Commander in Chief of the Army was off to an uneven start. He forced the British to retreat from Boston in March. Then he moved his army to New York with the idea of taking on the British, who were expected to be there in June. He set up a position on Long Island, but he had to abandon that to the British in August. He withdrew through Brooklyn to Manhattan and went north, along the Hudson, in a series of retreats. Finally, in November, he and his army were routed in White Plains and he surrendered Forts Washington and Lee. The British captured 2,500 men during the Americans' retreat across the Hudson River into New Jersey.

While the Continental Army moved through the New York area, an ambitious nineteen-year-old fatherless native of St. Kits, named Alexander Hamilton, left school and joined the ranks as a member of the artillery. He had studied the science for under a month but was among the best in the field. This young man joined because he saw this war as an opportunity for those with skill, fortitude, and ambition to prove themselves through the struggle. Ultimately, during the final major battle of the War, Hamilton was among the first over the ramparts that protected Yorktown. Two others who walked with Washington's army became prominent in the cause, Haym Salomon and Thomas Paine. Before joining the exodus Haym Salomon had been arrested in New York because of his revolutionary activities as a member of the Sons of Liberty. He had just recently left prison and was forced to leave all his possessions behind. The other, Thomas Paine,[70*] had come up with the Pennsylvania Militia.

The news of Washington's defeats reached France, and made the job of the American diplomacy much harder. Silas Deane wrote to Morris about this, and mentioned that Robert's brother Thomas was adding to the difficulties. Dean reported that Thomas had taken a trip from France to London and fallen in with such a "dissolute & expensive" group that he was harming the reputation of America as well as Willing, Morris & Co. The combination of these conditions was fueling speculation, promulgated by British spies, that Robert was "Negotiating, or giving up the Cause,

& the British Ambassador with other British Agents roundly assert it."[71] The British agents were wrong, of course.

Elsewhere in France, material support for the beleaguered American Army was secretly being made ready. By late November 1776, Beaumarchais had gathered four shiploads of war supplies in Le Hâvre, which included over two hundred pieces of field artillery. He also intended to send a unit of artillery officers to man the guns and assist the Americans in the proper use of these weapons in modern warfare.[72] The officer in charge delayed the sailing of these ships by going to Versailles to talk with the Admiralty to confirm these were legal shipments. Beaumarchais followed to hurry up that mission. With English spies everywhere such delays were not advisable. After getting back to Le Hâvre, Beaumarchais discovered that one of his plays was being performed in a local theatre. His vanity was impossible to suppress, and although he was supposed to be under cover as "Durand," he felt compelled to attend a dress rehearsal and that further compelled him to direct the cast. This revealed him to the British spies and three of the cargo ships were forced to stay in port.

Also in November, Robert asked Thomas to contact their mutual agents in London and close the accounts of Willing, Morris & Co, and to use the money to pay their debts.[73] Morris knew that their finances were under attack in that city because he had written, "good deal of pains had been taken & even ministerial influences used (as I am well informed) to do that previous to his [Thomas'] arrival."[74] As Deane noted earlier, Thomas went to London, himself, and took the money out of the accounts. Then he went out on the town drinking and gambling. He generated debts and expenses amounting to 1,000 sterling.[75] This horrified Willing, because Thomas had used company credit for his gambling binge. One wonders how it would have been possible for a well-known American patriot to travel in London, without the assistance of someone like Thomas' coworker, Dr. Bancroft, British spy. European intrigues and misbehavior continued.

Back in America, Washington's tired army continued its retreat from New York, through New Jersey, finally entering Pennsylvania on December 7th. They landed on the western side of the Delaware River, just a few miles north of Trenton. General Howe's British Army, and contingent of Hessians, were working their way south through New Jersey, and they seemed on the path to victory. They offered a general amnesty to New Jersey citizens who pledged allegiance to the British and not the Rebels. Many expected the uprising to end soon and accepted the offer.

Over in Europe, Beaumarchais had left his disallowed shipment behind, and made his way back to Paris by late December. When he arrived, he discovered that the political atmosphere had changed with the installation of the new American emissary, the famous and celebrated Dr. Franklin. Franklin was much beloved by France and many members of the French aristocracy visited him in Passy. Beaumarchais and Franklin did not seem to get along well, and this helped maintain Beaumarchais' cover.

Franklin was already familiar with his fellow Commissioners, Silas Deane and Arthur Lee when he took on his new role in France. He considered his situation and wrote to Morris after his arrival, "I remember that long before I was ordered here, you did me the Honor to say, you should not dislike being sent to France with me. Since being here, I have frequently wished that Appointment had taken place, I think I should have passed my time more comfortably."[76]

Just as the American ministers were establishing themselves anew in France, Washington feared the war was lost because his army was preparing to evaporate in less than a month. The British, and Washington, were well aware that the American troops' six-month enlistment was over on January 1st, 1777. Washington had no money, and no recent victories to his credit. Instead, the heavy losses in White Plains hung over his army and Congress. The promise of a short war, and easily won freedom was starting to ring hollow. The clouds were moving in on the sunshine patriots. Meanwhile Congress argued over the very existence of the Continental Army and the virtues of the citizen soldier. As Congress engaged in this interesting philosophical debate, they provided poor support for Washington's men in the field. Instead, they were taking steps to strengthen the state military forces.

With Washington's army in retreat, the Marine Committee sought to support Washington's situation. They ordered an attack on British supply ships to disrupt their hold on New York, and slow Howe's progress. General Howe's British Army was marching south through New Jersey toward Philadelphia. On December 10th Morris wrote from the Marine Committee,

> Sir, We have ordered the Captains of the Armed vessels now at Rhode Island Severally to proceed to Sea with all possible dispatch and to cruize for the Enemies Store Ships & Supply Vessels going to New York.
>
> You Sir will exert yourself to have these orders carried into execution as Quickly as possible."

We are sir, Your hble Servts.

William Ellery
Fras. Lewis
Robt Morris
Wm. Whipple
Richard Henry Lee[77]

This effort did not stop Howe's progress, but because of shortages he ordered his troops to forage for supplies. The result among the less disciplined was much stealing and some burning. This lawlessness degenerated to rape and other crimes committed by Hessian troops running wild. Naturally this behavior disturbed the inhabitants and alienated them to the point that they reversed their earlier decision to support Howe in return for an offered amnesty. Instead of a supportive citizenry, Howe encountered a renewed armed resistance from a growing insurgency of angry farmers, and other residents.

Some new war supplies came to Philadelphia when the Continental brigantine, *Andrew Doria,* successfully ran the British blockade. Morris used a portion of these supplies to create defenses in Philadelphia and to protect the city if the British entered. A second portion was sent north. During the first week of December Colonel John Cadwalader, a member of the Pennsylvania Committee of Safety, took a train of supply wagons north from Philadelphia and arrived at Washington's camp with the supplies and fresh troops. Among them was a new group of Associators from the Pennsylvania militia. Cadwalader was an occasional business associate with Willing, Morris & Co. John Barry, who at this point was without any ship, went north as his aide-de-camp. Cadwalader told General Washington about Morris' progress, and his intentions to send the ships to sea.[78] These supplies were put to good use in Washington's Christmas attack on Trenton a few weeks later.

Anticipating the arrival of Howe's British Army in Philadelphia, the Continental Congress retired, that is to say: ran away, to Baltimore during the second week of December. Morris sent his wife and children to her family's home in Maryland to protect them in the event the city was taken. The Morris family lost their house slave, Hero, during this confused time. He ran off, never to return. The Morrises let him go without launching any serious effort to find him as a runaway. Robert stayed in Philadelphia.

Congress left three of its members behind as an Executive Committee; Robert Morris, George Walton and George Clymer. They were expected to conduct the business of the Congress. Morris was keenly aware that Congress was jealous of its authority, yet at this critical time he was forced to make quick decisions on behalf of the body without their consent. Morris wrote, "The unfinished business of the Marine & Secret Committees I intend to confine myself to, but I hear so many complaints & see so much confusion from other quarters that I am obliged to advise in things not committed to me. Circumstanced as our affairs now are I conceive it better to take libertys & assume some powers than to let the general interest suffer."[79] A series of letters went back and forth that, in sum, allowed Morris to take executive actions on the behalf of Congress.[80]

It was during this time that he learned that his own interests were endangered by informers who told the British about his work to supply the American Revolution. A fellow member of the Secret Committee, Richard Henry Lee, wrote him a letter from Baltimore: "the British Ministry have an accurate account of every Vessel that arrives in every Port of Europe from America with the particulars of her returns and they know also of every Vessel that loads in Europe for America."[81] This information was coming, in part, from the Scottish merchants whose tobacco business had been interrupted by the Revolution and British blockade; and from spies who had infiltrated the American team in France.

More bad news arrived when Morris received critical intelligence from Washington that the British troops intended to mass at Trenton, and to cross above the falls on their way to Philadelphia. The ice and the falls at Trenton precluded the ships under Morris' influence from helping Washington, so he hurried to send the ships out of port to keep them from being harmed or captured. On December 13th Morris wrote to Washington for sailors to help sail the *Delaware* to safety. Morris also wrote to John Hancock, president of Congress, "As soon as I saw this authentic Account of the Enemy's design to Cross Delaware above the Falls, I waited on Genl. Putnam & proposed that the Frigate *Randolph* & Sloop *Hornet* shou'd be sent to Sea immediately as it was plain to me they wou'd be of no use here & I had received certain advice that there was not any British Men of War in our Bay. The General very readily Consented & I have this afternoon given Capt. Biddle & Capt Nicholson their Instructions signed by me on behalf of the Marine Committee."[82]

December 13th was also the day Washington started making plans[83] to attack the British in New Jersey, so he could not spare any of his troops. After Cadwalader arrived at camp, General Gates decided that instead of helping Washington engage the enemy in Trenton he would join the Congress in Baltimore. Colonel Cadwalader took command of General Gates' troops, and readied the men for the assault on the capital of New Jersey.

On December 16th the news arrived that General Charles Lee had been captured. Morris wrote to Hancock describing the event,

> ... some of the Tories have given notice to the Enemy that the General [Lee] lodged at a certain House 5 Miles distant from his Army. In consequence, a party of Light Horse about 50 Surrounded the House at day break. The Genl. had an aid de Camp & ten Men with him. They defended themselves in the House for two hours, when the Men offered to Surrender, alleging that the General was not there they answered they knew he was in that House & if he did not immediately surrender himself, they would burn the House & him in it. In short the Genl was obliged to appear & he promised to Surrender on Condition they would treat him like an officer & a Gentn. The moment they got him they mounted him on a Horse & Galloped off with him not even allowing him time to get his Hat, nor did they take any of his party but left them to do as they pleased.[84]

Lee, who at the time, believed the cause was effectively lost, spent the winter in unusually pleasant circumstances while under British guard, and has been suspected of collaborating during the period.

Morris outlined the situation to Silas Deane in France, and it looked bleak from Philadelphia,

> With a heavy heart I sit down to write to you at this time as the unfortunate case of American Affairs at this period leave [no] room for joy in the mind of a true friend to this Country.... But these unfortunate Events commenced with the loss of Fort Washington by the reduction of which the Enemy made about 2700 prisoners, & at this critical time, they by Treachery, Bribery or accident intercepted some dispatches from Gen Washington to Congress, also some of the Generals private Letters, particularly one to Ned Rutlidge in which he had fully laid open the unfortunate situation he was then involved in by the curs'd short enlistments of our army, for the times of most of them expired on the first of Decr. & the rest on the 1st of Jan., when the whole army would leave him ..."[85]

A somber Morris continued and said that

> Our people knew not the hardships & Calamities of War when they so boldly dared Britain to arms. Every man was then a bold

> Patriot, felt himself equal to the Contest and seemed to wish for an opportunity of evincing his prowess, but now when we are fairly engaged, when Death & Ruin stare us in the face and when nothing but the most intrepid Courage can rescue us from Contempt & disgrace, sorry I am to Say it, many of those who were foremost in Noise, Shrink coward like from the Danger and are begging pardon without striking a Blow.[86]

As far as Morris knew he was the only delegate left in Philadelphia on December 21st. A new supply sloop managed to slip past the British blockade and arrive from France with blankets and guns. Morris sent the blankets to Washington but moved the guns to a storehouse west of Philadelphia and out of the hands of the Associators.[87] He continued to prepare the remaining Continental ships for sea to escape, and implemented a plan to get them past the British blockade.

He wrote to Hancock,

> The *Delaware* is getting ready and I have ordered the *Fly*, Capt Warner, down the Bay to watch the Enemies Ships & bring us word if they should quit that Station. I have sent an express across the Jerseys to Capt Baldwin of the *Wasp* to Cruize outward of them to give Notice to inward bound Ships, and have Stationed the Hornet, Capt Nicholson, (who attempted to get out to Sea but could not) in Christeen Creeks Mouth to act in Conjunction with a large Galley of this State in defence of that Creek as there are many valuable Stores up it. I shall get the Sloop *Independence* hove down & some little damage she recd at Chincoteague repaired & then send her also to watch the Enemys Ships.[88]

The work of construction on the ships of the nascent Continental Navy was still underway in Philadelphia shipyards, and was becoming desperate. Morris had requested workers from among Washington's ranks, but was refused. Workers were so scarce that even math teachers and other volunteers helped get the ships to the point that they could escape.[89] Morris wrote to encourage Washington, "I have been told today that you are preparing to cross into the Jerseys. I hope it may be true and promise myself joyful tidings from your expedition. You have my sincere prayers of success and nothing would give me greater pleasure than to hear of such occurrences as your exalted merit deserves."[90]

A few days later, on December 26, 1776, Morris sent another message to Washington as part of his congratulations on Washington's victory in

Trenton, "Good news sets all the animal spirits to work, the imagination is heated and I could not help adding, that I suggested General Heath was to continue his march toward Brunswick which would draw the attentions of any troops posted there and at Princetown, while you would pursue the flying Heroes to Borden and Burlington where Ewing and Cadwalader can stop them and cut off their communication with the 2000 Hessians and Highlanders then come after Griffins, nay I almost promised them that you should by following up this finish blow, finish the campaign of 1776 with that éclat that your numerous friends and mine have long wished for and congratulate you most heartily on what is done."[91]

Morris continued to urge Washington onward. He wrote from the Executive Committee in Philadelphia, "We apprehend if your Victory is immediately pursued & no time allowed the Enemy to recover from their surprize you will have little difficulty in clearing the Jerseys of them. It is probable that those Troops whose times of enlistment are now expiring will follow their successful General altho they wou'd have left him whilst acting a defensive part.[92]

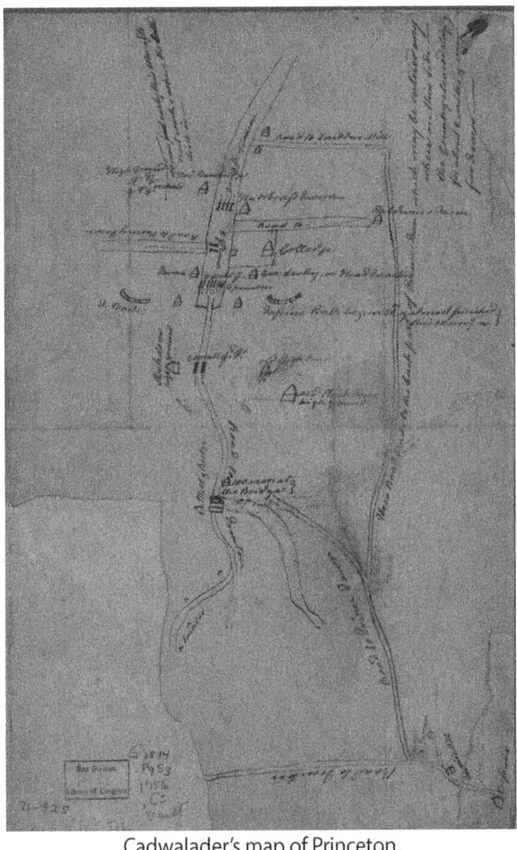

Cadwalader's map of Princeton, Library of Congress, Geography and Map Division[165]

Ice on the Delaware stopped Colonel Cadwalader and his men from crossing the river for the battle of Trenton on December 26th. Nonetheless, he undertook to gain intelligence about British positions in New Jersey and drew a map of Princeton before that battle. He provided this map to General Washington as a guide to his attack on that city.

After the battle of Trenton, Morris wrote to Washington about his continued concern for the small Navy,

> The Fleet has always been my particular care and at this time I am exceedingly anxious for its safety, but the difficulty of getting any thing done is inconceivable; most of the tradesmen necessary to finish the *Delaware* are all at camp. I have applied to the Council of Safety to order some few of them down and although they wish, they fear to do it, least the rest should follow. I have now under my care *The Randolph*, & *Delaware* Frigates, the Brigantine *Andrew Doria*, Sloops *Hanna, Independence* & Schooner *Mosquito,* all Continental armed vessels beside several valuable merchantmen. All wish to get out to sea, and think it might be affected if every man armed would exert himself in this department. I try to give them spirits to invigorate their exertions [with] all in my powers.[93]

Morris pledged to do his utmost. He worked to save the merchant ships that provided a lifeline for the Revolution and the tiny navy that was expected to protect them. On December 29th, 1776 he wrote to Congressman Richard Henry Lee in Baltimore, about the difficulties he faced,

> You cannot conceive how I am vexed & mortified to find after the deal of pains & trouble I have taken that the Randolph Frigate is still at the Piers & Ice making in the River but the Officers of that Ship show great reluctance to go away without being completely manned & that is not possible. She might have been at Sea before now had they exerted themselves for that purpose but they have had constantly in view to wait for more Men. This has its foundation in a Noble principle which has hindered me from complaining to the Marine Committee, altho I have scolded the officers like a Gutter-Whore for their dilatoriness; they say they wish to Fight & not to run. I tell them they must run until they can fight.[94]

The *Randolph* was captained by the same Nicholas Biddle who had been an able captain of the armed galley *Franklin* when that ship was part of Pennsylvania's gunboat navy. Sailors were so hard to find that eventually Captain Biddle resorted to using British prisoners as seamen on his voyage.

Washington replied to Morris and mentioned his need for money. Morris applied to the absent Congress for funds and then took it upon himself to find it. On December 23rd Hancock wrote that Congress decided to put $200,000 in the hands of the Pennsylvania Commissary for Morris to draw from.[95] Morris was unable to utilize the funds on that basis because Morris didn't control the Pennsylvania Commissary. In any case, many people's faith in America's chances of success was so low that they were not accepting continental currency. Morris pressed on with his duties in Philadelphia. He also kept up his communications with France via letters to Silas Deane.[96]

Morris maintained close contact with Washington during this period. He shared his thoughts about the current situation wherein the Army was practically out of money and the six-month enlistments were about to expire. He wrote to Washington on December 29th about Congress' actions to enlarge the role of states in recruitment and maintenance of state military forces to the detriment of the wider Continental Army,

> ... it is useless at this period to examine into the cause of our present unhappy situation, unless that examination would be productive of a cure for the evils that surround us, in fact those causes have long been known to such as would open their eyes, the very consequences of them was often foretold of the measures enacted by some of the best Friends of America; but it is vain, an obstinate practicality to the habits and customs of one part of this Continent had predominated in the Public Councils, and too little attention have been paid to others. To criminate the authors of our errors would not avail, but we cannot see ruin staring us in the Face without thinking of them. It has been my fate to make *ineffectual* opposition to all short enlistments to Colonial appointments of officers and to many of their measures that I thought pregnant with mischiefs, but these things either suited the geniuses & habbits or squared with the interests of some states that had sufficient influence to prevail, and nothing is now left, but to extricate ourselves from the difficulties in which we are involved if we can. Let us try to our utmost, man can do no more.[97]

Morris had not won the argument in favor of long enlistments in the Continental army during the early heady days of the Revolution. Those who thought the war would be over quickly had misunderstood the nature of the struggle and this had put the whole effort in jeopardy. Morris knew that the way to obtain a success in Congress was to obtain victory in the field of battle. That victory required troops, and the troops required money. Washington made a special plea to Morris for £150 in silver needed by "a certain set of People who are of particular use to us."[98] Among the spies due this money, Washington had hired John Honeyman to act as a disgraced patriot so Honeyman could flee to New Jersey and misinform the British about American intentions.

Morris was despondent over the lack of funds for the Army, and his inability to raise enough money to pay the informants Washington had in mind. The city was largely deserted, and only the Quakers and their families remained there. The British Navy was attempting to blockade the port. Commerce had come to a halt. Congress was in Baltimore. Washington's army was on the brink of evaporation. Morris was on the frigid early winter street in Philadelphia when he met an old friend. The Quaker gentleman asked Robert why he was so sad, and Robert told him of the conditions. He asked how he might help. Robert arranged a loan on the spot and pledged his own money, if repayment would not come from Congress. The Quaker gentleman went behind his house and dug up two canvas bags containing silver coins. Morris was able to send about £126 to Washington so he could at least pay his spies.

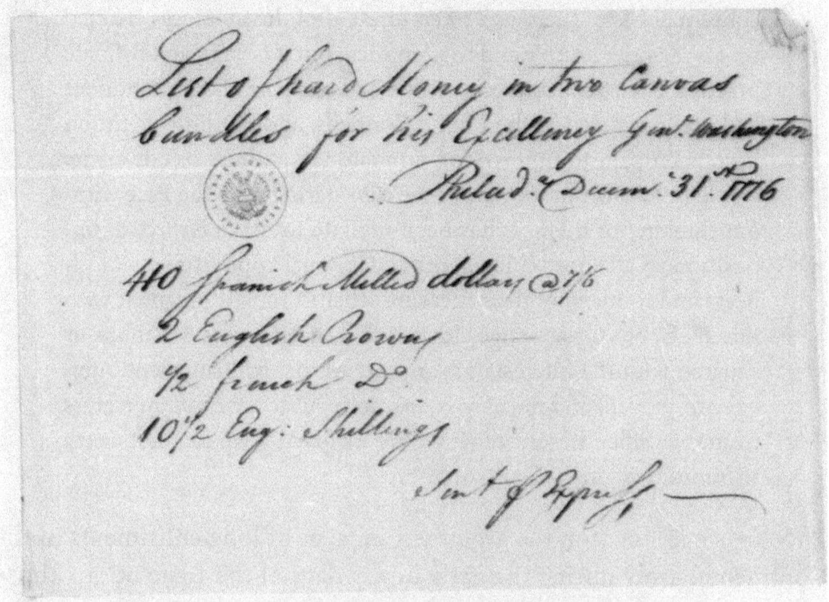

List of hard Money in two Canvas bundles for his Excellency Genl. Washington

Philad. Decem. 31st. 1776

410 Spanish Milled dollars @ 7/6
2 English Crowns
1/2 French Do.
10 1/2 Eng: Shillings

Sent p Express —

George Washington Papers at the Library of Congress, 1741-1799: Series 4. General Correspondence. 1697-1799. Robert Morris, December 31, 1776, Account of Specie Payment to George Washington, image 506

The next day Washington requested more. Without it, the troops would go home. He wrote:

> Tomorrow the Continental Troops are all at Liberty. I wish to push our Success to keep up the Pannick and in order to get their Assistance have promised them a Bounty of 10 Dollars if they will continue for one Month. But here again a new Difficulty presents

> itself we have not Money to pay the Bounty, and we have exhausted our Credit by such frequent Promises that it has not the Weight we could wish. If it be possible, Sir, to give us Assistance do it; borrow Money where it can be done we are doing it upon our private Credit; every Man of Interest and every Lover of his Country must strain his Credit upon such an Occasion."[99]

On January 1st, 1777 Morris sent $50,000 from Congress to Washington with this note: "It gives me great Pleasure that you have engaged the Troops to continue, and if further occasional supplys of money are necessary you may depend on my exertions either in a publick or private capacity."[100] George Washington was so pleased with the success of Morris' efforts that this episode cemented their friendship, a friendship that lasted until Washington's death nearly twenty-five years later.

The money Morris sent from Congress was just enough to provide a reenlistment bonus. This encouraged many soldiers to reenlist and the Army did not disband. The enlistment bonus was only a stopgap measure because it was not enough money for all their back pay and future operations. More was expected to come from Congress in Baltimore. Thomas Paine's stirring words *"these are the times that try men's souls"* provided spiritual strength, but a little cash in the pocket never hurt when a man was thinking of staying away from home or entering battle, and an important battle was about to begin. General Cadwalader and his men crossed the Delaware and joined Washington in winning the Battle of Princeton.

After the victories in New Jersey, a contingent of prisoners was marched through Philadelphia. Morris wrote to Hancock,

> We had yesterday the pleasure to see the Hessian Prisoners paraded in Front Street. They formed a line of two Deep up & down Front Street from Market to Walnut Street, and most people seemed very angry they shou'd ever think of running away from such a Set of Vagabonds.[101]

It was from this pool of candidates that Biddle chose his crew.

On January 3rd General Washington took his troops to winter quarters in what is now Morristown Pennsylvania, about a day's ride north from Philadelphia. In addition to the money, Morris was also able to send a quarter cask of wine to General Washington.

The victories in Trenton and Princeton went a long way to building credibility for the Americans in Europe. They were presented as successes in the national effort to defeat the British. The French considered they were supporting a national effort, as the loans they made to the United States demonstrate. Back in America it appeared that Congress had waited to see if Washington would succeed before actually providing the money to pay for the continuation of his army. Political maneuvering in Congress by those who wished to command the Army themselves, and by others who wanted to strengthen their state armies, caused the lack of Congressional support for Washington. Among those was General Gates, who was in the company of Congress during this period. He was jealous of Washington's role and he had the backing of the Lee brothers. They pointed to Washington's lack of success in battle and played on the desire of some states to enlarge their own control over military affairs. The *"genius & habbits"* that Morris mentioned was the thinking of Congressmen who habitually supported their states over nationalizing the effort. One of the results of this trend was the competition between states for soldiers needed to meet recruitment quotas. Civilians often waited for recruitment bonuses to increase before they enlisted. Sometimes they would cross state borders if the bonus were higher in a nearby state. Much money and energy were wasted in this way.

Maintenance of the Continental Army was central to the internal political effort of creating a unified nation. This army was the first place where a large number of people from different sections of the country worked together. This was the place where the leadership was forced to learn how to manage when faced with the regional cultural differences. Here it was necessary to deal successfully with the challenges of forging a unified force from people who actually had a greater allegiance to their home states than to a "nation" that had yet to be formed. The nationalist leaders tried to unite and coordinate the Army, but the structure of the supply system worked against this effort. Supplies from Pennsylvania were sent to the Pennsylvania troops with specific orders that they not go to troops from other states, and the same was true for other states. Individual soldiers who came from prominent families were easy to identify because they often had personal supplies while others did not. This system created uneven distribution of materials, and dissatisfaction among the troops.

After the Victory

Washington had stopped General Howe, for the moment, and proved himself in the eyes of Congress and America. His former adjutant, General Gates, who had gone to Baltimore and argued for Washington to act defensively, was dispatched to New York State to support General Schuyler's defense of the northern forts.

Washington's victories in New Jersey, and the continual applications to Congress for funding by Morris and his allies, finally resulted in Congress remitting enough to pay the soldiers. On January 7th Treasury Board member Thomas Nelson wrote from Baltimore, "There will be 200,000 dollars sent in two or three days at farthest, & Loan Office certificates to Mr. Smith to the amount 300,000 dollars."[102] Nelson went on to say the whole amount in the Continental treasury was $5,000,000 and that would soon be exhausted. He put his hopes in the success of the Loan Office certificates; but worried the interest rate was not sufficient to be attractive.

On Jan 14th John Hancock wrote to Morris from Baltimore that he hoped the money had arrived, and he added,

> I can assure you, your whole conduct since our Flight is highly approved, & happy I am that you Remained, many agreeable Consequences have Resulted from it, and your continued Exertions will be productive of great good. I must therefore beg you will continue as long as you can...The public are much indebted to you & I hope to see the Day when those public Acknowledgements shall be made to you.[103]

Morris kept Deane apprised of Washington's victory and how it happened. He wrote, "You'll observe in my former narrative I left the Enemy posted at all the little Towns & Villages in New Jersey that afforded them good quarters, ready however to form an attack against this place whenever the Ice should afford them a Bridge across Delaware. I then gave it as my opinion, this was a favorable disposition to attack them in. It seems Genl. Washington thought so too & meditated a heavy blow agst. them-such it would have proved had this plan Succeeded intirely & such has proved that part in which he did succeed."[104] The rest of the letter is a detailed account of the victories at Trenton and Princ-

Etching of John Hancock after a portrait by Copley

eton, which must have made interesting reading for British spies in the employ of the Americans in Europe. The next day Morris arranged a shipment of tobacco to France aboard the *Farmer*.

Morris continued his long letter to Silas Deane, which detailed the sad state of the New England economy. New England's economy was so disrupted that ships captured as prizes and brought to Boston were sent south loaded only with ballast because there was nothing of value to ship. This news was bound to disappoint Beaumarchais who expected something in return for the ships loaded with the weapons he had sent to America, if the ships could get through the blockade. Morris pressed Deane to get the French to commit their navy to help American commerce and outlined that a few ships of the line from France would break the British stranglehold on America. He continued to build the theme that it would be to France's benefit to protect American shipping as a way of getting products to France for their profit and as a means of supporting the war,

> Tobacco is to be sure a fine price in Europe and I hope we shall benefit thereby before long both for the Public & in some degree for ourselves also. Should you obtain a French Fleet to come out here, then will be the time to Speculate and I would have you to charter & send out some Ships with Salt for Virginia, Maryland & this place to carry Tobacco back. My Brother will conduct the Business & you & he must fix the Concern or Shares, but if no fleet, send no Ships, let us wait & look further first. The Congress give me too many employments & heap vastly too much on me for any Man living to do as it shou'd be. If they had left me to manage their Commercial matters & those only I could have done great things, but instead of that all their active business is pushed on me, much against my judgment although inclination prompts me to do what I can in any line that promotes the Service of my Country.[105]

Morris also wrote a more difficult and personal letter to his half-brother in France. Robert had not heard from his brother since Thomas had gone to London. He wrote to him, "these circumstances & your total silence to me, give me the most horrid presages of what I am to expect. Nevertheless it is possible that my friendly letter, & the unlimited confidence I repose in you, may have drawn forth the virtuous part of your Constitution into exertion, & you may have stepped forth & done your Duty to the Public & to your friends; happy will it be for us both if you have but when I look the contrary way the picture shocks all my feelings & I cannot bear it. Your follies as a boy I always forgave, expecting one day to see you despise them, & reap the fruits of your abilities; but if you have introduced them into the European World in the character of man and a merchant, I fear it will all be over & that your future prospects must be gloomy indeed."[106]

With the British army bearing down on Philadelphia, and with the other difficulties Morris faced, he often thought of his family in Maryland and wrote them. Mary was fifteen years younger than Robert, and at the age of twenty-eight she was three months pregnant with her fourth child. Her husband was far away and in the path of a mighty army. Mary and her three children went to stay with her half-sister, now Mrs. Hall, on the Bush River in rural Maryland near the western shore of the Chesapeake. This place was called "Sophia's Dairy." It was a house that had belonged to her father's first wife Sophia, and which was originally known to the family as Sophia's Dowry.

On January 15th Mary wrote to her husband,

> I have received five of your letters since my last, beside Mr. Hall's the content of which almost petrified us: - happy had we been had the petrifaction reached our hearts, and made them proof against our feelings in this day of Trial! I suppressed mine with all my power, and I wish to make myself agreeable as possible to this family, and as they had invited a party of young folks to a Twelfth Cake [an after Christmas celebration] I tried to be cheerful; how could I be really so when hourly in expectation of hearing the determination of so important a Battle, when the express arrived and pronounced Washington victorious, would you believe it, your Molly could not join the general rejoicing? No! Nor never can a victory be so dearly brought.[107]

She was holding in her fear as she looked after her family. She was so exhausted by pretending to be brave for the benefit of her children that by the time the news of Washington's victory arrived she could not rejoice. Instead, she could only remember the emotional cost. Morris' friends in Congress wrote to him about her distress and offered to provide whatever comfort they could. Everyone knew that victory was the only cure.

For his part, Morris took Washington's victory as an opportunity to keep using the port of Philadelphia. He focused on the ships under his "particular care," so he could get the tiny fleet to war at sea. Morris was familiar with managing ships and their associated captains because his merchant fleet was larger than the Continental Navy. From this he knew there is more to leadership than barking orders, and he worked to build a spirit of pride and optimism within the naval service. He wrote to Capt Biddle from the Marine Committee,

> For your encouragement in this service, I must observe that there are no Cruizing Ships an over match for you.... Any of their other single ships you need not fear, especially if you can persuade your men to board. Remember what a glorious exploit it will be, to add one of their frigates or 20 Gun ships to our navy in a few days after you get out, and if the *Randolph* has but Heels, I think you can and will do it; you will then get seamen Plenty.[108]

Morris connected with other captains. He wrote to the captain of the *Wasp* to settle the management of captured prizes and prepare him for a three-month voyage.[109] In February the *Wasp* went down the Delaware and met Esek Hopkins' small fleet at the Delaware Capes. Together they headed southeast to Nassau where they acquired some gunpowder and cannons. In March they arrived in new England and were received as heroes.

Morris wanted John Paul Jones (Little Jones, as Morris called him) to harass the British in the West Indies and draw their warships away from the U. S. coast.[110] On February 5th he wrote to Jones, "Therefore my plan is that you should take the *Alfred, Columbus, Cabot, Hamden,* and Sloop P*rovidence,* proceed first to the island of St Christopher's where a sudden & unexpected attack will carry that place being very defenseless. There is a number of cannon & stores there, as well as merchandize of various sorts that we are in want of and I fancy you will make a considerable booty. This however is not what I have so much in View as to alarm not only the inhabitants but the whole British Nation."[111]

Morris also suggested that Jones attack the British slave trade off the coast of Africa and at sea. The committee system made Morris' bold plan difficult to implement because committees require consensus. A vote of the whole Marine Committee, still in Baltimore, redirected Jones to France before he could lead this mission. Morris and a few business partners sent out a privateer to do the same work. He thought that attacking the slave trade would strike at the heart of British commercial interests.

Ten days later, Morris sent Captain Biddle a message instructing him to bring "Arms, Ammunition, Cloathing and other Stores" back from Martinique, where he could acquire them from William Bingham. Morris went on to say that if Bingham does not have enough Biddle should go to St. Eustatia and contact Samuel Curson, and if the stores there were insufficient he should continue to Curacao, and reach Isaac Governeur. If it turned out there still were not enough Morris directed Biddle to Cape Francois and his old associate Stephen Ceronio. Finally, if that failed then he should go to the Mole St. Nicholas in Haiti and take whatever he could from John Dupuy before returning to the United States.

Morris was sending Biddle to meet with all his trading partners and agents in the West Indies who might have received war supplies from Beaumarchais' company. He was careful to instruct him on the importance of good behavior and acting "for the honor of the American flag." Morris knew that the future of America hinged on building relations with other nations, and that each sailor was an American representative. The irony was that many of Biddle's sailors were British prisoners of war who had been pressed into service to get the *Randolph* to sea. This is just one of many letters Morris sent to instruct the Navy about the importance of proper conduct and how the behavior of the Navy reflected on America,

> As you command the first American frigate that has got out to sea, it is expected that you contend warmly on all necessary occasions for the honor of the American flag. At every foreign port you enter, salute their forts and wait on the Governor General or Commander in Chief, asking the liberty of their ports for the ships of the United States of America. Take care that your people do not molest their Trade nor Inhabitants nor in any shape disturb that good understanding we have with them.[112]

The next day Morris wrote to Bingham, in Martinique, that he had heard about the capture of a slave ship by one of Bingham's privateers. He also requested that Bingham stop sending Frenchmen to him because he did not speak the language. In addition, he mentioned that medicines were in short supply and in an appeal to Bingham's mercantile nature he said send molasses to America because great profits would arise, and that "much Money will be made if any Medicines &c have arrived from Mr Cathalante hurry them here among the first for they will be much wanted by the Publick." Finally, Morris cautioned Bingham not to communicate with Thomas Morris, about whom Robert had growing concerns, until Thomas and Robert had a meeting of the minds.[113]

The Continental Navy was small, but many American privateers were cruising the ocean. This generally aided the war effort, but, in some cases, they caused problems. It was not good news that one of congressman Hewes' ships had been taken by an American privateer. Morris wrote several letters to get the property back for Hewes. When those letters caused the owner of the privateer to attack the victim as being a Tory, Morris defended Hewes. Other American privateers were also acting in a way that discredited America. There were seizures of allied ships, and other American vessels. As a member of the Marine Committee, Morris was not pleased. He wrote,

> In all the Transactions of America nothing has given me more Concern than that kind of irregular Conduct on board the Am. Privateers that savours more of Moorish Piracy than Christian Forbearance. We have already many Instances that ought to be reprobated and the perpetrators brought to a Condign Punishment if the United States of America means to preserve a National good Character ... something I am sure must be done unless we wish to plunder one another & lay all the World under Condemnation as a lawless Set of Freebooters, which God forbid should ever be the Characteristics of the Country I love ...[114]

Morris continued to try and use the tiny navy as an efficient tool of war in a way that would honor America.

Morris sent various Continental ships to Baltimore for loading and fitting in December and January. The Secret Committee operating in that city, under Richard Henry Lee's control, had jurisdiction during that time. Ordinarily Lee would have records of these activities. Later, after a request was made for these records, it was discovered Lee had none. Lee was also busy working, however, on increasing Lee family influence in France and supplanting Thomas Morris with William Lee.[115] Congress was in their Baltimore exile, and Philadelphia was still under threat. The

The Wasp and the Frolic," by Thomas Birch, Courtesy of the Philadelphia Museum of Art

Lexington had been captured at sea but managed to get away with a few of the British sailors. Morris and Hancock worked out the details of the prisoner swap. The *Andrew Doria* captured a British ship, the *Race Horse,* which Morris proposed to buy for the Navy when it was condemned as a prize of war.[116] In those days a naval ship would capture a ship from the other side and the winning captain and crew would get a share of value in the sale of that captured ship. To enlarge the Navy the naval department would have to buy the ship as it was sold to satisfy the claims of the winning captain and crew.

As part of his duties for the Correspondence Committee, Morris made sure to send a packet of information to the Commissioners in Paris when a trusted ship was able to leave the eastern seaboard. Among the letters Morris collected for the current voyage was one sent from the Secret Committee in Baltimore that detailed the items required from Europe. In addition to impressing upon the recipient that the order was important and the voyage difficult the authors asked for blankets, tent cloth, "Stockings, Flints, & Muskets with Bayonets," they also included this information about the uniforms, "both the coats and waistcoats must be short skirted, according to the dress of our Soldiery, and that they should be generally for men of stouter make than those of France. Variety of sizes will of course be ordered."[117] Ordering uniforms instead of ordering material for uniforms that would be made more inexpensively in the colonies, might seem odd, but there was little or no manufacturing in the states at the time. There was no domestic sewing industry in America, and when seamstresses were finally hired, they were poorly paid. Morris included that letter and added one of his own. He outlined the progress of the Navy, Washington's success in New Jersey, and the expected strategy of the enemy. He wrote,

> We have at length got one of our Frigates the *Randolph,* Capt. Biddle, Cruising on this coast to meet any single frigates of the enemy and hope for good accounts from her. She sails fast, is well manned and appointed. Others will soon join her and our utmost exertions will be used to put the Navy on a respectable and formidable footing fast as possible ... General Washington continues to pen up the enemy in Brunswick from whence distress obliges them to send foraging once or twice a week, and although they come out 2 to 3000 Strong our people always attack and never fail to kill and take more or less of them. They have sent for reinforcements from Rhode Island and probably may render the Jersey War a little more

> serious again but our new enlistments go on so fast we shall soon be too formidable for them in the field unless they receive very great reinforcements from Europe, and I fancy they may not find that so practicable now as the year past.[118]

While the members of the secret committee in Baltimore were concerned with the cut of the uniforms, and the staffing of the agency in France, Morris kept the American agents in Europe fully informed on such topics as the state of naval affairs, to the status of the Continental Army, and expectations about enemy movements. Morris' letter shows that he put together information gained from the various committees upon which he served, and displays his administrative style, which was to keep information flowing amongst the interested parties.

Morris added this letter to Deane,

> I will not enter into any detail of our Conduct in Congress, but you may depend on this that so Long as that respectable body persist in the attempt to execute as well as to deliberate on their business it never will be done as it ought & this has been urged many & many a time by myself & others but some of them don't Like to part with power or to pay others for doing what they cannot do themselves.[119]

Morris' friends in Congress wrote him with agreement that much money had been wasted, and it would be good to have civilian executives in key positions. One member identified the areas of Finance, War, and Commerce as suitable executive departments.[120] James Wilson also urged the creation of executive departments.[121] Thomas Paine took the opposite side, and argued that representatives of the people, not paid factotums, should look after the people's interests. It took four years for the rest of Congress to come to see things Morris' way. Differences like this were the reason John Adams had said, Morris "does not always vote for what you and I should think proper, it is because he thinks that a large Body of People remains, who are not yet of his mind." Adams and Morris were rarely of the same mind and maintained their respective positions for years. True to his parliamentarian roots, John Adams' cousin Samuel was so against executive departments that he was one of only two people to abstain when Congress voted to make Morris Superintendent of Finance in 1781.

Political differences are common in democracies, on both the national and state levels. With that in mind, Morris wrote to his friend, John Jay, about the new Pennsylvania constitution, and the political climate in that state. He mentioned the fate of some of his old acquaintances, who chose to work with the British when the days were the darkest. Morris decried the sad fates of people he had known well and implied the dangers lurking for men like him when he wrote,

> What has happened is the fruits of that winters Cabals. Our Constitution is disliked, the People divided, unhappy, and consequently weak, the power if any there be, is placed in improper hands and in short the people seem to loose one day, the Confidence they placed in leaders of the day before.
>
> Where it will end God only knows. Dickinson & A. Allen have given mortal stabs to their own Characters & pity it is the wounds should penetrate any further, but they were men of property, Men of fair private Characters & what they have done, seems to pierce through their sides into the Vitals of those who have similar pretensions to Fortune & good Character. The defection of these men is supposed to originate in a desire to preserve their Estates & consequently glances a suspicion on all that have Estates to loose. I pity them both exceedingly. Dickinson's Nerves gave way & his fears dictated a letter to his Brother advising him not to receive Continental money. His Judgment & his virtue should have prevented this act of Folly, I call it such because I believe his Heart to be good & regret much that his exalted Character should be degraded, by what could hardly be called a crime at the time he did it, but he thought the Game was up. A. Allen deserves a better fate than he will meet with. Amiable in private character and deserving of the Felicity he has heretofore enjoyed he has rashly sacrificed it by a hasty resolution.[122]

Dickinson had been a mentor to Morris, and they both were members of the earlier Continental Congress. It was becoming clear that the new Pennsylvania government was going to act sternly with people whom they disfavored.

The Constitutionalists were active against their fellow Pennsylvanians, even while the British army was an imminent threat to their capital city. Howe's army held Burlington, New Jersey, and menaced Philadelphia. Morris cautioned both Congress and his family against coming back too soon. While this pleased Morris' opposites in Congress, namely Richard Henry Lee, and John Adams,[123] this caused many members of Congress to complain. Those Congressmen were not pleased with Baltimore with its muddy streets and high prices, nor were they happy with its scant and small accommodations. One member described the city as "this dirty boggy hole" where the devil had "reserved it to himself for his own chosen seat and inheritance."[124]

The continued printing of Continental currency, backed by nothing, and the resulting inflation, compelled Congress to look for ways to protect the value of their paper, and they hit upon Loan Office Certificates. Other states were already issuing their own bonds at 4%, Morris suggested to issue new loan office certificates at the higher interest rate of six percent per year. Later Morris repeated this request because he was still looking after Continental financing; and no one was buying the current issue at four percent. Congress was reluctant. The states that blocked this funding move were Rhode Island, Connecticut, Georgia, and both Carolinas. Dr. Benjamin Rush noted that it took just seven men to block the measure while states with over two thirds of the whole population favored it. This provided an example to the members that their governing system needed improvement.[125]

Brothers in Europe

During that same time period, in December 1776, Arthur Lee went from London to take up his role as commissioner in Paris. There he met with Franklin and Deane and stayed for a little over six weeks. Around the time of Lee's arrival, Thomas Morris returned from his drunken bender in London, and was successful in arranging the first of several loan contracts between the Americans and the Farmers General, the French tobacco monopoly and taxing authority.[126] Lee had no similar success. Instead, he focused on his unhappiness. He seemed to have taken his role as intermediary and conversations with Beaumarchais in London, his advanced education, and his social position in Virginia, as some kind of special entitlement to run American operations in France. It just so happened that the people with whom he worked did not see the situation in the same light.

The French thought Lee was a spy for Britain,[127] probably because he had not resigned his position as an alderman of London.[128] The American colleagues found him difficult to embrace. He abhorred Franklin, and Deane. He wrote against John Jay, who would become an American diplomat in Spain a few years later. He also disliked the Scots and wrote, "Beware of the Scotch ... whose perfidy you know can never be trusted."[129] This, no doubt, did not endear him to the many American patriots of Scottish descent including John Paul Jones, Alexander Hamilton, John

Knox, James Wilson, and the Livingston family. His personality was so odious to his American counterparts that they excluded him from much of the official business of diplomacy. In actuality, he had little to do with the treaties reached with France. Instead, Arthur made himself obnoxious by trying to get his brother, William, to take over the French Agency managed by Thomas Morris, even though William had been appointed commissioner to Vienna and Berlin.[130] As a result, Deane and Thomas Morris tried to keep Arthur at arm's length.

Among his other failings Arthur's choice of secretaries was poor. He employed "Major" Thornton, who was a spy for Lord North.[131] He dismissed Thornton and hired Hezekiah Ford, another British spy. As it turned out, both Deane and Lee trusted people who were revealed much later to be British spies. While it is widely acknowledged that these British spies read the mail, little has been said about any proactive role they played.

It would have been the spies' job to work in concert, and to drive a wedge between the American groups by playing on their prejudices and weaknesses. A clever agent would have easily manipulated Lee. The combination of his high opinion of himself, his ambition, and his lack of actual results made him a perfect target. Deane's business background and its attendant basis of trust, coupled with his long time association with Bancroft, would have exposed him as well. Thomas Morris' appetites made him easy prey for a calculating spy. After all, Lee, Deane, and Morris were all secret agents for America, and the British would have been remiss if they had not run a counterintelligence campaign against them. The Lee brothers suspected Bancroft, but they suspected everyone, so, like a broken clock, they were right sometimes. Nevertheless, being suspected by the Lees only put Bancroft more firmly in the Deane camp.

As events progressed in France, the Lee brotherhood and those working on Secret Committee business moved farther apart. Arthur felt he was not given the respect he deserved. He knew that he was not invited to participate in the Beaumarchais arrangement, and he started to make trouble.[132] Arthur's cousin, Francis Lightfoot Lee, told him, "to provide yourself with all the means necessary, both for attack and defense." Arthur took these words "to mean he should gather information on Deane, Franklin, and Morris ... as he directed his attention to those he considered to be his enemies."[133] Arthur's enemies list was well known at the time. It seemed to have escaped him that he was not on the Secret Committee and sharing its details with him would have been a breach of security. Little wonder that neither Thomas nor Silas Deane would tell Arthur the details of their official business.[134]

The lack of direct communication between these two American factions provided the British spies, who worked as secretaries for two American commissioners, with the perfect opportunity to form a back channel between Lee's office and Deane's office. A back channel such as this would have easily been used to send misinformation between the two groups. The record shows that for a man who was not "at the table," Lee had surprisingly detailed, but oddly skewed knowledge on the activities within Dean's department. However, the source of that information has never been made public. Arthur Lee maintained that he was being vigilant and virtuous as he accused Ben Franklin, Silas Deane, and by implication, Morris, of a wide variety of misuses of public money.[135] It was noted at the time, that, although Lee sent many letters to the Congress complaining of malfeasance, he did not offer any real proof. People at home believed in his sincerity because the tone of his letters was full of vigorous protest and righteous indignation. However, Lee's accusations were never borne out by the actual facts. No one has proven that Lee was a purposeful liar. It is, however, a sad reality that Lee had been duped by spies on more than one occasion.

Among the examples of Lee's reports of displeasure were slow rates of remittances from Cadiz, the lengthy stay of American ships in French ports, and the purchase of vessels as Continental cruisers by members of the secret agency in France. Deane, Ross and Thomas Morris had made these purchases because that was the quickest way to create an American naval force in European waters. It was during this time that Gustavus Conyngham, and William Hodge undertook their careers as American privateers operating from Dunkirk, a Danish city then under French control. They harassed British merchant shipping, horrified British citizens, and embarrassed the British Navy.

These Continental cruisers were purchased under direction of the Secret Committee, but they had to appear to the world as private vessels to protect French neutrality. To be seen as private vessels, private individuals had to invest in these ships, so the ships were publicly and privately owned at the same time. French authorities seized one of them, under the pretext of remaining neutral. Another proved too expensive to operate. Deane turned the money-losing ship over to John Ross, a partner of Morris', but there was no record of the payment showing the ship was transferred from public to private hands. In another venture Deane and Thomas Morris joined in using a ship meant to sail under a Letter of Marque which Robert Morris had gotten in America. Unfortunately, the American buyers were tricked into buying a useless ship. When it became clear that a fraud had been perpetrated Thomas Morris sought to cut his losses. A different ship arrived from the United States with private cargo from Robert Morris to be sold to raise funds for the privateering effort, and with other cargo sent on public account. Thomas appropriated the public money to pay for the publicly owned portion, and the private money to pay for his part of the private cost of the misadventure. This left Deane without a way to pay his portion of the fiasco, and with lingering feelings that Robert Morris owed him a debt. Deane turned to Beaumarchais for support. In a separate effort Ross bought a heavily armed ship as a cargo transport. Ross sold it to the United States as a cruiser when it became clear that it was not possible to ship enough cargo on this vessel because of its configuration. All of this buying, selling and blurring of the facts had been done without consulting Arthur Lee.[136] This did not please Lee at all. In mid-February he headed for Madrid.[137]

Back in America, the Continental Congress had been in Baltimore for nearly a month, and while Morris was in Philadelphia he had only an indirect influence on its deliberations. At the same time in France, Thomas Morris' interest in drinking and gambling started to outweigh his attention to business. When his fellow Americans tried to guide him, Thomas objected and complained loudly to his drinking friends. This started to color French views of the American efforts. Thomas delegated much of his business to a firm called, Messr. Pliarne, Penet & Co & J. Gruel. Mr. Penet & Co. had connections in Providence, Rhode Island, and a secret committee contract at the time. Later they did business with the Browns of Rhode Island and had a contract with the Board of War. Arthur Lee objected to the way that firm was conducting itself.[138] Once Penet & Co. were installed, Thomas relapsed, never to truly recover.

While Robert was hard at work in Philadelphia, Richard Henry Lee led the Secret Committee in Baltimore. In Robert's absence, Richard Henry continued his effort to insert his own brother, William Lee, into the same office as Thomas Morris.[139] When that was accomplished, Penet & Co did not accept William Lee as an equal to Thomas Morris, most particularly in allowing William to see what occurred in the agency before his appointment,[140] which only served to further infuriate the Lee brothers.

By early March, Arthur Lee's trip to Madrid was stalled in rural Spain. He was not welcomed at the Spanish Court because that would have meant that the Spanish Crown had officially recognized America. Lee could not proceed to Madrid and instead made commercial arrangements from the town of Burgos. While Willing, Morris & Co. had been working from the trading center of Cadiz for over a year, Arthur Lee was forced to stay in a small town, west of the Pyrenees, while he arranged a shipment of blankets from Bilboa.[141] Lee set up his shipping arrangements with Elbridge Gerry, of Massachusetts, who was an ally of the Adams, Gerry later, as governor of his state, lent his name to the term Gerrymander.

Arthur Lee's angry letters reached the Secret Committee in Baltimore. Committee member, Richard Henry Lee, then requested Morris provide an order and inventory check on articles sent from Europe.[142] Morris set about collecting the records from all his trading partners.[143] He also started to receive distressing messages from his contacts in Spain that his brother was again misbehaving to the discredit of all Americans. He asked Silas Deane to look into these allegations.[144]

Funding before Homecoming

Morris wrote from Philadelphia to Dr. Benjamin Rush, in Baltimore, about the continuing impasse in Congress over the interest rate of loan office certificates. The disagreements were based on different understandings in the subject of economics. Southerners understood so little about business and finance they suspected that if they paid interest on Continental loan certificates then eventually all the money in America would end up in the Mid-Atlantic states. Morris wrote, "I am told the Southern States object & think they shall pay the Interest & the others receive it, but this is a phantom, whilst they continue to raise such Valuable Commodities as Indigo, Rice & Tobacco, they will Command their share of the Riches of the Continent and discharge their debts with more facility than their Neighbors."[145] Morris had great faith in the resources of America, and he believed that American products would provide the means to pay for the interest, and the war, and by selling their products the South should become rich.

Hancock wrote that over the objections of the southerners, Congress eventually passed the interest change that Morris had requested.[146] He also expressed his desire to see his old friend again and inquired about city life and if Morris had been to the Oyster Club.[147] He closed one letter with an appeal that Morris find a few bottles of Madeira wine for him, and admitted the distance made him "feel awkward not to have it in my power to ask a friend to take a glass."[148] Hancock also promised to help Morris get Marine matters on firmer footing upon his return to Philadelphia. [149]

Once the city of Philadelphia was secured, Mary Morris returned home. Her trip was an ordered effort. On her arrival she wrote to her mother, "Last Wednesday noon I had the pleasure to arrive safe in dear Philadelphia, after a much pleasanter journey than I expected from our setting off, and it made me very happy to find myself at home after so long an absence, with the terrible apprehensions we fled with of never seeing it again."[150]

Congress' return to Philadelphia, however, was more like a rush from Hell than an orderly maneuver. Members were in such a hurry that wagons were in short supply. Men were left waiting in rented rooms as their belongings were sent ahead, and visa-versa. When Congress returned so did Morris' account books. Morris was relieved to see their return, "I have but just got back my books &c so that it will take me some time to enter & arrange the business I have been doing since they were sent away."[151] Much had happened since Congress and Morris' account books had gone to Christiana for safe keeping.[152] It would be difficult for anyone to reconstruct the whole record. As one author explained it, "Part of the problem was due to the nature of Secret Committee trade: because shipments of munitions violated neutrality agreements, virtually every Secret Committee cargo was loaded in haste and literally in the dark, and often without invoices… cargoes were frequently transferred from one ship to another, the contents left in jumbled confusion for the receives in America to sort out."[153]

Nevertheless, when the Secret Committee convened in Philadelphia they tried to harmonize their accounting with Morris' activities. It soon became clear that the Secret Committee, under the direction of Richard Henry Lee, had kept such poor records of the committee's activities. Morris wrote, "On examining the papers delivered [to] me, by the Committee on their return from Baltimore I find they did not keep any book of Minutes…"[154] The committee attempted to reconstruct the whole record using the available information, which meant Morris' vouchers, bills of loading, notes kept on loose pieces of paper, etc. This may have seemed an unimportant nuisance at the time, but over the years the gaps in this record made Morris' life difficult.

While Congress was focused on the recent past, Morris connected with a friend. He wrote to General Washington about the effects of some congressional policies that he saw as wrongheaded. He covered the topic of short enlistments, and that even though Congress had changed the time to three years, there was now a problem implementing that decision. Much money was being wasted on enlistment bonuses, called "bounties," as these bounties were often spent on harmful amusements. Even during the Revolution there were people outside the Army who were happy to take advantage of the soldiers.

Morris wrote,

> ...the Bounties, high wages & short Service has Vitiated the Minds of all that Class of People & they are grown the most mercenary beings that exist. Don't confine this observation merely to the Soldiery but extend it to those who get their livings by Feeding & entertaining of them, these are the Harpies that injure us much at this time. They keep the Fellows Drunk whilst the Money holds out, when it is gone they encourage them to enlist for the sake of Bounty, then to drinking again. That Bounty gone & more money still wanted, they must enlist again with some other officer, receive a fresh Bounty & get more Drink &c.[155]

Pennsylvania gets a Government

Nine months after the war started, the "Constitutionalists" in Pennsylvania finally managed to elect their first President of the Executive Council on March 5th, 1777, Thomas Wharton Jr. Many people with experience had avoided the honor because they did not want to be associated with the new government. People who had chosen the Tory side viewed the Pennsylvania government as "truly ridiculous." The new government in Pennsylvania did not inspire confidence in the members of the Continental Congress either. In expectation of further British offensive actions Congress passed a resolution on April 14th that stated, "The executive authority of the Commonwealth of Pennsylvania is incapable of any exertion adequate to the present crisis."[156]

Contrary opinions did not faze the creators of Pennsylvania's novel form of Government. Instead, they adopted increasingly radical methods and rhetoric to maintain their system even as it proved to be overwhelmingly incompetent in dealing with the State's problems. The people who defended Pennsylvania's direct democratic system with the greatest diligence were from German families now known as the Pennsylvania Dutch; and the Presbyterian Scots-Irish who were tradesmen, or who lived in the backcountry of Western Pennsylvania. They had been practically disenfranchised under the old proprietor rule of the Quakers that had been in effect for over 100 years before the Assembly was dissolved. Unsurprisingly, they were not interested in the Quakers regaining power, and so they instituted the Test Law. The Test Law was an oath of religious belief and fealty to the state and state constitution. The Quakers were constrained by their own faith and refused to swear oaths, so this effectively disenfranchised them. The Test Law disenfranchised many other religious minorities including the Moravians, Anabaptists, and Jews; and this amounted to nearly one half of the population of Pennsylvania.[157] The voting population was at most 50% of the whole population because only men with property could vote. The Test Law again halved this number, so in actuality only 25% of the population could vote under the new Constitution. That meant that one party could retain power with half of that 25%, or in simple terms: if just 13% of the total population voted for the "Constitutionalists" then they retained power. This was their version of Democracy, and they were going to hold on to it as long as they could.

The Test laws served a second purpose. In one of these provisions people had to swear to uphold the state Constitution. People who were against the Constitution would not swear to uphold it, so the Test Laws served to purge a range of people from political office. The state lost many experienced members from the state Naval Board, the Board of War, and the Assembly. The loss of experienced people was one of the reasons that Pennsylvania was so poorly managed.

As the political system in Pennsylvania went on, ad-hoc citizen committees were called to action, as an extension of the mode used during the earlier activist days starting with the Stamp Act protest. They were not official state organizations, but rather extra-legal organizations which were often directed by political leaders. There was no redress when they took action, and that eventually degenerated into a rough form of mob justice complete with property destruction, forced exile, and a general trampling of minority rights. This system provided an example not to follow when the U.S. Constitution was drawn up later.

The War goes on

Morris was too busy with Congressional business to do much about state politics. On April 1st, 1777 he contacted his friend in New York, John Jay, about the March arrival of some weapons that Beaumarchais and Deane had sent from France. Morris wrote,

> Last Week a Brig arrived here with 6800 Muskets & 2100 Gun Locks, another in Maryld with 633 bbls Powder, & this Ship into Portsmouth brought with her about 12,000 Muskets, 1000 bbls Powder, a number of Blankets & Cloathing.
>
> I fancy however, we must try our Strength alone for awhile longer, although I firmly believe a general War will & must eventually take place in Europe this Summer. I wish our army was in the Field, we want nothing else to make the day our own.[158]

Beaumarchais was left waiting for return cargoes.

Back in America, Washington's army was still in winter quarters. The British army confined itself to New Jersey where they suffered from desertions every day as the citizens denied them food for the soldiers, and hay for their horses. Even though the British out-numbered the Americans two to one, they still lost 3,000 to 4,000 troops and over four hundred horses during that winter. Morris thought that the only reason the British Army was not destroyed was because the American enlistment system did not allow for the development of a properly trained army to get the job done.

Morris wrote the commissioners in Paris,

> It is now evident to all America that if in the beginning of this Contest we had enlisted our army for a Number of Years or during the War, Genl Howe could not have wintered here unless as a Prisoner, but alas our army were disbanded by the nature of their enlistments when they could have been most useful & the militia are too much their own masters to expect from them a steady adherence to the extreme Fatigues of a long & hard winters Campaign. They turn out for a month or six weeks, show great Bravery whilst they stay, but curiosity once being gratified & some feat performed to make a good Story at home, they become impatient to return to their Families & neither persuasion nor principle can detain them.[159]

The difficulty in finding and retaining soldiers created a situation where the Continental Army started to recruit slaves without their owners' knowledge. Morris wrote the Army that until slavery was repealed by the Legislature the Army would have to stop the practice and return the slaves. There were similar hardships in the naval department. They had trouble finding and recruiting sailors. Captain Nicholson resorted, on occasion, to impressing sailors against their will for individual voyages. Morris wrote a stern letter from the Marine Committee to tell Captain Nicholson of Maryland that such impressments must stop. "The practice of Impressing Seamen cannot be supported on any other principle than Necessity and I am confident it is as pernicious to the Commercial Interests of a Country as destructive of the Civil Liberty of those Individuals who become its Victims. Under these opinions you will readily see I cannot advocate the measure."[160]

With characteristic forbearance Morris advocated nothing more than a reprimand for Captain Nicholson, if the captain realized his error. This Morris did not expect. He wrote,

> I think the dispute unfortunate because I have been taught to believe him an excellent & Capable officer, the loss of such a one will be a real misfortune to the Continent & yet I think he ought to be dismissed unless by satisfactory submission he atones for the offensive Stile of his letter which I suppose to have been written in warmth inflamed by the Violence of that Species of Whiggism that savours more of passion than true Patriotism, I am told he is of a high Spirit and that it is doubtful if he will make the Concessions he ought.[161]

The effects of his work were well know at home, where there was obviously a parity between spouses. His wife, Mary, wrote to her mother on the 14th of April,

> There are now three men of War in our Bay, which look as if they intend this way; Mr. Morris has met with a great loss, as well as the Continent, by them, the ship *Morris* with a most Valuable Cargo of Arms, Ammunition, and dry goods. She had provided Her self with guns, to keep off any common Attack, but was most Unfortunately beset by three, the Roe buck one of them, at our Capes, She defended her Self bravely as long as it was possible, and then the Captain run her on Shore, and very bravely blew her up, and poor fellow, perished HimSelf, in his Anxiety to do it Effectively.[162]

On April 17th, 1777, the Committee for Secret Correspondence became known as the Committee for Foreign Affairs.[163] Morris continued his role on that committee. Thomas Paine was made Secretary of it. He was given an oath which included this phrase: "to disclose no matter, the knowledge of which shall be acquired in consequence of such his office, that he shall be directed to keep secret."[164] Paine would later disgrace himself by breaking that oath as he fell prey to what Morris called "that Species of Whiggism that savours more of passion."

Endnotes

1. *Wealth of Nations*, pg. 711
2. *The Book of Philadelphia*, pg. 68
3. *The Works of Samuel Johnson*, published by Pafraets & Company, Troy, New York, 1913; volume 14, pg. 93-144
4. Letters of Delegates to Congress, 4:359-365
5. Letters of Delegates to Congress, 4:359-365
6. Ibid, 4:276
7. Ibid, 4:386
8. Letters of Delegates to Congress, 4:405
9. Ibid, 4:427
10. Letters of Delegates to Congress, 4:512
11. Letters of Delegates to Congress 4:512
12. Letters of Delegates to Congress, 4:603
13. Letters of Delegates to Congress, 4:543
13. "To John Adams from Benjamin Rush, 20 July 1811," Founders Online, National Archives
15. Ibid, 4:656.
16. Ibid, 4:656-8
17. Letters of Delegates to Congress 5:7
18. Letters of Delegates to Congress 5:73
19. Letters of Delegates to Congress, 5:74-5
20. *Journals Continental Congress*, August 29, 1776
21. Letters of Delegates to Congress, 5:224
22. Revolutionary Diplomatic Correspondence, 2:78-79
23. The Deane Papers, pg. 140
24. Letters of the Delegates to Congress, 4:623
25. *Pennsylvania History* (fall 1996), pg. 529
26. Deane Papers, 1:233
27. LOC- Papers of Robert Morris Correspondence reel 12 #336
28. Letters of Delegates to Congress, 6:586-587
29. *The American Revolution* and "A Candid World," pg. 40 – 84
30. *Journals Continental Congress*, Prefatory Note, pg. 6 by Worthington Chauncey Ford, Chief of Division of Manuscripts Editor, Herbert Putnam, Librarian of Congress December 18, 1905
31. Letters of Delegates to Congress, 3:270
32. *The American Revolution* and "A Candid World" Edited by Lawrence S Kaplan, pg. 40 – 84
33. Rappleye, pg. 84
34. Letters of delegates to Congress, 5:306-307
35. Ibid, 5:284
36. Revolutionary Diplomatic Correspondence, 2:151
37. Letters of Delegates to Congress, 5:273-274
38. Revolutionary Diplomatic Correspondence 2:1.52.
39. *The Annals of the Ancestry of Charles Custis Harrison and Ellen Waln Harrison*, pg.169
40. Letters of Delegates to Congress, 5:375-376
41. Morris Papers, Levis Collection, HSP #1957
42. *Diary of Richard Smith*, Pennsylvania Colonial Records x537,528
43. Naval Documents of the American Revolution, 4:548
44. Letters of Delegates to Congress, 5:375-376
45. Ver Steeg pg. 18
46. The Deane Papers, 1774-1790, 5:1887-91
47. American National Biography Online
48. Deane Papers, 1:145-146
49. Letters of Delegates to Congress, 10:707
50. Deane Papers, 1:290
51. Deane Papers, 1:299
52. Deane Papers, 1:136
53. Revolutionary Diplomatic Correspondence, 1:603
54. Deane Papers, 2:351-2; 370
55. Deane Papers, 3:171
56. Deane Papers, 1:165
57. Letters of Delegates to Congress, 6:155
58. Letters of Delegates to Congress, 6:195
59. *The Finances and Financier of the Revolution*, 1:165
60. Beaumarchais, pg.220
61. Revolutionary Diplomatic Correspondence, 2:171
62. Beaumarchais, p 220
63. *Henkels Catalogue*, pg.207
64. The Revolutionary Diplomatic Correspondence, 2:242
65. Deane Papers 1:331
66. Deane Papers, 2:94
67. Letters of Delegates to Congress, 5:373
68. *The Power of the Purse*, pg. 78
69. Letters of Delegates to Congress, 5:441
70.* Thirty-seven-year-old Thomas Paine joined the wave of English immigrants when he arrived in America in 1774. Prior to his arrival, he had been dismissed from his position in England as a tax collector. He had also superin-

tended the failure of the shop he owned with his wife, and the dissolution of his marriage. The Radical Whigs in England influenced his political thinking when he was there, and he gravitated toward the more radical factions in the American colonies. He took his letter of introduction from Franklin and attained a job with the *Pennsylvania Magazine*. Eric Froner, American National Biography Online.

71. *Henkels Catalogue*, pg. 60

72. Beaumarchais, 206-208

73. The Deane Papers, 2:296

74. Letters of Delegates to Congress, 7:266-268

75. Letters of Delegates to Congress, 6:181

76. *Henkels Catalogue*, pg. 1

77. Letters of Delegates to Congress, 5:595

78. Letters of Delegates to Congress, 5:604-605

79. Letters of Delegates to Congress, 5:611

80. Ibid, 5:643

81. Ibid, 5: 656-657

82.. Letters of Delegates to Congress, 5:604

83. The writings of George Washington from the original manuscript sources, 6:375-463

84. Letters of Delegates to Congress, 5:610

85. Ibid, 5:610

86. Letters of Delegates to Congress, 5:624

87. George Washington Papers at the Library of Congress, 1741-1799: Series 4. General Correspondence. 1697-1799 Image 308. Robert Morris to George Washington, December 21, 1776, with Invoice and Receipt

88. Letter of Delegates to Congress, 5:636

89. Oberlhotzer, pg.27

90. Letters of Delegates to Congress, 5:639

91. Letters of Delegates to Congress, 5:649

92. Ibid, 6:785-786

93. Letters of Delegates to Congress, 5:649

94. Letters of Delegates to Congress, 5:695

95. Letters of Delegates to Congress, 5:643

96. Ibid, 5:281

97. Ibid, 5:649

98. Washington, George, 1732-1799. The writings of George Washington from the original manuscript sources: Vol 6 December30, 1776

99. Washington, George, 1732-1799. The writings of George Washington from the original manuscript sources :Vol 6 December31,1776

100. Letters of Delegates to Congress, 6:12

101. Letters of Delegates to Congress, 5:699

102. Letters of Delegates to Congress, 6:147

103. *Henkels Catalogue*, pg. 5-6

104. Letters of Delegates to Congress, 6:59

105. Letters of Delegates to Congress, 6:83-85

106. Letters of Delegates to Congress, 6:179

107. "The Descendants of Colonel Thomas White" ref. *The Annals of the Ancestry of Charles Custis Harrison and Ellen Waln Harrison*, pg.163

108. Letters of Delegates to Congress, 6:168

109. Ibid, 5:694

110. Robert Morris, *Audacious Patriot*, pg.42

111. Letters of Delegates to Congress, 6:220-222

112. Letters of Delegates to Congress, 6:292-293

113. Ibid, 6:301-305

114. Ibid, 6:142

115. Rappleye, pg. 98

116. Letters of Delegates to Congress, 6:41-42

117. Letters of Delegates to Congress, 6:312

118. Ibid, 6:314

119. Letters of Delegates to Congress, 5:627

120. *Henkels Catalogue*, pg. 23

121. *Henkels Catalogue*, pg. 52-53

122. Letters of Delegates to Congress, 8:87-88

123. Rappleye, pg. 106

124. *Henkels Catalogue*, pg. 24

125. Letters of Delegates to Congress, 6:346

126. Revolutionary Diplomatic Correspondence, 2:300

127. *John Adams Diary*, 47:45

128. The Deane Papers, 3:314

129. Revolutionary Diplomatic Correspondence, 1:535

130. Ibid, I:135

131. Ibid, 1:§150

132. Letters of Delegates to Congress, 8:431

133. Ver Steeg, pg. 24

134. Letters of Delegates to Congress, 8:431

135. C. Ver Steeg pg. 25

136. *Power of the Purse*, 85-89

137. Revolutionary Diplomatic Correspondence, 2:267

138. Papers of Robert Morris, 2:321

139. Letters of Delegates to Congress, 6:103

140. Letters of Delegates to Congress, 8:431

141. Revolutionary Diplomatic Correspondence, 2:280

142. Letters of Delegates to Congress, 6:124
143. Ibid, 7:180
144. Ibid, 6:176
145. Ibid, 6:295
146. *Henkels Catalogue*, pg. 9
147. Ibid, pg. 7
148. Ibid, pg. 9
149. *Henkels Catalogue*, p.8
150. The Descendants of Colonel Thomas White ref. in *The Annals of the Ancestry of Charles Custis Harrison and Ellen Waln Harrison*, pg. 164
151. Letters of Delegates to Congress, 6:267
152. Letters of Delegates to Congress, 2:162
153. Rappleye, pg. 123
154. Letters of Delegates to Congress, 6:406-408
155. Ibid, 6:402
156. Oberholtzer, pg. 39
157. Robert L. Brunhouse, *The Counter-Revolution in Pennsylvania*, pg. 155
158. Letters of Delegates to Congress, 6:520
159. Letters of Delegates to Congress, 6:503-504
160. Ibid, 7:8
161. Letters of Delegates to Congress, 7:8
162. *In the Words of Women*, pg. 106
163. *Journals of the Continental Congress,* April 17, 1777
164. Ibid
165. Library of Congress, Geography and Map Division, Call number, G3814.P9S3 1776 .C3

IV

Changes in the Political Wind

North Carolina held an election in May. Mr. Hewes, a merchant, an author of the Articles of Confederation, and member of the Secret Committee, lost his seat in Congress. His ships had carried much of the tobacco, indigo, and other goods in the secret arms trade. He continued after losing office, but the trade was reduced as finances weakened and the political winds changed. The winning candidate was able to convince the voters that Mr. Hewes' time spent on Secret Committee business would have been better spent in Congress.[1] Hewes' loss was one of the early indications that the openness of the original revolutionary spirit was giving way to public opinion molded to suit older ideas. He was replaced by Henry Laurens, Vice President of South Carolina, plantation owner, and slave trader.

This use of popular prejudice against merchants signaled a political shift. The feeling grew that making money was somehow vulgar, and as an expression of the mentality found among many of the leaders in the South, they thought that merchants who did well were ill-equipped to be lawgivers. Southern elite eschewed labor for themselves, and thought their role was to manage others who managed workers, or to superintend. Being a lawgiver was the highest form of superintendence because it was the management of society. The high esteem with which they held themselves brought them to the conclusion that their cause was so right and so just that Europe would assist on the basis of their own virtue. Commenting on this mode of thought Morris later said,

> People have flattered themselves with a visionary idea that nothing more was necessary than for Congress to send a Minister abroad, and immediately he would obtain as much money as he chose to ask for.[2]

The lack of appreciation for the making of money to fund the war would take a toll on Congress' ability to win.

The British were threatening to take Philadelphia in the spring. However, the war supplies Gates had received in New England from Beaumarchais did not make their way south to Washington's army. Philadelphians readied a second retreat. Mary Morris spent those spring days preparing the family and their belongings for a move to Manheim, Lancaster County. Robert had purchased a house there that had been owned by Henry Steigel at the Iron Works. Mary was in Philadelphia looking after the packing of furniture and linens in The Hills. Everything had to be sent west by wagon to escape the British once again. She paused to consider that most favored spot from her home on Dock Street, "I am yet on dear Philadelphia ground, but expect soon to inhabit the Hills, where we shall remain, if possible, to the enjoyment of all that's beautiful to the eye and grateful to the taste: for, as if to add to our mortification, we are obliged to leave it, nature never appeared so lovely, nor promised such profusion of her gifts." She was able to spend the better part of the summer at the Hills because the British did not take Philadelphia until the fall.[3]

National Identity

Morris saw the navy's presence in foreign ports as a way of projecting to the world the image of America as a new and unified nation. Morris' words to Nicholas Biddle that he should "contend warmly on all necessary occasions for the honor of the American flag" speak volumes about Morris' intention. One problem with achieving this goal was the impulse that allowed each captain to fashion his own ship's flag. Captain Biddle's ship, the *Randolph*, flew colors that showed a coiled rattlesnake. The *Alfred* flew the Grand Union Flag.

An opportunity arose when Pennsylvania moved forward to create a flag for state ships. John Brown was the head of the State Navy Board of Pennsylvania when on May 29th, 1777 that board placed "An order on William Webb to Elizabeth [Betsy] Ross for fourteen pounds twelve shillings, and two pence, for making ship's colours…" At the time Brown was also a junior partner in Willing, Morris & Co. Betsy was related by marriage to Morris' business partner in France, John Ross. Another cousin of Betsy's, George Ross, had served with Morris on the Marine Committee.[4] All of these relationships and connections with Betsy Ross created an opportunity for Morris to use his influence so this flag might be more than a flag for one state's ships.

The following represents a good faith reconstruction of events that meets all the facts. Naysayers, and there are many, insist there isn't sufficient proof to support what they call the Betsy Ross Myth, but in each of their arguments they ignore the role Robert Morris played. However, the best proof is the flag itself. It exists; and had to come into being somehow.

Betsy Ross met with three men: her late husband's uncle George Ross, George Washington, and Robert Morris, about the creation of a flag.[5] Washington was in Philadelphia because he had not yet left for camp, which he did on the 3rd of June.[6] When the meeting started they had a design for the flag in mind that was similar in shape to the square naval flags of the day. However during their meeting Betsy suggested the flag not be square, but rectangular, that the stars be five pointed, not six; and that the stars be arranged in lines or in a circle.[7] She demonstrated an efficient technique for cutting a five-pointed star to support the idea. There is today an artifact that is purported to have come from the meeting. The Free Quaker Meeting House claims it has one of the first five pointed stars that Betsy made for the flag.[8]

After that meeting, Betsy visited Robert Morris in his Willing, Morris & Co. office. Robert provided a ship's flag from a chest where he had several flags so she could see the nature of the stitching. He also provided a drawing that had been made, considering her suggestions,[9] most likely supplied by Francis Hopkinson, who was a good friend of Morris'. She then returned to her task of sewing.

G. Washington -George Ross - Robt Morris - Betsy Ross[10]

The flag was finished on June 14th, two weeks after the Pennsylvania Naval Board started the project. Betsy took it to the committee members. The flag was run up to the top of the mast on one of Morris' ships, which was then tied up to the wharf. Later, John Paul Jones claimed he was the one to hoist the first "Flag of America."[11] The few bystanders and passers-by who saw the flag cheered and applauded. They took the flag down, and that day George Ross accompanied Morris to Congress.[12] Congressional business matters turned to the Marine Committee of which Morris was a member.[13] While conducting Marine Committee business Congress resolved, "That the flag of the United States be thirteen stripes, alternate red and white: that the union be thirteen stars, white in a blue field, representing a new constellation." Also during that meeting, Jones was put in charge of the *Ranger,*[14] so he was there during the Marine Committee action too. The creation and acceptance of the American Flag satisfied Robert's goals. The flag was most useful flying from the masts of American ships in European ports. At a time when the half-born country was in need of foreign support it projected the image of America as a real nation to countries around the world.

June 1777 was also the month in which "Gentleman" John Burgoyne began his campaign to cut the colonies in two. The British thought Burgoyne's campaign would finish off the troublesome rebellion for good. He left Montreal with thousands of British soldiers, and more than a few camp followers. They intended to take Albany, control the Hudson, and then join the British in Manhattan. While Burgoyne advanced, General Gates decided not to defend a hill that overlooked Fort Ticonderoga. This was in spite of the fact that a limping Benedict Arnold had gone to the top of it to demonstrate that the fort would be vulnerable if that hill were occupied by the enemy. With the enemy bearing down on his position, Gates left his army and went to lobby Congress in Philadelphia, leaving Generals Schuyler and Arthur St. Clair in charge. While he was gone, Burgoyne recaptured Fort Ticonderoga without firing a shot because Generals Schuyler and St. Clair had followed Gates' directive and not protected the hill, which the British took first. Gates blamed Generals Schuyler and St. Clair for the loss of the fort. He returned with a commission to lead the Northern Army and with reinforcements. Burgoyne's fatal decision to avoid Lake George on his way to Albany gave Americans under General Gates, Daniel Morgan, and Arnold, the opportunity to slow the British army in the thick forests of New York State. They used trees supplied by nature to clog the roads, and the weapons supplied by Beaumarchais to good effect.

The War Trade Continues

During those days in June, Arthur Lee was traveling in Europe before returning to Paris from his posting in Spain. He took side trips to

Vienna and Berlin where his brother William held sway. He had no authority from Congress to treat with the Germans, but he was conducting what he called "Militia Diplomacy." While he was in Germany having dinner with minister Baron de Schulenburg, his papers were stolen.[15] The contents were redirected to the English. Most of the papers and journals were returned and the Baron offered to sell guns to Arthur. Arthur bought a sample set of these fusils, but they were of such low quality he rejected them.[16] With this experience under his belt he arrived in Paris with the renewed idea that he and his family should control the American-French relationship. Others did not agree.

Back in Philadelphia, the Secret Committee enlarged its reach when it retained Oliver Pollock as an agent in New Orleans. Pollock had been working with the State of Virginia for some time. However, when he bought articles and leased ships for Congressional business, he pretended that he was working for Willing, Morris & Co. He was an agent for the company and had a personal friendship with James Willing, the brother of Morris' business partner. It was understood that the subterfuge was a good way to keep the prices down and to keep the English in the dark at the same time.[17] By June 18th, 1777, the Secret Committee had just two members: Philip Livingston and Morris. Two weeks later, the Congress created a new Committee of Commerce and intended to roll the business of the old one into the new. The old Secret Committee did not shut its books until October 1778 due to some difficulties in the accounts that Morris labored mightily to rectify.[18]

The nagging troubles in Europe never seemed to quiet down. Morris got a rude surprise near the end of June, when he learned that Silas Deane's office had given information about Thomas Morris' misbehavior to a man who made it very public. Robert wrote to Deane, "With respect to my Brother I shall deal very candidly with you, by declaring to you that I never was more shocked & hurt by any incident of my Life, than at the manner in which you Gentn Commissioners at the Court of France have been pleased to mention him in Public letters that you knew must be laid before Congress"[19] Robert felt compelled to defend his brother. He attributed the disagreeable news about his brother to the condition "that employment is sought for by others whom the Commissioners wish to gratify at his Expense. That Mr. Williams & others envy him &: that Relatives & Interested motives are united to remove my Brother to make way, for a Nephew, a Cousin & a Partner." All the while Robert was convinced that Thomas had improved and been misjudged, because he had closed a tobacco backed loan, and the Commissioners in France, whom he had asked to watch over Thomas, had not said more to him in private. Morris was so sure of his brother's merit that he wrote, "I had rather any man's Nephew, Cousin or Partner had the Employment, than that my Brother should give just cause for a single complaint."[20]

Morris informed Deane that a Mr. Bromfield, in whom Deane had entrusted some commercial information, was broadcasting ill news about Thomas Morris throughout the South, and discredited both Morris and Deane in the process. He explained how harmful the rumors had become to their mutual interests when he wrote that people would think, "private gain is more our pursuit than Public Good, for such unworthy suspicions are frequently taken up on less Grounds; however I shall continue to discharge my duty faithfully in the Public and pursue my Private Fortune by all such honorable and fair means as the times will admit of, and I dare say you will do the same."[21] He cautioned that the issue was not closed and he would wait to see if his brother got into any new scrapes.[22]

The story of Tom Morris shocked and hurt Robert, but it was just a small ripple in the larger world. By August 1777, American privateers were harassing British shipping from Ireland to the Baltic. Silas Deane reported that this "deterred the English merchants from shipping goods in English bottoms at any rate; so that in a few weeks forty sail of French ships were loading in the Thames on freight; an instance never before known."[23] Even so, American letters of Marque and Reprisal were not whole-heartedly accepted by European powers. Countries with agreements with Britain objected to American privateering, and when the Americans went to sell their prizes, these countries returned the ships to the English. On one occasion American captain Cunningham and his crew were imprisoned when they tried to sell their prizes.[24] They were eventually released instead of hanged for piracy, so there was some forbearance for American action. In most cases, however, the ships taken as prizes were sold well under their value. The privateering effort continued because, as Silas Deane wrote about the takings, "they have been of infinite prejudice to our enemies both in their commerce and reputation. Nothing can be more humiliating to those once proud lords of the ocean than the insults they receive in their own coasts and from those they so lately despised."[25]

In one case, Deane reported that two ships taken by American privateer captains had been brought into Nantes. He continued, that at the suggestion of a local merchant these ships were repapered by Mr. Lee and Mr. Williams, who then sold them privately,[26] contrary to the intent of privateering as a mode of fund raising for the cause. Somehow, there were no negative repercussions for the Lees. Later, John Paul Jones ran into some difficulty in Denmark when he tried to sell a prize he captured at sea. The Danes returned the ship to England, and after the war Jones protested to the Danish Crown. The Danes refused to admit error, and the episode harmed American Danish relations for decades.

All of this occurred because the British diplomatic corps was advancing England's interests in the ports of Europe. At the same time, American diplomats were not working together smoothly. Additionally, the administration of the Continental Navy was under the direction of a distant congressional sub-committee, which was not held in high regard by the men at sea. In October 1776, John Paul Jones wrote Morris that efficiency in naval administration could only be obtained by the appointment of a competent board of admiralty. Over the ensuing year various half-measures and weak attempts were made to correct the administration of the navy. The structure and membership of the naval committees was modified, but it took Congress three years and a debacle in New England before they actually improved this system.

In a related, but separate effort, Morris worked, throughout the summer, to manage the commercial trade of the United States. He kept the money mill turning and the war goods flowing past the British blockade. This placed upward price pressure on the local markets as demand for American produce increased in Europe, and in the French and Spanish Caribbean islands. By August, some states tried to keep prices low at home by creating legal barriers to trade called embargoes. This, and the lack of goods to export from New England, were among the many reasons Beaumarchais received empty ships in return for the ships full of arms he had sent to America. As a result, Beaumarchais' financial condition was in peril, and his credibility in France started to falter because, thanks to the efforts of Arthur Lee, he had not received a letter of agreement from Congress. Unfortunately for him, in early 1778, the French Government was beginning to make steps to take official action on behalf of America. That meant Beaumarchais' activities, as critical as they had been, were becoming superfluous.[27] It was around this time, in April 1778, that John Adams made his first official trip to France. The trip was largely unproductive, and he returned home a little more than a year later in June 1779.

At the time Adams was making his first appearance in France, state embargoes were starting to take their tolls in America. Morris wrote, I "am sorry to find every part of this poor Continent so exceedingly fettered in their Trade and convulsed about their Constitutions & Governments. We must have patience & let things take their Course."[28] These self-imposed state embargoes and the British blockade were creating shortages of goods inside the states. Rumors of mobs started to spread, and once again there were shortages of supplies for the Army.[29] Morris was asked to chair the new Commercial Committee, but he was hoping instead to wrap up the business of the old Secret Committee and then be relieved of public work. He wrote, "I have had a long spell, my own affairs suffering amazingly the whole time & having no Ambition to gratify I wish to resign my honors & powers to somebody that may be better pleased with them."[30]

Philadelphia is Lost

It became clear in Philadelphia, that Willing and Morris' business partnership was fraying. This was due to stresses caused by Robert's attention to Congressional business, and the behavior of Morris' brother in Europe. In September, when it was suspected that Howe was intent on taking Philadelphia, Willing decided to stay in town even if Morris left. He was worried that the English might seize his property in an effort to collect on some of the outstanding debts generated by Thomas' gambling in London.[31] Morris arranged for £500 sterling to be placed at Willing's disposal, just to ensure his old partner would not be without funds.[32]

Washington had won the battles of Trenton and Princeton, and he kept the British at bay in New Jersey, but the British were determined to gain possession of Philadelphia, this time from the South. They sailed around New Jersey's Cape May, moved their troops up the Chesapeake and north to Philadelphia over land. The British chose not to make a naval assault of Philadelphia because they knew that an able crew of Americans manned Fort Mifflin in the Delaware River, and that competent barriers lay within the river itself. Clearly an assault would have left their ships vulnerable to attack from shore, again.

Anticipating the overland arrival of the British, the Marine Committee decided on September 7th, 1777 to save what there was of the unfinished continental Navy. John Barry moved the uncompleted hull of the 32-gun *Effingham* up the Delaware River, and to hide the ship in the water so the British would not find her; he scuttled her near Bordentown, New Jersey. Washington attempted to stop the advancing British by positioning his troops between Baltimore and Philadelphia. This resulted in the ill-fated Battle of the Brandywine on September 11th, 1777, and another loss for Washington.

Battle of Germantown at Cliveden, By Schuessele, 1840

Washington's rout in the Battle of the Brandywine cleared the way for General Howe to take Philadelphia. When the British entered Philadelphia, on September 25th, they walked into a city that was mostly deserted, except for a few Tories and Quakers. The Revolutionary government had moved to York, Pennsylvania, and by September 30th they began to hold meetings. Morris had moved his family from the Hills, to Manheim, near York, PA. Washington made one last attempt to remove General Howe from Philadelphia, and on October 4th he attacked the English in the Battle of Germantown. Much of the fighting took place at Benjamin Chew's house, Cliveden. The Battle was close and well fought, but fog, and smoke from gunpowder conspired against the Americans. Expected reinforcements became lost in the fog on their way to the battle because of a poorly written and badly read map. The result was another defeat for Washington. After several skirmishes in the area, Washington went to winter quarters in Valley Forge, and General Howe set up camp in Philadelphia. The Americans in Fort Mifflin, on Mud Island, kept the British fleet south of Philadelphia until their fort was overwhelmed in December, at which point they had to burn and abandon it.

Once in possession of Philadelphia, the British set up their defensive perimeter right through Morris' countryseat, The Hills. They garrisoned their troops through his fields and quartered the officers in his house. They abused the farmhouse and the rest of the property in the process. Morris' friends thought it was no accident that the British acted with such calculated disregard for his favorite spot on earth.

Privateering

Naval Battle Between the *United States* and *The Macedonian* on Oct 30,1812

The British were in possession of his home on Dock Street, and his beloved Hills. Reports came to Morris, in Manheim, that British privateers were attacking his shipping fleet. At the start of the Revolution neither Morris nor Willing had been interested in privateering. Morris hoped that the war would be over someday soon and he would be doing business with the British again, so he thought it would be counterproductive to attack his future trading partners. However, after the loss of many merchant ships, some of which he owned, he was suffering from the lack of naval power. The loss of Philadelphia made it clear that building a Navy was going to be more difficult than anticipated. It also meant that Morris' ships would not be returning to that port for the foreseeable future.

He decided, as a private citizen in possession of ships, that he would challenge the British at sea. Willing never joined Morris in these efforts. Morris became involved slowly, first in December 1776 as a silent partner with William Bingham in a privateer that sailed from Martinique, captained by one George Ord. Morris wrote to Bingham secretly,

> You must know I had determined not to be Concerned in privateering but having had several Vessells taken from me & otherways

> lost a great deal of my property by this War, I conceive myself perfectly justifiable in the Eyes of God & Man to seek what I have lost from those that have plundered me.[33]

Ord's mission was to accomplish the goals Morris had set for J.P. Jones before Jones was removed to the European theatre.

Morris wrote again to his agent in Martinique, William Bingham,

> My scruples about privateering are all done away. I have seen such rapine plunder & destruction denounced against and executed on the Americans that I join you in thinking it a duty to oppose and distress so mercantile and enemy [as the English].

The letter continues to explore the division of Prizes due from the success of a ship that Morris was part owner.[34] Among the goods taken from British ships were hospital supplies, and other hard to import goods. Morris expected to get about nine percent of the total value.

William Bingham - PA Senate Collection

In the course of the partnership, Captain Ord sailed the *Rattlesnake* in coordination with the *Sturdy Beggar*, another privateer owned solely by Bingham.[35] Together the *Rattlesnake* and *Sturdy Beggar* took nine merchantmen.[36] They also took two British slave ships that were on their way from Africa to the British West Indies. The ships and the cargo were sold according to Morris' instructions. Morris had written Bingham,

> I have delivered Capt. Ord the Rules & Instructions of Congress and request that both he & you will closely abide by them, indeed I have given Bond that you shou'd do so. I think however that you may sell negroes, perishable Commodities & other Articles suitable for the Islands in Martinico if the General will give you leave without waiting a formal Condemnation in any of these States, but I think you had best send the Vessells & such parts of their Cargoes as are suited to the Continent to some part of it for Condemnation & Sale, & when you take out a Cargo or any part of it from a Prize you might Ship Salt or Mollasses, Rum &c in lieu thereof.[37]

There is no accurate accounting available for the total number of slaves involved, but the privateer that was owned solely by Bingham took a ship that held 353.[38] It is interesting to note that Morris did not want to bring the slaves to America where they would have brought a better price.

This act of war was sanctioned by the Congress, aimed at British commerce in general, and the slave trade in particular. The existence of the slave trade in the 18th century resulted in the slave ships becoming targets in the economic war at sea. Morris understood there was money to be made, but he maintained that was not the primary objective. As he wrote to J.P. Jones earlier, "... I fancy you will make a considerable booty. This however is not what I have so much in View as to alarm not only the inhabitants but the whole British Nation."[39] Ultimately the allure of privateering in England and attacks on the British slave trade by Americans slowed that trade to a halt; and resulted in fewer Africans leaving their native lands. In his own time, Bingham became well known for his part in this kind of trade, while Morris did not; however, after his return to Philadelphia Bingham supported the Abolition Society of Pennsylvania.[40]

Morris' interests in privateering were fraught with risk, material and political. In 1777, Captain William "Bloody Bill" Cunningham seized a Portuguese ship, the Phoenix, "a snow class vessel,"[41] and an international incident was started. There was some controversy over who fired first, and whether it was proper for an America Privateer to take a Portuguese ship at all, since America was not at war with Portugal. Even so, there was plenty of talk in Europe about the hostile behavior of the Portuguese towards the Americans because, at the time, the Portuguese were active allies of the British, and as such were likely to ship British cargoes. The controversy went on for nearly three years with effects in Congress and the Massachusetts Admiralty courts. Morris' name was attached to the ship because he owned a 4% interest in it. Political partisans made him a focus of the incident, even though Carter Braxton of Virginia was the leader of the project. On October 27th Morris commented on this topic in a letter he wrote to John Rowe:

> I can not help thinking that Captain Cunningham's conduct in seizing this snow if she is really & truly Portuguese property is extremely reprehensible for I do not believe that Mr. Braxton could or would give him orders to capture such property at a time when no Resolves of Congress authorized it but even if he has such orders, those who gave them are much to blame & I do suppose the Transaction will appear in this light to all the World.[42]

Endnotes

1. *Henkels Catalogue*, pg. 27
2. *Robert Morris and the Holland Land Purchase*, pg. 36
3. "The Descendants of Colonel Thomas White" ref. in *The Annals of the Ancestry of Charles Custis Harrison and Ellen Waln Harrison*, pg. 164
4. Journals Continental Congress, 6:894
5. The Huntington Library Folio 1 of Section H. HM41760
6. Letters of Delegates to Congress, 7:191
7. The Huntington Library Folio 1 of Section H. HM41760
8. *The Truth about the Betsy Ross Story*, pg. 116
9. The Huntington Library Folio 1 of Section H. HM41760
10. by Charles H Weisgerber 1893, https://lccn.loc.gov/2004669130
11. Papers of Robert Morris, 8:581
12. The Huntington Library Folio 1 of Section H. HM41760
13. Letters of Delegates to Congress 7:204-6
14. *Journals of the Continental Congress*, 8:464-5
15. Revolutionary Diplomatic Correspondence, 2:363
16. Revolutionary Diplomatic Correspondence, 2:804-805
17. Letter of Delegates to Congress, 7:185-188
18. Letters of the Delegates to Congress, 11:26
19. Letters of Delegates to Congress, 7:266
20. Ibid, 7:268
21. Ibid, 7:266-268
22. Ibid, 8:237
23. Diplomatic Correspondence of the American Revolution, 1:105-110
24. Revolutionary Diplomatic Correspondence, 2:381
25. Ibid, 2:381
26. Ibid, 2:382
27. Beaumarchais, p 228
28. Letters of Delegates to Congress, 7:429
29. Ibid, 7:558
30. Letters of Delegates to Congress, 7:603-4
31. *Pennsylvania History #36*, pg. 554
32. Letters of Delegates to Congress, 7:657
33. Letters of the Delegates to Congress, 5:573
34. Pennsylvania State Archives #84 Reel 21 Groupg.1546
35. Letters of Delegates to Congress, 5:573; 6:632
36. Ibid, 6:636
37. Letters of the Delegates to Congress, 5:573
38. Ibid, 6:303
39. Ibid, 6:220-222
40. Robert J. Gough. American National Biography Online
41. Letters of Delegates to Congress, 8:201
42. Letters of Delegates to Congress 8:201-202

V

Shift in Leadership

John Hancock resigned his position as President of Congress in October 1777. He claimed his departure was due to illness, but maybe he was just sick of the job. According to some sources Hancock resigned because he felt he was not given enough respect from his colleagues. He must have noticed that a movement to provide a memorial of gratitude for the service of this merchant was blocked by a fellow Massachusetts delegate, John Adams.

Robert Morris was asked if he would take the role of President of Congress. He replied that he had enough to do without this honor. At the time he decided not to accept the position he had a three-month-old infant son, Charles. Clearly the offer had made an impression at home. Mary Morris wrote to her mother from Manheim, "Don't you feel quite important? I assure you I do, and begin to be reconciled to independence."[1] Mary's earlier unease about the war seems to have dissipated, even though she had been chased from Philadelphia for a second time.

After Morris decided against accepting the offer to be the President of Congress, Henry Laurens took on the role. Before this, Laurens had been a member of the South Carolina Government during the attack on Fort Moultrie. Laurens was a successful southern planter. He had also taken a leading role in South Carolina's slave trade, bringing in 6,900 slaves. This stopped in 1774 when a non-importation agreement was reached in Congress. After that point he said he was against the business, but he continued to assist others in the trade.[2] He had two plantations in Georgia, and three in South Carolina.[3] Like many of the slave holding class, Laurens viewed himself in an unfailingly positive light. Laurens flattered himself, when he wrote to his son in 1776,

> My negroes [in Georgia], all to a man, are strongly attached to me - so are all of mine in this country [S. Carolina].

It was also in this letter he claimed to abhor slavery, and blame it on the English; all the while, he profited from it, aided it, and abided it.[4]

Laurens had a much more active administrative style than Hancock. Over time, he looked hard at Morris and his allies, whom he called the Property Men. He was suspicious of them for being insufficiently radical, because of their caution during the debate on independence. He was much more sympathetic to the Lee-Adams wing of Congress and acted accordingly. All three were champions of a stance they called "Republican Virtue," which translated, roughly, to a state's rights position, because they considered that they were not fighting to create a new king in America but to control their own destinies. Even so, all of them wished to have a weak central authority that would coordinate actions during stressful times, and so they participated in the Continental Congress with that understanding.

Coincidental to that faction taking control of Congress, military efforts in New York State, started during the previous administration, were going in the Americans' favor. "Gentleman Johnny" Burgoyne's campaign to cut New York State in two ended on October 10, 1777 with his loss at the Battle of Saratoga. That victory gave a much-needed boost to American credibility in Europe and demonstrated again to the European powers that the Americans could defeat the British in battle, even if it had taken most of the weapons sent from France by Beaumarchais.

The victory encouraged the French Crown to help the Americans on an official basis, but clearly France had England in her sights when support was offered. As that was happening, there was more shuffling of personnel in the American office in France. During November 1777, William Carmichael was officially named secretary to the Commissioners there.[5] He worked closely with Deane on the Beaumarchais contracts,[6] so naturally this did not endear him to Arthur Lee.[7] Carmichael was firmly on the side of the Morris-Deane bloc, and he often communicated to the Congress through Bingham in Martinique.[8]

Back in America, the competition for glory heated up after the victory in Saratoga. The record shows that the key work had actually been done by General Benedict Arnold, but General Gates and Lieutenant Wilkinson were both political operators, and they sought the credit. Colonel James Wilkinson had ingratiated himself to General Gates during the long campaign in New York by helping Gates hide his failure to protect Fort Ticonderoga properly three months earlier. In return, Gates praised and promoted Wilkinson over Arnold. Wilkinson, in turn, sang the praises of Gates. Gates' efforts to take Arnold's credit did not sit well with Arnold; and was one of the sore points that led him to turn on his fellow Revolutionaries.

The victory in Saratoga appeared to have been won by General Horatio Gates, and the loss of Philadelphia clearly occurred under General Washington. Gates lost no time in promoting himself as the superior commander to his southern friends in Congress. In the process, there was scant recognition for those who had provided the means for the victory, and little mention of uneven distribution of supplies from France, with Gates' army getting the benefit of the imbalance.

Political intrigues continued to emanate from France, while Gates' friends were at work in York solidifying their power. Arthur Lee maintained that the weapons Beaumarchais supplied were gifts, and he was believed in Henry Laurens' congress. Consequently, Silas Deane was denied his commission. On the other side of the Atlantic, Beaumarchais still expected to receive return shipments for cargo he had sent under the Hortalez name. However, Arthur Lee wrote,

> Upon this subject of returns, I think it my duty to state to you some facts relative to the demands of this kind from Hortalez ... The Minister has repeatedly assured us, and in the most explicit terms, that no return is expected from these subsidies.[9]

Beaumarchais was not the only target. Franklin was not spared as Lee painted him as a womanizing lecher. Unfortunately, the behavior of Robert's brother was making Arthur's case of general malfeasance more and more believable.

Arthur Lee's partisan campaign worked inside the Continental Congress, but it did not make him popular, even among those from his own state. Benjamin Harrison of Virginia wrote about the Lee brothers,

> You, who know them not, can form but an imperfect idea of those on that side of the water by what you have seen on this, they being much more designing, vindictive, and overbearing. Perhaps you may think this impossible, but be assured it is a fact, and that they are no more fit for the characters they bear than any man that can be thought on; however they are fixed, and I suppose America must suffer them for a season longer, as the cabal is at present too powerful to afford us the least prospect of their removal."[10]

The Laurens and the Lees were clearly in ascendancy. At the same time, many of the original delegates were missing from Congress because they had gone home to work on their own state constitutions. Morris wrote to his good friend, John Hancock,

> This seems to be the present business of all America except the Army. It is the fruit of a certain premature declaration which you know I always opposed.… My opposition was founded on the evil consequences I foresaw, or thought I foresaw, and the present state of several of the colonies justifies my apprehension.

He was uncomfortable with political developments in states like Pennsylvania, and not encouraged by the behavior of Congress. Noting the disagreements there about who got what office in America and in France he noted,

> We are disputing about liberties, privileges, posts, and places at the very time we ought to have nothing in view but securing those objects and placing them on such a footing as to make them worth contending for amongst ourselves hereafter.[11]

While various Congressional committees argued about the goings on in France, and the philosophical issues of rights and liberties, Morris argued for concrete actions to win the war.[12] He favored winning the war, then laying out a plan for the rights and liberties in the new country. If the war was lost, he reasoned, the philosophical issues became moot. The other side argued that a victory leading to a new tyranny was worse than defeat. While this notion may seem heroic, it was far from a practical solution to the problems encountered while waging an on-going conflict. Congress continued to argue the fine points of revolutionary philosophy,[13] and did not modify its structure in response to the conditions.

The Continental government, as a collection of committees, was used effectively by members to gain favor with their own local interests, instead of supervising executive departments that would have been effective in winning the war. As such, it was, and some say still is, prone to lack of action, and waste. Few of the high-minded discussions about serving the people and decentralized power resulted in the soldiers getting paid, clothed, or fed. The Marine Committee also suffered from these conditions. Morris continued to promote the idea of executive offices in the new Government.

> In short if the Congress means to succeed in this Contest they must pay good Executive Men to do their business as it ought to be & not lavish millions away by their own mismanagement. I say mismanagement because no Men living can attend the daily deliberations of Congress & do executive parts of business at the same time. I do

> aver here will be more money lost, totally lost, in Horses, Wagons, Cattle &c &c for want of sufficient numbers of proper persons to look after them ... [14]

A Bold Plan

James Willing, the brother of Robert's business partner, arrived in York in the fall of 1777. He had been living and working in Natchez, Louisiana for years, and came to Congress to promote a plan he and Oliver Pollock had developed.[15] They urged their friends in and out of Congress to launch a campaign against the British living along the Mississippi and in Florida. This campaign was modeled on the one launched against the British in Canada, and was supposed to be aimed at gaining support for the Revolution from the British in Florida. Congress, under Henry Laurens' leadership, had already considered and rejected their own version of this plan. They deferred on Willing's suggestion. Willing did not give up, and ultimately Robert Morris approved an expedition smaller than the one Willing had proposed. Morris supported this as a member of the Committee of Commerce, and after some effort[16] he secured Congressional approval[17] for a modified version. The mission was described as one to re-supply Fort Pitt with goods from New Orleans, but Willing also traveled with Letters of Marque and Reprisal so he might outfit some privateers in the Gulf. Various war supplies awaited the success of the mission and had been arranged by Oliver Pollock through his friend Sr. de Galvez, the Spanish Governor of Louisiana. All that was needed was for James Willing to pay for them and bring them north.

Pollock was a businessman with many interests. He was an agent for the Continental Government, a part time slave trader, a friend of the Spanish Governor, and a representative for a variety of trading houses on the Atlantic seaboard and in the West Indies, including Willing, Morris & Co. Pollock was one of the American traders who kept the economic relationship alive with Spain via his connections with Cuba, even when John Jay was shut out of diplomatic channels at the Spanish Court. He became involved in supplying the state of Virginia in their war effort on the western frontier, which embroiled him in a financial bind caused by trouble with credit from France. His communications with Morris about economic relations with Spain and his connections in Spanish Cuba introduced the use of the Dollar Sign "$" in messages sent to the American government. Merchants commonly used that symbol to represent the Spanish Milled Dollar. The first use of the "$" symbol in an official document occurred when Morris used it in his account books.

Hard to Leave

Morris' private business interests continued to suffer due to his work for the war effort. He hoped to straighten out the accounts that had become confused from the sporadic nature of the record keeping by his brother, his trading partners, himself, and Congress, particularly during the exodus to Baltimore where Richard Henry Lee somehow never kept minutes of the Secret Committee. Morris requested a six-month leave of absence to take on this accounting task. Morris was a representative of Pennsylvania, so permission had to be granted by that state. The Pennsylvania Council of Safety,[18] granted the leave in November 1777. However, Morris was not able to leave public service behind completely, instead he was required to attend to the public business upon demand. In addition to committee business, he felt compelled, on occasion, to rise to the defense of others. One such case involved his old associate and former member of the Pennsylvania navy board, John Brown of Philadelphia. Mr. Brown had headed to York from Philadelphia with a message from the British General Howe, who wanted to discuss terms of peace. For this, Brown had been arrested for treason by the State Government of Pennsylvania,[19] and thrown into prison. Morris petitioned for his release.

On November 15th the Continental Congress passed the Articles of Confederation, and Robert Morris went from his leave in Manheim to Congress in York and signed it. While it took less than a month for the Continental Congress to agree on a Declaration of Independence, it took about a year and four months for them to come to a consensus on how the former colonies would work together. It would take almost another three and a half years for the states to agree, and then that agreement was reached just as it became obvious that the war was nearly lost. Clearly, it was not inevitable that the United States would become united as a single nation. Considering the cultural differences between the "distressed cavaliers" found in the Southern plantation-based society, and the theocratic Calvinist puritans of New England, with their penurious ways and town meeting systems, it is most remarkable that they decided to become part of one nation after all. It was certainly a surprise to the British.

The Conway Cabal

While Washington was in winter quarters at Valley Forge, and shortly after Morris began his leave of absence, a tepid political intrigue started to brew in Congress. On November 27th, General Gates became the head of the newly reconfigured Board of War. On December 13th Gener-

General Horatio Gates

al Thomas Conway was placed in the newly created position of Inspector General of the Army. Generals Conway and Gates led a small group of like-minded men that used their influence in an attempt to remove Washington as the leader of the Continental Army.[20] This effort came to be known as the Conway Cabal. It involved the same General Gates who left Washington before the Battle of Trenton to talk to Congress, the same General Gates who left New York State before the loss of Ticonderoga, and the same General Gates who enlisted the assistance of Colonel Wilkinson in making a convincing effort to take credit for Arnold's success during the Battle of Saratoga. According to one report this "cabal" unraveled after co-conspirator, Colonel Wilkinson, divulged the plot during a moment of drunkenness while talking to a friend of Washington's in a Reading Pennsylvania tavern.[21] Others give credit to Henry Laurens for quelling this effort. In any case, the effort was discovered and to avoid blame Gates implicated Colonel James Wilkinson in the plot.[22]

Critical Consultations

Shortly after that supposed cabal was discovered, Morris was asked by the Board of War to go with two other congressmen and consult with Washington on the best course of action. The three-man committee was instructed to go from York to Valley Forge and to discuss a variety of topics including military strategy and the supply situation.[23] One of the key goals of this committee was to see if it was a good idea to launch a winter campaign against the British in Philadelphia.

From November 29th to December 12th, 1777, Morris, Joseph Jones, and Elbridge Gerry visited the encampment at Valley Forge. They all met with General Washington, and discussed the merits of attacking Philadelphia, but the idea was rejected. They determined the army should stay in Valley Forge for reorganization.[24] They wrote to Washington,

> That a reform may take place in the army, and proper discipline be introduced, we wish to see the Military placed on such a footing as may make a Commission a desirable object to the Officer, and his

> Rank preserved from degradation & contempt."[25] It was decided to have a "Committee of Board of War to Confer with a Committee of Genl officers for reforming the Army.[26]

News of Morris' involvement gave hope to the troops. On December 30th James Lovell wrote to John Adams,

> As a secret I tell you that there is the greatest risque that the army will be disbanded in a short season, for the Commissary's & Qr Master's departments are ruined. I hope Robt. Morris will take up the first himself immediately or as a Director; Buchannan is as incapable as a child and knows not how he can feed the army 3 Weeks from any parts, or how to feed them from day to day with what he has on hand. Mutiny is at present suppressed. The Clothier is little better & the Director Genl. of Hospitals is at his wits end. Trumbull would be deified if he was on the spot, send him from Boston if there.
>
> The Board of War with military drivers are Quarter masters owing to the Imbecility of the Govt. of this State which must be changed after the present glaring conviction of its Impotence. If at any day it musters courage to legislate it finds itself without any executive.
>
> Yr. frozen fingered Servt, J L"[27]

Keeping a five-thousand-man army in winter quarters stressed the supply system. Thomas Mifflin was the quartermaster for the army and has been the target of some blame for the condition of the troops. One of the little told stories of Valley Forge is that the poverty of the soldiers at the encampment was a direct result of changes in the supply system, made by the Continental Congress, under Henry Laurens' leadership. They took the quartermaster corps off commission and put them on a small salary. As a result of this new policy, most of the talented and able men went back to private enterprise where there was more money to be made. This was combined with the failure of the "Constitutionalists" in the Pennsylvania Assembly to supply the troops with materials that were nearby and going to waste. When materials did arrive in Valley Forge the quartermaster could not apportion them according to his judgment because they were often intended for certain groups according to the source. For example, when Pennsylvania did send shipments, the Assembly often required that their supplies go only to Pennsylvania troops, leaving others to go hungry.

One of the initiatives coming from Morris' trip to Valley Forge was the proposal of half-pay pensions for the soldiers. The idea was to encourage the troops to stay in the army till the end of the war, and then receive a pension in return for their trouble. Henry Laurens was vociferously against the idea, and he claimed it would create an aristocracy at the public expense. What it really would have done is empower a central government to administer the program. He supported an alternative plan, proposed by Rhode Island, to enlist slaves for the duration of the war, for free one presumes, and grant them their freedom in return for their services. This may have sounded like a good idea to someone who had imported 6,900 slaves, and owned well over 300, but it would have made these people *de facto* slaves of the state. It didn't happen. What did happen was, the issue of half-pay pensions became a point of a conflict between Henry Laurens and Robert Morris. Laurens characterized the struggle in titanic terms as "Virtue" against "Mammon,"[28] with himself on the side of "Virtue," of course. The issue was finally hammered out in May when, in a compromise, it was agreed that soldiers would get their half pay, but only for seven years, and those who stayed till the end of the conflict would get an $80 bonus. The issue would be revisited over and again during the course of the war. One thing was settled, though, Henry Laurens was on the losing end, and he was not pleased to see his opposite, Morris, carry the day.

While conditions were bleak at Valley Forge, the time spent in the encampment was not wasted. It was during this period that the Continental Army was transformed from an admixture of various militias into a unified fighting force, thanks largely to the work of Baron Friedrich von Steuben. Silas Deane had recruited von Steuben in France, with some help from Beaumarchais. Von Steuben was not a nobleman and had only obtained the rank of Captain of the infantry, but he had been given the honorary title "Barron" for his service in the Danish Army. Unfortunately, because some of the other French adventurers were becoming troublesome in America, new Europeans were not in demand. However, back in France, Beaumarchais contrived to hire two men to act as assistants to von Steuben, and he dressed von Steuben as a real Baron with the rank of Lieutenant General in the service of the King of Prussia. These theatrics were enough to convince the Americans agents in France that von Steuben was a real baron and send him to America to help.[29]

One of the first things von Steuben did before going to Valley Forge was to meet with Robert Morris in Morris' Manheim home offices. Morris was taken in by the pretense and wrote to the President of Congress and introduced the Baron,

> ...having served so long as twenty years under so great a Master as the King of Prussia one cannot but entertain expectations that the Baron must be capable of rendering important Services to this country."[30]

Von Steuben went to Valley Forge shortly after meeting with Congress.

Trouble in Trade

While Morris consulted with Washington in Valley Forge, the first, and only, return cargo arrived in France for Beaumarchais. It quickly became a bone of contention as the Lee brothers and Franklin endeavored, ungraciously, to assume ownership of it. Beaumarchais finally took possession of the goods, but not without some rancorous feelings for the American Commissioner, Arthur Lee.[31] At the same time, Robert Morris got more reports from Silas Deane that Thomas was misbehaving to the point of negligence and dereliction of duty. Morris had defended his brother earlier, so when it was clear to others that Robert was not going to make any changes in France, such reports became more and more public. Robert knew that if his brother were discredited in office it would hurt the nation and his personal business interests. He knew that if his brother were guilty of the charges made against him, the supply system for the Revolution would become compromised. After he discovered that the reports about Thomas were true, he acted in his capacity as a member of the Commercial Committee and dismissed his wayward half-brother, Thomas Morris, from his official duties in France.[32]

Thomas was not paying close attention to either Continental business, or to the business of Willing, Morris & Co. He had made arrangements with partners of dubious merit that Robert had to fire,[33] and it appeared that Thomas had converted some of the funds at hand to personal uses. His tendency to overindulge in a variety of vices made him a liability and a disappointment. Robert had been in personal denial about his half-brother's failings because the truth was very painful for him. Robert had taken on his half-brother, who was sixteen years his junior, as a son and educated him in the best manner possible. Thomas had more years in school than Robert ever did. He spoke several languages, and his social skills were unmatched. Yet his character was flawed. Robert was deeply hurt to learn that his half-brother was such a wastrel and that he was unable to do his job. Not only was Robert hurt on a personal level; he was also embarrassed politically and economically.

On December 27th, a humbled Morris wrote a letter to Henry Laurens, then President of Congress.

> These letters were written for the purpose of making me acquainted with the unworthy conduct of my Brother Mr. Thos. Morris in Nantes & their contents shocked me to the very Soul, I perceived instantly how grossly I had long been imposed on & deemed it my duty to have him immediately discharged from the Agency in which he was employed for the Public....
>
> Mr. Thos. Morris & myself are descended from a Father whose Virtue & whose Memory I have ever revered with the most Filial Piety. Our Mothers were not the same & this youth was born after our Father's decease, without any sufficient provision made for his maintenance. The tender regard I bore to the Parent, I determined when very young to extend to his Offspring, & no sooner had I fixed myself in the World than I took charge of this Brother. I gave him the best Education that cou'd be obtained in Philadelphia, & took as much care of his Morals as my time & capacity enabled. When he was arrived at a proper Age I took him into my Counting House to instruct him in the profession from which he was to draw his future support. [Flattery] first led him to seek improper Company, who readily granting him the preeminence he delighted in, soon carried him into the practice of their Follies & Vices.[34]

John Ross was asked to take over the Willing, Morris & Co. business for Thomas, and Jonathan Williams, Franklin's great-nephew, took over Thomas' official government position.[35] Robert tried to wrap up the business of the Secret Committee back in Manheim. Given the nature of the problem, and the fact that Arthur Lee had tried to supplant his own brother, William, into Thomas' role, it is hard to believe that Arthur was totally ignorant of the problems in the Nantes office. However, once Thomas was removed there was no political advantage in attacking him. Lee continued to attack Ben Franklin, Silas Deane, and by implication, Robert Morris.[36] Lee complained to Henry Laurens and to his friend John Adams, who in turn contacted his cousin Sam Adams.

Henry Laurens' ascension to the Presidency of Congress corresponded with Congressional trends to borrow and print more money, to encourage price controls, to support embargoes, and draw funds from Europe where there were none,[37] which was technically an act of theft by the Congress. During Laurens' tenure, loyalty oaths were instituted, and the Gates-Lee faction became more prominent in the Continental Government. This was also the period of the most prolific and least responsible spending done by the Congress, resulting in millions being lost to fraud and compounded by the lack of any credible accounting. Instead of correcting these practices during his tenure, Laurens took special interest in Morris' involvement with the questionable capture of the Portuguese Snow, the *Phoenix*. Laurens continued to ignore Virginian, Carter Braxton, who was the lead partner, and instead focused on Morris, who was often forced to defend his 4% interest as a silent partner in the venture.[38]

In January 1778, while factional differences were flaring in America, the British controlled two major mid-Atlantic ports, Philadelphia and New York. Inflation was rampant. Congress issued ten million dollars more in loan office certificates and encouraged the states to get their paper currency out of circulation. The British blockade worked to weaken American financial strength, and there were rumors that the British were distributing counterfeit Continental paper money to hasten the economic ruin of the Revolutionaries. When they thought they had the upper hand the British sought peace on their terms: with concessions, but not independence. The offer was refused. Times continued to be tense.[39]

The *Rattletrap* Embarks

After months of preparation, Captain James Willing embarked on his mission, contrary to the efforts of Henry Laurens. It was January 11th, 1778.[40] Willing had good reason to expect the Spanish to be helpful. In 1776 and 1777 they had agreed with Virginian, Richard Henry Lee, to work with Oliver Pollock and send supplies to Fort Pitt and to the posts on the Mississippi River commanded by George Rogers Clark. Willing had a large idea of his mission, but he only took about 30 volunteers. They traveled from Fort Pitt down the Mississippi on a boat called the *Rattletrap*. They harassed English Loyalists along the way and in western Florida. While it was never explicitly stated in Willing's directives, Willing did plunder Tory properties along the route to gain material to trade for the supplies. His group also managed to hoist the American Flag over the British fort at Natchez and secured a promise from that town to stay neutral during the war. This alarmed the British in Florida, who reinforced their defenses. James Willing went on to New Orleans and met with Oliver Pollock. Pollock arranged with the Spanish Governor to allow the public auction of the goods and slaves seized along the way. The money, more than $62,000, went to purchase needed supplies for the American forces at Ft. Pitt and in the western territories. [41]

Willing had accomplished his official mission, but he was not satisfied with that. He pressed on in the style of militia action. Using his letter of Marque, he operated from New Orleans, and he captured a British ship in the Gulf and renamed it *The Morris*. He used it as a privateer. In one successful foray he captured the British brig, *Neptune*, with its Jamaica bound cargo of lumber. In another sortie he captured the schooner, *Dispatch*, and its cargo of flour and fifty slaves.[42] Willing so harassed the English in the Gulf of Mexico that the British government complained to the Spanish government, and the British sent two frigates to close the port of New Orleans. The Spanish Governor became increasingly concerned over Willing's aggressive actions against the English because he did not want the English to seize the city of New Orleans in retaliation. De Galvez protected the Americans, but as part of the arrangement with the British, James Willing was not allowed to return north with the supplies through the Spanish Territories. Lieut. Robert George took the men and supplies on an overland route north under the protection of the Spanish flag. They met with Colonel George Rogers Clark's western army at Fort Kalkaska in the Illinois Territory. These supplies and the accompanying Spanish troops were most useful in the victories over the British at Ft. Kalkaska, Cahokia and Vincennes, all of which were in territory Virginia claimed. Eventually some of the supplies went to Fort Pitt. The British did reinforce western Florida, but they never captured Fort Pitt. James Willing headed back to Philadelphia on a sloop, and the English captured him before he could reach New York.[43] A little more than a year later, in 1779, Spain went to war against the British to assist their ally, the French. The British contingent along the Mississippi was no match for the combined forces of Pollock's men and de Galvez's soldiers.

De Galvez

The Price of Public Service

Thomas Willing stayed in Philadelphia during the English occupation, and this contact caused some concern among the more radical elements. On February 8th Willing contacted Morris in Manheim. He asked Morris to intervene in favor of Benjamin Chew, so Mr. Chew could return to his family. Benjamin Chew was a Quaker and co-signer of the non-importation agreements of 1767, but he was also a pacifist and therefore a suspected loyalist who was jailed at the Union New Jersey Iron works. Chew followed Willing's letter with one of his own, dated March 31st. He wrote that he was not sure what the purpose was for his imprisonment, and wondered if he should appeal to the Congress, or the government of Pennsylvania for parole to his family. He had been locked up for seven months and kept in the dark about his future.[44] He appealed to Morris instead of the President of Congress because he was sure Morris would be discreet and take the proper course. Benjamin Chew placed his fate in Morris' hands. Morris replied that it was up to the Pennsylvania Council, and that he would make a trip to Lancaster to meet with the state government and do what he could to help.[45] Morris added that, if that measure was not sufficient, he would bring the matter up to the Continental Congress. Benjamin Chew did gain his parole and was finally released from that parole on May 15th, as a result of Congressional, not Pennsylvanian, action.

Morris' partial leave of absence stretched from mid-December 1777 to mid-May 1778. During that period, he continued to be involved in ongoing Commercial Committee, and other Congressional business. He was also working on his private business and arranged shipments in France via John Ross.[46] At the same time, he kept trying clear the books of the old Secret Committee. There, the pace had been quick, and the paperwork did not always keep up with the business. Robert often hounded his half-brother Thomas, broker George Eddy, merchants Thomas Mumford,[47] John Langdon, and others for better documentation, but they were slow to respond. As a result, the record was spotty in places, destroyed in others, and generally confusing. The lack of clarity in the record haunted Morris as time went on. Henry Laurens added himself to the Commerce Committee, and suddenly became interested in the expedition of the *Rattletrap*, which he didn't favor from the start, and seemed to take some offence that it even occurred.[48]

Thomas Morris stayed in France after Robert fired him from his official positions. John Ross noted that Thomas looked ill and had become "a martyr to the most contemptible habit in the universe,"[49] meaning an addiction to opium, or as Ross put it, "the unconquerable habits to which he is addicted."[50] A few days after making these observations, John Ross wrote that Thomas died in Nance at 5:00 a.m., January 31, 1778[51] and said that his death was related to his dissipated lifestyle. One can infer that meant a drug overdose. Oddly, that happened on Robert's 44th birthday. Interestingly, some years later, another member of the American team, Silas Deane, died, also while in disgrace, and at that time his death was attributed to suicidal poisoning. An intimate acquaintance of both men was Dr. Edward Bancroft. Bancroft was noted as an authority in poisons and he had access to opium. Most critically, he had a second job as a spy for the British crown. At the time however, Bancroft was in Passy spying on Franklin and Deane. His fellow mole, Major Thornton, however, was in Nance,[52] and had just arrived there with a letter from the American commission, and perhaps a package from Bancroft for Thomas, just in time to celebrate Robert's birthday. Thomas' death was duly noted by John Paul Jones. He had his ship, the Ranger, fire a thirteen-gun salute to Robert's half-brother,[53] after Thomas was buried in a nocturnal ceremony.[54]

A week after Thomas' death, the relationship between The United States and France was put on firm footing. The military *Treaty of Alliance* and the commercial *Treaty of Amity and Commerce* were both signed in Paris on Feb 6th, 1778. On March 3rd John Ross informed Deane that shortly after Thomas died, William Lee went to Thomas Morris' apartment and took control of Thomas' private papers, including Willing, Morris, & Co. account books and Secret Committee papers. The papers were taken before any accounting could be done of them. John Ross called this an "unprecedented, unwarrantable and illegal measure." Writing to Deane he continued,

> ...you could exercise your judgment in the least on the consequences likely to attend Mr. Lee's posting expedition to seize and clandestinely search (upon the flimsy pretence of his powers as Agent) the books, papers & Secret Correspondence of Willing, Morris & Co., and that of Robert Morris, as well the correspondence of others with those gentlemen, in a public and private line...[55]

Contrary to the expectation of the Commissioners, William Lee moved the papers to Paris.[56] The Lee brothers then inspected the papers for several days and then attempted to get others to attest that the contents of the trunk had not been changed. No one would consent.[57] Arthur Lee insisted on his innocence, "I can answer for my brother and myself, that we expected as much to find treason in the Bible, as in the papers you mention."[58] Even with Thomas Morris' papers in hand, Arthur Lee's endless claims of malfeasance were never backed up with one bit of evidence.[59] The lack of evidence did not deter Lee, who addressed Adams,

"You know too that a person may be well satisfied of the truth of a thing without being able to produce legal proofs necessary for conviction."[60] While it has generally been assumed that the Lees returned all the papers to Morris in due course, it should be noted that even today papers from the Secret Committee, Morris, Ross, and Bingham can still be found among the Lee Family papers.[61] It never occurred to Lee that he had been duped into thinking the worst about his fellow patriots by a pair of British spies who were quietly working in France as trusted secretaries. He pursued his misbegotten beliefs to the end.

France, an Ally

France's entry into the war turned a civil conflict into a world war. The British finally sent a serious peace commission to America with generous terms. However, they arrived too late, maybe two years too late, and just as the Tories were abandoning Philadelphia. Morris received notice of this peace offer from the former British governor of West Florida, who proposed America accept terms that were short of complete independence. Morris had to ensure this letter would not compromise him, and sent word on to Congress. He wrote,

> ... the Government of Great Britain are alarmed at the prospect of our forming foreign alliances & from that apprehension has sprung Ld North's conciliatory measures.
>
> I thought it my duty to communicate such authentic intelligence to Congress immediately least they might not be apprized of any preliminaries being in their way from France.[62]

It was too late for compromise, and too early for peace. Neither side was ready to make the tough decisions required. In early May, Morris learned of the French-American alliance, but personal news came along with that message.

He wrote,

> "Mr. Deane tells me my Brother has paid the last forfeit of his follies by his death on the 1st Feby last. It is the happiest thing that could befall him but has in some degree renewed my feelings on his acct."[63]

It must have been a bittersweet time for him. His brother had caused him personal, political and economic embarrassment, and nearly ruined his long-time business partner, Thomas Willing; yet he was saddened to lose Thomas whom he had brought up, almost as his own son.

Britain reconfigured its fighting forces in response to the new alliance, and their fleet left Philadelphia shortly after learning the French might sail up the Delaware and attack them. The French fleet did arrive with Silas Deane and the new ambassador. The British decided to gather their mid-Atlantic land forces in New York and harass New England from the sea. They also wanted to move a portion of their ground forces to the South where they expected to get assistance from loyalists there. These considerations, and pressure from the French Navy on their possessions in the West Indies, caused the British to send part of their navy to the Caribbean to defend their islands. They realized that by seizing Philadelphia they had won nothing. The revolutionary government at the time was not to be destroyed by taking buildings, because the Continental Congress was small, the members traveled light. All they needed to conduct business was the papers they brought with them. Capturing the Capital, like defeating Washington's army, turned into an exercise in futility similar to the effort by Xerxes to defeat the nomadic Scythians in 600BC.

Never at Peace

On occasion, Morris received letters in Manheim asking for him to become more involved. He got one in March from a friend of his, William Duer, who wrote,

> The Consequences will in my Opinion, occasion its Dissolution very shortly unless both they [Congress], and the State of Penna. cease to interfere with the Military Departments.... Let me my dear Sir conjure you to attend Congress on the Return of the Committee from Camp. I am sensible private Convenience cannot operate upon your mind at this Crisis, provided you have a Prospect of being useful.[64]

Morris received another call to action, this time from John Penn, a congressman from North Carolina,

> ...almost every man would be glad to have you here. I hope my dear Sir you will excuse my being the means of giving you the trouble of coming to York as I really think it of great Importance to America to have a Gentn. of your abilities present when a Subject of such Magnitude is on the Carpet.[65]

Congressional problems were put into perspective by events in the war. Most particularly, when good men were lost. Nicholas Biddle died on March 7th, off the coast of Barbados, in an engagement between the

Randolph and the 64-gun *HMS Yarmouth*. The *Yarmouth* got off a lucky shot and hit the *Randolph's* powder magazine. The ship exploded and took all the men down with her.

Morris went to Congress in York to assist with the business of war supplies, most particularly in arrangements with the company run by Beaumarchais.[66] He moved other matters forward too; and was pleased to inform Bingham that Congress would repay him the 100,000 livres that Bingham had lent the Government in trade.[67] That was about $25,000 at that time. Others in Morris' network, Pollock, Beaumarchais, and Ceronio were being starved, or so it appeared. Beaumarchais had sent a representative to facilitate repayments. His name was Theveneau de Francey, and he had a lot of interesting details about the Secret Committee business due to his familiarity with the earlier trade. His knowledge was not complete; as such these half-truths provided ammunition for many of the aspersions later cast at Morris.

Aside from occasional trips to York, Morris stayed in Manheim until the British left Philadelphia. He got packets almost every day that included messages from ships across the sea and letters from people who needed Morris to represent their interests to Congress. He did what he could. As a member of the Committee of Foreign Affairs, Morris tried to increase the momentum for American alliances among the crowned heads of Europe. He moved to make a new office for Ralph Izard as minister to the Court of Tuscany.[68] Among the many items Morris got for the Army were the medical supplies he procured for Doctors Rush and Shippen. Morris also worked to operate his trading business. At the same time, he was unwinding his partnership with Thomas Willing. On top of that, the problem of having a wayward half-brother in Europe had aggravated the already difficult conditions inherent in running a shipping business during wartime, far from the port.

Morris said, "This affair of my Brother occasions me much business."[69] By that he meant he had to spend a good deal of time and effort dealing with the chaos left in his brother's wake, including the vast gambling debts from those binges in London. Before Thomas' death, Morris' partner, Willing, wrote that his bills of exchange, worth over £36,000, were being protested in London and such debts would sink him. In addition to real problems in Morris' accounts there were growing political problems as Arthur Lee stepped up his attacks on the merchants from the middle states.

Arthur Lee had his supporters. Both John and Samuel Adams defended him because they also had "Radical Whig" leanings. John Adams wrote, "

> I feel partial to Dr Lee. I confess I feel the strongest obligation to him for the eminent services he rendered to America when he was in England, and to the Massachusetts Bay in particular.[70]

Adam's noble feelings and motives lent weight to Lee's ignoble actions. Lee did not stop complaining "loud and long" to anyone who would listen, which included his brother Richard Henry, who was still in Congress. There was still no proof given by Dr. Lee, and ultimately the account books of the Secret Committee balanced, but Lee was looking for trouble and continued to send complaining letters.

Lee's ally, who was at that time the President of Congress, Henry Laurens, made another move against Morris' interests when he had one of Morris' clerks, Mr. Swanwick, arrested on suspicion of "unjustifiable correspondence between the said Mr. Swanwick & any person under protection of the Enemy."[71] It turned out that Mr. Swanwick had written a letter to his loyalist father, and not on a political topic. He was released and continued to work for Morris; and was eventually given a position in the Office of Finance. It could be said that the seeds of distrust between the merchants of the middle states and the slave holding planters of the South were sown in France, were nurtured for years by partisans in Congress, and bloomed over and over again until the Civil War.

From Mischianza to Defeat

When the British prepared to leave Philadelphia, they decided to punish the Pennsylvanians in a variety of ways short of burning a city they wished to control at some future time. On May 8th, 1778, the British raised and burned the ship the *Effingham,* which John Barry had tried to hide by sinking it eight months before. Ten days later, they held a grand party called the "Mischianza." This party entailed the conscription of every available young lady to accompany a British officer. According to Rebecca Franks, the daughter of loyalist merchant and slave trader David Franks, there was a river pageant that, with great show, ferried the citizens from Green Street Wharf down the river to what is now Washington St. They went to Joseph Warton's place where

> ...there was a tournament in which England's bravest soldiers appeared in honor of Philadelphia's fairest women, being divided into six Knights of the Blended Rose and six Knights of the Burning Mountain, each wearing the colors of his particular princess."[72]

This highly extravagant and frivolous event during wartime might seem a bit surreal, but it was an efficient and pleasant way to empty the stores of their merchandise, and to empty the houses of their best goods. For example, the peer glass mirrors at Clivedon, the Chew's house in Germantown, were moved to the banks of the Delaware to provide reflectance for the lights that brightened the river parade during the party. It was a rousing sendoff for the British who left Philadelphia without paying their bills. The city had suffered from their presence. For example, they had dug a mass grave near the State House for dead animals and people. Also, they had pulled up some of the floor-boards in that building and turned it into a latrine.

In June 1778, the British army was making its hot and heavy way from Philadelphia to New York, through the summer heat. Washington and his army followed and undertook one of the largest land battles of the war, The Battle of Monmouth. The Americans pushed Clinton's British army out of New Jersey at great cost to the British. This battle was almost lost by General Charles Lee who retreated against Washington's orders. General Washington reorganized the troops and saved the day. General Charles Lee was court marshaled. The remainder of the British Army made its way to New York.

A young woman named Mary Hays McCauly earned her place in history that day. She was the wife of an artilleryman and was traveling with the army. She placed herself in harm's way to assist the troops whom she knew well. She started by helping to refresh the fighting men with pitchers of water to slack their thirst in the hot summer sun. After the men fell from the heat, and she saw her husband shot down in battle, she took on his role as an artillery mate. She picked up his ramrod and in the face of heavy fire from the other side she kept the batteries firing at the British. This is the story of "Molly Pitcher" who was recognized in the field by General Washington with a warrant as a non-commissioned officer.

Endnotes

1. Oberholtzer, pg. 15
2. Documents Illustrative of the Slave Trade, 4:241,472
3. American National Biography Online
4. Documents Illustrative of the Slave Trade, 4:471
5. Letters of Delegates to Congress, 8:338
6. Ibid, 10:652
7. Ibid, 10:166
8. Ibid, 8:365
9. Beaumarchais, pg. 231
10. Anne Hollingsworth Warton ref., Diplomatic Correspondence of the American Revolution, 2:607-8
11. Letters of Delegates to Congress, 5:412
12. *The Financier and the Finances of the American Revolution*, 1:209-210
13. Ibid, 1:209-210
14. Letters of Delegates to Congress, 5:609
15. Ibid, 7:188n
16. Ibid, 10:499
17. Ibid, 8:298-299
18. Letters of Delegates to Congress, 8:249-250
19. Letters of Delegates to Congress, 8:284-285
20. *The Forgotten Patriot*, pg.65
21. *The Jefferson Conspiracies*, pg.92
22. *York Daily Record* 1777
23. *Journals of Continental Congress* 1774-1789 Nov 28, 1777 LOC
24. Letters of Delegates to Congress, 8:377-378
25. Ibid, 8:400
26. Ibid, 8:378
27. Letters of Delegates to Congress, 8:507
28. Rappleye, pg. 145
29. Beaumarchais, pg. 223-226
30. Letters of Delegates to Congress, 9:22
31. Beaumarchais p 231
32. Ibid, 8:428
33. Letters of Delegates to Congress, 8:428-429
34. Letters of Delegates to Congress, 8:475-482
35. *Power of the Purse*, pg. 91
36. Ver Steeg pg. 25
37. Papers of Robert Morris, 2:263
38. Letters of Delegates to Congress, 9:233-234
39. Jeremy Black, *War For America, The Fight of Independence 1775-1783*, Chapt 8
40. Naval Documents of the American Revolution, 10:267
41. Naval Documents of the American Revolution, 3:1336, 9:149
42. Natchez Historical Society, Mississippi July 4, 1976, the Mississippi Celebration of the Bicentennial of the American Revolution
43. *The Louisiana Historical Quarterly* entitled Willing's Expedition Down The Mississippi, 1778; by John Caughey in January, 1932
44. *Henkels Catalogue*, pg. 184-185
45. Letters of Delegates to Congress, 9:378
46. Ibid, 9:153-154
47. Ibid, 9:473
48. Ibid, 9:152
49. The Deane Papers, 2:344
50. Ibid, 2:156
51. Ibid, 2:345
52. The Deane Papers, 2:346
53. *Robert Morris, Audacious Patriot,* pg.51
54. Rappleye, pg.137
55. The Deane Papers, 2:386
56. Ibid, 2:427
57. Ibid, 2:463
58. Ibid, 2:426
59. William Graham Sumner, *The Makers of American History*, Jefferson / Morris, pg. 28-31
60. Ver Steeg, pg. 25
61. The Lee Family Papers, 1742-1795. Edited by Paul P. Hoffman. Charlottesville, VA: University of Virginia Library, 1966. 8 reels
62. Letters of Delegates to Congress, 9:505
63. Letters of Delegates to Congress, 9:567
64. Ibid, 9:243
65. Letters of Delegates to Congress, 9:232
66. Ibid, 9:222 & 280-284
67. Ibid, 9:568n
68. Ibid, 9:662
69. Letters of Delegates to Congress, 8:142
70. Ibid, 21:166
71. Ibid, 9:373
72. "Colonial Homes of Philadelphia" referenced in *The Annals of the Ancestry of Charles Custis Harrison and Ellen Waln Harrison*, pg. 179

VI

Partisan Homecoming

Congress returned to Philadelphia on July 2nd, and the capital began to reestablish itself. Morris came in from Manheim and joined the rebirth of city life. The 4th was celebrated with gusto in the retaken capital with a public dinner held at the City Tavern and cannons were fired over the river. A business opportunity also arrived at that public dinner when a new actor in town, John Holker, approached Morris and asked him if he wanted to work as an agent and factor. Morris initially declined because he was still a congressman, and his workload at the time would not allow him to take on any more projects.

Shortly after Morris settled in, he set up a Baltimore partnership, called Peter Whitesides & Company, to carry on his private shipping business.[1] July progressed, and the citizens of Philadelphia worked to get on with their lives and routines. This naturally resulted in the leading citizens hosting a round of parties and balls. Just as normalcy was being reestablished in Philadelphia, the British took Savannah, Georgia.[2]

General Conway, namesake of the Conway Cabal, retired from military service in early July. Afterwards he spent much of his time in Philadelphia disparaging Washington as a person, and his skills as a general. General John Cadwalader heard enough of his kind of talk and challenged him to a duel. General Conway suffered a gunshot to the mouth delivered by General Cadwalader in defense of Washington's good name. After this, Conway moved to France and became a General for the French Crown.

Working from the other side of the Atlantic, Franklin continued in his role in the Revolutionary cause. Arthur Lee was also still in France, spreading his own brand of malice. He and his brother attempted to control America's agent in Holland, Mr. Charles Dumas. William Lee even went to the trouble of pretending he was one of the American Commissioners at Paris in a meeting with Dumas, and other eminent leaders of Amsterdam, to trick them into taking the dangerous step of creating a Dutch alliance with America. When this effort failed, Dumas saw his commissions drop to about 15% of their former level. Dumas wrote Congress,

> It is with the most painful concern I mention to your Excellency [the President of Congress] this attempt of Mr. William Lee to undermine me in this manner.[3]

Lee still had his supporters, however, and foremost among them was Henry Laurens. Laurens continued to cast Morris and his efforts in the darkest light, from impugning him for receiving a letter from the British Governor of Florida, to insinuating dark deeds due to his brother's conduct in France, to wondering out loud why Morris could not finish his accounting for the Secret Committee. Laurens boasted he could clear up Morris' books "in nine days, or would forfeit two of his fingers."[4] Laurens got the opportunity – but was unable to make good on his boast.[5] He was not forced to surrender his fingers. Even so, no one questioned Richard Lee about his lack of record keeping during that same critical period when he was in charge of the Secret Committee in Baltimore.

Morris, for his part, kept insisting that his trading partners supply him with documentation to satisfy Congressional requests. It was slow in coming, if it came at all. Three months after Thomas' death Morris' business records were still in France. He wrote a letter to William Lee in an attempt to compel him to ship Thomas' papers back to America. Morris even had to apply to Congress for assurance that this would happen. He wrote to Lee,

> To prevent further altercation which I dislike exceedingly, I obtained an order of Congress for the delivery of the whole of those papers to my order and send a duplicate thereof by this Conveyance.[6]

William's brother, Arthur, continued to support Congress' refusal to pay Beaumarchais, which meant that Deane was still unable to receive the commissions he deserved. Deane arrived in Philadelphia on July 11th, on the same ship as the French minister, Gérard. After Deane's arrival he was often in Gérard's company,[7] but it was not really wise for Gérard to take sides in the internal American controversy between the Adams-Lee faction and the middle state merchants. An inquiry into Deane's conduct was engineered and conducted by Lee's friends in Congress, but they chose to do nothing to resolve the questions. Deane waited months for a proper hearing before Congress. While he waited, his allies worked to convince the French to admit the true nature of Deane's work with Beaumarchais. The French were reluctant to do so because they had denied the same before the Alliance was announced and did not want to appear dishonest.

A Turning Point

Life had been dramatically altered by the British and the war. Morris shared his thoughts on this to a friend.

> Philadelphia my Good Friend is vastly changed, the avowed Tories are I think more inveterately so than ever, our Circle's of Friends & acquaintance are all broke up and it is with difficulty we could patch up a little Social Club at Dick Peters' Spring during the hot weather, in short our greatest Society is now in the Company of Strangers. Should the British evacuate New York you will experience this & many other changes that I cannot spare time to tell you of. The Hills, poor Hills alas have changed, a Melancholy cast of Countenance covers the Face of Nature & the Works of Art exhibit Such Melancholy pictures in their present Views that Hospitality can no more cherish nor Festivity exhilarate the cheerful guest but I hope to see the day when the Scene again shall change & all be bright & gay.[8]

The attitude of the Tories rankled the Constitutionalists who, in turn, reinstated their mode of using citizen committees. They created the Patriotic Society, which started out well with both moderates, like Morris, and radicals, like Tomas Paine and William Bradford, on board. Soon enough, the more vigorous activists turn it into a witch-hunt society. They rounded up a number of Tories who had stayed in town during the occupation. Cooler heads prevailed for a while, and inquiries were made into each individual. Lawyers were put to work and almost all were acquitted. To the horror of many, four were convicted, two were chosen as examples, and they were hung in the public square.[9] This spectacle resulted in Morris, and other moderates, being elected to the Assembly in the next round, warding off the kind of terrors seen in France some years later. Citizens committees remained a fixture in Pennsylvania politics for a while, however. It was a volatile time.

The Morris family had the unpleasant task of rebuilding and refurbishing their country house, The Hills. Benjamin Harrison of Virginia commiserated with Morris on the topic.

> I am really concern'd for the dismantled condition of the Hills, tis but a pitiful kind of revenge to fall on houses and gardens for the offences of their owners, but such have been and ever will be the case with the low minded.[10]

John Holker kept after Morris and would not take "no" for an answer. Holker may have appeared to be among that crowd of French adventurers who were drawn to America during the war, as he was born an Englishman, but his family had moved to France because of their Jacobite sympathies. However, he was no ordinary fortune seeker. His father had previously assisted Beaumarchais in the arms trade during the Seven Years War. The French ambassador elevated him, and he was made the French Consul in America. From this position, and as Agent of the Royal Marine he was a purchasing agent for America's new ally. Holker finally convinced Morris to join in his schemes. He invested in numerous companies that supplied the American and French military. In the fall of that year Holker rented a house near the corner of Sixth and High StreetsStreets that had been owned by William Penns' grandson before Penn left Philadelphia with the Olive Branch Petition. Morris would later purchase after it burned under Holker's care.

Morris and Holker's partnership started off slowly, with Morris acting as his commercial agent. His local knowledge and political connections allowed them to find their way through the maze of local regulations and controversies. Morris never acknowledged that Holker was using him as a shield for Holker's more dubious trading activities; activities that contributed to high prices and much social discontent.[11] As time went on, Morris convinced Holker to invest in him and America in anticipation of realizing the many opportunities the new nation provided. This new association with Holker supplied Morris with capital to enlarge his commercial operations.

Official concerns were never far away however, and people kept connecting with Morris for assistance. When Anthony Wayne asked about uniforms, Morris had to inform him that the items were available in Europe, but they had to wait there until the committees of Congress reformed and ordered them.[12] Congressional delays were causing many hardships in the fields of battle. The early days of the revolution were long gone, and the brightest lights of the nation were back in their home states. Congress was weaker and more divided than ever. Morris harbored hopes that his friend John Hancock would come back from Massachusetts and take control of Congress once again.

On September 14th, Robert Morris wrote to John Bradford,

> I have been well employed in Committees on this [naval] & other business since joining Congress, so that although I got myself clear of the Standing Boards it makes little difference as nearly the whole of my time is taken from me & I never shall be master of it until I

> get quite clear of Public business, which I do most Ardently long for. Pray give my best respects to my Worthy Friend Mr. Hancock & tell him I hope he will come back by the end of next month & be ready to fill that Chair he before filled with so much Reputation & then my respect for it will again be as perfect as ever it was.
>
> We have a report that the British Fleet after showing themselves off Your Light House, have departed again, I don't think they have received Reinforcements and without them, they cannot block up the Count D'Estaing. I hope you will exert yrself to get the latter ready for Sea, & that he will immediately come this way to be Supplyed with Provisions.[13]

This was not to be. Morris' friend and fellow merchant, John Hancock, had responded to the call to arms in the fall of 1778. He became a Major General for a new campaign in Rhode Island that was to be the first Franco-American joint deployment against the British, and the fruit of the new alliance. On September 18th, Robert Morris' spirits picked up as he wrote to Hancock,

> I heard with great Satisfaction of your joining, as a Volunteer, the army at Rhode Island and was sanguine in my hopes & expectations that Mars would have been propitious and sent you home crowned with Laurels.... I hope they [the British] will not dare, to undertake an Expedition against Boston, or if they do, my firm perswasion is that they will smart severely for it, but the situation of the British affairs in general is such, that I cannot help thinking they must quit the United States very soon, in order to take care of those territories they have some title to.[14]

Morris was correct that some British naval forces were leaving the United States to protect their possessions in the West Indies; unfortunately, the Rhode Island campaign had already failed before the news had reached Philadelphia. D'Estaing's navy was blocked from entering and taking Newport so it was unable to make a decisive blow. A second contingent of the British navy had followed the French fleet to Newport, Rhode Island, and they attacked. The French Admiral d'Estaing and the Americans worked together poorly. Few Americans spoke French, so they spoke in Latin to communicate with their allies.[15] Just as the British fleet and Count d'Estaing engaged off the coast of Rhode Island in late August, a mighty storm came up with such force it broke the fight apart and ultimately sent Count d'Estaing's fleet to Boston for repairs.

The Americans were angry at the departure of the French and the subsequent loss of Rhode Island. Consequently, the Frenchmen were not well received in Boston. There were reports of street fights, riots, and brawls between Americans and their allies, the French. Some altercations resulted in deaths. America and France tried to minimize the disagreements over the failure at Newport and downplay the fistfights in Boston. Hancock never returned to the Continental Congress. Instead, he became that states' Governor, and much later helped that state ratify the U.S. Constitution.

While Morris focused less on Congress and more on his private business ventures, the new leadership in Congress changed long standing policies. Henry Laurens and his allies decided that now America had official recognition from France, Congress would abandon the trading system Morris had operated. The Secret Committee was officially disbanded on October 5th.[16] Congress ignored Morris' suggestion to continue his trading system under a Board of Commissions,[17] and instead they decided to rely more on loans and direct grants from European countries.[18] The business of closing the old accounts was placed in the hands of a clerk of the Committee of Commerce. The controversy Lee had generated over Beaumarchais was part of the reason the war trade was reduced, then abandoned by Congress; still, the Lees undertook trade with France as agents for Virginia. Arthur Lee's little poisoned seeds were doing their work and weakening Continental action in favor of state action. Ironically, when it turned out, in the 1780's, that Virginia could not pay for the materials that Lee had acquired, the Virginians applied for financial help from Congress and Morris as Superintendent of Finance.

Lee's partisan attacks resulted in a letter from Samuel Adams on November 23rd, 1778 which said, in part:

> Our Affairs says he [John Adams] in this Kingdom [France], I find in a State of Confusion & Darkness that surprises me. Prodigious Sums of Money have been expended and large Sums are still due; but there are no Books of Accounts nor any Documents from whence I have been able to learn what the United States have received as an Equivalent. And yet we are told by a Gentleman lately from France that the Accounts & Documents were left in the Hands of a Person in Paris. My Friend A. L [Arthur Lee] is called by those who dread his Vigilance "a dissatisfied Man." Having received many Letters from him since I last saw you, I know he is dissatisfied.[19]

It is difficult to understand why he would be dissatisfied. John Jay pointed out that by late 1778 there was a "family compact" at work, and that the Lee brothers held two seats in Congress, four foreign missions, and the French commercial agency, with the help of John Adams.[20]

Congress was still relying on individual merchants to finance their policies, and Morris tried to get them to pay Bingham more of the money he was owed, but Congress was always slow in that way. With money unavailable from Congress, Morris wrote to Bingham about their mutual private business, and placed the blame for the lack of cash squarely on him. Morris often delegated important decisions to aggressive junior associates, and sometimes this worked out poorly. He wrote to Bingham,

> I can not help thinking You have been somewhat to blame in suffering W.M. & Co. to be so basely treated by that Gentleman [Mr. Prejent]. You knew he had half of our Ship her Cargo & freight in his hands. You knew he was ordered to pay you the whole & I really think it was your Duty to have insisted on the payment whilst he had the Money instead of suffering him to fit out privateers with it & the more so as it was entirely owing to your recommendation that we trusted him which we did reluctantly at the time but depended on you to Insist on the payment.
>
> If you had done this you would have had little reason to write me in so pressing a style for remittances. I mention this affair that you may recollect the reasons of our being in your Debt, that it is in some degree unexpected & entirely your own faul*t.*[21]

It seems Bingham "doubled-up" on the deal and Prejent sent out a privateer, and that Prejent was not successful. Morris was having similar problems in his association with Peter Whitesides, who was buying salt against Morris' instructions. It was around this time that ominous rumors started to spread that Morris was driving the price of staple goods up by speculation. In fact, increased demand for American farm products by the French Army meant the growers were raising their prices, and that was affecting the whole market. Holker was buying these foodstuffs and Morris was blamed because Morris was Holker's agent. Morris was warned that if this continued, embargoes would be placed on these goods.[22]

While Morris and Holker increased their business ties, Morris' longtime partnership with Thomas Willing was strained. Willing's residency in Philadelphia during the English occupation, cast doubt on not only Willing's but Morris' loyalty, in the minds of some. Willing, Morris & Co.

went out of business late in 1778. Their partnership would resurface in different forms as Willing, Morris, Inglis & Co, and Willing, Morris, and Swanwick. Long after the war Willing and Morris sent the first American ship to trade in India, much to the surprise of Britain.

Morris looked forward to repairing the damage to his fortunes caused by lack of time and attention, but there were institutional problems in his way. There was little value to Pennsylvania state money. The state government of artists, artisans, and back country farmers was without any means to encourage an economy. There was no life in the market due to predation by the British fleet and the disruption of trade that occurred when they controlled the port. Philadelphia was bereft of cash and drained of goods. Pennsylvania was experiencing some of its worst ever grain harvests due to the extraordinarily long cold winters, so the local agricultural economy was not useful in stimulating the markets. These hardships plagued the citizens, who were well aware of the seemingly endless parties and balls enjoyed by the leadership. Epitomizing the resilient spirit of the Philadelphia merchants Morris looked elsewhere for the wealth needed to prime the system. He looked to the seas.

He created a trading relationship with Spanish "observer" Juan de Miralles, who in 1779, had been sent to Philadelphia by the King of Spain, Charles III. De Miralles acted as Spain's unofficial representative, but he was actually the Royal Envoy of the King of Spain. His true mission in Philadelphia was to remain under cover and to monitor and assist the Revolutionary War trade.[23] To avoid any appearance of an official diplomatic tie between Spain and the United States, de Miralles became a partner in various trading ventures with Robert Morris.[24] It is unlikely this went unnoticed by people who had only succeeded in getting as far as Burgos in developing a trading relationship with Spain. At this point Morris was in significant business partnerships with a French agent, and a Spanish agent, thus working closely with both of America's more powerful allies, official, and unofficial.

Morris and de Miralles conducted the first direct trade between an American and Spanish Cuba, carrying flour and correspondence. Spain appreciated the produce because Cuba was becoming a sugar growing area. The growing of sugar cane in Cuba replaced the growing of produce there, so the importation of food became more important. Morris increased this new commercial relationship through his agent, Oliver Pollock, and Pollock's friend, the Governor of New Spain, Bernardo de Galvez. In anticipation of improved relations with Spain, Richard Harrison moved from the island of Martinico, in 1779, where he had worked with Bingham, and opened a commercial office for America in Cadiz.[25] This would later become John Jay's point of contact when he went to Spain. Unfortunately for Morris, De Miralles died in 1780, and a new Spanish agent, Sr. Rendón, replaced him.

Morris found it difficult to purchase enough flour in Pennsylvania for his client in Cuba, so his buyers went up and down the east coast in search of goods to export. This had the effect of increasing demand for flour and that increased the flour prices in several markets at once. Morris did not reveal the identity of his client and this increased the mystery about Morris' activities in the popular imagination. The trade had the desired effect of improving relations with Spain, an important, but unofficial, ally; but the American people grew angry at the price jump, and suspicious of Morris.

The populace was not privy to the details of Morris' trading activities, but his other exploits were well known. Shortly after he left the Congress on November 2nd, 1778, Morris plunged into privateering with vigor, as he did with so many other ventures. He operated under Congressional Letters of Marque and Reprisal and, in the tradition of Sir Francis Drake, Morris got money the old fashioned way. He took it using private ships of war. A large part of the fortune Morris acquired and lost during this period of the Revolution was a result of privateering. There were eighteen letters of Marque and Reprisal issued to Robert Morris in Pennsylvania from 1778 to 1781. He was part owner of other privateers that left from ports up and down the coast, but the Letters of Marque for those ships were issued in other names.[26]

11/16/1778 – *Buckskin*
9/4/1779 – *Retaliation,* 8 guns
10/25/1779 – *Chevalier de la Luzerne,* 8 guns
11/9/1779 – *Lively,* 14 guns
7/3/1780 – *Havana,* 6 guns
7/4/1780 – *The Black Prince,* 12 guns
7/4/1780 – *Defense,* 18 guns
7/4/1780 – *Ariel,* 16 guns
9/22/1780 – *Gen'l Scott,* 8 guns
11/4/1780 – *Levingston,* 4 guns
11/8/1780 – *Queen of Sweden,* 8 guns

11/8/1780 – *Gustavus,* 2 guns
5/30/1781 – *Phoenix,* 8 guns
6/12/1781 – *Buckskin*
6/14/1781 – *Virginia,* 4 guns
6/20/1781 – *Maestrand,* 10 guns
9/29/1781 – *Molly,* 6 guns
12/15/1781 – *Charming Amelia,* 12 guns

Morris' interest and success in this legalized form of piracy, was well known. His private ships of war put men and treasure at risk to attack the British Empire at sea. Those on shore secure within the brick walls of their homes and without a stake in the game, saw him get rich while they toiled at labors without satisfying compensation. In his book *Chastelleux's Travels* M. Chastelleux, the former quarter-master general of the French auxiliaries in America noted that: Morris was

> ...in fact, so much accustomed to the success of his privateers, that when he was observed, on a Sunday, to be more serious than usual the conclusion was, that no prize had arrived in the previous week.[27]

This quote tells us more about what people thought about Morris' privateering than what Morris thought. However, it does indicate that Morris was involved to a significant degree and even though his thoughts may have been on the progress of the war, or even the behavior of his children in church, people on the street were inclined to assign motives to him that suited their own ideas.

Morris' help in managing naval matters was sought even after his term in Congress officially ended. Considering his absence from the Marine Committee, Captain Thomas Bell wrote to John Paul Jones,

> Mr. Morris has left the Marien [the Marine Committee] and Every thing is going to the devel [devil] as fast can.[28]

In early December, Count d'Estaing took his French fleet from Boston, and left the disagreements with the locals behind. He went to the warmer climate of the West Indies for action against the British and pursued the French agenda of gaining island territory. American ships joined the French Navy in naval battles around the Caribbean islands.

The State of the State of Pennsylvania

The Pennsylvania Assembly and the Continental Congress both used the Pennsylvania State House for meetings. This proximity facilitated communications between the "Constitutionalists" in the Pennsylvania Assembly and the members of Congress who disagreed with Morris and his associates. The "Constitutionalists" made a political alliance with the Adams-Lee faction in the Continental Congress, and over time, specifically with Arthur Lee.[29] The Adams-Lee faction found common ground as members of the Country Party with the "Constitutionalists" in their mutual disdain for merchants, "dealers in paper," and others the "Constitutionalists" cast as Tories. This alliance between the backcountry farmers and the more conservative members of the Tidewater elite formed an important part of the greater political force known as the Agricultural Interests. Later, that same political alliance encouraged backcountry Virginia farmers to move to Western Pennsylvania. As time went on, there was a growing reluctance among the farmers of both English and German descent, to relinquish their slaves in conformity to the Abolition Law of 1780, and a number of petitions were sent to the Pennsylvania Assembly for relief from those laws.[30] During the early days of the United States under the Constitution, the collaboration between western farmers and the Tidewater Elite provided the Virginians with some level of influence in Pennsylvania state politics, particularly with the involvement of Albert Gallatin in the Whiskey Rebellion.

In 1778, Morris was glad to be a private citizen back in his hometown. However, he was called upon by his fellow citizens and re-elected to the Assembly, as a reaction to the excesses of the Patriotic Society mentioned earlier. Afterwards he wrote to Holker,

> ...our fellow Citizens are determined not to leave me master of my own time, and as I cannot by our Constitution Serve longer in Congress they have Elected me a Burgess for this City in the general assembly.[31]

Morris was elected with the intent to cure the ills that had grown in Pennsylvania. The state's inability to provide for the troops at Valley Forge was symptomatic of greater problems within the state government. Back in the Assembly, Morris became the leader of a group of moderate reformers who called themselves the Republican Society. Eventually many members of this group became known as the Federalists and should not be confused with the Democratic-Republicans organized by Jefferson some years later. Morris considered the current state of affairs in Pennsylvania to be the tyranny of local mob justice, and that it was worse than the tyranny of a far-away king.

The people who controlled the Assembly felt differently. They encouraged citizen action to support the committees. Using a crude call to class envy they tried to rally support against the Republican Society whom they called "monoploizers, speculators, an infernal gang of Tories." An anonymous author wrote,

> But I call upon all, in name of our Bleeding Country, to rouse up as a lion out of his den, and make those beasts of pray, to humble, and prove by this days conduct, than any person whatever, though puffed like a toad, with a sense of his own consequence, shall dare to violate the least resolve of our committee, it were better for him, that a mill-stone was fastened to his neck, and be cast into the depth of the sea, or that he had never been born, Rouse! Rouse! Rouse![32]

This was just the condition Morris feared when he spoke out against independence during the debate on the Declaration a couple of years earlier. Morris had some experience with mob justice as a leader of the citizens committee that protested the Stamp Act in the previous decade. He was well aware of the nature of these citizen groups and how they can be used in a political setting. He did not like to see mob justice become a tool of the state. Morris joined with a group of like-minded citizens and together they wrote a letter that was published in the *Pennsylvania Gazette*. It expressed their concerns about Pennsylvania state government.

> We are convinced, upon most impartial examination, that its general tendency and operation will be to join the qualities of the different extremes of bad government. It will produce general weakness, inactivity, and confusion; intermixed with sudden and violent fits of despotism, injustice, and cruelty.[33]

After this letter was published in the newspaper Morris became subject to attack from his political rivals. Generally, their favorite tactic was to call anyone who opposed them a "Tory." Charles Lee wrote to Morris and commented on the "Constitutionalist's" tendency to justify their behavior by calling themselves Whigs and their political adversaries Tories. He wrote,

> ...they have no other means of charming down the voice of reason and truth than the epithet Tory...is the disenfranchisement of a great part of the Pennsylvanian Citizens a whiggish law? Is the confiscation of the property of innocent Absentees Men Women and Children; Friends and Foes indiscriminately, a whiggish law? Is the total suppression of the freedom of the press, or the felonious tender law by which property is at one slap trandfer'd from the right owners to those who have no claim to it founded in Whiggism? – if such Men are Whigs and such laws and principles Whiggism, I and my Associates are undoubted Tories, and we Glory in the name of it." He went on to say that they were living under a Mac-ocracy, "a Banditte [small band] of Scotch Irish Servants or their immediate Descendants (whose names generally begin with Mac) are our Lords and Rulers.[34]

In the political discourse of the early 21st century, similar techniques were used to partisan effect when one party defended their candidate by declaring his opponents were racist for using such words as "apartment," and "Chicago" and other words they deemed to be racist code words.

The "Constitutionalists" knew branding Morris as a "Tory" would not work because of his service to the Revolutionary cause. Instead, they proclaimed that he was a "War Profiteer," however a clear definition was never given of that term. The lack of definition for this term allowed it to be applied at the pleasure of the people who used it. The critics exhibited the tendency towards hyperbole typical of members of the old Country Party as they proceeded to make emotionally charged wild and false accusations against Morris. By doing this, they hoped to hamper his ability to succeed with his agenda of state constitutional reform.

In the Assembly, Morris, and his fellow Republican Society members, wanted to reform the state constitution and introduce checks and balances that would protect the rights of minorities and property holders from the "tyranny of the majority." To do this they worked to remove the Test Law, and thereby to return voting rights to nearly one half the voting population of the state.[35] Another part of the Republican Society's program was the protection of private property rights. They worked to stop the government from taking property from the people the "Constitutionalists" wished to chase out of the state. As part of that effort the Republican Society worked to bring about the return of the property of the University of Pennsylvania to the University. The University property was held by the state because it had been part of the Penn family's property, and that grant from the king was considered by the "Constitutionalists" to be a Tory holding. A few years later Dr. Benjamin Rush tried to convince the "Constitutionalists" to support Morris' program of reform, even though Rush had been and early supporter of the PA Constitution. During that campaign he wrote,

> The people here have been drinking with all their might, whiskey and bad rum all harvest. Though the Physician says it will destroy their bodies & the Clergyman, It will destroy their souls. They drink on. They *will* have the *Constitution* & the bottle at any hazard whatever.[36]

Morris was not the only target of the Radicals. First, they went after Benedict Arnold, who was a war hero at that time, and who held the position of Military Governor. Their complaint against Arnold was that they thought he was too haughty, and friendly with the Tories. The "Constitutionalists" compiled a list of infractions including allowing a young lady to pass through enemy lines to visit a friend. The "Constitutionalists" used the power of the State to demand that Arnold be court-martialed and maintained that relations between Pennsylvania and the Continental Congress hung in the balance. Finally, Arnold was censured for using a publicly owned wagon for private purposes and the "Constitutionalists" felt they had won their point by embarrassing General Arnold.[37] One can only conclude that such treatment did not make Arnold feel appreciated by the people for whom he was fighting.

"War Profiteer"

> *No foreign war of great expense or duration could conveniently be carried on by the exportation of the rude produce of the soil. The expense of sending such a quantity of it to a foreign country as might purchase the pay and provisions of an army, would be too great. Few countries too produce much more rude produce than what is sufficient for the substance of their own inhabitants. To send abroad any great quantity of it, therefore, would be to send abroad a part of the necessary substance of the people.*[38]
>
> –Adam Smith,

States in New England worked to curb inflation in their state currencies with a multi-state agreement to stop printing new bills, and to enact a set of price controls.[39] This worked adequately in Calvinist New England, with its strong community bindings and penurious ways, but results were uneven elsewhere. For example, consider Pennsylvania. The small-scale merchants who had enlivened the commercial scene before the British took over Philadelphia had vanished by the time the British left. A few large merchant-shipping firms had been able to survive the British, and they reestablished their positions in town when the coast cleared. Morris' partnership with Thomas Willing was in decline, but he endeavored to rebuild trade in Philadelphia and to profit in the process. He was not celebrated from every corner for his enterprising spirit. Many were suffering from the results of the economic privation, and looked for someone to blame, and the English were not there. Morris was often the subject of attacks in the press as anonymous writers went after him professionally, politically, and personally. The frequent attacks in the press must have stung him and his family, but he found it best to walk quietly through the noise, allowing the facts to speak for him. He relied on what he believed to be the objective correctness of his actions even when many others doubted him. His letters and diaries speak to his belief in the importance of his actions and put a mirror up to the puffery of others. It was during this period that Morris was most active as Holker's "agent and factor in a great variety of important public and private business."[40]

The "Constitutionalists" published their thinking about commerce and merchants during wartime, in the form of a broadside from their Committee of Thirteen. They stated that when they reentered Philadelphia, after the British had evacuated, there were no ships in the river, and that when the ships arrived they were full of goods that were too expensive and that expense was due to the greed of merchants. What they did not mention was that the Assembly had been printing money without anything to back it up, so the currency was losing value. This loss in value was the cause of the inflation that contributed to the apparent increase in prices of imported goods. Such inflation was not unique to Pennsylvania. E. James Ferguson pointed out in *The Power of the Purse* that during that period inflation of the Continental currency was running at a rate between 300 and 400% per year.[41] This was in direct contrast to the pre-Revolutionary experience of Pennsylvanians where the value of the currency remained nearly constant.[42] Instead of working to solve the problem of inflation by limiting the printing of currency and raising taxes to restrict the amount of currency in circulation, the Pennsylvania Assembly decided to print even more money and to create an elaborate system of price controls. The effort of merchants to get the port economy going again was undermined by backcountry thinking that merchants should consider their ships to be part of community property and that merchants should forgo making money for the benefit of all.[43] How the merchants were supposed to acquire items for import if they were constantly losing money was not addressed.

The merchants countered with the idea of free markets. They said if the market was free then more items would come in a response to higher prices, and that the increase in quantity of goods would result in prices going down. In other words, the merchants were trying to teach the backcountry "Constitutionalists" the laws of supply and demand. The "Constitutionalists" were having none of it, and they vilified the merchants and erected state embargoes. The farmers and the merchants were at loggerheads, and the farmers held the government. This period of increased political anger was the time in which Morris stopped being Holker's agent and factor and at the end of 1779 a separate company was formed to play that role.

Lee-Deane Affair Redux

The Lee-Deane controversy was revived in early December 1778. Silas Deane and his secretary, Carmichael, had been asked by Laurens to testify before Congress. Deane's hearing had been sputtering on in fits and starts, leaving little room for testimony or rebuttal. All that was happening was a slow death of Deane's reputation by accusation and delay. Before he was able to finally testify, and after many months of brooding, Congressional mistreatment, and commiseration with General Arnold, Deane published a piece in the newspapers entitled, *"To the Free and Virtuous Citizens of Pennsylvania."* In this article he not only attacked Arthur Lee, but also Congress for wasting so much time on unimportant matters, and for being ignorant about foreign relations. This caused a political firestorm of opinion and counter-opinion that threatened to shake the Franco-American alliance because the factions fell into pro and anti-French camps, with the pro-Deane faction also being pro-alliance. The French Minister fired off a letter to Congress with proof that the Deane-Beaumarchais contract was a standard commercial arrangement and not a gift as Arthur Lee had falsely maintained. When it became clear that Deane would prevail, Henry Laurens, who had tried and failed to get Deane censored, stepped down from his position as President of Congress, but he stayed on as a member. He wrote,

> I cannot consistently with my own honor, nor with utility to my Country, considering the manner in which Business is transacted here, remain any longer in this Chair, I now resign it.[44]

John Jay became President of that august body. Unfortunately, Dean's article made the partisan rancor of Congress visible to the public.

Thomas Paine responded to Deane's article with an article of his own on January 2nd, 1779 in support of the Adams-Lee faction. This article contained information that was a state secret, at least up to the point Paine published it. Two days later the French Minister lodged a formal request that Thomas Paine be removed from his Continental office because Paine had breached the confidence of his office as Secretary of the Committee of Foreign Affairs. Paine resigned. Most congressmen were convinced that Beaumarchais and Deane had been the victims of a vicious campaign of deceit. It was a political rout for the Adams-Lee faction. Deane left government work in disgust. He returned to Europe to reclaim his papers and became a private commercial agent for Morris and others, selling American lands in Europe for the Illinois and Wabash companies.[45] The Adams-Lee faction did not retire from the scene. Instead, they waited and looked for new opportunities to promote their agenda.

Thomas Paine

Thomas Paine attacks

The "Constitutionalists" in Pennsylvania had been conducting a long running campaign in the press against Morris and Deane with thinly veiled hints. With Deane out of the way, their attention turned to Morris. These attacks used innuendo as they complained about "commercial interests." One former mayor of Philadelphia coined a term "insinuendo" to describe the practice. "Constitutionalist," Thomas Paine, having recently been freed from any restraints he might have felt as a member of the Committee of Foreign Affairs, attacked the merchants in the press in an effort to turn public opinion against the more moderate, i.e. Morris. Thus, he hoped to weaken Morris' ability to change the Pennsylvania state Constitution, which Paine had helped create. Paine also had a secret financial arrangement with Henry Laurens to conduct this campaign.[46] Laurens supplied Paine with materials from the Lees to assist in the effort.

Paine raised his pen against Morris, and Morris replied in clear and authoritative prose, revealing more than perhaps he might have needed to. In his response he mentioned that the books of the Secret Committee had been closed and his company was owed money. He went on to say that he had not yet received the records taken from his brother's office in France,[47] even after the passage of eleven months. These missing records would help him close out the other committee work. He quickly learned the hazards of arguing with those who buy ink by the barrel.

Paine could not have been more pleased. He counted on people's general ignorance about international trade and the workings of the secret committees as he penned his new attack,

> Mr. Morris acknowledges to have had three private mercantile contracts with Mr. Deane, while he was a Delegate...To what degree of corruption must we sink, if our Delegates and Ambassadors are to be admitted to carry on a private partnership in trade? Why not go halves with every Quartermaster and Commissary in the Army?[48,49]

What Paine did not mention was as important to the subject as what he wrote. Paine did not mention that the Continental Congress had, in the recent past, appointed merchants to positions in the Quartermaster and Commissary Departments, and most, if not all had been commission agents.[50] He did not mention that Congress had agreed to the arrangement with Morris, Franklin, and Deane; nor did he mention that without such arrangements no one could afford to conduct the extensive war supply trade. The kind of arrangements about which Paine complained so loudly were normal accepted practice at the time, so much so that in the 18th century even individual sailors on board merchant ships had the ability to trade on their own account and were given limited space on the ship to do so.[51] Paine most certainly did not mention that the Lee brotherhood had both private and public roles in the war trade as well. These fine points somehow escaped Paine's attention as he succeeded in making his rhetoric heard by people who had no familiarity with these subjects.

Paine offered no indication how he expected the business of supplying the army to proceed. Neither was there any indication that Mr. Paine thought other members of Congress should give up their livelihoods. He did not argue that plantation holders in Congress should donate tobacco, flour, and meat. He did not indicate that officers or soldiers should fight without pay. Yet somehow in Paine's mind the people who supplied guns, ammunition, and blankets to the army should run the British blockade and risk everything they have to suit his aesthetic senses. Naturally, the evocative writing had an emotional appeal and resonated with those who wished to protect "American Virtue."

In late 1778 and early 1779 Paine's writing reflected the ambivalence or outright disdain felt by the Agricultural Interests toward merchants in the 18th century. Richard Henry Lee made that perspective clear when he said about merchants,

> ... such men are much fitter to be slaves in the corrupt, rotten despotisms of Europe, than to remain citizens of young and rising republics.[52]

These were the same impulses that the "Constitutionalists" in Pennsylvania followed. Backcountry farmers didn't value the merchant group because they saw them as far away greedy manipulators who were almost as bad as the Tories. These impulses resulted in the unintended murder of commerce.

Paine's writing called *"Common Sense to the Public"* was published in the *Pennsylvania Packet* January 12th, 1779. The ideas expressed in this version of *"Common Sense"* resonated with the public and brought an end to Morris' trading program. That program had supplied the army at a cost of a 2.5% commission per transaction. Paine's version of *"Common Sense"* sent Congress on the path of seeking greater and greater loans and grants from Europe. This resulted in a foreign debt of $25,000,000, as expressed in 1780's money. According to some accounts this was equal to six times the value of all the hard currency in America. The prevailing school of political thought maintained it was more virtuous for a new republic to go begging and borrowing from Kings and Princes in Europe than paying one's own way with trade. As events unfolded in that direction, America ruined her credit and could not get more loans from Europe until Morris was reestablished in office in 1781.

Henry Laurens took the publication of Morris' response as an opportunity to argue against Morris in Congress. Laurens came so close to accusing Morris of fraud that others had to silence him by insisting he make those charges in writing.[53] Morris most often proceeded with quiet dignity, sure in the knowledge that his course was correct, and time would prove this to be true. He wrote to Henry Laurens about public argument,

> You will observe that I have not chosen the Press as a Tribunal for the liquidation of Accounts but being charged Publicly by Name, I

> was under a Necessity of defending myself in my own Name publicly.[54]

Morris finally received a collection of Thomas Morris' papers from France and attempted to close the books on those operations. He had tried before, but had been unable to settle the accounts during his leave of absence in Manheim, PA. Some of the merchants involved in the trade still did not cooperate with Morris' requests for documentation. Mr. Nathaniel Shaw's brother claimed he was unable to help because of the destruction of his Philadelphia offices at the hands of the British occupiers.[55] Blair McClenachan, an ardent "Constitutionalist," could not be bothered with Morris' request until 1782 when it came time for McClenachan to make a claim for payment. In addition to reluctant partners, it ordinarily took up to a year and a half for all the paperwork to be done on one shipment and Robert's previous six-month leave was not long enough. Accounts left open due to this kind of delay would not be easily closed when the key participant had died in the middle of the business, as it was in Thomas Morris' case. The accounts of the "Indian Goods" project that Thomas Morris, Silas Deane and Dr. Bancroft worked on for the Secret Committee ultimately proved to be a problem for Robert.

The *Farmer* Affair

By early 1779, much distrust had developed within the American body politic, and partisan farmers, i.e., plantation holders, looked for a way to prove their point that the merchants were too wicked to be put into leadership positions. A controversy suddenly arose in 1779 over a 1776 deal conducted under Morris' war supply trading system. The ship *Farmer* was leased from a third party shortly after Washington's victory in Princeton. It was loaded with tobacco purchased on credit by Willing, Morris & Co. The consignment was made to Thomas Morris, and the *Farmer* sailed from Baltimore on January 9th, 1777. Richard Lee had been running the Secret Committee from Baltimore at the time, but, somehow, he kept no minutes of the meetings, and was not asked to help settle the matter. Thomas Morris was to be the receiving agent in France and the record of that transaction was kept in the Willing, Morris & Co. papers. While the tobacco was in transit, the ownership of five hundred hogsheads was transferred from Willing, Morris & Co. to the Continental war account.[56] A January 17th bill of lading showed that the tobacco was consigned to the United States after the ship had left port.[57]

The tobacco was purchased on private account and later transferred to the public account to keep ownership secret because the tobacco was being shipped to France to help the war effort. Another reason to keep the purchase secret was the behavior of tobacco sellers. They often overcharged government buyers; and this increased the cost of the war.[58] (As usual, this behavior was never questioned or called war profiteering.) The rest of the tobacco, fifty hogsheads, was kept on Willing, Morris & Co's. private account.[59] If the ship had arrived safely the war account tobacco would have been sold at the market price in France. The cost of the tobacco plus 2.5% would have been deducted from the sale receipts and the war account would get the profit.

However, in this particular case, the *Farmer* never arrived in France. The British took that ship and its tobacco at sea. Once the loss was confirmed Morris applied for an insurance payment for the tobacco Willing Morris & Co. had paid for and shipped on the Continental war account, but for which they had not been reimbursed after the loss. At the time there was no concern in Congress over the deal. However, nearly two years later, and shortly after Morris left the Congress, his political foes made the false claim that Morris was asking the Congress to pay for his private losses. This became known as the *Farmer* affair. Morris remarked,

> I believe it must be well known in Congress that all the attacks made on my character there happened during my absence.[60]

The attackers went to the press with their accusations. Morris could not defend himself in public without revealing the secret trading network he had set up to supply the American army. The former chair of the relevant committee, Richard Henry Lee, maintained his absence from the controversy.

The 1779 *Farmer* incident was made possible by a number of factors. Initially: when the *Farmer* contract was made in January 1777 Morris had been acting nearly alone in Philadelphia trying to supply Washington before the battles of Trenton and Princeton, getting the ships finished and to sea, and doing many other things for the Continental Government. Secondly: Morris kept the transaction records on loose pieces of paper in the Willing, Morris & Co. files, because the official Willing, Morris & Co. record books were in Christiana, Delaware at the time. The recording of the transaction into the company files did not take place until March 12th, 1777.[61] The Secret Committee, operating under Arthur Lee's brother, Richard Henry, was hiding in Baltimore at the time and did not keep any useful record for that period. Notations in the Secret Committee books were later delayed due to Morris' general workload, and while other committee members might have taken this on, they did not. Thirdly: the suspicions about Morris and his committee that Lee had spent years fostering had become well established in the minds of Arthur Lee's friends in Congress, like Henry Laurens. Lastly, the 1778 detention in France of Thomas Morris' private papers made the settling of all the Secret Committee accounts so difficult that neither Morris nor Henry Laurens were able to accomplish it on their own.

The genesis of this controversy was nominally a conversation between Henry Laurens and Francis Lewis who, in private, recalled to Laurens a previous conversation between Lewis and a sea captain. The captain told Lewis about the shipment. Lewis told Laurens. Interestingly, when Laurens asked Lewis to support the story, Lewis refused to cooperate. This left Laurens in the position of finding supporting documentation. He produced letters and extracts from the Committee records, but little could on the topic be found. Laurens admitted,

> The Clerk of the Office informs me that he has spent many hours seeking for these lights [documents that would illuminate] and can discover none of them nor any Papers concerning the *Farmer* excepting those before mentioned which were tyed up in one parcel and appeared to be all the documents relative to that Ship-but that he had not fully examined every Paper in the Office, it is possible therefore they may hereafter be found.[62]

Ultimately, Morris was able to supply the missing documentation from his own records, and once all was seen the affair was dropped and Laurens was satisfied that Morris had done no wrong. Morris was cleared.[63] The President of Congress, John Jay, wrote Morris a letter of apology.[64] People who distrusted merchants were satisfied they had managed to damage Morris' reputation with their false charges.

Morris was not about to let a little noise in the press and Congress slow him down. He pursued his private interests without great concern over the opinions of his adversaries. He knew how to get his ships to run the British blockade. This made him a valuable agent to John Holker, who looked to supply the French with food, and the Americans with European and West Indian goods. Morris also became involved in currency trading, and over the years he became a major partner in a number of firms up and down the Atlantic coast shipping such commodities as tobacco, indigo, and linen. By the mid 1780's Morris was involved to a significant degree with eleven of the seventeen largest firms in Philadelphia.[65]

Old friends, like William Duer, of New York, became involved in Morris' trading network. Many of the same people who had been part of the trading system while Morris was the Chairman of the Secret Committee became trading partners once he was back in private business. It is fair to say, however, that Morris' associates may have run the British blockade, and took large risks in search of opportunities, but Morris did not wish to act contrary to the various state embargoes or run afoul of local state authorities, because he knew his reputation was his empire, and without it he would be nothing. He wrote to one ambitious partner who suggested they circumvent state restrictions, "'even the most lucrative of trade' could not balance a 'sullied reputation and reproaching mind.'" [66]

Morris' interest in personal gain did not get in the way of his support for the war, instead his success in private business allowed him to assist the public effort. In one such case, Judge Richard Peters received a letter of desperation from General Washington that outlined the need for supplies. On that night a party was given by Don Miralles, the undercover Spanish minister, and occasional business partner of Morris. When Morris discovered that Washington's army had no lead for bullets he quickly arranged, on his own credit, for ninety tons of ballast to be delivered from one of the privateers that he and John Holker controlled. One hundred men were hired to form that lead into bullets over the course of one night. The bullets were on their way to Washington's army the next morning. Judge Richard Peters went on to say,

> I could relate many more such occurrences. Thus did our affairs proceed… [67]

This and other supply transactions are often characterized by modern historians as standard business deals, and what was once interpreted as generosity on Morris' part is now seen as yet another example of profit centered activity. The present "consensus" interpretation misses one critical element of the deals. He did not get cash, or silver, or gold. He only got a piece of paper from a nearly bankrupt government, an acknowledgement of a debt to be paid in the future, if possible. In the meantime Morris had to pay for the materials that were converted to military uses. A receipt or voucher from the Army would be of little value if America had lost the war. The record shows that many people who held these receipts were never paid; or were paid in devalued currency even though America did win. On the other hand, at the same time the civilian economy was going along. Morris could have used these materials in his commercial business, been paid in real money, and left the Army to look out for itself. Many other merchants took that path.

Another aspect of this interaction is the context that people like Morris, Don Miralles, and Holker were enjoying a long-running series of parties and balls, while many of the citizens in Philadelphia were struggling with a depressed economy, high prices, scarcity, and a political outlook that fostered envy and malcontent. This malcontent was largely based on the failure of their own ideas to solve the obvious problems, and their lack of willingness to modify their approaches.

Error upon Error

The government of the State of Pennsylvania was full of zeal to do everything differently from the way the Quakers had done it. The Quakers had used a form of state-run mortgages as the basis for a local currency during the time when English policy was to make the American colonies remain poor. The paper passed at par even though it was based on a yet-to-be paid debt, so there was little or no inflation. Adam Smith was familiar with Pennsylvania's old monetary policies when he wrote,

> To oblige a creditor, therefore, to accept of this [discounted currency] as full payment for a debt of a hundred pounds actually paid down in ready money, was an act of such violent injustice, as has scarce, perhaps, been attempted by the government of any country pretended to be free.[68]

The new government, on the other hand, just printed more and more currency. Inflation ensued, which was seen as an increase in prices at the market. The high prices were seen as unfair, so the state sought to control the markets with price controls. These controls discouraged producers from putting their goods into the market because the regulated prices did not easily adjust to the cost of producing the goods in those times of great inflation. To fix the inflation problem the State passed the "Tender" law. The tender laws required everyone, including the state, to honor the currency at its face value, and they made it illegal for others to discount the currency.

People discounted the state currency anyway because they had to buy items from outside the state. Once outside the state, the currency was valued outside the control of the state. This resulted in people in Maryland being able to buy a Pennsylvania pound for a half-pound and then resell it to the state for a full pound, once they were in Philadelphia. Obviously, the state lost money. The producers saw their costs go up because of currency discounting and because they needed inputs from outside the state. Unfortunately, the market was regulated so they could not make money selling their goods. In these ways the State Assembly's effort to regulate trade and establish the value of the currency by law had the effect of suppressing the markets, reducing the value of the currency, and nearly bankrupting the state. Naturally, the Assembly that had created this nightmare attempted to fix the system with more controls, including an embargo on trade with other states. They thought that by shutting the state borders they could control the economy of their own state. All this did was further depress the market and discourage producers who saw their only way of making money disappear. Large and small farmers refused to plant and reap crops for sale knowing they would only get worthless paper in return. The harvest also suffered from the brutal winters in 1778 and 1779. Artisans declared that they would not abide by the price controls until the prices of all commodities were set.[69] On occasion, the Assembly would lift their embargo to stimulate trade by allowing the importation of goods from the West Indies.

The distress in the market was the cause of much unhappiness and discontent. The population was not familiar with macro-economic theory, instead they worried when the market down the street was empty, and when the money they had was worth less and less. Robert Morris and James Wilson worked, while they were in the Assembly, to free the markets, end the embargo, and repeal the currency laws. Feelings ran high on these subjects and the general population chose to blame the individuals who worked to solve the problem, rather than the real culprit: the system their Assembly had created. To keep the Assembly's control firm, Morris and his allies had to be dealt with. The opposition's use of public humiliation had worked against Morris once and that success led others to try it too. The second time, the strategy was to focus public dissatisfaction with the whole economy on Morris. Thomas Paine and Charles Wilson Peale maintained that Morris was a war profiteer, and that Morris was unjustly enriching himself contrary to the laws of Pennsylvania. There was no proof given, but such niceties as proof in the press were not required in those times.

It was typical throughout the former colonies in America that the price of flour in the market rose when imported goods arrived, especially during times of inflation. In Massachusetts, farmers withheld flour until the prices rose so they could afford to purchase expensive goods imported from the West Indies and Europe. While this worked adequately up north, it was a disaster in Philadelphia, where the economy had not recovered from the British occupation. Farmers left the markets alone because the money was practically worthless, and there were not enough imported goods to attract the farmers. The flow of imports had been stopped by state embargoes and the British blockade.[70]

Farmers often chose to barter with millers for imported goods instead of marketing in town. Philadelphia's market went into hibernation for the winter of 1778 as everyone waited for spring and the arrival of ships from the West Indies. The spring of 1779 came, and a flotilla of ships arrived. Trade blossomed for a while and as supply increased, prices declined.[71] Spring also brought a new member to Morris' growing family. His second daughter, Maria was born on April 24th. The family was still living in their old house on Front Street below Dock St., with six children ranging from newborn to ten years, that must have been a lively place.

The prices rose again, and a public meeting was held on May 25th, 1779, featuring inflammatory speeches by former General Daniel Roberdeau, who had been militia leader and a prominent member of the Pennsylvania Assembly. As a result of this meeting a Citizens Committee empowered itself to set tariffs and investigate individuals without sanction from any state agency. The Committee used off-duty militia men for enforcement[72] and claimed the power to threaten property and personal rights.[73] The Committee movement became so odious to farmers one wrote,

> Your regulators or mob has put a stop to my sending flour until I know whether its mine or theirs.[74]

The Committee set about its work of mob justice urged on by radical members of the Pennsylvania Assembly and Executive Council. Thomas Paine was a member of two of these extra-legal committees.[75]

Mob Justice, Pennsylvania Style

The committee investigated Morris' activities with the intent of proving he was a war profiteer. The focus of this committee was the polacre *Victorious*. (A polacre is a kind of ship ordinarily found in the Mediterranean.) The *Victorious* sat in the

lower Delaware Bay while the other ships offloaded. The firm, Sr. La Caze and Mallet, owned the ship and they named Morris as agent.[76] Morris wrote,

> It was many days in this port before I had the least idea of a connection with it, and when it did come into my view, it was upon the application of other people to me.[77]

Morris then quickly sold a large quantity of the material on the polacre to the Continental Army. It turned out that Sr. La Caze spoke only Spanish, and the translation of the terms had been so poor that Morris' understanding was not the same as Sr. La Caze. Morris had sold the material to the Army *under* the price the importers had paid. There was more cargo on the ship, so they renegotiated the deal. Morris had the importers accept the existing sale to the army as a condition of going forward. The sale of the rest of the cargo went ahead, and according to the pricing system of the day.[78]

The new effort to defame Morris failed, once the facts were known. Undaunted, the citizens committee went after Morris for his work with John Holker. Morris was buying large quantities of flour for the French Fleet, and having the flour moved from the countryside to the port by the means of wagons. The wagon rates were set by the state at this time, as so many prices were. The farmers hiked their prices according to their usual practice, so they might get the most for their flour. The subsequent rise in all flour prices enraged citizens,[79] and Thomas Paine was chief among those who excoriated Morris in the press, and advocated seizing Morris' property. Again, Paine did not blame the farmers for charging high prices. The Wilmington citizens committee seized the flour from Holker's ship.[80]

Morris was not the owner of the flour or the ship and acted only as agent who arranged the sale. He had arranged to supply the flour to America's only ally, the French, and by doing so Morris managed to enrich the farmers at the expense of the French. None of that mattered to the critics who had contrived, somewhat theatrically, for a pair of women to go to Morris' home with empty sacks and beg at his door for flour. Morris was called in front of the Citizens Committee to account for his actions. They had set up their tribunal in the park behind the Pennsylvania State House so all could attend. He went before them respectfully, and addressed the disgruntled crowd gathered on the green right behind the building were Morris had signed the Declaration of Independence nearly three years earlier. He calmly explained exactly what happened and pointed out that of all the people involved in the shipping business only he had been singled out, and this was probably due to his opposition to the Pennsylvania Constitution. In response to his critics on this account he wrote,

> ...that a freedom of opinion on such subjects is essential to a free government, and that to act in conformity with our opinions where the object is public good is the duty of a good man.[81]

Considering the nature of the proceedings, a calm presentation of the facts to this mob would have taken an extraordinary amount of self-control. Morris felt an address to the committee was not sufficient and he published a letter in the press. It annoyed Morris' political adversaries, but the French minister to the United States, Conrad Alexandre Gérard wrote to Morris,

> I have perused with great satisfaction your address to the citizens of Pennsylvania, which you did me the honor to leave with me. All what refers to my Court in the transaction you relate is stated with the greatest exactness and I am ready and determined to support your conduct in this respect at proper times and places, in a measure consistent with my public character and with the Justice which is due to your zeal for measures intimately connected with the most essential interests of the united states and of the Alliance.[82]

After the Wilmington mob took the 182 barrels of flour from Holker's ship, French minister Gérard became involved on an official level. Holker relied on his role as a French Consul for protection, as the French turned to Congress for help.[83] Gérard protested to Congress, and to the State of Pennsylvania.[84] Congress intervened because this incident involved American relations with her only ally, France. When the facts were known the "Constitutionalists" quickly dropped the whole issue, but Morris' reputation had been unjustly damaged, again. This episode was among the many lessons Morris learned about the importance of the rule of law compared to the dangers of mob rule. This also served as a turning point for Thomas Paine, who decided from that moment to support economic laissez faire, as activities conducted by free men that would bring prosperity to all.[85]

The local power play by the "Constitutionalists" in the Pennsylvania Assembly had far reaching repercussions. The French were trying to buy 1,500 barrels of flour to feed their sailors, who had been in the West Indies since the preceding December. American mob justice did not favorably impress the French. Minister Gérard thought the controversy between farmers and merchants was ridiculous because the farmers were receiving rare and much needed hard money for their crops.[86] These incidents made the people of the United States look like amateurs in the eyes of the French Crown, and the French started to pull back on their support for the war.[87] As a result, Gérard spent much of the remainder of his tenure in Philadelphia promoting French interests, instead of mutual interests. For example, he attempted to convince Congress to limit American territorial expectations, and not to insist on extending American fishing rights off the Grand Banks. This was not well received by the New England delegates, who were not very pro-French in any case.

On June 16th, 1779 John Holker placed a new order for food from Virginia and Maryland through Robert Morris. This business was making Morris' life difficult because Henry Laurens and his allies suspected, but never proved, that the official trade to supply France was being used as cover for a parallel private trade. It became Gouverneur Morris' duty to tell Council Holker that the bread, flour, and pork would be unavailable because the Army needed these materials.[88] When the food was clearly unavailable the remaining part of the French fleet stayed in the West Indies until September, far away from the American coast which needed their protection. The supply of basic foodstuffs in the mid-Atlantic region was low, due to the war, the lack of a reliable currency, weather conditions, and a Citizen Committee system backed by mob violence.[89]

La Luzerne Arrives from France

French minister Gérard had been suffering for months from fevers, possibly even malaria. His replacement, Chevalier de la Luzerne, and his first secretary Barbé-Marbois, left France for America in mid-June 1779. They sailed on the same ship as John Adams, and all of them arrived together in Boston. The six-week voyage provided Adams with the opportunity to make the new minister sympathetic to the Adams-Lee perspective. Luzerne was feted in Boston for a month, and then traveled to Philadelphia. Shortly after Luzerne's arrival, Gérard left Philadelphia for France. It was October 1779. Luzerne was received by Congress on November 17.

Luzerne remained tolerant of internal divisions in America and publicly maintained that all Americans favored liberty and supported the French alliance. He was well received in Congress and society, but he still had to contend with anti-Gallic sentiment in New England. Other than lingering suspicions he had about Henry Laurens, Luzerne worked to build support for French diplomatic efforts by appealing to the Southerners and the Middle state delegates while not openly antagonizing the New England block.

Naval Warfare

As political squabbles continued, the War was still being waged on land and at sea. Congress had dismissed Commodore Ezek Hopkins in March 1779 for what they saw as lack of success at sea, general disregard for Congressional oversight, and because Congress thought Hopkins was too timid in pursuing the enemy. In June, the British left Rhode Island and redeployed to New York. They soon turned their ships around and used them to bombard Stratford, Fairfield, Milford and New Haven along the Connecticut coast, and to harass American shipping.

In September, there was a joint mission under the control of the Massachusetts Navy to strike back at the British. They combined State and Continental vessels, and pursued the loyalists, who fled from Boston to the Penobscot Bay, in what is now the state of Maine. During the course of the engagement the tables were turned on the Rebel fleet, and the Americans were chased into the tight confines of the mouth of the Penobscot River. They attempted to form their ships into a kind of fort by clustering them together. This failed to protect the American fleet and the wooden fort of ships was an easy target for the British Navy. The Americans burned their own ships to avoid capture. Britain controlled the Gulf of Maine for the remainder of the war. The effort left 3,000 men in rural Maine, cost nineteen armed ships, and about twenty merchant vessels for a total of nearly $7,000,000.

Hopkins may have seemed timid, but he did maintain the navy as a fighting force. The failure in the Gulf of Maine effectively removed Massachusetts, the former hot bed of revolutionary zeal, from the war effort for the rest of the Revolution. There was little hope of rebuilding the fleet, and the British blockade was increasing in effectiveness. The fighting would not be over for years.[90]

In July 1779, a congressional committee, encouraged by Henry Laurens, was still investigating the seizure of a Portuguese snow class vessel that had been taken in 1777 by the privateer, *Phoenix,* and sold in Boston. The Portuguese were sympathetic to the British, and their ships carried British goods, but their ships were not proper targets of American privateers. The owner wanted his money back and worked through Congress for this. Morris, who owned four percent in the venture, had been too busy with Congressional committee work and too distant at the time to manage a ship sailing from Spain. The partnership was being represented by Carter Braxton of Virginia, but Morris was nearby, and he was repeatedly called before Congress. When he suggested Congress discuss this with the group's representative they did not, and instead they criticized Morris and all his partners. Then they empowered all the states of all the owners to seek redress from the individuals.[91] John Penn, of North Carolina, objected but was overruled by Congress.

John Paul Jones was cruising European waters, taking British ships and harassing the coast of England during that September, when the French Crown lent him a merchant ship. He refitted her and renamed her the *Bonhomme Richard* in honor of "Poor Richard" a character of Ben Franklin's invention. Jones led four other American ships and two French privateers against British commercial shipping. Among the American ships was the *Alliance.* On September 23rd, 1779 this small fleet encountered the British Frigate *HMS Serapis.* The *Serapis* was faster and more easily turned, because she was a ship designed for naval warfare. The *Bonhomme Richard* was a converted merchant ship; built to carry, not to fight. During the fight captain Landais, of the *Alliance,* surprised everyone and opened fire on both *Serapis* and *Bonhomme Richard.* The *Serapis* was getting the best of Jones' ship in a close sea battle when the captain of the *Serapis* asked for Jones' surrender. Jones refused to and replied,

> I have not yet begun to fight!

Jones took possession of the *Serapis* through a series of bold actions, and the bravery of his men who fought at close quarters while the ships were grappled together. The *Bonhomme Richard* was so damaged that she sank on the spot and Jones sailed away in his new prize. Jones and Franklin told captain Landais, of the *Alliance,* that he was relieved of duty because he had fired on an American ship. Command of that ship was transferred to John Paul Jones. On October 13, 1779 Jones wrote to Morris that he released the *Serapis* to the French Crown, and that the King had given him a ceremonial sword, which is now in the Naval Academy Chapel in Annapolis. He also mentioned that Arthur Lee tried to enlist Jones in Lee's campaign against Franklin.[92] That failed, and after Jones arrived in *L'Orient* he was tasked with ferrying Arthur Lee back to America, which Jones disdained. Lee then tried, and failed, to convince Jones to take a large amount of personal baggage back to America.[93] Jones went on to Paris for guidance on how to deal with Lee.

On June 29th, 1779 the Spanish declared war on England, but even so, they did not "officially" recognize the American states. Their claim was more in support of the other Bourbon state, France. The Spanish Crown saw that an independent America would compete with Spain in the new world, but a weakened England would not. The Spanish Governor of Louisiana, Don Bernardo de Gálvez began his own attack on the British in western Florida. By October 5th his Spanish forces occupied much of what is now Louisiana including Natchez, Baton Rouge, and Fort Bute. Earlier de Gálvez had offered Congress an opportunity to cooperate in this effort, but Congress refused. The result of Congressional inaction and Spanish success was expanded Spanish control of the Lower Mississippi, which helped during the latter part of the Revolution, but the eventual closure of the Mississippi at New Orleans bedeviled America until Pinckney's treaty in 1795.

During this period the British made gains in the South as they took possession of much of Georgia. Farther north, Washington and his army held their position in New York State. General Anthony Wayne won the Battle of Stony Point. General Benjamin Lincoln contacted Admiral D'Estaing, who was patrolling in the West Indies. These two devised a plan to retake Savannah, Georgia. The resulting siege and Battle of Savannah was a bloody loss for the American side. America lost 800 men, including Count Casimir Polaski. Admiral D'Estaing returned to France in December. International events were not going well; and local political controversies continued in Philadelphia.

Mob Justice II

> *"Here the People are bewitched. They seem to have not one Idea of Virtue and Patriotism left – Motives of private gain swallow up every laudable Principle. The Merchant against the Farmer, the Farmer against the Merchant."*[94]

The radicals who created the Pennsylvania Constitution were resolute in their defense of the system they made. Those who wished to modify their new government were not treated lightly. James Wilson, for example, was a member of the Pennsylvania Assembly who, like Morris, sought to reform the system created by the radicals in 1776. Wilson was an eminent lawyer who had signed the Declaration of Independence, but he was also the lawyer chosen to defend the supposed Tories who were accused by the mob associated with the Patriotic Society, earlier. A situation developed that clearly shows how volatile things had become. A handbill was circulated that called for people to "drive off from the city all disaffected persons and those who supported them,"[95]

On October 4th, a Philadelphia street rabble made up of supporters of the "Constitutionalists" in state government, who were considered "idle militiamen, and street loiterers,"[96] met at Byrne's Tavern and decided amongst themselves that James Wilson was a war profiteer, and loyalist sympathizer. They left the tavern and started traveling in the city as a large disgruntled group. The mob attacked Wilson's house and managed to break down the front door. In the ensuing fight five people died and seventeen were wounded. It was dubbed the "Ft. Wilson riot."[97] Just before the rioters could get a cannon aimed at Wilson's house, the First City Troop arrived at the scene. This Troop, known to some as the "Silk Stocking Brigade," had been training as a military unit in case of mob actions, and was part of the state militia system. Tempers cooled after this event but not before a separate incident wherein a gang threatened General Arnold in the street, only to be chased off by his pistols.[98,99] The First City Troop kept its status as a private militia well into the 20th Century. They had a private fort, an armory, and before the first World War they sent members to support General John Pershing's efforts to fight Pancho Villa along the Texas border.

In 1779 the war was in its third year, and where were the people who demanded independence now? Richard Henry Lee, who had proposed the Declaration of Independence in Congress, was in Virginia attending to his private life. Thomas Jefferson was in Virginia rewriting the Laws of the State. John Hancock was in Massachusetts working on a new Constitution. He became the Governor of Massachusetts in 1780. John Adams was in Massachusetts also working on the new Constitution for that state but was to leave for Paris in the Fall. In October, John Jay left his position as Chief Justice in New York State, and went on a diplomatic mission to Spain as a minister plenipotentiary to the court of Charles III. His mission was to gain official recognition for the United States. However, he was largely ignored because the Spanish court would not "recognize" him and by extension the United States, as a country separate from Britain. Benjamin Franklin was in France working for the Revolutionary cause. Morris was in the Pennsylvania Assembly, working to solve the state's financial problems, and there he hoped to rework that state's constitution. He continued to promote free trade and open markets as the solution to the state's economic problems. On Nov 10th, 1779 Congress acted to rid the nation of mob-run committees through a multi-state pricing plan.[100] The Armies went to winter quarters, and the war slowed for several months.

Morris ended his controversial agency for John Holker, and passed the business to William Turnbull and Co., a company in which Morris maintained a financial interest.[101] On November 23rd, 1779, Congress was hard at work attempting to draw £200,000 from Europe by writing bills of exchange when there were no funds to support them, and no means of generating those funds.[102] In other words Congress was so desperate for funds they were willing to commit fraud.

On Dec 3rd, 1779, the Board of Admiralty folded due to lack of support from Congress and apparent disinterest among its members. They could not even muster a quorum.[103] During this period, ships in the Continental Navy spent long periods of time at dock because it was difficult for the Navy to attract sailors. This stemmed from the growth and allure of privateering. Sailors could make much more money on a privateer vessel than in naval service. However, the Navy was necessary, and so with Morris' endorsement, John Brown, of Pennsylvania, became the Secretary to the new Board of Admiralty. Brown had been a junior partner in Willing, Morris & Co, and he had worked on the Marine Committee with Morris in 1775.[104] This was also the same John Brown who had been the head of the State Navy Board of Pennsylvania when Betsy Ross was hired to make "ship's colors."

Disorder in the Navy found its way to Europe in the spring of 1780. Arthur Lee was looking to get himself, and his huge amount of personal baggage, back to America from France. With Jones in Paris, he approached the disgraced Captain Pierre Landais. Arthur Lee did not relish the idea of sailing with Jones, who was the actual captain, and convinced a willing Landais that only the Marine Committee could take away his command. Lee was able to convince the disgraced captain to ignore Franklin and Jones. On June 12th Landais took command of the *Alliance*. Once in command, Landais took Lee back to America. The trip was not serene. One of the first things Landais did was to imprison the brave sailors who had sailed with Jones on the *Bonhomme Richard*, and who had helped Jones win the Battle of Flamborough Head. After that, there was much strife on board; including the episode during dinner one evening when Landais threatened Arthur Lee with a carving knife in an argument over a cut of pork. Landais was relieved of command before the ship arrived in Boston.

Back in Philadelphia, the campaign of lies and demagoguery against Morris by the "Constitutionalists" in the Pennsylvania Assembly was so successful that Morris and his allies were voted out and the "Constitutionalists" took complete control. Morris was out of Government, and knowing that his reputation was his fortune, he acted to reclaim it. On March 31, 1780, Morris wrote to Benjamin Franklin in France:

> After four years of indefatigueable public service, I have been reviled and traduced for a long time by whispers and insinuations which at length were fortunately wrought up to public charges, which gave me an opportunity to show how groundless, how malicious, there things were; how Innocent and honest my transactions. My enemies, ashamed of their persecution, have quitted the pursuit, and I am in the peaceable possession of the most honourable station my ambition aspires to, that of a private citizen in a Free State.[105]

For all their other failures, the "Constitutionalists" did have some successes. On March 1st, 1780, the Pennsylvania Assembly, led by urban Radicals, passed the Act for the Gradual Abolition of Slavery and Pennsylvania became the first state to adopt an abolition law. It became the model for other states. During that time John Jay, Morris' friend and ally, wrote to Egbert Benson:

> An excellent law might be made out of the Pennsylvania one for the gradual abolition of slavery. Till America comes into this measure, her prayers to Heaven for liberty will be impious. This is a strong expression, but it is just. Were I in the legislature, I would prepare a bill for the purpose with great care, and I would never leave moving it until it became law or I ceased to be a member. I believe God governs this world, and I believe it to be a maxim in His and in our court, that those who ask for equity ought to do it.[106]

The Southern Department

The British thought that they would have better success in the southern states than in the North, where they were stalled. They understood the more conservative nature of the Southerners and expected help from the Tories in the South. They also estimated that the Southern Rebel leadership would not be able to muster an effective defense. On April 13th, 1780, British General Henry Clinton arrived from Newport, Rhode Island, and laid siege to Charleston, North Carolina. The Americans surrendered in May. The British took the city, and Clinton took the captive American leaders north to New York, leaving Lord Charles Cornwallis in charge. Among the captives was General Lincoln, who had been in charge of the whole Southern Department. Congress appointed General Horatio Gates to replace General Lincoln. Gates finally got the command he had sought for so long.

Back in Pennsylvania, the English had gone, but it seemed the state was its own worst enemy. By late spring 1780, the fiscal policies of the "Constitutionalists" were pushing their state into bankruptcy. The money became worthless, and Pennsylvania was not able to fulfill its commitment to the war effort. In response, a group of private citizens, calling itself the National Merchants' Association, was formed at the urging of Elbridge Gerry to help supply the army in their time of distress.[107] Morris might have been out of office, but he did not turn his back on the war effort, and he became an active participant in this volunteer association. In July 1780, General Washington's headquarters applied directly to Philadelphia Merchant's Association for help.[108]

> The Merchants are however roused. Mr. Robert Morris is at the head of an Association for the purpose of furnishing the Army with three Millions of rations, for which the public is to reimburse them as soon as their finances will admit. They have yesterday sent on five hundred barrels of Flour.[109]

The land war in the North was near a stalemate. A division of French land forces led by the Count de Rochambeau arrived in Newport Rhode Island on July 11th. After their arrival, the British in New York were more conservative in their actions. They seemed content to maintain their positions and watch the American economy self-destruct. The French presence was too weak to undertake any offensive military action against the British in New York. Rochambeau promised that at least one more division was going to arrive. Unfortunately, the British blockade was effective against the French navy, so it would be another year before De Grasse could make good on that promise. Washington and Rochambeau met several times to make plans, but little came of them. The main benefit of their presence in Newport was the money they spent to support themselves. In the meantime, the British made gains in the South. The Continental Army there was near desertion for lack of supplies and pay and there were occasional mutinies over these issues. The Revolution was four years old and there was no victory in sight.

The near collapse of the Pennsylvania state economy caused the "Constitutionalists" to lose political power. The voters re-elected Morris, and soon he was back leading the Republican Society in the Assembly with a narrow, but new majority. There was an initiative by the Constitutionalists, headed by Reed, to issue another round of state currency which was supposed to revive the economy. Morris was very much against this, but it went ahead anyway. The currency lost value almost as fast as it was printed, so the second traunch was not issued. This provided an opportunity for Morris to implement his market-based reforms. During his terms in the Pennsylvania Assembly Morris worked to repeal the penal and legal tender laws, open the currency to Market forces, repeal price controls, repeal the state's embargoes, and open the ports to world markets.[110]

Morris personally provided $80,000 in loan guarantees to overcome the current deficit. He became the Agent of Pennsylvania, which was a specially created office that allowed him to oversee the state's financial transformation. His next step was to create an independent bank, The Bank of Pennsylvania, to take over the role of the Merchant's Association. A plan was adopted for raising £300,000, in Pennsylvania money, to capitalize the bank. Morris pledged £10,000.[111] With more than 90 subscribers pledging, the required amount was raised in a short period. Morris was able to send 500 barrels of flour to Washington almost immediately.

From this office as Agent of Pennsylvania, Morris used money from the small bank to buy even more supplies for the Army and make good on Pennsylvania's commitment to support the war effort.[112] On June 21st a Congressional committee was appointed to "confer with the inspectors and directors" of the bank and the following day Congress agreed to reimburse those who pledged capital.[113]

The success of the Republicans was a bitter pill for Joseph Reed and his fellow "Constitutionalists." Even so, Reed still held the position of President of the Executive Council.[114] The factions were evenly balanced in the Assembly so no large changes could be made. The Republicans in the Assembly, led by Morris, attempted no structural changes that would require a rewrite of the Pennsylvania Constitution. Instead, they used the existing system to make good on the State's commitments, to moderate the programs of "Constitutionalists," and to grow their majority.

Over time, the Republicans would not only keep the Abolition Act in place, they defended it against various petitions for repeal sent in by German farmers and members of the Scots-Irish "Constitutionalists" from Back Country Pennsylvania.[115] The moderates "from Philadelphia City and County generally opposed every attempt to modify the law."[116]

At the same time Pennsylvania was starting to put its economic house in order, the Continental Congress was learning that securing sufficient grants from European Powers was more difficult than anticipated. This was particularly true when it was discovered that Congress had tried to get money by passing bad bills in Europe. The Spanish and the French considered the military losses in the South, particularly the loss of Charleston, as important indicators of American impotence in the face of British advances. These losses and the American financial problems made the job of American diplomats in Europe next to impossible. If there ever were indications that Spain was about to recognize America, these vanished. There was continued talk about a loan from Spain, but it receded into the mists of diplomacy. The only connections the Spanish were willing to make were along commercial lines.

Congressional Committees were muddling along as the currency became worthless. The states were able to make some contributions to the cause with goods, but the goods did not reach the army because they were difficult and expensive to transport. The shortage of wagons and wagoneers was matched by the poor quality of roads. The roads were dirt, rutted and poorly maintained, so they were just passable in dry weather and almost impossible after the rains. The cost of the war was increasing, and the states were helping but the results were not good; supplies spoiled, while elsewhere soldiers starved and froze.

By March 18th, 1780, the Continental Congress could no longer pay the interest on their loans, so the country BECAME bankrupt. They devalued the money at a ratio of 40:1. It was as if every dollar were suddenly worth two and a half cents. Silas Deane was still in Europe where he worked on selling Loan Office Certificates as part of the war finance effort. These early war bonds were not easy to sell once it became known that the Continental Congress could not even pay the certificate holders the interest that was due to them. Silas Deane wrote to Morris:

> Loan Office Certificates are in no kind of credit in France; that the very worst construction has been made of the resolutions of Congress of March last, and that in consequence public credit is gone, and private very low, and that no loan has been made… [117]

The British continued to make military gains in the South under General Banastre Tarleton, and Lord Cornwallis. On August 16th, General Gates was routed by the British at Camden, South Carolina. General Horatio Gates fled well beyond the margin of safety, by about 60 miles. Then he retired to his plantation. It was three days after that, when Arthur Lee and Captain Landais arrived in Boston, where Landais was again relieved of duty, this time by the Eastern Naval Board.

September 3rd proved to be a fateful day of unfortunate ineptitude at sea. The British captured a ship carrying Henry Laurens to Europe. He had been appointed to represent America in Holland. As usual before being captured, the American's threw the bag of secret papers overboard. Unfortunately, it did not sink, and it was fished out of the water. It turned out Laurens was carrying, among other things, a document created by one of his allies, the roving American agent, William Lee. That document outlined a proposed alliance between America and Amsterdam. This was the alliance to which Mr. Dumas referred when he complained to Congress that William Lee was misrepresenting himself as an American Commissioner at Paris. Even though neither Lee nor his Dutch interlocutor, de Neufville, had the power to join nations in an alliance, this document was used as a pretext for Britain to declare war on the Dutch.[118] As soon as the Dutch were in the war, the English attacked the Dutch West Indies and those islands stopped being useful as transshipment ports, which further damaged American economic prospects. Henry Laurens was sent to prison in the Tower of London where he had plenty of time to reflect on his actions, get a very nice portrait painted, as well as to meet his former English partner in the slave trade.

The failure of American finances encouraged the imperial courts in Europe to develop their own post-war plans. The Great Powers of Europe, including the Empress of Russia, Catherine the Great, and the Emperor of the Austrian Empire, and the Crowned heads of France and Spain, were planning a meeting to mediate the peace between England and her colonies. The American ministers were not invited. These monarchs were not interested in the success of a potentially dangerous republic in America. They saw that possibility in the light of their own interests and plans. As America became weaker, the efforts by this group became more ominous. Their plan was to partition America to suit their own designs. One of the first concrete efforts that came forth was the Armed Neutrality, which was intended to protect neutral European ships at sea. The effect was quite different, and it was later hailed as the "Armed Nullity" since it did little more than nothing other than encourage smuggling.

Back in Boston, Captain John Barry took control of the *Alliance*, leaving the disgraced Captain Landais without a ship. A new low point was reached in New York when on September 23rd, 1780, Benedict Arnold's betrayal was discovered in West Point. Three days later, Cornwallis occupied Charlotte, North Carolina. Elsewhere, down south, revolutionary militia leaders Thomas Sumter and Morgan harassed British troops in a continued guerrilla campaign. The British were waging a counter-campaign to encourage the Tories to rise up against the revolutionary governments. They also attacked the economy of the South by freeing slaves. These two policies worked against one another because the loyalists didn't want their slaves freed. Many of the slaves who left the southern plantations, and went with the British on promises of freedom, were in for a rude surprise when they were sold to British sugar cane plantation owners in the West Indies. Thousands and thousands of slaves left with the British. Two weeks later, on October 7th, the militia defeated the local Tory forces at the Battle of Kings Mountain in N. Carolina and removed the Tories as a military threat.

The Southern Department had been without a leader since Gates had fled in the middle of August. On December 2nd, 1780, Nathaniel Green moved from being Quartermaster General in Philadelphia, to Commander of the Southern Department. Green was replaced as Quartermaster General by Timothy Pickering, another Morris ally. Green found an Army low on supplies, food, clothing, and morale. He had to split his southern army into two, just to ensure their physical survival, because one large Army would decimate local provisions.

Nathanael Greene, by Charles Wilson Peale[120]

The traitorous Benedict Arnold led the British troops in raids against Virginia. He landed twenty-five miles below Richmond on January 3rd, 1781. The Constitution of the State of Virginia gave the Governor control of the state militia, but Governor Thomas Jefferson had difficulty countering the invasion by the English. It seems that only white people were allowed to join the militia, but the white population was not highly concentrated because they were dispersed among their plantations. There were so few of them in Richmond who were willing or able to put aside their private concerns, i.e., leave their slaves whom the British might free, that only about two hundred Virginia militiamen were left facing almost one thousand British troops. Jefferson was forced to surrender Richmond. There was no military reason for the British to keep Richmond after Arnold had provisioned his troops and burnt the local stores of tobacco, so Arnold left the city and moved the army to Westover.[119] On January 17th the Battle of the Cowpens resulted in a much-needed American victory over Tarleton's troops.

Endnotes

1. Letters of Delegates to Congress, 10:257
2. *War For America, 1775-1783*, Chapt 8
3. The Revolutionary Diplomatic Correspondence, 3:567
4. *Journals of the Continental Congress*, 13:50
5. *Power of the Purse*, pg. 200
6. Letters of Delegates to Congress, 10:618
7. *The American Revolution and the French Alliance*, pg. 39
8. Letters of Delegates to Congress, 10:608
9. Rappleye pg. 163
10. *Henkels Catalogue*, pg. 18
11. Letters of Delegates to Congress, 13:110n
12. Letters of Delegates to Congress, 10:641-642
13. Ibid, 10:609
14. Letters of Delegates to Congress, 10:661-662
15. *War for America*, pg. 168
16. Letters of Delegates to Congress, 11:26-27
17. Letters of Delegates to Congress, 11:7
18. *Robert Morris*, Sumner pg. 27
19. Letters of Delegates to Congress, 11:238
20. Revolutionary Diplomatic Correspondence, 1:551
21. Letters of Delegates to Congress, 11:5-12
22. Ibid, 11:13
23. *The Catholic Encyclopedia*, Volume V Copyright © 1909 by Robert Appleton Company
24. Jan 26, 1779 entry Pennsylvania State Archives, Willing Morris & Co Records Manuscript grouping.84 record group 27
25. APS, Benjamin Franklin Papers, ALS XIV, 163
26. Pennsylvania Archives, 5th Series, V1 (F-146/P41) printed 1906
27. *Biography of the Signers*, 5:366-367
28. *Robert Morris, Audacious Patriot*, pg. 53
29. *The Counter-Revolution in Pennsylvania*, pg. 60-62
30. Journals of the Assembly 1781, pg. 570, 573, 581, 586, 591, 594, 595, 601, 690, 693
31. Letters of Delegates to Congress, 11:79
32. *Life in Early Philadelphia*, pg. 259
33. Pennsylvania Gazette, Item # 27033
34. *Henkels Catalogue*, pg.144
35. *The Counter-Revolution in Pennsylvania*, pg. 155
36. Ibid, pg. 160
37. *The Counter-Revolution in Pennsylvania*, pg. 66-67
38. *Wealth of Nations*, pg. 499
39. Rappleye, pg. 108
40. Papers of Robert Morris, 9:410
41. *The Power of the Purse*, pg. 44
42. *The Power of the Purse*, pg. 13
43. The Committee of Thirteen Reply, *Pennsylvania Packet*, September 10, 1779
44. Letters of Delegates to Congress, 11:313-316
45. American National Biography Online
46. Letters of Delegates to Congress, 11:425n
47. Letters of Delegates to Congress, 11:430-435
48. The Deane Papers, 3:268
49. Common Sense to the Public, *The Pennsylvania Packet* Jan 12, 1779
50. Chernow pg 13
51. *The Early Republic and the Sea*, pg. 105
52. *Power of the Purse*, pg. 75
53. Letters of Delegates to Congress, 11:440n
54. Letters of Delegates to Congress, 11:453
55. Papers of Robert Morris, 5:177
56. Letters of the Delegates to Congress, 6:387
57. Letters of the Delegates to Congress, 6:475
58. *Journals Continental Congress*, 13:165
59. Letters of the Delegates to Congress, 6:387
60. *Journals Continental Congress,* 13:172
61. Letters of the Delegates to Congress, 5:612
62. Letters of the Delegates to Congress, 11:475
63. *Journals Continental Congress*, 13:176
64. Letters of Delegates to Congress, 12:75
65. *A Vigorous Spirit of Enterprise*, pg. 241
66. Ver Steeg, pg. 32
67. *Biography of the Signers*, 5:203-204
68. *Wealth of Nations*, pg. 367
69. *The Counter-Revolution in Pennsylvania*, pg. 72
70. *In Irons*, pg. 139-141
71. *In Irons*, pg. 141
72. *The Counter-Revolution in Pennsylvania*, pg. 70
73. *Makers of American History Jefferson and Morris* by William Graham Sumner, The University Society 1905
74. *In Irons*, pg.141-142
75. American National Biography Online

76. HSP Misc. letters folio, Robert Morris papers Levis collection call # 1957, letter May 5, 1779
77. *The Pennsylvania Gazette* ITEM #64999, December 15, 1779
78. Ibid
79. *In Irons*, pg. 141
80. HSP Robert Morris letter to the Citizens, Robert Morris papers Levis collection call # 1957
81. *The Pennsylvania Gazette,* December 15, 1779, item #64999
82. Letters of delegates to Congress, 13:165n
83. Letters of Delegates to Congress, 13:110
84. *The American Revolution and the French Alliance*, pg. 37
85. American National Biography Online
86. Ibid
87. Revolutionary Diplomatic Correspondence, 10:324-347
88. Letters of Delegates to Congress, 13:103-104
89. *In Irons*: 137-143
90. *The American Heritage Book of the Revolution*, pg. 290-291
91. Letters of Delegates to Congress: 13:158
92. American Philosophical Society Collection
93. Joseph Callo. 2006, *John Paul Jones*, pg. 112
94. Letters of Delegates to Congress, 14:12
95. Letters of Delegates to Congress, 14:16
96. *Counter-Revolution in Pennsylvania*, pg. 76
97. Ibid
98. Ibid
99. Harry M Tinkom. 1982. *The Revolutionary City in 300 Years of Philadelphia History,* Barra Foundation, pg. 147
100. *In Irons*, pg.143
101. Papers of Robert Morris, 9:410
102. Papers of Robert Morris, 2:263
103. *Journal Continental Congress*, November 26, December 3, 7, 8, 1779
104. Papers of Robert Morris, 2:208-209
105. APS, https://founders.archives.gov/documents/Franklin/01-32-02-0122
106. Henry P. Johnston, ed., *The Correspondence and public Papers of John Jay*, 4 vols (New York 1890-93) 1:406-407
107. Letters of Delegates to Congress, 15:293-294 15:294n
108. Ibid, 15:417
109. Ibid, 15:345
110. Ver Steeg, pg. 70
111. The Papers of Robert Morris, 1:73
112. Burnhouse, *The Counter-Revolution in Pennsylvania*, pg. 86
113. Letters of Delegates to Congress, 15:346
114. *The Counter-Revolution in Pennsylvania,* pg. 90
115. *Journals of the Assembly 1781*, pg. 570, 573, 581, 586, 591, 594, 595, 601, 690, 693
116. *The Counter-Revolution in Pennsylvania,* pg. 102
117. The Deane Papers, 4:214
118. *The Peacemakers*, pg. 25
119. *Pictorial Field Guide to the Revolution*, 1:434
120. National Park Service, Independence Hall Nat'l Park Collection

VII

1781

WINTER

Morris' economic plan for Pennsylvania started to work and that allowed the state to meet its war-funding obligations. While he was in the middle of this, Continental finances demanded his attention. In the year 1780, the states sent Congress a combined total of $422,000. That amounted to less than 4% of the Congress' debt to those who had purchased loan office certificates. Unfortunately those certificates were issued at a 6% return. Continental Congress was unable to meet its loan interest payments because of this 2% gap. The failure to meet the interest payment was, and is, the definition of bankruptcy.

In addition, the bankrupt Congress owed the French Crown about $9,000,000. On top of international debts, there were state debts, requisitions from individuals, and back pay for soldiers. The total war debt owed by the Continental Congress was well over twenty million dollars, and this did not include the continuing costs of the war. Congress responded by declaring it would no longer pay the interest, and then they devalued the currency.

The path to insolvency started with the seminal disagreement over the role of, and support for, Congress as an institution. For his part, Morris supported the Continental Congress when he responded to the first request for gunpowder and built a trade system to support the Continental effort. In 1778, the Morris brothers helped arrange the first tobacco-backed loan from France to the United States. However, Robert was unable to support such loans through trade, not due to British warships, but because after he left office, the Continental Congress canceled his trading program to protect "American Virtue."

This shift in the political winds aligned with theories promoted by Thomas Paine, who was paid by Henry Laurens to portray Morris' trading system as "corrupt." After Congress lost its source of independent income, it became beholden to the states. 1778 was also the year Congress removed Silas Deane from his official role in France, right after the alliance was formed, and the year Congress returned to the strategy of controlling markets at home, while seeking expanded loans and direct grants from European powers. This was the direction Samuel Adams, Arthur Lee, Henry Laurens, and their faction favored. They promoted the idea that America was entitled to free money and endless loans from the Princes of Europe. After all, Lee was able to convince Congress that a private French citizen, Mr. Beaumarchais, simply gave away millions in military assistance before the Battle of Saratoga. Their public stance was accepted as reasonable because people thought they were protecting American Virtue from the corrupt policies of the past, and their cause was just and worthy of support. Simultaneously, members of the faction spinning that yarn attempted to operate a modified trading system for the benefit of themselves and their respective states. They operated Congress the same way. The political winds shifted back only when failure became obvious.

The nationalists became ascendant once again as financial collapse stared America directly in the face. With the soon-to-be ratified Articles of Confederation on the way, Congress revisited ideas set aside three years earlier. Congress turned away from its beloved committee system, and towards the creation of the first executive offices in government.

A Momentous Invitation

On February 7th, 1781, "Congress then resumed the consideration of the plan for the arrangement of the civil executive departments of the United States; and thereupon, Resolved, That there be a Financier Superintendent of Finance, a Secretary at War, and a Secretary of Marine."[1] Morris eventually held two of these positions, Finance and Marine. The third office was the War Department, which was ably manned by Morris' good friend, Judge Richard Peters; in time, General Lincoln took over the role. Six months later, Congress created and filled a fourth, the Office of Foreign Affairs.

Victory was highly uncertain when Congress appealed to Morris to become the Superintendent of Finance. The American government was poor. Congress had no power to tax; and had lost its ability to borrow money. There was no market for American Loan Office Certificates after Congress had decided to stop paying the interest on the existing debt. The Southern Army was in tatters. The British occupied New York City, and Charleston, South Carolina. Massachusetts was effectively removed from the conflict by the British blockade, and by their losses in the Penobscot Bay. British troops roamed the countryside and remained garrisoned in the western frontier. The Navy had been reduced to just three ships, and these were kept at port. Commercial shipping had stopped because the British blockade seized American merchant vessels from the Gulf of Maine south to the Carolinas, almost at will. This meant that supplies could not flow to the war zones, and nothing could be brought in from Europe.

Under these circumstances, Morris did not jump at the opportunity to take a step that might well be equivalent to putting his head on the chopping block. During lengthy negotiations with Congress, he demanded the right to pursue his own economic interests. He had lately emerged from controversies in Pennsylvania that were based on his private business dealings, and he didn't want to repeat that on a national scale. While the discussions continued, Morris was busy getting Pennsylvania on a firm economic footing. According to economic historian Clarence Ver Steeg, Morris would not take the oath of the Office of Finance until his goals for Pennsylvania were met.[2] Historian Ellis Oberholtzer observed that Morris intended to use his Pennsylvania solution as a model for improving the finances of the Nation.[3] Also, Morris demanded control of his work, without interference from committeemen and appointees from the failed Treasury Board. Morris insisted that he should be able to hire and fire people in his department, that he would not be involved with the debts incurred before he entered the new office, and he would control the flow of the money that went to and came from the Continental Government. Finally, he needed to ensure that Congress supported his efforts.

It took some time to work out the details. His Congressional opponents decried his "dictatorial powers." Today we call it executive authority. Morris held the upper hand because Congress wanted him more than he wanted the position. Finally, Congress accepted Morris' terms. On February 20th, he was officially and unanimously elected by Congress to the Office of Finance. This unanimity was achieved just as it had been for the Declaration: those who objected abstained. One of the two people to abstain was John Adams, that inveterate supporter of Arthur Lee.[4]

The Superintendent of Finance was the first American governmental executive to function on a "continental" scale. The War Department managed the Continental Forces; the Foreign Affairs department coordinated the diplomatic efforts, but everything required money. Morris used his understanding of finance and human nature to put the administrative wheels in motion that eventually brought the states together as a nation. There were many obstacles in his way, including prejudice, ignorance, secrecy, duplicity, misinformation; self-interest masquerading as virtue, and narrow parochialism. In other words, the typical political conditions prevailed.

The first entry into the *Diary in the Office of Finance* was an expression of Morris' thoughts on the offer to be Superintendent of Finance. His trepidation was almost palpable. He wrote:

> Received a letter from his excelly Samuel Huntinton Esqr. President of Congress enclosing their act of the 20th. Whereby I was unanimously elected the Superintendent of Finance of the United States of America. This appointment was unsought, unsolicited, and dangerous to accept, as it was evidently contrary to my private interests, and if accepted must deprive me of those enjoyments, social and domestic, which my time of life required and to which my circumstances entitle me; and a vigorous execution of the duties must inevitably expose me to the resentment of disappointed and designing men, and to the calumny and detraction of the envious and malicious. I was therefore, determined not to engage in so arduous an undertaking. But the solicitations of my friends, acquaintances, and fellow-citizens, a full conviction of the necessity that some person should commence the work of reformation in our public affairs by an attempt to introduce systems and economy, and the persuasion that a refusal on my part would probably deter others from attempting this work, so absolutely necessary to the safety of our country; - these considerations, after much reflection and consultation with friends induced me to write a letter to the President of Congress ...[5]

Morris maintained the proposition that an entity, the United States, had incurred a huge debt during the Revolutionary War, therefore it was up to the United States to pay that debt. As Superintendent of Finance, he worked to create a unified national economic system to meet that goal. However, Congress could not bestow upon Morris the authority required for the job, because they could not give what they did not possesses. They had to rely upon those holding the financial reigns, the states. Morris, however, had control over one thing, his department. That was where he began the long path to get the states to pay for a war their delegates had started almost five years earlier. He was aware of the fact that the old Treasury system cost more than it collected. He took a page from the playbook of the French Crown's finance minister, Jacques Necker, and one of his first official acts was to dismiss over one hundred and fifty of the political appointees who had been on the government payroll of the Treasury Board. This did not make him popular among those who favored the old system.

Once Morris was back in Continental service, it became necessary for him to reclaim his reputation from the damage it had received at the hands of the "Constitutionalists" in Pennsylvania. Morris wrote to his old ally, Charles W.F. Dumas, the U.S. agent in Holland,

> After serving my country in various public stations for upwards of four years, my routine was finished; and no sooner was I out, than envious and malicious men began to attack my character, but my services were so universally known, and my integrity so clearly proved, I have, thank God, been able to look down in contempt on those that have endeavored to injure me; and what is more, I can face the world with that consciousness, which rectitude of conduct gives to those who pursue it invariably.[6]

This was the same Charles W. F. Dumas who had been so badly used by the Lee brothers, and to whom John Adams later turned when he appealed to the Dutch for loans and official recognition of the United States. The Dutch government was fighting Britain, but in 1781 it was not yet ready to take an official position on American independence.

When Congress reached out to Morris, they did so because of his previous roles in managing Congressional finances, his expertise with naval matters, and his economic prowess. Morris did not need a government job. According to economic historian Barbara Chernow, "by 1781 Morris was the most influential merchant in the former colonies."[7] Morris' ability to influence events was directly related to his good reputation. His reputation was won through deeds. He had moved hundreds of thousands worth in goods for the war. As a private merchant, he helped supply Washington's Army when Congress failed. As an owner of privateer ships, he had the money to back up his word. He used his understanding of finance to get Pennsylvania out of bankruptcy. With his reputation intact, he could provide creditworthiness to the United States. Without it, he could not have conducted the business of his office. If the "Constitutionalists" of Pennsylvania had been successful in destroying Morris to the extent they intended, it would have been much more difficult, if not impossible, for him to accomplish his new task. He was asked to use his special skills, and knowledge, to bestow upon the United States "the Jewel of Public Credit."

Establishing "the Jewel of Public Credit" was critical because money had to be borrowed to pay for the war. It would have been impossible to restart the trading program, because of Britain's naval supremacy, and the slow nature of ships carrying bulk goods. Additionally, the American states were struggling to implement a failing pay-as-you-go method to fund the war through internal taxation, and the requisition of specific supplies. This approach had impoverished the states, and at the same time, it failed to meet the requirements of the Army. On the other hand, public borrowing was the source for war funding for England and all the great powers of Europe. Unfortunately, America had just ruined her credit. Morris had warned them, not to "lavish millions away by their own mismanagement,"[8] but back in 1777 Congress was unreceptive to that message. By 1781, an infusion of money was needed to pay for the continuing military efforts that would win the war. The "Jewel of Public Credit" was the key to borrowing that money, but that key had been thrown away in a flourish of righteous political rhetoric, and partisan fervor.

The only way to secure a loan has always been by assuring the lender that he will be repaid and rewarded. America had defaulted in the recent past, so this assurance had to be reestablished. The states had yet to pay requisitions, so there was no revenue. Morris realized he would have to substitute his own creditworthiness for America's; thereby rebuilding the latter based on his own. By closely associating his reputation with that of a bankrupt confederacy Morris put his fortune and sacred honor directly at risk. America had everything to gain, and Morris had everything to lose in this transition. If the nation failed to become worthy, the individual states would remain, but Morris would be brought down in the process.

In the eighteenth century, a person was judged by his ability to meet his obligations. This was particularly true in the merchant community, where fortunes were staked to the word of a buyer, seller, or broker. The risks of trade were too high to also introduce moral hazard into the equation. Merchants would simply not do business with a discredited individual. Morris had internalized these values. It was natural for him to extend this idea of personal and professional responsibility to explain the obligations of the nation, while he discussed America's willingness to borrow for the war, as well as the states' reluctance to pay for it. He said that if people had no proof the Government would pay its debts, then those people would have no faith in such a Government. He held governments to a higher standard than individuals, because the repercussions to a nation for having an irresponsible government would be far broader than the simple failing of an individual.

Morris said that a dishonest government would never be founded on "the solid basis of justice," by which he meant, "being just to individuals, to each other, to the Union, to all; Morris opined that once faith in the government and nation was restored,

> ...these States must expect to establish their Independence and rise into power, consequence and grandeur.[9]

Morris saw his job in the Office of Finance as laying the cornerstone of a just society upon which a great nation would be built. Localist politicians, who fought his programs, thought he was just interested in accumulating power; after all, that was their goal and they saw the political world in their own terms.

Spring

Congress had proposed the drafting of Articles of Confederation, and the Declaration of Independence on the same day back in 1776. Congress accepted the Declaration quickly, but it took over a year for them to pass the first form of a loosely knit multi-state government in November 1777. However, these Articles were not in effect until they were ratified by all of the individual states, a process that took until March 1st, 1781. That was four years and seven months after the war started. Obviously, the states were more willing to go to war with Britain, than to agree with one another in the pursuit of victory; an idea that was, at the time, being crushed on the field of battle.

Ratification had been held up over arguments about the Northwest Territories, even though the Americans did not control them. In 1781, the British still believed it was British land and filled it with their forts and soldiers. Nevertheless, states without a claim to those territories foresaw themselves taxing their inhabitants to pay for the war, and at the same time they thought the other states would pay for their share of the war by selling off land in these territories. States with interests in what became the Northwest Territory had been haggling over the fate of that vast area long before they held clear title to it. Squabbles over the contested region stretched back for decades; for example, allegiances to different land companies developing the Western Territories had been a cause for conflict between Arthur Lee and Franklin, while they lived in London in the late 1760's.

The expense of defending the western frontier mounted for Virginia, who claimed the largest part. Oliver Pollock did what he could to arrange funds for their efforts, but in 1781 Virginia finally ceded its claim to the Congress, and that broke the political logjam. The date of ratification was also a little more than a week after Congress acted to create the executive departments of Finance, Marine, and War.

By ratifying the Articles, the states agreed to send money to the Congress according to Congressional requisitions. Each year Congress determined a budget for the war, and each state was assigned its share as a requisition, to support the war. The size of these state payments was calculated using a formula based on the amount and value of land in each state. In keeping with the prevailing system, the value was based on the acreage itself, and on the improvements made to that land. By 1781, the states wanted adjustments because of damage to property caused by the war. This did not speed the payments of state requisitions.

The Articles provided for a very weak form of government, under which the Congress was an organizing committee representing the interests of independent states. Other than Pennsylvania, each state tended to be run by descendants of the same people who founded the colony over one hundred years earlier. The cultural differences between the states were real, well established, and continual. Those differences reinforced the economic, and the political ideas that worked to keep the states apart; for example, as described in *Albion's Seed* by David Hackett Fischer, there was little agreement about the definition of the "Liberty" for which they were all fighting. The New England states saw liberty as freedom to form a consensus, and to act within it. In the backcountry, Liberty was very individual and meant being left alone to do as they pleased. The Old Dominion saw liberty as freedom for the leaders to do pretty much as they always had done without outside interference; and this included their freedom to enslave others. For his part, Morris had internalized the values of the Quaker establishment that had run the state of Pennsylvania since its inception. Morris embraced the idea of reciprocal liberty based on the Golden Rule, which he extended to the relationship between individuals and the government. He described this approach when he said,

> That every operation which can have the slightest connection with public credit, ought to be conducted on the principles of equal and reciprocal Bargain; so that the object be performed with the perfect consent of the party, as well as of the Government.[10]

As Morris organized his administration, he knew he would need funds from all the states to pay for the war. This would require him to cement together the interests of many different states, people, groups, and cultures. The only way to overcome the existing multitude of perspectives and special cases was to create a single overarching system based on consistency, regularity and uniformity in process and conduct. That meant he had to make hard choices, affecting friends and foes alike. The policies he made were in accordance with policies set forth by Congress, and not the personalities involved. Morris' efforts to rationalize and nationalize American finances put him in direct conflict with men who had been friends, for example, Governor John Hancock of Massachusetts, and Governor Benjamin Harrison of Virginia. Morris prevailed to some degree, but their friendships were damaged. He also took the opportunity to invite participation from former critics, like David Rittenhouse and Thomas Paine. He acted without being vindictive as he moved his agenda forward, though it may have seemed otherwise to people who disagreed, or whose needs were great. At the height of his power, it was widely reported that he could move his vast political influence and personal wealth to destroy an opponent. Appealing though this myth may be, there is no evidence that he ever did.

Just as he embarked on his new role in government, Morris' past as an arms dealer, privateer owner, and a runner of the British blockade, were about to catch up with him. His acceptance of this executive office in the new Confederation coincided with a bold attack by the British on his commercial interests. On February 3rd, 1781, the British Navy made a direct assault on the Americans and Dutch when Admiral George Rodney, the British naval commander in chief in the West Indies, seized the Dutch island of St. Eustatius. St. Eustatius was called "The Golden Rock" because for years it had been a trading center for items and slaves going to the West Indies and South America. It had also been a politically neutral trading center used by American firms such as Willing, Morris & Co. in their efforts to avoid the British blockade. Many American merchant ships stopped there as they supplied the American forces with goods from Europe. Dutch neutrality had previously protected the island, but the obvious and vigorous trade that had been going on there was well observed by the British Navy. Henry Laurens' and William Lee's clumsy attempt at freelance, a.k.a. "militia," diplomacy, provided the pretext for British hostility toward the Netherlands, and it did not take long for the British to reach out with an iron hand. St. Eustatius was not well defended and quickly fell. British predation was severe. Goods of all sorts were taken. Warehouses, homes, churches and synagogues were ransacked; even graves were dug up in the search for treasure. They also found plenty of treasure from America, in the form of tobacco. Stephen Ceronio was a Willing, Morris & Co. agent who made frequent trips to that island.[11] Mr. Samuel Curson was there on a more permanent basis as a Secret Committee agent. He, and his compatriot, Mr. Isaac Gouverneur, who was stationed on Curaçao, were arrested and hauled off to an English prison in chains.[12]

On March 26, 1781 Admiral Rodney wrote to Germain,

> I may speak within bounds when I say that since taking this island upwards of two hundred thousand pounds[£200,000] in value of [American] tobacco has fallen into our hands.[13]

Admiral Rodney hid behind the Dutch flag to fool approaching American Ships. He reported that he took 150 vessels. It is unknown how many of these vessels belonged to Morris and his associates. Morris demurred when asked, because he did not want to seem to brag. Some estimates put Rodney's total take between £3,000,000 and £4,000,000 sterling, in 1780's currency. Morris refocused his Caribbean shipping efforts to Cuba.[14]

Morris took his losses and redoubled his efforts to win the war. His first priority was to support the Army in the field. His earliest decision was to pay only for the ongoing costs of the war, and to delay payment of past bills until the war was won. He knew that he could not afford to repay the old debts from the time before his administration, and also fund ongoing war efforts. This policy did not endear him to many debt holders who felt their special needs were worthy of greater consideration. He was constantly deluged with demands from individuals who wanted money. These supplicants frequently had wrenching and tragic private tales of misery, brought on by the failure of the government to pay its debts. Such pleadings weighed on Morris as he worked through his day, but he had to keep trying to get enough money to pay the interest on existing loans so new loans could be arranged. The years of incessant pressure of the office was so unremitting that it may well have been the cause for the suicide of one of Morris' clerks.

When Morris started out as Superintendent of Finance, the two most obvious sources of funds were taxes on Americans, and loans from Europeans. Unfortunately, in early 1781, the states were falling behind in their commitments, and Europeans expected America to fail. America's financial problems were well known in Europe, so people were unlikely to throw good money after bad. William Carmichael wrote from Cadiz about American credibility,

> ... what I have been able to collect from the Public Prints [papers]. It is the general opinion here and I believe in Europe that it will be impossible for the States during the war to retrieve the credit of their paper and of consequence that their military operation must become more languid every day.[15]

This apprehension in Europe meant that Americans would have to provide greater support for their own war.

The French had been helpful with loans to America during Morris' tenure in the Pennsylvania Assembly. Then they saw an advantage in supporting America because it was popular with the French people, and at the same time, America weakened Britain. The French continued their financial support until the Continental Congress declared bankruptcy in March 1780 and devalued the currency at the rate of 40:1. However, their level of active military support had long since declined as a result of the earlier tomfoolery in Pennsylvania, a few high-profile losses, and because British naval movements endangered the French island colonies.

Morris' appointment as Superintendent of Finance reinvigorated the Franco-American alliance. In an April 30th, 1781 letter, Alexander Hamilton wrote that the French once again believed the Americans were serious about winning, because Congress had put Morris back into a position of authority.[16] John Jay's wife was with Jay in France while her sister, Kitty, lived with the Morrises in Philadelphia. She wrote to Mary Morris that America's friends in Europe were glad to hear of Robert's appointment.[17] James Madison shared a similar view.[18] This flicker of optimism in Europe was based on the belief that Morris could revive American creditworthiness. They were counting on him to re-establish the American commitment to repay its debts, and for America to pay for its own war. Morris worked to do this by encouraging the creditors at home to support his proposals. He offered the idea that they would be paid if funding was arranged according to his nationalist plans. He reasoned that with support from the existing creditors, his plans could be realized, more money could be raised to win the war, and all the creditors would eventually be paid, even the ones in Europe.

Before a nation was deemed to be creditworthy it had to have a viable economy, but in 1781 the American economy was really the sum of thirteen failed state economies, and many of the available resources were being spent on the war. The states had to contend with enemy land forces, depreciating state currency, interstate trade restrictions, and the British blockade. As a result of these combined forces, the American economy had moved backwards into a primitive mode. The bankrupt condition of the local and the national economies resulted in the revival of a kind of barter system in America. In realization of this, and prior to Morris' arrival, Congress voted in favor of using "specific supplies" to equip the Army. Under this system, each state was required to supply products instead of money. Those products could have been hay, tobacco, wheat, beef, or even shoes.

Under the system of "specific supplies," materials for the Army were accounted for in a patchwork of arrangements. In one such case the Continental Army would buy items from a farmer with a Continental note. That farmer might hold on to the note or trade it for goods to a third party who then would want to redeem it, but these notes lost value over time. In another kind of deal, the state took supplies from a farmer as a tax, and then gave that farmer a state tax receipt. Then the state would make the Congress aware that the state contribution to the war effort should be reduced by the value of that tax receipt. The Congress had no way of knowing the real value of the goods, so disputes arose from these kinds of arrangements. By the time Morris arrived in office the farmers felt cheated, and the states felt they had done more than their share. While this system allowed the states to discharge their obligations, it was the source of much waste, fraud, and confusion. Even so, when the material was provided, it was often low in quality and many miles away from any army post or military hospital.

Long gone were the early days of the war; by the time Morris took office in 1781, the bloom had faded and the spirit of patriotic sacrifice had waned. The states sought advantage from the system of "specific supplies," and they were reluctant to part with hard money. They wished to get rid of surplus products, and to account for their contributions according to their own needs. Morris wanted a single system so he could avoid the inevitable conflicts that would arise when a bushel of wheat was sold to a neighbor for $1, and the same bushel was valued at $2 when it supplied the Army. To that end, Morris undertook the mammoth and thankless task of creating a unified financial structure for the entire Confederation.

Morris envisioned a sweeping transformation of the economy from one that relied on barter and state-controlled markets based on depreciating paper currency, into a national system based on free enterprise and hard money. A key step in realizing this vision was the creation of a protocol that would not allow for a thousand special cases, and instead would rely on one rule: the value of currency backed by silver. Morris intended to apply that rule broadly, so every individual would be treated in the same way, and thereby a form of economic justice would prevail. He reasoned that his approach, based on equality and reciprocity, would go a long way to reestablishing people's trust in the Continental government. However, that alone would not be sufficient. He needed all of the colonies to thrive. Unfortunately, a period of economic depression had settled upon the United States. This depression was a result of a variety of forces. Obviously, new trade patterns had to be created because the largest traditional trading partner was currently the enemy. Other than trade between the states, the most promising potential new partners were the existing European Monarchies. These were vertically integrated monopolies that controlled internal markets of their own, which they did not wish to disturb by opening their doors to unpredictable "free trading" Americans. In any case, when buyers could be found, conducting trade was highly risky with the naval blockade, British privateers, bad roads, and uncertain prices, but when unreliable state currencies were thrown into the mix, along with harsh winters, state embargoes and price controls, trade slowed to a crawl. After all, who would risk life and limb to deliver a load of flour, just to lose money because the currency had devalued, or possibly to be thrown in jail for breaking an embargo?

These were the conditions in the states at the time. One might think that the states would reconsider their policies in light of the near collapse of the Revolutionary War, and that they would look forward to taking a new path to success. Instead of cooperation from the states, Morris was faced with stiff resistance. In hindsight, it is not hard to see how Morris' sweeping economic reforms and the development of a federal funding system would be resisted by a set of states that saw themselves as sovereign countries. During this period, each state printed its own currency, collected its own import duties, had its own "gunboat navy," and levied its own taxes. Even so, it was not long before their state currencies fell in value, just as Pennsylvania's had. Morris was familiar with state currency problems; that was why he planned a system based on hard money.

Morris' insistence on this policy came from his experience as a merchant. Merchants favored hard money because it was useful at any port of call, just as it would be useful in any part of the Confederation. Before the Revolution, the colonial economies were somewhat closed, and tended to rely on paper money systems that consisted of fiat currency and land banks. These forms of money reinforced the value of real estate, and so were familiar to and favored by the descendants of the old fashioned English Country Party as it existed at the time in agricultural America.

A land bank was a kind of government-run mortgage system. For example, the Pennsylvania Assembly would offer loans to individuals. The individuals would put up their property as collateral. The land was effectively mortgaged to the state, and in return the owner got notes. The owner used the notes as currency to improve his land, pay debts and buy things, so they circulated as a medium of exchange. This was so successful in Pennsylvania, before the Revolution, that during some years there were no other taxes. The state made money because the interest payment was paid upfront with a discount, but the issued notes could not be cashed for years and were traded at face value. The present value of such a note would be about 40% of its nominal value upon issuance, so basically the state made 60% interest on the money lent.[19] Adam Smith had a low opinion of making people accept these notes at face value because it socialized the debt. In other words, a farmer who traded his wheat for such a note was not the recipient of the loan; instead he was taking on the obligation of the discount, in trade for goods that were 100% valued. No wonder the farmers were hard pressed while the state made money.

There was a second method: when a state printed money (fiat currency), and the paper was not backed by gold, or silver. It was theoretically backed by the state's ability to support the value with the taxes they received. However, unless the taxes were at a 100% rate, there would always be a difference between the paper currency that existed and the state's willingness to convert all the notes into gold and silver. That is why fiat currency always lost value.

By the time Morris was in the Office of Finance, the states saw a new benefit to paper money: its tendency to become devalued. This allowed debtors to repay loans with devalued currency, like paying for a $10 horse with ten fifty-cent dollars. Morris saw this as an injustice to the seller; the others saw it as a way of saving money. To protect their ability to pay with cheap currency, Morris' political adversaries were quick to associate his hard money policies with the monarchy of George III. They cast Morris' plans as not only being as oppressive as the King's, but also being the first step in establishing a new monarchy through the control of wealth. This resonated with many because the King supported much of his Empire with trade, and that trade relied on hard money. These people held thinking which Morris called "the genius & habbits" a few years earlier. What the adversaries did not mention was, their familiar colonial system was devised to keep them weak and to benefit England. If the United States were going to be strong enough to be free and independent, Morris figured, they needed to learn from a system that worked.

Morris had seen free markets work to the benefit of Pennsylvania. He considered economic freedom to be the means of releasing the great potential of America and advocated the end of state market controls. He put economic freedom on par with political freedom and sought to build a nation that relied on both,

> I ask no embargo, no regulations, on the contrary I wish and pray that the whole detestable Tribe of Restrictions may be done away,

> and the people be put in possession of the freedom for which they are contending.[20]

Morris was aware of difficulties ahead, so his mission as the Superintendent of Finance was focused on the one single point of agreement among the states. That was the prosecution of the Revolutionary War. Morris worked from this point to build a system that would be accepted by all. He offered an alternative to the system of "specific supplies," which was obviously not helping the Army. He offered to change that confused *ad hoc* barter scheme into an efficient system that worked to benefit the men in the field. He needed two things, money and a practical method of spending it.

The states were pledged to help the Continental Congress, but in practice, the states had sent Congress only about 5% of the money they had promised. Instead, the states were backing the war in a way that suited them, or as they said, according to their "ability." They provided for their own military movements within their state borders; for example, Virginia had used Oliver Pollock's help to underwrite their campaigns in their western territories. When states supported the Continental Army these "localists" sent money to their own troops within the Continental Line. This created unevenness and dissension in the Continental Army, as some soldiers were paid while others were not. It also undermined Congress' authority by making them look useless.

Morris reasoned that the voluntary nature of this system was encouraging the mutinies that had already happened. At the same time, it was ruining the Congress' ability to pay the continuing costs of the war and destroying American creditworthiness overseas. He believed that Congress needed a way to get funds that did not rely on intermittent, voluntary contributions from the states. The only way to accomplish this was to change the recently ratified Articles of Confederation and allow the Congress to collect taxes directly. Congress voted to pass an impost, which was an import tax that the Continental government would collect at the ports. Congressional action was not sufficient because, under the Articles of Confederation, all the states had to agree and allow the Congress to collect the tax without state involvement. State governments were reluctant to empower the Continental Congress to get that job done because that meant giving up some of their sovereignty, and income. They had declared, but not yet won, their freedom from Britain and were not in a hurry to give power to anyone else. They preferred to send "their share" of the debt to the Congress, according to a schedule of their own making.

Morris Notes & The Bank

Morris intended to create a bank as an integral part of his hard money program. It would be run, somewhat, like the new crop of banks sprouting up in Scotland and England at the time. The basic idea was to collect a suitable amount of silver, and then to issue notes based on the silver, and those notes would pass as currency among the citizens. The expected result was to expand the economy and provide a trusted medium of exchange for internal use as well as international trade.

On May 17th, 1781, Morris proposed the creation of the first congressionally chartered bank, The Bank of North America.[21] He proposed to sell shares to the public, and to capitalize the bank with $400,000 Spanish milled dollars. There would be twelve directors elected by the stockholders. There would also be inspectors who would report the Bank's business to the Superintendent of Finance. Naturally, there were those who didn't want the Continental Congress to charter a bank. Proponents of the bank, most of whom also favored the impost, noted that if the Continental Congress were to collect money with an impost it would need a place to put it. As part of the negotiations, Congress decided that as far as they were concerned, bank notes would have to be accepted only as payment for taxes to the Continental government, or as payment of duties.[22] This meant the bank notes were not necessarily legal tender so there was no compulsion for private individuals to accept them, even though many were happy to do so. The Government was still bankrupt while the organization of that institution was under way. On the 28th of May, the Congress passed the resolution and the bank was formed. This was done over the objections of Madison and some others,[23] who thought it was outside Congress' power to incorporate entities. They argued that the Congress was a committee, and not a sovereign entity; they feared creating a force beyond their control. The genesis of their fear can be found in the medieval history of British Country Party experience where the King incorporated towns to counterbalance the power of the lords and barons. The contemporary "lords and barons" in America were traditional landholders who did not want any interference in the way they ran their states.

For their part, the states considered their internal economic needs to be their most important responsibility, and besides, they claimed they had already sent more than their share to the Congress. Morris had to demonstrate to the states that each was being treated fairly by his office. He started an accounting of each state's inputs to the Continental treasury, balanced against the amount requisitioned from that state, according to the agreed framework under the Articles of Confederation. The states were willing to wait for this settlement to be completed before doing more for the Continental effort. It seemed to escape their notice that the war was not actually over at this point, and that doing nothing would lead to failure. Their apparent lack of concern was reinforced by the convenient misconception that foreign loans were paying for the war.

In addition to trying to gather money for the war effort, Morris had to control expenses, primarily by reining in military spending. He needed General Washington's help to reduce these costs, so they arranged an organizational meeting at his encampment near Dobbs' Ferry, New York. Before the meeting, Morris began reorganizing the supply system, and insisted that it must be designed to support the troops, not to exist for the convenience of the states. He started selling materials where they were not needed and using the money to buy supplies where the troops were actually located.

To overcome the wasteful system of "specific supplies" Morris moved ahead to make a radical change in military procurement. He borrowed the idea of military contractors from the British system and modified it. He planned to use the money, expected from the states, to pay private contractors who would fulfill the needs of the Army. These contractors were expected to win the government's business by competing within an open bidding system. He would make agreements to control costs because these contracts would be for specific amounts, and under the proper terms these would allow for deferred payments.

Before Morris' innovation, the Continental Government ran its own sprawling supply system with no financial controls. In one such case there was a "Continental Barn" which was supposed to be used to feed the "Continental Horses." To the dismay of one observer,

> The Horses after being worked to the Bone, become neglected because it is nobody's business to take care of them, the Feed is stolen, wasted and destroyed, because nobody can tell who is entitled to it, and who is not, every Officer in the service Crams his Horses into the Public Stables and calls him Continental, every Team that is hired and ought to find their own feed, say they are Continental and demand it as a right from the Public.[24]

Morris' new bidding system brought the cost of the war down by 60%,[25] and is still in use today throughout all levels of government in the

United States. What Morris did with these steps is turn the Government into a market, and suppliers into competitors.

An intended consequence of Morris' program was the creation of an interstate system that would bind together the economic interests of all states. In theory, when the contractors were paid hard money from the Continental treasury they would use the funds to buy produce from the local farmers and suppliers near the Army. Once the farmers and suppliers received cash, they would use some to pay taxes to their respective states. Once the states had collected the tax money, they could send their requisitions to the Continental treasury, which in turn would continue to pay the contractors according to the agreements. Without willingness on the part of all the States to tax for this purpose there would be no way to pay contractors, and the system would fail. This approach to creating a system of circulating hard money was the key step in moving away from barter and worthless state paper.

Morris knew that even though the states had not acted, there were currently thousands of soldiers in the field who needed food and supplies. He decided to hire the contractors as the first step in his program, and that the Continental Congress would have to be liable for payments, but they had no funds. Leading by example, he stepped into the financial breach and volunteered to use his own notes as a way to get the financial system going until the tax money came in. Once the Bank of North America was formed, he could use bank notes in addition to his own notes. Adam Smith wrote about the use of notes,

> When the people of any particular country have such confidence in the fortune, probity, and prudence of a particular banker, as to believe he is always ready to pay upon demand such of his promissory notes as are likely to be at any time presented to him; these notes come to have the same currency as gold and silver money, from the confidence that such money can at any time be had for them.[26]

Morris figured that once the states saw the advantages of hard money, and the benefit of growing free markets, they would enact taxes to support the continuation of the new system. After all, it was clear that the old system of specific supplies, had not, in actuality, resulted in materials being delivered to the Army. Instead, these goods were pre-positioned, and there they sat and spoiled in storage far away from any soldier or battle. There were many reasons for this waste. Primarily, goods such as flour, hay, and meat are bulky. In the 18th century, the volume and mass of the materials made their transportation difficult, even without a naval blockade. This was particularly true when it came time for supplies to go from New England to the battlefields of the South, where active fighting was still under way. Secondly, the nature of the militia system, favored by the States, made long range planning impossible because militias were called up in reaction to enemy movements. This reactionary nature made the location of any militia encampment unpredictable, at best. As a result, even if the right supplies were in the area, the chance that they would be at the exact spot they were needed was slim to non-existent.

Those who suffered the most were the soldiers in the Southern Division. In one letter, General Greene noted that some soldiers had so few supplies that they would not leave their tents because they were literally naked. Nevertheless, on March 15th, enough soldiers in General Greene's army did leave their tents to meet Cornwallis in the battle of Gilford Courthouse. After this General Greene wrote to Lafayette,

> We fight, get beat, rise, and fight again.... The whole country is one continuous scene of blood and slaughter.

Greene lost, but this was a pyrrhic victory for the British. When the news reached England, Charles James Fox exclaimed in Parliament,

> Another such victory would destroy the British Army.

After this battle Cornwallis withdrew to Wilmington, North Carolina.

A few weeks later, in April, General Andrews Pickens and Colonel Elijah Clarke started a military siege of Augusta, Georgia. Greene took his ragtag army into the backcountry of the Carolinas and proceeded to attack a series of forts that the British were using to occupy the territory. Near the end of the month, on April 25th, they met the enemy at the Battle of Hobkirk's Hill and lost. Greene's lack of success on the battlefield can be attributed, in part, to the lack of material support he received from the southern states within which he fought. These agrarian states were poorly organized to help General Greene; meanwhile, armies from both sides foraged, and waged war though the very farms and fields needed to provide food for the soldiers. At the same time, the barns in New Jersey and Maryland were full of produce, but there was no obvious way for Greene to utilize these resources because of the success of the British blockade, and the shortage of wagon teams.

Back in Virginia, Thomas Jefferson's term as Governor expired in May. He had been criticized for his lack of support for Greene's army, and resigned on June 1st. His state was still occupied by the British when he retired to Monticello. Peace was not found there. The British tried to capture the ex-governor at his home. Jefferson kept his freedom by escaping through a window, just five minutes in advance of General Tarleton's troops.

The British still held Augusta, Georgia. Fort Ninety-Six was across the Savannah River from that southern capital. In an effort to regain the city, the Americans began "The Siege of Ninety-Six" on May 22nd. It ended in Greene's retreat on June 20th, but later he returned and won the fort. Greene held the fort as militia leaders, Col. Elijah Clarke and Col. Andrew Pickens worked with Continental troops under "Light Horse" Harry Lee to take Augusta. Eventually it fell to the Continentals. This allowed Greene to break the British supply lines, and backcountry Georgia slowly fell into the hands of Greene's Southern Army.

While General Washington is credited with winning the Revolution with very few victories on the battlefield, General Greene excelled in turning defeat into a means of victory. He used his knowledge as a former quartermaster to attack British supply lines, and he forced the British to expend their supplies so rapidly that even though the British won the battles, they could not afford to hold the territory afterward. His efforts did break the British hold on the South and he eventually took the forts. The British were far from England and their supply system was stretched as much as, if not more than Greene's. He may not have won the battles, but he succeeded in splitting the British army and bottling them up in Charleston, South Carolina, and Wilmington, North Carolina. Guerrilla action against British regulars continued in the field; executed by the local militia under Thomas Sumter, and Francis Marion, "The Swamp Fox."

Back in Philadelphia, people had remade their lives during the two years following the British occupation. They were far from the fighting and it was springtime. That meant if Morris' wife Mary was not chatting with Kitty Livingston in the second-floor parlor of their home in Philadelphia, then she and the children were spending more time at the Hills overlooking the Schuylkill River, or perhaps visiting the Livingstons at Springetsbury.[27]

On June 12th, 1781, Robert's first daughter, eighteen year old Polly Morris, was married in Baltimore to Charles Moale Croxall. Morris had made sure Polly was well educated, and that she was seen as a suitable bride for a respected member of society. Charles was a member of the prominent Croxall family of Baltimore, and he had previously been in the

Continental army, but he had suffered at the hands of the British through years as a prisoner of war. There is no record that Robert attended the wedding, but he sent his well wishes later, at the arrival of their first child.[28]

Instead of attending weddings, Morris worked to reestablish American credibility. The French allies still had a dim view of American prospects. Just six months earlier, various members of the French court had investigated a separate peace with England, without the permission of the Crown. They were concerned over the cost of the war to France, the likelihood of failure, and they were not enthusiastic about a republic sprouting up in America. These people were more interested in a flawed peace that would stop France's financial bleeding, and would, at the same time, create future difficulties between England and her American colonies. One of those who supported a separate peace was Jacques Necker, the French Director General of Finance.[29] These secret dealings were unknown to Morris. Still, he did consider that France was not going to throw good money after bad, and that as an ally, France must have wanted to know what steps the new Superintendent would take to solve the fiscal mess that had nearly destroyed the nation before it was born. Necker was well known for streamlining the French treasury system through a series of economic steps which saved the king a lot of money.[30] Morris was about to do the same thing for America.

Summer

In a June 15th, 1781 draft letter to Jacques Necker, Morris set forth his views on the cause of and cure for the financial distress of the struggling country. The pace of communications from Europe made it impossible for Morris to know that Necker had been forced to resign nearly a month earlier because of his unauthorized peace overtures to England. Ultimately, Morris never sent the letter, but in this draft, Morris described the course of the American economy. He related that, initially, the states were accustomed to issuing short term notes, called "Country Paper Money," that were valued as gold or silver, and that this currency was backed up by their ability to collect taxes, but in some cases, it was backed by real estate.[31] After Independence was declared, Country Paper Money was still used, and it retained its values. Morris wrote that as time went on, the states fell under the influence of "projectors" who "insisted that they could dismiss the bad and practice the wisest systems of other nations ... to these projectors is to be attributed the Acts of Congress for stopping our commerce when we stood most in need of it, for laying embargoes on provisions until the want of a market prevented the raising of them, and the scarcity that ensued compelling the arbitrary measures of seizing private property for the substance of our Armies had nearly put the finishing stroke to industry and agriculture. In short I might give you a long list of those follies we have been guilty of from too high an opinion of our own Wisdom."

Morris went on to explain that Congress' Treasury Board had hired an excessive number of officers, but they cost more than they collected. After that, money was printed without any backing, and quickly fell in value to a point equal to the cost of printing the bills. He said, finally "the projects tried on this paper, tricks played with it, the injustice individuals were subjected to by it, all conspired to destroy the confidence of the people in their rulers." Morris continued and explained that the mismanagement of the economy was at an end, and the people of America were still rich in spirit, resources, and ability. He explained that his program would be to change the current direction and create,

> ... a free and open commerce, and unrestrained liberty of disposing of private property at the pleasure of the owner, a few wholesome laws, and the exercise of real economy in our expenditures will very soon, bring the minds of the inhabitants to cool reflection, encourage their Industry, and restore the necessary confidence to invigorate the measures of Government.[32]

In this, Morris outlined his program of economic liberty.

Morris needed to use all the means at his disposal to arrive at his goal. He was able to bring along two large assets when he went from his position in the Pennsylvania government into the Continental government: his title as Agent for the State of Pennsylvania and his control of £340,000 in Pennsylvania money, which was the amount Pennsylvania owed Congress as its requisition.[33] Morris combined these funds with his own reputation to generate an aura of wealth and credibility. It was said at the time,

> The State have made large assessments & placed their revenue in the hands of Mr. Morris.... His personal credit here, as well as in Europe, is very extensive.[34]

To these assets he adopted the role of booster and promoter of the United States, and he used his reputation as "richest man in America" to great effect during this period.

It has long been a matter of some disagreement whether or not Morris was actually the "richest man in America." Curiously southern planters with their multi-thousand-acre plantations, numerous houses, and hundreds of slaves are often mysteriously excluded from the competition, but ultimately what mattered was that his reputation served the important function overseas of boosting American credibility.

Summer had started, and Morris had yet to convince the state governments to cooperate in paying current expenses. That part of the task would wait, as he kept his attention on communicating with his counterparts in Europe. Much of the effort related to Morris' efforts to get silver into the Bank of North America from France and Spain.[35] Sending the secure letters abroad was, however, a challenge, so Major David S. Franks was hired in July to act as a trusted courier carrying dispatches to Franklin in France and Jay in Cadiz. Major David S. Franks, originally from Quebec, was not known to be related to the Tory merchant and slave trader David Franks who had left Philadelphia for New York in 1776.[36] Major Franks was instead a patriotic American soldier and former aide of Benedict Arnold, who had been cleared of suspicion by a through congressional review.

News of Morris' new position reached Europe, and on July 26th, 1781, Robert's old friend Ben Franklin wrote a letter of congratulations. With typical insight, Franklin was able to foretell the difficulties that lay ahead for Morris,

> I have just received your friendly letter of the 6th of June announcing your appointment ... the business you have undertaken is so complex in nature, and must engross so much of your time, and attentions necessarily to hurt your private interests, and the public is so niggardly even of its thanks. While you are sure of being censored by malevolent critics and bug writers, who will abuse you while you are serving them, and wound your character in nameless pamphleteers, thereby resembling those little dirty, stinking insects that attack us only in the dark, disturb our repose, molesting and wounding us while our sweat and blood are contributing to their substance....
>
> For besides my affection for the glorious cause we are both engaged in, I value myself upon our friendship and shall be happy if mine can be of any use to you.[37]

Franklin was just one of many Americans in Europe. Adams had gone back there; he was commissioned in 1780 to negotiate with the Dutch for loans. He was sent in place of Henry Laurens, who Congress first chose for the post, but who was subsequently incarcerated in the Tower of London. One of Henry Laurens' close associates, Commodore Alexander Gillon of the South Carolina state navy, was also in Europe. There he chartered the ship *South Carolina* from Chevalier de Luxembourg and promised him a share of the prize money, which the Chevalier never received. Gillon's misdeeds haunted American efforts in Europe for years to come. Adding to the difficulties, various state agents were attempting to procure supplies on non-existent funds, or to borrow money from European financiers, without collateral to offer. Elsewhere, Deane's former secretary, William Carmichael, was in Cadiz making steady progress in his cautious commercial dealings with the Spanish. There he acted as John Jay's secretary in America's mission, and Morris' commercial agent.

Silas Deane was back in Europe. He had been released from the public service and had gone there to find the documentation necessary to clear his name. During this time Deane needed money, and since Arthur Lee had convinced Congress that Beaumarchais had given free weapons to the Continental Army, it was impossible for Deane to get his commission for the deal.[38] Unfortunately for him, he was not able to find all the vouchers he needed, even though (or perhaps because) he had reconnected with his old secretary Dr. Bancroft,[39] who was still a British spy. His difficulties with Arthur Lee appeared to have weighed him down. Many of his contemporaries were led to believe that Deane ultimately sought help from the British ministry of Lord North. Most Americans thought North paid Deane to write letters to several leading Americans to convince America to quit the war. One went to Morris, and a copy went to a Loyalist in New York who made sure it was published in the press.

Thomas Paine told Morris that Deane's letters had been seen in the Press,

> I am very apprehensive they were written for the purpose of publication, and not with a design of being sent to the persons they were directed to.[40]

This did not endear Deane to Morris, and that did not speed the payments that Deane thought were due him.[41] From this point on, Deane was considered to be as much among the enemy as Arnold. Morris cautioned Deane not to return to America. Morris later wrote that he was very disappointed in Deane, and had no faith left in him. One has to wonder if Deane put his secretary, and British spy, Dr. Bancroft in charge of the letters' safety.

Back in America, financial efforts were coordinated by Morris at home, and Franklin in France;[42] diplomatic efforts were under the supervision of Congress, Franklin, Jay, and Adams. There was no Secretary for Foreign Affairs until August, so it occasionally fell to Morris to organize a diplomatic reception or party. He was also called upon to discuss naval matters and finances with the foreign ministers from France. He had a history of commercial relations with Spain and maintained an office in Cadiz. The Spanish Crown continued to be interested in the success of the American Revolution, but only up to the point that their stake in America was not put at risk. Many suspected that Spain wished to make the Gulf of Mexico into a Spanish sea by controlling all the land around it.

Morris put a good face towards Europe, still he had to contend with the unpleasant fact that the impost bill had been in the hands of the states for five months, and ratification was not in sight. He knew that aid from Europe would be possible only if the states agreed to pay their debts, so on July 27th, 1781, he wrote to exhort the Governors to pass the measure,

> In the moment when none others dared oppose Great Britain in her career towards Universal Empire we met her ambition with our fortitude, encountered her Tyranny with our Virtue and opposed her credit with our own.

Morris went on to make the point that even though the effort had gone well, it would go better if that credit were maintained by the willingness of the states to support the war by paying for it. Morris continued to say that an import tax would make domestic production more attractive, and reduce the consumption of *"foreign Superfluities,"* (a term that might be understood as a code word for slaves, among other imports). He pointed out that no vendor or customer would be favored because all who bought the imported goods would feel the effects of the impost equally. Next, he warned the Governors against interstate jealousies,

> It is a Truth that the Enemy does not even pretend to hope any Thing except from sowing discord among us.

Morris wanted the impost to bring the states closer together, not to fracture the delicate confederacy.[43] One of the problems he had to contend with was the tendency of states to have tariffs of their own. The impost would have cut into that form of state revenue, so the states haggled and delayed to protect their own interests. Morris tried mightily to advance a policy that he saw as necessary, even though that legislation would have harmed Morris' personal financial interests. It was not only a tax on imports, and he certainly was in the shipping business; but it also mandated a 5% tax on prizes taken by privateers, and he was involved in that as well.

While Morris was pressing the states for passage of the impost, the Army was in a quandary. In late July and early August 1781, Washington's army was encamped along the Hudson near Dobbs' Ferry, New York. The General was keenly aware that the troops, and Congress, expected him to use the army at his command, and that he had to take some form of action before winter set in. He and his French counterpart, Rochambeau, were considering an attack on New York City, which was just a few miles away, but they were expecting Lord Rodney to arrive there with his fleet.[44] They were also thinking about refocusing their joint efforts in Virginia, because much of the active fighting was in the South at that time. Washington wrote to Morris for information about how the troops might be moved to Virginia by water.[45]

While Washington cogitated, Morris was in Philadelphia. The many demands on his time had forced him to postpone the long overdue planning meeting that he intended to have with the Commander in Chief of the Army. Morris had an eye on expenses and wanted to cut military funding to a sustainable level. He needed to know what the future requirements of the Army were expected to be, so he, as "The Financier," could devise a way to meet those needs. He prepared for that eventuality by working on getting silver coins into Bank of North America. For this purpose, he sent the Continental Navy ship, *Trumbull,* down to Havana with flour, along with the bills of exchange backed by the promised French loan. The ship was supposed to return with Spanish milled dollars.

During this period, Morris continued a modified commercial relationship with the French Council John Holker, who was acting as a supplier to the French forces. Morris had been Holker's agent in 1778. When he became Superintendent, they formed a new company called Turnbull, Marmie & Co. Morris' role in this partnership was passive and he did not exercise operational control. Still, he retained his close association with the French Council. Morris was also in frequent contact with French ministers, Chevalier de la Luzerne, and Barbé-Marbois, as he maintained communication with America's best ally and largest backer, the French. This gave him access to information on French strategy and activity.[46]

Yorktown Campaign

On July 28th, Morris had a meeting with Minister of France, Chevalier de la Luzerne, "on the subject of my intended visit to [Washington's]

Camp which he urges strongly."[47] A week later, on the morning of August 6th, Morris met again with la Luzerne, and then in the afternoon he convened with the members of the American Board of War.[48] The next day, Judge Peters of the Board of War, James Wilson, and Robert Morris went together to Washington's headquarters near Dobbs' Ferry, New York. Col. Ephraim Blaine, from the Commissary General, joined them en route. They all went to discuss the reorganization of the Army and the next year's campaign.[49]

As they were traveling on the 11th, news reached Philadelphia that two days earlier, the ship *Trumbull* had been taken by the British Navy.[50] She had departed for Cuba at night to evade the blockade, but just when she was off Cape May, a summer squall suddenly came up and broke the ship's mast. *HMS Iris* then out-paced and captured her. The loss of the *Trumbull* represented the loss of one third of the Continental fleet, and a lost opportunity to get ready money to America. Morris and company arrived at Washington's camp on the 12th during the General's regular levee and took dinner with him that evening.

The next day, Gouverneur Morris was in the Office of Finance when he received a coded message from a ship that had just arrived in the port of Philadelphia. He sent "a letter to Mr. Morris with intelligence from Europe in Cypher" from the Office of Finance to Dobbs Ferry,[51] one day away for an express rider. Even though the letter was in code, it became known in Philadelphia on that day, that Sir Rodney and his ships were in possession of St. Eustatius, and that French privateers had captured at least thirty of the ships Rodney had loaded with loot and tried to send back to England.[52]

On the 13th, Morris and Peters held planning meetings with Washington to chart the course of the Army in regard to its needs for future campaigns. He wrote,

> Mr. Peters and myself had a long conference with the General... This conference branched out into various other Articles respecting departments, Expenditures, Oeconomy, &Ca &Ca and therefore was considered by Mr. Peters and myself as a general conversation.[53]

Morris followed this meeting with a letter to Washington, stating it would be impossible to rely on the states for many more soldiers or much more money for a new campaign. He suggested, for example, reducing the size of the officer corps by relieving the officers who were no longer in command of soldiers.[54]

General George Washington

On the following day, news from Rhode Island reached Headquarters in Dobbs Ferry. The French frigate *La Concorde* reported that instead of attempting to take New York by sea, Admiral De Grasse's fleet would leave Cape Français in Saint Domingue and be available to help the Americans in the Chesapeake area.[55] Washington was initially furious that François-Joseph-Paul de Grasse would not be available to help in the New York campaign. As Judge Peters put it, Washington was "violently exclaiming against the breach of faith on the part of the French admiral" when the commissioners left him. However, when they joined him again, a short time later, they found him calmly making notes and plans for the new campaign.[56]

Historian B.J. Lossing presented this discussion between Morris, Judge Peters, and Washington.

"'What can you do for me?' said Washington to Mr. Peters. 'With money, everything, without it, nothing,' he replied, at the same time turning an anxious look toward Mr. Morris.

> "Let me know the sum you desire," said Mr. Morris; and before noon Washington's plan and estimates were complete. Mr. Morris promised him the amount, and raised it upon his own responsibility.[57]

Washington wrote to de Grasse,

> In consequence of the dispatches received from your Excellency by the Frigate *La Concorde* it has been judged expedient to give up for the present the enterprise against New York and to turn our attention towards the South.

He let de Grasse know they would meet in Virginia.[58] It seems that with de Grasse available to cruise the Chesapeake, and Rodney unavailable to reinforce the English in America, the decision was made to go South.[59]

Morris was back in Philadelphia a few days after the fateful decision was made. On August 16th he met with the French leadership to discuss logistics and supplies for the movement of both Armies to Virginia. The new southern campaign was not the only business at hand. He encountered, among the French, a mood similar to that found elsewhere in the wake of Mr. John Holker. Jean-Baptiste Rochambeau and his staff were unhappy with Holker's treatment of them because they thought he was overcharging them. Morris had to calm their concerns. He said,

> I took occasion to explain the same and assure them over and over of what I do most sincerely believe, vizt. That Mr. Holker is as honest a man and zealous for the King's service as any that ever came from France.[60]

Morris was not about to undermine the credibility of a business partner; however, he used his position as Superintendent of Finance to provide the French with further assurances. As the Financier he was able to supply the French without charging a commission for his services, unlike Holker, and he was able to provide American farm products to the French Navy and Army. As unofficial quartermaster to both the French and American forces, Morris could avoid competition from French agents for scarce resources. Morris told the French,

> I would not undertake this business unless the affairs of the Navy as well as the Army were put under my direction otherwise I should assume much trouble and fatigue for the service of one part of the force without effect as the affairs of the other would operate to overset my plans.[61]

Instead of directing the French leadership to purchase from his own business partner, Holker, Morris undertook to reduce the expense of the goods and supply them at cost through the Office of Finance.

When Morris originally took his office as Superintendent, he declared he would not act as quartermaster to Washington's army, however when the chips were down, he reversed himself. As Washington's Army moved south, Morris acted as unofficial quartermaster for both the American and French forces. He arranged supplies and transportation as Washington's troops marched towards Maryland, and as they traveled by water from Maryland to Virginia.[62] Before Washington's arrival in Philadelphia he wrote to Morris about their mutually formed plan,

> I have in confidence imparted to you the alteration of our late plan and made you acquainted with our intended operations... it will be necessary to give the American Troops destined for southern service one month's pay in specie.[63]

Robert worked to arrange that payment.

When the Army passed through Philadelphia, Washington used Morris' Dock Street home as his headquarters.[64] This was for security purposes. In offering his house Morris said,

> ...too many people have for some days past seemed to know Your Excellency's intended Movements.
>
> This city is full of strangers, so that Col. Miles cannot procure private lodgings, and my Family being at Springetsbury, affords me the Opportunity of appropriating my House in town for your use.[65]

During Washington's stay, Morris met again with the French leadership. With them he made initial arrangements to meet Washington's request for transportation. After the Army left the city, both Robert and Gouverneur Morris rode down to Chester and met Count Rochambeau with the news that the French Fleet had arrived in the Chesapeake Bay. There, Morris arranged with the Count to borrow the hard money needed to pay the soldiers according to Washington's request, and pledged to back the new loan with his personal credit.[66] Next, Morris arranged for the deputy paymaster, Philip Audibert, to distribute the "one month's pay in specie" (silver) when it arrived.[67] The French did not have the silver on hand, so it had to be brought by de Grasse's Fleet, which was stationed in Rhode Island at the time.

While Washington's army was on the move, the Morrises returned to Philadelphia, where Robert continued to run the Office of Finance. In the latter part of August, he wrote to raise specific supplies from Delaware to feed the troops. He also worked with Haym Salomon to convert the funds lodged safely in French banks in France, into ready money for use in America. Salomon worked as an independent broker who sold bills of exchange for both the French, and for Morris' office. In this particular case, they had to replace money expected from the sale of the bills lost during the capture of the *Trumbull* on the night of August 8th.

Most of the activity of the Government came through Morris' office in one way or another because nearly all aspects of government require money. It was hard to come by, but that did not stop people to whom money was owed from seeking it. Morris wrote,

> A thousand Applications, and my Refusals, for Money which become very troublesome and disagreeable to me; the Parties ought to have their just Right, but it is not in my power to give them any relief.[68]

Morris regretted not being able to pay the amounts due, so he continued his effort to convince the states to pay their shares. Unfortunately, each state awaited the settlement of their states account before contributing more. Morris wrote,

> ... until it [settlement] be completed the States will persuade themselves into an opinion that their exertions are unequal. Each will believe in the superiority of its own efforts, Each claim the merit of having done more than others, and each continue desirous of relaxing to an equality with the supposed deficiencies of its neighbors. Hence it follows that every day they become more and more negligent."[69]

The pressures were great, and the expectations were high as well. At this early point in his tenure Morris had the support of Congressmen, even from Samuel Osgood from Massachusetts, who wrote about the expected financial settlement,

> I have no doubt but Mr. Morris will render us great service, and I hope we shall use our utmost endeavors to support him.[70]

While Morris was scraping together every dollar he could find to support Washington's trek south, he encountered interstate jealousies that made him long for a more national system. The states used the slow process of settling their accounts to put off making payments to Congress. Some worked to delay the process and took years just to appoint a commissioner. There is irony in the fact that the states fought this effort as a way to protect their sovereignty, because in so doing they increased the financial pressures that ultimately pushed them together. The settlement Morris started was meant to determine the size of expected State contributions under the Confederation requisition system, but little money was immediately forthcoming. However, years later, the amounts resulting from the settlement process became the center of the 1789 debt assumption argument that took place during the Washington Administration. It finally turned out that Hamilton's Treasury Department assumed responsibility for the money owed by states. That became the glue holding American finances together during the first years of Government under the new Constitution, and part of the deal that resulted in the creation of "The Federal City," Washington, D.C.

While Washington's army was on the march, events in Europe moved at their own pace. Morris' friend and commercial agent in Spain, William Carmichael, wrote to tell Morris that the Armed Neutrality, designed by Catherine the Great to protect neutral shipping, was useless. He added in a positive note that the English loss of Pensacola to the Spanish was cheering Europe. He continued that the French gains in India, and the presence of the French Navy around the British coasts were keeping them on their toes around the world. He rounded off his letter by saying that even though Spain had many pleasures to offer, "I pine now and then for Mr. Morris' society, corn beef and Madeira."[71]

The Armed Neutrality was supposed to be a way to protect neutral ships from the privateers in European waters. The policy stated that goods and ships that were not involved in the conflict must pass without harassment, but if they were attacked, the neutral nations would defend their ships. This worked against American interests because the English started shipping their supplies on the ships of other nations, which America could not attack. America shipped goods only in its own ships. Morris explained,

> The British will not adopt the same rule. Consequently Neutral Ships cannot protect American property against British capture, although Neutral Ships will cover British property against American Capture.[72]

The Empress of Russia eventually conceded that the Armed Neutrality was not working as intended.

On August 28th, 1781, Morris wrote to Franklin that he was eagerly anticipating the arrival of Lieutenant Colonel John Laurens and his ship carrying the silver from France.[73] Morris thought he might use some of this silver to repay the French for the money he had borrowed and used to pay the American troops.[74]

Clearly, coordination with the French Navy was needed to get Washington's men from Elkton because Continental Naval affairs were in disarray at the time. Administratively, the Naval Committee of 1775 had given way to the Marine Committee. The Marine Committee held operational control of the Navy until 1779 when the Board of Admiralty took over. The Board of Admiralty organized naval matters for about eighteen months, but in the end failed to take action due to lack of a quorum. Congress created the executive office of the Agent of Marine in February 1781, but they were slow to fill the position. The position had been offered and refused at least once, and it soon became clear that the executive who filled it would have to have command of the Navy itself, not just have responsibility for it. While the office was being reconfigured, the Navy continued to operate under the Board of Admiralty, Continental Agents, and state navy boards. It became apparent that Congress was courting Morris for the role during this period. On June 28th, Congress dissolved the other boards, and after a series of small steps, they gave more and more authority over naval affairs to Morris.[75] In August 1781, John Brown, of Pennsylvania, stepped aside as Secretary of the Board of Admiralty to make way for his former employer, and sponsor, to take over naval affairs. Morris asked for and was given authority for executive action by Congress. Anticipating the expected formal action by Congress, Morris enlisted John Hancock, John Bradford, and Tench Francis to get the existing vessels to sea; and sent cruising orders to Captain John Barry. Thusly, Morris got the *Deane* sent out under orders, and prepared the *Alliance* for service. He also urged Congress to supply funds to finish the seventy-four-gun ship *America*.[76]

On September 7th, Morris became acting Agent of Marine by an act of Congress.[77] The office was analogous to the modern office of Secretary of the Navy. There is a great difference, however. In 1781, the Continental Navy consisted of only two useful ships, the *Deane* and the *Alliance*. There was a third ship, *America*, under construction. It had languished in the Portsmouth boat yard, unfinished. There was a fourth, *The Bourbon,* which was also incomplete, and she sat in a Connecticut boat yard. A fifth was later discovered in Massachusetts; and in 1784, a sixth was found in a similarly useless state near Poughkeepsie, New York. These last two had been ordered in 1776 and never completed. There were so few seaworthy ships, that Morris decided running the Navy would not be a full-time occupation requiring a complete department. He claimed that saving money was his main reason for taking this position. Morris recalled, "I accepted the Marine Agency simply with a view to save the Expense of the Department." He took on the role of Agent of Marine; but did not collect any salary for the position. Even so, considering his experiences with the Naval Board back in 1777, being able to use the Navy as he saw fit, without the influence of other parties, may have been a net positive in his mind. He was authorized to "fit out and employ all Continental ships of war 'in such a manner as should appear to him best calculated to promote the interest of these United States.'"[78] Morris commissioned John Brown, of Philadelphia, to go to Boston and straighten out the Naval Accounts.

Morris, as Agent of Marine, continued to be in charge of the administration of naval affairs until after the end of the war. These duties included being a point of contact for navies of other countries, command of the small American fleet, supervising the administration of naval justice, including dealing with British citizens who had been captured at sea, the distribution of Letters of Marque and Reprisal, and the settlement of prizes.

September 7th was also the day Robert Livingstone was appointed Secretary of Foreign Affairs. A friend wrote to congratulate Livingstone, and in that note he also indicated Morris was moving his family into their new house at 190 High Street,

> No body is better pleased with your Promotion to the office of Secretary for foreign affairs than his Lady [Mary Morris]. It is on her hint that I mention that there is a house opposite to Mr. Morris' intended residence.... It is large enough for your family conveniently & healthfully situated; Conveniently because it is near the State house, Financier's, & French ministers-Healthily because it is in a high & open part of the Town ... Mrs. Livingston's Comfort will be much promoted by the neighborhood of Mrs. Morris, as she has no Friend who will pay her more attention. She interests herself deeply in your making the purchase as she assured me this morning at breakfast.[79]

The Morrises set up their household and entertained a great number of dignitaries in a style all their own.

> Dinner company, well chosen, frequent, and elegant, was the style of the time. It was in this style that the home of Mrs. Morris was distinguished. Besides its essential household of table-servants, coachmen, footmen, &c., her establishment had its housekeeper, butler (a fine old Frenchman named Constance), its confectioner, and all the retinue of a mansion in which dinner company is frequently and elegantly entertained. Unlike most of the menial servants of that day, in Philadelphia, Mrs. Morris' were all white, and they all wore the Morris livery.[80]

-|-

Back in 1780, nearly five thousand Americans, including General Lincoln, had been captured in the surrender of Charleston, South Carolina. In 1781, many of those leaders were released from their New York captivity as a result of negotiations between British and American authorities. General Lincoln went to New York to serve with Washington, but others applied to Congress for money to pay for their return to the South. Congress quickly instructed Morris to make funds available for this.

Congress wanted to give each of the newly freed captives hundreds in hard currency and free transportation. Morris saw this as an opportunity to get much needed funds to General Greene and his starving army. He suggested that once the former prisoners got home, this money should be repaid as part of South Carolina's war finance effort. This was done, and when these gentlemen returned to the South the money was sent to George Hall, tax receiver for S. Carolina. He, in turn, gave it to General Greene, thus refreshing the army before the critical Battle of Eutaw Springs, on Sept 8. The Battle of Eutaw Springs was among the bloodiest battles of the war. General Nathanael Greene drove the British forces from South Carolina with the help of Anthony Wayne, Harry (light horse) Lee, and the militia commanders. After the loss, Cornwallis and the bulk of the British force went from the Carolinas to Yorktown, Virginia.[81]

The lack of support for the Southern Division by the Southern State governments, the minute trickle of funds for state remittances, and the reluctance of the states to pass the impost, as Congress had requested, all contributed to this expression by Morris in a letter to General Greene,

> That more power ought to be given to Congress is evident now to many, and will probably become soon very apparent to all. The disobedience [to Congress] of many states, and the partial obedience of others, discontents every one of them; and that will, in itself, be a reason for enabling the sovereign representative to exact a compliance with its requisitions, but as you observe all these things are in the womb of time…[82]

Morris worked to aid the Army as it moved south,

> I have been obliged to advance to the Paymaster Genls. Department all the money I had to complete the payment of a Months pay to the troops under Genl Lincoln.[83]

Morris concentrated on raising funds to pay to get the Continental Army to Virginia, and on directing Continental finances close to home. This would be difficult in the best of times, but the conditions were dire. Still, the interruptions never stopped. He wrote in the Office of Finance diary,

> It seems as if every person connected in the Public Service entertain an opinion that I am full of money for they are constantly applying even down to the common express Riders and give me infinite interruption so that it is hardly possible to attend to business of more consequence.[84]

The movement of an army is difficult to keep secret for long. After the British learned that Washington's Army was on the move south, they spread the rumor that the British might attack Philadelphia again in order to divert the attention of the Continental Congress. Morris commented on that rumor,

> Sir Henry Clinton threatens an attack on Philadelphia, by way of diversion, in favor of Lord Cornwallis; this has a little intimidated some few ladies of my acquaintance.[85]

He was referring to the timorous members of Congress and the Pennsylvania Assembly.

While the final large battle of the war was in the making, Congressional behavior caused alarm in Europe. Franklin became concerned that Congress was once again about to ruin American credit. Just as France had regained enough confidence to send silver to America, Congress resolved to draw on the credit of the Minister at Versailles, "funds or no funds," and there were none.[86] Franklin refused to cooperate with this. Congress was again trying to spend money it did not have. Even so, Morris was able to apportion a small amount of supplies and provisions for the Oneidas, America's only native ally within the Six Nations.[87]

Morris was looking for a long-term cure for America's economic ills, so he kept working to capitalize the bank. Unfortunately, the sale of shares in The Bank of North America was going very slowly. There was little money in the North, and less in the south where much of the military action was underway. The available funds there supported the militia. There was meager support for the Southern Continental Army, and less for a far away and very controversial bank.

In the midst of this activity, Morris took the time to assist individuals. He wrote to General Washington in favor of a *"Romish"* young man who was a friend of Thomas Fitzsimmons. This man had been convicted of desertion and sentenced to death. Washington granted him clemency.[88] Morris also tried to encourage General Gates to overcome the mortification he felt from his defeat at Camden and to rejoin the war effort. In what looks like a practical guide to Morris' own philosophy, he told Gates,

> Repair to the busy scenes of the world, call loudly for the Justice you think your due, insist on being heard, and appear again a champion for fresh Laurels and renewed Glory.[89]

Gates ignored this advice and stayed on his plantation, stewing.

Morris put aside old disagreements and reached out to Thomas Paine, whom he had characterized as writing, "Common Sense and other performances." Morris understood that Paine's popular writing style could be put to use and

> ...proposed that for the Service of the Country he should write and publish such Pieces respecting the propriety, necessity and utility of taxation as might be likely to promote the public service of America.[90]

While he tried to galvanize public opinion to favor the funding plan, he worked to get Captain John Barry to sea. He trusted Barry to harass the enemy, and he needed only to give the Captain the broadest outline of the mission.

> It is my Intention that you should go upon a Cruize and therefore you will when ready sail from the Harbor of Boston and use your best efforts to distress the enemy ... I do not need to fix your cruising ground nor limit the length of the cruize because I expect you will know the most likely course and will be anxious to meet such events as will do honor to the American Flag.[91]

He delegated management of naval affairs in Europe to Franklin.[92] Franklin used Morris' commercial connections in Nance, Cadiz, New Orleans, Gibraltar, and Martinique as key resources for the American cause. These contacts proved to be quite useful when the American merchant ship, *The Aurora,* and her crew were captured by the Brigands in their Algerian Corsairs and held in North Africa as slaves. Morris' Gibraltar agent, and Franklin in France, conducted successful ransom negotiations for the crew. Unfortunately, the ship was lost.[93]

West View of Gibraltar by John Mace (1782)

Clearly, one of the challenges Morris faced was to raise a credible naval force to counter the growing British Navy. During the year 1781, the number of vessels of all classes in the British navy increased from 538 to 551.[94] It was impossible to expect a bankrupt nation to buy and launch a competitive Navy, so the merchant community was brought into the action. Five hundred fifty Continental letters of marque and reprisal were issued to private armed vessels in 1781, even more were issued by state governments. This was a much larger number than in any other year and an increase of 249 over the figures for 1780.[95]

The army had its militia and citizen soldiers. The Navy had privateers. This "Privateer Navy" focused its energy on the British merchant fleet. At one time, there were as many men under sail in the service of America, as there were men at arms in the field. Privateers were used to attack British commercial interests at sea and prosecute the economic war against Britain, one of the world's great trading nations. These men fought the American Revolution as an economic war, which it was, as well as a military and political one. In the meantime, the English were turning their merchant fleet into privateers as well. As a result of these two factors, British shipping slowed so much in 1781, that early in 1782 the leaders of Liverpool petitioned King George III for peace with the Colonies.[96] One casualty of this economic battle at sea was the British slave trade; so, before Britain officially ended their slave trade in 1834, this was the only time British slave ships had not gone to or left from Africa since the concessions were won from the Dutch in the 1600's.

One privateer ship that sailed out of Philadelphia in 1781 was the *Royal Louis.* She had a complement of 200 sailors, 20 of whom were free Blacks. The majority owner of record was Stephen Decatur. Decatur's privateering was a sign of the times. It showed that in 1781 opportunity was the guiding force behind action: that self-interest was in the national interest and that there was a possible reward for all who participated. On her first cruise, *Royal Louis* seized a British Naval brigantine as a prize. It was unusual for a privateer to go after naval vessels, so there was great jubilation when the *Royal Louis* came home with a British warship under its lee. The second trip did not go as well, and she was taken in a skirmish with three ships, the *Amphylon,* a British frigate, and two other warships. Among the crew was

James Forten

James Forten, who at the age of 15, was a powder boy on the American privateer. He had been a drummer boy for the Army, but serving on a privateer meant a share in the prize money, and that was one of the few ways people could improve their economic situation during the Revolution.

After the Revolution, James Forten bought the sail loft where he worked, and to do this he borrowed money from Morris' former business partner, Thomas Willing. Forten's sail loft became the most prosperous in Philadelphia, and James Forten became the richest African American in the nation. He used his wealth and position to support the abolitionist movement. Perhaps a future historian will investigate how many sails Morris' shipping companies bought from Mr. Forten's sail loft.

Some modern historians evince disdain for the privateers because the privateers made money in the fight. This odd aversion overlooks the obvious facts that the men in the army also expected to be paid; and held out for large "enlistment bounties." These sneering hindsighters forget that the private ships cost money; that men need to be paid to leave the safety of home and hearth; and that the chance of riches was just one of many motivations luring men to the sea during wartime. In any case, many captured privateer sailors spent years awaiting the end of the war in England's Mill Prison.

Back on land, the armies under Generals Washington, Lincoln and Rochambeau were still making the long trip from Dobb's Ferry, New York, to Elk, now Elkton, Maryland before going to the Yorktown peninsula in Virginia by sea. Washington wrote Morris,

> I have written to Count De Grasse and have requested him to send up his light vessels of every kind to Elk, but I would never therefore wish to have all that may be at Baltimore and the upper parts of the bay summoned. I shall therefore be obliged to you to take measures at a proper time for the purpose. When that time will be and when you shall give orders for the deposit at Elk I will hereafter inform you.
>
> I shall order the Quarter master in due season to take up all the small craft in Delaware for the purpose of transporting the troops from Trenton to Christiana. Should he have reasons for advice or assistance from you upon this occurrence I must request you to give him both.[97]

That was how Morris was asked to look after the transportation of the troops, and that meant coordination with the French Navy, American sea craft on the Chesapeake, and the arrival of the American and French Armies at the Head of Elk. First, Morris moved ahead to aid the French fleet by finding the best pilot in the Chesapeake; a man who was familiar with the coasts of Virginia, the Carolinas, and Georgia. He arranged for that pilot to accompany the Chevalier de La Luzerne.[98]

All the while, Morris received daily calls for cash from suppliers and officers. Much of his time was spent arranging the payments he could manage, often for amounts as low as £35 or £150. He focused on the tiny details of covering the continuing commitments of the United States in his efforts to supply Washington's army deployment to Yorktown. This gave the impression that he would continue to oversee the military supply system. He arranged flour, meat, wood, clothes and rum for the troops in different garrisons in different states. These requests came to him because he held the ability to pay, but while he helped, he also directed that the supplicants go through the quartermaster department.

Battle of Virginia Capes, 1781 by V. Zveg

From September 5th to the 13th, the Second Battle of the Virginia Capes was conducted in a series of engagements between the French and British Fleets. This battle was fought at and near the mouth of the Chesapeake Bay, just as Washington's army was moving south. This sea battle allowed Comte de Barras to slip a small group of French ships into the Bay with French siege cannons onboard. These cannons were later used in the Battle of Yorktown. Once inside the Chesapeake Bay, the French ships carried Washington's troops from "the Head of Elk" Maryland, south to Virginia. The rough treatment the British Navy received at the hands of the French fleet caused them to withdraw to New York City at this critical juncture. The English captains seemed oblivious to the movements of the two armies, while at the same time, their expected reinforcements had been otherwise occupied on the island of St. Eustatius.

Lord Rodney had finished his plunder of St. Eustatius. He had stayed on the island for months, seizing so much property and so many ships that he sent them back to England in a series of convoys. Rodney had been so busy looting St. Eustatius and seizing ships that he sailed back to England before he could intercept Comte De Barras and his cannons. He was unaware that French Admiral De Grasse's ships were on their way to Virginia from Saint Dominique. Instead of helping Cornwallis, who was left waiting in Yorktown for assistance, Rodney returned to England with the last of his booty.[99]

Unfortunately for Rodney, his convoy of treasure ships were, in turn, seized by the French before they arrived in England.[100] When Rodney finally arrived home, King George III refused to see him. Rodney had to answer to Edmund Burke in the House of Commons.[101] Ultimately France retook the island and gave it back to the Dutch, Rodney was sued in court by non-combatants for their losses.

Edmond Burke characterized Rodney's behavior as

> ... a general confiscation of all the property found upon the island, public and private, Dutch and British; without discrimination, without regard to friend or foe, to the subjects of neutral powers, or to the subjects of our own state ; the wealth of the opulent, the goods of the merchant, the utensils of the artisan, the necessaries of the poor, were seized on, and a sentence of general beggary pronounced in one moment upon a whole people.[102]

After De Grasse's French Fleet brought the silver coins Morris had borrowed, they were unloaded and sent to the paymaster to pay the troops. The paymaster, Audibert, sent the order for the kegs of money to be put into wagons and the lids broken open so the troops could see the silver pieces. This raised the morale of the American troops. While the French were present, the support of the Spanish Crown was also critical to the battle of Yorktown. Spanish ships protected the French Caribbean colonies, allowing the French Navy to help the Americans.[103]

After much heroic action, including Colonel Alexander Hamilton's charge over the British defensive wall, the Battle of Yorktown was won on Oct 19th. Still, the War was not over. On the topic of bringing about the "miracle" of the Yorktown campaign, Morris said, "I advanced not only my credit, but every shilling of my own money, and all which I could obtain from my friends, to support the important expedition against Yorktown."[104]

Judge Richard Peters wrote, years later in 1818,

> The expense of provision for and pay of the troops, was accomplished on the personal credit of Robert Morris, who issued his notes to the amount of $1,400,000, which were finally all paid."[105] He continued, "It may be truly said that the financial means furnished by him [Morris] were the main-springs of transportation and supplies for the glorious achievements which effectively secured our independence, and furnished the foundations for the present prosperous and happy condition of our nation.[106]

Surrender of the English Army commanded by Mylord Comte de Cornwallis to the combined armies of the United States of America and France under the orders of Generals Washington and Rochambeau to Yorktown and Glocester in Virginia, October 19, 1781 by Mondhare.

Autumn

By the middle of October, nearly eight months since the formation of the Office of Finance, Morris observed that the cost of the war was about $20,000,000, but during his tenure he had received only $750 dollars from Pennsylvania and nothing from any other state. With so little income, he looked to control the debt situation. Morris requested that the unissued loan office certificates be sent back to Philadelphia. This action resulted in the unpleasant discovery that some of the former Treasury agents had been paying the interest on old loan office certificates with new loan office certificates. Morris was horrified and ordered an end to that practice.

Morris' experiences in trying to gather money for the Battle of Yorktown, and the low rate of voluntary state remittance, led him to send a second appeal for funds to each governor. In this "Circular to the Governors of the States" he attempted to focus the minds of the state governments, so everyone saw the situation in the same way. The first thing he did was to dismiss the false notions that were commonly held, notably that there was plenty of money coming to America from all over Europe.

> People have flattered themselves with a visionary idea that nothing more was necessary than for Congress to send a Minister abroad, and immediately he would obtain as much money as he chose to ask for.

He asked, why would they want to give us money? And answered, they did not. Sending money into a war zone was much riskier than a safe investment at home. He explained,

> ...could it be imagined that the disorders necessarily incident to a great Revolution would be considered as a better source of trust and confidence than the regularity and consistency of ancient establishments?[107]

He continued that there was just $1,000,000 left in the treasury, and that the French expected Americans to participate in paying for their own liberation. He was worried about the kind of national character that was developing when he wrote, "While we do nothing for ourselves we cannot expect the assistance of others" and that finances were so bad that, he said,

> The neglect of funding the public debt, had introduced the practice [by former treasury board officers] of issuing Loan Office Certificates for the interest due on other Loan Office Certificates. This is absolutely forbidden, nor will I ever consent to it.... This would be such a fraud, as would stamp our national character with indelible marks of infamy, and render us the reproach and contempt of all mankind. It is high time to relieve ourselves from the infamy we have already sustained, and to rescue and restore the national credit. This can only be done by solid revenue... By the bounty of the Almighty we are placed in a situation where our future fate depends on our present conduct. We may be happy or miserable as we please. If we do our duty now the War will soon be brought to a close...nothing more is necessary than a proper system of taxation.[108]

Morris pointed out that the enemy was hoping the poor financial condition of America would cause the Revolution to fail. He proposed as a cure, the establishment of the Bank of North America combined with the willingness of the states to pay taxes to the Continental Congress. This way, he argued, the Congress could pay for the war. The response by the Governors was tepid. On October 17th Morris wrote to Washington on this reaction,

> I do not perceive in the States a desire to furnish revenue; on the contrary there is a degree of torpor and lukewarmness which nothing can justify.[109]

The states were simply implementing a technique on Morris that they had used in the years before the Revolution against royally appointed Governors. They were well versed in the art of starving the executive branch.

Morris used the few remaining funds at his disposal to capitalize the new bank. He used money from the Bank of Pennsylvania to buy shares in the Bank of North America. This made Pennsylvania a shareholder. This also maintained the value of the Pennsylvania money, because if he had dumped them all on the market, the value would have plummeted. Morris kept looking for individuals to buy bank shares as well. By the end of October, the sale of bank stock raised $70,000.[110] In November, Colonel John Laurens arrived in Boston with the much-anticipated silver from France. Morris arranged for Tench Francis to transport the $470,000 in French silver from Boston to Philadelphia over land. The money casks had been damaged during the sea voyage, so Morris suggested that a thousand crowns be counted and the rest weighed and compared against that known amount. Morris ordered most of the silver to be sent by wagon, but also that some bills of exchange be brought, just in case the silver was stolen. In typical Morris style, he described the method of overland shipment. He detailed the type of cart, the size and construction of the boxes, and he even suggested the use of four six-year-old oxen and one seven-year-old horse.[111] Morris also requested that the Board of War grant a military escort.[112]

When the silver arrived, Morris, as Superintendent of Finance, used it to buy bank shares worth $254,000 on the Government's account. The Continental government instantly became the largest stockholder in the Bank.[113] This capitalized the Bank sufficiently so it could start operating. Thomas Willing was elected President of the Bank of North America. Being a bank president was new to Willing, so he and his board of directors move ahead with caution. He wrote,

> The business ... was a pathless wilderness, ground but little known this side of the Atlantic.... Established as merchants, we resolved to pursue the road we were best acquainted with. We established our books on a simple mercantile plan.[114]

Americans and their money were an important topic in France. The French administration was getting nervous that the Americans were overdrawing their lines of credit, which they were. Franklin refused to honor any notes that were not covered by real funds. Even the American ambassadors were embarrassed by their personal poverty during this period. The French king helped out and backed a ten million livre loan from Holland; and warned the United States not to draw more from the loan deposit than the actual amount.[115] By the time that new loan came in, much of it had already been spent.

In America, the Chevalier de Chastellux had promised a loan to the state of Virginia. Morris cautioned de Chastellux to remember that lending money to the state of Virginia was not the same as lending it to the Continental Congress. Instead of allocating the money from the old loan, Chevalier de Chastellux had created a new one. This was more money than he was allowed and caused some chagrin on his part. Morris convinced the Frenchman he had to be good to his commitments, even if he overstepped the bounds set by the French Court.[116]

Congress attempted to make good on its promises to an ally in New York State. They had committed to help the Oneida because that tribe was the only member of the Six Nations to help America. Congress allowed them to have food from the "specific supply" system. This would not have concerned Morris, except that the State of New York was not happy to comply, and instead New York demanded that the state get credit for the supplies. That demand triggered adjustments to be made by Morris. The letters took a long time to get back and forth between Albany and Philadelphia. In the meantime, winter set in and the Oneida went without.

John Brown was still in Boston trying to make sense of the situation regarding the Eastern Naval Board. There seemed to be some question about the sale of the *Argo's* cannon and stores to pay a foreign debt due to the influential Brown family of Rhode Island.[117] Morris instructed his agent to sell the marine supplies that were not needed, but not to pay the Browns of Providence, and instead to focus on getting the *Alliance* ready for sea. Morris intended to settle the Brown's claims along with others who were owed money by the same source, Mr. Penet, of France; the same Mr. Penet with whom Thomas Morris had contracted years earlier. This did not make Robert popular with the Browns of Rhode Island.

It soon became clear that there was not enough money to hire sailors for the *Alliance* or the *Deane.* Morris proposed that sailors should be offered assurances that they would receive their wages, but the money would have to come from prizes taken at sea. In addition to that, they would also get their regular share of the prize money.[118] At the same time, the privateer navy was encountering difficulties on the high seas because of the Armed Neutrality, and there were continuing disagreements with neutral European countries over ships taken as prizes by Americans.

Back on the home front, Robert, and presumably his wife, were conducting a survey of the local schools. It was decided to send their two eldest sons to Europe to be educated. Morris asked a trusted friend, Matthew Ridley, to guide them to France, and then into a suitable boarding school. He wrote,

> It is my intention to give them a liberal education, to open their minds to every science, and channel of knowledge, that in future times, they may choose for themselves their walk through life upon terms of advantage equal to any.[119]

Robert never finished secondary school and did not attend a day of college. This letter indicates he knew the role of education in a person being *"equal to any."* His willingness to send his half-brother Thomas and his illegitimate daughter, Polly, to private schools, also shows this understanding. With the act of sending Robert, at the age of 12, and Thomas, at the age of 10, to Europe, both Morrises made a real commitment to preparing their boys for the future. Washington understood, and helped arrange for the boys' passage on a French warship. He wrote,

> I have had the pleasure to take your two boys by the hand and welcome them to Virginia. For my countries sake, I rejoice in the sacrifice you are making to your own feelings for the education of the young gentlemen, your sons, in whose behalf I have taken the liberty to enclose your letter to the Count de Grasse, and have interested myself with him to show them every civility and accommodation in his power, which I dare say he will readily do, for your own same, and as well as on my account.[120]

De Grasse wrote to Morris that the boys had left for France on the French Naval vessel, *Andromaque*.[121]

On November 3rd, Washington's army re-entered Philadelphia. This time they carried the flags of surrender from Yorktown, and the enormity of the war was brought to the doorstep of Congress. The occasion is best described by a witness. Morris wrote,

> The City Troop of light Horse went to meet them [Washington and his aides] and became the Standard Bearers as 24 Gentlemen privates in the Corps carried each of them one of the Colors displayed, the American and French Flags preceding the Captured Trophies which were conducted down Market Street to the Coffee House thence down Front to Chestnut Street and up to the State House where they were laid at the Feet of Congress; who were sitting, and many of the members tell that instead of Viewing this transaction as a meet matter of Joyful Ceremony which they expected to do, they Instantly felt themselves impressed with ideas of the most solemn and awful nature. It bought to their minds the distress our Country has been exposed to, the Calamities we have repeatedly suffered, the perilous situation which our affairs have almost always been in, and they could not but reflect the Threats of Lord North, that he would bring America to his Feet on unconditional terms of Submission, but Glory be unto thee Oh Lord God, who hath Vouch safed to rescue from Slavery and from Death these thy Servants.[122]

Even this solemn occasion was not enough to compel members of Congress to get their respective states aligned in support of Morris' programs. Life went on as before. Robert continued to attempt to "make bricks without straw," and he was keen to get John Barry to sea, so Barry could attack the blockade. Instead, Congress directed John Barry to take the Marquis de la Fayette to France on November 27th. Morris added he should cruise European waters and take prizes there.[123] This voyage by Barry also provided Morris with an opportunity to send new letters. In one, Mary Morris ordered a dress from France, and she wanted assistance from the American women in France to purchase one in the latest style. Matthew Ridley waited in France for his wife to arrive from America to fulfill that request. Robert arranged payment for the dress from his French banker,[124] and at the same time allowed his banker in France to be used as a conduit for some Continental funds, if necessary.

Morris also brought Franklin up to date on the conditions in America. In a phrase Morris would have done well to heed in the following years, he wrote,

> A Revolution, a War, the Dissolution of Governments, the creating of it anew, Cruelty, Rapine and Devastation in the midst of our very Bowels, these Sir are Circumstances by no means favorable to finance. The wonder then is that we have done so much, that we have borne so much, and the candid world will add that we have dared so much.[125]

Morris continued that he was not sure what to do about the Army, since there was money to feed and pay them, but not for munitions or horses.[126] His experience in providing material to the French army gave him a new perspective on his business partner, Mr. Holker. He wrote to Franklin,

> I am not disposed to criminate, but it is right that I should inform you of my opinion, which is that the French Troops in this country have cost much more than necessary.[127]

For their part, the French agents started to complain that they were being cut out of their commissions because Morris had taken over temporary management of their supply system.[128]

Morris' role as one of the first executive officers in the Continental Government gave him a uniquely national perspective on the citizens, and their habits. He noted that Americans were quick to respond in their own local interest when the British attacked; but would relax as soon as danger was no longer visible. He thought this made coordinated efforts difficult in a large country,

> An application is then made immediately to the feelings of the people, but when the inroad ceases, when the enemy retires, the storm subsides, each man returns to his domestic pursuits and employments, and thinks no more of the scenes which had just passed before him. It is true that this is only changing the Field of Battle, but America is so extensive that a shock given at one extremity is lost before it reaches the other.[129]

This observation led Morris to conclude that America was too large an area to have a single, all-powerful central government. That, however, did not stop him from reflecting that more order was required,

> This is the period of weakness between the convulsive Labors of Enthusiasm, and the sound and regular Operations of Order and Government.[130]

Morris received a letter from John Jay who said, he had "little hopes of loans or subsidies from Spain."[131] Morris had to inform Congress that they were running out of money.

Meanwhile in the South, one might suppose that the Virginians would be pleased to see the victory at Yorktown and the liberation of their state, but apparently there was a tinge of embarrassment as well. Earlier, the militia leader and state governor, Thomas Jefferson, had done little to assist Generals Greene or Gates, when they were most in need. Next, the Virginia militia had been routed from Richmond when the traitorous Benedict Arnold led British troops into the state. Their ineffective resistance and the resulting surrender of the state capital seem to have mortified the proud leaders of the Old Dominion. Finally, Jefferson resigned at the end of his term, with the British still holding the state. A year later, when he declined to serve in the Virginia Assembly, he admitted that he was not really well suited for military leadership. After the war there was an investigation into Jefferson's actions, which resulted in a document that praised his leadership. As proud Virginians, and promoters of state sovereignty, it must have been a bittersweet deliverance to see the Continental Army come to their rescue. Their behavior, after Washington's victory, demonstrates Virginia's effort to recover its "honor" by attempting to retake control of the trade in its precious tobacco.

The Battle of Yorktown ended with a negotiated surrender by the British, which cost Cornwallis the loss of his treasure to the United States. One of the articles of capitulation provided for a transaction that would enrich the American treasury by $24,000 Spanish milled dollars. A tobacco contract was drawn up that allowed the loyalist New York merchants, who had followed the English to Yorktown, to sell all their goods to Virginians in return for a total of six hundred and eighty-five hogsheads of Virginia tobacco, (six hundred and eighty-five thousand pounds). That tobacco was to be transported to New York. After it was resold in New York, half of the profits would go to the American treasury.[132] This whole business was supposed to be finished within three months. The man the British chose as their agent was George Eddy. Eddy was a contractor to the British who was already involved in feeding American prisoners held in New York.[133] Previously, he had negotiated the release of various British prisoners of war.

The British were concerned that the tobacco would be seized on the way from Virginia to New York by French or American privateers. They appealed to Congress for protection. Congress turned to Morris, as Agent of Marine. Britain proposed to use half of their half of the proceeds to benefit American prisoners of war held on British prison ships in return for Morris' help, on behalf of the Continental government, in assisting in the safe passage of the tobacco. Morris, and then Congress, accepted this deal.[134]

Virginia citizens started to complain that the New York merchants were selling their goods for cash payments instead of taking tobacco in trade. The governor, Benjamin Harrison, worried about the loss of precious hard money from Virginia, as well as this kind of use of state tobacco by the Continental Congress. Just as these issues became apparent, the Lee brothers interjected themselves into the deal. Arthur and Richard

Henry started to portray this whole business as "trading with the enemy" in the Virginia Assembly. They ignored Congress' role and focused on Morris. They worked up popular sentiment against him for even allowing the trade.[135] As the Virginia Assembly moved against the Morris-Eddy deal, the Lee brothers supported a nearly identical Virginia-based tobacco contract with the same New York merchants, private sellers, and a Virginia agent. This latter effort was outside the agreement between the British and Congress. The hypocrisy of this was not lost on James Madison who noted that it was a "copious topic for the Anti-Virginia critics."[136]

With the willing cooperation of Virginia sellers, Eddy did eventually send one ship, the *New York*, carrying the privately owned tobacco. Once Morris realized the private deal would go through anyway, he offered the services of his personal agent in Virginia, Daniel Clark, as the official buyer, and Morris arranged to have Eddy deposit the funds into the Bank of North America. Instead of using the hard money to buy the Virginia tobacco, Morris had Eddy use Bank notes. That way, the Bank had the use of Eddy's funds until the deal was settled. Still, Morris considered that tobacco trade to be beyond the scope of the contract with Congress and was not willing to ask for official protection from the French fleet for that ship. Morris' lack of interest in misusing his government office to get the French to protect private tobacco shipments aggravated Governor Harrison of Virginia to the point that he made shipping the Continental tobacco difficult. Morris' political adversaries wasted no time in besmirching Morris' name over his involvement in this deal, while at the same time not acknowledging his contributions to success of the Battle of Yorktown.

Morris' Office did not have the luxury of focusing on one deal to the exclusion of all else. It was also conducting a settlement of the accounts within the old Treasury department. He had John Brown, of Philadelphia, in Boston working to organize the business of the Navy, which was still suffering from the misadventure in the Penobscot Bay. Morris was promoting the capitalization of the first Bank. He was working on building the new supply system for the Army, which in turn, he hoped, would start a national economic system using hard currency. He also began to coordinate activities between the new executive offices, the commanders in the field, and Congress. He suggested, and held, regular "cabinet" meetings every Monday for that purpose. He noted in the record that he

> Held a conference with the Secretary of War, Secretary of Foreign Affairs, the Commander in Chief, the Secretary of Congress, and my

> Assistant Mr. G. Morris, wherein proposed that the same Persons should meet every Monday Evening for the purpose of communicating to each other whatever may be necessary and for Consulting and Concerting measures to promote the Service and Public Good.[137]

By this time, Morris' circulars had arrived and been read in statehouses up and down the Atlantic coast. State Governors did not receive Morris' message enthusiastically. They preferred the existing system of local control and continued to use the unfinished settlement as a delaying tactic. They were not shy about taxing their own populations for their own purposes, but they were reluctant to send cash to the Continental Congress. They maintained their support for state units within the Continental Army and sent their surpluses as "specific supplies" as an offset to their requisitions. Morris had to explain, yet again, that instead of giving credits for specific supplies, he wanted the states to send money as their requisition, and that money would go to pay contractors who in turn would buy from local farmers, whom the states could, in turn, tax.

Gouverneur Morris and Robert Morris by Charles Wilson Peale - PAFA

Morris moved forward with his program to replace the failing specific supply system. He engaged Comfort Sands & Co. as contractors to supply Washington's Army in New York. He wrote to Governor Clinton of New York,

> Your Excellency will perceive that I am now about to supply the Troops by Contract, wherefore a ready market for their Produce must immediately be opened to the inhabitants of your state. This will enable them to obtain hard money, and that will enable them to pay taxes." Morris also volunteered an opinion about the state's practice of giving enlistment bounties, "I am sure I need not observe to your Excellency the impracticability of carrying on a War where it costs as much to enlist a man as it does to feed and pay him for six months. [138]

As might be expected, the Governors were sure they were better qualified to run their states than Morris was.

Morris was determined not to pay hard money to any state, without a reciprocal effort on the part of that state to send hard money instead of specific supplies. However, one state in particular was unwilling to pay, but was still successful in getting money from Morris' office. British prisoners from the surrender at Yorktown were being held in Maryland, but Maryland was not remitting money to Congress. Morris considered Maryland's economic condition; and asked the Governor to feed the prisoners with specific supplies. He allowed the value of those supplies to be deducted from the state's commitment of requisitions. The Governor refused, and even though he was not willing to pay taxes, he wanted Morris to pay in hard currency for the food of these prisoners. The Governor was willing to hold them hostage until Morris agreed.[139]

As Morris worked on his grand vision, occasionally some personal news would come to him. He learned that his sons arrived in France by the middle of December. Matthew Ridley wrote Morris about their educational options. He suggested that they should first learn French, and to comport themselves in polite European company before going to school in Switzerland. For that purpose, Ridley suggested tutors be employed.

> All I want is for them to acquire a manner of going into and leaving a room and which will on their first appearance at Geneva create a favorable impression – much depends on the first impression.[140]

The boys were on the first leg of their European era. It would be years before they returned to America.

Back in Philadelphia, Robert continued to focus on clearing up past mistakes and poorly executed good ideas. Contrary to his better judgment, he was drawn into finishing the business of the Continental Lottery. It was originally intended to be a fundraiser, and a way to remove excess currency from circulation. Tickets were sold as early as 1776. Unfortunately, the Continental Government was chased out of Philadelphia before the pay-out could be conducted. Then it was delayed because the Congress wanted to reserve the bulk of unsold tickets for the United States, so the government might get the profit and the proceeds. A third attempt was completed in 1780, but a fourth drawing was postponed due to currency depreciation and lack of funds for the prize. Morris agreed to pay the winners if Congress wished, but only in the new Continental currency at the depreciated rate of one new for forty old.[141]

Philadelphia was a great distance from the Southern Army. That, and the slow speed of communications in the 18th century, convinced Morris to empower General Greeen to negotiate contracts and run the Southern Army's finance arm. But first he wanted the states of North and South Carolina to remit hard cash. After all, what was he expected to pay the contractors with otherwise? He wrote,

> Should the States of North and South Carolina adopt the present Plan and lay the tax and set about collecting it in earnest I wish you to endeavor at a contract for supplying your troops with rations for six Months...[142]

To help Greene, he wrote to the Governors of North and South Carolina, and Georgia.

> The delegates from North and South Carolina thought the plan eligible, but one of the delegates of Georgia was disinclined to that part of it which requires the previous passing of a law to raise the quota of taxes called for by the United States.[143]

After Georgia's action, South Carolina fell away. These states wanted to promise to tax after the contracting began, but Morris refused to agree,

> As Superintendent of Finances of the United States it is my duty to urge a compliance with the requisitions of Congress, and therefore to facilitate the compliance, but I should betray the trust reposed in me, if by any expedient whatever I assisted in eluding those requisitions.[144]

Morris' national vision was in conflict with the localist tendencies of the southern governors. Rhode Island presented a similar problem. They maintained that they already had remitted more than their share.[145] Morris had to remind them that even if they had paid in the past that was not enough to win a war that was not yet over,

> I feel it my duty to observe that nothing but a continuance of active exertions, on our part, can possibly assure these objects [fruits of victory], for which so much has already been done and suffered.

The lack of cooperation by the states was also felt in Maryland, and Delaware. Morris wrote to Yates, the quartermaster there,

> If they and their fellow citizens instead of uttering complaints on every occasion would exert themselves in paying their own and influencing their neighbors to pay their taxes for the Continental Service I should soon hope to see our affairs on such a footing as to silence all complaints but whilst people are grasping at every farthing the public possesses and no measures are taken to replenish the fountain from whence payments spring what can they expect?[146]

A thread of exasperation can be seen in some of the messages Morris sent to sympathetic readers, but the states were not ready to come into line with Morris' program. Congress moved another piece of business onto Morris' desk. There were three "Indian boys," George Morgan White Eyes, and two brothers, Thomas and John Killbuck, who were attending a public school in New Jersey. They had been put in the care of Congress by the Delaware Tribe as part of a cooperative arrangement, whereby the Indians promised to pay the expense in land after the war.[147] Morris asked the New Jersey representative, a Dr. John Witherspoon, to pay for their food and clothing with money he had collected as part of a British prisoner exchange. If the Doctor refused, Morris said he would look after it. Dr. Witherspoon did refuse and another man offered to put them into trade instead. Morris wrote,

> My opinion is against this measure as I apprehend the United States mean to educate these lads in such a manner as to attach them to the interest of the United States and so instructed as to understand those interests & etc therefore desired they might be kept at the public school but if not properly attended to then to inform me that I might lay the same before Congress.

Morris didn't want second class citizens to be made of these "Indian boys."[148]

Economic War

Even though the peace had not been ratified, many people thought the war was won after the victory at Yorktown. Contrary to this opinion, the war was actually still very much on. The mode of battle had changed from guns and bullets, into an economic war. During this period, much of Morris' time was spent arranging the finances so that the troops had food, clothing and medicine; even if they did not have munitions. The shooting may have stopped, but the army was still needed to keep the British at bay. Just at this time, bad news came in from Europe. Franklin warned that France was becoming firmer in their conclusion that they had done enough for America, and that America had to do more for itself.[149] This could only have confirmed what Morris already knew from his dealings with the French in Philadelphia. The same packet also included news from Matthew Ridley that "Deane has lost himself."[150]

Morris reconsidered the prospects. He contacted John Brown of Philadelphia, to devise a way to get a boatload of silver from Havana, Cuba. More silver was needed this time than in the previous attempt, so it would be a double voyage. The *Active* would take its first trip south to bring American flour and iron to Havana, in return for their sugar, and salt. This sugar and salt would be traded for American food products and naval supplies, which in turn would be sold in Havana for silver. The plan was set into motion on January 10th, 1782.[151] This was just another example of how Morris was willing to engage the spirit of his training as a Philadelphia merchant and double up the risk when the rewards were most needed.

Clearly, Morris was scrambling to attend to the small and large pieces of Continental business. He paid for government obligations to individuals for as little as £10; and solicited loans of millions. As Agent of Marine, Morris ordered the sale of marine supplies, designed naval missions, and arranged to pay the sailors. As Superintendent, he promoted the Bank of North America, and lobbied the governors with a vision of a national economy that would bring them out of penury, while rescuing American honor. As the patriotic fellow that he was, Morris put his own money into that system to demonstrate the benefits of his ideas. He wrote,

> … my own notes, which I issued only as a prelude to the others by way of opening the Public Eye to their utility was well to apply my personal credit to the public service.[152]

At the same time that Morris looked after his sons, he made sure the Oneida got their due, and insisted that the trio of Indian Boys were not turned out of public school and sent to the trades. If there is any thread running through this whirlwind of disparate acts, it is that he did what he must to keep the continental effort going forward, to realize the promise of the freedoms for which all were contending.

As the Revolution evolved into an economic war, a suitable new fortress was necessary, and it was under construction. The Bank of North America had existed on paper since May. It had been capitalized since November. All it needed was a charter of incorporation to operate. There was a long and bruising fight in Congress about the ability of the Congress to incorporate an entity such as a bank. One side argued that the power of incorporation was not explicitly granted to Congress in the Articles of Confederation, and since the Confederation was a collection of sovereign states, only the states themselves had this ability. Conversely, the other side maintained that the Confederation was a sovereign state, as evidenced by its ability to raise an army, and all sovereign states had the right to incorporate entities. These interesting legal and philosophical arguments continued for months, but no action was taken. The establishment of this federally chartered and privately owned bank, was one of the pillars of Morris' plan to reestablish the creditworthiness of America. Morris finally made it clear to Congress that the Bank of North America was the centerpiece of his program, and that if they intended for him to do his job, the bank was required. Understanding that the practice of banking was new to America, to buttress his arguments, Morris offered his copy of Smith's *The Wealth of Nations* to a member of Congress.[153] Ultimately, it was agreed that the United States had generated debts, and the practical solution was for the United States to have a bank that could be used for the payment of those debts.

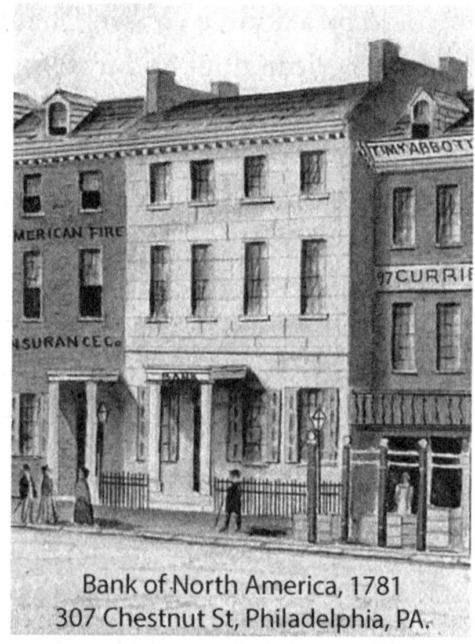

Bank of North America, 1781
307 Chestnut St, Philadelphia, PA.

On December 31st, Congress approved the charter of the first national bank in the American history, the Bank of North America. Pennsylvania and Delaware were two states that confirmed the institution's charter. The Bank of North America was capitalized by the sale of stock in the first initial public offering in American history. The basic idea was to fill the bank with silver, and then use bank notes backed by that silver to pass as currency. This is called a hard money system. Through the use of fractional reserve banking techniques this system would magnify the wealth of the country and encourage the growth of the economy.

In his volume, *The Wealth of Nations,* Adam Smith explains the benefits of banks like the one Morris intended. He asserts that the establishment of Scottish banks in 1695 and 1727 contributed greatly to the increase of wealth in that country. Smith was not just writing about the growth in bank deposits, but the value of the whole Scottish economy.[154] It is useful to remember that the wealth of a nation is not the sum of the money held in the banks, but rather it is the sum of all the assets in the country plus the production of new items for the market. Money in itself is a medium of exchange through which people transfer value in the acquisition of produced items, or the disposition of them. A solid medium of exchange encourages the production of items for trade because one can predict how worthwhile it will be to invest the effort in new production. That is the true engine of growth, not the printing of currency.

For his part, Morris had to develop a system that allowed for the creation of an expanding economy in America, because he had to deal with a condition of expanding indebtedness. As part of his solution Morris saw the need to use a hard money system, because it was the basis for sustainable national and international trade, and he understood the importance of trade as an engine of growth. Morris also sought to free the markets as the second part of the solution.

Not only were there numerous recently enacted interstate trade restrictions, but individual Americans had little hard money. That scarcity was a hold-over from the former Colonial economic system; wherein the home country would loan hard money to colonists, but the colonists could never get out of debt because the home country controlled both the money supply and the market for the colonists' goods. This resulted in the money going back to England and many colonists living their whole lives in debt to English investors. On more than one occasion, those investors would "call in" the total due, and thereby take possession of the life's work of that unlucky colonist. It should not be a surprise that paying such debts after the war would cause concern among the most indebted, the southern planters; nor should it be surprising that during the war, the southern planters and other farmers associated the English hard money system with oppression. They were more comfortable with locally controlled state paper currency, largely based on real estate, and they worked to maintain that system.

To understand the role of the Bank of North America, it is also useful to see it in terms of Morris' ultimate goal to create a national economy based on good credit, and a reliable currency. The Continental Congress had given Morris the mission to maintain the United States under the Articles of Confederation, so his job as Superintendent of Finance was national in nature. Moreover, Morris had experienced the pettiness of state administrations, and he thought that a national system would be more broad-minded. He was well suited to this because he had long seen the current Confederation as the United States of America, and he was concerned that a loose confederation of independent states would fight amongst themselves and fall prey to European power politics. Morris undertook an effort not just to rebuild the various failed state economies, but rather to build a truly American economy for the first time. His preferred means was to draw the states into closer economic cooperation by focusing on the shared goal of winning the war.

Where does one start with such a project? Morris started with the weakest link in the chain, the currency. There are two forms of money: hard money, and paper money. Hard money, or specie, is made of an amount of a precious metal that is valued, more or less, universally. Generally speaking, a gold coin of a certain weight has a known value, regardless of the design stamped on its surfaces. The term, Hard Money, refers to the specie itself and the notes that are explicitly backed by gold and silver. Paper currency, or state notes, on the other hand, is just a promise that one can use the paper in exchange for items valued at a certain rate. The state paper currency was backed by the state's expectation of tax revenue, or by a land bank mortgage. Neither form of state paper was suitable for a growing economy because both tended to zero out. That is, the paper money was equal to the taxes collected, and the land bank money was equal to the value of the land and any interest went to pay the costs of government. This limited the ability of the colonial economies to grow. Additionally, each state had its own currency, and that hampered trade between the states. From his viewpoint, Morris needed an expanding economy to help pay off the increasing debts; all he had to do was get cooperation from the states.

It had been five years since 1776, when the Revolutionaries threw out the old colonial governments. Still, the new state governments tried to keep the familiar old colonial monetary system. However, they did not have the backing of a larger empire to support it, and they didn't seem to realize the colonial system was designed to keep the colonies poor and the mother country rich. To make matters worse, over time the states lost their fiscal discipline due to pressures upon the elected officials to provide money to voters. When the states needed more money, they would just print it, often without increasing taxes to cover the liability. Inflation resulted. What we call inflation today, because we have to spend two dollars for what used to cost one, was called discounting in the 18th century, because they saw each dollar as being worth 50 cents. To stop the inflation, states passed their tender and penal laws. These laws provided criminal penalties for people who refused to honor the money at its face value, i.e., discounted the money. This did not stop the discounting, because people needed economic inputs from outside their states, and the monetary laws had no effect away from the legislative state. The use of local paper made buying items from other states and countries difficult under good conditions, and when the discounting started, things went from difficult to nearly impossible. People resorted to using hard money from foreign countries. The states' response to this problem was to enact embargoes so interstate trade would not be able to affect the value of the currency any longer.

Aside from the world of state currencies there was a parallel world of private paper. One type was the note, and these were similar to a kind of personal check. They represented promises from individuals that some responsible person would make good on converting that note with an item of agreed value, like silver bullion or coin. In a slightly different circumstance, a merchant would buy a shipload of goods, and he would issue a bill of exchange, which would be honored in foreign ports. The seller often held this bill of exchange until the merchant sold the shipment to a third party. When that sale happened, settlement would be made to the original seller.[155*] Commerce was rarely so simple, and people would often pass these bills of exchange to others as payment on different accounts, similar to countersigning a check today, so it frequently took over a year and a half for one deal to clear. In the meantime, these bills of exchange acted as a trusted means of transferring value and a kind of second tier currency. When the finances of the Confederation collapsed, Morris stepped in with his notes, and they were accepted because there was an existing system to accommodate that kind of financial instrument.

A nation could not rely on the private checks of an individual for an extended period of time, so an institution that could play a similar role was required. A bank was one such institution: they issued their own notes, backed by real assets. The bank would not issue more than they could honor, because that would endanger the bank and its officers would be liable for the shortfall.[156] The real benefit of a bank becomes clear when one considers the following question: What would a merchant in Spain do with a Maryland three-pound note when the continental notes were discounted at 40:1? Basically, he would avoid the whole business and want to be paid in silver, tobacco or some other tangible product.

The problem with barter is that there is no leverage to it. In other words, you cannot expand your economy when you have a zero-sum system like barter. All you really do is transfer economic power to the growers of commodities and shut everyone else out. Naturally, the largest growers were the slave-holding elite who routinely used their money to buy more land, even if they did not use it. This reduced opportunities among those without slaves and plantations; and caused dissatisfaction. It also created conditions wherein the plantation owners planted too much, say, tobacco, to make even more money in trade; yet this had the contrary effect due to the law of supply and demand. More tobacco ends up bringing less money per pound, so the result is a market that swings wildly, and if it does not collapse it is necessarily affected by uncontrollable conditions like weather and insects. Banks and hard money policies offer an alternative approach that is based on the efficient use of assets. It rewards those who add value to what they already have. This gives rise to such things as manufacturing, the automation of farming, and the importance of intellectual property.

Capital collected in a bank allows for the magnification of value by the careful understanding of risk. Before banks existed, rich men might lend money to their friends, on occasion. In such cases, a rich man with $100 might loan $20 to five people, but then there would be no money to lend again until it was all paid back. If you were not personally favored by the acquaintance of such a man, your ability to get capital was very limited. What a bank does with that $100 is lend $20 to five people, but it requires each of those people to pay a portion of the money back in a timely fashion. If they do not pay on time, the loan is called, or the items are repossessed. In that way, depositors have access to some of their funds when they want, the rest grows with interest, and borrowers have the use of the funds over time. It also allows the bank to lend money to other people, because as partial payments come in the money becomes available again. It works out as long as the bank lends to people who pay back the loans on schedule, so this system relies on the responsibility of individuals, not slavery, real estate, and the weather.

The key element to the system is faith in the value of it. When Morris created the Bank of North America, it was known that he was behind it. People who bought shares believed in the Bank because they believed in Morris, so he was able to use his reputation as the "richest man in America" to bestow credibility onto that bank. It was also known that the United States had invested in it, so the bankrupt United States gained in standing because of the association with Morris. Morris reinforced American creditworthiness, by advertising the combination of the American spirit with the abundant natural resources as the ultimate source of American wealth. Morris' reputation, and the creation of a private bank, outside the pressures of political forces, made a potent combination. Together, they established that the United States government and foreign governments could rely on the notes drawn on the new bank without fear of inflation. The bank was able to make that value stick: initially on the basis of Morris' reputation, then on the silver in its vaults, then because of the quality of loans they made. Morris was aware of this when he wrote to Governor Harrison of Virginia:

> My personal credit which thank heaven I have preserved throughout all the tempests of the War, had been substituted for that which they had lost ... I am now striving to transfer that credit to the public.[157]

He continued, and told Governor Harrison of Virginia that paper money was of such little value, that a hard money system was the only one that would work. The transformation from paper to "hard" currency was a difficult and painful one for many. All this economic theorizing was tested in the cauldron of the ongoing economic war. Morris intended each step to be based on hard money values, and that value was often transferred with Morris notes, and bank notes.

Autumn passed as the Bank issue brewed. The onset of winter brought the cold, and that increased the need for wood, particularly for soldiers in the field, and prisoners of war in New York.[158] Morris attempted to fulfill the will of Congress and move forward with the Yorktown Tobacco deal,[159] which he expected to benefit those prisoners held in New York. He wrote Governor Harrison, of Virginia, about his involvement in what was unfolding to be an unpopular effort,

> ... it is my duty, to protect the Interests of the United States, and guard their property entrusted to my care.[160]

Shortly after that, he got a letter from Gov. Harrison of Virginia explaining that the state was not interested in participating because

> ... the Confederation gives Congress a right to call on the States, for their respective quotas of the national Expense, but leaves it to them, to raise the money as most convenient to them.

Harrison objected to the Confederation taking control over Virginia's most precious resource because

> ...that whenever the Continent come to be settled, that it will be found that we are far from being indebted, however it may appear on your books...

... and he continued in that vein to explain how generous Virginia had been.[161] The Governor of Virginia objected to Continental use of Virginia tobacco valued at its market price in hard money. A committee of Congress was empowered and agreed to let the sale go through.[162] Using funds available from the victory in Yorktown, Morris made arrangements to repay the French for the silver that he had borrowed to pay the troops before the battle, so Morris was thusly released from his loan guarantee.[163] He moved on and kept up the search for money, and used his role as Agent of Marine, to gain funds for the United States by settling prizes taken by privateers.[164]

After passing the bank bill, Congress moved at its stately pace and started to investigate the question of currency. They instructed Morris that his office should provide a table of rates for foreign coins. Gouverneur Morris was given the job of analyzing the currency tables and learning the secrets of coinage metallurgy. In response, the Office of Finance devised a system of domestic coinage that could be used across state boundaries. It was in this effort that Morris' Office proposed a national monetary unit based on the decimal system that would serve as the basis for a new series of silver coins. The resulting report, Gouverneur Morris penned, was based on his earlier work, but it was clearly the work of both Morrises in the Office of Finance.[165] They proposed a currency comprised of several denominations: A *mark* which contained one thousand units, a *quint* of five hundred units and a *cent* of one hundred units. (see appendix, Coinage) There was no proposal for a one-unit coin because the "unit" mentioned in the report was a value derived as a common denominator from all the useful currencies of the day. Robert also used this opportunity to begin the organization of a national mint.

The mint was his solution to the problem of unstable state currencies. The values of the various state currencies changed within the states according to how far one was from the capital, or how much had been printed lately. The exchange rates between states were inconsistent. This meant that individual buyers and sellers had to negotiate the price of the goods and the price of the money at the same time. It was simpler and less risky to use foreign coins or barter goods under those circumstances.

Merchants and farmers often used foreign currency instead of state currency to overcome, or at least reduce, the uncertainty and risk in their business. A foreign currency acted as a trusted intermediary between two state currencies, but foreign currency was not always available, which is the reason Morris undertook to create a domestic currency that would play the same role. He figured that if there was one United States currency that was accepted across state boundaries, as foreign currency was at the time, this would help overcome the economic stagnation that gripped the separate States. Morris also thought that if the United States were to present themselves to other countries as a reliable trading partner, it would need a stable currency which would be accepted overseas. This was the reasoning behind the creation of a mint, and why Morris, using private funds, contracted with Benjamin Dudley,[166] to devise a machine for striking coins, and why he proposed his mint plan in July 16, 1781. On February 21st, 1782 Congress approved the project.

Endnotes

1. *Journals of the Continental Congress*, 19:126
2. Ver Steeg pg. 70-71
3. Oberholtzer pg. 59
4. *Journals of the Continental Congress*, 19:180
5. Papers of Robert Morris, 1:8, 9
6. Diplomatic Correspondence of the American Revolution, pg. 455
7. Chernow, pg. 17
8. Letters of Delegates to Congress, 5:609
9. Papers of Robert Morris, 6:38
10. Papers of Robert Morris, 8:491
11. Rappleye pg. 56
12. Rappleye pg. 272
13. Report on the manuscripts of Mrs. Stopford-Sackville, of Drayton House, Northamptonshire, pg. 207
14. *In Irons*, pg. 190
15. Papers of Robert Morris, 2:56
16. Papers of Alexander Hamilton, 1: 604
17. *Boogher's Repository* pg. 35
18. Letters of Delegates to Congress, 17:384
19. *Wealth of Nations*, pg. 367
20. Papers of Robert Morris, 3:415
21. Papers of Robert Morris, 1:66
22. Papers of Robert Morris, 2:181
23. *History of the Bank of North America*, pg. 26-29
24. Letters of Delegates to Congress, 6:79
25. Ver Steeg pg. 106-107
26. *Wealth of Nations*, pg. 325
27. Papers of Robert Morris, 1:193
28. Nuxoll, *Illegitimacy, Family Status, and Property in the Early Republic; The Morris-Croxall Family of New Jersey*, 1995
29. *The Peace Makers*, pg. 95-111
30. Rappleye, pg. 223
31. The Papers of Robert Morris, 1:149
32. The Papers of Robert Morris, 1:149-152
33. Papers of Robert Morris, 1:181
34. Letters of Delegates to Congress, 17:376
35. Papers of Robert Morris, 1:287-209, 295
36. Papers of Robert Morris, 1:255
37. B.F. Robert Morris papers - Pennsylvania Historical Society - Levis Collection # 1957
38. Papers of Robert Morris, 2:239
39. Deane Papers, 4:505
40. Papers of Robert Morris, 3:257
41. Papers of Robert Morris, 1:128-139
42. Papers of Robert Morris, 3:264-283
43. Papers of Robert Morris, 1:389-400

44. George Washington to William Greene, August 7, 1781, https://founders.archives.gov/documents/Washington/01-03-02-0007-0004-0004

45. *The Diaries of George Washington*. 3:405 Donald Jackson, ed.; Dorothy Twohig, assoc. ed. The Papers of George Washington. Charlottesville: University Press of Virginia, 1978

46. Papers of Robert Morris, 2:141

47. Papers of Robert Morris, 1:409

48. Papers of Robert Morris, 2:25

49. Papers of Robert Morris, 2:74, 86

50. Papers of Robert Morris, 2:61

51. Papers of Robert Morris, 2:50

52. Letters of Delegates to Congress, 17:511 - Oliver Ellsworth to Richard Law; 17:515 Samuel Livermore to Meshech Weare

53. Papers of Robert Morris, 2:75

54. Papers of Robert Morris, 2:52

55. Papers of Robert Morris, 2:81, ref Washington Diaries, II, 253-254

56. *Biography of the Signers*, V5 Pg. 293-294

57. B.J. Lossing. 1848. *Lives of the Signers of the Declaration of Independence*

58. *The Diaries of George Washington*, 3:410 n

59. *George Washington Diaries 1748-1799*, 2:253

60. Papers of Robert Morris, 2:77

61. Papers of Robert Morris, 2:78

62. Papers of Robert Morris, 2:68-209

63. Papers of Robert Morris, 2:68

64. Papers of George Washington, *Washington's Revolutionary War Itinerary and the Location of His Headquarters, 1781*, UVA

65. Papers of Robert Morris, 2:147

66. Papers of Robert Morris, 2:199

67. Papers of Robert Morris, 2:172-3; 2:180

68. Papers of Robert Morris, 2:120

69. Papers of Robert Morris, 2:125

70. Letters of the delegates to Congress, 17:567

71. Papers of Robert Morris, 2:256-57

72. Papers of Robert Morris, 3:33

73. Papers of Robert Morris, 2:125

74. Papers of Robert Morris, 2:308

75. Papers of Robert Morris, 2:215

76. Papers of Robert Morris, 2:157

77. *Journal of the Continental Congress*, 19:127-8, 21:916, 21:943

78. Papers of Robert Morris, 2:217

79. Letters of Delegates to Congress, 17:498-499

80. Rufus W. Griswold, 1867 *The Republican Court, or, American Society in the Days of Washington*, D. Appleton and Company, New York, pg. 313 ref https://librarycompany.org/women/republicancourt/morris_mary.htm

81. Papers of Robert Morris, 2:151, n2

82. Oberholtzer pg. 221

83. Papers of Robert Morris, 2:244

84. Papers of Robert Morris, 2:244

85. Papers of Robert Morris, 2:254

86. Papers of Robert Morris, 2:261

87. Papers of Robert Morris, 2:269

88. Papers of Robert Morris, 2:201, 212

89. Papers of Robert Morris, 2:280

90. Papers of Robert Morris, 2:281

91. Papers of Robert Morris, 2:318

92. Morris, Robert to Benjamin Franklin, November 23, 1781; 12:20 APS

93. *Naval Documents of the American Revolution*, 4: 112

94. Hannay, ii, 211; Schomberg, ii, 36, iv, 376-384

95. Naval Records (calendar), 217-495{**}

96. Baines' History of Liverpool, 1852, pg. 462

97. Papers of Robert Morris, 2:68

98. Papers of Robert Morris, 2:188

99. J. Franklin Jameson, 1903, St. Eustatius and the American Revolution, pg. 707, The American Historical Review American Historical Association

100. Allen, *Naval History of the Revolution*, 2:572

101. Hansard, 22:18-262, 769-785, 1023-1026

102. Hansard, *The official report of all Parliamentary debates*. 22:221, 222

103. Maryland State Resolution - 16 March, 1996

104. Oberholtzer pg 90

105. *The Revolutionary Diplomatic Correspondence of the United States* 1:601 n3

106. Papers of Robert Morris, 2:81

107. The Papers of Robert Morris, 3:84

108. Papers of Robert Morris, 3:87

109. Papers of Robert Morris, 3:73

110. *History of the Bank of North America*, pg. 33

111. Papers of Robert Morris, 2:246

112. Papers of Robert Morris, 2:230

113. Papers of Robert Morris, 6:346n

114. *Robert Morris, Audacious Patriot*, P 89

115. Papers of Robert Morris, 3:249

116. Papers of Robert Morris, 3:234, 243, 254, 256

117. Papers of Robert Morris, 2:232, 2:322

118. Papers of Robert Morris, 3:124
119. Papers of Robert Morris, 3:53
120. Papers of Robert Morris, 3:115
121. Papers of Robert Morris, 3:122
122. Papers of Robert Morris, 3:131
123. Papers of Robert Morris, 3:260-261
124. Papers of Robert Morris, 3:255
125. Papers of Robert Morris, 3:268
126. Papers of Robert Morris, 3:269
127. Papers of Robert Morris, 3:275
128. Papers of Robert Morris, 3:519
129. Papers of Robert Morris, 3:281
130. Papers of Robert Morris, 3:282
131. Papers of Robert Morris, 3:301
132. Papers of Robert Morris, 4:405-6
133. Papers of Robert Morris, 4:511n
134. Papers of Robert Morris, 4:404-407
135. Papers of Robert Morris, 5:295
136. Papers of Robert Morris, 5:295
137. Papers of Robert Morris, 3:317
138. Papers of Robert Morris, 3:270
139. Papers of Robert Morris, 3:390, 393
140. Papers of Robert Morris, 3:372-3
141. Papers of Robert Morris, 3:389
142. Papers of Robert Morris, 3:407
143. Papers of Robert Morris, 3:411-415
144. Papers of Robert Morris, 3:412-3
145. Papers of Robert Morris, 3:465
146. Papers of Robert Morris, 3:460
147. Papers of Robert Morris, 3:498
148. Papers of Robert Morris, 3:416
149. Papers of Robert Morris, 3:518
150. Papers of Robert Morris, 3:519
151. Papers of Robert Morris, 3:524
152. Papers of Robert Morris, 4:267
153. Rappleye, pg. 247
154. *The Wealth of Nations*, pg. 330-333
155. This system is descended from the ancient hawala system, first devised in India centuries ago, to transmit value along the silk road and also avoid theft.
156. *Wealth of Nations*, pg. 352-353
157. Ver Steeg, pg. 87
158. Papers of Robert Morris, 4:6
159. Papers of Robert Morris, 4:7
160. Papers of Robert Morris, 4:9
161. Papers of Robert Morris, 4:186-187
162. Papers of Robert Morris, 4:215
163. Papers of Robert Morris, 4:330
164. Papers of Robert Morris, 4:16
165. Papers of Robert Morris, 4:24-27
166. Papers of Robert Morris, 1:304n

VIII

1782

Winter

Most of the shooting had stopped on the American mainland, but the war called the American Revolution was still causing repercussions around the world. Shortly after the American victory at Yorktown, Britain suffered a series of losses to the French in parts of Dutch Guiana, and the West Indies including St. Eustatius, St. Christopher, Nevis, and St. Kitts. This was followed by the loss of Minorca to Spain. With Britain in a weakened position, Spain tried to use the peace negotiations, underway in Europe, to their own advantage, as they sought to regain Gibraltar, and to control the Mississippi and the Gulf of Mexico. The French wanted to win possession of islands in the West Indies, trading rights in India, fishing concessions on the Grand Banks, and islands off the Maritime Provinces. Peace negations see-sawed back and forth as conditions on the ground changed. On January 26th, 1782, The British and the French fought the decisive Battle of Frigate Bay off St. Kitts in the West Indies, which the British won.

Their victory over the French navy commanded by Admiral de Grasse, was the beginning of the decline of France's influence in those islands. This increased the importance of the remaining French possession, Saint Dominique, because in 1782 the economic output of that island was greater than the economic output of all the New England states combined. Thereafter, the French ministers in Philadelphia attempted to influence the instructions Congress sent to the American diplomats abroad in ways that would benefit France. While America's nominal allies were working hard for their own sakes, the British considered it would be impossible to maintain their control of the North West Territories, so they negotiated those territories away to America. The ultimate result was a greater success and brighter future for America at the hands of our enemies than our allies had hoped for.

As wrangling among the Great Powers continued in Europe, Morris focused on winning the economic war for America. He began to appoint tax receivers for each state. He did this in anticipation that the states would actually pay taxes, which at this point they were not. He encouraged the receivers to lobby the state governments to "lay on" a tax so the Continental Government would have some funds.[1] The lack of funds did not stop the need for funds, so Morris borrowed $100,000 for the Continental Government from the Bank of North America.[2] To reduce expenses, he arranged for the quartermaster to shut military posts that were not needed, and to move horses to where they could be used, or to sell them. Morris also sent the *Active* out on her mission to gain silver from Cuba, but the silver remained elusive because the sailors jumped ship after the second leg of the journey.[3]

During the winter of 1782, the large and small matters of administration continued to flow across Morris' desk in the Office of Finance. The settlements of state accounts were being organized, and an audit of the major departments had begun. Morris proposed this to Congress because he knew the states needed proof they were not overburdened and, as he wrote,

> I have reason to believe that many fraudulent Practices have happened and that in some Cases considerable Balances are due to the United States.[4]

One such case, the unofficial audit of the Eastern Naval Board, caused a great deal of enmity. Morris' agent in Boston, John Brown, conducted the audit. Neither the Naval Board nor Brown was happy with the other, and all sent complaining letters to Morris.

There was also friction between the contractors and the Northern Army. Morris learned that the contractors tried to be true to the letter, if not the spirit, of the contracts, and ultimately the soldiers were hungrier than intended. Money problems limited the ability of the contractors to supply food. Lack of funds also meant lack of pay for soldiers. Morris started to receive messages from Thomas Paine that the soldiers were increasingly discontented for lack of pay.[5] The army officers needed uniforms, but the uniforms could not be issued because officers were supposed to pay for them. The officers had no money, and the government had no money. As a short-term solution, Morris gave the officers six-month Morris Notes that they could exchange for their uniforms.[6] Then he arranged for John Holker to accept these notes and to provide the uniforms in return. In so doing, Morris was able to delay the payment to Holker for six months.[7] The much-anticipated loan from Holland came through in the summer, just in time to pay that debt; unfortunately it had already been spent on other things.

General Greene was concerned about the finances of the Southern Army. In late January he wrote to Morris,

> Capt. Pearce has arrived with the money you sent me for which I am much obliged to you. But when I consider how little the sum and how great our wants I cannot look forward with but great anxiety... the distress of the officers is great and many of them have drained every private resource in their power. Men may bear their sufferings to a certain degree, beyond which it is dangerous to push them nay ruinous.

Greene understood that lack of support had enlivened a mutinous spirit in his army, and he worked hard to suppress it. He concurred with Morris that the fault lay in the agreement between the states, the Articles of Confederation.

> We have no mode to restrain any State in its local policy however prejudicial to the common interest nor can we compel them to such exertions as are requisite for general security."[8]

General Greene also mentioned that there was no ammunition.[9]

Morris was aware of this state of affairs when he wrote to Washington to encourage his officers to lobby the states to make the payments that Congress requisitioned. He wrote Washington,

> I hope therefore the Gentlemen you employ will join me in urging such grants, with all their force and abilities.[10]

He also wrote about paying Thomas Paine in a secret public relations effort to change the minds of the state legislators.[11]

The distress of the marine, and the two American armies, was not universally shared, as some individuals put their needs before others. For example, Captain Landais made his way to Philadelphia after his freelance trip on the *Alliance* from France to Boston with Arthur Lee. He was aggressively petitioning the American Government for the payment of prize money he felt was due to him. Morris insisted that Landais appeal to the prize agent who settled his prizes. Landais was displeased by this and went with "a Frenchman" to Morris' office to gain satisfaction. Landais recalled the experience in a letter to Congress,

> We went in, by the first door on the right and going in the entry, into the Office, where usually keeps one of the Clerks, they were four men in, Dressed gentleman like, I delivered said letter to the

> one clerk who kept in that Office, telling him it was a letter directed and for the Honble Rt. Morris; he answered he had his orders to receive none from me, and holding said Frenchman by the arm, put it into his hat, the French man put it back upon the clerks arm; I told the French man to come away, what we did, without saying a word, the clerk and others followed us, as far as the threshold of the entry door, where they stood bawling and calling me all the French bouger they could; they threw the letter I had remitted to the Clark for the Superintendent of Finance in the street and continued to abuse me thus 'till I was about fifty yards from said office.[12]

Morris continued his weekly cabinet meetings to seek solutions to the continuing problems. To quell desertions from the Army, they developed a way for Washington to enlist a military police force.[13] They also began to work with the British to settle the prisoner of war problem. Gouverneur Morris was sent to New Jersey, as part of the delegation, to discuss that issue with the English. During their February 10th, 1782 meeting, Washington agreed with Morris to employ Thomas Paine on a secret basis at the rate of $800 per year. This was done because Paine had been so successful in galvanizing public opinion earlier in his career.[14]

Morris hoped to encourage states, like Virginia, to pay money to the continental government instead of specific supplies and proceeded with his plan to pay contractors in states who were willing to comply with that mode. States unwilling to remit tax money were told they were not going to get contracts, but instead of working with the system, they became jealous. In January, Morris was clearly concerned about the future of his cash-based system.

> I cannot find that a single State has yet laid on taxes.

He hoped money from that tax would be the first step to reinvigorating the Army for a spring campaign. Considering the current bleak condition of the Army, Morris proposed an enlistment bounty system that would discourage soldiers from enlisting during the winter when they were fed; but did not fight. His proposal would encourage enlistment in the spring for new campaigns. He also considered it to be counterproductive for states to raise state armies that did not operate under Continental control, and he suggested that a national army would be less expensive and more useful in winning the war.[15] The states were not immediately receptive to these suggestions.

February 12th, 1782, was a rare day in the Office of Finance. The State of Pennsylvania sent £30,000 in silver.[16] Morris approached David Rittenhouse of the Pennsylvania Assembly. Morris wrote,

> I went to see Mr. David Rittenhouse he being sick, and offered him the Appointment of Receiver of the Continental Taxes in this State. I pointed out to him candidly my reasons and told him honestly and truly the pleasure it gave me to make him the offer.

Morris did this despite the long-standing policy differences he had with Rittenhouse, who was a staunch defender of the "Constitutionalist" faction.[17] Rittenhouse declined Morris' offer, evidently because of State regulations against holding two positions, and Rittenhouse did not want to leave his state office, or so he claimed.

Other state governments reacted to Morris' program. The government of Connecticut nominally supported Morris' substitution of cash for specific supplies, and though they would not accept Morris Notes they were willing to accept bank notes from the Bank of North America. They realized the importance of protecting this paper, so they developed punishments for bank note counterfeiters:

> ...all persons who may be consern'd in counterfeiting the Notes of the Bank, or in passing them, knowing them to be counterfeit are subjected to the same penalties as were formerly ordain'd for similar crimes by a statue of the State, which are, cutting off the right ear, branding with the Letter C on the Forehead, perpetual imprisonment, and confiscation of Estate.[18]

Connecticut's Assembly was willing to protect the Bank notes, but they were still divided over Morris' tax program. The old habits of local colonial governments were not set aside easily, however supporters of Morris' programs were optimistic that once the system started to work people would be convinced of its merits. General Huntington wrote about the goings on in the Connecticut Assembly,

> The well wishers to Mr. Morris' system have had to combat almost invincible prejudices. Those however daily gain ground and I doubt not the operation of his plans will evince their goodness and gainsay every opponent.[19]

Acceptance of Morris' programs went slowly in Virginia. There were grumblings about the Yorktown tobacco deal, and the lack of appreciation for efforts made in good faith by the Old Dominion. They pointed to their efforts with Oliver Pollock to support George Rogers Clark's work in the western borders. The validity of these efforts as real expenses would come into question when it was learned that Virginia made excuse after excuse not to pay Pollock. The lack of hard money coming from the Office of Finance to Virginia was falsely used as evidence that Morris' Office was favoring some states over others. A committee of delegates from that state consisting of Arthur Lee, Joseph Jones, and James Madison went to visit Morris on that account. Morris reminded them of the workings of his plan, and that the states receiving money through government contractors were the same ones who paid money instead of specific supplies. Morris wrote in his diary,

> In short I believe the delegates were perfectly satisfied of my impartiality and desire to serve the United States. I told them that ... whatever I can consistently do for the relief of Virginia from her present difficulties I certainly shall do but they must ultimately expect to supply me with money.[20]

These interstate differences aside, European powers continued to expect America to pay for its own war; and would supply no more funds.[21]

Morris anticipated that the Yorktown tobacco deal would yield some money to help the American prisoners held in New York. He tried to move the process forward when he set the price to be paid for the leaves.[22] Just as everything was ready to proceed, the Governor of Virginia became more adamant that even though his state would not levy taxes in the form of money they would also not allow Morris' office to dictate the form of specific supplies, i.e. tobacco.[23] This delayed the shipment, and more effort was required.

Morris' insistence on sticking to the money value of bulk goods slowed compliance by Virginia, but his program of requiring cash payments instead of items in barter was useful in funding the purchase of supplies through contractors. However, it was not going to be sufficient to pay for much more than that. With a huge debt hanging over every expense, and with peace still elusive, Morris proposed a new finance and tax system. He thought the new system would be sufficient to pay the debt, settle the accounts of the states, and fund the ongoing business of government. He had not yet published his work "On Public Credit," but on February 27th, 1782, he was willing to share the general outlines.

> I shall propose the following Taxes to wit.
>
> 1st A land tax of one dollar for every hundred acres of land
>
> 2ly [secondly] a Poll tax of one dollar on all freemen and all male slaves between sixteen and sixty, excepting such are in the federal Army, and such as are by Wounds or otherwise unfit for Service, and
>
> 3ly [thirdly] An excise of 1/8th of Dollar per Gallon on all distilled Spirituous Liquors."[24]

This letter was read in Congress and referred to a committee made up of Arthur Lee of Virginia, Samuel Osgood of Massachusetts, and Abraham Clark of New Jersey, all of whom were habitually against Morris' nationalistic programs. At that time, all the states levied taxes on their own citizens. Massachusetts elected their tax authorities. Pennsylvania's tax system was administered by locally elected officials who also tended to be responsive to the local population. Virginia also had a tax system with a tax on slaves, land and other items, but it was collected at the direction of people appointed by the Assembly according to whatever system the appointee chose to follow. There was no small amount of chicanery in that state. In one famous case the state treasurer, who was supposed to collect and destroy state paper currency as a move against inflation, decided it was preferable to distribute it to his friends instead.[25] It was routine for tax collectors to press harder on yeoman farmers than the large planters who were also members of the Assembly. The system was ripe for abuse because the tax collector was the same person who was empowered to take property when taxes were not forthcoming. Virginians were no strangers to abusive tax collection systems, and they were not interested in a federal system that they could not control.

Virginia had over 200,000 slaves in 1782 and a federal head tax paid on slaves, and a tax on real estate would not please slave-holding committee members like Arthur Lee. His family had over 250 slaves and 30,000 acres of land. On March 25th Lee's committee reported against the proposal, and their report was read months later, on August 5th. They thought the mode was "too exceptional" and would fall unequally among the states.[26]

Morris could not let disappointments in Congress halt his efforts completely. He still had an office to run, and daily expenses to manage. He had to refuse raises for his clerks, who were on the civil list.[27] He could not justify raising their pay above a subsistence level when soldiers in the field were going without. In other business, he bought special paper for printing bills of exchange so there would be security and value in the notes.[28] Washington wrote that Von Steuben wanted money.[29] Of course Morris knew this from his own meeting with Von Steuben.

Morris got word from Ridley in Europe. Young Robert and Thomas had arrived in Europe but were not yet enrolled in a proper school. The original intention was to enroll them in a school in Geneva, but war in that country had made that dangerous and unappealing. Ridley still looked after them and volunteered to find a proper tutor if a suitable school was not found soon.

Morris hires Paine

Morris moved forward with the secret plan to hire Thomas Paine. He provided Paine with a list of goals for a public relations campaign. Morris hoped Paine would galvanize public support for his programs and reinvigorate the patriotic spirit.

> ... we want the aid of an able pen to urge the Legislatures of the several States to grants sufficient taxes; to grant those taxes separate and distinct from those levied for State purposes; to put such taxes, or rather the money arising from them, in the power of Congress, from the moment of collection;
>
> To grant permanent revenues for discharging the interest on debts already contracted, or that may be contracted;
>
> To extend by a new confederation the powers of Congress, so that they may be competent to the government of the United States and the management of their affairs;
>
> To prepare the minds of the people for such restraints and such taxes and imposts, as are absolutely necessary for their own welfare;
>
> To comment from time to time on military transactions, so as to place in a proper point of view the bravery, good conduct, and soldiership of our officers and troops, when they deserve applause and to do the same on such conduct of such civil officers of citizens, as act conspicuously for the service of their country.[30]

Public support would be welcome as Morris' economic programs were being considered and fought over in State Houses up and down the Atlantic coast. In the Pennsylvania Assembly, Morris' Republican faction was able to get the Assembly to agree to pay the state's whole requisition in hard money, but the "Constitutionalists" made sure that most of the taxes would be apportioned to, and paid by, the counties which supported Morris' program, namely Philadelphia and Chester Counties.[31]

While Morris' grand strategy was playing out, Franklin was working to send military supplies from France to America. He wrote to say he could not find ships to sail through the British blockade, so while there were war supplies awaiting shipment there were no ships available to carry them. On a positive note, he mentioned that the French promised a loan of 6 million livres at 1,500,000 per quarter.[32] Promises aside, getting the money from France to America past the blockade was a problem. The Office of Finance was the point of contact in gaining funds from other European countries as well. Gouverneur Morris was assigned to communicate with

Spanish agent Rendón to get a Spanish alliance on track, and to support Jay's efforts. The best Rendón could do was appeal to the Spanish King for the protection of American commerce.[33]

The daily demands continued in the Office. The President of Congress applied for a pair of horses.[34] Eleven cannons were brought from Virginia to Maryland to be sold.[35] Morris directed Timothy Pickering, the quartermaster general, to sell 1000 barrels of salted provisions in Rhode Island for Morris notes, or Bank notes; and then to buy supplies for Fort Pitt in Pennsylvania with money Pennsylvania remitted.[36] He continued to work with the military contractors, and to be deluged with requests for funds by individuals of all kinds. Among them was former general Charles Lee. He needed money after his court martial from the Army, so he sold his plantation. The people who contracted to buy it didn't pay for it. Morris advanced his own money in the form of a mortgage to help Lee get the sale relinquished so Lee could sell to a party who would pay.[37]

Morris had been in office for about a year and the states were far from unanimous in their support for his programs. New Hampshire wanted to pay its requisition in old Continental currency at a decreased rate, and to have its requisition lowered.[38] They were also dealing with a group of armed citizens who wanted to split the state and form Vermont, so that state was busy with a threatened armed struggle within its borders. Massachusetts, Connecticut, and Rhode Island were acting to grant part of Morris' request. New York was suffering internal conflicts and claimed it was "much exhausted and impoverished by the war." New Jersey seemed to be willing to try to help but were unsure how to generate the cash. Pennsylvania and Delaware were expected to pass tax laws to raise the funds. Maryland and Virginia were sticking to the system of specific supplies. Georgia was still occupied by the British. According to General Greene events in the Deep South were not progressing in an orderly direction. Greene wrote about the ravages of war and the gangs of insurgents that roamed the south and hampered all efforts at establishing regularity in people's conduct. He wrote,

> What can be expected from those States who have been ravaged continually and who are still torn to pieces by little parties of disaffected who elude all search, and conceal themselves in the thickets and swamps from the most diligent pursuit and issue forth from these hidden recesses committing the most horrid Murders and plunder and lay waste the country.[39]

Morris considered the slow adoption of his system and the continuing need for money. On March 8th he borrowed another $100,000 from the Bank of North America to refill the treasury.[40]

New Hampshire's proposal to send old paper money to Morris was not accepted. The state was not sure how to meet its obligation to send hard money to the federal government. Morris wrote,

> Now sire if the citizens of New Hampshire will sell their beef and other produce of their country on reasonable terms it will command either hard money or these notes [Morris notes or Bank notes], and your Government should immediately order all the tax gatherers to receive them in payment. Your beeves [beefs] may be sold to the contractors who undoubtedly will buy where they can buy cheapest. The ship America will cost a good deal of money...

Morris went on to encourage New Hampshire to cooperate in the tax plan so the money could be spent in New Hampshire and the *America* would be finished. He outlined his program and explained how he was willing to use his own notes to get the system started. He also had to contradict the popular notion that he was busy working on his private business by replying to a gentleman from New Hampshire that he was in fact, too busy on Continental business for any new private ventures.[41]

Morris was running an efficient operation in the Office of Finance. He had kept the Army in the field over the year and spent under $500,000 in cash.[42] That was just in payment of obligations incurred from the time Morris took office. Morris' policy of paying only the current costs had repercussions. Suppliers were starting to sue purchasing officers for amounts due from before Morris' tenure.[43] This made those purchasing officers even more reluctant to part with any of the supplies they had on hand. They wished to sell those supplies and pay the suppliers and avoid punishment. Morris refused to allow them to do that because a contested item is better than none. He insisted the money go to the army via the contracting system. He worked to get Congress to pass a law that would put off such lawsuits until the accounts of the states were settled.

An unhappy discovery was made in Europe. Supplies that Col. John Laurens and his associates had purchased in Amsterdam, turned out to be English made.[44, 45] It was illegal to buy English products during the Revolution and they had to be sold immediately. Morris was less interested in finding the guilty party than getting things straight. He wrote,

> As these Matters are not clearly stated, it would be useless to go at present into an Enquiry who had been or is to blame and therefore any particular observations from me would be both unnecessary and improper.[46]

Working from Passy, Franklin followed Congress' directive to settle the accounts of American agents in Europe. He arranged to pay requests for funds from John Ross and William Bingham, but he thought that Holker's request would go unpaid for a while. This was due to caution on the part of Morris' French banker, who was also acting as Congress' banker in France. That French banker said Congress was not paying what it owed, and he would not honor their checks until they did. Morris' reputation was at stake in this affair since he had convinced his French banker to take the bankrupt America as a client. If the states would only pay their share, Europe would be more helpful.

Franklin wrote Morris about events unfolding on the diplomatic front. He pointed to changes in the political winds in England,

> ... the sense of the nation is fully against the continuance of the American War. Petitions of the Cities of London and Bristol were unanimous against it...

He cautioned,

> That nation is changeable. And tho' somewhat humbled at Present, a little Success may make them as insolent as ever. I remember that when I was a boxing boy, it was allow'd even after an adversary said he had enough, to give him a rising Blow. Let ours be a Douser.

That Quaker gentleman saw that the road to peace was for the strong.[47]

Special interests kept knocking on Morris' door. Arthur Lee went to Morris' office ostensibly to discuss the tax proposal, and ended up asking if his brother, William, would be paid for his work in Europe. Captain James Willing, who had been released by the British from prison in New York, went to Morris in search of support for his proposed return trip down to the Mississippi. Morris replied,

> I told him his conduct had been improper when there formerly and that I thought it probable he might meet with trouble on that account.

Morris refused to give him letters of recommendation for passage.[48]

Morris received word that horses were starving in Maryland. The President of Congress wanted money to pay the rent on his house. Morris learned that there were 450 prisoners in Mill Prison in England, and they were ill fed and needed supplies.[49] He continued to be informed on the topic of the Bank, as his meetings with the Bank's directors were conducted on a regular basis.

Spring

Clearly, it would be necessary for America to develop trade relations with as many countries as possible, but most were reluctant because of their own internal policies, and the status of America as a rebel colony. Morris already had private trading relations with Spain, Italy, and the Levant. Utilizing his habit of seeking new opportunities, gained though his years as merchant, he tried to open Prussia to American trade through Baron d'Arendt. He said his Prussian Majesty should take advantage of the new freedom of America,

> ...the Importance thereof can be easily estimated from the Riches it poured into Britain while she enjoyed the benefit of monopoly. All that is needful to be done is to set open his Ports to our Vessels and protect them whilst there.[50]

The Prussians did not respond in the affirmative. Morris had to look elsewhere.

Long term plans took a back seat to immediate cash needs. Now that a new loan was coming in from the French, Morris started to sell bills of exchange through broker Hyam Salomon.[51] When these bills of exchange were sold it amounted to an individual buying a check written on an account in France, for example, and in remitting hard money to the seller. The rate of these exchanges varied according to people's ability to buy, and their interest in owning these checks. For example, a person could buy a check worth $100 for $90, and that would be a 10% discount. The buyer would do this because he could collect the $100 from the bank and make $10. Sometimes there was no market because no one had the money, or because the people with money had enough of these bills already, or because the buyer didn't believe the seller could guarantee the value of the bill, or it was impossible to get to the foreign bank due to something like the British blockade.

Most of the money that Morris raised went to supporting the troops. General Washington also needed money to pay the expense of maintaining his headquarters. Morris offered him some in the form of his personal notes; however, he insisted that Washington use them at their face value in silver. While Morris was trying to establish sound currency as the basis of trade, he continued to contend with remnants of the system that had failed earlier. It was a system that he suspected was full of corruption. In one such case, he had to deal with a reluctant Continental loan officer in Rhode Island who was stalling and not settling his accounts. Morris was not accepting any more excuses, and he expected the man to wrap the business.[52] More locally, Morris got word that the price for bills of exchange was improving, and Hyam Salomon asked if there were more to sell.[53] Meanwhile, Morris continued working on the mint with Wheeler and Dudley.[54] When a difficult mechanical problem arose they brought David Rittenhouse and Francis Hopkinson into the effort.[55]

During this time, Gouverneur Morris was in New Jersey negotiating for the care and/or the release of prisoners of war. The English wanted their prisoners released. America wanted the English to follow customary procedures and pay for the care of Englishmen captured as prisoners during Saratoga and Yorktown. The last thing the English wanted was to give hard money to the Americans, instead they wanted to subtract the amount they had spent on maintaining American prisoners who had been captured on privateers and held in England. These Americans were not Continental navy personnel, so America argued that the Continental Congress should not pay. No prisoner exchanges were possible until these accounts were settled, and there was a stalemate. Washington decided to offer the Germans prisoners the opportunity to enlist in the American army instead of allowing them to languish in prison at the expense of America.[56]

Robert used the continuing discussions with the British to get Captain John Green released from Mill Prison in England. He wrote Gouverneur Morris,

> ... he was a master of a ship in which I was part owner when taken, and had been many years in my employ. He has a Numerous Family here and is a deserving man.

Morris offered to pay a lawyer in England to do this, or to swap an English prisoner for him.[57]

While conferences continued, various state assemblies argued, and American soldiers went hungry in camps in the north and south, America's economy was staggering from the effects of the British blockade. The land war was quiet, but things were different at sea. British frigates and ships of the line were cruising the coast and taking eighty percent of the ships that tried to trade in American ports. In addition, there were small boats in the Delaware River which Tory sympathizers used to attack American merchant ships.[58] This too, was crippling trade. In a private effort to protect and encourage trade Thomas Fitzsimmons, a director of the Bank of North America, and a Mr. Nesbit offered to buy a naval frigate from the French so they could use it to patrol the Delaware. Morris contacted the French council general to arrange this.

Considering the blockade, Morris concluded America needed a competent navy, but that would be impossible under the current conditions, especially up north. Marine matters in New England were still unresolved, because administration was never as simple as giving orders. It always required managing the relationships between people. In the eighteenth century that was a slow process of letters and conferences. John Brown and the former members of the Eastern Naval Board were feuding. Morris tried to get them to work together, and not allow personal animosities get in the way of the mission. The members of the Eastern Naval Board did not want to sell Naval stores and send the money to the federal government. They were concerned about being sued in Massachusetts courts for non-payments on public accounts. They wanted the accounts of the State of Massachusetts to be adjusted for their value, or for the items to be sold to pay Massachusetts. Morris would not allow this because these items belonged to the Continental Navy, and not the state of Massachusetts.

Morris told Brown to prepare to leave Boston.

> I will not detain you longer in Boston on that account. Messrs. Warren and Vernon [of the Naval Board] have surprised me much by declining to deliver those Stores and more by withholding an Inventory of them. You must remember that I always considered them as Gentlemen of respectable Character and that I placed confidence in them ...[59]

Morris sent John Brown from Boston to Connecticut to see if the *Bourbon* could be launched, or if it should be sold. Even if it were finished, there were few sailors to get it to sea. He heard from Captain John Barry that out of the two hundred and twenty men and boys on his ship "there are not 12 Seamen." The shortage of competent seamen was due to continuing allure of privateering. Additionally, the capture of many sailors by the British continued to plague the small Continental Navy.[60] To make matters worse, The Armed Neutrality continued to make privateering and naval interdiction efforts difficult to conduct. England sent all her war goods on neutral ships,[61] and this put the contents out of bounds for the Americans.

Morris wrote to the Navy Board of the Eastern Department, and he tried to defuse the disagreement by providing the recalcitrant managers with a way out.

> Probably you forgot that it was my desire that the Money for fitting those ships should have been furnished by the State of Massachusetts in Part Payment for the Balances due to the United States on the former requisitions of Congress...

Morris was letting them know that these supplies would be sold and the money spent in Massachusetts; but he could not allow the items to be seized.

> If this practice was to be admitted how is the Public Service to be carried on, is the cause of America to be lost because those debts cannot be immediately satisfied and if all the public stores can be withheld from the public Service under such pretences it is easy to see that all our operations must cease.

Morris addressed the concerns in Massachusetts about looming lawsuits by suppliers against government purchasers for non-payment.

> You will find that all actions brought against the Public Servants for debts actually contracted for and on behalf of the United States must be discontinued or meet a stay of judgment on due proof being made.[62]

Finally, when John Brown returned from New England in May, Morris noted,

> ...from his representations it appears that the Navy Board of Boston have much misbehaved themselves.[63]

Just as John Brown and the Naval Board were arguing, so were John Paul Jones and John Langdon. Langdon had been sent to Portsmouth, New Hampshire, to help complete the construction of the *America*. Jones had the same goal in mind, but he thought it was going too slowly. Morris wrote to Jones,

> He [Langdon] is a respectable Gentleman, his Country confides in him and you must not listen to every thing you hear. Public Men are too much subjected to abuse in Republics especially if they have any thing to do with Money Matters. I cannot yet spare funds for this ship as fast as I could wish but expect to do it in the progress of the season, in the mean time Colo. Langdon must only Proportion his force to the Means.[64]

He then wrote to Langdon,

> ...with respect to the coldness between Capt. Jones and you I most sincerely wish it were done away. Harmony between Gentlemen engaged in the same Cause and particularly whilst employed on the same Object is absolutely necessary if they mean to promote and serve the Public Interest.[65]

Morris supplied Langdon with $10,000 in Morris notes, and cautioned,

> ...these you must keep until they will command the money dollar for dollar in your state or Massachusetts and when you get the money then drive on and I will supply more.[66]

It seemed friction and discontent were everywhere in America. Morris worked to convince Governor Harrison of Virginia to remit tobacco instead of other specific supplies, and Virginia continued to resist.[67] Elsewhere, disagreements with contractors in New Jersey nagged at Morris' attention and hurt the Army's morale. The prime contractor in New Jersey, Francis & Slough, was having difficulty with a sub-contractor. The sub-contractor was out of Morris' direct control. The problems lingered and finally the contract was dissolved in May.[68]

Then there was the case of a man with a real problem. Morris responded to a seaman who had lost his leg on the *Alliance.*

> I lament the loss of your limb and am extremely sorry that it is not in my Power to pay the money at present.[69]

Congress had not yet created a pension system for disabled veterans, and Morris could not act without that kind of authority. Instead, Morris encouraged him to join other individuals and to lobby the states to pay their share and create a national funding system so deserving individuals would be compensated.

Among the many pieces of news that crossed his desk, Morris received a report that the militia in Burlington New Jersey had destroyed an orphanage. He sent someone to inspect the situation. Also, he learned that General Charles Lee was successful in getting out of his bad real estate contract. Lee wrote,

> ...was it not for the friendship of Mr. Morris and a fortunate purchase that I made (more by luck than by cunning) I might be begging on the streets without much chance of being relieved.[70]

A letter from France offered a change in the pace of business in the Office of Finance. Franklin wrote Morris to bring him up to date on events in Europe,

> No demand has been made on me by Mr. Wm Lee. I do not know where he is; and I think he did so little for the 3000 Guineas he receiv'd that he may wait without much Inconvenience for the Addition.

Franklin seemed to think that William Lee was getting more than he deserved, but then William Lee had been waging a political campaign against Franklin since 1778. Franklin went on to say,

> I do not know whether this will diminish your expense for the coming campaign, because while they have an army in our Country, I do not think their proposed Inactivity is to be trusted, tho' it is said that after such resolutions of Parliament, no Minister will dare to order offensive operations.

Rumors of quiet were not enough to convince Franklin, who still had the difficult job of forging a real peace at the negotiating table. He also reported that troops were no longer being sent from Ireland, and recruits from Germany were not being sent to the sea for any voyage to America.[71]

Clearly, uncertainty prevailed in diplomatic circles. This meant Morris must keep working to supply the needs of the Southern Army. When the hope of getting hard money from that quarter was gone, Morris was willing to take specific supplies at their cash value, in order to help General Greene.[72] As the Southern Department struggled to find supplies in the Carolinas, Morris implemented his policies in the north. He had advertised for a new contract to supply the Moving Army, which encompassed much of the military force north of the Mason Dixon Line, including Washington's Army. Among those who responded was a company in which Morris and John Holker held an interest, Turnbull, Marmie & Co. On April 2nd, 1782, another group headed by Daniel Parker won the bid.[73] It was soon discovered that Parker had bid in a different currency from the other bidders, and that made the bid seem lower than it really was. No one would vouch for Parker in the business so finally his bid was rejected. A New Yorker, Mr. William Duer, then won the contract.[74] Daniel Parker was not quick to go away, and eventually worked as a sub-contractor under the Moving Army contract. Later he tried to become a prime contractor in Morris' supply system. Morris asked George Washington to help by telling the contractor where to put supplies so they would be most useful.[75]

These first contracts were written as good faith documents, and as such were not absolutely specific about all the details. This probably seemed reasonable because Morris and Duer were well acquainted from Duer's earlier days in the Congress, and Morris was godfather to one of Duer's children. The contractors, however, appeared to take advantage of the loose contract. Morris had to learn how to operate this new system of contractors. He decided that to deal successfully with them he needed an on-site arbitrator who would quickly resolve differences between the army and the contractors.[76]

New York State was the recipient of much of the money spent in this Moving Army contract so Morris focused on getting the Government in Albany to contribute to the effort. New York was, and still is, a large state. Even if the British held New York City, there was plenty of territory in the hands of the American patriots. Morris communicated with his friend John Livingston, who was a member of the New York state government even though he was also serving as Secretary of Foreign Affairs at the time. Morris wrote,

> The State of New York has plead Poverty and Inability for twelve months that I have been in the Office, I have never received one Shilling of Money from it to this day, and the Agent stopped all supplies to the Army long since, so that in Fact nothing has been contributed ... to the support of the War for more than a year, altho the greatest part of the Money expended during that Time has been sent thither.

He went on to ask Livingston to stop the Governor of that state from using their money outside the Confederated system. Morris had learned that the Governor had sent money specifically to support the troops from New York. The problem with this approach was "there are States that will pay better than she can, and of course her line will become discontented."[77] Morris was worried that discontent would lead to mutiny.

The most discontented American soldiers were prisoners of war. To resolve their plight Gouverneur Morris continued negotiations with the British. To bolster their side, Robert counseled Gouverneur that in negotiations he could tell the British that,

> ... from one end of this Continent to the other I can obtain whatever is wanted for the public Service, by a script of the Pen.[78]

Robert told Gouverneur that support for the British prisoners would cost the British $1000 per day, and if money was not forthcoming he should work to get specific supplies from the British. The British could easily get goods through their own blockade.[79] Shortly after this, the prisoner conference reached an impasse. Gouverneur Morris came back to Philadelphia.

The cost of maintaining these prisoners was high, so it was again suggested that the Hessian prisoners be able to earn their freedom and become American citizens.[80] Two months later, in July, the committee on prisoners made a deal with the owner of a local iron foundry to take German prisoners as indentured workers. Morris proposed to the Secretary of War that the German prisoners be allowed to take an oath of allegiance to the United States and pay $80 each for their freedom. The secretary agreed to act.[81] Morris' plan to have the German prisoners buy their freedom and become Americans resulted in a net gain of $27,840 for the Continental Treasury.[82]

Morris kept focused on the income side and worked to appoint tax receivers. He installed Lowell in Massachusetts, William Churchill Houston in New Jersey,[83] and George Read in Delaware.[84] Morris wrote the Governor of South Carolina and requested that he appoint a receiver of taxes in that state.[85] He expected these receivers to be active agents as well as tax collectors. He encouraged them to help overcome localist objections; and supported them with a new circular to the states. Morris tried to overcome each state's feeling that it had already contributed more than its share so they would send their requisition. He wrote,

> No determination of quota's which Congress can at this time possible make, will create a difference for or against any State, equal to the expense which will arise either by disputing its quota, or by delaying to have it fixed.

Morris pointed out that a settlement would be made, and that fighting the quota would just cost extra money on top of what was requested by Congress.[86]

It was difficult for the states to contribute, even if they wanted to, because of their own expenses and the British blockade. That blockade was not only costing the Office of Finance in its ability to utilize the French loans, and the merchants in lost revenue; it also made military supplies hard to deliver. Goods and equipment for the army had to be moved by ox teams instead of by ship. In anticipation of a new spring campaign Morris provided Quartermaster General T. Pickering, with $40,000 to buy ox teams in New England so goods in New York could be transported to the south.[87]

In an effort to help the soldiers in western Pennsylvania, Morris was willing to take specific supplies delivered at Ft. Pitt in lieu of money for the same fort.[88] He was flexible enough to see the benefit of taking specific supplies when they were delivered at the point where they were useful instead of insisting on blind adherence to his own directive of accepting only hard money. He said he would only accept the flour if it were of high quality and in barrels, and if it had been valued at its hard money price. He decided that if there was extra flour it should be shipped on riverboats to New Orleans for sale.[89]

The far-flung armies were not the only ones in need of aid; so was the Navy. To encourage public support for countering the blockade, Morris encouraged Thomas Paine to write an article in support of defending American Commerce. Morris hoped this would aid his effort to convince Congress of the importance of a navy. An anonymous letter was published that reflected Morris' views on the subject.[90] Morris started an initiative to review and settle Marine accounts.[91]

The services needed support, and so did many individuals. Supplicants continued to come into Morris' office. Some were more deserving than others. Morris had to determine the validity of the claims. The investigation of the aforementioned Orphanage was completed, and it turned out that instead of being laid waste by the Army it had been converted to a hospital for continental soldiers and wounded militiamen. This put it into a different category and onto the list of impressed articles. In a personal case, one Mr. Wynkoop was in the Continental Army when he took command of the "gunboat fleet" in the lakes of New York. This was a state navy, so Morris told him that he would not receive Continental Navy pay or benefits and should apply to New York for his pay as a member of their state navy. Morris continued that he would allow him to apply for his pay during that time as a member of the Army, right along with the rest of the members of that armed force.[92]

Early patriots waited many years for these long-delayed payments to be made. However, in April 1782, Morris still expected the states to make good on their commitments, and so he was confident that the Continental Government would be able to repay Americans who had supported the war, and ultimately the French.[93] The loan money that the French had put into Grand's bank in France was being turned into cash through the sale of bills of exchange sold through commission brokers like Hyam Salomon. Salomon was getting notes and selling them. He remitted an agreed value for the note and kept the difference. Morris asked Hyam Salomon to adjust his business with the treasury, and to account for the forty-two notes of which he had taken possession.[94]

French money helped keep the country on a war footing while news from France hinted at peace. Franklin wrote to Morris that things were looking up in England because a new ministry had just been installed.

> Since my last [letter] of the 30th past we hear that the old ministry are all out to a Man, and that the new Ministry have, kiss'd hands, and were about to enter on their respective Functions.... They are all of them Men who have in Parliament declar'd strongly against the American War as unjust.[95]

The regular flow of business continued to move through the Office of Finance. Members of the Pennsylvania Assembly sought Morris' advice on matters of state finance.[96] General Greene told Morris that the south was so disrupted that it was difficult to supply any army, his or the English; that money from other states was not valued so please send supplies.[97] The plan for minting money that would retain its value went slowly, Dudley wanted a horse so he could travel and see the mechanic.[98] Morris received a letter from his French banker asking him to help Mr. Thomas Beer and his family. Mr. Beer was a rope maker who had helped many Americans escape Mill Prison in England and was forced to flee to America when he was caught in the act.

Morris continued to appoint receivers of taxes in anticipation of remittances to the Continental Government. After some haggling, Alexander Hamilton accepted the role of tax receiver in New York State. It took some convincing because Hamilton did not think New York would pay enough into Morris' national funding system to make his effort worthwhile. By the middle of April 1782, Morris had most of his tax receivers in place. He sent a letter to them to establish policies and keep everyone headed in the same direction. Morris wanted his hand-picked agents to be above reproach and to lobby the states into compliance with the wishes of Congress, and with the details of his program. They were his front line in this first effort to nationalize the economy.

He wrote,

> 1) "you must use the most tremendous and unremitting Efforts, by all the lawful and just Ways and Means in your power to urge the collection of taxes.
>
> 2) Urge a compliance with the Resolutions of the Congress of the eighteenth of March 1780 and such other measures as may tend to call in all paper emissions." He exhorted them to also fight emission of new state paper.
>
> 3) To "pursue the strict maxims of Integrity and Oeconomy in your own official Character and Conduct" and take measures to stop frauds."
>
> 4) "if you see tendencies to prefer local interests to general interests you must prudently oppose that."
>
> 5) and to "keep me regularly informed." [99]

As a last step he advised,

> If no payment is made that you declare in one of the news papers published in that state that you have not during that month received any money for the use of the United States. Let your publication be made in terms that will make known the facts without giving offense.

Morris also instructed the receivers to accept his notes in payment of tax money.[100]

Once that was underway, he turned his attention back to long-standing business in the Marine department. Morris urged the completion of ships: *America* in New Hampshire, and the *Bourbon* in Connecticut, so American ships could break through the British blockade. He wanted to get as many ships to sea as possible, but that required the assistance of Congress. He appealed to them,

> I cannot help observing that from present appearances it may become immediately necessary to bend our attention and exertions to the accomplishment of a naval force for the protection of that commerce which is to enable the payment of taxes throughout the United States.[101]

Morris' office was the front line in the new economic phase of the Revolution, but America's economy relied on the sea for food and trade. The Congress was drowning in debt. Growers could not make money because they could not get their goods to market, and merchants could not carry goods for fear of British privateers. Fishing fleets were grounded, and trading centers were shut. The British were choking the trade of the United States and making it difficult for the states to recover their financial footing. At the same time, they offered Americans items for sale in New York, and this brought in an illegal trade. The Bank of North America was feeling the pinch because the illegal trade with the British in New York had depleted the Bank's supply of silver. They stopped making loans and cashing notes. Morris knew two warships would not be enough to protect the commerce of America from the British blockade. He offered a solution. In May 1782 he requested that Congress authorize the construction of a navy starting with six ships a year.[102]

Morris saw that the United States, as he called them, were subject to attack because of their military weakness and exposure to thousands of miles of seacoast. He noted that nineteen out of twenty American ships that tried to run the blockade were lost to the British.[103] He contended a strong Navy would protect commercial shipping; and pointed out a Navy would protect American neutrality in times of wars between European powers. It would project the American presence around the world, and this would also create awareness of America outside of Europe.[104] Such awareness would be beneficial to the trading interests of the United States and the resulting growth in trade would generate income for the payments of the debts of the Congress by way of the impost.

Considering the effort spent by the European powers on their navies, it is striking that the American Congress was so disinterested in building its own Naval power. However, the people in Congress represented state governments that wanted to protect state power. Localists argued that the states should be responsible for defending their own coasts with the "Gun Boat" defense system, even though that system had failed miserably. In response to Congress' disposition to do nothing, Robert Morris and John Dickinson acted personally to outfit the schooner *Delaware* to protect ships in the Delaware Bay and River from the British.[105]

Morris did not have the luxury of focusing only on the marine issue. Next, he wielded his greatest weapon in the war of finance. He lifted his pen to appeal to those who could help in creating a national funding system. Morris wrote the continental loan officer of Massachusetts Nathaniel Appleton,

> We cannot be called a Nation, nor do we deserve to be ranked amongst the Nations of Earth, until we do justice to those who have served and trusted us. A public debt supported by Public Revenue will prove the strongest cement to keep our Confederacy together.[106]

Morris planned to attach the interest of the debt holders to the nationalization of the economy, and the debt holders included the members of the Army and Navy, who were owed money for their service, as well as the rich and not-so-rich who had purchased loan certificates.

The states had committed to pay requisitions under the Articles of Confederation they had recently ratified. However, when they were asked to pay for the cost of the war, even with the enemy at hand, they were slow to comply. Morris was using his own money, foreign loans, and delayed payments to acquire food and clothing for the Army. At the same time, states like Connecticut were selling provisions in Continental storehouses and pocketing the revenues. Then they would account for this in their books by substituting supplies that were scattered through the countryside. This ruse shifted the cost of transport of goods to the Continental expense account and made it harder for Morris to sell the supplies to raise money for the Southern Army.[107]

Nathaniel Greene, who was working hard to keep the Southern Army together, was feeling the lack of coordinated action by the states. He wrote about the effect of the Associators from Pennsylvania,

> The seeds of discontent and mutiny which have been deep rooted among the Pena. troops they are endeavoring to spread through the whole army and not without the appearances of success. I have not been able to fix the crime on more than one person who is a sergeant and of much influence. I shall order him executed immediately and hope they may be deterred from accomplishing their scheme which we nightly dread.[108]

The cost of each state's localist thinking was high in life and treasure. Morris considered that the cost of the war was increased by 25-50% because everything became an emergency.[109]

Back in Philadelphia, good news came when the Chevalier de La Luzerne announced to Morris that the French crown had decided to make 6,000,000 livres available to America, but there would be no more after that.[110] Morris sought to keep this news quiet because he knew that if the states learned the French were supplying money, that would make it even more difficult to convince the states to pay their quota into the national system. In a separate acknowledgement, France also agreed not to confuse an agreement with the State of Virginia with the deal with the Continent. The French crown was not pleased to learn that Virginia was acting alone in arranging their loan, because they thought the Continental treasury would back that state.[111] Morris wrote the Governor of Virginia about his hope that states would stop seeking independent aid in Europe, and to please inform his office of Virginia's payment plans so he could help and take measures to "preserve her [Virginia's] Credit and not be injurious to the United States." He also noted that in an accounting of the deal between Virginia and France, Mr. William Lee had spent 66,853 livres in unspecified supplies for that state.[112] Naturally, W. Lee expected a commission for his troubles. 2.5% of 66,853 is 1,671.32 livres, or 417.83 Spanish milled dollars. Virginia was not alone in seeking loans in Europe. Maryland also tried to negotiate a loan from Holland. They hired Matthew Ridley as their agent. Years later, Ridley did arrange a loan, but the process was halted when it became clear that the state's credit was so bad, that the best terms he could arrange were unacceptable to the Maryland Assembly.[113]

The endless flow of supplicants kept arriving at Morris' door looking for money. A Philadelphia merchant and ardent "Constitutionalist," Blair McClenachan, wanted a quick settlement on old Secret Committee business. It was against Morris' policy to pay old debts, and he was not quick to go back to work on that account after McClenachan had not provided information when Morris requested it in 1778, when he was trying to settle those same accounts.[114] French Captain, Landais, petitioned Congress for a settlement. Morris said Landais had threatened the Secretary of his Office and

> ...drove out of his lodgings with abusive language threatening to beat him with a stick, which he picked up for that purpose."

Morris continued to say that Landais should wait with everyone else who had a valid claim on the Government, and noted that if they make a special case of Landais then many more petitioners will come forward and all their time will be taken with paying people when there is no money to do so.[115] In other business, Turnbull proposed a contract in Connecticut for forage to feed extra horses and cattle over the winter,[116] and at Fort Pitt, General William Irvine was arranging boats to take expected surplus flour to market in New Orleans as a way getting money to supply his restless garrison.[117]

The New York merchants pressed ahead with the Virginia tobacco deal, and George Eddy arranged passports for the Virginia State tobacco traded on Continental Account. As a measure of good faith in America, and as a way of safekeeping for money they expected to spend on their own troops, the French deposited 300,000 livres into the Bank of North America.[118] This deposit allowed the Bank to restart its policy of discounting and ended their short term cash shortage. The Southern Army needed money, so Morris sent $5,000 in silver and $20,000 in his own notes by way of Colonel Edward Carrington of the Quartermaster corps.[119] Carrington turned Morris' notes into specie at the Bank of North America before going to South Carolina. This meant that Morris had just personally donated another $20,000, in silver, to the war effort, which would be over half a million dollars today.

Relief from the endless pressure would occasionally arrive in the form of a letter from Europe. John Jay wrote from Spain that Ridley had arrived there with Morris' boys. They had not been sent to Geneva because of the shooting there, and he wrote that,

> "Caty's [Catharine Livingston] late letters have given us reason to be anxious bout her health, and to be grateful for your and Mrs. Morris' attention to her. She is a valuable and affectionate friend, and I am happy that in these unsettled times she has a pleasing retreat in your friendly and hospitable Family.

The Morris' had taken Catharine Livingston into their home on High (now Market) Street as a guest until she regained her strength. Mrs. Morris was writing back and forth to Jay's wife in Spain. When Jay wrote Morris, he usually covered various diplomatic topics and in this letter, he discussed the nature of living in Spain with soldiers posted everywhere and how oppressive that seemed.[120]

By the spring of 1782 the Morris family was living in their newly rebuilt house on Market Street. The icehouse was cooling drinks for guests. The French cook made meals for children and dignitaries alike. The liveried indentured servants looked smart in attendance in the house and on the coach. Morris continued to help his illegitimate daughter, Polly. He told Charles Croxall that he had set aside a trust of $500 for Polly Morris and he may use it for their family. Unfortunately, two years later, in 1784, Mr. Croxall was deeply in debt and Morris stepped in and assumed his debts. This happened a few times, and ultimately in 1795 Morris provided an estate in New Jersey to be held in trust for Polly and her children, so Mr. Croxall could not harm the financial future of his family.[121] Mary Morris kept up correspondence with the Ridleys in Europe and wrote, "Mr. Morris' good constitution still supports him in health tho' more emerged in business than ever."[122]

Personal respites were rare, far more so than personal attacks. The "genius & habbits," or thinking of the past, was at it again as various localist interests in the state houses in the former colonies tried to defeat Morris' programs by launching a series of allegations. Morris had to defend himself in Virginia, and in New Hampshire. The distance between these cities and Philadelphia, the national scope of Morris' programs, and the fact that people were not personally familiar with Morris became obstacles. He had to explain himself over and over again. He wrote,

> By accepting the Office I now hold I was obliged to neglect my own private Affairs. I have made no speculations in consequence of my Office and instead of being enriched I am poorer this day than I was a year ago.... I have totally quitted commerce and commercial Projects to attach myself wholly to a business which requires my whole Attention.[123]

The states were reluctant to send money, but they knew all about getting money, and were active in pursuit of it from Morris. When they requested money for their previous expenses he responded that he would pay only according to what was actually owed from the start of his administration. He promised a special commissioner to settle accounts of individuals holding continental currency and loan office certificates in South Carolina. This commissioner was to be empowered to "determine on the Justice of every claim which appears against the United States," and that payments would be made from the proceeds of the impost. The impost was yet to be ratified, and Morris looked to increase the number of people who were interested in making it pass.[124] The needs of the army grew as the states delayed. At Fort Pitt in western Pennsylvania, General Irvine used every bit of money on hand to get contractors to buy food from Virginia. The soldiers were getting restless. Irvine wrote, "for seven Days together the latter end of April they had not one ounce of Meat."[125]

Protection of Commerce

Morris worked to build a navy in support of commerce, because of commerce's role in generating funds to support the army, and ultimately pay the debt. He directed the *Bourbon* to be completed and advertised for the contract bids.[126] He also sent $1000 in his own notes to fund the completion of that ship. He wanted to purchase the *Fantastique,* which had been captured as a prize and was up for sale. He intended to strip her "for her stores" and use them to finish the *Bourbon.*[127]

The state of South Carolina wanted to sell one of its ships to the Continental Marine Department. The brigantine *South Carolina* was brought to Philadelphia. Morris and a committee, which included Joshua Humphreys, inspected the vessel. The ship was not purchased for the Navy because a financial agreement could not be made,[128] but Humphries learned a few new techniques during the inspection, which he put to use in his subsequent design for the *USS Constitution, USS Constellation* and the four other frigates built for the United States.[129] In 1782, Congress was leery of building a Continental Navy and the proposal Morris made that year for the construction of six new ships was put aside for nearly ten years. Congress was also slow to support the completion of several currently unfinished ships. They considered sending money to a couple of New England states to be an unpopular business, especially knowing that able seamen were hard to find and that the ships might be destroyed on their first days at sea.

Morris reported to Congress,

> ...the Navy of the United States is not in a situation to afford protection to their commerce nor can be rendered equal to the object for some considerable time even if the necessary funds could be procured. That there means no mode of obtaining such protection unless from the allies of the United States...

Following up on the offer of protection from the Spanish representative, Rendón, Morris requested that Congress ask him as Agent of Marine to apply to France or Spain for protection of the American commercial fleet.[130] At the same time a group of merchants, who had just met with Morris on the subject, followed his advice and petitioned Congress to protect trade. Congress took up the petition and asked Morris to write up a plan.[131] Morris proposed that a convoy system be established.

On May 4th, 1782 Congress resolved:

> That the Superintendent of the Finances [Morris] prepare a state of the commerce of the United States, together with a plan for the protection thereof; And that the Superintendent as Agent of Marine [Morris] make application to the commanders of the fleets of France and Spain in the West Indies for such protection as may be in their power to afford.
>
> That the Agent of Marine [Morris] prepare a draught of an application to be made by Congress to the Court of France for the protection of the trade of the United States, and report to Congress.[132]

The British blockade was still highly effective at strangling America. Consequently, the local economic tide changed for the worse, and Hyam Salomon informed Morris that bills of exchange could no longer be sold in Philadelphia. Morris sent other bills to James Lovell in Boston where they might be easier to sell.[133] At the same time, the brisk, but illegal, trade between individual Americans and the British in New York continued. The British only accepted hard currency and that caused hard money to leave the States. In desperation Morris used an agent who tried to sell the French-backed bills of exchange in British-occupied New York.[134] Morris could have sorely used the hard money that was filling British coffers in that city.

Just after the bad news arrived from Salomon, Morris got the estimate for the Army from General Lincoln. He had to tell Lincoln

> ...that the two million[dollars] payable by the several states on the first of last month I have not received a single Doit [penny] neither do I know when I shall receive any. My engagements are very numerous and extensive so that I am daily subjected to calls for

> considerable sums and should I advance any thing on the Quarter Master's Estimates I might be forced into a violation of my pecuniary engagements the consequence of which would be ruinous. Of the two evils the least must be chosen which is that the operations of the campaign stand still.[135]

On the other side of the blockade, in Europe, the French wanted their loans to be used in the fight against the British. Consequently, they refused to pay the expenses of American diplomats in Europe and requested America make other arrangements. This task fell to Morris. Morris worked to maintain the appearance that the United States was economically and politically viable while the negotiations continued overseas. He knew that it would embarrass the United States to have a set of threadbare diplomats begging in Europe, so he made their support a priority. Working through Mr. Carmichael in Spain, Morris was able to supply funding for the Ambassadors with money loaned from the Farmers General, which was the French tax and tobacco agency.[136] This work went on behind the scenes as the diplomatic effort progressed.

At the same time, the French were still annoyed to learn that they had lent money to the state of Virginia instead of the Continental government, as they had thought. To express their annoyance the French requested assurances from the Congress that Franklin was the official representative and not a free-lancer. William Lee had previously played the role of free-lance diplomat, so this gambit was also their way of objecting to "militia diplomacy." To sooth French nerves Morris advised Congress to "transmit to Dr. Franklin full powers finally to execute the proper obligations for securing debt and fixing the periods of payment."[137] Congress, in turn, allowed ministers to borrow on the credit of the United States for their salaries on a quarterly basis. Franklin's foe, Arthur Lee, objected and wanted to control the funds from the Treasury. Lee did not win the point. Franklin was able to draw the money he needed.

On May 10th Morris submitted his official plan for the protection of commerce, which he had managed to get Congress to request of him. Knowing the Congress was not going to fund a navy Morris intended to coordinate with France and Spain; and create a convoy system. The proposal was to use one French ship of the line and four frigates to break through the British line off the American coast, and a similar number of French ships on the other end of the voyage at L'Orient, Brest, Nantes and Cadiz. Morris considered the ships were as safe as possible on the open sea, and warships would be better used to get merchant ships into the sea lanes. Unfortunately for Morris' plan, the British had already won the Battle of the Saints in the West Indies. This reduced de Grasse's fleet, and France's ability to supply ships for the proposed American convoys.

In those days, even the defeat of an ally provided enterprising citizens with opportunity. Rumors of Admiral de Grasse's capture reached Philadelphia five months after the battle, and a large gambling operation started at the Coffee House in Philadelphia with nearly £100,000 at stake on the topic of de Grasse's fate.[138] Other than this, the economy stagnated. War stopped the ships, but rumors of peace stopped the commerce as well. No one wanted to buy goods at high wartime prices, only to sell them at newly depressed peacetime prices.[139] The French government was reeling from the economic consequences of De Grasse's loss, and began conducting an audit of their own expenses. The Marshall du Castres, of the French Marine department, insisted that John Holker produce an accounting of his business as the Agent of the Royal Marine, and "the inspector general of trade and manufacturers." In response Holker started to seek a settlement from Morris for their various dealings reaching back four years to 1778. This effort would take years to conclude.

The Continental government's financial situation was not improving. On May 16th Morris drafted another circular to the states. He was clearly becoming frustrated and suggested he would quit rather than be a fraud. He sent this one to Congress for approval.

> I write Sir to apprise you of the Public Danger and to tell you I shall endeavor to fulfill those Engagements which I have already made that I may quit my Station like an Honest Man. But I will make no new Engagements so that the public Service must necessarily stand still ... I again repeat that I am guiltless for the Fault is in the States. They have been deaf to the Calls of Congress, to the Clamors of the public Creditors, to the just Demands of a suffering Army and even to the Reproaches of the Enemy who scoffingly declare that the American Army is fed, paid and clothed by France. That Assertion, so dishonorable to America, was true, but the Kindness of France had its Bounds, and our Army unfed, unpaid, and unclothed will have to subsist itself or disband itself.[140]

Congress suggested that the letter should not be sent, but rather Congressional emissaries would go to the states and plead the case. It was difficult to do this, and at the same time, to keep Congress at work; because a quorum was required in each state's delegation. People had to be chosen for their ability to convince, and also to be absent from Philadelphia.[141]

Congress would not allow Morris to scold the states for money, so instead he looked to take direct action and moved the matter of naval protection forward. He offered to hire the Pennsylvania state ship, *General Washington,* to take messages to the French and Spanish in the West Indies on the subject of protecting commerce. He then went, in his role as Agent of Marine, to the Ministers of France and Spain to arrange a convoy for one trip out.[142] After the *General Washington* left on its mission, the Pennsylvania Executive Council asked Morris' office to pay $4000 for the expense of the trip, and for outfitting the ship. Morris paid this amount from official funds. The ship took two prizes during the trip and Morris argued that the money from those prizes, and not Office funds, should be used to pay for the voyage, and Morris wanted a refund. The state refused, and because of the way the prize money was divided, Morris' office ultimately got the worst of the deal. By the end of August Morris arranged to buy the ship from Pennsylvania to use it as a packet vessel to Europe.[143]

In cooperation with Morris' request for a convoy system, the French minister, La Luzerne, coordinated French and American Naval movements from Philadelphia. La Luzerne suggested the French frigate *Emerald* meet with the *Alliance* and go together to Santa Domingo. Morris agreed, and wrote Captain Barry to prepare for the voyage. Unfortunately, the *Alliance* was unable to leave port. Barry was in New London having a hard time getting food for a sea voyage, or sailors to man his vessel.[144]

Morris was endeavoring to get the states to support the Continental war effort, with mixed results. Pennsylvania was collecting its old continental money to discharge its quota, but they gave it to the Loan Officer instead of sending it to Morris' office.[145] In June, the Massachusetts Assembly overcame Governor Hancock's objections and dropped their insistence on specific supplies. They soon started to pay silver to the Continental Treasury.

With such meager support from home in mind, Morris made arrangements with Ferdinand Grand, the United States' French banker, to insure the French loan was handled properly. He told Grand to expect a total of six million livres to be paid from the Court of the King of France in monthly amounts at the rate of 500,000 every month for the year of 1782. He instructed the banker to expect Franklin to pay into the account all the United States' money in Europe including funds in Amsterdam and Cadiz, where Morris had sent it.[146] Once the money was collected Morris could sell, in Cuba, bills drawn from this account, and in this way, he planned to get much needed silver coins into America as possible. Capt Barney, of the *General Washington,* was underway to Hispaniola to join with the French and Spanish in a convoy to Havana for the collection of hard money for America. Morris cautioned Barney not to take any risks, prizes, or delays.[147] In accordance with an act of Congress, Morris also instructed Grand to pay the money due to American agents John Ross, William Bingham, and the French council John Holker.[148]

Foreign debt, Spanish silver, and European promises were all far away from Washington's camp in New York. It was there he had to contend with day-to-day operations of the military contractors who seemed to pursue their own ends without consideration for military needs. Washington complained that the contractor in New Jersey was not satisfactory, and it would be good if Morris would appoint an arbitrator soon, especially considering that dissatisfaction there led to a mutiny in the Connecticut line. The ringleaders were executed for it.[149]

While Morris looked for a suitable arbitrator, news reached Philadelphia that Morris' April circular to the states had been intercepted and published in the *Freeman's Journal* on May 1st. He had not originally intended to publish the circulars, but he was unable to change that fact. So, Morris thought that it would not really harm the cause anyway because the enemy already knew the information, and the publication of the circular should spur the states into action. At least one congressman thought Morris had published the letter to embarrass the state of New York and could not understand why Morris thought New York could pay its requisitions anyway.[150]

Morris had already put forth a good amount of his own money in anticipation of repayment from taxes by the time he wrote to the tax collector in Rhode Island, Olney,

> I confess I am not a little surprised at the backwardness and dilatoriness which is evidenced in the laying and collecting of Taxes.[151]

William Whipple, Morris' collector in New Hampshire, pointed out that the granite state had not collected a farthing. He continued that New Hampshire was only willing to pay in specific supplies, and in any case that would not help because they were too far from where they were needed.[152]

Morris must have been pleased on June 25th when the legislature passed a resolution to accept Morris' notes as payment in taxes and to remit £40,000 for their 1782 quota.[153] Shortly after this event, Morris started to consider that the publication of the collection information was going to help him raise funds by embarrassing the states. He noted,

> Men are less ashamed to do wrong than vexed to be told of it.[154]

He thought public exposure would allow all the citizens to see that their own state had not over-contributed and that fact would make states more likely to contribute. Morris seemed immune to the idea that public humiliation of state officials was going to make him unpopular, and that might make his programs more difficult to fulfill. He pushed ahead with his plan to embarrass the states into compliance, even though he had thousands of his own notes at risk; and annoying the states might make it impossible to cover his personal exposure. This is another example of Morris' personal tendency to "double up" or increase the risk when the stakes were high and the goal was important. The technique was somewhat effective; but did not warm the hearts of the states' leadership to Morris.

In Europe, minister to the Netherlands, John Adams had been seeking help from Charles Dumas. After consultation with him, Adams decided to make a direct appeal to the Dutch people and published an article in the newspapers of several Dutch cities. This article galvanized popular support for America among the citizenry,[155] and their government did officially recognize American independence in 1782. On June 11th, that year Adams and Dumas contracted with a Dutch financial house for a subscription loan of five million guilders. News of this loan would not arrive until September. It would take even longer for the subscription to fill. Maryland passed a hard money tax on June 14th to be paid to the Continental Treasury.[156] As time went on, it became clear the implementation of that law was uneven.

Virginia kept working to compel Morris to send money into their state. They wanted a military hospital where there was no need for one, and they were disappointed to learn it would not be funded. They wanted Morris to supply the Southern Army with contracts, even as they also continued to block cooperation with the Yorktown Tobacco deal, and to block the collection of money or even bank notes for taxes.[157] The Virginians were under the impression that Morris was trying to do the same thing the English were successful at; that is, absorbing all the money in the land. Morris had to counter the false impression that the tax was intended to drain the states of resources. He replied,

> Those who consider this matter will see clearly that my plan is calculated to supply you with a solid medium instead of draining it from you.[158]

Morris had already sent thousands in his own notes to the states, and he thought that fact would be enough to make the critics realize their error. This point of view might have won the day if the criticism of Morris were based on rational fact instead of displaced "Country Party" political rhetoric, emotion, and economic notions that were almost medieval in nature. In any case, he worked to include Virginia in the contracting system so they would see money coming to their state. He told the deputy quartermaster in Virginia to negotiate contracts there. The Secretary of War agreed with Morris to concentrate the Army in Virginia in a small number of posts, so the contracting system could work.

This was not enough for the Old Dominion, and the Congressmen from that region continued to press Morris to supply the Southern Army through contracts. Over the next few months their continued insistence on this course resulted in a Congressional investigation into why supplies were not reaching the troops under the system Virginia favored, and to find the

> ...causes of delay, embezzlement, and other circumstances which have so frequently arrested the supplies for the southern army.

Morris proposed Zephaniah Turner to settle accounts with Virginia.[159] By the end of June, Morris sent a report to Congress explaining why contracting in the South was more expensive than it was worth, and the experience of Greene's army provided proof of his conclusions.[160]

There was never enough money, and any knowledge about the little bit sent from France seemed only to discourage the states from contributing their due. Morris wrote,

> I have only to lament that the Situation to which our affairs have been reduced is such that the greatest exertions which our ally can make in our favor is barely sufficient to satisfy present engagements and that the knowledge of such aid only confirms the inattention of our own citizens to more distressing circumstances which it does not relieve.[161]

This condition was about to overtake the loan that Morris had hoped to keep secret. On May 25th, Morris was informed that the news on the French loan was out. It was reported,

> ...his Majesty to grant to the United States a loan of 6 millions for this year was revealed by letters recently arrived from France.[162]

Arthur Lee learned that the French had promised six million livres for the year. He concluded it would somehow end up in the hands of Beaumarchais. Arthur Lee was not one to allow any personal enemy even the smallest advantage, including, apparently, repayment due on a loan. He proclaimed,

> …that large sums of money were reserved in France for certain purposes; that in his opinion some of these purposes did not require so large a sum and was reserved for them, and that others were not proper; [and] that the situation of our treasury required and examination into this matter.

This effectively stopped any further payments to Beaumarchais.[163]

Morris asked Franklin to look into the Beaumarchais deal because it seemed mysterious. He wrote,

> Mr. de Beaumarchais certainly had not funds of his own to make such considerable expenditures, neither is there any reason to believe he had credit. If the Court advanced money it must be a secret … the whole might be managed by the passing of paper receipts from you to the Court to him…. The diverting from a loan for the Service of the current year so considerable a part as that due to Mr de Beaumarchais will defeat the object for it as granted.[164]

Over time it came to light that there was the mystery of the "missing million." As part of the debt settlement process America received an accounting from the French. It showed that, at one point, the French had supplied four million livres to America. It was subsequently discovered that Beaumarchais had not deposited one quarter of the money into the American account. This was because the King of France had given money to him as an initial investment in Hortalez & Co.[165] A clerical error in the French ministry was the reason the money was credited to the Americans, and not Beaumarchais. Beaumarchais was unaware of the clerical error, so he could not address it directly. He claimed that he had spent his own money on war supplies as part of his trade arrangements because he knew the money had been part of the start-up funds supplied secretly by the king, but no one else knew exactly what his arrangements were.[166] Morris hoped that a pair of accounting entries in the books of the Court of France would settle the Beaumarchais issue.

Even with the loan in the French bank, the blockade was effective in keeping the funds from America. There was no money in the treasury to get the *Alliance* to sea, so on May 24th Morris appealed to Thomas Mumford, a patriotic merchant and privateer from Connecticut.

> I must therefore request that you will supply Capt Barry with such things as are necessary and Capt. Barry with only such sums of money as are indispensable…. You may depend that I will re-

> imburse you speedily and I believe it will be done partly thro Mr. Thomas Russell of Boston.[167]

Russell was the deputy Agent of Marine in Boston. Morris contacted Russell to prepare him to repay Mumford and to help John Barry, who was supposed to go to Havana with the *Alliance.* Captain Barney was also in on the mission as captain of the *General Washington,* and Morris wrote to de Grasse (who had not been captured) that the more help de Grasse could provide these two captains the better. The news had not yet reached Morris that the *Alliance* was stuck in port. He was still focused on getting that silver from Cuba.[168] Morris wrote to Robert Smith, the U.S. Agent in Havana, to draw on an account owned by the house of Harrison & Co., a trading firm located in Cadiz in which Morris had an interest, to the "extent of one hundred thousand Mexican dollars." In turn, Mr. Richard Harrison was to draw on the account in Grand's bank in Paris, which held the money the French had loaned America. Morris expected the Governor of Havana to realize this was all paid by the French loan in the American account in Paris, so the money was good.[169] [170]

Back in Philadelphia, Congress knew all about the French loan of six million livres, so Morris had to explain his actions, especially since Arthur Lee was complaining in Congress about Morris' secrecy. He wrote,

> I should earlier have communicated my intelligence of the loan in question but I wished to receive the details which would enable me to judge how much of it was at my disposition. I confess that I did not expect they would been so unfavorable. [Much was owed on other loans and overdue charges.] I was restrained also by the apprehension that the exertions of the States would relax when they should learn that any foreign aid could be obtained. And the situation of our commerce was such that if I had enabled to draw for larger sums it would have been of no avail as I could not have got the money for the bills.[171]

Even though the French had made this loan, it did not matter, because the money was out of reach. No one could sell bills of exchange to realize the funds, and Morris' efforts to get the silver from Cuba had yet to yield the desired result. Morris still needed the states to pay tax money so he could pay the contractors and build the Navy to protect the coast. Once that was done, he could sell bills of exchange and get the money that the French had lent. However, when the states heard about the loan from France, they relaxed their efforts to pay. The ships to protect commerce remained un-built and the money remained elusive. The only practical effect of the news about the loan was that the states became even more reluctant to contribute, and money was even harder to get.

The cacophony of concerns continued to echo in the Office of Finance. General Lincoln wanted to hire some wagons, but Morris didn't have the money to pay for that. He replied to General Lincoln,

> ...we ought not to make more Contracts until the states would pay taxes to enable a compliance with them, of which there was no present appearance.[172]

In New Jersey receiver William Harrison bemoaned the state of commerce and the resulting lack of funds to pay into the Continental coffers. He wrote,

> The people in general are willing and forward; their barns are full; a means of changing what they have into money is alone wanted.[173]

Walter Livingstone, brother to John Livingstone who headed the Foreign Affairs branch, was concerned that if the French Army or Fleet started buying supplies from individual farmers then that would compromise Morris' contractors' ability to buy at a price they could afford. The French usually paid in silver, while America was forced to pay with Bank notes or Morris notes. These notes were discounted more and more as the seller moved farther from Philadelphia. Morris hoped to expand the Moving Army contract to supply the French, but it did not work that way. Eventually this competition with French buyers contributed to the destruction of the Moving Army contract.[174]

Morris was forced to fire a trusted employee, Mr. Broadhead, because he had revealed the intended destination of the *Alliance.*

> I am persuaded that this was an act of mere inadvertency, but the consequences of imprudence or indiscretion in things of the nature may be as pernicious as if they proceeded from bad designs, therefore I dismissed him instantly from this office – sorry however for the necessity he had laid me under to do so.[175]

Morris' old friend, Samuel Bean of South Carolina, wrote Morris to say that he would be happy to participate in a tobacco monopoly once the war was over. There was one problem. Bean was a Tory sympathizer and not to be dealt with. Morris told him as much.[176]

General William Irvine, commander at Fort Pitt, wrote about the success he had with sending flour to New Orleans,

> I am glad that you gave permission to the boats to carry down flour. The opening of a market for that article is sure and certain means of rendering it plenty and cheep there and hereafter.[177]

Good news was hard to find. Mr. Mumford was not helpful to John Barry in Rhode Island. Barry wrote,

> I have press'd Mr Mumford ever since my arrival here to get me what stores I wanted, but all I have had from him is fair promises. In shore there is no one here that cares a curse for anything but their own interest.

He needed a bowsprit, two rowboats, spars and men. He continued, and with some hurt pride, to expound on the subject of his rank and working with the French in convoy,

> I should rather suppose the honbl. Robert Morris would be more tender of the Rank of a Continental Captain – as their rank and honor is all they expect, or at least all I have got for serving my country.

He went on to say he would work with the French Naval Lieutenant; but would find "it very hard to be subject to his orders."[178] Morris was still trying to find a market for his bills of exchange and one of his brokers, Mr. Hill, complained he could make more money selling French bills.[179]

Morris' agent, Daniel Clark, was in Virginia trying to compile tobacco for shipment on the Yorktown Tobacco deal. He was deluged with slanders about Morris. 1) That Morris was robbing the eastern states of their hard money. 2) That he was partial to Pennsylvania. 3) Partial to the disaffected, i.e., the Tories. 4) That he established a bank for sinister purposes. 5) That he aimed to keep Virginia poor. 6) That he engaged in speculation with the secretary of Congress. None of these claims had an iota of merit, but all this was in keeping with the general tenor of the work of Arthur Lee, who had gone from Philadelphia down to Virginia to join his brother Richard Henry Lee and fight the tobacco deal to which Congress had agreed,[180] as they simultaneously promoted a parallel arrangement outside the scope of the official agreement. Morris was compelled to write to Clark on these points and refute them one by one. David Ross notified Morris that the state of Virginia had refused to comply with the

> "...views of Congress in the exportation of tobacco by the capitulants of New York.," and that "every obstruction of that sort is a reflection upon our national character, therefore I request your kind assistance in forwarding the business."[181]

The atmosphere around Morris' reputation had been made so poisonous by his enemies in Virginia that he had to respond to letters from his southern friends,

> As to the infamous insinuations made by those designing factions enemies of all good and honest men, I despise them and the authors alike.... If as my friend you feel yourself hurt by these tales, discharge the idea at once and assure yourself that I am most perfectly clear of every imputation.[182]

Morris suggested that members of Congress, Mr. Clymer of Pennsylvania, and Gov Rutledge of South Carolina, visit Richmond and settle the tobacco matter with the State of Virginia. Morris wrote to Ross about the culture of the Old Dominion,

> ...the character and description you gave me of the people of Virginia gives me much concern although I had too much reason to believe in the justice of it before. Until some great change takes place nothing can be expected but Poverty, Imbecility, and those murmurings which all men make in distresses which arise from their own misconduct .... they complain all the specie is gone out of their country and this complaint is not founded in an anxiety either to pay their private debts or contribute to the public service, but arises from the want of means to purchase foreign superfluities [silks, slaves, billiard tables, etc] and administer to luxurious indolence.[183]

Morris wrote David Ross in Virginia,

> I am in hopes that Governor Rutledge and Mr. Clymer will be able to remove those unfounded prejudices so that the public service may be performed and that you will soon find it in your power to load the ships *New York* and *Fame* with the quantity of tobacco already ordered.... I am indifferent to the intended attacks on my measures; if those ingenious gentlemen can point out such as are more eligible to the public good, I am ready to pursue them or to give the opportunity of doing it to themselves – provided they can prevail on America to trust them with my Office which I wish were placed in other safe hands.[184]

With the tobacco deal in limbo Morris looked to other administrative business. He and Washington continued to write back and forth about paying the civil list. Morris wrote,

> I can easily suppose that military men should murmur to find the salaries of the civil list more punctually paid than their own ... I am persuaded that your Excellency must be of opinion with me that without the civil list ... neither civil nor military can exist at all.[185]

Daily business continued. The Treasury was collecting and burning the old paper Continental money as a way of reducing the supply, thereby controlling inflation and defeating counterfeiting.[186] As Agent of Marine, Morris pointed out to the Congress that legal matters were stalled in that department because there was no means to conduct a naval court martial. He suggested that the rules be changed to allow them to go forward. The prevailing rules required the attendance of more officers than were available. The rules were modified.[187] He was able to gain some money from settled prizes sold in the West Indies.[188] The Secretary of Congress suggested that the vessel named *Deane* be renamed, since Deane had "by his perfidy and defection forfeited all title to every mark of honor or respect."[189] This was not immediately done, but eventually the *Deane* was renamed the *Hague*. Morris looked for but could not find a pilot for Barry's ship.[190] Meanwhile on the high seas, three deserters from a British truce ship took possession of a second vessel and were using it to seize ships at sea. These men were apprehended by the British and prosecuted in New York as pirates.[191]

Morris learned that his notes were being discounted in New England, and he wanted to keep their value up. He put a good face on the situation when he said,

> ... the former possessors will shortly be convinced of their folly by seeing these notes exchanged at par then they will regret having disposed of them for less value, and their credit will thereby eventually be established.[192]

He continued using his own notes as a kind of currency that could be used before tax money was collected from the states. To do this he had to turn his notes into something of real value. He instructed James Lowell to accept up to $6000 in Morris notes when the notes came into the office in Massachusetts, and to redeem them at face value by using the tax money Lowell had collected.[193] Then Lowell would forward the Morris notes to the Financier in Philadelphia as part of Massachusetts' requisition. Once returned, the Morris note would be retired. When one kind of note was not accepted Morris was willing to use a note from the Bank of North America to maintain the value of the first. With this understanding in place, Morris sent $20,000 of his own notes to the deputy Agent of Marine in New England, Thomas Russell, to pay for the completion of the *Alliance,*[194] and to supply Captain Barry with the full complement of sailors.[195]

Similarly, Morris was willing to pay £1,000, in his own notes, as part of the Moving Army contract if the receiver of taxes in New Jersey would remit them as tax to the treasury instead of cashing them at the Bank of North America.[196] It was with such techniques that Morris endeavored to maintain the value in his notes. This was all because there was a shortage of hard money and Morris needed his notes to trade at par.

In addition to the difficulties of trying to start a national economy without any funds, there were many distractions in his daily routine. Morris wrote

> ... the greater part of my time is now taken up with hearing of peoples' distress without a possibility of affording them relief until the taxes are collected.[197]

The people who approached Morris did not seem to understand that he would only spend money on current operations. One such person was Richard Butler, a retired officer of the Pennsylvania 5th regiment. He applied to Morris because he was in great financial distress. He wished to borrow £6000 (PA) and give Morris the mortgage to his property. Butler pleaded,

> When I entered the public service I had money, and property in lands and stock. The former I have obliged to subsist on, the lands are yet my own, but my stock is destroyed by the Indian wars and want of proper people to take care of it.[198]

Morris was unable to help, and he even approached the Bank on Butler's behalf. There was no money to be had. Morris eventually told Mr. Butler to join the ranks of the creditors and await a settlement.

An old friend contacted the Office of Finance when Beaumarchais wrote to Morris for payment, saying that Silas Deane had settled his account from the days of the Secret Committee. Unfortunately, Deane was out of favor and his settlement was dismissed as being unofficial. Morris tried to get the Court of France to take on Beaumarchais' payment, but they would not.[199]

It was difficult for Morris to manage his time because supplicants kept interrupting his work.

> Finding that the daily interruptions which I met with by persons making applications on various matters that chiefly relate to them-

> selves, prevents my getting through the business of this office in the satisfactory manner I could wish ...[200]

He changed his schedule to meet with individuals who wanted money. He set aside two hours a day for three days a week.

While Virginian Arthur Lee worked to stop payments to Beaumarchais from his position in America, his brother, William Lee, continued to work hard to collect money for his work as an Agent in Europe. William petitioned Congress. Congress told Morris to pay him. Morris told Franklin to pay him, and Franklin wrote back about arraigning the payment to his former nemesis, "I do not know where he is."[201] Lee confronted Franklin with whom he often bickered and told him he was not "Disposed to be trifled with any longer." Later William confided to Arthur that, "The trick you see evidently originates with R. Morris."[202] William was wrong as usual, but he did get paid. With such behavior within the leadership of Virginia, Morris was not surprised to learn that state would not take his notes in payment of taxes. Morris did not care what money they paid with, as long as they paid with some kind money.[203] They seemed only marginally willing to part with tobacco.

The pressure for money only increased. Private individuals in France began pressuring America through La Luzerne to get America to pay the interest on the Loan Office certificates they had purchased in Europe. France had previously stated that it would not allow its loans to be used to pay interest on these debts, and the states were not yet sending Morris tax money to make the payments.[204] The Quartermaster General wanted Morris to pay for 1500 cooking kettles, 1000 oars, some boats and wagons, but if that was not possible, at that moment it was most important to pay for feeding the horses.[205] The Moving Army contract was still making the army miserable, and there was little meat for the troops. Washington wrote, "No magazines of salted provisions have yet been placed in the deposits of West Point."[206] The Southern Army was not in better shape. It tuned out that they were low on uniforms because the short enlistments resulted in men returning home with new clothes supplied by the Army; and this left the new recruits without uniforms; in short, the Army was clothing the South.[207] There was, however, a ray of hope that Morris' long-term plans would work. He received word that Maryland had passed the impost. The fate of the funding plan rested with Rhode Island.[208]

Morris suggested that tax collector, Mr. Hall, allow Morris' notes to circulate as cash in South Carolina, and to be collected from the state as a tax. This would allow the quartermasters and commissaries to have the notes to spend on provisions, and then the provisioners could remit them as tax for later collection.[209] He put more of his notes into circulation when he paid $10,000 to the contractors for the Moving Army, which he expected would be cashed in New Jersey in the form of tax receipts.

On June 11th and 12th of that year Morris moved the location of the Office of Finance to the northwest corner of 5th and Market. It was less than two blocks away from his new house near the corner of Market and 7th, so work was a short walk away for the large man who walked with a cane.[210] It was during this move that Morris received a visitor.

He wrote,

> On coming to the office I found the honorable Mr Maddison [Madison] and gave him my opinion in favor of having committees appointed twice a year to examine into the management of this and the other great offices, as nothing will be done more agreeable to me than to lay the whole of my proceedings and management before congress as frequently as practicable from a conviction of my constant desire and exertions to promote the honor and interests of the U. States.[211]

Morris was interested in silencing his critics by opening his administration to review, and thus began the policy of openness and accountability of an executive in government to the national legislature. Madison introduced a bill to Congress to create such committees, with the idea that this would show Morris' critics how well he was running that office. Lee complained that the members of the committee were too friendly to Morris, and progress of their work was slow.

George Webb took the Virginia office of Receiver of Continental taxes.[212] Shortly after that, Virginia passed an act that levied new state taxes on land men, slaves, horses, cattle, carriages, billiard tables, and licenses. They were payable in specie, new emission Virginia state currency, tobacco, hemp, or flour. Clearly the states were not shy of placing taxes on their citizens. Continental taxes, however, were collected by the state collector, and applied after state tax obligations. In that way, Mr. Webb was kept outside the process and little went to the Continental treasury.[213] Morris also discovered that New York was collecting a tax, nominally for the Continental effort, and then spending it for their own purposes instead of sending any to the Continental treasury.[214] Unhappy discoveries like this convinced Morris that the taxes should be paid directly to his receivers.

Always taking the nationalist view, Morris wanted to create some kind of pressure on all of the states to pay their share of the war costs. He had already instructed the tax receivers to lobby the state legislatures in favor of his policies. He sought to channel the interests of the creditors so they would become a lobbying force as well. He didn't have the money to pay the interest on the Loan Office Certificates, and he would not have it until the states paid into the system. He decided to pay interest on Loan Office Certificates only with money collected from the states;[215] thereby he was able to demonstrate to the Certificate holders, why they should lobby for his program. Morris announced the appointment of commissioners to settle the accounts of the loan offices to determine what was owed, thinking this would show support for their claims.

Morris met with a loan office certificate holder, Colonel Walter Stewart, on the topic of the lack of interest payments. Morris informed him that the French would not allow their loans to be used to pay interest on these notes. Stewart determined that a meeting of loan office certificate holders must be called to pursue measures to protect their interests. Blair McClenachan, who had been disappointed by Morris' refusal to dig up records from 1778, took the lead in organizing this group of creditors, who went on to petition Congress. Morris made it clear that he saw this as the fault of the states, not Congress, and that he would help all creditors to get repaid.[216] He wrote to Congress that he would not sell any more bills of exchange for money to pay interest, and that interest must be paid from the money collected via the impost. He did this to apply pressure on the states to pass and implement the impost as he directed the creditors to pressure the state governments to work with Congress. All was waiting on Rhode Island to pass the impost. In a separate meeting with other public creditors, who also were no longer getting interest payments, Morris encouraged them to lobby the states to pay tax money into the Continental treasury.[217]

It was June 12th and there was uneven progress on a variety of fronts. Captain John Barry still could not find sailors to man the *Alliance*. He told Morris that he would come to Philadelphia to find them.[218] Morris reviewed the last request from the Quartermaster General and wrote,

> Colo. Pickering called for money. His wants are most pressing, and equaled by nothing but the poverty of the treasury. I have however granted him a warrant of Mr. Hilliagas [US Treasurer] for $800.[219]

The Governor of Connecticut sold supplies gathered for continental use; Morris requested that he send the money gained from that sale.[220] Back in

Philadelphia there was no money to print, so there were no press runs. Morris shut the office of the Inspectors of the Press and saved a little money.[221]

America had the poorest government on earth, while America itself was bountiful. Many private citizens, who were not owed money by the Continental government, seemed to have enough for their own purposes. There was discussion in Congress about the large illegal trade with the British in New York. The trade was already illegal so Morris didn't see that another law would stop it. He wrote,

> The history of human affairs demonstrated the inefficiency of penal laws to prevent such a commerce, when the temptation is great.[222]

He noted that the trade was being helped along by the British as part of the economic warfare against the United States.

> This commercial intercourse forms a part of the system of the enemy at present, and they make any sacrifice to give it success.[223]

Food from New York state and supplies from New Jersey were found in the British garrisons of New York City and in the holds of British war ships. Morris noted that the only way to stop it was to compete with it economically, but that was difficult. The British were dominating the currency in the way that Arthur Lee accused Morris of trying to do, while at the same time Morris was hard at work sending his currency into the local economies. He hoped to appeal to the citizens on a patriotic basis, pointing out that if New Jersey sent hard money to the Continental Treasury they would be getting it out of the hands of the British in New York.[224] New Jersey passed a hard money tax bill on June 22nd. That state would send 80% of the hard money to the continental treasury and used the state paper for its own purposes.[225]

A little farther north, the Army was still encamped in New York. Washington wrote Morris on the difficulties he was having with the contractors and included a further observation of paying the civil list and not the officers:

> ...your observation that without a Civil list neither civil nor military men can exist but I beg to leave to all to it as my own that if the military should disband for want of pay (while the war continues to rage) a period will very soon be put to the civil establishment under our present constitution. The civil and military then having a reciprocal dependence upon each other taxation of the property of one being equal to that of the other and the wants of both the same it is worthy of some consideration whether the first is to receive all and the other no part of their pay.[226]

Washington was dealing with the grumblings of his officers, some of whom were not so gentle in their expression. Colonel Armand reported that

> ...others in the civil line are paid exactly because they have the means in their hands...[227]

The $8000 Morris was getting paid as an annual salary was small when compared to hundreds of thousands in credit he extended on his own account, and the tens of thousands in silver sent to the south. He sent even more of his own notes to his deputy in the Marine department in Massachusetts to help get the *Alliance* to sea.[228] Unfortunately, the Franco-American naval convoy was held up in Boston due to the slowness of outfitting and manning the *Alliance*.[229] Morris wrote Barry that he would not be expected to join that convoy. This freed the French fleet to leave Boston, and Barry to come to Philadelphia. Later, when Morris met with Captains Nicholson and Barry about sailors, he told Barry he could offer an enlistment bounty of $10 to get the men he needed.[230]

The small navy was becoming more active. John Paul Jones reported that the *America* was being finished. The un-renamed *Deane* had been out on a cruise and captured the *Mary* with her stores, and £5,000 in silver. The goods went to Hispaniola for sale. The *Deane* also captured *HMS Jackall*, and that was taken to Boston along with 50 prisoners and various packets of British mail. Next, the *Deane* captured the privateer *Swallow* with fifty-three men and fourteen cannons. The *Deane* also captured the Brig *Elizabeth* with tobacco and barrel staves from South Carolina. The captain sent that back to Boston. The *Deane* captured the privateer *Regulatro* carrying eighteen cannons and seventy-five men. Morris used this recent history to encourage Congress to reconfigure the awarding of prize money because after all the prizes are divided up and the bounties paid the Congress would owe the sailors $10,000 from the prize money. Morris suggested this was not a suitable system and a simpler approach was needed: half to pay the sailors and half for the Continental government. This of course required Congress to pay the sailors a regular salary instead of using the bounty system that had gotten the ships to sea, but which also caused the financial problem.[231]

On June 22nd New Jersey collected $4,000, and Morris told his receiver to put it into the Bank of North America and get a treasury note for it.[232] That way New Jersey would be credited for its requisition due to the Treasury, and the Bank would have money to lend. The Governor of South Carolina wrote Morris to explain that his state was not going to levy a Continental tax any time soon,

> ... but as soon as our affairs can be reduced to order I flatter myself due attention will be made to that important business.

The Governor went on to list the difficulties in managing a state with an active insurgency, requirements for troops, supplying General Greene's army and the burden the state tax was on rich and poor alike.[233] Contrary to a law passed in Maryland, that state kept trying to pay their portion in the form of specific supplies. One way or another, they looked for ways to make good on their commitment.

On June 23rd, the tobacco for New York was finally loaded in Virginia.[234] George Eddy wanted to know if Morris would help send even more tobacco from Virginia. Morris replied

> I answered in the negative having already had too much trouble and plague with that business, but I told him if he thought proper to Commission my Agent Daniel Clark Esq. I would engage him to execute his orders on the best terms in his power."[235]

Morris made it clear to Clark that he must not ship more tobacco than Congress authorized on the ships traveling under a truce flag.[236] By this time Morris was tired of squabbling with the Virginians over their tobacco and desired not to be involved in any new tobacco deals "until I see the end of Mr. Eddy's affairs." [237]

News from Europe arrived in the form of a letter from Matthew Ridley. He wrote (partially in code) to say that the English ministry "can only exist for making peace ..." Ridley also noted that he was in Amsterdam to solicit a loan for Maryland, and that some in France thought Morris should pay for their loan to Virginia. He went on to ask what to do with Morris' boys since Geneva seems so dangerous and morally corrupt. He continued that a new friend of the boys was a spoiled child; and they might be picking up some bad habits from him, so this would be a motivator to remove them from the tutor to a proper school. Finally, he mentioned that Mr. and Mrs. Jay were now in Paris, and William Carmichael had stayed in Spain as the American Charge D'Affairs.[238]

Morris replied to Ridley that while it was nice to hear about the boys' activities he would only be relaxed after they were enrolled in a proper school. He was not happy about the lack of determination about which school they were to attend, and the fact that Ridley, who was so close, was looking to Morris for advice when he was an ocean away. Morris provided broad guidelines for Ridley to consider.

> The difference of expense between one place or another is of no consideration but it is of consequence that they should have proper care taken of the Religion, morals, manners and habits as well as their learning and that no time be lost in placing them where they are to acquire the whole...[239]

Franklin's first letter from France since January arrived in the beginning of June. He said the war supplies that had been purchased for export still had not been shipped from Europe because of the British blockade. He added that he was slowly selling off those British goods that had been bought by the southerners and was buying soldiers' uniforms. He was also considering buying a ship for transport. He cautioned himself not to go over the loaned amount as a way of cautioning Morris to do the same. He was successful in negotiating with the French Crown to allow for the repayment of the debt over time after the war. He tried to gauge English intentions and corrected his previous observation about the German troops. They did disembark because there had been a change of orders.

He stated

> ...that tho' the English a few Months since seemed desirous of peace, I suspect they now intend to draw out the negotiations into length, till they can see what this campaign will produce. I hope our people are not deceived by fair words, but be on their guard, ready against every attempt that our insidious Enemies may make upon us.[240]

Conversations via the overseas mail took time, and Morris was finally able to reply to Washington's last letter on the subject of paying the "civil list" while the army went without pay.

> I know well the connection which ties together all the public servants, and lament every comparison which implies a distinction between them. The civil list consists chiefly of persons whose salaries will not do more than find them food and clothing. Many of them complain that with great parsimony they cannot obtain even those necessities.[241]

He continued on this sensitive topic to say that food and shelter were just what he was trying to provide the soldiers in the field and if he added pay to the soldiers then the civil list would go without.

Washington decided that West Point should be the storage site for supplies and notified Comfort Sands and Co., the contractors for the Moving

Army.[242] The difficulties between Washington and the contractors were growing. Washington felt the contractors were shorting the Army and pocketing the difference. The contractors had been promised hard money in payment. There was none, so Morris offered his own notes instead and insisted that they be valued as hard money. When Comfort Sands and Co. tried to pay for supplies with these notes, and went to convert them into hard money in New York, or elsewhere in New England, the notes were not accepted at face value and were discounted. Sands and Co. could only supply the Army with the food they bought with these discounted Morris notes. Morris insisted that he had paid in hard money because he knew his notes could be converted at face value at the Bank of North America. He insisted others should convert them at the same rate. Everyone was trying to do their best with the conditions that prevailed, but the men were still hungry and Washington had to look after their interests. The friction continued. The states kept sending money to soldiers from their own state, and this made the discontent in the ranks grow. Morris tried to manage relations with the contractors because he hoped money would soon come from the states in some form of tax.

There was a change in the economic climate, and Hyam Salomon was approached by people who wanted to buy bills of exchange.[243] Salomon quickly sold some and this generated much needed cash. Morris kept the business with the French on firm footing as he communicated with the U.S. Banker in France, Grand, and told him which bills of exchange to honor.

It must have seemed to Morris that he was fighting on many fronts at once when he replied to each of the various states according to their particular natures. Morris wrote the Governor of Rhode Island to discourage him from paying his own soldiers in the Continental line, and instead encouraged him to pay a tax to the Treasury. This way Morris could use his system to prevent irregularities and dissension among the troops.[244] He told his receiver in Rhode Island to accept nothing but money in taxes, and he regretted that Rhode Island was not remitting to the Continental treasury in the amounts previously agreed.

Morris responded to the Governor of Maryland's letter in which that Governor listed his laments and difficulties as excuses for not paying into the Continental Treasury,

> No proposition can be clearer than this that the salvation of our country must depend upon such grants and it will be a matter of wonder to future generations how a people who once showed such enthusiastic ardor for freedom should at the moment when

> it is within their grasp put every thing to the hazard by omitting to make the little exertion which remains.[245]

Maryland's difficulty in raising money and Morris' disinclination to take specific supplies were the reasons Morris, Quartermaster Pickering, and Morris' Maryland receiver were evaluating Maryland's latest offer to transport materials to South Carolina as a way to defray Maryland's tax liability. They decided to take the offer and ship the materials to the Southern Department. It was better that than nothing, but still those supplies were valued at their market prices.

Earlier, Congress had asked Morris to find contractors for the Southern Army. He issued his report in June, explaining that it was not a practical possibility to do this. There were no suitable contractors; the areas were so depleted the goods would have to be carried too far to make them inexpensive; the nature of the Army was such that they could not defend any territory they inhabited so they would have to move with the supplies they had; and that if a supply depot were created it could not be defended and the goods would be lost.[246] Southerners grumbled because they thought the contracting system would bring hard currency to their states.

The South was still very hard-pressed due to the agricultural nature of their economy and the predation of that agriculture by British and American Armies fighting through their crops. To relieve the financial distress of the congressional delegates from Georgia, and North and South Carolina the Congress was paying their salaries. This news excited the jealousy of some people in New Jersey who did not want to pay delegates from the South. This complicated the tax collector's job. He wrote to Morris,

> I have often heard repeated with some uneasiness, that under all our pressures and difficulties to obtain money, several of the southern delegates are still maintained on expensive appointments, out of the public treasury.[247]

Summer

On July 4th, 1782, Morris shut the office early "that they might be at leisure to indulge those pleasing reflections which every true American must feel on the recollection that six years are now completed since that decisive step was taken in favor of freedom of their country, and that they might each partake in the festivity usual on holidays."[248]

A few days later, with the long-gone heady days of 1776 on his mind, he wrote to the receiver of taxes in Virginia when he learned that Virginia was not going to send any money to the Continental treasury until December,

> Not until December will Virginia give any thing you say towards the service of the current year. How then are we to carry on those operations which are necessary? How is the country to be defended? How is our Army to be supported? Is this what is meant by the solemn Declarations to support with Life and Fortune the Independence of the United States?[249]

The demands of his office, the feeling that he alone was able to accomplish the task, and the lack of support from the states finally began to weigh on him. He wrote to Washington:

> There is scarce a day passes in which I am not tempted to give back into the hands of Congress the power they have delegated, and lay down a burden which presses me to the earth. Nothing prevents me, but a knowledge of the difficulties I am obliged to struggle under.[250]

On July 11th, 1782, the British evacuated Savannah, Georgia.[251] They took with them thousands of slaves by offering them freedom. According to some reports the British turned around and sold a number in the West Indies. Many were with the British as prisoners of war. Others still considered themselves British loyalists and recipients of a promised British amnesty.[252] This last group became a point of discussion in 1783 during the British evacuation of New York and was associated with the prisoner exchanges. After the war, Southern planters complained about the loss of their property and sought compensation from the British. They based their arguments on a provision that was inserted into the peace treaty at the last moment. This dispute was the nominal reason southerners later blocked the payment of debts due to the British. Their lack of compliance with the terms of the peace treaty was used as an excuse by British fur traders who stayed in the North West Territory to continue their fur trade, and to occupy the old English forts and settlements. In response, the British maintained that the Southerners should pay the debts owed to them from before the war. This disagreement over the payments of debts from before and incurred during the Revolution resulted in border fighting, sea battles, and eventually in Jay's mission to England and Jay's Treaty years later, in 1795. All this death, destruction and disagreement for the most part, can be traced to a last minute change made to the peace treaty by paroled former slave trader and South Carolina grandee, Henry Laurens.

However, back in 1782, General Greene needed money to support the Southern Department, during that hot southern summer. The chronic difficulties there, convinced Morris that he could use a better line of communication with the Southern Department. He hired, at the rate of $100 per month, an express rider to communicate with General Greene. The rider had to supply his own horse.[253] Among the problems Greene faced was the fact that all the goods sold to the Army were 150% more expensive than the same goods sold to neighbors.[254] Even so, there was no outcry in the Philadelphia press about war profiteering by Southern farmers. There were no public demonstrations. There were no seizures of private property. Whatever animus there was during the Revolutionary war about pricing was uniquely focused on the merchant class, and particularly those who favored nationalism.

That other example of north-south harmony, the Virginia Tobacco deal, was closed, and Morris finally put Eddy's $20,000 in British silver into the Bank of North America.[255] Also, as part of the deal, Eddy returned a bill of exchange that he had hoped to resell, but could not, thus saving the cost of the discount. It had taken ten months to do a simple cash-producing business transaction with the state of Virginia that was supposed to be finished in three. It would take even longer to get them to send their own money to Congress for the quota to which they had already agreed. Lack of support from the states and the cash crunch, caused by the blockade, continued to be a concern. Morris started to recall unused Morris notes he had placed with trusted third parties because he was worried for their value and his liability. When news came back to him that these third parties did not have his notes because they were circulating as currency, he claimed that he never intended them to be used by a select few. Initially however, he had been sure to place them with people who would not discount them. Again, he turned to Hyam Salomon to see if he could raise any more money by selling bills of exchange on the French account.[256] For his part, Salomon was looking forward to peace, and a new career as an auctioneer in his old town, New York, where his father-in-law had a slave importing business.[257] Salomon asked for, and Morris granted approval that Salomon might advertise himself as "Broker to the Office of Finance." Salomon also acted as "Broker to the Council General of France, and to the Treasurer of the French Army."[258]

With a steady eye on protecting commerce,[259] Morris, as Agent of Marine, wrote to Captain John Barry that now he had collected enough men he should "as soon as possible proceed to a cruise and as to the places where you cruise and to which you send your prizes you will be governed entirely by your own discretion in which I have confidence." Morris supplied a list of approved locations for Barry to use when he captured a ship at sea and was able to sell the ship and its contents.[260] Morris also sent $5,000 more in his own notes to help outfit the *Alliance* in New London when he knew that the men were available to sail the ship.[261]

Just as Morris increased his personal financial risk, Maryland tried a new way to satisfy its quota, and at the same time, to avoid putting their own money into the treasury. This time they tried to borrow the funds from the Bank of North America. Morris told Maryland's treasurer that the Bank of North America was not going to lend that state money to pay its requisite amount to the continental treasury, and that the state had to sell its products and tax its citizens to come up with the funds.[262] Maryland continued the practice of sending money to their troops, just as other states did. To avoid growing discord in the ranks, Morris told the Governor of Maryland that any money sent to the troops would not be used to offset the amount the state owed the Continental Treasury. He considered Maryland's situation, and decided they needed assistance in selling their products. Morris helped Maryland by placing an advertisement in the Pennsylvania papers for Maryland tobacco and wheat, held on the public account. These were to be sold for

Captain John Barry

> ... ready money, the Financier's Notes, bank notes, or the Pay-master General's notes.[263]

While Morris was helping the states meet their quotas, he quietly helped individuals as well. He maintained his private effort to restore General Gates from his ignominy, and informed Gates that he had contacted General Lincoln on Gates' behalf and that Lincoln would help Gates restore his honor. Morris also kept up his efforts to assist General Charles Lee to get the best deal for his property. He introduced John Vaughan as a worthy buyer for Lee's plantation. Once the property was sold, Morris would be able to recover the money he had earlier lent Lee and to release the mortgage. Later, Morris heard from Charles Lee that he had met with Mr. Vaughan about the property sale. Lee looked to Morris for his opinion on the value of his plantation, and for help in closing the deal.[264]

There are no soul-searching memos or diary entries on the motivation for these activities. The general tendency in Morris' life was to include people and bring them along when possible. His interest in the Indian Boys in New Jersey, the disgraced Generals, his struggling son-in-law; even his willingness to help William Lee get paid, shows a consistent pattern of reaching out to others, no matter what their political views, and helping them as much as he could. Morris often expressed concern about the "disaffected" so these efforts may be seen in terms of Morris' larger goals of creating a unified nation with a variety of participants working together. Even so this takes a certain kind of personality. While some people, like Arthur Lee, seemed to live for revenge, Morris said that people may dislike his policies and politics, but he did not believe they really disliked him. Often, people unconsciously see in others what they are themselves, so Morris' hopeful assessment speaks more of his character than the motivations of others.

Nationalist policies were falling out of favor in the political and financial realms. Accordingly, Maryland and Virginia demonstrated their staunch defense of state's rights. The state of Connecticut acted similarly. It was not using Morris' continental tax receiver. Instead, the person collecting state tax was collecting the Continental taxes, and he was applying them as he saw fit.[265] It seems he did not see fit to send them to the Continental Treasury. Not surprisingly, progress on the mint was going slowly, and Dudley wanted money. Morris suggested that Dudley would be better off if he delayed plans for the mint, and instead assist in the creation of a brass cannon foundry in Springfield.[266] The mint might have to go begging, but there was money to celebrate the French alliance. That evening there was a great ball with an international flair. Morris, Washington, the French ministers, and about seven hundred other people celebrated the first birthday of the Dauphin, the young prince of France.[267]

Two days later, Captain Barney returned from his voyage to Havana and reported to Morris' office. Barney's ship, *General Washington,* was anchored in the Delaware River off of Chester, Pennsylvania. The *General Washington* had come under fire and lost her masts in the West Indies. She had then been refitted and traveled under convoy to Havana with the French sixty-four gun ship *Evillie.* On the way back to America, the convoy fell under attack by two British frigates. After nearly getting the best of those two, the *General Washington* had to leave the scene when a British sixty-four-gunner hove upon the horizon. The *General Washington* outran the British and made it safely into the Delaware Bay. Morris' plan to get specie from Havana finally worked, but not as completely as Morris had hoped, because the

Alliance was not involved, and the *General Washington* could not carry all the silver Morris wanted. Nevertheless 60,000 Spanish milled silver dollars came to America. More silver could have been loaded, but it was judged that the *General Washington* would not sail well if she carried so much weight. The money was a welcome addition to the Bank's coffers and the national condition. The mission had not been an easy one.[268]

In July, Morris was using the sale of bills of exchange drawn on the French loan to pay for much of the war effort. Hyam Salomon sold nearly half of them during this period. On July 15th, Salomon told Morris of his concern that the price of bills of exchange was about to fall because there was no market for them. Morris scoured the states for tax revenue. He was able to get some income from the sale of captured ships, and the occasional sale of supplies, but as a last resort Morris used his own money. When that was impossible he worked to delay payments. Morris wrote,

> ... my time is principally consumed in forming contrivances to pay some debts and to parry the payment of what I cannot accomplish.[269]

By the latter part of July the Moving Army contractors held $20,000 in Morris' notes.[270]

"On Public Credit"

On July 29th, Morris sent another circular to the governors of the states. He wrote,

> Judge of the situation in which we are placed and be not surprised at any consequences which may follow from that universal neglect which is alike unaccountable and inexcusable.[271]

Morris considered he was "preaching to the dead" and did not expect much to come of it. He wanted a better system, and so he designed one. He unveiled his bold plan for federal funding in a document entitled, *"On Public Credit."* Within this plan lay the lessons Morris had learned as an observer and former participant in the financial system that was developing in England. There were many other sources for Morris' plan as well. Members of his office had a role; of course, Gouverneur Morris added much. Robert Morris also drew on the works of the famous Scotsman, Adam Smith, and Jacques Necker the Swiss/French economist. Morris incorporated the views of David Hume who, like Morris, believed in directing men's self-interest toward the public interest. Morris had books in his library from British political economist Thomas Mortimer, Sir James

Stewart, and the duc de Sully. He also conversed with American economic thinkers like Pelatiah Webster and William Barton, and he was the recipient of letters from Alexander Hamilton. Hamilton was full of ideas, observations, and opinion. There is no teacher like experience, however, and Morris' personal history as a merchant and participant in the controversies in Pennsylvania over free trade and the monetary laws provided a model of violence and failure that he wished to avoid. As a member of a small group of wealthy individuals he had first-hand knowledge of how the wealthy see the world, and did not have to guess at their motivations. Such guesswork is often the reason for failure in other systems, like Marxism.

It has been said an optimist is one who turns lemons into lemonade. Morris figured out a way to turn the debt, which was generally thought to be onerous and oppressive, into an engine of wealth that would bind the nation's interests. On July 29th, 1782, the Superintendent of Finance issued his report, *On Public Credit*, to the President of Congress.[272] This event occurred in the midst of a debt controversy generated in large part by Morris and his Office of Finance. Morris had stopped making all interest payments. He did this for several reasons, first he needed the money for current expenses, and second, he did this to put all creditors on the same footing to unite them as an interest group behind his plan. Finally, he offered his plan as the solution to the funding problem. He hoped the creditors could pressure Congress and the states into adopting his plan, or at least enough of the plan to keep America from losing the War of Finance that had begun after the Battle of Yorktown.

Morris proposed an economic system that would benefit both the agricultural and the merchant communities, each of which saw the other as a political opposite. He sought to engage the interests of the rich, the middling and the poor; of the yeoman farmer, plantation owner, tradesman, shop keeper, merchant, and banker; of creditors, contractors and suppliers – all of whom would participate in an economic system resulting in growth and expanding markets based on an invigorated citizenry, circulating hard money, good credit, and free trade. Above all, Morris proposed a federal economic system, and to answer his current needs this required support in the form of taxation. He wrote,

> In every society also, there must be some taxes, because the necessity of supporting Government and defending the State always exist. To do these on the cheapest terms is wise. ... it would be wise to carry taxation to a certain Amount, and expend what should remain after providing for the support of Government and the national defense, in works of public utility, such as opening roads and Navigations.[273]

Once a funding system for a central government was in place, Morris saw that it would be possible to secure political stability because public creditors would wish to maintain a system that insured repayments of money owed. He saw taxes as a way of funding the debt and encouraging private industry. Morris envisioned public debt, in the form of government bonds, providing bond holders with low-risk interest income, to become a

> ... medium of exchange, a source for business capital, the foundation for banking, and a profitable investment for otherwise idle funds ...

...which would be invested in generating even more wealth. He thought that people generally work only as hard as necessary, so if they had to pay a tax they would work to do so, and this would spur greater activity. He also thought that if rich men were taxed then they would be forced to seek higher returns on their assets. This would spur investment and industry while putting fallow resources to work. At the same time, he saw his proposal as discouraging wasteful public spending. He reasoned a wasteful Government would soon be voted out of office. All this would result in the "inestimable Jewel of Public Credit" and allow the nation to defend itself in times of war and also to prosper in times of peace.[274]

Morris demonstrated that an impost alone would not cover the whole amount due because he estimated that it would only raise about $600,000 per year.[275] He sought a land tax as a way to raise revenue that would not over burden the small farmer but would force the large landholder to incur a high cost for the idle lands. He reasoned this would break up land monopolies and increase the development and productivity of existing properties by making property available to more people for cultivation in small farms. On the land tax Morris wrote,

> Yet a large proportion of America is the property of great landholders, they monopolize it without cultivation; they are (for the most part) at no expense either of money or personal service to defend it; and, keeping the price higher by monopoly than otherwise it would be, they impede the settlement and culture of the country. Morris considered the "industrious Cultivator" to be "the most valuable part of a community.[276]

Morris sought a poll tax of one dollar a year from each citizen as a small contribution by individuals, and a good way for the government to know the size of population. Morris said about the poll tax,

> But in America, where three days of labor produces sustenance for a week, it is not unreasonable to ask two days out of a year as a contribution to the payment of public debt.[277]

Morris also favored a poll tax on slaves, which would have cost slaveholders a dollar per slave while others would only pay for themselves. One might consider this Morris' way of using tax policy to combat slavery, however this is the only part of the tax plan upon which Morris makes no comment. Robin Einhorn pointed out in her work, *American Taxation, American Slavery,* that the Impost as enacted under Hamilton, neatly sidestepped the issue of slavery because it was formulated without any use of "property" within the borders, as did all federal taxes until 1860. The Southern states did tax slavery to some extent, but never in a way that would jeopardize that "peculiar institution." Southern planters were keenly aware that national tax policy could be used to destroy the slave system and used every method at their disposal to defeat the idea. Some years later, during the arguments over federal taxation in the process of ratification of the Constitution, one former Governor from Virginia put this issue in plain terms, "They'll free your ni--ers!"[278]

Morris sought an excise, or sales tax on liquor, as a way of

> ... compelling vice to support the Cause of Virtue ... and will draw from the idle and dissolute that contribution to the public service, which they will not otherwise make.[279]

One might wonder if the behavior of his long dead alcoholic half-brother Thomas was in his mind when he wrote this. Internal taxation was never popular with citizens, and shortly after a federal Whiskey tax was enacted in 1795, there was the infamous "Whiskey Rebellion" in western Pennsylvania.

Morris sought to defend the freedom of financial markets. He thought that a free market finds its own balance, and his experience with controlled markets in Pennsylvania convinced him that the Government would not do a better job. He said that a Government whose courts defend private rights to collect debts should not refuse to pay its own debts. In arguing for payment of Continental obligations at their face value he pointed out that the Government should not be concerned with the trading value of those debts in the open market because the Government had already agreed on the value of the debt it owed. He pointed out that any depreciation in the value of those certificates in the marketplace was caused by uncertainty stemming from the very funding problems he was trying to solve.[280] Morris contended that if the United States developed a way to pay the debt, then the debt certificates would have value. The people who had risked their own money would be able to use that newly revalued asset to build future assets. Morris expected the free market to work and create long term benefits for all. Once the certificates were backed, he anticipated that they would be collected and

> ... monied men would purchase them up (tho perhaps at a considerable discount) and ... by distributing property into those hands which could render it most productive the revenue would be increased, while the original stock continued the same.[281]

Monied men were those who knew how to make the most of money, in contrast to Landed men who, supposedly, knew how to make the most of their land. Morris had observed that when farmers and tradesmen had money at hand, they tended to spend it in the shops and taverns. He hinted that when members of the Southern Aristocracy had surplus money, they spent it on idle lands, indolence, and "foreign superfluities." It was his opinion that monied men knew how to make money work and would invest money into development projects, and that in turn would build more value than could be built by consumption at the store or tavern, or by the Southern elite's taste for luxuries. Some people in Morris' time considered this to be an aristocratic attitude, while such characterizations might have been satisfying to those who made them, they served to mask the plain fact that Morris' observations were well founded.

Morris was not alone in his thinking. Adam Smith wrote on this subject,

> If they employ it [money] in purchasing foreign goods for home consumption they may either, first purchase such goods as are likely to be consumed by idle people who produce nothing, such as foreign wines, foreign silks &c; or, secondly, they may purchase an additional stock of materials, tools, and provisions, in order to maintain and employ an additional number of industrious people, who reproduce, with a profit, the value of their annual consumption.
>
> So far as it is employed in the first way, it promotes prodigality, increases expense and consumption without increasing production, or establishing any permanent fund for supporting that expense, and is in every respect hurtful to society.
>
> So far as it is employed in the second way, it promotes industry, and though it increases the consumption of society, it provides a permanent fund for supporting that consumption, the people who

> consume reproducing with a profit, the whole value of their annual consumption.[282]

Some of Morris' political rivals reacted to his proposal by contending that it was his intention for the poor to become poorer. They noted that people who held a few Loan Office Certificates were apt to sell them as soon as they could get anything for them, and that it was not until the monied men held them all that the value increased. There is little in the record to indicate that was Morris' intent; instead his consistent point was that the Government must pay these debts at their face value. It was his expectation, however, that people would sell their notes to get some value from them, as soon as they could, simply because government paper had gone up and down in value for such a long time. Morris' rivals did not mention that their policies were responsible for the low value of the certificates, nor did they admit that if they had consistently backed the certificates with a tax, then the "poor" would have been well served by their belief in the Continental government. Morris often explained that it was his policy for the Government to treat all certificate holders the same, and the open market would set the exchange value from day to day. The existing state of affairs was caused by lack of support for the debt, and that in turn resulted in the situation where only monied men had the cash on hand to buy up the certificates and hold them in anticipation of repayment from the government. If instead of holding these notes, the monied men had demanded immediate payment, they would have forced the Continental Government into a deep bankruptcy, and this would probably have led to the dissolution of the only existing form of national government. By holding these notes, the "monied men" supported the policies of the nationalists at great risk to themselves.

Morris said that in the name of Justice all of the holders of these bonds must be assured repayment from the proceeds of the proposed tax system. These bonds and bondholders became the source of much controversy and demagoguery by opponents of Morris' national funding plan. Those who risked their money to support America were portrayed as vile speculators. Morris' call for "Justice" on the behalf of these bond holders fell on the deaf ears of many in Congress and the States.

There was clearly a cultural clash over the nature of money, wealth, and what was to become of the assets of the nation. Morris' plan relied on the very things that the Southern elite did not like. They actively disliked the business of trade. They were not interested in investments or other "dealings in paper." There was very little thinking about manufacturing.

According to Morris' observations, they did not like to work and instead spent their money on their own delights and indolence. This was all directly at odds with Morris' vision of hard work, investment into productive enterprises, trade, new technology, banking, and risk taking. The fight over Morris' programs and policies was really a fight over the future of the nation. As it turned out the South won the battle and lost the war when they defeated Morris' plan. Over the next sixty years, the path they chose led to their defeat during the Civil War, and the near ruination of their culture.

In this report Morris was neutral on the topic of the "Back Lands" which later formed the North West Territories. His position was that Congress had authority over the issue, and he would leave it up to their wisdom. He was polite enough to omit the glaring fact that the English still controlled the area. Morris considered that sales of Western lands would not bring much money. There were also many unsettled issues of land title ownership in that area, as the members of the Six Nations would attest. Uncertain title was not the road to wealth in real estate. The development of the Western Lands had been one of the original sore spots between the Lees and Franklin.[283] When the report was issued, Morris held 1/84 of one Western Lands development company, the "Indiana Company."[284]

Congress debated the merits of Morris' proposal. James Madison thought that the Confederation should "assume" the debts of the States and repay those debts from centrally collected funds according to a quota arrangement. This suggestion was approved of and modified by the Financier, Morris, such that the states would become creditors to the central government. This became part of his plan. With this addition, Morris' plan was clearly the basis for the economic plan proposed by Hamilton some ten years later.[285] Hamilton observed the reaction to Morris' plan, and so Hamilton proposed, as Secretary of the Treasury, a scheme more politically sensitive to the sovereignty of the states. It did not initially call for a poll tax, or land tax, because the states were using these direct tax methods. As Hamilton's plan worked out, the Federal tax system was less visible to individuals because it relied mostly on an import tax collected at the ports, out of the view of most citizens.

While Congress was considering Morris' plan, he sent a budget message to Congress outlining expenditures amounting to eleven million dollars for the year 1783. This pair of documents contained the basis of a national governmental system. One proposal covered the income side of the equation, and the other provided detail on the expenditures Morris envisioned. Of course, it was easier to write reports and proposals than to get these policies enacted into law, so he worked to build a political constituency to support his initiatives. Morris designed a grand national architecture, but meanwhile the states had not agreed even to pass a modest import duty as a way of keeping the soldiers from starving.

Congress replied to Morris' budget by slashing the proposed amount for almost every department. Civil and Military staff was cut by 33%. The Clothing Department was cut by 85%. There was a total elimination of the promised half-pay pension provision Morris proposed to pay soldiers who fought in the war. The Marine Department was cut by 88%. The Congress reduced the budget by an overall amount of 30%, and then reduced the amount requested from the states from Morris' figure of $5 million to $2.8 million.[286] The requisition was later reduced to $2 million. Morris had to postpone his plan of creating a naval force, starting with six ships.[287]

Morris had engaged the "genius & habbits," or thinking of the past, on the great topic of national funding and gotten little more than the chance to put his ideas on the record; at the same time, real expenses demanded his attention. On July 30th, Morris was looking for the money to pay the six-month notes turned in by the officers in payment for their uniforms. He worried,

> ... I am likely to be disappointed of upwards of 22,000 dollars.[288]

He had hoped Henry Hill would have sold more bills of exchange (maybe in British occupied New York), but Hill managed to raise only £8,750. This was about half of Salomon's total for the period.[289] By August 1st, Morris managed to convince the uniform supplier, Mr. Pierce, to redeem the $140,226 in Morris Notes given him six months earlier, minus some that Pierce had transferred to Mr. Sands of the Moving Army contract. Morris expected to pay almost all of those notes with money collected by the sale of French bills of exchange, leaving a balance of $15,320 dollars, "which I think will be ready before payment is demanded." He was pleased to make note of his success. He wrote,

> So that the hopes and expectations of the malicious and disaffected will in this instance be disappointed.[290]

When it came time to settle the final balance on the account of the officers' uniforms, Morris made up the difference with $4,000 in his own notes.[291] One might see this as paying one debt with another, or maybe as paying a bill with a post-dated check, but Morris considered he was personally liable for these notes, and never expressed a contrary opinion nor did he try to weasel his way out of backing them.

He finished up another piece of old business. After much delay and going back and forth on the topic, Morris supplied Congress with the winning numbers of the Lottery and then proclaimed,

> ... the lottery is among those things, which on my entering into Office I stipulated that I should have nothing to do with.

He continued to insist that he was done with the business and Congress must take care of it from this point on.[292]

As the summer of 1782 moved towards fall it became increasingly clear that sufficient money was not going to be coming in from the states. At the same time Morris' notes were nearly due. He stepped up his efforts to solidify the interest groups into one force to lobby the states. Among those groups of creditors were found the vendors of supplies to the Continental efforts before Morris' tenure, the people who had supported the war when they purchased loan office certificates, and a host of other parties including the armed forces.

One of the largest groups to whom the Congress owed money was the Army. The officers and the soldiers were just subsisting on their rations. Other than officers who had gotten vouchers for new uniforms six months earlier, none had seen anything like a salary for a long time. Since the days of Valley Forge, Morris had supported a proposal to provide half pay for the life of any soldier who stayed in the army until the end of the war. This proposal served three purposes, which Morris supported. It insured the continuation of the Army until the end of the war; it encouraged long term loyalty to a Continental system of government; and it joined the interest of the Army with support for Morris' funding programs. In a telling detail, this provision had been removed during Congress' review of Morris' proposed budget.

Congress was not totally obtuse; and was aware of discontent in the army. Congress agreed with Morris' suggestion that an intermediary to settle differences between the Army and the contractors was needed. They directed (allowed) him to appoint an inspector for the Northern Army.[293] Morris started to search for the right individual for the job. Even so, the effort to supply the Northern Army was chronically hampered by the lack of funds from the states. It was immediately threatened by the limits of Morris' personal credit and financial resources because he was relying on his own notes to pay the contractors. The contractors in turn used the notes to buy the food and other supplies for the army. Growers did not accept Morris' notes at face value when the contractors used them to buy food. The growers discounted the notes; and this reduced the amount of food the notes would purchase. This disappointed the contractors, and the Army, and was a major cause for the disagreement between the two groups. Morris claimed he was up to date in his payments. The contractors claimed they did their very best to fulfill the contract with the resources they had. The end result was short rations for the soldiers even though everyone did what he could, everyone but the states who were not contributing.

In summing the situation, one contractor, William Duer, noted his disgust with what he saw as the negligence of the states. He advocated that Morris stop issuing his notes. He said, it would be

> Ultimately for the public good, both for yourself and the contractors to declare their inability to subsist the Army any longer. Such a Declaration may rouse a stupid, unthinking peoples (scarcely deserving the object they are contending for) from their present lethargy.

He continued by warning that Morris' private exertions gave a false sense of ease that would lead to disaster for him and the war effort. In his opinion only a shock would wake the people from their "delirium."[294] Morris did not heed this advice. Within the next two days he had given the quartermaster another $45,000 in his notes. By this time Morris was using timed notes, so he could control the rate of redemption. Morris expected the quartermaster to redeem these notes for money collected by the regional tax collectors in New England. This was not to be. They had no money to send because they were not collecting the tax for the continent. New York offered to redeem the notes at a discount. Morris declined. Instead, the quartermaster used them to purchase food for the Army's horses and held onto the majority of those notes.[295]

Additional pressure was felt when the French approached the same growers with silver instead of notes. This resulted in a majority of the available supplies going to the French, and a resulting lack of food for the American Army. Morris tried to add the French forces as clients to his contracting system because he wanted to bank their silver and stop the competition for resources. He claimed he could save them money by not competing with them. They were not willing to change their supply system, and this effort failed.

Matters from Europe also called Morris' attention. He and Ridley still had not settled on a school for Morris' boys. Ridley was taking them around Europe with him as he worked on various business arrangements. He began to think European schools were no better than American. Morris was growing tired of Ridley's procrastinations and outlined the kind of education he expected the boys to have. Another indeterminate effort was the prisoner negotiation. They were on again and off again without any firm resolution.

Matthew Ridley and Gouverneur Morris also kept in touch across the Atlantic. Both of these men wanted to see the United States become a unified nation, and both decried the efforts of localist interests who worked to thwart that goal. In a private letter Gouverneur expressed his thinking that the progress in creating a national system was going slowly. Considering the forces that were at work he thought that the war was useful in forming a nation. He wrote,

> Nothing remained but vigor, organization, and promptitude to render this a considerable Empire. These can only be acquired by a continuance of the war which will convince people of the necessity of obedience to common councils for general purposes. War is indeed a rough nurse to infant states and the consequence of being committed to her care is that they either die young or grow up vigorous. We have at least lived thro the cradle and are familiarized to her looks of horror.[296]

Another nationalist, General Greene, reported from the Southern Department that the English were expected to depart Charleston, South Carolina in late August.[297] Naturally, the states were aware of the lack of aggressive military action on the part of the British, and they also heard the rumors of peace from Europe. They were not inclined to build a central government if peace was on the way. To overcome their reluctance, Morris continued to publish the monthly totals sent by the states, and this did embarrass some into action. Nevertheless, the states were uneven partners. Morris had some allies in a few state houses, and fewer in others. Each state determined its own level and mode of support, regardless of what they had agreed to under the Articles of Confederation, or of what Congress or Morris said. The composition of the state delegations to Congress changed over time. Fewer and fewer members remained of those who had unanimously voted for Morris in 1781. The success of Morris' solutions reduced Congress' feeling of imminent financial collapse, and this in turn reduced their willingness to take measures necessary to ensure the continued success of Morris' program.

With peace hovering overhead and waning support in Congress, the states objected to Morris' taxation policies. This happened just as their help was needed the most. The states saw loans coming from France and Holland, so their representatives in Congress asked the states for much less than Morris thought necessary. Unfortunately for all, in the 18th century a loan banked in Paris could not immediately feed an Army in New York or the Carolinas. The bills were mounting, and there were reports of soldiers in mutiny. In the face of these conditions, Rhode Island looked inward; it still had not acted on the impost proposal of 1781. Rhode Island was a state with a large merchant fleet, and they considered the impost to be an excessive burden on them. They suggested using the North West Territories, which did not belong to them, as an alternative funding source. Borrowing on such a dubious asset was unlikely to bring in much, and at great expense in terms of acres used. All of this resulted in Morris turning again to France for yet another loan and seeking ways of importing more silver from Cuba.

Alexander Hamilton observed from Albany, New York, that the problem with getting money from the states was the effect of the new democracy on the members of the legislature. The legislators were not used to the difficulties of making unpopular decisions and also keeping elected office. He wrote,

> Here we find the general disease which infects our constitutions, an excess of popularity. There is no *order* that has a will of its own. The inquiry consistently is what will *please* not what will *benefit* the people. In such a government there can be nothing but temporary expedient, fickleness and folly.[298]

Morris and Hamilton shared the same dream of seeing the United States become a true nation. Morris wrote to Hamilton,

> A firm, wise, manly system of federal government is what I once wished, what I now hope, and what I dare not expect, but what I will not despair of.[299]

Elsewhere in New York, Washington and his army were still waiting for someone to be appointed to deal with the contractors. Washington felt the need urgently, mostly because much of his time was taken up with these concerns and he felt that was not the best use of his energies.[300] Also animosity was growing between him and the contractors. The contractors went to New Hampshire for supplies. There a farmer sold $3,000 worth of cattle to the suppliers of the Moving Army contract. That farmer received Morris notes, and those notes eventually found their way back to Morris. That meat was the only contribution made by New Hampshire for the year.[301] Morris got some favorable news from his old business partner, Thomas Willing, who was head of the Bank of North America. Willing visited Morris and told him that the bank was willing to extend the payback period for the outstanding loan of $100,000, but he would not be able to do this again.[302]

In an unexpected event, Philadelphia merchant, Joseph Wilson, approached Morris on August 9th and agreed to buy 200,000 livres in bills of exchange for the amount of £6,000 (English money), and to take delivery in December, but to pay in monthly installments of £2,000 starting on the 15th of August. Morris worked with John Chaloner on this arrangement. Morris supplied half of the bills, and Chaloner the other half. They also split the proceeds.[303] Chaloner was a merchant, and agent for the supplier to the French forces. He had his French bills of exchange on hand for that reason. The deal with Chaloner started off well but became a problem. Morris was in such need of cash he borrowed against the whole amount expected from the sale, and so later on he not only had the interest to pay the bank, but half the money that was due Mr. Chaloner. Morris already owed Chaloner $20,000 from a separate May loan to the U.S. which Morris backed, and that amount was due soon. Morris turned to his old trading partners Holker, Bingham, and Ross. Holker and Bingham did help.[304] Ross was busy lending his money out at 5% per month; and was not inclined to spare any for Morris' shortfall.

No matter how much time went by in Europe, the old Lee/Franklin animosity never seemed to cool. Franklin wrote that he was still disinclined to pay Mr. William Lee because the congressional order stated, "as soon as the state of public finances would admit" and Franklin did not judge the state of finances to be sufficiently strong to allow that payment.[305] Franklin seemed to take some pleasure at Lee's expense, but when it came to helping America, he was very competent. He succeeded in freeing hundreds of captive marine prisoners. Among them was Captain John Green, who arrived in Philadelphia on August 12th. Green had been captured as a captain for the Continental Navy and held in Mill Prison in England. Morris sought his release before Franklin traded American sailors for British prisoners. The first ship held 216 prisoners, and the second carried 132, eleven of which died in transit due to illness on board[306]. (The loss of 9% in transit is roughly equivalent to the losses experienced during the slave trade.) Green brought information about a British convoy of 200 ships heading to America.

After consultations with Morris, Captain John Green went to New York to move the prisoner negotiations ahead. Sir Guy Carleton wrote Morris that he was willing to receive the number of British prisoners equal to the number of American naval prisoner released under the deal struck with Franklin a few months earlier.[307] Washington wrote to Morris acknowledging that Gouverneur was not going to attend the prisoner exchange meetings, and that he, Washington, would appoint a Mr. Skinner as commissioner.[308] Washington picked Generals Heath and Knox as prisoner negotiators, and arranged for them to meet at Orange, New York, now Tappan. He appealed to Morris for $500 in specie for their expenses.[309]

With this underway, Morris, as Agent of Marine, worked from Philadelphia to make the most of his tiny navy. He wanted to provide John Paul Jones with the means to launch the *America* from its birth in Portsmouth, New Hampshire, but work was proceeding slowly.[310] He also worked to purchase the *General Washington* by agreeing with state treasurer Rittenhouse that as Agent of Pennsylvania the state of Pennsylvania would promise to pay for the ship in nine months. He planned that the Continental treasury would repay Pennsylvania within that period.[311] This way Morris was able to add a new ship to the Continental Navy without formal Congressional approval. Just a few months earlier Congress had reduced his proposed budget for Naval funding by eighty-eight percent, and Morris' earlier efforts to fund the navy had been met with much resistance. Morris planned for the *General Washington* to play a critical role in the American victory.

One Mr. Raguet had purchased some bills of exchange in Philadelphia but did not have the money to pay for them. He and Morris entered negotiations. In an effort to make good on his commitment Raguet offered goods from his store. These were not suitable for the Army. He then offered a ship he was having built, *Duc de Lauzun*. At first Morris declined, but when several other businessmen offered to take the ship with Morris, as Superintendent of Finance, in a kind of creditors' partnership, Morris accepted. Eventually Morris bought out the other partners with bills of exchange and converted the ship to a Continental Navy ship. Morris' efforts to increase the size of the Navy did not go unobserved by members of Congress who had objected to funding the Navy.

Morris took control of the *General Washington* on August 28th and began using it as a mail, or packet, ship to Europe. This was timely because of the growing need for communications in light of the critical diplomatic efforts and peace negotiations underway in France at the time. Commercial activities were almost at a standstill, but there was some excitement at the Coffee House when Morris' messenger announced that the French

Navy was in the Delaware Bay.[312] The merchants readied themselves to travel in convoy with them when the French left port.

Back in the state house, the Congressional representative from New Hampshire, a Mr. Gilman, made it clear to Morris and Congress that it would be next to impossible to finish the ship *America* for the United States, and if finished it would be impossible to find a crew. Morris, for his part, requested a meeting with a committee of Congress and suggested that the *America* be presented to the French.[313] Congress agreed to present that ship to America's best ally.[314] Morris hoped transferring the *America* to the French would be a good way to start a ship building business for the French Navy. Morris, as agent of Marine, contacted the Minister of France, Chevalier de La Luzerne, and offered the *America* to the French Crown. The minister was pleased at the news but needed the King's approval.[315] Morris had to tell John Paul Jones about the fate of the *America.* John Paul Jones wrote from New Hampshire to Gouverneur Morris that he was not happy about the French getting the *America*. John Brown, of Philadelphia, was still evaluating the work of the Eastern Navy Board, and he found it lacking in detail as well as effectiveness. He suspected foul play. He sent an auditor's report to Morris and suggested that Morris contact the members of that board, "... and give them an opportunity to supply the defective vouchers."[316]

The details of the Office of Finance kept rolling through. Morris bought paper for Eleazer Oswald, the printer, to use for official printing. He talked with Mr. Wheeler who had made rollers for the stalled mint. Morris supplied five hundred dollars to the hospitals in Virginia in the form of a note.[317] He met with Oliver Pollock about the money Pollock was owed.[318] He met with General Gates, who wanted Morris to see him in a positive light after the publication of a negative message in the press.[319] Major David S. Franks wanted to be paid for his work in Europe where he had been sent with important letters to the diplomats.[320] Morris arranged for Major Franks to be paid.[321] Haym Salomon could not sell any bills in late August. Arthur Lee wanted the Treasury to control the settlement of accounts of those who served in Europe. Morris wanted an independent commissioner for that.[322] Rumors were circulating that Morris had allowed British naval prisoners out on parole, but that was not true because they were being sent to New York as part of the exchange program.[323] Morris heard from Timothy Pickering, the Quartermaster General, that Morris' notes could not be used to raise money and pay for supplies in Hartford, Connecticut. The tax collector of Connecticut wrote that,

> There is little money raised here in taxes. In this town perhaps as able as any, only twenty dollars has been collected in money.[324]

Mr. Bradford, a Boston man, bought items for the United States from Connecticut. He bought them on credit, and when the bill came due, he appealed to Morris such that the amount would be credited to Connecticut's balance. Morris denied this because he did not want individuals in the middle of the interstate tax system. He requested that Connecticut not charge Bradford, and instead that they assume the debt and make that part of their contribution.[325]

Letters between Morris and Washington, in August 1782, show a mixture of the embarrassment, frustration, and resignation they both felt in their positions. There was embarrassment because they both knew each was doing his best, but that there was still not enough to go around. There was frustration because Morris was unable to get others to contribute, and Washington had to live with the suffering soldiers. There was resignation that they had to maintain their positions, because without their combined efforts the whole long War would quickly end, and not in their favor. They opened their lives to one another, and in one letter to Washington Morris outlined his financial exposure on notes: $45,000 to the Quarter Master General, $20,000 to Langdon for the ship *America*, and $50,000 for the contractors to the army.[326]

Morris had a plan to get money to Washington's army via George Eddy. Eddy was supposed to show up in Morristown, NJ with $10,000 from the sale of some of the tobacco from the Yorktown deal, but Eddy could not be found. The money was needed for the contractors and had to be replaced, somehow.[327] It soon came clear why George Eddy was missing. The two tobacco ships from Virginia had been captured. Only one was to be protected by a flag of truce. Both were finally released. In the meantime, Morris wanted to be repaid for the stalled official shipment.[328]

The lack of money was felt everywhere. There was no money to buy more horses for the Virginia cavalry, and the clothing account was paid with 60-day Morris notes. Morris wrote to the leader of the cavalry about those notes,

> I have no doubt that you can readily negotiate them for specie and in payments without any discount. This not only saves the expense of transporting silver but enables me to extend my means of payment and to anticipate the taxes.[329]

There was not even money for cannon balls "without diverting money from services which are indispensable – many such services are now suffering."[330] All the available funds went to feed and clothe the Army, or for ships to get prizes, goods from Europe, silver, or news of the negotiations.

Money was needed for the backer of the new Moving Army contract. Mr. Chaloner demanded payment of the $20,000 Morris owed him as Superintendent of Finance. Morris turned to Salomon to raise funds by selling bills of exchange to Bingham and John Ross for cash. Both agreed to help, but neither had the ready cash to hand over. Bingham also mentioned that there was much already owed to him by the United States and that he would appreciate a deposit into his account. Morris replied that a commission was underway to determine the balance of such accounts.[331]

Congress recommended to the states that they grant a stay to all lawsuits against public officials until the end of the war.[332] Morris sent the resolution along with one of his circulars to the Governors. He hoped that the people who had been justly worried that state suppliers would sue them for non-payment would now be able to send newly collected tax money to the Continental Treasury.

That vigilant congressman, Arthur Lee, managed to get himself put onto the oversight committee Madison had proposed in agreement with Morris.[333] Lee frequently arrived in Morris' office under the auspices of membership on that committee, even when other committee members were not present.[334] On occasion he took those opportunities to advance the interests of himself, his brother, or his nephew.[335] In addition, Arthur Lee used his position on that and later committees to great partisan effect. His written notes are found in the margins of many documents that originated under Morris' administration, and have been considered by various historians as valid entries in the documentary record. As a result, some historians have taken Arthur Lee's notes as a guide to interpreting the record of Morris' tenure without taking the time to review the overall context. Thus, Arthur Lee's point of view has survived long after the particular arguments have been forgotten. The irony is that Lee's contemporaries did not trust him. They saw him as a vicious partisan and sought to exclude him from important tasks; yet somehow over the intervening 200 years Lee's partisan sniping has become the default perspective in many modern historical interpretations of Morris and his work.

Lee, as a member of the oversight committee, questioned Morris on the need to hire tax receivers instead of retaining the former loan officers to perform the same job. Morris responded that new receivers were required because any income from states paid to the old loan officers would have gone directly out as interest payments; and would not be available for the continuing costs of the war.[336] What Morris did not mention was that the loan officers had been using new loan office certificates to pay interest on old loan office certificates, a practice Morris held in low regard. Morris was also silent on the topic of fraud in the old treasury board, of which Lee had been a member. Lee questioned Morris' employment of Mr. Swanwick, on whom Morris relied for disbursing the Morris Notes. Lee considered that Morris was using Swanwick to bypass the Treasury in handing out Continental monies.

The record shows that Morris called on the Treasurer, Mr. Michael Hillegas, to issue notes from the Treasury when there was money, and he used Swanwick to issue Morris Notes for Continental purposes when it was necessary. Morris saw his notes as a short-term method of backing American creditworthiness. They were like loan guarantees that he would cover if the United States could not pay. The first Morris Notes were issued wholly on Morris' credit, and these were payable on demand. The second round of Morris Notes were timed notes, so he could control the rate of redemption. The amount of his notes, for which he felt personally liable, increased to well over $1,400,000 (in 1780's dollars).[337*] What started as a way to buy time to build a national funding system was becoming a huge personal liability, precisely because people like Arthur Lee were so successful in fighting Morris' efforts to create a national funding system.

In keeping with Morris' plan to transfer his personal creditworthiness to the United States, and because he was increasingly worried that his personal liability was too great, Morris started to issue his notes on behalf of the United States. This made Morris a co-signer of American notes and that meant that if the U.S. could not pay, he would. This transition from originator to co-signer was the way Morris transferred his creditworthiness to America. This transitional condition also gave some measure of credibility to Lee's charges about Mr. Swanwick, but particularly in the minds of his partisans.

While Lee fought Morris' efforts to get money to the Continental treasury from Virginia (or even tobacco for that matter) and while Lee fought Morris' efforts reduce fraud and waste in government; Lee was quick with his hand out for special treatment in the Congress if it meant getting paid, or money for his family. Lee's disappointments in France, plus his distrust and dislike for Franklin, Deane, and the general class of merchants from the north, all served to fill his mind with suspicion and misapprehension. Lee concluded about Morris,

> The accumulation of offices in this man, the number of valuable appointments in his gift, the absolute control given him over the revenue officers, his money, and his art; render him a most dangerous man to the Liberty of the country, as his excessive avarice does to the treasury.[338]

Lee never explained how Morris' current liability of over $1,400,000 in support of the war effort amounted to "avarice" but his word was accepted without question by fellow partisans, and dismissed as ridiculous by people at the time who knew the facts.

Morris carried on with his program, which included settling the accounts of the states and the various Continental departments. Contrary to the implications within Lee's assertions Morris did not have the power to appoint commissioners to settle the accounts. He did, however, have the ability to propose individuals whom the Congress could then approve or disapprove.[339] This process was somewhat like the nomination process founded in America under the Constitution, whereby the President nominates individuals; and the Senate confirms or rejects the nominee.

The never-ending effort to supply the troops in the South, and General Greene's use of the techniques Morris introduced, revealed the nature of the problems inherent in the system of specific supplies. General Greene wrote Morris,

> I find the State of North Carolina want to furnish specific supplies at the old rates, when the articles can be had by contract at least 60 or 100 percent lower.[340]

Greene agreed to take specific supplies, but only if the agreed value was at the cash price. If that was not acceptable, he would take the articles and let the state and the settlement agents figure it out later. Morris continued to scramble to find money to pay the Moving Army contract. He expected that by the end of August the contractors were owed another $13,000. Before this time, he had sent agents to New York to convert some of the bills of exchange backed by the French loan into hard money. Unfortunately, that conversion never occurred. As soon as Morris discovered this shortfall, he sent $5,000 from the treasury and $2,000 in his own notes. Morris planned that these notes would be convertible to hard money at the tax collectors' offices.[341] Morris looked again to his old business partners for money. He borrowed $10,000 from John Holker.[342] Officers of the Bank of North America requested repayment of some of the loans made to the Office of Finance.[343]

Morris was aware that tax collection was not proceeding according to his expectation. He had to prepare Washington for the eventuality that the whole contracting effort might fall apart. Morris knew that both he and the contractors would outlive the war, and so they both had to act in a way that would not disqualify them from future business. He told Washington that,

> I am determined to act justly and therefore when I find that I shall be unable to pay the contractors I will give them due notice that they may retire in season.[344]

Morris continued to warn Washington of the impending failure of the contracting system because of lack of support by the states, and summed up the note with an expression of his frustration,

> I have done all that I could and given repeated warnings of the consequences but it is like preaching to the dead.[345]

Washington continued to be displeased with the current contractors and requested Morris to compel them to supply the agreed articles. Morris had told him that the contractors had been paid (even if each payment had not been as timely as hoped) so Washington assumed the lack of supplies was due to the contractor's greed.

> I must say, that Mr Sand's whole conduct plainly indicates an intention to make every thing to himself at the expense of the army and the public.[346]

Unfortunately, Washington and his troops were experiencing the effects of the loss of purchasing power due to the discounting of Morris' notes by farmers and other suppliers to the contractors. Additionally, prices for supplies were high due to competition from French contractors. Morris was not only competing with the French contractors in the purchase of supplies, but also in the sales of bills of exchange, as brokers were also selling bills drawn on French banks. The French were underpricing their offerings and Morris told Salomon not to compete on that basis.[347] Morris encouraged his agent Lowell, in Massachusetts, to sell bills of exchange if the rates were favorable.[348] He reminded Lowell not to pay old debts with newly collected revenues. That money was needed for the continuing effort, and the old debts would be settled after the war.[349]

On September 6th, William Duer, of Comfort Sands & Co. wrote to tell Morris that the lack of money due on the contracts made it impossible for him to buy any more from over-stretched suppliers. He attempted to quit the contract,

> I am no longer master of the price of any article, and scarcely in a situation to furnish the supplies from day to day. I am therefore bound in Justice to myself to declare that I consider myself totally freed from the contract, which I can no longer execute on the present terms without ruin to the Concern.[350]

He stated he would supply the troops until the end of September. The slow payments to the contractors had to be admitted as a way of explaining the contractor's behavior to Washington. The desperation of the situation is clear in Morris' letter,

> Already I am in arrears [de]spite all my efforts. I am determined however to continue those efforts to the last moment, but at present I really know not which way to turn myself.[351]

The Moving Army contract started to fall apart shortly after Duer, of Comfort Sands & Co. threatened to quit, but some individuals from that company wished to continue in a different form as Sands, Livingston & Co. Instead of working with a reconfigured Comfort Sands, & Co. a new contractor was engaged. This company, Wadsworth and Carter, was one of the contractors to the French army. They were willing to give Morris long-term credit as they supplied the rations. The trade-off was that each ration was more expensive, demonstrating once again how the negligence of the states was driving up the cost of the war.

After looking for months on a related matter, Morris was finally able to announce to Washington that General Cornell had accepted the Office of the "Inspector of the Contracts etc." for the Army. This happened just as Washington's Army had to be fed between the end of the Comfort Sands & Co. contract, which was over on September 30th, and the beginning of the new Wadsworth and Carter contract, which was due to start on Oct 15th. Wadsworth and Carter was a contractor to supply the French forces; and had been competing with Morris' contractors for food stuffs. John B. Carter was married to Governor Schuyler's daughter, who happened to be Alexander Hamilton's sister-in-law.[352] Morris wanted Cornell to talk to the contractors and help to bridge the gap between the two contracts.[353] He wrote,

> I am reduced therefore to this point that unless means can be devised to feed the army at a long credit I must desire the contractors to desist and desire the General to subsist his troops by military collection.[354]

Sands' former partners, including Daniel Parker, in the form of Sands, Livingston & Co., offered to bridge the two-week gap if they were given sufficient cash to make the necessary purchases.[355]

The earlier business with Chaloner and the French bills of exchange became entangled with the new contract for the Moving Army with Wadsworth and Carter because Chaloner was an agent of that new contracting firm.[356] These gentlemen were willing to give the United States ninety days' credit, but they needed money to buy the food, and that was to come from the repayment of the old debt. By wheedling borrowed funds from Bingham,[357] Morris was able to cover the debt on September 25.[358] The contract would be signed in October.

Morris wanted to have a reliable currency. To that end, he reported to Congress on September 7th that he would like to direct the states to collect and destroy their old discredited currency, but to account for the amount destroyed so that amount could be credited to the States at the 40:1 rate as if contributed as part of their requisition.[359] It seems Morris was trying to reduce the amount of currency in circulation as a way of ending inflation, while at the same time easing the burden on states during future settlements. He chose the 40:1 rate because that was the last expressed will of Congress. Congress was against Morris' proposal because it overvalued the discredited currency in some states; it hurt states without a circulating currency because they would have to send a silver dollar instead of forty pieces of paper, and at the same time reduced the chance anyone would send silver when they might send old paper. Some states worried they would have to buy currency at artificially high prices to pay the requisition and thus enrich speculators. In brief, Morris' suggestion was rejected because of the uneven economic status of the various states.[360] The issue was left unresolved during the Confederation period because Congress decided to decide later.

Morris maintained his effort to keep hard money in the bank, and use notes as a circulating medium. This way the specie was available only in the most critical cases. In one case, Morris convinced the contractors to the French forces to use Morris Notes to purchase cattle in New Hampshire. He sold $12,000 in his notes to the French Contractors for them to use in New England.[361] Similarly Morris worked to keep Eddy's silver in the bank. His Virginia tobacco agent, Daniel Clark, was still trying to close up the Virginia Tobacco deal and he expected to hear from Eddy.[362] Morris had acceded to southern wishes that Eddy could buy tobacco on private account over and above the Congressional limit, using Clark as the purchasing agent. In return Eddy had to put cash into the Bank of North America to cover the transaction, while Morris sent $2,000 in his six-month notes to Clark in Virginia and cautioned him to keep careful records of all transactions.[363] The intended result was that the "Public" would have use of Eddy's cash until the deal was finally settled.[364] By mid-September the intended beneficiaries of the tobacco deal, the American prisoners held by the British, had been traded and so they didn't need support from the deal, which explains why the funds were free to go to Washington's Army. Morris released the British marine prisoners, and they sailed to New York. He also sent a list of the prisoners and expected the British to settle their America percentage because the British were supposed to pay for the prisoners' maintenance.[365] Shortly thereafter, George Eddy reappeared and announced that the second tobacco ship *New York* had arrived in the city of the same name. Morris made it clear he expected Eddy to clear up his account with the Bank.[366]

Bits of news filtered into and out of the office. Officers of the Bank of North America again requested repayment of some of the loans made to the Office of Finance.[367] Hamilton resigned as Continental tax receiver to pursue a career in the Law. Morris replaced Hamilton with a Mr. Tillotson in New York. He told his business partner, Whitesides, to move indigo bought for the United States from Baltimore to Philadelphia. He received a pleasant letter from Matthew Ridley with news about the Jays, Franklin's illness, and the state of the boys' progress in Europe.[368]

Morris had not heard from Maryland since he started helping them sell their goods with advertisements in Pennsylvania. Good news came from Daniel of St. Thomas Jenifer, the intendent of revenue of that state. He wrote,

> ...very considerable sums have been advanced by this state on Continental Account since the 1st of January last to the 3rd of September – to wit – 45,497 Specie, 816.2.16 Ct Flour, 105,500 lbs tobacco, and 76,162 rations.... There is in the Treasury six thousand pounds specie subject to your order.[369]

Morris sent Captain Green to collect the silver from Maryland.[370]

On September 9th, Congress acted to stop the use of bills of exchange drawn on France, for the payment of interest. This step helped to put all the creditors on equal footing and worked to encourage all creditors to lobby the states to pay their requisite amounts to the Continental treasury. Morris officially asked Congress to agree that a new loan for 4,000,000 livres should be applied for.[371] Congress agreed that day.[372] Morris and the Secretary of Foreign Affairs, Livingstone, arranged a loan of five million livres from the French, and on September 14th, 1782, Congress responded to Morris' request and agreed to accept that loan.[373]

In early September a group of leaders from Pennsylvania's military and civil establishment asked Morris how much the Office of Finance would be able to pay of the expected £5,000 (PA currency) that their intended western expedition against the Indians would cost. Morris said he had no funds for that, and if Pennsylvania wanted to underwrite it that would be fine, but if they wanted the Continental Treasury to pay they would need a positive balance in their Continental account and approval from the Secretary of War for the expedition.[374] A delegation from Pennsylvania forwarded the matter to Congress on September 10th. Later, Congress agreed to allow the Continental Troops to join the Pennsylvania troops. Morris asked Pennsylvania to provide provisions for Continental troops, but Morris agreed to pay the cost of rations for the troops at the contractor price. He promised to supply blankets and the state agreed to pay for them.

The mission to Pittsburgh was never launched because on September 23rd Washington announced that in his communications with Sir Guy Carleton, the British agreed to stop Indian incursions into American territory. Washington argued against the American mission because it would probably start a series of actions based on "defense and revenge" and the British would allow that to continue under the belief that the Americans had started it.[375]

Once the mission had been stopped, Morris tried to recall the money he had borrowed from the Bank and had sent to Fort Pitt to finance the Continental portion of the mission. When that failed, he decided to credit that amount as Pennsylvania's contribution to the war effort and repay the loan with money Pennsylvania sent as requisition to the Continental Treasury. The "Constitutionalists" in Pennsylvania were pleased to get hard money from Philadelphia to Fort Pitt, and not pleased to learn they would be charged for it as Morris suggested. This effort by Congress to defray the costs of an unnecessary adventure against the Indians was viewed by partisans as an example of the Eastern interests taking money from the Western frontier, when actually the "Eastern interests" (Morris) had sent them money to help with their initiative and the money was expected to be repaid.[376]

In mid-September, the clothing which had been bought by a contingent of Southerners in Amsterdam a few years earlier, and which sat in warehouses for years awaiting shipment, finally arrived in Philadelphia on board the ship *Herr Adams.* Morris directed the clothes fit for officers to be sold to them, as the policy in those days was for officers to supply their own uniforms.[377] Also with that ship came the news of Adams' success in arranging a subscription loan of 5,000,000 gilders through a group of Dutch bankers, Wilhelm and Han Willink, Nicolaas and Jacob van Staphorst, Jacobus de la Lande, and Hendrick Fynge. Morris wrote to Adams:

> I do myself the pleasure to congratulate you on the success of your patriotic labors in Holland.[378]

In a loan of this kind, people in Holland would buy a portion of the loan in expectation of getting increased revenues when the loan was repaid. It takes time until all the money is raised in this kind subscription of loan. Morris was overly optimistic about the rate this loan would "fill" and expected the money to arrive quickly. The loan Congress approved on September was over and above this amount.[379] The ship *Herr Adams* was to be sold as a way of paying for the trip.[380] The state of Pennsylvania decided it would not allow the supplies from Europe to be unloaded in Philadelphia until the state duties on those goods were paid.[381] Morris provided a bond for the duty and reserved the right to bring the matter before Congress.[382] Shortly after that the Attorney General of Pennsylvania decided that the ship *Herr Adams* could be unloaded without the payment of duties because the goods belonged to the United States.[383]

Congress began investigating the business of the newly arrived Dutch-bought supplies, many of which had been replaced previously in Europe because the originals were English made. The participants of record in this business were Colonel John Laurens of South Carolina, his secretary, William Jackson, and Alexander Gillon of the South Carolina Navy. The committee decided to fault Franklin's conduct for the business, somehow overlooking that Franklin was in France at the time. James Madison was not favorably impressed; and he said the report was "one of the most single monuments which party zeal had produced."[384]

Everyone was looking for cash. The market for the French bills of exchange was nonexistent in Philadelphia.[385] Holker was short of money due to his loans to the US. Morris got a loan from the bank to pay a portion to Holker.[386] Morris sought repayment for a $4,000 loan to Francisco Rendón, the Spanish emissary.[387] Morris was approached by a gentleman, Mr. Tillinghast, who had been a former prize agent for the old Secret Committee, where his job had been to convert ships captured at sea into funds for the war. Tillinghast contended that he was owed money from before 1779 and wanted repayment from funds gained by the sale of the ship *Polly* that had recently been captured by a privateer. Tillinghast hoped to clear some of those balances with the sale of new prizes, but Morris stuck with his policy of not paying old debts and Tillinghast had to wait.[388]

Morris continued to use money as the basis for supplies in the South, and especially in the Carolinas, where the pricing was irregular. He wrote the tax receiver in South Carolina with the news General Greene had given about the high prices of commodities in that state. He wished to make it known that price gouging would not be tolerated. He wrote,

> I am persuaded that no gentleman in your state can wish the continent to be charged more than a thing is worth and therefore I attribute any overcharge to misinformation which will I am sure be readily corrected on further consideration.[389]

He sent a bill of exchange of the $266 drawn on the governor of South Carolina, with General Greene as the intended recipient. This transferred tax money collected by that state to General Greene. Morris sent another note for $800, which was to be converted into cash upon arrival. This amounted to $1,066 for General Greene and his army.[390]

Quartermaster General, Timothy Pickering, wrote with news from New England that the French were buying up as much of the forage as they could, but he was able to get assurances that he could get specific supplies at the same rate as the farmers sold to the French, if it was agreed that Connecticut would be credited.[391] He also stated that the frigate *Bourbon* was to be finished, but to stay in the boat yard. The shortage of sailors and money to supply the ship continued to weaken the navy.

The great task of settling the accounts of the Continental departments was about to start. Congress had concurred with Morris' choices for the Commissioners of Accounts for the five great staff Departments. Congress had charged these people with settling the accounts of Departments from the time before Morris took office. He sent a letter to them and outlined their work. He wrote,

> You can not be ignorant that the public Officers in the several Departments have been charged with Peculation, Fraud, and speculating with the Public Money. These charges are of the most serious nature and therefore whether true or false they ought be enquired into.[392]

He went on to suggest ways of determining if undue enrichment at the public expense had occurred.

> ... such are great and unusual expense of living beyond the bounds either of the public salaries and allowance or the private fortune of the party also sudden acquisition of wealth without any visibly adequate means to which may be added the neglect of public duties connected with an attention to other business and the consorting with those characters noted for being concerned in speculations. Under such circumstances it will be proper to make more close examinations.[393]

Morris was willing to have government inspectors review the work of his office, but the same cannot be said about those who went before him.

-|-

There was, at that time, no mint and a general lack of reliable currency. To solve the problem, Hamilton suggested that if Morris were to issue his notes in smaller denominations they would more readily enter into circulation.[394] Morris responded to Hamilton's suggestion and agreed that his notes might be useful. However, the basis upon which Morris issued his notes was in anticipation of tax remittances, and not really for use as currency. A tax note could be retired by the Office of Finance, but currency would only have value if it could be turned in for silver. Morris knew the silver would probably come from his account, and he knew the notes were not supported by any laws except when they were ultimately used to pay taxes. He did not really expect low denomination tax notes to hold their value. He wrote,

> ... Farmers will not give full credit to money merely because it will pay taxes, for that is an object they are not very violently devoted to; but that money which goes freely at the store and the tavern will be sought after as greedily as those things which the store and the tavern contain.[395]

Morris added that he was worried about counterfeiting and that counterfeit notes would pass among illiterate men who could not tell the difference between real notes and fakes.

The matter of the supply ship *Franklin* lingered on Morris' desk. He informed Barclay, the American council in France, that the ship *Herr Adams* had arrived and was sold for $20,000. The money was to be used to pay for the trip and any profit went into general revenues. He also noted that Congress was contemplating the settlement of accounts for those in service in Europe, including Silas Deane. Morris said of Deane,

> Justice is indeed due him in common with all other men but his conduct has been such as to preclude the idea of any thing like favor.[396]

Morris sought to use American products as a way to pay Continental debts. On September 23rd Morris sent $60,000 in his notes to Daniel Clark, his agent in Virginia. This was to buy tobacco, and supply Virginia with Morris notes for them to use in payment of their Congressionally mandated specie requisition. Clark seems to have been confused as to whether this was a private or public purchase, and when he went to make the purchase it was rejected because the people in Virginia thought it must be a private venture. Morris had to clarify that it was a public measure, and the sale finally went through. In early 1783, much of the tobacco went to Holland and the money from the resulting sale went to pay interest due on a previous Dutch loan that Adams had arranged. The rest of the tobacco was sold via La Caze and Mallet to raise needed cash.[397]

On September 23rd the Governor of Virginia, Harrison, had debts on his mind. He wrote to Morris asking him to take over the loan that his state had arranged with the French,

> ...we shall be obliged to you to take them off our hands and take the debt so far as they go on to the states.[398]

Morris contacted Barclay the next day, and requested that he send all the Virginia supplies to America immediately and to do so using American credit.[399] He informed his banker, Mr. Grand, that if the American account was overdrawn in France then Grand should look to the Dutch loan to cover any gaps.[400] He made arrangements with his contacts in Cadiz and his private banker in France, Le Couteulx and Co., to bring the remains of the Dutch loan through Havana as silver. In the process he outlined how careful purchases of various currencies would increase the size of the account to the benefit of the United States,

> I am informed that Bills on Cadiz at thirty days sell at the Havana for an advance of eight percent, and that bills on Paris sell at Cadiz for an advance of nine percent and there is also an advance on bills drawn from Paris on Amsterdam to which may be added that a considerable time is also gained in these various negotiations and therefore if any benefit can be derived to the United States from that circumstance you will govern yourself accordingly.[401]

The market had soured again, and bills of exchange were not selling in Philadelphia. Morris decided to sell the cloths that came in on the *Herr*

Adams to pay some of the debts owed by the Clothing Department.[402] After all his cost cutting and trades, he seemed to be pleased to provide his friends in Europe some relief from their financial embarrassments. He wrote to the peace commissioners in France, Franklin, Adams and Jay,

> I hope and believe that while I am writing this letter...you will be freed from the Torment and perplexity of attending to Money Matters ... I have long since requested the Secretary of Foreign Affairs to ... appoint an agent or Attorney here to receive and remit your salary which will be paid quarterly.[403]

Morris had reached the limit of his personal credit; and refused to write any new notes because the states were not collecting taxes to pay the holders. He wrote,

> I am very unwilling that new debts should be contracted for the shameful and I think I might say treasonable negligence of those (whoever they are) whose duty it is to compel the collection of taxes takes away the hope of being able to pay them and it is my determination not to promise where I do not see the prospect of performance.[404]

Morris needed action from the states.

Washington was not pleased to be encouraged by Morris to lobby the states. He felt that the states would think he was out of line, reject his input and embarrass him.[405] He suggested that if the states would not pay in hard money it might be best to revert to the system of specific supplies just to ensure that supplies were on hand for winter quarters.[406] Morris replied. He used an example to make clear the need for participation by state government. He said that he could only pay to feed the Army and that even though there was enough linen to make 30,000 shirts the clothier could not afford to make them, because the nation owed the seamstresses much already. He continued, "while people who live in ease and even in Luxury avoid under various pretexts the payment of taxes a great portion of the public expense is borne by poor women who earn their daily bread by their daily labor."[407]

Money troubles surrounded Morris, and the challenges never went away, but Morris did not advertise the poverty of America. As a result, most people thought there was money for their special needs, particularly those who had a history with Morris. Oliver Pollock and his associates from the 1778 expedition of the *Rattletrap* and privateer *Morris* looked to Morris for payment and settlement of their accounts. It was not to be. Morris was only able to settle the business conducted for the Continental

Congress. Other matters became tied up with Pollock's role in supplying George Rogers Clark's western frontier forces of Virginia. This confusion originated because the expedition's organizer, Captain Willing, had not accompanied the supplies north. As a result, the majority of the supplies ended up with Clark in the Western territory instead of Fort Pitt as originally planned. There was also the matter of various dealings Pollock had with the state of Virginia regarding repayment in silver for bills of exchange drawn from a French account owned by a man who had gone bankrupt.

Morris reported to Congress on the subject of Oliver Pollock's application for repayment. He noted that Pollock was due $59,355 from loans he made to the United States in 1781. However, Morris was not able to make this payment because an act of Congress required him to learn from Spanish Governor, Don de Galvez, about the money de Galvez loaned to Pollock. That information had not arrived by October 11, 1782, so he could not act. He continued and concluded that the money Pollock spent for articles used by the Virginia military in the western areas would finally be chargeable to the United States, and since de Galvez had not responded, Pollock's account with the United States should be left open until his account with Virginia could be settled. Morris then respectfully suggested that Virginia settle Pollock's account. Morris wrote a supporting letter to the Governor of Virginia. Governor Harrison asked the Virginia assembly to look into Pollock's claims, and this was to be done before any further settlement could be made by Morris office.

Amid the demands, investigations, wrangling, power struggles and desperation Morris took the time to share his thoughts with a friend in Europe. He expressed his hope for the future and his understanding of the present when he wrote to Franklin:

> Twenty years hence when time and habit have settled and completed the federal constitution of America Congress will not think of relying on any other than that being to whose justice they appealed at the commencement of their opposition [to Britain]. But there is a period in the process of things, a crisis between the ardor of enthusiasm and the authority of laws, when much skill and management are necessary to those who are charged with administering the affairs of a nation.[408]

Considering the performance of the states, which by September 27th had paid less than 2% of the $8,000,000 requisitioned by Congress, Morris remarked that,

> Many who see the right road and approve of it, continue to follow the wrong road because it leads to popularity. The love of popularity is our endemical disease and can only be checked by a change of seasons.[409]

He was judging the nature of the new democracy that was being fought for, and the problems it created for the few productive members of the government. He wrote to Franklin,

> Your enemies industriously publish, that your age and indolence have unabled you for your station, that a sense of obligation to France seals your lips when you should ask their aid, and that (whatever your friends say to the contrary) both your connections and influence at Court are extremely feeble. I need not tell you that messieurs Lee and company are among the foremost who make these assertions, and many others not worth mention.[410]

Autumn

As the peace treaty drew closer, Arthur Lee's old jealousies came forward again, more viciously. He objected to the way the Americans were conducting the peace negotiations. He proclaimed that Franklin was operating "by the absolute order of France" and Franklin was a "both dishonest and incapable man." Lee went on to say that Franklin's interests in Western Land companies made him a dishonest broker of the peace, and that the way Franklin had handled the Gillon affair amounted to "an absolute robbery." Lee also complained that Morris and Franklin abused their power over the money from both sides of the Atlantic.[411]

On November 18th, 1782, a committee consisting of Arthur Lee, John Rutledge, and James Madison instructed the United States Council General to France, Thomas Barclay, to collect all the information about Morris that Barclay could find in Europe. This act of investigation, coupled with the response by demagogues in America to Morris' economic plan, restarted the rumor mill about Morris as a corrupt man. Rumors of this sort made it difficult for Morris to advance his plans, which may have been the intent. Naturally, the "Ancient Regime" of France was no stranger to political intrigues, and their American ministers kept close watch over Arthur Lee and his associates in Congress. Among these associates were Ralph Izard of South Carolina, Theodorick Bland, Jr. of Virginia, and William and Richard Henry Lee of Virginia.[412]

In such times it was good to have an ally. Hamilton did not lose contact with the Office of Finance just because he had resigned as tax receiver. He still supported Morris' goals. He wrote to Morris that the public creditors were starting to organize in New York State, and that he expected to see a national convention of people to whom Congress owed money for the war.[413] Morris was pleased to learn that the creditors were organizing themselves. He wrote Hamilton, "their numbers and influence joined to the justness of their cause must prevail if they persevere."[414]

Morris' receiver of taxes in New Hampshire, William Whipple, had little to do because of New Hampshire's lack of remittances, so he accepted Morris' invitation to settle a disagreement between Pennsylvania and Connecticut over the status of the Wyoming Valley, in what is now Pennsylvania.[415] This controversy became known as the The Pennamite Wars and was based on overlapping claims by the English and Dutch in the 17th century , and a later both colonies bought the same land from the Native Americans. Whipple attended a meeting in Trenton, New Jersey, to settle that dispute.

The state of civil society was such that in 1782 the post offices in Hartford and Fishkill, New York, were delaying the mail by two or three days so they could print, in their newspapers, information found in the letters. This was unacceptable to Morris. He noted, "This unnecessary detention increases the credit of those newspapers; but it lessens in a much greater degree the value of the post office; for no man will now send his letters by the post if ... he can expect to read his mail in the newspaper before the letter arrives in his hand.[416]

Occasionally there were little signs of progress for Morris' programs and policies. The Congress passed a resolution that no articles sent directly to state troops could be used to reduce the requisition of money from the states. Of course, Morris had to enforce the will of Congress, so he informed the intendent of Maryland that because the sums the state had sent to their troops had not been forwarded to the Continental receiver they were not applicable to their current requisition. Morris went on to say Congress might make the adjustment, but he could not.[417] In another little step forward, Morris moved ahead with his plan to use the ship *America* as a way of encouraging the ship building industry when the minister of France approached Morris on the topic of American shipyards building ships for the French Navy.[418]

Still, old business dogged his efforts. Trade with Europe was on his mind when he wrote to Franklin about Virginia's buying spree in Europe,

> I confess that I disapprove of those [purchases] he had made: for the purchase of unnecessary things, because they are cheap, ap-

> pears to be a very great extravagance. We want money as much as any thing else, and the world must form a strange idea of our management if, while we are begging to borrow, we leave vast magazines of clothing to rot at Brest, and purchase others to be shipped from Holland. I have said nothing of this to Mr. Barclay, because the thing, having been done could not be undone, and because the pointed resolutions of Congress on the subject will prevent any more such operations.

Morris encouraged Franklin to speed Barclay's efforts to ship the goods purchased in Europe.

He also noted that Congress was supposed to appoint a commissioner to settle the accounts of Americans in Europe, but no one had been appointed. He ended the letter by writing,

> I hope measures will be taken by our public ministers in Europe to prevent the people from falling into the snares which the enemy has laid. Undue security in opinion is generally very harmful in effect, and I dread the consequences of it here if the war is to be carried on, which is not improbable.[419]

Morris asked Franklin to assist in arranging a convoy using French ships to accompany the *George Washington* in her voyage carrying silver from Havana.[420]

News of the shipment of supplies from France reached camp in West Point. Washington asked Morris to send the shirts that arrived in the cargo.[421] Morris replied,

> That part of the late arrival of clothing which is unfit for soldiers use is now selling to pay off debts contracted by the clothing department during my administration. Among these debts are twelve thousand dollars for needle work done by people in extreme indigence. The clothing which arrived fit for the officers wear is inadequate for the purpose of clothing them all.

He explained that it was necessary to sell the clothes, because there was no other source of money to pay the seamstresses.

> My credit is already on the brink of ruin. If that goes all is gone, but if it can be preserved there will in the last necessity be some chance of making advances on credit to the army as well as to others ... if the states cannot be prevailed to make greater exertions it is difficult to foresee where the thing [the Revolutionary War] is to terminate.[422]

In his never-ending quest for funds, Morris encouraged the French to make a new loan to the US. He wrote to the Chevalier de La Luzerne,

> I am to entreat sir that you will represent to your Court the necessity of the applications which Congress have directed their ministers to make, for a loan of four million dollars.[423]

In an effort to maintain good relations in America's allies, on October 3rd, Morris invited the delegates from France, Spain and Holland to meet with him, and the President of Congress, for a dinner. They celebrated the Dutch acknowledgement of American independence.[424] Later, it was reported that Morris had served as host to the complete Congress during the event.

Morris observed another kind of social obligation. On October 4th, Morris noted in his office diary, that he and Gouverneur Morris had attended the funeral of Charles Lee. Lee had come to Philadelphia to close the real estate deal Robert had arranged. Unfortunately, Charles died in Philadelphia from the sudden onset of a disease. Morris noted,

> ... the late Major General Charles Lee who formerly rendered considerable service to America, but who by an eccentricity of character had been latterly led into a conduct unworthy of his talents and abilities and by means whereof he had lost the esteem even of those who wished to be his friends. He was buried with the honors of war and the funeral attended by his Excellency the President of Congress and other respectable characters.[425]

Morris found himself in the awkward position of being a creditor to the estate of Charles Lee. Morris held the mortgage on Lee's plantation, and he wanted the loan repaid. He was not interested in taking possession of the property, and requested Lee's lawyers to look into and resolve the matter.[426]

Morris sent a new circular to the state Governors. He clearly was tired of their shirking.

> Now Sir, it is a matter of perfect indifference by what subterfuge this evasion is effected, whether by voting against taxes, or, what is more usual, agreeing to them in the first instance, but taking care in the second instance to provide us no competent means to compel a collection; which cunning device leaves the Army at least as a kind of pensionary upon the voluntary contributions of good Whigs, and suffers those of a different complexion to skulk and screen themselves entirely from the weight and inconvenience.[427]

Morris was sure to send a copy of this circular along with an act of Congress to Generals Washington and Greene to show them that he and the Congress were working on their behalf.[428]

Morris could not spend what the states did not send, so instead he kept building the basis for eventual payment, which he expected would be made in the future. Consistent with his general view that all people should be treated with equal justice, Morris issued a report that officers of the Marine were entitled to the same depreciation adjustment as the members of the Army. This adjustment was created to be sure that the value of their salary was maintained in the face of inflation. By doing this he hoped to unify them with other creditors and gain their support for his programs.[429] He also advanced his ideas of justice when he put together a list of articles of clothing wanted for the Oneida and other tribes in New York State, so that clothing could be bought and sent north.[430]

There must have been some relief to learn that a crisis had been averted in the commissary department, albeit briefly. General Ezekiel Cornell negotiated an arrangement to supply Washington's Army between the end of the Moving Army contract, on October 1st, and the middle of October, when the new contract would start.[431] However, there was just a small matter of a disagreement between a meat-supplying subcontractor and the prime contractor. Morris was advised to authorize payment for the difference because it was feared that a lawsuit would result if he did not. Morris refused to pay "hush money" because he thought any deviation from his strict adherence to the contract would open the floodgates, and all controls would be lost.

Poor, poor, Arthur

Arthur Lee complained that he, alone among the American representatives in Europe, had not been paid according to the August 6th,1781 resolution authorizing such payments. He claimed he was "the soul object of neglect"[432] and complained that others had been paid, but he was carrying a "mark of the displeasure of Congress."[433] Morris was prepared to make payments to Arthur Lee until he found out that the former Treasury Board had already paid Lee in the form of interest bearing loan office certificates. He discovered this when the Register of the Treasury wrote Morris that Lee's account for his salary, the money he spent on clothing shipped on the public account, and his expenses, both ordinary and extraordinary, had been closed and that Lee had received payment in the form of Loan Office certificates.

> His demand is now resting on the public security of the specie Loan Office Certificates on the amount of nine thousand nine hundred and fifty dollars, fifty-five ninetieths of a dollar.[434]

As soon as Morris saw that Lee was a loan office certificate holder, he put Arthur in that category of creditors. After Lee's continual complaints, Morris sought Congressional approval to treat Lee differently from the vast number of other people who held similar certificates. Morris proposed that Congress allow him to "exchange Lee's loan office certificates for the equivalent in bills of exchange on France."[435] Before Congress had time to act, Arthur Lee wanted Morris to give Lee's nephew $200 from the amount Lee felt he was owned.[436] Morris took that opportunity to point out that Lee had already been paid in Loan Office Certificates,

> ...you will see that it is not in my power to make you any payment without a special resolution of Congress for the purpose, until funds are provided for paying other Loan Office Certificates which are become due.[437]

When Morris wrote the Congress to encourage them to pass a measure to allow Lee to change the debt into money, he happened to omit any reference to Lee's earlier complaints about people who demanded payment in cash.[438]

Morris turned from a political enemy when he wrote to a friend, Matthew Ridley, that the dress and other items sent to Mrs. Morris from France were lost in transit when the ship *L'Aigle* (the *Eagle*) was captured. He went on to say that he was displeased to learn his sons had not yet been placed in school. He repeated that "a proper place should have been sought and determined on immediately" and when a school is found only enough money should be used "to put them on a footing with the general run of boys at the same school." Just to add a bit more pressure he added,

> Mrs. Morris puts great dependence on your attention to these Boys, she had your promises, believes in them, and will exact a rigid performance, so see what trouble you have brought onto yourself by the offers which a friendly disposition prompted you to make.[439]

On the topic of the state of the United States, Morris noted that privately he wished the peace would come at a very quick pace,

> But was I to confine myself to the language of a Patriot, I should speak in another manner and tell you that a continuance of the War is necessary until our Confederation is more strongly knit.[440]

Ridley wrote to Gouverneur Morris on the topic of Morris' sons.

> Bob's application for a boy his age is really astonishing. Tom is not so steady but possesses an acuteness and talents that make me flatter myself that he will become a shining character.

He went on to say it was nearly impossible to find a suitable school, and

> I do not think the advantages to be acquired in education in Europe will by any means repay the anxieties of parents in parting with them, or the not having a proper person properly attached to them.[441]

Ridley continued on to topics of interest from the natural tendency of America to become a marine power, to observations on war and peace. He wrote,

> War begets poverty, Poverty peace, Peace makes riches flow, war ne'er doth cease.

He pointed out that Spain's expected effort to capture Gibraltar "... has thrown a little damp in the ardor of the Spaniards."

The contest was still in their future, but it was expected that Howe would use all his might to keep the fortress island, and then he may go after Cadiz, Spain. Ridley was not impressed with the Dutch military efforts, which were hamstrung by internal division.[442]

Later, in reply to Robert's letter, Ridley took Morris' tone seriously and wrote a long letter about the boys. He proclaimed his attachment to them, and maintained that he was looking after their interests, even going so far as to hire an additional tutor for English studies. John Jay wrote Morris on the topic of the boy's education, and his general opinion was that it was better to raise them in America.[443] On the mutually interesting topics of diplomacy, Jay wrote to Gouverneur Morris that the King of England had "authorized Mr. Oswald to treat with the Commissioners of the United States of America." This was an important step and required England to recognize that there was such a thing as the United States of America, and not just a bunch of unruly colonies. He went on that America must remain strong and ready for war "... until every ideal of hostility and surprise shall have completely vanished."[444]

Ridley wrote back to say that he had been in Holland during the last 4th of July and

> ... we had an elegant entertainment given by Dutch patriots, well wishers to the liberties of mankind, and who were not without hopes the wisdom of America may extend herself over great part of Europe.

There had been toasts and cheers aplenty. He referred Morris to "other channels" for news of politics, meaning Gouverneur Morris, and kept to a social tone. He mentioned that he hoped the carpet and other items he had shipped to Mrs. Morris had arrived. He continued, the boys were well, and they were sending a fine doll to their sister Hetty. As usual he sent his well wishes to Miss Kitty Livingstone and expressed a fond hope to see them all soon in their Market Street home.[445]

The effort to relieve the plight of the German prisoners of war, and at the same time, make a little money, was proceeding with mixed results. Morris decided that because Mr. Samuel Hodgdon's iron foundry had been so useful in supplying the cannon balls used in the battle of Yorktown, that Morris was willing to accept Hodgdon's personal note as payment for the liberation of the German prisoners employed at that factory. Morris collected $6,000 for the treasury from Hodgdon.[446] However, the now infamous Commodore Gillon, of the South Carolina Navy, approached Morris with the proposition of using captured German Soldiers on board his state-owned ship. Morris was not in favor of that, and said he expected a bond be held on the basis of $80 per German in Gillon's service. Gillon refused; but offered to make such payments out of prize money gained in the voyage. Morris reminded Gillon that he still expected him to pay Colonel Laurens the money Gillon owed, and that Morris was being compelled to file suit against Gillon because of Gillon's lack of other payments.[447] Morris wrote to the Secretary of War, Benjamin Lincoln, for his thinking on the subject of Commodore Gillon's efforts to get German prisoners as sailors on board his ship.

> I assure you that nothing would induce me to go into this measure but the respect I have for your opinion, and my idea that it was the intention of Congress that it should be adopted.[448]

-|-

Governor Harrison of Virginia asked Morris to arrange transportation from France for clothing, shoes, and blankets for about six thousand soldiers. These items had been purchased by Virginian agents in Europe some time ago; but were never shipped to America because of the British blockade. The Virginia agents used the money la Luzerne had lent the state of Virginia thinking he was lending it to the United States. After consulting with Congress,[449] Morris wrote to the Governor of Virginia that he would accept the goods purchased in France by Virginian agents as goods belonging to the United States. Next, he suggested,

> ... it might not be as well to omit the importation of arms which would be a great Risque of much Property and probably they would be useless after their arrival.

In his way he was telling Governor Harrison that the war supplies had sat around in Europe too long to be useful, and that it would be better to sell them and use the money in other ways. He was trying to bring Harrison to that point without being too blatant about it.[450] Harrison wanted them sent, and Morris asked Barclay to ship the goods from France. Morris asked Barclay to ship the goods so freight would be payable upon arrival, thus avoiding payment for a shipment that may not survive the blockade.[451] Ultimately, the supplies arrived, to a disinterested peacetime market, and most were sold at depressed prices to cover the pressing need for cash, all of which gave rise to more complaints by Arthur Lee.

It was during this period that Jay and Franklin were negotiating with England while not informing France of the work, a practice that had been the source of much heartburning by Arthur Lee. The diplomats had decided to ignore the instructions Congress sent, and which the French had worked so diligently to influence. The hard work of Jay and Franklin bore fruit. The first draft of a peace treaty was conditionally signed and sent back to England on October 8th. Negotiations would continue in that way until November 30th when the provisional treaty was signed by Jay, Adams, Laurens and Franklin. After this England and France had to come to terms, only then could the final treaty be agreed to.[452]

As long as that peace deal remained secret, it had no practical meaning in America. The troops stayed in the field that fall, and much work was done to see they were fed and clothed in their winter quarters. For General Washington, the end of September meant the end of the Comfort Sands contract for the Moving Army. That transition was not as smooth as anyone would have liked. Some money was still due to Comfort Sands & Co. but it was slow in coming. While they waited for payment they wished to be indemnified against suit by their suppliers.[453]

The remnants of the Moving Army contractors, who were providing provisions between contracts, kept complaining about the price they had to pay for the beef. They wished Morris to indemnify them or make up the difference. They thought the way the contract was being handled was ruinous to their interests, and they offered to quit the business if Morris wanted. They wrote,

> Should it be your wish that the contract should be given up, declare it as such, and give us an explicit assurance that we shall be placed on the same footing as we were before the contract commenced, and we will cheerfully renounce it.[454]

Cornell, who acted as intermediary, replied that indemnification was impossible and a shortage of money was the only reason that payments were late;[455] then he asked them to tell how long they would continue to supply the garrison at West Point. They wrote back that they would continue until the 15th and could go to the end of the month, but someone else would have to supply flour for the last two weeks.[456]

Morris wrote the contractors on Oct 10th with his reasons not to pay their extra expenses,

> The object of a contract is, to substitute a certain to an uncertain expense. Had I agreed to your propositions [over the beef expense] that object would have been lost. No distress would have induced my consent: nothing but absolute necessity.[457]

Morris pointed out that even though he was sorry the contract had not worked out well for all concerned it was his job to adhere to his obligations, and if the contractors could prove harm came to them because he failed to do his part they were welcome to use the courts. Cornell agreed that the arrangements between the contractor and the subcontractor for beef were not the business of the office of finance.[458]

Morris wrote to Congress asking them to approve the new contract to supply the army. The old contract was defunct due to lack of payments from the states, the demand for payments that could not be made, and animosities between the contractors and the Generals. Morris wrote,

> If it be asked whether this be a good bargain, I answer at once that it is not. But I believe it to be the best which could be made. In a situation where only bad things can be done, to adopt the least pernicious is all which can be expected.[459]

On Oct 12th Morris formalized the new contract for the Moving Army with Wadsworth and Carter.[460] The benefit of this contract was not in the price, at a 30% increase or thirteen cents[461] per ration, but in the payment terms. This contract eventually worked out so the whole amount was paid over a year later, by a 1783 loan from the French. The payment terms of the contract allowed a grace period that lasted until that loan was made. After Congress reviewed and agreed to the contract, Arthur Lee objected because he thought it was too expensive. The contractors did make a fair bit of money, but Morris considered the deal worth the money because it relieved the endless pressure to pay on a monthly basis with money that did not come easily.[462]

At this point, Comfort Sands and Co. decided to ignore its own previous offer to quit the business and objected to the end of the contract. They wrote,

> We can never consider an answer to the question put to us by General Cornell as a voluntary surrender of the contract on our part: to the contrary, we protest...

They went on to admit that they could not control the prices, but it was only because the Office of Finance would not pay them more than they were due under the contract that their efforts were unsatisfactory. They promised to seek a quick and equitable solution. It was not resolved in the courts until the 1830's.[463]

The contracting system was difficult for all, but it worked better than the old system of specific supplies. The Office of Finance moved ahead and looked for contractors to supply the military for the following year, 1783. They advertised for bids on seven contracts:[464]

1) Eastern States, i.e., Connecticut and Massachusetts
2) New York and New Jersey
3) Pennsylvania
4) Delaware and Maryland
5) Virginia
6) North Carolina
7) South Carolina and Georgia

Each was to be paid six months after the contract start date. January's bills would be paid on the first Tuesday in May, February's in June and so on.

Just as Morris was enlarging his contracting system to encompass the whole confederacy, alarming news arrived. Some of the Morris Notes that Morris had supplied General Greene returned to Philadelphia for payment. Morris did not want to pay personally, and the Continental Treasury did not have the money because the states were not paying into the system, so he offered bills of exchange on the French account instead. This was accepted.[465] Considering this turn of events he wrote to Franklin that if the Havana plan failed to work, then Franklin should

> ...endeavor to obtain the shipment of a considerable sum in Europe on board some of the King's frigates. At any rate, we must have money and I think you may venture fifty thousand Crowns by this vessel. [the *George Washington*].[466]

Money from Europe would help, because the states were still up to their old tricks. James Lovell was not having much success collecting the requisition from Massachusetts. They had paid only 6% of what was expected, and in September they remitted just $1,703.25.[467] New Hampshire did little better. Against his better judgment, Morris received some beef for taxes from New Hampshire. He was not surprised to learn that the meat was thought to be of low quality. He opined,

> ...it being not unreasonable to suppose that those who are to pay in that manner will be more attentive to private than public interests.[468]

If the states had been more cooperative the Continental Navy could have done more. However, there was little interest in it outside the Marine Department. Thomas Russell wrote Morris from Boston to tell him that one of the ships that was originally started in 1776, as part of the first naval expansion program, was still unfinished and sitting in a boat yard in that city. Morris suggested that the ship be sold as soon as possible, and that any leftover timber should be sold as well.[469] As Agent of Marine, Morris finished the purchase of the *General Washington* on October 17th, but he had to discharge the captain because Morris made the ship into a Continental Navy vessel, and that required a captain with a continental commission. The newly dismissed captain understood and left without protest.[470] Up in New England, Captain Nicholson had been embroiled in a dispute with some of the sailors on the *Deane* (renamed *The Hague*). The court martial had been held in Boston, and the sailors were released, but Nicholson was convicted. Morris, as Agent of Marine, thought the

> ...irregularities of the proceedings of the court must be considered as void and altho the witnesses appear to have been on oath yet as the Judge Advocate who certifies the depositions was not on oath the whole can only be taken as mere allegation.

Morris also rejected the cross examination and other testimony and a new court martial was eventually ordered.[471]

The Continental Navy was not just under fire from partisans in New England, there were also live rounds being fired at sea. Captain John Barry wrote from France about the results of his cruise in the *Alliance*. He had captured a brigantine shortly after leaving New London, Connecticut, and sent her to port as a prize. He sailed for Bermuda and along the way captured a schooner and a sloop, which he sent to Cape Français because the captured ships and goods were of little use to the war effort. Next, he headed for the banks off Newfoundland and along the way he captured a whaling ship. He sent that to Boston. A few days later he captured a Brigantine loaded with rum and sugar. He sent that, too, to Boston. From the crew of that vessel, he learned the Jamaica Fleet was to the east and he sailed for that and captured three more ships and headed with them to France for more crew and repairs.[472] Morris directed John Barry to go from Martinique to Havana where "further orders will meet you." He was still trying to set the stage for another silver cruise from Havana.[473]

Following up on his note to Barry, Morris wrote Washington that he planned to send the *Alliance* to Havana to fetch some silver for the cause. His intent was to cash some bills of exchange for Spanish silver. He wrote,

> If I succeed a part of the money shall be applied as pay. If the plan should fail, the army will not be the only persons who will have reason to lament the failure.

Morris thought that winning the war was only the first step to building a nation, and it was a useful step, but the pressures of war were helpful in uniting the various states.

> You observe in your letter, that a Peace is necessary; but if I were to hazard an opinion on the subject it would be, that war is more likely than Peace to produce funds for the public debts, increase authority to Congress, and vigor to the administration of the union as if its component parts. These things all appear necessary to our future prosperity, safety, and happiness.[474]

Morris not only theorized about nation building. He had allies around the country working to implement the shared dream. They kept in contact, each with his individual concern. The contractor to Fort Pitt needed money and noted that the inhabitants could not be counted on because of Indian attacks.[475] Morris wrote the deputy Quartermaster of the Southern

Dept. that items were so expensive in the South because of the depreciation of the paper currency, and that he was right not to accept specific supplies at the rate of depreciated paper and then value that paper as silver.[476]

Quartermaster Pickering wrote from the South that the horse teams from Massachusetts had not been paid for, and that had left the owner in a financial bind. Additionally, many of the horses died in the heat of the Virginia summer, yet there had been no payment at all. He suggested selling the ox teams and the horses, and then repurchasing them in the spring to avoid feeding them over the winter at Continental expense.[477] Washington wrote that he had spent some money to provide a spy for the French, and he would like the French to pay him back.[478] Morris wrote to the Quartermaster that he agreed it was a good idea to sell off the livestock before winter, but it would be best to consult with Washington before doing so.[479] Morris provided another $4,000 to the hospital department.[480] Whipple, Morris' receiver in New Hampshire, could not cure that state of sending specific supplies, no matter what he said or did. He told Morris that beef was going from that state to the Army, but "I can not ascertain the amount."[481]

Morris' unique role in the Office of Finance put him in the position of dealing with the particular conditions of each state. He figured that if North Carolina wanted to pay in specific supplies, they could, but doing that would not be considered a response to the requisition from before Morris' tenure. The state was still expected to pay in hard money for the later requisitions from Congress for money.[482] Morris had to explain this to the Governor of North Carolina as well. He added,

> It is by this means alone that oeconomy can be established, order restored and confusion that parent of fraud (too apt to introduce itself into public accounts) be banished and destroyed.

He also recommended that the governor stop the state policy of embargos, and instead allow merchants to ship goods from that state.[483]

He used his position as Superintendent to contact the states and attempt to get them to cooperate with his initiatives. Morris wrote to the Governor of the newly liberated state of Georgia to encourage that state to pass the impost,

> ...the state of Georgia has been so recently delivered from invasion, that the neglect there can only be imputed to the distracted state of the country, but I hope before this letter shall reach your excellence both Rhode Island and Georgia will have complied.[484]

He also enclosed a resolution of Congress calling on the states for "an immediate definitive answer."[485]

Morris wrote again to the Governor of Rhode Island to encourage that state to pass the impost, because he knew that the world expected the Americans to pay for their war. It was also well known in Europe that the states had not paid the requested amounts, and this made loans from Europe impossible to arrange. He noted, "Now the fact is that no body will lend upon the promise of such requisitions."[486]

The Governor of Maryland wrote that his state was compelled to revert to the specific supply system and supply clothes and shoes for the soldiers because the soldiers

> ... are almost naked ... and unless clothing can be sent to this place ... we shall be obliged to supply such things as cannot be done without.... We mention this to shew you, that however essential it is that the regulations obeyed by Congress be strictly adhered to, yet from the nature of things, then must be broke through in some instances ...[487]

It is a sad irony that these goods were just the kind that Virginia had purchased in France, only they arrived too late to be useful.

Sometimes, Morris interceded on behalf of individuals. Acceding to his suggestion to the Secretary of War, General Lincoln intervened and returned General Gates to service. Gates rejoined the Army in New York,

> I am well and as happy as an old soldier can be, in a tent to latter end of October, we move in a day to winter quarters, where I hope to get warm for once.... The enemy Sir Guy [Carleton] is so damn'd close, that he must be doing something he's ashamed of; for everything offensive on his part is at an end ...[488]

Morris wrote to the President of Delaware, John Dickinson, in favor of Mr. Shields, a river pilot. This pilot had fallen on hard times during the war. He could not gain permission to go to sea, so he resorted to working for the English. He had been captured by the French, for whom he piloted ships until his subsequent captured by the British again. His release during the prisoner exchange put him in danger of arrest and punishment by the Americans. Morris wrote,

> I can also from personal knowledge say that previous to the war Mr. Shields supported the character of a sober, orderly, honest man and a good pilot in which capacity he may, if permitted, become again a useful citizen.[489]

There were various efforts to pardon him through the Delaware legislature, but the records of the final disposition of the case are missing.

The individual pleas for money kept coming into Morris' office with heartbreaking regularity. Morris' friends often noted the distress he felt. People like Arthur St. Clair suffered, while Rhode Island continued to mull, and to consider, and to delay the impost. St. Clair wrote to Morris,

> I am about four hundred pounds in debt, and I am not possessed of one shilling in money in the world. I have spent a very considerable amount in the service and have in the course of the war disposed of a most valuable plantation and three houses ... the sacrifices I have already made which amount to seven thousand pounds...I have a large family fast pressing forward into the world, and who very justly look up to me for light and assistance.[490]

Morris could not give him more than promises and he wrote,

> The states do next to nothing and thereby expose their most faithful servants to suffer for their cruelty and injustice.[491]

St. Clair was not alone in his misery, but he was lucky enough to get some personal help. Morris loaned General St. Clair $320 to be collected later as back pay was given to the military.[492]

The proposed solution to all this pleading and wheedling was the impost bill of 1781. However, everyone was still waiting for Rhode Island to act. After it was known that the twelve other states had passed the impost, the value of the Loan Office Certificates held in Rhode Island doubled in anticipation of the state's consent. A number of speculators in Providence saw an opportunity. Together these men held about $250,000 in Loan Office Certificates. One merchant, and member of the state Assembly, John Brown of Providence, owned $100,000 in Loan office Certificates. While the market was good, he sold some of them for a profit of $30,000. Then he worked against the Impost to increase the value of his holdings in state securities.[493] This group of speculators supported David Howell, the delegate to Congress from Rhode Island. It just so happened that David Howell was an in-law to slave trader and Assemblyman, John Brown.[494]

David Howell led the opposition to the Impost. He published various articles against the measure in newspapers owned by the merchants of Providence. Howell used the pseudonym, A Farmer, A Countryman, and A Freeholder as he resurrected the old familiar "Country Party" arguments with great effect. He warned against centralized power, placemen and pensioners. Instead of arguing against the King, Howell argued against Congressional taxation, and it worked. Howell added to his argument that the money was not even needed by Congress because the loan from Holland made it unnecessary. Popular feeling went against the Impost, and in favor of the state supporting its own debts. The Rhode Island assembly voted against the impost on November 1st, 1782. The value of state debt certificates increased, and various speculators were pleased. Unfortunately, by 1787, state taxes, used to support the state debt, became so high that many of the debt holders, who were supposed to benefit from repayment, were forced to sell their homes and farms to pay the tax.[495] Citizens who were not interested in taxing themselves to death promoted the adoption of the Constitution in 1789.

Without a source of income, Continental finances in November 1782 went along at the pace of the previous months. Horses needed feed. The Army needed wood, and blankets, shirts, and stockings. The American Commissioners in Europe needed money. Contractors needed payments. The unfinished ship *the Bourbon* was covered in the shipyard so the coming winter would not damage it. There was a dispute about prize money for a ship taken earlier in the war. Morris made arrangements to get the *Duc de Lauzun* to Havana for the importation of silver dollars.

Morris also had to deal with those who operated outside of his system. This included one former loan officer who wanted the position of receiver of Continental Taxes; but was refused. Morris had told him that Continental officers needed to be free of state attachments usual to the former loan officers. The former loan officer replied,

> ...the Financier had too much power already, and that Congress had better curtail him.[496]

A former ally of Colonel John Laurens, Commodore Gillon, was the focus of some attention as the public claims against him grew, and his friends tried to paper over the issues with a bond.[497] In other uniquely Southern business, Morris informed Arthur Lee that Congress had acted on his request and as soon as Mr. Lee sent in the loan office certificates Morris would authorize the delivery of bills of exchange from France that Mr. Lee could then convert to cash. Mr. Lee's clerk also awaited payment in the same fashion.

In addition to the various personalities who stalked the countryside there were practical problems. Morris was primarily concerned about covering his notes with bills of exchange from France in the event the state taxes would not cover them. On the other hand, Morris' notes were in such large denominations that they were difficult to convert to hard money in states with little hard money. People applied to Morris for smaller notes so the notes might pass as a form of currency. Morris continued to decline because he had learned about some counterfeiting of his notes.[498] As debts mounted in America, the Dutch loan subscription was slow to fill in Europe. Adams wrote a cautionary letter,

> If you suppose that my Loan of five Millions [gilders] is full, you are mistaken. There are so many loans open from France, Spain... that I cannot promise you any success.[499]

A far away America, with its low credit rating and uncertain prospects, was competing with the kings and princes of ancient nations in Europe.

Morris was slowly implementing his plan of unifying the debt as he continued to nominate people as commissioner of accounts for various states. These individuals were being put into place to settle the accounts between the states and the Continental Government. Morris sent directions to the commissioners selected by Congress to settle the accounts of the states. These commissioners were to "settle all accounts between the United States, and each particular state." He supplied a detailed list of instructions, duties and methods to be followed. These instructions included the way to lay out the account books, which accounts to open for the various currencies, the categories of expenses and how to deal with expenses that did not easily fit into categories.[500] Morris also supplied a list of questions and answers, which could be used in the process either to answer the queries of the commissioners, or to answer the queries of the various state officers they would meet.[501] This document was sent along with guidelines from the Comptroller of the Treasury. The monumental task of settling these accounts would continue for years and the result acted as the basis for the debt assumption arguments that echoed in Congress, long after 1789.

Among the many state interests there was also the matter of Morris' role as "Agent of Pennsylvania." He had never relinquished this office, even after he took on the job of Superintendent of Finance. He had been supplied with £500,000 in Pennsylvania currency. The state had intended for Morris to use that to purchase supplies for the state's quota of specific supplies due to the Continental Congress. Morris was wary of the currency depreciation that would occur if so much state paper were to arrive suddenly in people's hands, and he had purchased some Bank of North

America stock for Pennsylvania with a portion of the money. The time came for him to remit state money to the Continental Loan officer, but to avoid the resulting depreciation he used continental funds for that purpose, arguing, "the united states would benefit from preserving the value of the state currency already in circulation."[502] Then, he endeavored to raise the value of Pennsylvania state money and managed to lift it from 5:1 to 2:1 specie. He did this by using it to purchase French bills of exchange and currencies from other states, thus he established the value in relation to other known items of value. By raising the value of Pennsylvania money, it was not necessary to spend as many Pennsylvania Pounds on supplies, so when the time came for Pennsylvania to settle its debt with the Continent, Morris proposed that the surplus value to the money be used by Pennsylvania to offset part of that state's debt to the Continent. John Nicholson, the state Comptroller, did not agree and the haggling began.

The states hemmed and hawed; delayed and sought advantages; but the ultimate recipient of this effort was the Army. It is hard to imagine the life led by the soldiers and officers in the field. The officers were not given their "subsistence money." They had used these small sums to maintain their dignity as officers and gentlemen. The pleasures in the field were few and far between, but the officers at camp had been able at least to invite each other over for a meal, or to entertain a friend without embarrassment. Once this ended, their mortification caused them to lash out at Morris, and these expressions of unhappiness found their way to the press.[503] Morris was aware of the anger this embarrassment caused, and in November he and General Lincoln proposed to issue cash to officers so they could reestablish a form of the "subsistence money." [504] In addition Morris worked to get their past allowances paid to them. The shortage of cash resulted in the use of "subsistence notes" that could be used to buy suitable goods for their entertainments, but the notes had little value outside the military contracting system. It took Congress a few months to agree with the plan and during that time the unhappiness grew in the officers' ranks. Morris was not able to print and sign the notes until December. The dissatisfaction of the officers eventually developed into the difficulties Washington had to face in Newburgh, New York.

Washington appealed to Morris, as Agent of Marine, to appoint someone to deal with the matter of marine prisoners. He was being deluged by various states on this account and he wanted relief from that pressure.[505] After Morris became involved, he learned that American Marine prisoners, still held by the English in New York, needed wood to keep them warm. The English suggested that they would come across enemy lines to cut the wood and bring it back to New York where the prisoners were being held. Their proposal opened up many forms of mischief including increased opportunities to trade with the enemy, spying, the excessive cutting of wood for British troops and more. Morris told Washington of his concerns about the English desire to get this wood and proposed that the wood be cut by Americans and carried to New York on vessels flying a flag of truce.[506] Washington concurred that it would be unwise to let the British behind American lines to cut wood for use in New York City, and that it would be better to sell the wood to them. Then it was suggested that U.S. and British maritime prisoners be exchanged instead. The English replied that they wanted to trade American maritime prisoners for their soldiers. Washington also repeated his objection to trading American Marine prisoners for seasoned British troops held as prisoners.[507] The negotiations stalled.

Morris moved forward where he could and continued to arrange the importation of silver coins from Havana. He instructed John Brown, of Philadelphia, to act as supercargo and to take the *Duc de Lauzun* to Cuba for the conversion of bills of exchange into Spanish silver. He agreed to pay Brown $4000 at Havana for this risk and trouble, and made it clear to Brown that if he or his ship were captured, he "would have no claim against the United States for any sum whatsoever."[508] Morris cautioned the captain of the ship not to chase enemy vessels, and to stay with the plan and do the job quickly. Morris also wrote a letter of introduction to the Governor of Cuba to prepare him to facilitate the transaction, which was expected to amount to $200,000.[509]

Even with this effort underway in Cuba, one continental captain, in particular, was feeling very under-utilized. John Paul Jones returned to Portsmouth, New Hampshire, where he observed the launching of the ship *America*; a ship he had worked hard to complete. He noted the transferal of that ship to the French Navy; and wrote Morris to ask that he be allowed to join the French in their next campaign so he might learn from them and that would "enable me to better serve my Country hereafter." Morris wrote Congress in favor of this move by Jones, and it was allowed by that august body. Jones sailed to the West Indies and stayed with the French Navy until word of peace reached him at sea.[510]

Elsewhere in New England, Rhode Island passed a regulation that delegates could not accept any "post or place of profit under Congress, or any servant of Congress" until six months after leaving the Rhode Island delegation. This resolution was aimed squarely at Ezekiel Cornell who then tendered his resignation as inspector of contracts, noting that he was charged with "having been guilty of every kind of villainy while I was at Philadelphia" and that he was forbidden from continuing in the position because of the six-month rule.[511] Morris had been relying on this gentleman to manage the relations between the contractors and the Army. Earlier such relations had taken much of Washington's and Morris' time and it had taken a long time to enlist Cornell's help. Morris concluded that Cornell was being pressured by his state to leave the office he had just taken.

Morris wrote,

> I am not ignorant that many people employ themselves in defaming men whom they do not know, and measures which they do not understand. To such illiberal characters and to all which they can write or speak the best answer is to act well. Believe me sire, I sincerely lament the conduct which your legislature has lately pursue. I will not censure them because I suppose their motives have been good although their view of things differs much from mine.[512]

Cornell retired to his farm in Situate where he stayed until his death in 1800.[513]

In the meantime, Arthur Lee had made himself so odious to the people in Congress that Virginia threatened to recall him as a representative. Lee went home, and with the help of his brother, kept his seat; but while he was there, he surreptitiously managed to get the Virginia assembly to remove their support for the Impost, mostly to foil Morris.[514]

The behavior of Rhode Island was in the minds of many in Philadelphia. Thomas Paine proposed to Morris that it may be best to encourage Rhode Island to adopt the impost as a temporary measure, in the hopes that such an act would carry the finances past the current point of despair.[515] Congress moved toward convincing Rhode Island to change its vote and authorized a delegation to travel to that state. Morris met with Congressman Osgood to prepare him for the trip to Rhode Island. The next day, December 22nd, news arrived that Virginia had reconsidered its support for the impost and was now in opposition to it.

The trip to Rhode Island was canceled. Congress was so furious at Howell for his misrepresentation of the financial situation between Europe and America, that the Congress considered censuring him. As Howell argued the virtues of Free Speech, and the correctness of his information, he was embarrassed to learn, with the rest of Congress, that America was overdrawn in Europe and the French declined to offer further assistance. Howell and Morris continued to argue over finances, and Paine published articles about the need to reform the confederation in a way that would empower the Congress to collect money and repay the debts it had incurred.

Rhode Island's worries about direct taxation were not only based on ceding sovereignty to a centralized authority. The impost was an import duty, and it was seen by some as an anti-slavery maneuver. In the 1760's the Pennsylvania Quakers had used a local import tax to stop the importation of slaves into that state. Morris' fellow Pennsylvanian, George Clymer, believed the 1789 impost would act as an anti-slavery measure.[516] Rhode Island was deeply involved in the slave trade with between 60% and 90% of the slaves entering the U.S. on American ships coming in on Rhode Island ships.[517] Their position as a key point in the "Triangle Trade" is well documented. Their opposition to this impost was certainly rooted in their reliance on importation as a mainstay of their state economy. Once Virginia removed support for the measure it became clear that Morris' efforts towards funding the nation with an import duty collapsed because of action taken by states that had pro-slavery interests. Morris remarked the Articles of Confederation gave Congress the "privilege of asking everything" while giving the states the "prerogative of granting nothing."

Soon both Maryland and Massachusetts removed their support for the impost and then a large number of states followed.[518] In desperation, some members put forward the notion of implied powers for Congress. They reasoned that reform was not required because Congress must already have the right to raise money from the states to pay the debts it incurred on behalf of the states. This argument did not win the day.

The creditors, whom Morris had encouraged to organize, became aware that the impost did not become law. Morris hoped political pressure from the creditor groups would push the states together into a stronger Federal union, but once the impost failed the creditors applied to the state governments for either repayment or at least the payment of interest. The unifying force was about to become a divisive one. Pennsylvanians held a third of the Continental loan office certificates.[519] The creditors asked the Pennsylvania Assembly to start payment of the interest on their loan office certificates. This represented a major counter force to Morris' intention. Creditors were relying on the interest payments to pay their taxes to Pennsylvania, so it was in Pennsylvania's interest to take over the interest liability. It was assumed by Morris' political adversaries in Pennsylvania, the "Constitutionalists," that Morris worked behind the scenes to defeat the creditors' effort.

> I fear Congress with the assistance of his high mightiness, the Financier, have so managed matters as to prevent any thing capital being effected for the relief of the sufferers at this sitting of the Assembly.

It was clear that Morris was against state assumption; and opposed it in principle when New Hampshire acted in a similar fashion, but Pennsylvania politics were close and combustible. Morris stood aside and let his allies engage in this battle.[520] He was on record in his continuing efforts to arrange a unified settlement with all the states, as he continued with the slow process of putting commissioners in place.

None of this was good for America's image overseas. Matthew Ridley wrote from France that Europeans were laughing at the states' refusal to pay for its own war, while at the same time threatening to fight England as the English were loudly pursuing peace.[521] On a personal note he wrote that he was disappointed to learn the carpet, dress, and pictures he had sent to Mrs. Morris had not arrived due to the sinking of the *Eagle.* He went on to say that he continued to look after the education of Morris' two sons. He reported they were learning Latin, French, dancing, drawing and arithmetic. He also disclosed, in a separate message to Gouverneur Morris that,

> ... every loan we make, every favor we ask only serves to increase obligations in Europe and render us, for the time, pensioners.[522]

He considered it to be contrary to America's stated aim of being independent to remain dependent on handouts.

Dissatisfied Army

The Army was becoming more restive. At the same time the civilian creditors were seeking repayment from whomsoever might have the money. For their part, Army officers made it clear that they expected their subsistence money, back pay, and many expected the half-pay pension they had heard about, but which had been removed from Morris' budget by Congress. In dealing with the issue of Army salaries, Morris was put into the position of attempting to deal with debts due from before his administration, contrary to the agreement he had with Congress from the start of his appointment. Yet, to solve the crisis he suggested that the size of debts due the officers should be determined, and that these officers be given interest bearing certificates so the money due to them would be payable as the rest of the national debt was paid.[523] Discussions about arranging payment to the troops quickly became subsumed into the larger issues of the war debt, that is, who would pay the debts and which country would supply new loans. However, chances of Congress paying for a nationalized debt were receding with the memory of the impost.

INDEPENDENCE HALL, 1776.
(PHILADELPHIA, PENNSYLVANIA.)

As peace neared, the state Assemblies became less and less interested in a national union. The political calendar rolled along, and there was a new election in October. Morris' party, the Republicans, won in Pennsylvania. In defense of the "Constitutional" faction, and their hold on state power, a member of the 9th Battalion of Lancaster voiced his concerns to the Assembly. He wrote,

> Let us not then coolly and simply suffer any of our Rights to be taken from us by any men especially as our Constitution invests us with full power to oppose any such attempts.[524]

This man and his allies were worried about the ascendancy of the Republican faction in the State House, and that faction's tendency to favor a more nationalist view. There was a meeting among the Pennsylvania army officers as a result of this letter, and it was learned that the vast majority of them were pleased with the Republican victory. The more radical elements were thus unable to mount a credible threat to the elected officials.[525] However, such highly visible efforts pushed the State of Pennsylvania to argue more aggressively that their money be used by Morris, as Agent of Pennsylvania, in particular ways of their choosing. Morris was generally disinclined to follow these instructions.

Considering this inward looking trend among the states, General Greene said,

> All insist on their being complete independent sovereign states, forgetting that the powers delegated to Congress are so many retrenchments essential to their sovereignty.... The genius of the people here [South Carolina] is much better suited to monarchy than republicanism; and yet they are by far the most democratical of any part of the United States...It will take a long time for civil government to recover a proper tone in this country [S.C.] and I am thus explicit that you may have some idea of the footing on which part of your revenue rests.[526]

Just as the critical question of how a fracturing confederation was going to pay a restive army was heating to a boiling point, it occurred to Arthur Lee that he had left some table linens in Paris. He wanted Morris to arrange for their shipment. Lee did not ask Morris directly. Instead on December 5th, 1782, he had the President of Congress write a note to Morris to instruct him on this matter.[527] Any other person would have been accused of using public resources for private matters, but Arthur Lee was mysteriously immune from such observations. Implicit in Lee's request was an insult to Morris, the merchant, by Lee, a leader of the Old Dominion. Lee acted to reinforce the social differences between them by requesting Morris to act as his personal shipping agent in the important business of napkins.

Worthy or not, the Continental Government still relied on Morris. They did not have the money to repay the first $100,000 that was now due from an earlier loan from the Bank of North America. Instead of supplying funds from nearly non-existent revenues, Morris sold back to the bank, the five hundred bank shares owned by the Continental government. Then he used the money from that sale to cover the loan. That also made those shares available to interested buyers, of which there were many.[528]

Simultaneously, Franklin waited in France to hear about the fate of a newly applied for loan of 4,000,000 livres. Peace negotiations were at a critical phase, and the French Crown was not sure if the loan would be needed in peacetime, or if a larger one was needed if the war continued. As they considered these realities, they told Franklin nothing could be done until a particular letter from America was found, and this prompted a paper chase within the American camp. The "required" papers were discovered and delivered. Meanwhile Franklin delayed Captain Barney's exit from France because he hoped to send the treaty with him to America.

Franklin also noted that Virginia's agent, Thomas Barclay, was preparing the Virginia goods for shipment from Europe, and that a different agent who represented Virginian interests, Pierre Penet, was totally without personal funds. When it became clear the French Crown would not make more loans to individual American states, like Virginia, Penet, as agent for Virginia, headed off to points unknown.[529] Penet's exit from the scene hurt Oliver Pollock because Pollock had counted on bills of exchange drawn on Penet in 1779, and the failure of those bills was the source of Pollock's legal troubles. Governor Harrison launched a special commission in December 1782 to conclude the business of Pollock's supposed debt.[530*]

Matthew Ridley wrote from Europe to congratulate America on King George III's acknowledgement of American independence. He noted that Jay and Adams had acted with honor, and Henry Laurens had arrived after his parole from the Tower of London just in time to sign the preliminary peace accord.[531] Laurens had been freed in return for the freedom of Cornwallis. True to his status as a slaveholder and former slave trader, Laurens managed to insert one clause into the accord, which was to ensure that the English remove no slaves from America without reimbursing the slaveholders. This caused much difficulty later.

John Barry was still in France. He reported that several of the men on his ship refused to ship out to America until they were paid their salaries. Barry responded that money for salaries was not available and they would be getting a lot of money from their settlement of prizes. The men still refused, and so Barry had them locked up, and their prize money was withheld until their court martial.[532] These insolent sailors remained in confinement until they went before the court, in May 1783.

Congress also had European affairs on its collective mind and resolved to name a commissioner in Europe to settle American accounts there. Thomas Barclay was chosen, so Morris wrote him to settle the accounts of "all servants of the United States who have been entrusted with the expenditure of public monies in Europe."[533] The process included the adjustment of Beaumarchais' account, and the business of the Secret Committees including the involvement of Willing Morris & Co. and specifically Thomas Morris. Ignoring any implications that may have arisen from Barclay's role as Agent for Virginia, and his role as an intimate of the Laurens/ Lee contingent, Morris respected Barclay's experience as a merchant and hoped for a quick settlement of the old Secret Committee business with which he had been involved.

Back in the Office of Finance, the money hunt continued, and Morris worked with his team. The continental tax receiver from New Jersey told Morris that he had sent $5,947 in Morris Notes as payment in taxes from his state and that he submitted them to the treasury.[534] New Hampshire sent in $3,000 in Morris Notes to Joseph Whipple who was acting as receiver while his brother William worked to settle the territorial dispute in Pennsylvania's Wyoming Valley.[535] Morris wrote Lovell in Massachusetts to exchange up to $8,500 of the money they had on hand from tax collection for any Morris Notes that came into the office. Over that, Lovell was to send the money. Morris also arranged finally to settle the amounts due to Ross and Bingham, in a manner similar to the way he had settled Arthur Lee's account. He offered them bills of exchange drawn on the French loan. Getting money to Ross and Bingham at this point would come in handy later when it came time to cover bills drawn on the Dutch loan.

A few dollars came in, but the military expenses never seemed to stop. Von Steuben's accounts were still in the process of being settled.[536] News came in that a robbery of Morris Notes had taken place in Albany, New York. No one was able to solve it or recover the lost funds. Quartermaster Pickering was able, however, to get $5,000 to the Army at Newburgh to pay the teamsters who brought in supplies,[537] and he wanted to repay a Lieutenant for the loss of his horse.[538] Washington had to sell all unnecessary horses because the Army did not have food for them. By the middle of December, the remaining horses were not well fed, and in some cases were starving. Washington wrote the Quartermaster in Philadelphia, and Pickering returned with enough Morris Notes to buy whatever forage was available at that time. Feeding the Army's horses continued to be a problem as long as the Army was in the field.[539]

The Northern Army was being fed because of the relationship between Morris and the contracting firm Wadsworth and Carter. Morris started up another contract in December 1782. This one was for feeding the Army in New Jersey during 1783. The contractors were William Duer and Daniel Parker. They had both been active in the Comfort Sands Company, but this was a different configuration of individuals. This contract gave the inspector the right to reject supplies of low quality and demand the money instead. This provision had been lacking in earlier contracts and that resulted in low quality food being delivered.

Feeding prisoners of war cost money every day. Washington forwarded a letter from Sir Guy Carleton to Morris, as Agent of Marine, on the subject of Marine prisoners. Morris proposed a bold solution to the unpleasant situation that would achieve Washington's goal of keeping British troops as prisoners. He wrote to the British Rear Admiral, Robert Digby,

> Let us liberate all marine Prisoners on both sides taking proper receipts. Let us come to a settlement of the account as speedily as possible. If the balance is against us I will pay you in money immediately according to the terms of cartel existing between England and France.... In the mean time I shall be glad to have your permission to send in some wood which I am told the prisoners want. If you want I will lade one or more vessels and send them in under protection of flags of passport.[540]

It took some time, but this offer was eventually accepted.

The old Yorktown tobacco deal, which was supposed to support American prisoners of war, never seemed to be finished. By this point Morris was disinclined to help the Virginians who had shipped tobacco in excess of the congressional agreement. When asked about it, he wrote,

> The ship has been seized and libeled in New York. What will be the result in any case I am very indifferent. This however I am convinced of, that it will be impossible to serve the People of America until they have learnt to believe in the possibility of Moral Honesty.[541]

He was clearly disgusted with the shenanigans of the Virginians. Time was coming to settle the account with the Virginians for the tobacco shipped to New York, and they wanted more money than they had agreed earlier. Morris refused,

> The labor I shall readily consent and the insinuations I can despise, but I cannot consent that the public sustain a loss and therefore I cannot agree to give more than the market price.[542]

Virginia's behavior did not escape the attention of General Greene. He wrote to announce that the British evacuation from Charleston, South Carolina, that had been expected since August, had finally occurred in December. He went on to note that Virginia was spending money on their own civil list that they had collected for continental purposes. Greene expected other states to fail to support the Continental Army as well. He detailed the use of notes to pay for clothing, and to pay officers who were released from service. He confessed that he also had to give some notes to officers who stayed in the service, even though he was aware that this was not what Morris might have liked. To relieve the financial pressure, he dismissed the new recruits from North Carolina except for one regiment. He did mention that the rate of sickness was five times higher in the southern army than in the north, and that the expense of the hospitals was a priority. They used rum, vinegar and wine as medicines and so these were consumed at a higher rate in the South. Bowing to the inevitable, Morris allowed South Carolina to have credit for the specific supplies they provided the Southern Army. The rate was not as favorable as the Carolinians might have liked, because Morris kept to the market rates.[543]Back in early 1782, Greene had used Morris Notes in supplying the Southern Army. Greene asked Mr. Pettit, a business partner of his, to sell the notes and to retain some of the funds as a contingency in case of future needs. Later, when Greene requested the remainder of these funds, Pettit claimed he needed them to offset losses he sustained earlier as a supplier to the Army. Pettit cautioned Greene not to mention this to Morris, and he hoped to return the funds because he expected Congress to pay for the earlier contracts. It became clear that this payment was going to be a long time in coming. In April 1783 Greene finally revealed the situation to Morris because he wanted Morris' help in solving the problem. Morris was not pleased to hear about Pettit's self-payment. Morris contacted Pettit and it took many years for the matter to be resolved.

Back in Philadelphia, Morris worked to protect what little money there was. Delays on the part of Congress on the subject of the mint, and the continuing exodus of silver to the British in New York, prompted Morris to propose that Congress fix the exchange rate between Spanish Milled Dollars, and the Light Silver coins of the English, the French, and Dutch. The idea was to artificially overvalue the Spanish dollar in relation to these other coins and make it unattractive to convert and spend the money in New York. The Congress did not act, but the Bank did, and that helped the situation.[544] In other, favorable news, local commerce got a boost when merchants left the Delaware River in mid-December under the protection of a French convoy. The British blockade had become less severe by this point, but everyone welcomed the protection anyway.[545]

Morris sought to protect individuals as well. He asked the Governor of New Hampshire for relief in the case of a Mr. Isaac Tichenor. Between 1776 and 1780 Mr. Tichenor had spent his own money and used his own credit to purchase supplies for the Army in New England. Creditors were suing Mr. Tichenor for the money still owed. Congress had no money to reimburse Tichenor; but had already passed a resolution to ask states to stay these lawsuits in state courts until final settlement could be reached. New Hampshire had not acted to protect Mr. Tichenor, and the creditors had attached his property. They were moving to imprison him for non-payment.[546]

-|-

Franklin wrote to Morris that Spain was clearly interested in confining America to the area east of the Allegheny Mountains, and that he hoped Congress would insist on the extension of America to the Mississippi.[547] In his next letter he revealed that after a "little misunderstanding" he had procured a new loan commitment of 6,000,000 livres from the French. He planned to send this to America on the *General Washington* with the preliminary articles of peace. What Franklin called a "little misunderstanding" was the discovery by the French Court that, contrary to Congress' instructions, the American commissioners had negotiated a preliminary peace with the English without the involvement of the French. Franklin admitted that he had not acted in strict compliance with the Franco-American understanding, but if the French ruptured the alliance over it, then only the English would prosper, and this would undo all the years of hard work. The French had to overlook this bit of sneakiness by the Americans and proceed as if the alliance were as firm as ever, because the French still had to negotiate their part of the peace with the British.[548]

On the day after Christmas 1782, Morris finally got 100 newly printed sheets of subsistence notes for the hard-pressed officers in Washington's Army. He was still waiting for 3,900 more notes to be printed. He gave the 100 to the treasurer, Mr. Hillegas, "desiring that he would immediately sign the same and be prepared to deliver to the Paymaster Genl. notes to the amount of subsistence for the Month of January."[549] A few days later Morris discovered the remaining notes had not been printed and he told the clerk to "go instantly and urge the Printer [Eleazer Oswald] to finish them being absolutely necessary at Camp on the 1st of January when the new Contract commences."[550]

The end of the year did not mean the end of money troubles. In late December Morris' agent in New Jersey, William Churchill Houston, wrote that the New Jersey Assembly had adjourned without passing a tax bill to meet the Congress' requisition for 1783. It was not passed until June 9th, 1783. New Jersey still did not make payments to Houston, but rather kept the money in the hands of the state receiver who favored the holders of state notes over Congressional requests.[551] The lack of money from the states forced Morris to turn to two of his old trading partners. Acting on Morris' request, William Bingham lent the government $60,000. Morris used it to make a payment to the bank for money owed by the United States. John Ross lent $10,000 for the same purposes. Both were to be paid back on the 1st of July, 1783.[552]

How did the United States make it through 1782? There were three elements to this: foreign loans, private loans, and notes. Notably absent was any significant contribution from the states. The French made two loans. One loan for 600,000 livres was made. Unfortunately, Congress had already spent the money in Europe, so this new loan was used to pay off old loans and was unavailable to the Financier. There was a second loan from France, and this was the basis for the sale of French bills of exchange sold by Haym Salomon in Philadelphia and James Lovell in Boston, among others. Morris' notes were used as currency, and were put into circulation, in addition to some notes from the Bank of North America. The Bank of North America's notes were mostly used to keep the wheels of commerce rolling, and in addition the bank made loans to the Congress. Finally, Morris relied on his friends and trading partners for support. Wadsworth and Carter fed the Army without pay for three months, and Bingham and Ross helped cover Continental debts to the Bank with their personal funds. They did so because of their belief in Morris' ability to get them repaid, not because of the good past practices of the Continental Government.

Endnotes

1. Papers of Robert Morris, 4:63
2. Papers of Robert Morris, 4:23
3. Papers of Robert Morris, 4:254
4. Papers of Robert Morris, 4:251
5. Papers of Robert Morris, 4:107
6. Papers of Robert Morris, 4:121,148
7. Papers of Robert Morris, 4:126, 135
8. Papers of Robert Morris, 4:109
9. Papers of Robert Morris, 4:14
10. Papers of Robert Morris, 4:119
11. Papers of Robert Morris, 4:142
12. Papers of Robert Morris, 4:129n
13. Papers of Robert Morris, 4:178
14. George Washington Papers, series 4 LOC: image 196
15. Papers of Robert Morris, 4:207-213
16. Papers of Robert Morris, 4:223
17. Papers of Robert Morris, 4:225
18. Papers of Robert Morris, 4:276
19. Papers of Robert Morris, 4:307
20. Papers of Robert Morris, 4:299
21. Papers of Robert Morris, 4:191
22. Papers of Robert Morris 4:315
23. Papers of Robert Morris, 4:312-313
24. Papers of Robert Morris, 4:317-318
25. *American Taxation*, p 34-36
26. Papers of Robert Morris, 4:318
27. Papers of Robert Morris, 4:325
28. Papers of Robert Morris, 4:334
29. Papers of Robert Morris, 4:346
30. Papers of Robert Morris, 4:328
31. Papers of Robert Morris, 4:337
32. Papers of Robert Morris, 4:340

33. Papers of Robert Morris, 4:346, 351-2
34. Papers of Robert Morris, 4:348
35. Papers of Robert Morris, 4:349
36. Papers of Robert Morris, 4:364
37. Papers of Robert Morris, 4:339
38. Papers of Robert Morris, 4:395
39. Papers of Robert Morris 4:383
40. Papers of Robert Morris, 4:366-367
41. Papers of Robert Morris, 4:453-454
42. Papers of Robert Morris, 4:369
43. Papers of Robert Morris, 4:373
44. Papers of Robert Morris, 4:341
45. *Power of the Purse*, pg. 84
46. Papers of Robert Morris, 4:377
47. Papers of Robert Morris, 4:381
48. Papers of Robert Morris, 4:400
49. Papers of Robert Morris, 4:412
50. Papers of Robert Morris, 4:417
51. Papers of Robert Morris, 4:421
52. Papers of Robert Morris, 4:431
53. Papers of Robert Morris, 4:448
54. Papers of Robert Morris, 4:429
55. Papers of Robert Morris, 4:436
56. Papers of Robert Morris, 4:439-440
57. Papers of Robert Morris, 4:447
58. Papers of Robert Morris, 4:60
59. Papers of Robert Morris, 4:449
60. The Papers of Robert Morris, 4:140
61. Papers of Robert Morris, 4:202
62. Papers of Robert Morris, 4:452
63. Papers of Robert Morris 5:225
64. Papers of Robert Morris, 4:458
65. Papers of Robert Morris, 4:459
66. Papers of Robert Morris, 4:460
67. Papers of Robert Morris, 4:465, 476
68. Papers of Robert Morris, 4:477, 478
69. Papers of Robert Morris, 4:484
70. Papers of Robert Morris, 4:492
71. Papers of Robert Morris, 4:486, 487
72. Papers of Robert Morris, 4:495
73. Papers of Robert Morris, 4:496
74. Papers of Robert Morris, 4:508
75. Papers of Robert Morris, 4:511
76. Papers of Robert Morris, 4:584
77. Papers of Robert Morris, 4:499
78. Papers of Robert Morris, 4:510
79. Papers of Robert Morris, 4:510
80. Papers of Robert Morris, 5:90
81. Papers of Robert Morris, 5:547-8
82. Papers of Robert Morris, 5:564
83. Papers of Robert Morris, 4:514
84. Papers of Robert Morris, 4:534
85. Papers of Robert Morris, 5:64
86. Papers of Robert Morris, 4:519-520
87. Papers of Robert Morris, 4:522
88. Papers of Robert Morris, 4:513
89. Papers of Robert Morris, 4:516
90. Papers of Robert Morris, 4:535-536
91. Papers of Robert Morris, 4:571
92. Papers of Robert Morris, 4:424
93. Papers of Robert Morris, 4:540
94. Papers of Robert Morris, 4:545
95. Papers of Robert Morris, 4:548
96. Papers of Robert Morris, 4:563
97. Papers of Robert Morris, 4:565
98. Papers of Robert Morris, 4:570
99. Papers of Robert Morris, 4:573
100. Papers of Robert Morris, 4:578
101. Papers of Robert Morris, 4:580
102. *Journals of the Continental Congress*.--Tuesday, May 14, 1782
103. Papers of Robert Morris, 5:193
104. Papers of Robert Morris, 6:94-96
105. Papers of Robert Morris, 5:298
106. Papers of Robert Morris, 5:4
107. Papers of Robert Morris, 5:15
108. Papers of Robert Morris, 5:36
109. Papers of Robert Morris, 5:8
110. Papers of Robert Morris, 5:38-39
111. Papers of Robert Morris, 5:54-55
112. Papers of Robert Morris, 5:73
113. Papers of Robert Morris, 8:509n
114. Papers of Robert Morris, 5:40-41
115. Papers of Robert Morris, 5:47
116. Papers of Robert Morris, 5:67
117. Papers of Robert Morris, 5:81
118. Papers of Robert Morris, 5:82-83, 107
119. Papers of Robert Morris, 5:56-57
120. Papers of Robert Morris, 5:60-61
121. Papers of Robert Morris, 5:129-130
122. Papers of Robert Morris, 5:236
123. Papers of Robert Morris, 5:96
124. Papers of Robert Morris, 5:95
125. Papers of Robert Morris, 5:103

126. Papers of Robert Morris 5:49
127. Papers of Robert Morris, 5:131-2
128. Papers of Robert Morris, 5:105
129. *The Early Republic and The Sea*, Chapter 1
130. Papers of Robert Morris, 5:103
131. Papers of Robert Morris, 5:90-91
132. *Journals of the Continental Congress*, 22:238
133. Papers of Robert Morris, 5:110
134. Papers of Robert Morris, 6:xxxiv
135. Papers of Robert Morris, 5:121
136. Revolutionary Diplomatic Correspondence, 6:271
137. Papers of Robert Morris, 5:127-8
138. Papers of Robert Morris, 5:156
139. Papers of Robert Morris, 5:145-148
140. Papers of Robert Morris, 5:191-2
141. Papers of Robert Morris, 5:203-204
142. Papers of Robert Morris, 5:189
143. Papers of Robert Morris, 5:181-2
144. Papers of Robert Morris, 5:246-7
145. Papers of Robert Morris, 5:177
146. Papers of Robert Morris, 5:207
147. Papers of Robert Morris, 5:218
148. Papers of Robert Morris, 5:221-222
149. Papers of Robert Morris, 5:209-10
150. Papers of Robert Morris, 5:227
151. Papers of Robert Morris, 5:229
152. Papers of Robert Morris, 5:230
153. Papers of Robert Morris, 5:230
154. Papers of Robert Morris, 5:417
155. *The Peacemakers*, pg. 204
156. Papers of Robert Morris, 5:410
157. Papers of Robert Morris, 5:237
158. Papers of Robert Morris, 5:228
159. Papers of Robert Morris, 5:257
160. Papers of Robert Morris, 5:238
161. Papers of Robert Morris, 5:251
162. Papers of Robert Morris, 5:264
163. Papers of Robert Morris, 5:253
164. Papers of Robert Morris, 5:281
165. *Power of the Purse*, pg.196
166. Beaumarchais, pg. 294-295
167. Papers of Robert Morris, 5:255
168. Papers of Robert Morris, 5:258
169. Papers of Robert Morris, 5:259
170.* Note: Harrison & Co. had been in Cadiz since 1779. Richard Harrison went to Cadiz from Martinique where he had helped Bingham run Secret Committee smuggling operations from 1775 to 1779.
171. Papers of Robert Morris, 5:271
172. Papers of Robert Morris, 5:275
173. Papers of Robert Morris, 5:261
174. Papers of Robert Morris, 5:268
175. Papers of Robert Morris, 5:280
176. Papers of Robert Morris, 5:265
177. Papers of Robert Morris, 5:282
178. Papers of Robert Morris, 5:283-4
179. Papers of Robert Morris, 5:287
180. Papers of Robert Morris, 5:295
181. Papers of Robert Morris, 5:302
182. Papers of Robert Morris, 5:305
183. Papers of Robert Morris, 5:303
184. Papers of Robert Morris, 5:330
185. Papers of Robert Morris, 5:332
186. Papers of Robert Morris, 5:340
187. Papers of Robert Morris, 5:300
188. Papers of Robert Morris, 5:307
189. Papers of Robert Morris, 5:337
190. Papers of Robert Morris, 5:351
191. Papers of Robert Morris, 5:331
192. Papers of Robert Morris, 5:311
193. Papers of Robert Morris, 5:348
194. Papers of Robert Morris, 5:356
195. Papers of Robert Morris, 5:359
196. Papers of Robert Morris, 5:350
197. Papers of Robert Morris, 5:310
198. Papers of Robert Morris, 5:315
199. Papers of Robert Morris, 5:327
200. Papers of Robert Morris, 5:414
201. Papers of Robert Morris, 5:353
202. Papers of Robert Morris, 5:354
203. Papers of Robert Morris, 5:351
204. Papers of Robert Morris, 5:357
205. Papers of Robert Morris, 5:360-362
206. Papers of Robert Morris, 5:367
207. Papers of Robert Morris, 5:372
208. Papers of Robert Morris, 5:369
209. Papers of Robert Morris, 5:373
210. Papers of Robert Morris, 5:375
211. Papers of Robert Morris, 5:385
212. Papers of Robert Morris, 5383
213. Papers of Robert Morris, 5:384
214. Papers of Robert Morris, 5:392

215. Papers of Robert Morris, 5:396
216. Papers of Robert Morris, 5:83-84
217. Papers of Robert Morris, 5:548
218. Papers of Robert Morris, 5:394
219. Papers of Robert Morris, 5:395
220. Papers of Robert Morris, 5:403
221. Papers of Robert Morris, 5:412
222. Papers of Robert Morris, 5:442
223. Papers of Robert Morris, 5:415
224. Papers of Robert Morris, 5:449
225. Papers of Robert Morris, 5:416
226. Papers of Robert Morris, 5:419
227. Papers of Robert Morris, 5:420
228. Papers of Robert Morris, 5:435
229. Papers of Robert Morris, 5:450
230. Papers of Robert Morris, 5:475
231. Papers of Robert Morris, 5:453
232. Papers of Robert Morris, 5:460
233. Papers of Robert Morris, 5:463
234. Papers of Robert Morris, 5:471
235. Papers of Robert Morris, 5:483
236. Papers of Robert Morris, 5:490
237. Papers of Robert Morris, 5:519
238. Papers of Robert Morris, 5:446-7
239. Papers of Robert Morris, 5:545
240. Papers of Robert Morris, 5:477-9
241. Papers of Robert Morris, 5:502
242. Papers of Robert Morris, 5:528
243. Papers of Robert Morris, 5:507
244. Papers of Robert Morris, 5:485
245. Papers of Robert Morris, 5:551
246. Papers of Robert Morris, 5:492-3
247. Papers of Robert Morris, 5:541
248. Papers of Robert Morris, 5:530
249. Papers of Robert Morris, 5:553
250. Papers of Robert Morris, 5:552
251. Papers of Robert Morris, 5:561
252. *Letters of Delegates to Congress*, 20:249-250
253. Papers of Robert Morris, 5:556
254. Papers of Robert Morris, 5:560
255. Papers of Robert Morris, 5:556
256. Papers of Robert Morris, 5:562
257. *The Transatlantic Slave Trade* CD-ROM
258. Papers of Robert Morris, 5:569
259. Papers of Robert Morris, 5:578
260. Papers of Robert Morris, 5:569-570
261. Papers of Robert Morris, 5:577
262. Papers of Robert Morris, 5:572
263. Papers of Robert Morris, 5:600n
264. Papers of Robert Morris, 6:213
265. Papers of Robert Morris, 5:600
266. Papers of Robert Morris, 5:584
267. Papers of Robert Morris, 5:585
268. Papers of Robert Morris, 5:593
269. Papers of Robert Morris, 6:26
270. Papers of Robert Morris, 5:605
271. Papers of Robert Morris, 6:35
272. Papers of Robert Morris, 6:56-76
273. Papers of Robert Morris, 6:58
274. Papers of Robert Morris, 6:43
275. Papers of Robert Morris, 6:65
276. Papers of Robert Morris, 6:66
277. Papers of Robert Morris, 6:67
278. Einhorn pg. 170, 178-179
279. Papers of Robert Morris, 6:68
280. Papers of Robert Morris, 6:70
281. Papers of Robert Morris, 6:63
282. *Wealth of Nations*, pg. 328
283. Papers of Robert Morris, 6:456
284. Papers of Robert Morris, 5:294
285. Ver Steeg, pg. 175
286. Papers of Robert Morris, 6:93
287. Papers of Robert Morris, 6:95
288. Papers of Robert Morris, 6:87
289. Papers of Robert Morris, 6:117
290. Papers of Robert Morris, 6:118
291. Papers of Robert Morris, 6:167, 227
292. Papers of Robert Morris, 6:122
293. Papers of Robert Morris, 5:573
294. Papers of Robert Morris, 6:128
295. Papers of Robert Morris, 6:135
296. Papers of Robert Morris, 6:148
297. Papers of Robert Morris, 6:185
298. Papers of Robert Morris, 6:188
299. Diplomatic Correspondence of the Revolution, 7:250
300. Papers of Robert Morris, 6:143
301. Papers of Robert Morris, 6:144
302. Papers of Robert Morris, 6:152
303. Papers of Robert Morris, 6:158
304. Papers of Robert Morris, 6:228
305. Papers of Robert Morris, 6:170
306. Papers of Robert Morris, 6:175
307. Papers of Robert Morris, 6:297

308. Papers of Robert Morris, 6:299
309. Papers of Robert Morris, 6:315
310. Papers of Robert Morris, 6:178
311. Papers of Robert Morris, 6:294
312. Papers of Robert Morris, 6:136
313. Papers of Robert Morris, 6:303
314. Papers of Robert Morris, 6:302
315. Papers of Robert Morris, 6:311
316. Papers of Robert Morris, 6:329
317. Papers of Robert Morris, 6:222
318. Papers of Robert Morris, 6:233
319. Papers of Robert Morris, 6:235
320. Papers of Robert Morris, 6:252
321. Papers of Robert Morris, 6:288
322. Papers of Robert Morris, 6:257
323. Papers of Robert Morris, 6:261
324. Papers of Robert Morris, 6:247
325. Papers of Robert Morris, 6:259
326. Papers of Robert Morris, 6:231
327. Papers of Robert Morris, 6:262
328. Papers of Robert Morris, 6:269
329. Papers of Robert Morris, 6:263
330. Papers of Robert Morris, 6:265
331. Papers of Robert Morris, 6:267
332. Papers of Robert Morris, 6:159
333. Papers of Robert Morris, 6:3, 87, 105, 118, 133, 137, 275
334. Papers of Robert Morris, 6:16, 226, 235, 288, 304
335. Papers of Robert Morris, 6:137
336. Papers of Robert Morris, 6:275
337.* If this large amount were updated to the early 21st century according to its relative percentage of the Gross Domestic Product, which was very small at the time, the equivalent amount would be over $95,000,000,000 {http://www.measuringworth.com/calculators/uscompare/index.php}
338. Papers of Robert Morris, 6:276
339. Papers of Robert Morris, 6:560
340. Papers of Robert Morris, 6:291
341. Papers of Robert Morris, 6:281
342. Papers of Robert Morris, 6:284
343. Papers of Robert Morris, 6:305
344. Papers of Robert Morris, 6:282
345. Papers of Robert Morris, 6:282
346. Papers of Robert Morris, 6:316
347. Papers of Robert Morris, 6:317
348. Papers of Robert Morris, 6:339
349. Papers of Robert Morris, 6:349
350. Papers of Robert Morris, 6:325
351. Papers of Robert Morris, 6:345
352. Rappleye, pg. 323
353. Papers of Robert Morris, 6:417
354. Papers of Robert Morris, 6:420
355. Papers of Robert Morris, 6:357
356. Papers of Robert Morris, 6:265
357. Papers of Robert Morris, 6:267
358. Papers of Robert Morris, 6:429
359. Papers of Robert Morris, 6:335
360. Papers of Robert Morris, 6:337
361. Papers of Robert Morris, 6:311
362. Papers of Robert Morris, 6:308
363. Papers of Robert Morris, 6:309
364. Papers of Robert Morris, 7:388
365. Papers of Robert Morris, 6:382
366. Papers of Robert Morris, 6:384
367. Papers of Robert Morris, 6:305
368. Papers of Robert Morris, 6:321
369. Papers of Robert Morris, 6:327
370. Papers of Robert Morris, 6:375
371. Papers of Robert Morris, 6:343
372. Papers of Robert Morris, 6:353
373. *Journals of the Continental Congress* Saturday, September 14, 1782
374. Papers of Robert Morris, 6:331
375. Papers of Robert Morris, 6:333
376. Papers of Robert Morris, 6:333
377. Papers of Robert Morris, 6:351
378. Papers of Robert Morris, 6:443
379. Papers of Robert Morris, 6:353
380. Papers of Robert Morris, 6:371
381. Papers of Robert Morris, 6:378
382. Papers of Robert Morris, 6:381
383. Papers of Robert Morris, 6:384
384. Papers of Robert Morris, 6:397
385. Papers of Robert Morris, 6:365
386. Papers of Robert Morris, 6:407
387. Papers of Robert Morris, 6:409
388. Papers of Robert Morris, 6:390
389. Papers of Robert Morris, 6:355
390. Papers of Robert Morris, 6:394
391. Papers of Robert Morris, 6:405
392. Papers of Robert Morris, 6:398
393. Papers of Robert Morris, 6:398-9

394. Papers of Robert Morris, 6:413
395. Papers of Robert Morris, 6:500
396. Papers of Robert Morris, 6:418
397. Papers of Robert Morris, 6:419
398. Papers of Robert Morris, 6:421
399. Papers of Robert Morris, 6:431
400. Papers of Robert Morris, 6:423
401. Papers of Robert Morris, 6:424
402. Papers of Robert Morris, 6:429
403. Papers of Robert Morris, 6:432
404. Papers of Robert Morris, 6:435
405. Papers of Robert Morris, 6:415
406. Papers of Robert Morris, 6:416
407. Papers of Robert Morris, 6:436
408. Papers of Robert Morris, 6:448
409. Papers of Robert Morris, 6:449
410. Papers of Robert Morris, 6:455
411. Papers of Robert Morris, 6:456
412. Papers of Robert Morris, 6:456
413. Papers of Robert Morris, 6:460
414. Papers of Robert Morris, 6:603
415. Papers of Robert Morris, 6:461
416. Papers of Robert Morris, 6:483
417. Papers of Robert Morris, 6:468
418. Papers of Robert Morris, 6:463
419. Papers of Robert Morris, 6:464-6
420. Papers of Robert Morris, 6:471
421. Papers of Robert Morris, 6:477
422. Papers of Robert Morris, 6:601
423. Papers of Robert Morris, 6:477
424. Papers of Robert Morris, 6:479
425. Papers of Robert Morris, 6:490
426. Papers of Robert Morris, 6:524
427. Papers of Robert Morris, 6:497
428. Papers of Robert Morris, 6:498
429. Papers of Robert Morris, 6:491
430. Papers of Robert Morris, 6:516
431. Papers of Robert Morris, 6:501-502
432. Papers of Robert Morris, 6:507
433. Papers of Robert Morris, 6:507
434. Papers of Robert Morris, 6:525
435. Papers of Robert Morris, 6:507
436. Papers of Robert Morris, 6:507
437. Papers of Robert Morris, 6:531,353
438. Papers of Robert Morris, 7:50
439. Papers of Robert Morris, 6:511-512
440. Papers of Robert Morris, 6:512
441. Papers of Robert Morris, 6:545
442. Papers of Robert Morris, 6:557
443. Papers of Robert Morris, 6:577
444. Papers of Robert Morris, 6:579
445. Papers of Robert Morris, 6:596
446. Papers of Robert Morris, 6:597
447. Papers of Robert Morris, 6:515
448. Papers of Robert Morris, 6:525
449. Papers of Robert Morris, 6:534
450. Papers of Robert Morris, 6:651
451. Papers of Robert Morris, 7:135
452. Papers of Robert Morris, 6:580
453. Papers of Robert Morris, 6:529
454. Papers of Robert Morris, 6:543
455. Papers of Robert Morris, 6:544
456. Papers of Robert Morris, 6:545
457. Papers of Robert Morris, 6:552
458. Papers of Robert Morris, 6:553
459. Papers of Robert Morris, 6:637
460. Papers of Robert Morris, 6:565
461. Papers of Robert Morris, 6:637
462. Papers of Robert Morris, 6:567
463. Papers of Robert Morris, 6:641
464. Papers of Robert Morris, 6:549
465. Papers of Robert Morris, 6:515
466. Papers of Robert Morris, 6:519
467. Papers of Robert Morris, 6:536
468. Papers of Robert Morris, 6:537
469. Papers of Robert Morris, 6:599
470. Papers of Robert Morris, 6:608
471. Papers of Robert Morris, 6:617
472. Papers of Robert Morris, 6:625
473. Papers of Robert Morris, 6:582
474. Papers of Robert Morris, 6:604
475. Papers of Robert Morris, 6:605
476. Papers of Robert Morris, 6:609
477. Papers of Robert Morris, 6:619
478. Papers of Robert Morris, 6:626
479. Papers of Robert Morris, 6:646
480. Papers of Robert Morris, 6:647
481. Papers of Robert Morris, 6:668
482. Papers of Robert Morris, 6:610
483. Papers of Robert Morris, 6:613
484. Papers of Robert Morris, 6:614
485. Papers of Robert Morris, 6:615
486. Papers of Robert Morris, 6:656
487. Papers of Robert Morris, 6:662

488. Papers of Robert Morris, 6:661
489. Papers of Robert Morris, 6:623
490. Papers of Robert Morris, 7:60
491. Papers of Robert Morris, 7:60-61
492. Papers of Robert Morris, 6:379
493. *We The People*, p 324-326
494. Rappleye , pg. 320
495. *We The People*, p 327
496. Papers of Robert Morris, 7:10
497. Papers of Robert Morris, 7:26
498. Papers of Robert Morris, 7:28
499. Papers of Robert Morris, 7:21
500. Papers of Robert Morris, 6:585
501. Papers of Robert Morris, 6:587-591
502. Papers of Robert Morris, 7:30
503. Papers of Robert Morris, 7:76
504. Papers of Robert Morris, 7:105
505. Papers of Robert Morris, 6:520
506. Papers of Robert Morris, 7:137-8
507. Papers of Robert Morris, 7:193-4
508. Papers of Robert Morris, 7:112
509. Papers of Robert Morris, 7:121
510. Papers of Robert Morris, 7:134-5
511. Papers of Robert Morris, 7:127
512. Papers of Robert Morris, 7:126
513. Papers of Robert Morris, 7:127
514. Rappleye pg. 327-328
515. Papers of Robert Morris, 7:183
516. The Gilder Lehrman Institute of American History, Document Number: GLC04769
517. Coughtry, Jay. *The Notorious Triangle: Rhode Island and the African Slave Trade, 1700-1807*. Philadelphia, 1981
518. Papers of Robert Morris, 7:79-86
519. Papers of Robert Morris, 7:144
520. Papers of Robert Morris, 7:147
521. Papers of Robert Morris, 7:93-6
522. Papers of Robert Morris, 7:99
523. Papers of Robert Morris, 7:151
524. Papers of Robert Morris, 7:178
525. Papers of Robert Morris, 7:179
526. Papers of Robert Morris, 7:155
527. Papers of Robert Morris, 7:168
528. Papers of Robert Morris, 7:202
529. Papers of Robert Morris, 7:204
530. This was the same Mr. Penet with who had a secret committee contract in 1776, and with whom Thomas Morris had dealt in 1778, to the displeasure of the brothers Lee; and who, under contract to the Board of War, failed to establish a gunsmithery in America; and with whom the Browns of Providence dealt unsatisfactorily until 1781. The Browns were more fortunate than Pollock, in that they were able convince Congress to sell some continental cannons to cover a bill they had drawn on Penet. Papers of Robert Morris, 2:321;2:322. This sale was one source of the controversy between the Eastern Naval Board and Morris.
531. Papers of Robert Morris, 7:207-8
532. Papers of Robert Morris, 7:181
533. Papers of Robert Morris, 7:168
534. Papers of Robert Morris, 7:182
535. Papers of Robert Morris, 7:227
536. Papers of Robert Morris, 7:215
537. Papers of Robert Morris, 7:199
538. Papers of Robert Morris, 7:228
539. Papers of Robert Morris, 7:238
540. Papers of Robert Morris, 7:215
541. Papers of Robert Morris, 7:187
542. Papers of Robert Morris, 7:211
543. Papers of Robert Morris, 7:220-222
544. Papers of Robert Morris, 7:196-199
545. Papers of Robert Morris, 7:190-191
546. Papers of Robert Morris, 7:235
547. Papers of Robert Morris, 7:200
548. Papers of Robert Morris, 7:230
549. Papers of Robert Morris, 7:238
550. Papers of Robert Morris, 7:243
551. Papers of Robert Morris, 7:244-5
552. Papers of Robert Morris, 7:246

IX

1783

Winter

Morris' effort to get silver from Cuba was well underway. John Brown, of Philadelphia, was in Havana where he arranged the sale of bulk products in trade and negotiated bills of exchange from Harrison & Co. in Cadiz. The resulting shipload of Spanish silver got past the British blockade, and back to America. To stimulate economic activity in the mid-Atlantic region, Morris requested a French convoy for the merchant ships, and at least twelve tobacco ships readied to sail from Baltimore to France. Even so, not all the ships made it safely to sea.

Both commerce and finance were under pressure in the North; Morris' notes were being discounted in Massachusetts, against his wishes that they trade at par. As usual, financial matters continued to be difficult between states and the Congress. New York was still not paying their quota to Congress, and neither was New Hampshire. In frustrated disappointment Morris wrote to his receiver, Joseph Whipple,

> I may venture to ask if this be the result of those professions so often repeated of a willingness to sacrifice life and fortune for the freedom of America.[1]

The spirit behind the early pledges had dissipated. The state commitments had not arrived, and the resulting unsettled condition of the Army was on the minds of many. Washington wrote to Congress about growing dissension in the ranks. He was aware officers from his camp had gone to petition Congress, and he wanted to ensure they got a fair hearing. He argued,

> Up to now the officers had served as a buffer between the troops and the public, quelling mutinies when they had arisen, but if the officers' grievances should be suffered to raise equally high, I know not what the consequences may be.[2]

A delegation of officers from Washington's army met with Robert Morris two weeks later, on New Year's Eve. The next day Gouverneur Morris wrote to John Jay, who was serving as a peace commissioner in France,

> The Army are not disciplined and their wants as to food and clothing are relieved but they are not paid. Their back accounts are not settled. If settled the balances are not secured by competent funds. No provision is made for the half-pay promised them. Some persons and indeed some states pretend to dispute their claim to it. [For later encoding] (The Army have swords in their hands. You know enough of the history of mankind to know much more then I have said and possibly much more then they themselves yet think of.)[3]

Gouverneur Morris echoed Washington's sentiment, and he gave some of the first dark hints on the dangers involved in dealing with a dissatisfied Army. He continued,

> I pledge myself to you on the present occasion, and although I think it probable that much of convulsion will ensue, yet it must terminate in giving to the Government that power without which government is but a name."[4]

Gouverneur was an ardent nationalist, as was Robert. However, while Robert counseled patience and encouraged the army to lobby the states, Gouverneur thought the threats implicit in the Army's petition might be a constructive force in cementing the confederation into a real national government. He wrote to Matthew Ridley,

> ... I fear the legislature will not derive much good from the fermentation [of the Army]. However that may be I shall not be sorry to see some thing which may draw forth general attention to our affairs and then perhaps order may be drawn forth from confusion.[5]

On January 6th the officers petitioned Congress and urged

> ... an immediate adjustment of all dues" [and putting the rest] "on such a footing was will restore cheerfulness to the army, revive confidence in the justice and generosity of its constituents, and contribute to the very desirable effect of re-establishing public credit.[6]

Later the officers testified before Congress, with Morris looking on. They aired their grievances about lack of current pay, back pay, and the half pay pensions. They shared the common concern that many officers would be returned to civilian life in "reduced circumstances" after winning a war for a seemingly ungrateful nation.

During the meeting between the Army officers and Congress, Madison worried that if Congress suddenly paid the Army as a result of their petition, then it would look so successful that endless petitions would follow. This faded quickly when the delegation pointed out the enlisted men would feel justified in mutinying, and the officers would be disinclined to stop them because the country had failed to honor its commitments.[7] Congress decided that making some payment arrangements would be wise. In a small gesture, Congress authorized Morris to pay the traveling expenses of the military delegation. Later, the officers met with the Superintendent, and they all devised a report delivered to Congress on January 20th. In turn, Congress asked Morris for ways to come up with the money. It seemed to have slipped Congress' notice that they might have appealed to the states to make good on their commitments, and thereby support Morris' efforts.

America was not alone in wanting to put its financial house in order. As peace neared, John Holker was ordered back to France for a review of his dealings. Before he could return home, Holker needed to settle his accounts with Morris, accounts that stretched back to 1779 through a variety of ventures. He contacted Morris with a high degree of urgency. However, Morris was fully occupied with various crises. He told Holker he would supply the requested settlement, but it would have to wait. The timing of France's request suggests that suspicions were generated in the French Court when they became aware of the inquiries Arthur Lee's committee made through Thomas Barclay.

Arthur Lee was not just investigating Morris' actions as Superintendent of Finance, even though this was the impression that Lee created. He was also scouring Europe to find traces of Morris' work on the Secret Committees, some five years earlier. The curious aspect of this effort is that Arthur Lee was aware of the existing record. He had seen Thomas Morris' private papers in Paris back in 1778, because his brother William Lee had removed those papers from the dead man's abode. In actuality, it was Arthur Lee who opened these records to the same people in France to whom he now looked to provide the information he had already seen. A suspicious mind would conclude that Lee was not interested in discovering new information, but rather he was making sure that any holes he might have secretly created in Morris' business records could not be filled by the surprising discovery of any new information. If Arthur Lee had one thing it was a suspicious mind. Madison's dislike of Lee was compounded by the Lee vendetta against Robert Morris, whom Madison supported.

Madison later wrote,

> My charity cannot invent an excuse for the prepense malice with which the character and services of this gentleman [Morris] are murdered. I am persuaded that he accepted his office from motives which were honorable and patriotic. I have seen no proof of misfeasance. I have heard of many charges which were palpably erroneous. I have known others somewhat suspicious vanish on examination. Every member in Congress must be sensible of the benefit which has accrued to the public from his administration. No intelligent man out of Congress can be altogether insensible of it. The Court of France has testified its satisfaction at his appointment which I really believe lessened its repugnance to lend us money.[8]

The French Crown's interest in Holker's actions was a renewal of a six-month-old query. Holker had operated with a free hand for years, even though he held an official position as French Consul in America. His operations had given Morris' contractors problems in their efforts to supply American forces. The French Army and Navy had complained, since 1781, that they felt overcharged by Holker. This was the main reason the French ministry had asked for an accounting from him six months earlier. In January 1783, Holker would not be put off, and demanded an accounting from Morris. He started off by requesting "the most speedy settlement of your accounts with the Royal Marine." Holker had previously taken a proprietary interest in a variety of American military supply companies in addition to the partnerships with Morris, but the record shows these were not the roads to riches. Instead, the credit of all involved was sorely tested. These difficulties resulted in financial hardship for many and Holker was being accused of being a "public defaulter, a character too odious to be supported by any man of principle or feeling."[9] As events unfolded it became more and more clear that Holker somehow hoped to deflect these aspersions onto Morris.

While Holker fumed in the wings, Morris looked after feeding the army. He made a single and final payment to the New York contractors. In January Wadsworth and Carter received a three-month bill of exchange for 1,038,000 livres, ($192,222) that could be drawn from the American account in France on the 3rd of March. The Amount was so large that when the bill came in during March, the French banker requested they draw smaller amounts in a series of transactions until the sum was reached.

Morris had arranged payment for the time being. He still had to consider the lack of support he was getting from the states, and the faction who fought his programs. As he did, he became increasingly concerned about the ruination of his personal credit, but he was more concerned about the army. The only source for funds to pay the army came from the French loans, and he would not learn about Franklin's success in securing the last loan for several months. In anticipation of a shortfall, he asked for permission from Congress to sell bills of exchange on uncertain funds. In other words: to write bad checks. Congress was concerned about overdrafts in Europe but remained publicly silent. As events unfolded over the course of the year, the bills Morris sold were actually covered either by the French or the Dutch. However, in January Morris did not know what the future held. What he knew was that the Army was clamoring for money, and he told Congress they must exert themselves to pay the forces.

Morris focused on the Army. Holker focused on Morris, and he became more insistent to achieve a settlement. Holker's actions began to alarm Morris, who said he

> ...discovered that there was something on his mind with which indicated suspicion of my having other reasons for delaying the settlement, other than the declared one, of an interference with my public duty.

At this point Holker became more vocal and in an apparent desperate bid for attention, started to contend that Morris owed money to the King of France.[10]

The Commander in Chief of the Army, Washington, wrote Morris on a different topic. He shared his disappointment that there was still no Agent of Marine Prisoners to attend to the details of the prisoner exchange. He also wanted money to buy some land for himself; and mentioned that it would also be good to have some funds for the secret service. He repeated his contention that Comfort Sands & Co. had contrived to make money with "dirty tricks" and that he expected better from the current group of contractors.[11]

Supplying the northern army continued to be difficult, but it was even more so in the south. Captain Nat Irish spent over $6,000 of his own money to supply troops in Virginia and wanted repayment, but the Continental coffers were bare. Considering the state of Virginia's failure to support the Continental Congress in favor of their home state, Morris wrote his agent, George Webb,

> Your State is but beginning to feel the effects of bad policy and the baneful consequences of suspicion. They will, I suppose, like the rest of the World adopt what is wise and just when they have smarted from impudent conduct.[12]

Morris clearly had faith that the Virginians would eventually see their best interests lay in the development of cooperative policies. It appears he thought a little harsh medicine would bring them around, and they would give up on their negativism and distrust. He misjudged their cultural habits; instead, they just thought Morris was arrogant and annoying.

Morris kept in touch with America's friends in Europe. His boys were still not in a proper school. He wrote to Jay on the topic, and while he allowed another course might have been taken, the fact was the boys were in Ridley's care and the goal was to be sure they were "instructed in all those things which they ought to learn." He went on to express the thoughts of many parents who understand that money spent on education is better spent than money sent to maintain children who are ignorant. He said,

> I do not desire to save one farthing of money as a deduction from the learning of my children. The more they cost me the less I shall give them but Instruction at this Age is of infinitely more consequence than the Money it Costs can be hereafter. Upon these principles I wish them without Regard to expense to be placed where they can acquire the most perfect Education.

He went on to ask John Jay to keep an eye on his boys who were so far away.[13]

Next, he turned to Franklin and expressed his regret about the financial predicament of the United States,

> Imagine the situation of a man who is to direct the finances of a country, almost without revenue (for such you will perceive this to be) surrounded by creditors whose distress, while they increase their clamors, render it more difficult to appease them. An army ready to disband or mutiny, a government whose sole authority consists in the power of framing resolutions." Even in these circumstances, he still believed in the success of his mission, "I would not draw one more bill, and would boldly hazard every consequence of omission, if I were not persuaded that they would be paid.

With that he entreated Franklin to press for further loans from France.[14] Finally he wrote,

> In my turn, I rely on your promise of exertion to pay my drafts. If one bill should be protested, I could no longer serve the United States.[15]

Morris worked to maintain European support for his financial program. He wrote his banker in France, Grand, to ensure his credit would last. He also wrote a long, complicated, and somewhat embarrassed letter to the Minister of France Chevalier de La Luzerne. In this letter he explained how it came to be that the United States were overdrawn in their French account. He noted that amounts he requested from the French Crown were not supplied; the states were uncooperative; unbeknownst to Morris, Franklin was drawing on the same account; the much-anticipated Dutch loan was slow to fill; and the U.S. really needed the money anyway to be ready for more war in case the peace negotiations broke down, which was why Congress authorized the overdraft. He ended with this thought,

> If, however, I have incurred censure on the present occasion, it must be because I was ignorant of what I could not know, and did not know. And did not perform what was not in my power.[16]

Morris followed this letter with a document entitled *Observations on the State of Affairs.* This work was a collaboration of both Morrises and was intended to provide a rationale for a hoped-for peacetime loan from the French. It was also an outline of the Morrises' thinking on the subject of the United States becoming a nation instead of a Confederation.

> ... the states (if closely united) will become important and respectable; but otherwise they will be miserable at home and contemptible abroad.... The country is too large to be one Republic, anarchy would ensue, and then despotism.... Congress should have at least have an authority competent to general purposes of Commerce and War, also to decide disputes between different states.... Their influence should be such as to lead the states ... and to procure obedience to their authority without military coercion ... influence may be obtained by funding the public debts, on general revenues. A large part of the community would be thereby interested to support national authority.... The demand for permanent funds for the public debt, is most likely to succeed.... If the collection [of revenues] be given to Congress a prudent exercise of that trust would facilitate every subsequent measure. The possession of money will acquire influence. Influence will lead to authority, and authority will open the purses of people ... but the favorable moment both to gain and establish power, is at the close of a war....
>
> England will certainly attempt, either to deprive France of her new ally, or to render that ally useless.... It is natural that the British Court should have a faction in America, and that the National Council should adhere to France...the relative force [of that fac-

> tion] must be estimated by a comparison with the powers of [the National] Government
>
> The present union of America is from necessity. It is a vessel whose parts are kept together by exterior compression. It is therefore ... important to obtain for Congress the influence and authority which they stand in need of.

The document concluded with the idea that the necessary "compression" might be maintained by the various interest groups, including the Army, pressuring the states to grant Congress the power to tax. Of course, money from France would be needed in the meantime to keep the Congress going, and an operating Congress could supply

> ... the power which is alike necessary to perpetuate the alliance and promote the happiness and greatness of America.[17]

-|-

The war was practically over; so its ability to keep the army together had waned. After consultations with a Congressional committee headed by Hamilton, Morris had another meeting with the representatives from the Army. Morris told them,

> I am however willing to make an exertion to advance one month [pay] to the Army.[18]

Later he expanded on this meeting in a letter to the President of Congress wherein he said he told them...

> ...that the money would not only be taken from other essential service, but that the amount exceeded any finds which I could rely on and that of consequence if the measures I have taken to procure money did not succeed the most serious evils would be produced."[19]

Morris did not have the money on hand and had to stretch out the payments, so he counseled patience.[20] He was gambling on help from the French, and the hoped-for arrival of silver from Havana on the *Alliance*. The delegation seemed satisfied, and one of the officers offered to go the camp and propose this to his constituents. The following day Morris met with the paymaster to devise a method of arranging the month's pay. After he received La Luzerne's reply to his request for further funds from France, he wrote,

> ...this day I received a letter from his Excellency the Minister of France... the contents of which I regret, &c. &c [etc.].

Luzerne had considered Morris' plea and discussed it within his councils, but France would not make the peacetime loan. French losses in the West Indies not only weakened their navy, but their economy as well. Ominously, Morris had a meeting with Swanwick and Salomon, and told them not to sell one more bill. There would be no money to cover them.

With an eye to covering existing commitments, Morris wrote to Adams and encouraged him to see that the Dutch subscription loan had been filled. The Dutch loan was America's last financial lifeline; yet this urgency had no effect on the slow movement of Dutch risk takers. Morris then wrote Franklin to expedite the shipment of the weapons Virginia had purchased in France; one supposes they might otherwise have been seized in payment for American overdrafts. On the topic of state intransigence, he wrote to General Greene,

> ... the states seem to consider as the most precious part of the separate sovereignty the power of doing injustice. And to this I might add that they seem to fear lest their successors should be deprived of it under the idea that it has by non-usage become obsolete.[21]

On January 20th he instructed the paymaster to start the process of providing one month's pay to the Continental army and treated the question about payment as if it were a decided fact. It would be a few days before Congress came to the same conclusion. Previously, Greene had decided to give the Southern Army one month's pay, which made Morris' move more natural and in tune with his often-stated goal of treating all according to one rule. The plan was to pay half a dollar a week to the enlisted men until the total amount for each was reached, and to pay the officers in Morris notes, payable in 60 days.[22] Congress ratified a resolution on January 25th authorizing Morris to pay the army. Morris wrote Washington to ask him to discuss, with the contractor, the possibility of accepting Morris' notes in payment for articles when the officers gave those notes to the contractor.[23] He wanted to create a system where he could pay officers with his notes, and the officers in turn could buy articles from the contractors, in a form of military script.

Morris risked even more of his own funds, in the form of his notes, and he looked to the states to cover them. Pennsylvania had done more than most states in meeting its requisition, but it was still slow to send money to the Congress, in this late period. Morris' patience was clearly nearing an end when he wrote to them on that subject,

> It is of little avail sir that the army, who are the immediate sufferers, or the people of America, whose national existence is so imminent-

> ly hazarded, should be told that a law has been enacted for raising the sum required. Laws not executed, or which from their nature are not executed only substitute deception in the place of denial.[24]

As states attempted to deceive their citizens, military financial problems became personal for individuals. Quartermaster Pickering found himself in a lawsuit. It happened that in 1780 Pickering had been empowered by Congress to issue notes to purchase supplies. An enterprising fellow named Melanchthon Woolsey had purchased these notes at great discounts; and was suing Pickering for their value in gold. Woolsey did not sue Congress, which was also liable, nor did Congress help Pickering to solve the problem. It took some time, but the state of New York passed some legislation to provide Pickering with relief.[25]

The daily business continued. The work on the ship *Bourbon* needed to be paid for. The purchase of cannons was declined. People wanted British prisoners of war as workers. The bills of exchange Congress had written, in 1779, to be paid by loans Jay never got from Spain, had been protested, and still had to be paid. Nevertheless, small forward steps were taken in a variety of areas. Morris worked to alleviate some of Washington's complaints. As Agent of Marine, he directed the Commissary of Marine Prisoners to appoint an agent at Dobb's Ferry and asked Washington to advise him. He also promised Washington that the paymaster would have some funds available for the purposes of the secret services.[26]

Morris finally got some cooperation from Virginia. George Webb, in Virginia, was starting to use tobacco as payment for the Continental requisition. Morris instructed Webb how the notes were to be redeemed for tobacco and then submitted to Webb as the Continental receiver.

> Let the officers or others bargain with the Treasurer and buy the public tobacco [with their notes]. You will receive the notes given by them in payment from the state and the whole matter is finished.[27]

A little help from one state was not going to solve the crisis, as efforts to gain the much-needed public support stalled in the North. Thomas Paine reported from Rhode Island that the political opposition was blocking his work in favor of the 1783 impost. Members of that faction owned the newspapers. Paine wrote,

> I find that the persons who are at the head of the opposition in this town are endeavoring to prevent the publication of any more of my

> pieces. They set out claiming the privilege and freedom of the press and now want to suppress it.[28]

Actions of such reluctant states made the pursuit of silver from the Caribbean even more important. Just at this time, John Barry was being chased around the Caribbean Sea by the British, as he tried to get to Cuba and bring the Spanish silver back to America. Morris hoped to use part of that silver to pay the restless Army.[29]

"Minister of Injustice"

Finally, on January 24th, 1783 Morris had enough. He tendered his resignation, valid as of May 31st, 1783. In hindsight, the activities undertaken a few days preceding this step point to a man who was moving to close up shop. His resignation was in keeping with his stated intention of working as long as he was useful, and his plans had been thwarted. It was in keeping with his need to protect his reputation: he often said that he would not sign a note that would not be honored. It was in keeping with his distaste for being attacked in the press, and on the floor of Congress, for doing what seemed clear and obvious as the right steps to take. It was in accordance with his stance that the Government practice Moral Honesty in dealing with the citizens, and he had witnessed countless occurrences of irresponsible actions by a variety of governments. It was in accordance with many declarations he had made including a statement to the governors that he would quit his station and make no new engagements if money were not forthcoming. He had lent his own money. He had convinced his friends to lend money. He had wheedled generous terms from suppliers and ultimately paid them with notes and loans. He came to realize that the states expected he would pay, but they would not reimburse him. When the foreign loans stopped coming, but the expenses of government did not, he found himself in an impossible position. He had once said,

> I wish most sincerely and ardently for peace that I may get rid of a most troublesome office … but I must confine myself to the language of a patriot … and tell you that the continuation of the war is necessary.[30]

Now that peace was coming, he was clearly looking to leave his troublesome office in a way that would protect his reputation.

It was bad enough to be attacked with false charges in the Press, it was worse to be someone who was actually untrustworthy. His reputation was his life, and he needed a way to make sure his work for America did not ruin him. In his resignation letter, Morris objected to being obliged to buy for the government on credit, while at the same time, the government had no intention of paying.

> I should be unworthy of the Confidence reposed in me by my fellow citizens, if I did not explicitly declare, that I will never be the Minister of Injustice.[31]

Congress decided not to make Morris' resignation public because they feared it would hurt the public credit. Morris wanted it released, because he needed to be sure that his personal reputation would not be destroyed by those who did not do their duty. Congress held on to the news and entered into an odd state.

Madison wrote the event made "a deep and solemn impression" on Congress. He said that Morris would leave a "vacancy which none knew how to fill, and which no fit man would venture to accept."[32] Morris' ally James Wilson knew the seriousness of the act, but Congress would not deign to ask Morris to reconsider. After all, that might make them look as powerless and inept as they actually were. Congress had grown accustomed to delegating most of their work to the Office of Finance. Historian E. James Ferguson wrote, "Morris soon possessed the greatest influence of any man in the country except, perhaps, Washington. Whatever the subject under consideration in Congress – whether military matters, foreign affairs, or relations with the states – the main problems usually related to finance... General Irvine wrote that

> ...the most trifling thing can not be done in any department but through Morris.[33]

Still, nothing really changed as a result of Morris' proposed resignation except that Congress revisited the idea of an impost and greater requisitions from the states.

Morris' resignation was not going to be effective until May, and there was still much work to do. He helped Jefferson prepare for his voyage to France as peace commissioner, a voyage that never took place because peace came first. He reviewed the estimates to pay the Army. He worked with the state of Pennsylvania to clear up his account as Agent of the State of Pennsylvania. Oliver Pollock came back from Virginia where he had finally obtained a settlement of his account with that state. When Congress approached Morris about Pollock's accounts Morris stepped aside saying,

> I told them I wished to be excused, and I never desire to meddle in the accounts of those gentlemen with whom I had connections in friendship or business.[34]

Virginia finally decided that Pollock should be paid on his claims, but they did not have the money at the time. There was still no money from the Yorktown tobacco deal. The final disposition and status of the Virginia Tobacco flag ships was so uncertain that the Agent for the British, George Eddy, was unable to give Morris any useful information on the topic. Also during this period, Morris' effort to get Arthur Lee's table linens continued. Morris had gotten an order from the Treasurer to send to France on Lee's behalf. When he asked Lee to sign it Lee refused, saying he had already contacted a gentleman in France who would manage the business from there.[35] True to form, and in the typical languid language of the Old Dominion, Virginia claimed it was too incapacitated to comply with Congressional Requisitions. Morris surveyed the conditions and wrote,

> I am heartily tired of Financeering.[36]

-|-

When Morris and the Secretary of War, Lincoln, drew up the estimates for the army contractors they tried to predetermine the number of rations that would be supplied to all, including the women known as camp followers. He put that figure into the contract as a way to insure that the women would be fed, but not to the extent that the Army would be feeding the whole local population. Washington objected to this because he had not been consulted, and he felt that this was an unwarranted and potentially harmful intrusion into his management of the Army. Washington noted this in a way he characterized as a "free, friendly and confidential communication" that,

> I was obliged to give provisions to the extra women in these regiments or lose by desertion – perhaps to the enemy – some of the oldest and best soldiers in the service.... But if from misconception, mis-information, or a partial investigation, the interior of my business is taken up by others at the distance of 150 miles, it is easy to conceive the confusion and bad consequences which must ensue.[37]

Down south, General Greene was faced with changes and challenges in the operation of his Army. The English had left the Carolinas, and so the danger they posed subsided. This resulted in Green receiving even less cooperation from that state than before. He wrote,

> Ever since the enemy have been gone we have been obliged to subsist ourselves at the point of the bayonet. All the state agents quitted the business the moment the enemy left Charlestown.[38]

The contractor for the southern contract, Mr. Banks, was the only bidder on the army contract. He won the business at terms he set, and still he wished to quit. Greene lobbied the governments of Georgia and South Carolina to support Congress' plans. He told both that if the Army was not supported it would go north or disband.

Morris had been working for some time on a plan to provide the Northern Army with one month's pay. He was finally able to sign the warrant to make the payment. Just at that time, news of a general peace started to make its way across the Atlantic to Philadelphia. It came in a letter sent from Morris' banker on February 4th, 1783. His banker was arranging for the payment of bills expected to arrive from Cuba. He had followed Morris' suggestion that he buy the Spanish silver in Cadiz at a favorable rate, and the difference of $5,755 allowed Morris to have a little extra to work with.[39] The Bank of North America sent notice that the United States was due to repay an obligation of $100,000. Morris sought to delay payment.[40] No payments were actually made until ten months later, in December 1783, and only because the Bank deferred to Morris after he reconsidered his resignation in May. Ultimately the United States could not repay the debt to the bank and Morris bought it, along with his friends, Ross, Whitesides, and Hazlehurst.[41] Then they hoped to be repaid.

Financial arrangements between Pennsylvania and the Office of Finance remained unfinished. The comptroller of Pennsylvania, Nicholson, was still dickering with Morris over the accounting for his purchases as Agent of Pennsylvania. Meanwhile in an effort to help an ally, Morris worked to protect Haym Salomon from an unscrupulous purchaser who had defaulted on payments for Bills of Exchange. To that end, Morris held a meeting with an old associate, de Mars, and informed him that the purchaser was understood to work for de Mars. De Mars denied this, and after a lively discussion de Mars suggested Morris resort to the courts for satisfaction.[42]

As Morris scrambled to find money for America, Virginians continued their efforts to get money into Virginia. Morris responded to a letter from Arthur Lee and explained why there were no new military contracts in Lee's state. He informed Lee that the War Office had not requested any for that state and that he

> ...was the less solicitous to frame one for Virginia because it was highly probable that very few rations would be consumed there.

He explained that only new recruits (of which there were none), passing soldiers (of which there were few), and newly captured prisoners (of which there were none) would be likely to benefit, and there was no way to supply such groups with a contract.[43] The Virginia delegation to Congress then wanted assurances that any money the state spent there supporting these groups would be considered as part payment of the requisition of 1782.[44]

Greene kept up his efforts to supply his Southern Army. The Governor of South Carolina forbade the Southern Army to impress goods, and allowed contracting as the only mode of supply, but the state would still not pay into the system. Greene noted to Morris,

> I am astonished at the independent principles the Southern States assume when I consider how unable they are to support themselves. It appears to me they are little disposed to examine their real situation.[45]

Part of Greene's problem lay in suspicions generated by the Army's dealings with Mr. Banks, the contractor to the Southern Army. Rumors circulated of corruption in the business of supplies, and of course the name Robert Morris was whispered along with Greene's; after all, Morris was sending General Greene money to buy supplies and that was proof enough, for some. The truth was more mundane: Robert Forsyth, a deputy of the commissary general of purchases, had made a secret partnership with Robert Banks who acted as an independent supplier of clothing. Banks could not buy enough clothing from Virginia because it did not exist there, and so Banks ended up buying clothes where he could find them, from the English who held Charleston at the time. Cries of "self-dealing" and "trading with the enemy" were heard again. Greene had to prove his innocence. He did, but his operations suffered.[46]

Large and small matters never stopped coming through the Office. George Washington complained about the food being sent by the contractor, and he told Morris that he had appointed a new food inspector. Back in Philadelphia, Morris started to take formal legal action against de Mars in favor of Haym Salomon, even though Salomon was officially the owner of the notes when those notes were sold. Morris employed William Lewis, Esq. to defend Salomon.[47] A geographer, Erskine, wanted payment, as did every other member in a host of other supplicants who passed in front of Morris' desk every week;[48] for example, he wrote to General Gates that he may not be able to repay Gates' wife for some of her expenses.

Morris' resignation letter was still unpublished, and American creditworthiness had not improved. Despite all the work, planning and risk, Morris' effort to sell bills of exchange in Havana was not as successful as hoped. Captain John Brown wrote,

> I have not sold the amount of bills of exchange, which I was authorized to draw... owing to a want of confidence in the people of this place. Had I been authorized to draw for your private account I should have found no difficulty in making a sale of any sum... and at a very favorable exchange.[49]

Captain Brown did manage to sell beef and flour in Cuba. He was able to net $16,328 for the United States from the trip, and he also brought back $50,000 in private silver for the merchants with items for sale.[50]

Spanish businessmen supplied more to Continental coffers than most states. The state interests would only support a modified impost to pay the foreign debt. They were not interested in the nationalist policies coming from the Office of Finance or Congress. They fought the nationalist efforts to pay the Armies, and to build a navy. John Rutledge, of South Carolina, Arthur Lee, of Virginia, and like-minded individuals wanted the states to pay their own soldiers. This meant not supporting the half-pay pension the Army expected. It also meant not supporting the one month's pay offer that Morris had made to the Army delegation, and not supporting Hamilton's plan of "commutation" that was suggested as a substitute for the half-pay pension. To further his ends, Rutledge tried to uncouple the Army, and the Foreign Debt, from the other creditors, notably the loan office certificate holders and those who held notes used to pay for supplies.

Those who supported state assumption of the debts made some political progress. The Secretary of War, Lincoln, was working behind the scenes to establish the amount of the obligation to the Army.[51] He planned to support payment by the states, mostly because he believed the states were most likely to make the payments. Considering the financial position of Congress this was not a bad assessment. The state of Pennsylvania was also starting to move toward assuming their portion of the debt. The Pennsylvanian debt holders, whose most vocal advocates were members of the Radical faction in Pennsylvania politics, drove this move.

On the other side Alexander Hamilton and James Wilson worked in Congress to

> ...unite the influence of Congress with that of the Army and the public Creditors to obtain permanent funds for the United States which will promise most ultimate security for the Army.[52]

A fight ensued in Congress as the state funding faction tried to shift the army payments to the states. La Luzerne noted in a letter to France that the operations of Congress were somewhat absurd since a small but vocal minority in that chamber easily thwarted any progress.

The Army was not silent on its own fate. General Alexander McDougal, one of the members of the Army delegation who had met with Congress, and with both Morrises in the Office of Finance, wrote to General Knox on February 12th, "the sentiment is daily gaining ground that the Army will not, nor ought to disband till Justice is done to them."[53] Francis Mercer, a Virginian Congressman who had voted against the impost, and who wanted to separate Army payments from other debt payments, made a similar statement when he wrote,

> ...the Army would not disband until satisfactory provision should be made.[54]

From the nationalist side Gouverneur Morris promoted the idea to General Knox that the Army should

> ...connect themselves with the public creditors of every kind and unremittingly urge the grant of general permanent funds ... the army may now influence the [state] legislatures...[55]

This had been the position of the Office of Finance for some time. Knox replied that he was not sure how the Army was supposed to lobby.

> But they are yet to be taught how their influence is to effect this matter. They may assist, they must be directed in the mode by proper authority.[56]

Washington made it clear he thought it unfitting for him to lobby the states. It would have clearly been improper for Morris to start commanding Army officers to lobby the states, so he was only able to make general encouragements. Knox might have followed General Greene's example, but apparently this did not occur to him. On February 24th Morris met with a congressional committee consisting of delegates from northern and southern states to work out a financial plan.[57] The congressional delegates who met with Morris that day were generally favorable to the idea of federalizing the debt; but were unable to muster support from their states.

Congress had yet to respond to Morris' formal proposals, made nearly seven months earlier in July 1782. Their eventual response was far from what Morris had hoped. After this meeting "Morris probably concluded that there was little prospect of securing a funding plan that would enable him to stay in office under honorable terms."[58]

Congress could not agree with itself, but American diplomats reached agreement with its enemy. On February 20th, 1783 the American ministers to France signed the "Declaration of the Cessation of Hostilities" with Britain. This was the agreement that ended the overt shooting part of the war. Shortly thereafter, far across the Atlantic, Morris concluded that his resignation letter should be made public. This was a few weeks after Morris made the arrangements for the first payment for the Army; and after his state, Pennsylvania, started to move to assume the debts; and after his meeting with the Congressional delegation on the 24th of February, which failed to produce any new national funding initiative. His letter appeared in the *Independent Gazetteer* on March 1st, 1783.

The effect of the announcement was electric. There was excitement in Congress, in the Press, on the streets, and in the embassies. Morris' letter laid the blame on Congress and the states, so it was only to be expected that even his allies in Congress would find the letter to be "reprehensible."[59] Arthur Lee, and his ally Theodorick Bland, immediately proposed the reconstitution of the Treasury Board, that instrument of decay and corruption from the recent past. Congress voted this down on March 5th, and instead worked "to devise the most proper steps to be taken."[60]

Henry Laurens, a long-time adversary of Morris' policies, wrote that he felt "no unhappiness" about Morris' coming departure.[61] Morris' resignation provided his political opposites with a perfect opportunity to discredit him. The anonymous Lucius took great pains to make the most of this opportunity and wrote copiously on this very subject. Working against Morris was the fact that America's poverty had been a well-kept secret. Congress' authorization to draw funds from France, where there were none to draw, was still an official secret, and many believed America was blessed with hearty support from overseas due to Howell's completely fabricated arguments against the impost. Morris had worked hard to hide the financial crisis so the nation would look creditworthy. This masked the true state of affairs so well that when the state of the finances was finally revealed, the lack of financial support by States and America's allies was seen as the effect rather than the cause of Morris' resignation. Morris had done such a thorough job in putting "lipstick on the American financial pig" that Washington wrote Hamilton,

> So far was I from conceiving that our finances was in so deplorable a state at this time that I had imbibed ideas from some source or another, that with the prospect of a loan from Holland, we should be able to rub along.[62]

Spanish and French representatives in America were unaware of new loans.

Reflecting on the Financier's resignation Von Steuben recounted an allegory, recalling the time when he came to America from France in 1776. He brought along a famous chef. When they arrived, the provisioners brought the food, but no cooking tools. The cook looked for the "utensils, indispensable, in his opinion for preparing a meal, and finding none" he asked the provider of food for cooking tools. The provisioner told him the food was usually prepared "by hanging it up by a string, and turning it before a good fire till sufficiently roasted." A few days later the frustrated cook left the camp, explaining to Von Steuben that anyone "was just as able to turn the string as I am." Von Steuben summed,

> ...the Treasury of the United States is just as empty as my kitchen was at Valley Forge; and Mr. Morris wisely retires, thinking it of very little consequence who turns the string.[63]

Friends and foes alike had lively discussions on the topic, but much of the speculation died down less than two weeks later. On March 12th, the *General Washington* arrived in Philadelphia with the Articles of Peace, and enough of the last French loan to avert a complete financial disaster. Morris warned Congress not to relax their exertions to create a national funding system because of the predictable results.

One hundred and fifty miles away, a series of dramatic events unfolded. Copies of Morris' resignation letters arrived in Washington's camp at Newburgh, New York. Morris sent along a personal note to Washington,

> I do assure you that nothing would have induced me to take this step but a painful conviction that the situation of those to whom the Public are indebted is desperate.... From my soul I pity the Army, and you my dear Sir in particular, who must see and feel for their distress without the power of relieving them... For the assistance which you have kindly afforded me, I pray you to accept my thanks, and be assured that I shall ever retain for it the most grateful Emotions... I hope my successor will be more fortunate than I have been, and that our glorious Revolution will be crowned with those acts of Justice, without which the greatest human Glory is but the Shadow of a Shade.[64]

Upon receiving the news about Morris' resignation Washington wrote,

> I have often reflected, with much solicitude, upon the disagreeableness of your situation and the negligence of the several states, in not enabling you to do that justice to the public creditors, which their demands require. I wish the step you have taken, may sound the alarm in their inmost souls, and rouse them to a just sense of their own interest, honor, and credit. But I must confess to you, that I have my fears - for as danger becomes further removed from them [i.e., news of peace] their feelings seem to be more callous to those noble sentiments, with which I could wish to see them inspired - mutual jealousies, local prejudices, and misapprehensions have taken such deep root, as will not easily be removed.[65]

The news quickly circulated in camp at Newburgh, New York, and many people in camp concluded that, "the Army would not disband until they had obtained Justice." Justice had become a political code word for payment. This view was supported by General Gates.[66] Gates, it seems, had been in communication with Alexander Hamilton on this subject. Earlier, Gouverneur Morris had made oblique statements in private coded letters to his confidants in Europe that the Army's swords were sharp and it should seek justice, but he softened his tone when actually addressing the Army. Gouverneur's letter to General Knox advocated working with the state legislatures, but it was misused by partisans to indicate complicity in the "Newburgh Conspiracy" on the part of the Office of Finance. This idea was advanced by Colonel Ogden, who had also been part of the Army's delegation to Philadelphia. He told Major John Armstrong, General Gates' assistant, that the Office of Finance wanted "the officers to prepare their minds of some manly, vigorous association with the other public creditors."[67] Colonel Ogden did not mention Morris' admonition to be patient. Ogden's representation would not be the first example of an activist misusing, or perhaps misunderstanding, the policy objectives of a third party in a way that misdirected a subordinate individual into making a dubious choice.

Ultimately, it was Major Armstrong, General Gates' aide-de-camp, who wrote the Newburgh position paper. A few days later, Colonel Brooks revealed the paper to Washington. On, March 15th, Washington interrupted a meeting of General Gates and the so-called conspirators. In a heartfelt speech to the officers, he unraveled the "Newburgh Conspiracy" by pledging his support for Justice, and counseling faith in Congress.

Headquarters at Newburgh

Essentially the "Newburgh Conspiracy" was an effort to make an ill-advised appeal to the officers and is proof that General Knox was right when he said the Army did not know how to use its influence. The address Armstrong wrote was a call for the officers to demand respect in the form of the long-promised payment from Congress. If that was not granted, then they were urged not to disband without payment if peace came, and if the war were to continue then to walk away from the ungrateful Congress. Armstrong wrote,

> If peace, then nothing shall separate you from your arms but death; if war, that courting the auspices and inviting the directions of your illustrious leader, you will retire to some unsettled country, smile in your turn, and mock when their fear cometh on.[68]

The actual threat was not a military takeover, but rather solidarity in peace or abandonment of the cause in war.

Major Armstrong did such a good job writing the address that it was the general opinion in Washington's camp that the anonymous paper must have been written by Gouverneur Morris;[69] and brought to camp by Colonel John Brooks along with Gouverneur's letter to Knox. What was omitted from this analysis is that along with the letter to Knox the courier, Colonel Brooks, also brought Congressional resolves and part of the first payment Morris had promised; money intended to keep the Army from mutiny.[70] Behind this ill-considered threat called "The Newburgh Conspiracy" one finds the same person who was behind the Conway Cabal back in 1776. In both cases General Gates wished to characterize Washington as a weak and unworthy leader so he, Gates, could lead the Army.

One can only wonder what Morris' opinion of this must have been since he labored mightily to support Washington, but he had also worked with General Lincoln to encourage Gates to stop fretting on his porch and return to the field and regain his honor. This act firmly established Gates as one who was capable of embarrassing himself with and without help from co-conspirators. After the flare up in Newburgh, Congress approved a kind of lump sum payment called "commutation" to the soldiers instead of the half-pay pension.[71]

The influence of the Morrises and the Office of Finance was such that Robert Morris' hand was seen to be behind almost every event on Earth at the time. Sometimes this was true; in this case only suspicions support the claim. Historian Richard H. Kohn argued in his *Eagle and Sword* that the Federalists had conspired with the Army to force Congressional and State acceptance of the national debt funding plan. This is exactly the position taken by Morris' long-time nemesis, Arthur Lee, and the state interests. It is just one example of many where Arthur Lee's work haunts the legacy of Robert Morris.

To accept the contention that Robert Morris was somehow behind the "Newburgh Conspiracy" one would have to believe that the same man who would leave the most powerful office in the United States government to protect his personal integrity would lie to his long-time friend George Washington and secretly support the effort to remove Washington from command. One would have to believe that when Morris urged patience, he secretly meant the opposite. One would have to believe that when Morris finally, and with great difficulty, scraped together money as part of the "one month's pay" to fend off a looming mutiny it was done secretly to support the mutiny. Finally, one would have to believe that Morris had suddenly, and secretly, abandoned years of work spent trying to keep the Army together so it could protect the United States, and instead decided to secretly work against his own goal while at the same time relying on the success of the initial policy and simultaneously resigning from power to keep it.

Unfortunately for this theory there is nothing but shabby circumstantial evidence and wishful thinking to support it. But such things as lack of evidence never stood in the way of Dr. Arthur Lee. As early as January 29th Lee had written to Samuel Adams that Morris was in league with the Army. If Morris was in league with the Army, the Army did not think so. Washington suspected that Morris and members of Congress were just using the Army as

> ...mere puppets to establish continental funds...and that rather [than] not succeed in this measure, or weaken their ground, they would make a sacrifice of the Army and all its interests.[72]

The French had noticed Morris' long-time effort of encouraging the Army to lobby the states and reported rumors that Morris was behind some effort to foment unrest. Rumors, no matter how interesting, are not evidence.

Instead of turning to a truly dark and Byzantine interpretation of Morris' involvement in this episode that hinges on a complete reversal of everything Morris was or stood for, one can look at it from a simple perspective. It was then, as it usually is now, that in times of uncertainty people tend to interpret events according to one of the oldest questions we know, "What about me?" Morris was worried about his personal reputation and creditworthiness being dragged down by his work for America. Washington was worried about his army being misused in the struggle between the states and Congress over the states' refusal to pay what they had promised. State interests worried about their sovereign power, and they held onto their money, thus precipitating the whole problem. When the states answered the question, "What about me?" they responded, "We're innocent, it was the other fellow." In keeping with the nature of political debate the State Power interests were quick to point the finger at Morris. It was easier to cast blame on a highly visible individual like Morris, who used the press to scold the states for irresponsibility, than to take the blame themselves, especially because they nominally represented the will of the people. So, Morris was cast as a despot trying to use the terror of a mutinous army to increase his political power. That was a much more sensational and politically popular posture than admitting your state had failed to support its own people during the war. Morris never relented in informing the population on the low level of contributions from the states with such statements as, "The publications of nothing must however continue until the cause of them be removed."[73]

This redirection of blame was successful with people who were predisposed to support the Agricultural Interests or State Power faction. The work of the anonymous writer "Lucius" was published to support the State Power side. The true author of the "Lucius" letters is not known – and may not be the work of a single author, but the letters were all anti-nationalist in position, and often personal in nature. The editors of *The Robert Morris Papers* conclude,

> "...the Lucius letters of 1783 were commonly believed to have been inspired by him [Arthur Lee].[74]

This view was particularly held among Morris' defenders. Arthur Lee admired the publication of Lucius' letters so much he sent copies of the newspapers to his friend Samuel Adams in Boston.[75]

Morris did not publicly answer Lucius' letters, yet their contents displeased him mightily. On March 12th, 1783 he wrote in his office diary,

> ...and on this day also appeared a virulent attack on my public and private character signed by Lucius in the *Freemans Journal,* replete with the most infamous falsehoods. Assertions as base and infamous as envy and malignancy could suggest. I think I know the author and if my conjecture is right, he is of that baneful character which brings dishonor to those whom he means to befriend and the reverse to whom he opposes.[76]

Morris clearly believed in the power of the facts; and misunderstood the willingness of some historians to look anywhere for material to support their foregone conclusions.

Without giving Lucius more attention than he deserves, it is good to know the tone and some of the content of his letters because they appealed to Morris' opposites and provide a sampling of their political thought. Lucius implied Morris was involved in fomenting the "Newburgh Conspiracy."[77] He attacked Morris for ruining America's credit by offering his resignation and for defaming Congress. He attacked Morris for speculating in government securities, even though there has never been any proof for this claim. He accused Morris of threatening "...vengeance upon authors that write with the freedom of Lucius."[78] He never did. Lucius used Morris' letter to the President of Congress when he accused Morris of using the war to enrich himself at the expense of his fellow citizens, when in fact Morris had extended credit of hundreds of thousands in 1780's dollars to the US. He accused Morris of "rotting in Asiatic luxury," and being surrounded by "the incense and adulation of surrounding parasites" while others could

> ...hardly purchase the crumbs which fall from your luxurious table.

He scolded Morris for

> ...rotting in voluptuousness, gorged with honors, profits, patronage, and emoluments.[79]

So it was with such putrid language that Lucius painted the image of Robert Morris, and moved forward the agenda of the State Power faction to disintegrate the United States. While Lucius railed against the "parasites" in Morris' command, and railed against his power to fill positions with patronage, the actual civil list shows[80] that Morris had fired over 150 officers in the old Treasury Board, yet he conducted the whole national business with sixty-three, less than half the former number. There were ten people in the Office of Finance (including Morris), three in the Marine Agency, twelve tax receivers, and thirty-eight men in the Treasury, including all the commissioners appointed for settling state and department accounts.

These vivid words portraying Morris as a voluptuary may have alerted him to the idea that his critics in Congress would use this false image as an excuse not to cover his notes, once he left the Office of Finance. Congress did eventually renege on America's commitment to repay the United States loans to France;[81] they allowed Silas Deane and Dumas to go unpaid and fall into poverty, and years later the Jefferson administration financially ruined Federalist, Arthur St. Clair, by making him personally responsible for government expenditures in the Northwest Territory. Clearly Morris was wise to stay in office until he covered his commitments.

Lucius also included a kind of threat towards Morris. It was a threat that struck at Morris' humble origins and demonstrated Lucius' aristocratic nature,

> Remember sir, what your were and think what you may be. This admonition is the salutary admonition of a friend. There was a time, sir, and it is not long past, when you were compelled to atone, not only to Congress, but to individuals, by the most abject submission, for the injurious insolence of your conduct. Beware of similar humiliation.[82]

Whether the mention of atonement was a reference to Morris' apology for the conduct of his brother six years earlier or not, one might consider the chain of events that lead to Morris' ultimate fate in the light of this threat from persons unknown.

Always quick to point a finger, Arthur Lee picked up Lucius' points and suggested that Robert Morris was using the "terror of a mutinying Army" to obtain permanent funds for Congress. Morris was put in the position of having to make a denial of any intent to raise *"civil Commotions"* in a letter to Washington.[83] While the focus of many has been on the Office of Finance, few seem to have noticed that Major John Armstrong, who wrote the letters behind the "Newburgh Conspiracy," was embraced by the "Constitutionalists" in the Pennsylvania Assembly and given the job of Secretary of the Executive Council when he returned from the camp. These were the same "Constitutionalists" who had troubled Morris and his allies for years. Armstrong was given a position similar to that the "Constitutionalists" had given Thomas Paine when he was writing articles they liked.

Spring

Before the peace was signed, Jefferson arrived in Philadelphia, and was getting ready to join the Peace Commissioners in Paris. He intended to leave for Europe in a style befitting his position. "He wore a long waisted white cloth coat, scarlet breeches and vest, a cocked hat, with a black cockade."[84] This was a more authentic ensemble for him than the one he later wore in 1803 and again in 1805 as President when, to prove his Republican *bona fides,* he met the British and then the Tunisian Ambassador in sloppy old clothes and ragged slippers. To fill out the voyage to France, David S. Franks, who had been so helpful to Franklin and Jay, was prepared to travel with him. They expected to travel on the *Romulus,* but the ship was caught in the twin grips of the remaining river ice and the British blockade. Jefferson was so delayed in Baltimore that the peace was signed without him. Consequently, Congress canceled his mission, and his $11,000 annual salary. Morris' salary was $8,000. A year later, on March 5th, 1784 Jefferson's Congressional committee reviewed the civil list and suggested that the Superintendent of Finance be paid only $2,000.

The work of the Office of Finance continued despite the background noise from Lucius and others. Dr. Franklin wrote about the last loan from France, and added a thought which touched on the work of the Lee-Adams faction as it played out in Europe,

> I hope the ravings of a certain mischievous madman here against the French and its ministers, which we hear of every day, will not be regarded in America…[85]

Morris kept up his efforts to move forward the business of his office, with some success. He kept in contact with his network of state tax receivers. However, he was experiencing delays in installing the nominated commissioner of accounts in North Carolina. It was not until 1785 that one was eventually installed. By that time the state had assumed almost all of the debt, thus mooting the effort. In a separate matter, Morris met with Haym Salomon and advanced the de Mars litigation to protect the broker. He also kept the pressure on George Eddy, who could not seem to finish the tobacco deal in New York.

When Morris was at his political weakest, in early March 1783, Congress finally responded to his July 1782 report wherein Morris had asked Congress to vest in itself the authority to collect taxes. Their response made it clear that no matter what efforts were undertaken by Morris' allies in Congress, Congress was only willing to get the states to enact a weakened impost and reevaluate state contributions. Congress was moving away from the idea of centralized taxation and to back state funding plans. Morris' reply to this anemic effort sounded familiar themes: The creditors deserve Justice. The Congress must have the ability to collect revenues to pay for debts it incurs. The states have proven themselves unsuitable to the task of remitting money to Congress. He also urged the settling of accounts with the states.[86] To a man with one foot out of the door it must have seemed like yelling at the tide.

On March 17th Morris wrote the President of Congress to inform him that before his resignation, it was learned that the loan from Holland had not lived up to the hopes Adams had held. Only half the expected amount was forthcoming. He went on to detail that the French loan, that had arrived with the Peace Treaty, when added to the Dutch loan, would only cover the current expenses including the Army's one month's pay and their food. He did not dwell on the sorry state of taxation; but faulted himself for not coming up with plans that were more widely adopted, and hoped abler minds might be put to the task. He derided his critics and put his faith in Congress' true knowledge of the situation. He finished,

> I knew that until some plan and rational system should be adopted and acceded to the business of this office would be a business of expedient and chicane. I have neither the talents nor the disposition to engage in such business and therefore I pray to be dismissed.[87]

Reaction to the gradual payment scheme, with the one month's pay offer, started to come in from the Southern Department. General Greene wrote,

> ... many of the principal officers of this Army are on opinion it will be rather disgusting than pleasing to the troops. They think it will be treating the men too much like slaves. That the men have a right to expect and demand a different mode.[88]

He also mentioned that the Southern states were disinclined to adopt Congress' approach because

> Too many appear to be impressed with an idea that most of the public arrangements are made in favor of Pennsylvania.[89]

It appeared that the best Congress would do was not good enough.

All the while, worthy supplicants stood in line at the Office of Finance for non-existent money. One Lieutenant Thomas Liston's South Carolina unit was disbanded. He had been held prisoner, was left destitute, and he applied for help. Morris wrote,

> That the claim of the Memorialist [Liston] to Pay due to him appears to be just and that in common with all others having such Claims upon the United States he ought to be paid. But that there are no funds for the purpose.... That altho the memorialist appears to be in very distressing circumstance which is unfortunately the case with many others. And although he only asks a part of what is due to him, Yet the Prayer of his Memorial cannot be complied with.[90]

Distress in the Army was not limited to the soldiers. Washington wrote asking how he could pay his expenses when the local people in New York State would not take the subsistence notes.[91] The money hunt continued.

The long planned for effort to bring in Spanish silver was still underway. Captain Barry joined Captain Brown in Havana, where he was given his secret orders. The two of them were able to convert bills of exchange on public account and put $72,477 in public money into the holds of the *Alliance* and *Duc de Lauzun.* The ships had to wait for two weeks in the Havana harbor until their convoy was arranged with the Spanish fleet. The Americans sailed with that fleet on March 6th and then went their separate way. While en route, they came under attack by the British, but with the help of the French warship *Triton* both American ships survived what has been called the last sea battle of the Revolution. Then it was decided to transfer all the silver to the *Alliance* because the *Duc de Lauzun* was slow and not made for war. The ships became separated in a dense fog on their voyage back. The *Duc de Lauzun* found her way to the Delaware Cape. The *Alliance* finally arrived in Narragansett Bay on March 20th. After the *Duc de Lauzun* arrived in Philadelphia there were complaints that Captain Brown had shipped too much under his captain's privilege. An investigation ensued.

Finally, on March 25th, 1783, after the safe arrival of the silver, and in accordance with the arrival of the peace treaty, Congress spoke, and Robert Morris, as Agent of Marine, recalled the fleet.

> To all Captains, Commanders, Masters and other officers of armed vessels, commissioned by the United States in Congress assembled, and to all others whom it shall or may in any wise concern:

> According to the orders of the United States in Congress unto me given on the 24th day of this present month of March, I do hereby recall all armed vessels cruising under commissions from the United States of America, whereof you will please to take notice. Done in the Marine Office of the United States of America, this twenty-fifth day of March, in the Year of our Lord, one thousand seven hundred and eighty-three.[92]

Morris had observed the supposed controversies over "Captain's privilege" and acted to protect other members of his team from political troubles. Ever vigilant, Arthur Lee complained that John Swanwick's position in the Office of Finance was not approved on the Congressional civil list, Morris asked the Treasurer to determine his pay so Morris would avoid the appearance of improperly employing him.[93] In the business of protecting Salomon, Mr. de Mars awaited trial for his role in defrauding Haym Salomon, and he did so from prison under Morris' orders. Morris attended the trial of de Mars vs. Salomon in April, which Salomon won. Morris directed Salomon to demand immediate payment from de Mars.[94]

Now that the Revolution was nearly officially over, members of the Office of Finance started to look towards their futures as private citizens. Robert entered into his first private contract since the time he took public office. Robert Morris and Gouverneur Morris entered into a land speculation agreement with John Vaughan, a member of a prominent English Family, who had bought Charles Lee's property.[95] They were unable to secure the funds needed, but Robert was not deterred from making even more spectacular plans later on in his career. Sensing other opportunities, English trading partners started to approach Swanwick in his capacity as Morris' clerk for private business.[96]

It was too early for Morris to focus exclusively on private matters. Recalling the fleet wasn't enough to end marine business. The Spanish Governors of Louisiana and Cuba complained to Morris, as Agent of Marine, about an American privateer who had taken a brigantine, which they argued, was Spanish, not English. The matter went to a Massachusetts state court and became an example of the interference individual states may exert in international affairs.[97] Morris collected information on the matter of Captain Brown's conduct. He arranged to have the *Alliance* repaired and ready for sea.[98] Then he moved forward to appoint a commissioner to settle the accounts of the Marine Department,[99] and to further reduce expenses by selling the ship *Duc de Lauzun*. With an eye to the future,

Hamilton contacted Morris and asked him if he would participate in the formation of a new Naval Department. Morris declined the offer; pointing out that he was trying to leave government service, not join a new one.

The juggling of priorities was never ending. News of peace had a positive effect on the price of bills of exchange in Boston. Morris offered to repay some of the money loaned by Ross and Bingham, but neither accepted the rates.[100] He arranged for payments to the secret service. He worked to get payment to the soldiers, using some of the money brought back from Havana for that purpose.[101] He contacted the Clothier General and requested shutting down the effort to clothe the troops. The matter of the two Indian boys came up once again. Colonel Morgan wanted payment for clothing worn by the three Indian boys in his care. Morris sent them down to Congress with a note for Congress to assist them, but to their disgrace, Congress took no action.[102]

As part of his effort to wrap up the duties of his office, Morris insisted the Quartermaster, Timothy Pickering, submit a settlement of his accounts. Pickering was unprepared for such a massive undertaking. He had been in the service for seven years, and he said,

> I see that the final settlement of the numerous and intensive accounts of my department, scattered from one end of the continent to another, will but be accomplished in six – perhaps twelve months.[103]

Pickering went on to explain his embarrassed financial condition, and that he had owed his friends $1,900 for the support of his family, and so sold off his family's land to pay his creditors. After reading the letters from Timothy Pickering, Morris offered to pay him $5,000 for his past service as a member of the board of war, due to him since 1781. This was possible because that payment was payable from the civil list under Morris' control. Pickering answered,

> ... while I receive the benefits of your indulgence, I wish it to be the least possible inconvenience to you ...[104]

In sharp contrast to Pickering's behavior, Pierre Landais, was able to convince the Treasurer that he was owed nearly 15,000 livres, or about $3,000. Morris authorized him to draw a bill of exchange for that amount. Landais refused the offer and held out for more.[105]

Morris tried to finish his commitments to his home state. On April 1st he transferred the shares in the Bank of North America to the State of Pennsylvania to pay a debt due from the Office of Finance to Pennsylvania from Morris' tenure as Agent of Pennsylvania.[106] Finally, on the positive side, after much delay and engineering, the very first coin struck as American Coin was delivered by Mr. Dudley to Morris' office on April 2nd, 1783,[107] and sent to the Congress for approval.[108]

The English in New York received news of the peace on April 5th and contacted the head of foreign affairs, Livingston, in Philadelphia. Livingston drafted a proclamation and asked Morris to make it public.[109] Morris deferred to Livingston who announced the

> ... cessation of arms, as well by sea as by land, agreed upon between the United States of America and his Britannic Majesty, and enjoining the observance thereof.[110]

Congress passed this on April 11th, 1783 and the war was over.

As soon as the war was over, worries shifted from keeping men in the field, to getting them home with money in their pockets, and by doing so avoid mutiny and disorder. Uncertainty settled upon the Southern Army as the date of Morris' resignation neared. General Greene wrote,

> Every mind seems to be impressed with the most awful consequence. The doubts upon war and peace, the hopes and fears in mattes of revenue, the discontents of the army and the consequences [of] all that these may produce upon our domestic policy, and in the measures of British administration, fills every mind who feels for the tranquility of this country with no small anxiety.[111]

Morris was still present and trying to move his plan forward as a way of keeping the peace without foreign intervention. He wrote the tax receivers that eventually,

> Surely the pride and good sense of the people will combine in stimulating them to exert themselves so as to stand on their own feet and not owe a support to the precarious bounty of foreign powers.[112]

He was always an optimist.

The Southern Army was not alone in its quandary. Morris could not pay and support the soldiers at the same time, because he did not have enough money in the treasury. Congress was unsure if they could convince Morris to stay in office, or even if they wanted to. The group that was least unsure was the one that should have been the most worried. Those who supported greater sovereignty for the states felt that the weakness of Congressional authority would only benefit them. They did not foresee that the growth of their power would lead to economic dislocation, European intrigues, riot and insurrection. Only the hard lessons of experience would teach them.

Morris informed Congress that it would cost $750,000 to provide the Army with the three months' pay deemed *"indispensable"* by General Washington. He continued that, since such a sum was neither forthcoming from the states, nor available through the sale of government property, it was therefore only possible through a "large paper anticipation." Meaning, notes payable in the future should be given to each soldier instead of the three months' salary in hard money. Morris offered his own notes for the task. He went on,

> In issuing my notes to the required amount it would be necessary that I should give an express assurance of payment: and in doing so I should be answerable personally for about half a million [$500,000] when I leave this office and depend on the arrangements of those who come after to save me from ruin.[113]

Clearly Morris was not interested in being ruined in return for his service to the country, and he mentioned that it would take time to make this plan work.

With an eye to the future, Morris made an effort to build a new life in private enterprise. He contacted the Baring brothers in England, and told them he had been a silent partner with Samuel Inglis and Co. He wanted the Barings to consider doing business with that firm. One of these brothers, John Baring, went on to found Barings Bank, which in the 1790's helped Bingham finance the separation of Maine from Massachusetts, but also figured prominently in Morris' financial difficulties. In 1783, however, the opportunity to ship great quantities of Maryland tobacco presented itself.

Morris Reconsiders

Captain Barney, who had brought the peace treaty from France, was accused, by detractors, of bringing back too much under "Captain's Privilege." Morris asked him about that.[114] Oddly, these detractors were nowhere to be found when Arthur Lee brought back a large amount of baggage upon his return from France with Captain Landais aboard the *Alliance.* However, in keeping with the new trend to question all things

Naval, Theodorik Bland took a page from his friend Dr. Lee's book, and wrote Morris questioning the authority under which Morris had acquired the *Duc de Lauzun.*[115] This step was very similar to the tactic used by Arthur Lee in France when Lee complained about Silas Deane's acquisition of ships during the Lee-Deane affair in 1777.[116] The use of this familiar tactic gave new depth to Lucius' threat to humble Morris.[117]

Morris replied to Congressman Bland that he found it impossible to get funds by selling bills of exchange in American markets and needed to get money to do his job. It was for that reason he acquired the *Duc de Lauzun* as a vessel for secret missions to Cuba in search of silver. He wrote

> ... it was necessary to have a ship belonging to the public because it was necessary that she should wait both the Event of the operation and until Convoy arrived as also that she should be kept in order for Sailing without taking on Board a Cargo as is the practice of common Merchantmen and above all it was necessary to keep the operation secret.

He emphasized that by saying the whole business had to be secret, otherwise the bills could not have been sold because an agent from the other side would have discredited the bills of exchange before they could have been converted in Cuba.[118]

Fortunately for Morris, the French minister wanted to use the *Duc de Lauzun* to transport the French troops in their exit from America. He offered to sell the ship in Europe and credit the account of the United States.[119] Converting a ship that had become a political liability into a debt repayment would have been a helpful step, considering Morris' critics in Congress. He agreed to this arrangement.

Morris planned to put the tiny navy to work again, because the time had come for the United States to make an interest payment on the Dutch loan. He made arrangements to use American tobacco for a debt payment. He contacted the same buyer in Virginia, with whom he had worked during the Virginia tobacco deal, to purchase five hundred hogsheads of tobacco, and he notified John Barry to ready the *Alliance* for the trip. He trusted the Dutch creditors to sell the tobacco, and to send the money in excess of the interest payment to America's banker in Paris.[120]

Marine Department matters continued to demand Morris' time. He wanted to conclude the matter of Captain's privilege in the Navy. He was finally able to review the records of the shipment from Havana, and the shipment from Paris. He was annoyed to find that both Captain Barry and Captain Green, respectively, had taken excessive advantage of the "Captain's privilege" and told them they had to submit to arbitration to determine the freight they should pay.[121] Morris sent a letter to Congress asking them to determine whether captains could exercise this privilege, which was common on private ships, and not mentioned in any Continental Naval regulation at the time. This issue in the navy was clearly driven by factional differences. Gouverneur Morris observed the growth in partisanship and wrote Ridley,

> We are as is usual in free Governments immerging into party as we emerge from danger.[122]

General Greene was also well aware of the growth and effect of "party politics" in an appeal he made to Morris not to leave office. He wrote,

> But low jealousy and mean suspicion mingles too strongly in private life and public measures as to leave little room to hope for any radical cure to our political evils or reform from the public confusion and injustice which prevails. But where is the man that can conduct this business to the same advantage you can; and we must not desert our country.... Never forsake unfinished what you have so nobly attempted.... Let people say what they will candor will oblige them to confess you gave them the clue which has brought order out of confusion...[123]

Morris replied,

> Sir: I received the other day your letter of the 2d of February last, and am very much obliged both by the pains you have taken and the sentiments you have expressed in favor of a department which I shall shortly be obliged to abandon. You will before this reaches you have seen in the newspapers my letters of resignation. I shall not, therefore, go into a detail of the reasons for taking that step, which was as painful to me as you can easily conceive. But I had no alternative. I saw clearly that, while it was asserted on all hands our debts ought to be paid, no efficient measures would be adopted for the purpose; no good plan agreed on. I felt the consequences of my resignation on the public credit; I felt the probable derangement of our affairs; I felt the difficulties my successor would have to encounter, but still I felt that above all things it was my duty to be honest. This first and highest principle has been obeyed. I do not hold myself answerable for consequences. Those are to be attributed to the opposers of just measures, let their rank and station be what

> they may. I expect much obloquy for my conduct, because this is what I knew to be the reward for any conduct whatever which is right. To slander I am indifferent, and still more indifferent about the attempts to question the services I have rendered, but I feel most sensibly for your situation and for that of every other officer.
>
> The Congress have now, and have long since had under their consideration a due provision for the public debts; when they will conclude it, and what it will be, God only knows. If it is such as in my opinion will do justice, I shall stay somewhat longer in office to know the decisions of the States, and if their proceedings are what on such an occasion they ought to be, I shall spare no labor and regret no time in completing the business, so that my successor may receive it from my hands as clear and simple as it was confused and embarrassed when it was undertaken. But if these things do not happen, you and every other good man will, I hope, acquit me for leaving a post in which I am totally unsupported, and where I must be daily the witness to scenes of poignant anguish and deep injustice without the possibility of administering either relief or palliation. While I do continue in office rely on every support in my power, and always, whether a public or private man, believe in my esteem and affection. I am, very respectfully, &c.,Robert Morris[124]

A Congressional committee met with Morris in late April on the subject of his resignation. Morris said that the state of American credit in Europe had to be considered, and he made no more commitment. His investigation into the state of American finances revealed that the current loans would only cover current expenses, and that meant the offer to supply the Army three months' pay was not funded. In response to Morris' proposal that Congress devise a plan to secure a stream of revenue, Congress developed the "System of General Revenue" funding plan, which they recommended to the states on April 18th, 1783. This system was as ineffectual as earlier voluntary systems recommended by Congress. Regrettably, it was adopted. After operating under this plan for several years Congress agreed with what Morris had said all along when, in 1786, they observed,

> In the course of this enquiry it most clearly appeared, that the requisitions of Congress for eight years past have been so irregular in their operation, so uncertain in their collection, and so evidently unproductive, that a reliance on them in future, as a source from whence monies are to be drawn, to discharge the engagements of the confederacy, definite as they are in time and amount, would be

> not less dishonorable to the understandings of those, who entertain such confidence, than it would be dangerous to the welfare and peace of the union.[125]

Shortly after Congress passed their 1783 idea of a funding plan, Morris met with the same committee of Congress that had asked him to reconsider his resignation. The topic of paying the Army was one of the issues. He said he supported the idea of disbanding the Army, now that he had arranged to give them his notes. He offered to stay in office until those notes were covered.

He wrote,

> ...that no man can be better disposed that I am to satisfy the army or more desirous of serving our country but that my own affairs call loudly for my care and attention &ca. however being already engaged in this business and willing to oblige congress if they think my assistance essential I will consent to remain in office for the purpose of completing such payment to the Army as may be agreed on as necessary to disband them with their own consent &ca. [etc.] but praying of Congress to excuse me from even this service if they can accomplish their views in such other way as they may approve.[126]

He placed a condition on staying. He wanted Congress to pledge to support his efforts. He wanted a vote of confidence. The committee withdrew.

The official minutes from that meeting with the Congressional committee came to Morris' attention. He was not pleased to see that his offer to stay in office was noted incorrectly. He contacted Mr. Osgood "that they had misconstrued my sentiments." Osgood agreed to have Morris' corrections entered into the record.

While Morris negotiated with Congress for support, Lucius made his opinion clear in the press. Making plain the attitudes of the landed elite, he allowed that Morris was an able accountant, and a successful merchant. He continued to address Morris from the pages of the newspaper. His words dripped with arrogant condescension,

> ... but from whence, in your confined sphere of education and of action, you could have drawn that liberal, vast, and extensive knowledge of the interests of nations, and the most approved systems or taxation, or the various sources of revenue, and the productive powers of the state, all which, together with a mature and able judgment, are necessary to constitute a capable financier; was to me utterly incomprehensible.[127]

Implicit in this was a condemnation of Morris' background and lack of formal education. In his own way Lucius told the world that someone of Morris' class was simply unacceptable in a position of leadership.

The discussions over Morris' incumbency went on. The Congressional committee went back to Morris to convince him to stay in office. Morris noted in his official diary they wanted him to stay

> ...until the Army were disbanded and Peace arrangements take place &c. To all their arguments I opposed my observations on the conduct of Congress towards me; and I wish for nothing so much as to be relieved from the cursed scene of drudgery and vexation.[128]

The resulting report of the committee did little more than grant him permission to hold his office; and did not include any pledge by Congress to support his efforts. This pledge was Morris' condition of continuation, not to mention that he did not seek permission to keep an office of "drudgery and vexation." Congress refused to acknowledge that they had asked him to stay so they could continue to rely on his skills, contacts and credit. To the degree that Lucius' letters displayed the attitudes of Morris' critics in Congress, it was clear why it was politically impossible for the whole Congress to admit the obvious.

At this moment, Morris' old enemy, Arthur Lee, took it upon himself to cast Robert in the most despicable light. He wrote to Samuel Adams:

> The resignation of Mr. Morris, & the manner of it are a great shock to public credit. At bottom it is certainly a maneuver to force the system of funding upon the States, in which Mr. Morris & his friends are so deeply interested as to hazard the destruction of this Country, rather than not realize the immense wealth, which large purchases of Loan Office Certificates [certificates that Lee had just recently turned in for bills of exchange] at an infinitely low depreciation, has offered to their hopes. I hope the good sense & discernment of the Public will see this factious measure in its true light. This only can prevent its malignant operation here; but abroad the full mischief of it must be felt, & I fear will put an insurmountable bar in the way of Loans, upon which only we depend. This Morris could not be ignorant of, & therefore the injury done is a deliberate Act, & deserves exemplary punishment.[129]

Arthur Lee said that Morris' friends were "deeply interested" in the funding system, and they were because they had extended their own money and wanted to be repaid; something that seemed to be an anathema to Lee, just as he was against repaying Beaumarchais. Like any good partisan, Lee mixed a bit of truth in with a batch of confusion, and he was particularly adept at reversing cause with effect.

While he talked to Congress about his future role, Morris was still in office and working to accomplish his goal, which required the passage of the 1783 Impost to provide funding for the Continental debt. In its support he wrote,

> I know not what representations or misrepresentations are made with respect to my conduct, but I know that my greatest enemy [A. Lee] having had an opportunity fully to investigate it has not been able to shew any color of impropriety. If my own reputation alone was concerned I should be totally indifferent but it is extremely painful to think that the publick service should be injured by personal malice.[130]

Morris had faced these forces for years. Now the difference was the fact that he no longer thought he would be able to meet his obligations. Other than that, the pressures on Morris to withdraw from public office were not obvious. It would be easy to conclude that he was simply tired of the abuse, or that he was just trying to save his reputation. However, he had much to risk by leaving, because there was no reason to believe the Continental Congress would protect him from the financial exposure he had. He often wrote about the personal toll of the job, and the pressing nature of his private affairs that he had left unattended so long. However, the exact nature of these pressures can only be surmised. He had left the business of running his various shipping firms in the hands of others. It was not exactly a blind trust, but clearly Morris put trusted people in charge so he could conduct the business of the Office of Finance. Prominent among the concerns directly affecting Morris was Holker's effort to force him to settle accounts with him, accounts that covered their mutual private business arrangements. Holker had been pressing Morris for almost five months, and Morris did not have time to attend to his request. At the same time the French crown was pressuring Holker for a settlement of his work for the Royal Marine.

An opposing pressure came from his old friend George Washington and General Green, who together symbolized a suffering Army. Washington was disappointed to hear of Morris' resignation. They had both been in the war effort from start to treaty, and Washington had grown to rely on Morris' ability to do the impossible when it was necessary. There was also a very real possibility that the contractors Morris had arranged for the Army would simply abandon their work once Morris was gone. This would leave the Army without any means of survival, which might well lead to riot and insurrection by experienced soldiers. In addition, there was Morris' connection with the Bank of North America and the United States' unpaid debts there. Finally, there was that matter of the promised Morris Notes that were soon to be in the hands of soldiers all over the various states.

The Bank, his friends, his contracting system, and his money all pulled him back into Government service, but only if Congress would support his work, and limit it to settling the business of his time in office. He had exposed himself to a huge liability because the Congress had been unable to provide for its own funding, funding he had supported many times over with his notes. Even so, Congress had misrepresented his meetings with its committees, and withheld support. When he wrote Congress on the status of his office he said, "I had a right to expect Congress would pledge themselves for my support, when I have entered into such deep engagements for theirs." Congress had not provided a resolution of support by May 1st and he told them

> I must add that under the resolution in its present form I cannot stay.[131]

There were many reasons that Congress was slow to act on Morris' vote of confidence. A positive vote would mean they supported the funding proposals Morris had submitted. More broadly however, the same old arguments, made since 1777, about the respective roles of the Continental Congress and the states had never been settled. This lack of resolution allowed all to gloss over their differences and proceed toward the common goal of defeating the British. However, there was no principled decision to guide matters in peacetime, so events took over and forced action. The people who were not in favor of a permanent standing army figured peace was at hand so the Army would soon disband and go home. They also thought that by funding a standing Army they would create a potential threat to the new civilian government; ironically the resulting mutinies prove that they nearly caused what they feared most.

There were two more meetings with the Congressional Committee, and on May 3rd Morris reconsidered,

> I find all my friends so extremely anxious on this subject that I have considered it maturely and as Congress have pledged themselves to support me and to enable me to fulfill all engagements taken on

> public account, I have concluded to continue so much longer as may be necessary to disband the Army and fulfill my Engagements already taken as well as those to be made for the above purposes.[132]

He wrote the President of Congress,

> ...the affairs of the Marine Department occupy more time and attention than I can easily spare. This Department will now become important, and I hope extensive.[133]

He asked that a full time Agent of Marine be appointed in his place.

Morris had a series of conferences with his allies inside and out of Congress before his announcement was made final. On May 3rd Morris announced he would stay in office. It is generally considered that he stayed to fulfill his existing engagements, and that meant figuring out a way to cover his financial exposure, however it is not hard to see from his letters that he had the future of a nation in mind as well. He was resolute in his conviction that his financial system would lead to the formation of a Just nation, but he was not sure how long it would take for the rest of the Continental leadership to come to the same conclusion.

It had been some years since 1781, when he had been installed with a unanimous vote of Congress. The make-up of Congress had changed dramatically. Shooting had stopped and the final peace treaty was expected to be ratified by Congress. Unfortunately, the bills had yet to be paid. Debts were owed to thousands of Americans, and Morris needed Congress to step forward and commit to support the development of a national financial system that, up to that point, had been based on his personal credit, and future promises of bulk commodities. This was the reason he insisted on a "vote of confidence" from Congress, before he went ahead and took an even greater personal financial risk by signing hundreds of thousands in notes that were to be used to pay the Continental Army. If Congress failed to secure funding from other sources, he was going to be personally responsible for those notes. He went forward as he tried to arrange his support system.

Morris may have been thinking about leaving office, but he was not about to give up on his project of creating the United States Mint. He took the sample coins created by Dudley and forwarded them to the President of Congress. Meanwhile, the work of selling the idea of a national system of coinage was underway. Gouverneur explained the plan to Congressman Hemsley wherein he detailed that the current Spanish dollar contained

365 grains of silver, while the old Spanish dollar had 3% more silver at 376 grains. Since both old and new dollars were in use in America, he went into great detail on the importance of reaching a common denominator that would allow the old and new dollars to fit in with the various state currencies. That common denominator was 1/1440. He then used that number as the basis for the coinage, but no one ever proposed an actual coin of that value. Instead, the new coin proposed by the office of finance was worth 25 grains of silver for the lowest valued silver coin, 250 grains for the second, and 2500 for the next highest, thus creating a decimal proportion between them at 1, 10, 100, and 1000, and finally using a 10,000 version as a gold coin.[134] The coins of the lowest two values were coppers. It would take years before Congress agreed to a national currency and to funding the mint.

The Navy, the impost, debt assumption, and Morris' national economic program were seen by the states as unwanted intrusions into their rights. While Morris saw his job as national in scope and worked to strengthen the bonds that held the states together, the states sought to weaken them. While Morris was familiar with international relations, state governors were used to near horizons surrounding a homogeneous group of interests. It took years of uncertainty and a constitutional convention to resolve the conflicting ideas around statehood and nationhood. The arguments of record on the ratification of the Constitution reflect the forces with which Morris had to contend during his tenure as Superintendent of Finance. In the meantime Morris continued to work towards making the United States into a nation. Consider the image of a foundry where the blacksmith hammers different pieces of metal together in the forge. In this case Morris is the blacksmith, the metal is the states, and the forge is the fire of debt and dissolution. In the years 1781 to 1784 the fire just wasn't hot enough to make the pieces stick. It is not difficult to understand why Morris' tone changed after these events. He became a bit harsher in correspondence. He was less generous in spirit toward those who opposed him, and he became far less active in proposing new solutions. In short, he kept the office open and worked to reward an army that had served the nation, but he was not looking for new challenges. He wished for the day when he could make sure his notes were covered, and he could get back to private life.

As Morris was laboring to wind up the business of the Office of Finance, there were a number of matters to be dealt with: feeding the Army, paying the soldiers, selling off the ships, closing the hospitals, settling the prisoner of war issues, administering naval justice, covering the loans, settling the state debts, raising revenue, and opening trade with other nations. In addition, Morris looked for personal business opportunities. He had the ability to do this throughout his administration, but he waited until after the question of his resignation was settled before he acted to any great degree.

His first responsibility, however, was to his country. Others had different priorities, and the business of collecting funds from the states moved slowly. In May 1783, Virginia made its first payment towards the requisition of 1782. Morris had to return $140 as counterfeit.[135] His tax receivers were anxious that once he left office they would no longer be paid; and were ready to quit if he did. Congress never addressed their pay, so Morris told them to take their pay directly from the taxes collected.[136] They got paid, but this did not please the Congress and the issue remained unsettled until Hamilton's time in Treasury some eight years later.

Morris picked up all the financial threads he could find. He put John Barry in charge of the slow work of fixing the *Alliance,* so he could carry tobacco to the Dutch and pay the interest on the Dutch loan. Morris later arranged for the conversion of Virginia taxes into the Virginia tobacco that was to be shipped to Holland, and for insurance to cover the risk of the voyage.[137]

He approached the French minister for a loan from the money the French Army was keeping in America.[138] He contacted his French banker to tell him about the money gained from the sale of the *Duc de Lauzun* and instructed him to apply that to bills that he expected to arrive from America.[139] He wrote again to inform that Henry Laurens' friend, Commodore Gillon of the South Carolina Navy, had left large debts in Europe, and that South Carolina was responsible for them. This meant that an American ally who had trusted Gillon, Monsr. De Luxemborgh, was left with nothing more than recourse through South Carolina courts.[140] Congressional action had limited the size of the navy, but Morris had to provide transportation for General Greene's Southern Army back to the middle states. In mid-May he advertised for the transportation contract.[141]

Morris met with the Secretary of War about disbanding the Army, and they wrote a joint letter to Congress to learn Congress' disposition on the topic.[142] He sent a very different letter to the Continental Agent of Rhode Island. Post office officials there wanted repayment for their outlays in that state. Morris agreed to repay them even though they were supposed to be repaid from Post office profits. He did this because "according to the

Confederation it is to yield no Revenue." Obviously, no organization can pay expenses from profits that don't exist.

The old business of unfunded Congressional bills of exchange drawn in 1779 continued to linger in Morris' office. He wrote to Adams that he could not get reliable information from Congress on the topic.[143] He mentioned to Thomas Barclay that such Congressional actions were making his department difficult to manage,

> The Bills drawn by order of Congress as a long sight on their ministers as well in Spain and Holland as in France have involved the affairs of my department in a labyrinth of confusion from which I cannot extricate them and I very much fear that many of these bills will have been paid twice.[144]

If this turned out to be true it would unjustly enriched one party and leave others without funds.

Well-known individuals moved their private cases forward. Oliver Pollock busied himself with trips to Congress and Morris' office in his effort to be repaid for his early contributions to the War effort.[145] Pollock asked Morris to apply to Congress on his behalf so he might become the Continental Agent at Havana.[146] Morris paid half of Haym Salomon's legal bill.[147] Though his work was done, Thomas Paine considered himself uniquely deserving and continued to apply to Morris for funds.[148]

The Pennsylvania comptroller, John Nicholson, pressed Morris for more payments in silver for the aborted effort to defend western Pennsylvania in September 1782. Morris' office had pledged funds in hard money under duress, when it seemed an attack was likely. Once the danger receded Morris attempted to convert that pledge into a payment with the Pennsylvania currency the state had given Morris, as Agent of Pennsylvania, for use in the purchase of specific supplies. Nicholson wanted the hard money instead.[149]

By this time, Daniel Parker was a prime contractor under Morris' army supply system. Parker told Washington that he would sell supplies to soldiers who chose to go home. He suggested that he would accept the soldiers' credit for the three months' pay certificates expected from the Financier, and he would supply goods from his storehouse. Parker was traveling back and forth between Washington's encampment and New York City in search of supplies when he was appointed by Washington to "help supervise the evacuation of British forces from New York."[150]

In New York, on May 5th, General Washington and Guy Carleton had a meeting about the British evacuation of the city of New York. It was during this meeting that Carleton revealed that the British were in the process of evacuating nearly six thousand Black loyalists who had been promised protection by the Crown of England.[151] Most of these Black Loyalists were former slaves who chose freedom in English territories after the war, instead of returning to bondage in America. Sir Guy Carleton took it as a point of honor to insure these people were not returned to places where they might be punished or killed.[152]

Word of Carleton's plans for the Black Loyalists in New York traveled to Philadelphia. There was heated discussion in Congress about this. Slaveholders were aghast that their "property" was being taken contrary to their understanding of the Peace Treaty. Carleton said that a registry was created; and compensation would be made.[153] Others were less concerned, and arguments in Congress resulted in no Congressional determination other than to insist on compensation. The Americans decided to send commissioners who would verify the contents of the registry. On May 8th Washington named Parker to an official commission to verify the exodus of Black Loyalists. Interviews with former slaveholders were conducted, and this process eventually resulted in the creation of the "Book of Negroes." It was signed by chief negotiator, Colonel Smith, and by Nathaniel Philips, Samuel Jones, Captain Wilbar Cook, Daniel Parker, and both William Armstrong and T. Gilfillan of the Quartermaster Corps, for the United States. Three thousand identified Black Loyalists whose names were entered into Sir Guy Carleton's book were transported to Nova Scotia, Quebec, and other parts of Canada. In July, George Plater, of Maryland, wrote to Gouverneur Morris about several of his slaves, who had left with the British, upon their evacuation from New York.

> I know not upon what pretext they detain them especially as the same treaty stipulates in express terms that no Negroes shall be carried away from the United States of America.[154]

Mr. Plater was well aware of the item slave trader, Henry Laurens, had inserted into the treaty, but would not get a satisfactory letter in return from Gouverneur, the abolitionist.

During the process of sending the Black Loyalists out of New York, Parker used his persuasive abilities to gain a contract to supply the British in Nova Scotia with 20,000 barrels of flour. Nova Scotia was a destination for many hundreds of the Black Loyalists who left America under British protection. The funds from this sale provided Parker with the means to buy the goods he exchanged for Morris notes given to him by individuals in the American Army. So, in this way, Parker's work in the exodus of the Black Loyalists paid for the supplies sold to American troops who headed home from camp. While Parker was in New York he was also actively working on a private project of great interest to Morris, developing the China Trade. He was reported to be in that city looking for ships to accomplish that venture. While Parker was there, he assisted General Carleton in breaking up a counterfeiting ring.[155] Morris noted,

> General Carleton's just proceedings on the occasion [of dealing with the counterfeiting ring] correspond with the opinion which his former conduct [in dealing with the Black Loyalists] had inspired.[156]

Morris had to focus on developments in Philadelphia. It was up to him to produce the physical notes that would go to the soldiers. On May 6th, Morris arranged for Benjamin Dudley to make five thousand sheets of specially watermarked paper in anticipation of their use as Morris Notes to pay the Army. The production of the notes was slow. The soldiers had to be fed and kept in camp in the meantime. They grew restless and wanted to go home, however the soldiers had decided not to leave the service until they were paid. The finances were so tight that there was only money to feed them or pay them, but not both. Washington's answer was to grant them furloughs. This way they were technically in the Army, but they did not have to be at camp.

The issue of disbanding the Army continued to be a topic of discussion in Philadelphia. On May 15th, after a meeting with members of Congress and the secretary of war Morris wrote,

> I opened the business and stated very fully the necessity of disbanding the army in order to get clear of an expense our resources were unequal to ... but which if continued any longer will consume the only means now left for making a payment to the Army when disbanded.[157]

By the middle of May there had been an expenditure of $1,096,386 for that year, and there had been only $259,682 in receipts for the same period.[158] The shortfall for the first five months in that year was $836,704. This did not include paying the troops, because that was yet to happen.

Also on May 15th, the Governor of Cuba was in Spain, and the acting Governor took a bold step. He reimposed trade restrictions in Cuba, and America lost trading rights there. Trade between the Spanish colony of Cuba and America had been opened as a war measure. Morris, Holker and their business associates, notably William Turnbull, had been busy in this trade. This allowed them to supply flour to the sugar cane plantations and opened the door to bringing home silver for the war effort. Once the war was over, Spain reverted to the pre-war conditions. Spanish representative, Rendón, assured Morris and the Congress that trade with Cuba was fine, as long as the Spanish Crown had not made an official statement. It was under that unofficial status that various American merchants conducted trade with Cuba. The kind of trade that developed, without sanction, began to take on the irregularity that Morris thought would "bring America into disrepute."[159] He sought to change that for the better.

Morris advanced the idea to Congress that Oliver Pollock should be made the American Agent of Council in Cuba. Morris wanted to encourage American trade with Cuba and thought that the reputation of Americans was worth protecting because, as he said

> ... if sentiments injurious to our national character should be imbibed it may operate to an exclusion from all commerce with that part of the Spanish dominions.[160]

Pollock's account with Virginia had been settled before he went, but there was still an open question. Did Spain see the $74,087 debt owed in New Orleans as a personal one due by Pollock, or was it a debt that was owed by America? Morris wrote to the Governor of Spanish Cuba for an answer. This had to be settled because the creditors were starting legal action against Pollock for non-payment of bills drawn on Penet, Virginia's agent in France.[161] Pollock wanted to go to Cuba, in any case.

While Pollock waited for an answer from Spain, events in the Army once again called Morris' attention. Quartermaster Pickering informed him that the owner of the land around the Army base in New York wanted payment for his fences, wood and use of the property. The owner suggested that payment might include keeping some of the buildings built by the Army during their stay.[162]

Morris tried to settle other matters of military expenses. He wrote General Greene in the Carolinas that he had no more funds, and that Greene should sell the public property he had and use that money to subsist the Army.[163] John Nicholson of Pennsylvania was still looking for hard money to be sent to the western part of the state, but Morris insisted the value of the uniforms already sent had to be deducted from the total Nicholson presented.[164] Ultimately, Morris had an assistant working on settlement of the account of the Pennsylvania Bank with Treasury, and he stated that if there were any payments to be made Morris would make sure they were.[165]

On May 21st the soldiers in Newburgh, New York, decided, with the urging of their paymasters, to trade their expected notes for goods and other considerations. Unfortunately, without official action on payment to the soldiers, these transactions took place at a significant discount. Almost a week later Congress, back in Philadelphia, resolved to furlough the soldiers who had enlisted for the whole war. They also instructed Washington and General Greene to send the troops home with supplies for their homeward journeys.

The next week, General Lincoln took Congress' furlough resolution from Philadelphia to Washington's Army. By the time he arrived, the camp was in disarray caused by friction between soldiers and officers. There was a swirl of speculation arising from the imminent arrival of the notes, and allegations about pressure placed on soldiers by regimental paymasters to make bad trades using the non-existent but expected notes. At the same time, Parker and company were having trouble supplying all the needs of the Army because some soldiers were staying, others were going, and the ones who left wanted enough supplies to get home. This nearly put Parker in breach of his contract to supply the Army because he had supplies to maintain the army at a certain consumption rate, but not stockpiles to supply some for long trips and others to stay.

Further south, the effort to move back home by the Southern Division of the Continental Army was under way. In the middle of May, Morris contracted with Daniel Parker to supply transportation, by sea, for Southern Army troops who wanted to move north from the Carolinas. Unfortunately, Congress' furlough orders of June 3rd reached the Southern Army before the transport ships. Greene had already contracted two ships on his own authority and sent his wife, some Virginia troops, and some Pennsylvania troops north so they could get back home as quickly as possible. As events unfolded later, these Pennsylvanians arrived in time to join in a mutiny already in progress,[166] much to the growing horror of Congress.

In the south, General Greene was still trying to wrest the funds from Mr. Banks, of Charleston, who had appropriated them to himself. Greene had written to Morris. Morris had no Continental money to pay Greene while the matter was unsettled, so he sent him $500 of his own money. Morris wrote that repayment of those funds would be "suspended until the final determinations are taken with respect to the

Army."[167] Generous terms indeed, considering Morris' experience in moving that matter forward.

Gouverneur Morris tried to put General Greene's mind at ease on the topic of disorder in the newly free states. On May 18th, 1783 He wrote,

> In every state shortly after the enemy leave it or are driven away there succeeded a season of moral anarchy, in which they are sure to act wrongly, but there succeeds again another season in which as the minds of men tranquilize the orders and ranks become more clearly designated. The people … look around for those who ought to hold the reins. These are to be found only among the more elevated ranks and the graver order of citizens…. Such as these will therefore by degrees endeavor to cement the American Union.[168]

Such thoughts were best shared among friends who had lived through disorder and repair. The accuracy of Gouverneur's viewpoint was immaterial when compared to the emotional impact it would have had if presented to the members of the "less elevated ranks."

Morris alerted his receiver of Continental taxes in Maryland, Mr. Harwood, to expect the arrival of unhappy Maryland troops from South Carolina. He reinforced his appreciation for their efforts, even though there had been an obvious lack of support from the state. He wrote,

> Your line have already (as I am told) mutinied … and I hope they will not be called on there to witness the ingratitude of their country. Whatever may depend on me shall be done for I respect their courage, fidelity, and sufferings but unless the States do more than many of them seem inclined to my sphere of utility will be narrow indeed.[169]

Robert noted, optimistically, that Congress was in the process of passing the 1783 Impost, but he thought it was insufficient,

> There is indeed a plan adopted by Congress, and if agreed by the states it may procure to the public creditors some temporary prospect of relief, but in my poor opinion it is not well calculated to obtain general adoption not to give (when adopted) a perfect security however I shall not impede tho I cannot in my conscience strongly recommend it.

The weakness of the impost of 1783 came from Congress' desire to write legislation that would overcome Rhode Island's objections to the last impost. As part of the proposed changes an amendment to the Articles of Confederation was under consideration. That amendment offered the idea of using population as part of the means of apportioning state requisitions. After the Southern states objected to being taxed on every slave, the population of slaves was to be accounted for at three-fifths of their number for the purpose of taxation. This amendment never passed. The three-fifths idea was used in other ways within the Constitution, five years later.

Realistically, Morris had low expectations for the impost, and so he continued to sell off excess military supplies. He suggested, however, to be sure to allow the cavalry officers to keep the horses they brought, but, in the case of Lee's Legion, which was made up of government horses, Morris wanted to auction those horses to get the money he needed to pay the troops. Those officers were not happy with the thought that the horses they rode into battle would now be sold from beneath them.[170]

It seemed a thousand voices were trying to be heard at the same time. Thomas Paine was still busy trying to find a way to be paid for his contributions. He eventually got the Congress to award him $3000, half the sum he thought was his due.[171] Congressman Theodoric Bland wanted Morris to find money to pay the lottery winner, but when Morris attempted to correct Bland's thinking about the availability of money from Europe, Bland was "rather unwilling to go into the investigation."[172] Morris was approached by a Dr. Lochman, because of Morris' role in overseeing the Hospital department. Dr. Lochman was in desperate need of money, like so many others. Morris gave him cash from his own pocket and advised him to apply for funds as a Foreign Officer, perhaps because he knew there was money in that account.[173]

Personal matters had a way of becoming international events, even in the 18th century. Morris had protected the interest of Haym Salomon and the Office of Finance from the fraud of Mr. de Brassinne, who was associated with de Mars, and now he found it necessary to protect his own reputation from the slanders of the same Frenchman. He wrote to the Chevalier de Chastellux,

> The gentlemen who are concerned in the transaction there mentioned took no little pains to defame as well as defraud me. In neither could they succeed here, but it may perhaps form a theme for their conversation in Paris. It is of little importance to any man in France whether I am a knave or honest, but you will I hope pardon a solicitude on the subject in me.[174]

Adams wrote from Europe and bemoaned the progress of the Dutch loan,

> In general, it is now sufficient to say the private interest, party spirit, factions, cabals and slanders have obstructed, perplexed and tortured our loaned in Holland as well as all our other affairs foreign and domestic.

He went on to advise borrowing money from England as a means to encourage the Dutch to close the loan as a form of competition.[175]

Naval matters were being wrapped up, and John Paul Jones looked to Europe for employment. He also tried to convince Morris to continue as Agent of Marine. Elsewhere, the offenders from the *Alliance* mutiny were being sentenced. In Philadelphia, Morris had to deny the former captain of the ship *Confederacy,* Harding, any special treatment, even though Harding had served bravely, been captured, released, rehired and retired. It was not until Harding's financial difficulties resulted in his arrest for debt that Congress was moved to act on his behalf. Unfortunately for Harding he was not able to keep consistent records through the loss of his ship and subsequent imprisonment, and so Congress did not settle his accounts until 1788, five years later.[176]

Morris was willing to mix the personal and political in one case of importance: to gain trade concessions in Cuba. The widow of Don Miralles sought payment for her husband's services from both the Spanish crown, His Most Catholic Majesty, and America. Don Miralles had been a Spanish representative in Philadelphia before he died during the early days of the Revolution. Morris was unable to help because of the behavior of Spain. He wrote the widow,

> I am sorry to observe that an order of his Excellency Governor Unzaga for shutting the port of Havana against American ships may probably obstruct remittances being made to his family...

He continued and suggested that Senora Miralles ask the Governor of Cuba to allow two or three more American ships to enter the port so they could bring in the remittances.[177]

Morris put the interests of individuals aside and focused on the larger issue of paying the Army. He knew that more money must come from somewhere. On May 26th he turned again to France. He wrote Franklin,

> The Army expect a payment which will amount to seven hundred thousand dollars. I am already above half a million dollars in advance of our resources by paper anticipation. I must increase this anticipa-

> tion immediately to pay monies due on the contracts for feeding our army and I must make them the expected payment by notes to be discharged at a distant day. Now sire if these notes are not satisfied when they become due, the little credit which remains to this country must fall and the little authority dependent on it must fall also. Under such circumstances it is that you are to ask aid for the United States.[178]

The new Morris notes were not yet backed with funds, but the creation of them went forward. The next day Dudley told Morris that the paper for the notes was made, but it was not yet dry. Time ticked away as the army in camp grew restless. Unfunded, and unfinished, the notes were already in demand. Meanwhile, Quartermaster Pickering was selling the Army horses in Newburgh. He was able to get about $50 for each because he was willing to take advances on the payment the officers expected to receive from the notes Dudley was making. The total received was about $4000, and Washington was able to keep "about twenty of the best" horses for future use.[179]

On May 29th Morris wrote to Washington and explained his plan with the new series of Morris notes.

> I shall cause such notes to be issued for three months pay to the army and I must entreat sir that every influence be used with the states to absorb them together with my other engagements by taxation. The present [tax] collections are most shameful and afford but a sad prospect to all those who are dependant upon them.[180]

If it were possible to convince the soldiers to pay their tax with his notes, or to exchange them at the state tax offices for cash, and next to convince the states to pay their requisitions with the collected notes, then Morris could collect them and retire them, perhaps in a bonfire. As it was, Morris was about to be responsible for funding another $700,000 obligation. He was still working to meet the interest on the Dutch loan and was able to pay 108,000 florins.[181]

In anticipation of his new commitment, and the dangers ahead, he wrote to John Jay in Europe,

> I have made an effort to get clear of this troublesome and dangerous office but as yet I am not permitted to retire. On the contrary I must of necessity increase my engagements to a degree that renders it entirely uncertain when I shall have it in my power to see them discharged. If you can obtain me aid, for Heavens sake, or rather for the sake of our country, do it.

John Jay also wrote that he had seen Ridley and the boys. The boys were in good shape and finally on their way to school in Geneva.[182]

Robert Morris, like Gouverneur, foresaw difficulties in the near term after the peace,

> The blessings of peace flow in upon us spontaneously but it requires the full exercise of more virtue and good sense than had yet appeared in our councils to secure the continuance of them.[183]

Summer

Washington was concerned with the uncertain conditions at his encampment. To avoid mutiny, he issued a furlough order on June 2nd. On the same day in Philadelphia, the new watermarked paper was ready; and Morris sent it with the text to the printer. On that day, while he was about to put himself on the line for hundreds of thousands, he received $220 from the State of Massachusetts, and amount he called "pitiful collections" from "one of the first states of the union."[184]

Morris had decided to stay in office and wrap up his commitments. He wrote,

> Nothing would have induced me to continue in office but a view of public distress. These distresses are much greater than can be easily conceived.[185]

He stepped again into the financial breech because, as he wrote, he was

> ... willing to risk as much for my country as any man in America.[186]

While the soldiers had risked life and limb, he worked for the cause according to his own abilities, well after the shooting stopped.

However, his was not a suicide mission. He wanted to make sure that his notes were paid, and that his fortune was not at the mercy of his political adversaries. He wrote to the American Minister to Spain, his old friend, John Jay,

> My engagement and anticipations for the Public amount to a Million of Dollars. It racks my utmost invention to keep pace with the demands ... I hope, my Dear Friend, that you and our other Ministers will be able to procure some farther assistance from France and Holland ... Our Government is too weak, bad men have too much sway, there are evils afloat which can only be avoided or cured by wise and honest measures, assisted by the lenient hand of time.[187]

Adams arranged assistance in the form of a new loan from Holland, at a higher interest rate to lure investors, but the local financial news was not as good. Morris learned from the Chevalier de La Luzerne that he was "unable to give you the slightest hope of success on this subject" of a new loan from France. Instead of a new loan, La Luzerne requested immediate payment of $12,000 for bills of exchange that Barbé-Marbois tried to cash at the local tax office in New England for funds needed to get the *America* ready for sea.[188] Morris instructed his agent Lowell to send money collected in Massachusetts to the French agent in Boston so the *America* could be supplied and sail to France. After he informed La Luzerne that payment would be available, La Luzerne pressed for settlement of Baron de Kalb's account. De Kalb's widow was pinched for funds, but as a victim of the war, and a dead one at that, de Kalb was unable to provide the necessary documentation that Congress required. Morris told La Luzerne that only Congress could allow a payment to de Kalb's widow under these circumstances. Later, near the end of August, the Chevalier de la Luzerne suggested a solution to the account of the departed Baron de Kalb, "It appears that one can easily make up for this lack of documents by supposing that the 226,000 continental dollars remitted in May 1780 to the Baron de Kalb were used up by the division which he commanded." La Luzerne was attempting to help de Kalb's family out of their financial embarrassments.[189] The matter was not resolved until 1854 when de Kalb's heirs were awarded $66,099.76.[190]

Morris looked forward to life outside public service, and hoped to set up a private real estate business with John Vaughan. Vaughan was in Europe looking for backing. He found a general economic malaise instead. He wrote that loans in Europe were available only at very high interest rates. The risks seemed too great for real estate speculations in America, and as Vaughan put it,

> ... the rich are rich enough, and also old and distrustful; the young would have been sanguine, but too poor, to which add that all the rich were not American in principle, and many of those who were so, understood the public, but not the private question relative to our Country.

Clearly, the behavior of the American States convinced Europeans that private citizens were not good credit risks, just as Morris had repeatedly warned. Vaughan continued about his experiences with the Dutch,

> They had suffered also by the [loss of] conquered islands and they had lost immensely by loans to their own colony of Surinam, and the word America is applied to all.

He finished by saying private loans to local European groups "look safer and which are nearer and better understood, as well as shorter and more transferable." He concluded by saying that he had tried the most likely investors under the veil of secrecy so at least if the effort failed it would not be widely reported.[191] That way, the effort could be retried when conditions changed.

The situation in America was on its uneasy way from war footing to peacetime. The Oneida Indians were still being supplied with rations from the United States. By June 1783 they were consuming $1,231 in supplies per month. Mr. Fitzsimmons argued in favor of maintaining the subsidy.[192] Morris supplied the quartermaster corps with $5,000 but wished to remove the Oneida from the public payroll. Then he wrote to the Governors on the topic of sending state tax money to the Continental treasury,

> I hope the urgency of the case will produce the desired exertions and finally enable me to preserve the credit and honor of the federal government.[193]

The money was not forthcoming.

Morris contacted his agent in Maryland about a notice in the newspaper that Maryland was applying taxes collected for Continental purposes to be used otherwise in the state. The Maryland Intendant of Revenue, Daniel of St. Thomas Jennifer, had diverted these funds to pay the Maryland troops instead of allowing Morris to use the funds to finance the payment of the whole army. Jennifer claimed that Morris' notes were not going to be due for six months and he would be able to make the payments by then.[194] Jennifer felt free to use Continental funds for his own purposes just because he had it in his possession at the time, while others were quick to put out their hands for it.

Captain Landais was still convinced he was owed more money than anyone else thought he was owed. He had refused the settlement Congress offered. Morris received a letter from him on this topic, and he determined to start ignoring subsequent letters. He wrote to Lowell in Massachusetts that the first letter he opened

> ... was conceived in such a style as determines me never more to trouble myself about that man ... If he will not endorse the warrant

> be pleased to return me both the bills and the warrant and give yourself no further trouble about him.[195]

Acting as Agent of Marine, Morris tried to resolve outstanding issues in the Naval Department. He allowed an aggrieved party to sue the captain of an American privateer who took a Portuguese ship. In a different case, Captain John Manley, of *The Hague,* was to undergo a court martial. This would put him in the company of Captain Nicholson, who was found innocent, and Captain Green who was suspected of abusing his "captain's privilege." Considering how few ships there were in the Navy, the percentage of captains under investigation was extraordinary. The only captain of an active Continental Navy ship to escape this fate was John Barry, simply because he was just suspected of abusing captain's privilege and never charged. Jones was sailing with the French at the time. Oddly, a friend of Arthur Lee's, Captain Landais, had appropriated a Continental Ship after he was removed from service, yet he managed to not only escape court martial, but he felt entitled to bother the head of the navy, Morris, with a series of disagreeable letters. Another Captain who escaped American justice was Commodore Gillon from the South Carolina Navy; he had bought English goods in wartime, been involved with alleged misdeeds over prizes in Europe, and later insisted on using prisoners of war as sailors for free. He was traveling somewhere in Europe with debts to the United States, and the debts to Prince of Luxembourg hanging over his head. Never mind, all that – he was a friend of Henry Laurens.

Down in South Carolina, Greene was signing notes that he could not cover; and he hoped Morris could help. One of his colonels wanted to sell the horses, but he could not get enough money to make it worthwhile. The troops decided they had a right to discharge from the Army and were difficult to manage. Greene wrote, "One part of the Cavalry have mutinied and gone off to Virginia."[196] This group became known as Baylor's Regiment of Dragoons.

While other soldiers were waiting anxiously for the much-anticipated transport ships, these mutineers left the Army with their horses. They claimed that they were promised thirteen months pay and never received it. They wrote,

> The general report was they intended to dismount us and leave us to shift for ourselves or to be carried round by water which would so been very disagreeable to most of the men.[197]

In actuality, they were offered the opportunity to buy the horses they rode, with the money they were owed.

Under contract to the Marine Department, Daniel Parker's troop transport ships sailed to the Carolinas and picked up soldiers to bring them home. The clothes Colonel John Laurens and his associates purchased in France back in 1780 finally arrived in South Carolina, just in time to miss the troops who had recently been evacuated. South Carolina had been supporting the Army and was not about to buy uniforms they did not need. The merchants in Charleston were not interested in uniforms either; instead, they wanted payment for the items credited to the Continental cause. Back in Philadelphia, Morris planned to put up his own notes to fend off a large-scale mutiny, so it was natural for him to look to the states for the money he needed to cover them. On June 3rd he wrote Rhode Island about the army,

> I am pressed on all sides to make them a payment of three months wages. Want of money compels me to do it in Notes, and a vigorous collection of taxes throughout the states is indispensable necessary to enable to discharge of the notes as they fall due.[198]

Instead of helping to pay the army, and contributing to Morris' plan, Rhode Island wanted to be credited for clothing certificates from 1782. In the process, the state paid only $346 in the first six months in 1783. This would not go far in covering the anticipated $800,000 in notes.

Washington knew about Morris' plan to use his notes. He wrote,

> I am extremely apprehensive that insuperable difficulties and the worst of consequences may be expected, unless the notes you mention shall be paid to the officers and men before their departure from this cantonment … I send the messenger who is the bearer of this – pray do not delay him a single instant, but if all the notes should not be ready, forward the remainder by the earliest possible opportunity, and be so good as to inform me when they may be expected.[199]

Among the pressures to disband the Army was the economic consequence of opening the port of New York. Peaceful trade would resume, but first the British would need to buy supplies for their departure, and the citizens would want fresh products from the country. This would drive prices up for the suppliers to the Army and make it even more difficult to keep the soldiers fed. Dissatisfaction with the contractors was almost always high, so disruptions due to price fluctuations only made things worse and accelerated the breakup of the West Point camp.

$800,000 in Morris Notes for the Troops

Morris approved the proof sheets for the notes and ordered the immediate printing of them on June 4th.[200] Then he wrote to keep Washington abreast of the developments because there was great concern about the timing of the notes' arrival. Two days later, the printing was done, and Morris started the process of signing thousands of notes. He had $60,000 ready that day and signed another batch of $50,000 by June 9th. Once printed and signed they were delivered to the paymaster.

The paymaster, John Pierce, seemed a bit confused about what to do. He waited for further instructions about the notes, and he wondered if he should consider accounts closed because the notes were delivered, and what about the clothing accounts, and on and on. Morris considered the notes to be the result of the commutation agreement and could not answer these questions without Congressional approval because the answers rested on their authority to settle accounts. Morris delivered the first batch of notes to Pierce's assistant, Mr. Audibert. Audibert, in turn, gave them to Paymaster Pierce without telling him a second batch was to arrive soon. Audibert said that the notes were to go to the officers who were to be furloughed because he understood that paying the officers and men sent on furlough was meant to clear them from camp so the remaining men would have supplies. The short count seemed to support the idea that there were not going to be enough notes for everyone. The situation was interpreted in camp as meaning only the men who accepted furlough would be paid. Since Pierce did not know about the second series of notes he was at a loss to combat that impression. Audibert waited for the second batch and sent both batches together. This delayed the distribution by a week. The notes did not reach camp until June 15th. By that time nearly two weeks had passed since Washington first mentioned the furlough plan and there had been much uncertainty. In disgust, some of the soldiers who had already taken the furlough left instructions that their pay should be sent after them.[201]

With the urging of various unscrupulous regimental paymasters, many soldiers sold their notes below face value, even before the notes arrived in camp, just to get provisions for their trips home. Desire to leave, and speculation over notes decimated the supply system in camp. The contractors, including Parker, accepted the notes in return for goods in their store houses. Many of the soldiers needed money immediately instead of waiting for the six-month notes to mature, so these soldiers sold their notes at a discount. This discounting forced down the value of the notes further.

In addition to the contractors, several of Morris' friends eventually held large quantities of these notes for two main reasons. First, there was a chance the notes might someday be worth more than their purchase price. Secondly, none of them wanted Morris to be called upon suddenly to pay huge sums of money he did not have on hand.[202] Forcing Morris into bankruptcy would only insure their own financial demise. Certainly, the Government could not cover them at the time. So, while the contractors and Morris' friends protected him by holding these notes, Morris' political adversaries labeled them all as vile speculators. They used people's ignorance about the government's finances to manipulate their fears and jealousies by making it appear that Morris was enriching himself and his friends at the expense of the soldiers. As events evolved many of the soldiers, who felt cheated, found it easiest to understand the emotional appeals of Morris' political adversaries and adopted their position.

Everything the critics did was aimed at destroying the value of the notes. These notes were the last vestiges of the Continental Army, an organization that some in Congress had tried to undermine since 1776. From their perspective, the Congress did not really have the authority to raise an Army, or a Navy, because to them Congress was just a coordinating committee for state actions. First, they denied the Army funding, which almost worked until Washington's victory at Trenton and Princeton. After they failed to kill it, they tried to take it over. After that failed, they largely ignored Morris' attempts at a unified financial system and maintained the strategy of state support, which led to dissension and mutiny. If they managed the failure of the notes, that would finally prove the Continental government was incapable of being trusted; and would destroy any remaining faith in a unified Continental effort that existed in the minds of the soldiers. It would also mean the destruction of Morris, because Morris was liable for their value, and it would mean the destruction of his allies. All of this effort was aimed at increasing the power of state governments and realizing the localist dream of creating their own mini-nations. It was just a side benefit, to the critics, that Morris was denied any praise from those he helped; just as he had been denied any recognition for his effort in getting Washington's Army to Yorktown.

Far from ruining the dream of creating a single unified nation, Morris' allies, a.k.a. the "vile speculators," held the Morris notes and lobbied for a federal funding plan. Over time, a market in these discounted notes developed and their value rose and fell with the debate over debt assumption. Of course, if the Congress and States had agreed to a funding system from the start, the soldiers would have gotten full pay. If these critics had not spoken against the notes the soldiers would have gotten more value from their sale, but none of that was the focus of the public debate, because that debate focused on the supposed wickedness of the man who had risked $800,000 in his own funds to pay the Army. Few, if any, acknowledged that Morris had put himself at great financial risk for the benefit of an army he did not control; an army that showed no gratitude to the man who stepped in when all else had failed. General Washington's address to the officers halted the Army uprising at Newburgh. The payment Morris arranged insured it did not reoccur.

While anonymous partisans used the *Freeman's Journal* to whip up the ill will of the emotionally driven, the real work of the Office of Finance continued. Captain William Pickles, who in 1778 had sailed out of New Orleans on the *Morris* as a privateer Captain under the direction of the disgraced Major Willing, and who later had been captured with Henry Laurens, came to Morris "respecting his rank in the navy."[203] Morris suggested that Captain Pickles petition Congress for recognition.

Morris discovered another $340 in counterfeits sent in from Virginia.[204] He requested Hezekiah Merrill, the state tax receiver of Connecticut, to pay cash for Morris' notes out of the state tax coffers, otherwise the *Bourbon* would not be able to sail from that state.[205] Elsewhere, Thomas Barclay was hard at work in France trying to reach a settlement of the foreign accounts, including the old Secret Committee business.[206]

While Morris attended to the details of his office, Baylor's Regiment of Dragoons neared their destination of Virginia. The Governor thought that Congress had ordered all the troops to go north long before their mutiny, and he concluded that the cavalrymen would be pardoned if they agreed to behave. Virginia hastily arranged provisions for the mutineers to avoid witnessing a change in their mood from discontent into anger, plundering and bloodshed. When the news of the mutiny of Baylor's Regiment crossed Morris' desk, he agreed with the Secretary of War that the Secretary could proceed according to the Articles of War. He added,

> ... except that the Secy. At War may pardon by proclamation such as surrender themselves and horses within the time he shall limit.[207]

The two of them requested permission from Congress to offer such a pardon to the soldiers.[208] Governor Harrison of Virginia, who had nominal authority over the militia, was embarrassed by their behavior and blamed the Virginia Assembly for their negligence and lack of attention to the needs of the soldiers.

Threats of mutiny came from other quarters as well. On June 12th part of the Maryland line, which had been furloughed from New York, passed through Philadelphia. They had started home before receiving their pay and were not happy about it. While the Maryland paymaster was in Philadelphia, he applied for Morris notes to pay his troops. The Pennsylvania line, stationed in Lancaster, was still not furloughed, and they were uncertain about the status of their pay. When these two groups of soldiers talked among themselves the feelings of inequity, and the uncertainties hardened into resentment and anger. Sergeants from the Pennsylvania line petitioned Congress in the language one might expect from enlisted men. Such harsh tones offended the delicate sensibilities of one Congressman who said it was "of so insolent a nature as to forbid any answer."[209] John Armstrong, who already had some experience in mutiny, considered the petition from his position as the Secretary of the Executive Council, and thought the material was suitably direct. In an effort to even the scales, Arthur St. Clair issued "After Orders" that indicated Washington's furlough offer was available as an option to the Pennsylvania line. The paymaster indicated that they could have one month's pay in cash and three months' pay in notes. Unfortunately for all, there was not enough cash until Morris pressed the board of the Bank to find it. For reasons unknown, the paymaster decided to give notes only to soldiers who accepted furlough. At this juncture Pennsylvania troops coming home from the Southern Division started to disembark in Wilmington. They were supposed to march to Lancaster, away from a volatile situation in Philadelphia.

Picking up the theme of mutiny, Sergeant Nagle of the 3rd Pennsylvania Regiment assumed leadership of the group of soldiers in Lancaster that was intent on marching on Philadelphia. They left Lancaster without the payment notes that were due to them. Morris learned from the President of Congress of the "…mutinous disposition in the troops at the barracks who had written a letter to Congress with threat &c."

Robert had also received reports of agitation by members of the "Constitutionalists" in the Pennsylvania Assembly.[210] He and others were concerned the soldiers might force themselves on the Bank and demand money that was not there.

For his part Morris had long since made plans to be out of town that weekend. He spent the weekend in Bethlehem, Pennsylvania, where among other activities he expected to talk with Gouverneur Morris on the topic of the mutiny. He set out on the trip with his wife and John

Holker, probably to escort Kitty Livingstone home to Elizabeth, New Jersey. Likely topics of conversation would have included the contract between Holker's partners, Duer and Parker, and the United States, and also the planning of a bold venture to send the *Empress of China* to the Far East.[211]

Rumors of mutiny in the Pennsylvania line were confirmed on June 19th when reports came in from Lancaster that the soldiers were heading to Philadelphia and intended "to seek justice &c."[212] On June 20th Morris met with Peters, Hamilton and Ellsworth. Together they decided to offer pay to the soldiers if they would return to Lancaster.[213] It was also decided to send Alexander Hamilton, G. Morris, and William Jackson to the Philadelphia barracks for a talk with the soldiers.

As it turned out, G. Morris was not the best choice for a mission to calm the soldiers. He and Hamilton attempted to convince them to stay in Lancaster until pay arrived, and G. Morris annoyed them greatly by saying,

> ... that the soldiers would in a few days be happy as they would receive one month's pay, which would carry them home in a genteel manner.[214]

The soldiers were irate at the thought that one month's pay should suffice for men who had spent years in the field of battle. They were inspired to protest. Finances were stretched thin as it was; with Morris' efforts to pay Washington's Army he had little to send to the Pennsylvania line. He was forced to turn to the contractors as a source of goods to be used as pay for those troops.[215]

By June 22nd, the President of Pennsylvania Executive Council called on Morris and told him that the soldiers were in mutiny. Morris suggested calling out the militia.[216] The Executive Council argued that there was no way to know if the militia would join the mutiny or help the Congress.[217] This was a quandary similar to the one Washington had confronted back in 1776, about the same organization. The Executive Council declined to call the militia and suggested a conciliatory approach. Then Morris contacted Thomas Willing, Mr. Hamilton, and Mr. Fitzsimmons at the Bank, and told them "of the dangerous temper of the soldiery in order that such precautions be taken as the directors should judge proper."[218] He also looked after his family. "I went over to my house to apprize my family and prevent alarms, from thence I went to a friends house to wait the event..."

What was feared to be a violent episode was little more than a disorganized protest. The soldiers surrounded the State House in a threatening manner while the Congress remained inside. On the outside there was drinking and some shouting of rude remarks, but ultimately the soldiers dispersed without doing any harm. The lack of protection from this mob made members of Congress feel very vulnerable.[219] No arrests were made. The only time a similar event occurred in American history was on January 6th, 2021, when an amalgamation of groups surrounded and forcibly entered the US Capitol Building in protest of the Presidential election of 2020, resulting in destruction, physical harm, and several deaths. Hundreds of participants have been hunted down and many were criminally charged for this.

During the 1783 demonstration Morris went to stay with David Conyngham at Woodford, about a mile down the ridge road from Morris' own country seat, the Hills. Conyngham noted,

> They stayed until the alarm was over, which there were sorry they had dreaded, or had been alarmed about.[220]

Morris went back to Philadelphia. He recalled,

> ...after the Soldiers departed from the State House I returned to this Office, sent to the President of Congress to know if Congress had any Commands, there being none I went agreeable to engagement to Club, returned in the Evening, waited on the President of the State and Strongly urged the calling out of the Militia to quell the Riot, &c."[221]

News of the mutiny was sent to General Washington, who was in Newburgh with paymaster Pierce attending to the business of distributing Morris' notes to the soldiers there. That process was held up by Pierce, who wanted Morris to answer the questions Pierce had asked Morris two weeks earlier, on June 6th. Even without these answers Pierce reported that, according to his information, much of the Pennsylvania line was still in the South. Nevertheless, he had instructed Arthur St. Claire, commander of the Pennsylvania line, to look after the accounts of those men. He had also given Philip Audibert instructions on settling their accounts. He did admit that since he was in New York he did not know if his instructions had been carried out, and that he could not be sure of the result until he was in Pennsylvania again and the whole line had returned from the south.[222] Pierce learned on July 1st that the comptroller knew of no accounts that had been actually presented by the paymasters. Morris noted in his report to Congress on the day of the mutiny,

> That the settlement of accounts generally is delayed not only by the want of authority [from Congress] for the purpose but the difficulty of obtaining an account of the advances made by the several states and public departments to officers of the line.

To solve part of that problem Morris requested authority from Congress to empower the paymaster to settle and adjust accounts.

As it so often is with governments there was plenty ofblame to go around, particularly when there is money involved. The states, the Congress, the paymaster, and the Office of Finance were each attempting to pursue their own course, and the soldiers were left in the breach. Several weeks after the crisis, on July 4th, Congress agreed with Morris' proposed resolution.[223]

While the more populist elements of Philadelphia society cheered the troop's mutiny there was much discussion about the behavior of the Pennsylvania line, and the state's refusal to defend Congress. Morris met with,

> Mr. Fitzsimmons, Mr. Wilson, Mr. Hamilton, and Mr. Peters on the business of the Revolted Soldiers. These gentlemen gave me notice to prepare myself for departure from this city with Congress as it appeared probable that they will remove this afternoon no steps being taken or promised by the Executive of the State to protect them from a repetition of insult.

The Congress decided to move to Princeton, New Jersey, and to keep the movement secret because of the possibility that the mutineers might kidnap some members to extract concessions. Morris left town and told his office to suspend operations until further notice.[224]

Once Congress had vacated the city of Philadelphia the attitude of the Executive Council suddenly changed. They took immediate steps to protect the Bank and suppress the mutiny.[225] By June 26th the Lancaster troops had put down their arms and gone out of Philadelphia. In the ensuing investigation the troops blamed G. Morris for his insensitive approach, and that was enough to cause the partisan press to blame the whole business on the Office of Finance.[226]

Arthur Lee seconded this idea. He wrote,

> It is much speculated that he & his friends have been the prime movers of all the disturbances in the Army, for the purpose of enforcing the 5 per ct. in the shape most parental of a corrupt influence in Congress of which he with reason expected to be the prime Minister.[227]

Arthur Lee, and his allies in Pennsylvania, shared the same perspective on Morris. They both believed that the Office of Finance held too much influence over Congress, and that separating the Morrises from Congress would be of some use to the provincial factions they supported. During the mutiny the mutineers avoided confrontation with the Executive Council and directed their energies at Congress. Armstrong, the Secretary of the Executive Council and former mutineer, had the opinion that Congress had passed its usefulness, and was "like their paper currency, in a state of depreciation, having no solidity or real worth."[228] Even some of the officers seemed to take secret satisfaction in knowing the enlisted men had scared off the Congress.[229]

With Congress in Princeton, Morris often found himself shuttling between that temporary capital and Philadelphia, but that did not depress his spirits. On July 4th Morris wrote,

> Finding on my return from Princeton that no public entertainment was provided for this day, I invited a company of forty gentlemen, consisting of foreigners, military and civilian officers, citizens, and spent the afternoon and evening in great festivity and mirth.[230]

The next day Benjamin Dudley delivered the last packet of three thousand sheets of notes for Morris to sign, and so the total of 15,000 sheets had been printed. Each sheet had three notes printed on it. Morris spent the better part of July 5th signing notes to pay the soldiers.

Mutinies did not galvanize the states to support Congressional plans. Instead, the states kept their money at home to protect themselves. Maryland decided to pay their own troops and leave it at that. Eventually Congress moved to censure them for their failure to live up to their commitments. The Maryland delegation to Congress managed to have the motion tabled indefinitely.[231]

Quartermaster Pickering acknowledged a £16,000 debt to the Massachusetts supplier of wagons and oxen to the Army.[232] He noted that the man who was owed so much for his wagons and oxen was disinclined to pay tax because of the debt owed to him. He observed,

> That the non-payment of public dues in general affords a pretext for refusals of paying taxes ... [233]

New Jersey did not remit any money in the month of June 1783.[234] Payment was also slow from New York. Morris had instructed his receiver, Tillotson, to publish the amounts of salary paid to New York legislators next to the amount paid to the Continental treasury.

Morris learned that Tillotson was thought to be spying on New York. He wrote,

> I should rather call it an Inspector on the part of the Union to take care of its interests in the state.

He defended his policy of embarrassing public officials when he wrote,

> To place the conduct of such men in a conspicuous point of light rendering the public opinion a test of their proceedings is a general as well as a particular duty of society.[235]

This desire for transparency is the same thinking that brought about the first amendment's guarantee of freedom for the press. For his own part, Morris was very familiar with being the subject of articles in the paper. Clearly, he was not wishing on others what he did not have to endure himself.

Down south, Virginia met the arrival of its soldiers with supplies. They were aware of events in Philadelphia, and the appearance of the mutinous dragoons from South Carolina was cause for some trepidation. A short time later Secretary of War, Lincoln, arrived in Richmond from Philadelphia. He brought three months' pay for the soldiers according to the plan to treat all soldiers alike. Morris wrote Benjamin Harrison, Governor of Virginia, that supplies given by Virginia to returning soldiers would be paid for by the Continental system.[236]

The disbanding of the Army was a chaotic and dangerous time. Angry soldiers filtered back to their respective states and homes. State governments worried about riot and mutiny upon their arrival; the states that had supported the soldiers poorly during their last two years of service and were not able to muster the resources to pay them properly in the end. The only payment they had, Morris notes, became the topic of much misinformation by Morris' enemies. The soldiers heard little else, and as the notes lost value, they disparaged the Financier's efforts. Over time this negative reaction to what Morris believed to be a valiant gesture to do Justice, and a great risk to his personal fortune, discouraged him and caused him to rethink his efforts.

However, he did not turn his back on individuals whom he thought deserved Justice. On July 5th Morris recommended a pension for three disabled veteran sailors. Congress took no action until September. Congress, in its wisdom, did agree with Washington's recommendation to put Major General von Steuben in charge of taking possession of the western forts, supposedly evacuated by the British according to the preliminary peace agreement. Von Steuben's aide informed Morris that the Major General should appear in the style of a gentleman commensurate with his rank, and he would also need a staff, and our course money to fund the venture to the western forts.[237] Such expenses were not in the budget, and Morris approached the Bank for another loan of $100,000 based "on the general security [creditworthiness] of the United States." Thomas Willing told Morris that the directors did not think that sufficient and refused the loan.[238] In a separate effort, various citizens of Philadelphia, including Thomas Willing, Thomas Paine, Tench Francis, and Gouverneur Morris drafted an address to Congress petitioning for the return of that august body to the City of Philadelphia.[239] Congress did not move.

-|-

Adams wrote from Europe to Morris in Philadelphia on the confusing matter of Congress' bills of exchange from 1779. He was sure he had not allowed any bills of exchange to be paid twice. Then in typical fashion, for Adams, he took that opportunity to underscore his contributions to the success of the diplomatic efforts, and how his life in Europe was really quite difficult, and how his fellow diplomats did not always inform him, but it was nice to hear congratulations on the peace. He went on that it was all very hard work, and complicated really, and there was the question of signing the peace individually or as a group; waiting or not, when waiting would have given time for the ministry in England to change, but he thought they had done well. In a somewhat poetic fashion, he summed,

> When frail vessels are navigating among innumerable mountains of ice, driven by various winds and drawn by various currents, if that one improves the moment and sets the example, it will not do to stand upon ceremonies and ask which shall go first, or that all may go together.[240]

Back in Philadelphia, the Marine Department begged for attention. Captain Landais continued to make himself unpopular by threatening to publish a letter he felt to be useful to him. Morris replied,

> With respect to Capt. Landais I am perfectly easy whether he publishes it or lets it alone. I pity the man who seems to be more his own enemy that any body else can be.[241]

Captain William Pickles took Morris' advice and petitioned Congress for recognition of "such rank as you in your wisdom might think justice entitled him to." Congress rejected the petition. A few days later Pickles was killed in a knife fight. Morris asked Captain Barry to make sure Pickles received a military funeral and that the flags were flown at half-mast for him.[242] A new court martial proceeding was being organized in Boston. This time it was against the captain of the *Hague*. During July, Morris had ordered the arrest of Captain Manley, and that he stand trial.[243] The inadequate supply of available officers delayed the trial until August.

Morris was still trying to determine the right amount of "captain's privilege" for a Continental Navy ship. Captain Barry wanted to extend it to the boatswain and carpenter, but Morris limited it to the Captain, and to other officers at the discretion of the captain.[244] Morris also petitioned Congress for the right to sell the *Hague*, formerly the *Deane*. He said it would reduce expenses in a distressed time, and

> The ship never was a good one and not being American built is for that reason also unworthy a place in our Navy.[245]

He continued to say that until there was funding, there was no hope for a Navy or an Army. He did not forsake the idea of building a Navy, but did not see the time as being right, just yet. He wrote,

> Every good American must wish to see the United States possessed of a powerful fleet, but perhaps the best way to obtain one is to make no effort for the purpose till the people are taught by their feeling to call for and require it.[246]

The sale of naval vessels by auction created some controversy. Morris put a number of ships up for sale and made it possible for bidders to make payment with the Morris notes he had used to pay contractors and others. He was also willing to accept notes from the Bank of North America. People who had remained outside his funding system objected to these modes of payment and wanted to use Loan Office Certificates, which Morris consistently eschewed as being from before his administration, highly depreciated, of dubious value because they were not funded, and therefore only useful after the large debt settlement was completed. Morris' use of his notes in these sales was part of his overall plan to maintain the value of his notes and Bank notes by allowing them to be redeemed for something of real value, like a ship. Taking depreciated and unfunded Loan Office Certificates would have defeated his plan to establish a national currency based on hard money. Morris' political adversaries, who wished to pay in Loan Office Certificates, which they seemed to have no intention of funding, focused their complaints not on monetary policy, but on the easier to understand and more emotionally evocative issue of the personalities involved. Since Morris' military contractors were holding many of his notes the adversaries pretended outrage that the system was a prime example of corrupt self-dealing.

It is understandable that his enemies would object to his programs, but Morris even had trouble focusing the minds of his political allies so they would understand the hard money system. Continental tax receiver of South Carolina, George Hall, had been accepting specific supplies from that war-ravaged state. Those supplies were accepted as part of the requisition of 1782. Supplies accepted over the 1782 quota were to be converted to their hard money value in accordance with the 1783 requisition. Morris wrote, "if the excess you mention is credited against the requisitions of 1783, it must be at the rate such things would sell for." Morris realized that the states were placing values on their supplies that were much higher than the market value for the same articles. This price inflation was just a method of reducing the amount of goods sent to the Continental government. It would be like paying your taxes with one pound of salt and trying to maintain that the salt was worth $1000. Morris refused to accept this. His refusal did not please the states. Morris was not happy to learn that the deputy quartermaster for the Southern Army had accepted a private note for one of Morris' notes sent south to buy supplies. While this was similar to the private business practice of buying bills of exchange with a note, it was not acceptable to Morris, who told his agents to accept only goods or hard currency for his notes. When that fellow's note failed to clear and a second one was offered Morris became angry,

> If by this you mean that I should in any wise alter the general mode of procedure in this particular instance I think you have not fully considered the consequence. If individuals can by their pertinacity alter the course or stop the current of public measures there is at once an end of all rules and orderly management.[247]

Morris was having similar difficulties with the state governors who were still not paying taxes to the Continental treasury; taxes that would go to convert Morris' notes into money for the soldiers. He considered their actions toward honoring America's debt to the soldiers to be tantamount to fraud. Morris wrote,

> And on this occasion I take leave to observe that the moment is very fast approaching which is to determine whether America is entitled to the appellation of just, or whether those who have constantly aspersed her character are to be believed.[248]

His insistence on valuing state contributions of bulk goods at their market value made sense abroad, even if Americans behaved as if it did not matter. News about Morris' intention to pay the interest on the Dutch loan with Virginia tobacco reached Adams. He was pleased to learn about the plan. He knew that the French were not the financial lifeline of Europe, and in the long run American fortunes rested in the credit markets of Holland. He also knew that America needed to pay its debts, because the world saw refusal to pay as a form of theft. A nation's moral character was seen in terms of its willingness to be something other than a nation of thieves.

The post-colonial states in America, however, were more concerned with their own interests than the ideas of European money merchants, and the States continued to resist repayment. Their habit, under colonial rule, was to use depreciating fiat currency, but the protective umbrella of the British Empire was gone. They failed to grasp the ramifications of that. Adams wrote,

> All depends, however, upon the measures to be taken by Congress and the states by ascertaining their debts and a regular discharge of the interest.... The thirteen states in relation to the discharge of the debts of Congress, must consider themselves one body, animated by one soul.... Every hesitation, every uncertainty about paying or receiving a just debt, diminished that sense of the moral obligation of public justice which ought to be kept pure and carefully cultivated in every American mind.[249]

Down south, General Greene was confronting a lack of integrity on a much more personal level. Greene needed about $4,000 to pay the soldiers one month's pay. He wrote to Morris,

> Mr. Banks owes besides this balance [for clothing] about four thousand dollars upon a set of bills drawn last spring for 6,000 dollars for which he was to advance me money occasionally to the whole amount by the time they became payable. On these bills he has advanced something less than 2,000 dollars.[250]

Back at home, Morris was still unable to close the books on the Yorktown tobacco deal, even after the passage of over a year and three months. George Eddy tried to claim that some of the tobacco sent under that agreement was substandard, and he wanted a reduction in its price. Morris refused this gambit by pointing out that Eddy had bought the tobacco as it was always sold, under the auspices of the Tobacco Board of Trade,

> Your tobacco had been bought in the common and usual manner, the money has been paid and you cannot call on me nor I on any other person for recompense under the idea of loss.[251]

Economic confusion reigned in many quarters. Troops who had left camp in New York started to arrive in Boston, and they sought payment from the Assembly there. The soldiers and the legislature were generally unaware that regimental agents were settling the soldiers' accounts with the continental government, and after this was done, the pay would arrive in the form of six-month Morris notes, exchangeable for money at the office of the Continental Receiver. Localist interests saw this plan to be one that favored speculators, and the Massachusetts General Court ordered its delegates to the Continental Congress to see to it that the money for the Continental requisition of 1782 be paid out to the soldiers. The money was supposed to be paid in a form of state currency that could be used to pay state taxes. Such a large payment of state script would have immediately flooded the economy with paper money, and that would inevitably result in inflation, so the state plan favored payment in a rapidly depreciating currency over Morris' plan of a timed payment in hard currency. One problem with this plan was the state of Massachusetts had not paid enough in the 1782 requisition to support it. Out of the total quota of $1,307,594 Massachusetts paid only $332,677 or about 25%. After that became clear, Massachusetts delegates to the Congress tried to get laws passed to favor their soldiers. The rest of Congress acted to support the part of Morris' program that treated all soldiers alike. Other states attempted to substitute direct payments of state script to their soldiers for their pledged requisitions to Congress.[252]

Morris tried to maintain the integrity of his system by suggesting to Governor Hancock of Massachusetts that his state could accept his notes from the soldiers and convert them to cash. He wrote,

> If they give good encouragement from the State the officers and soldiers will probably bring in those Notes and thus you will be able to make immediate payment of a considerable part of your quota with very great ease to the people.[253]

Doing this would have required that Massachusetts make a large current outlay, and then hold the note until it matured in five months.

Reacting to assertions by Morris' adversaries that the plan to provide a way to convert the notes held by the soldiers was "known to a few only, and not to the soldiers and other holders of these notes,"[254] Congress sent instructions from Princeton to Morris asking him to explain why the soldiers had not received their pay in notes or instructions about what to do with them. Morris replied that he had sent his notes, and his policies had been unchanged for years, so he had no idea why people were unaware of them. Congress supported the idea of a general advertisement on the subject of redeeming the notes. Morris replied that a general advertisement to send Morris notes immediately into state receivers for conversion to cash would create a flood of notes before there was money to cover them, and that flood would result in empty coffers at the receivers' offices long before the flood subsided. This would reduce the value of the remaining unconverted notes and make holders even more miserable.

In response to continued Congressional interest on the topic, and to comply with their wishes, Morris published, in late August, an advertisement to the public saying,

> That the receivers in the several states have long since been instructed to take all notes signed by the Superintendent of Finance in payment of taxes and also to take up all such notes whenever tendered if they have public money in their hands.

This notice was published in New York, Virginia, Pennsylvania, and other states.[255] Instead of a flood of notes, this approach allowed the receivers to pay at full value on a first come, first served basis.

During July, Morris contacted the paymaster in the New York camp and forwarded Congress' request for a report on the delivery of notes to the soldiers. This resulted in the regimental paymasters revealing their settlements and showing that most of the soldiers in the Massachusetts line were due no more because they had traded their notes for supplies before they left camp.[256] These were the same regimental paymasters who had been accused of encouraging the troops to engage in this trade of discounted notes before they physically arrived.

Ultimately Morris hoped to cover the notes with money from the Dutch loan, but that loan needed to be supported by interest payments. In July 1783, Captain Barry was in Virginia loading the *Alliance* with an interest payment, made in tobacco, which was bound for Holland. Haggling proceeded according to pattern. Suppliers wanted more money; the state of Virginia wanted to set the value. Morris instructed his Continental receiver to stick with the market rate for the tobacco. Rhode Island was taking small measures by supplying the continent with £20,000 in hard currency. Morris was unwilling to comment on these little actions considering they were expected to pay $1,200,000 and that Rhode Island also refused to pass the impost of 1781.[257] Morris was careful when dealing with such adversarial states as Rhode Island and Virginia.

In an administrative action, he supported his team by finally placing Swanwick under the jurisdiction of the Treasury Department, thus protecting him from Arthur Lee's complaints. Swanwick still performed the same functions for Morris, but his position was accounted for in a way Lee would have to accept. Morris relied on Swanwick for a wide variety of tasks, and ultimately brought him into a business partnership. He was so useful to Morris that instead of receiving a salary he was provided with a percentage of the official business he conducted. It came to about 2.5% per transaction. Once Swanwick was out of risk, Morris moved the process of settlement with the states forward and requested settlement documentation from Virginia. He also proposed a Commissioner to South Carolina. South Carolina accepted the commissioner seven months later, but he was not in office until a year had passed. By that time South Carolina had substantively assumed nearly all their war debts.

The work of Morris' adversaries reverberated in the body politic. The public outcry about the manner in which the soldiers departed the army caused the Congress to seek answers. Morris responded to Congress' request for information about the payment of soldiers. Morris started his response by pointing out that Congress never actually ordered him to arrange payment of the soldiers. He reminded Congress that paying the soldiers was the job of the paymaster and the paymaster was part of the War Department. The Office of Finance voluntarily took on the responsibility for supplying the paymaster with the notes. He continued by pointing out that in the seven weeks from the 9th of April, when the topic of military pay and furloughs arose, to the 26th of May, when Congress finally decided to furlough the soldiers, Morris was not able to act due to lack of any determination by Congress. If the Congress had not ordered the soldiers furloughed they would had to have been supported at camp and that activity would have consumed the financial resources that eventually went to pay them. During the two weeks between the 27th of May and the 6th of June Morris had the special watermarked paper made, the notes printed and six thousand were signed and delivered to the paymaster. Delivery of signed notes continued until July 18th.[258] After the delivery of $500,000 in notes Morris reasoned his next job was finding a way to pay for them, and it was up to the paymaster to use the notes. By July 20th the six and twelve month notes started to make their way back to Morris' tax receiver in New Jersey.[259] The paymaster responded that he had held back some of the notes because, "I was disappointed by a sum expected from Rhode Island…" Morris continued as he explained that the Massachusetts paymasters did not get notes because they had not called for them, and any unevenness in distribution came from the behavior of the troops; some of whom took greater stores before their furlough than others.[260]

Such queries from Congress in Princeton indicated the influence of southern partisans. Not surprisingly, they directed the Secretary of War to build supply magazines on the James River in Virginia. They needed £500 in Virginia money, and justified this by saying the supplies would be ruined without cover.[261] Morris replied that the best solution was to sell the supplies. He pointed out that doing that would raise money instead of requiring the expense of it.[262] These letters were sent to Arthur Lee and a committee of his allies in Congress. They determined to build the storehouses anyway, using Virginia money instead.[263] Quartermaster Pickering sold similar material in New Jersey.

Selling off a few supplies would not help Morris cover his financial exposure. His repeated attempts to get loans from Europe were becoming less popular after the war than during. John Jay wrote from France. He cautioned that the King of France felt as if he were being treated as Morris' cashier, but Jay said the King was pleased that Morris decided to stay in office anyway. He cautioned Morris not to expect his experience in the Office of Finance to improve. He wrote,

> Your office is neither an easy nor a pleasant one to execute, but it is elevated and important and therefore Envy with the inseparable companion Injustice will not cease to plague you.[264]

Morris responded to John Jay,

> My situation as a public man is distressing. I am cursed with the worst of all political sins, poverty. My engagements and anticipations for the public amount to a million of dollars. It racks my utmost invention to keep pace with demands, but hitherto I have been able to preserve that credit which kept our affairs alive until you have the opportunity of concluding a glorious peace, and now a little exertion on the part of the states would enable me to make payment and quit the service with reputation.[265]

Morris' wife Mary kept up correspondence with Mrs. Jay. Her life was busy with domestic activities and that included being hostess to a parade of strangers whom her husband would bring to the house on a regular basis. She wrote, that at

> ...dinner time I generally have the pleasure of Mr. Morris' company and often two or three guests, strangers who swarm in our city from all parts of Europe and numbers of them are recommended to Mr. Morris' particular attention, and which we find most agreeable this warm weather to see in a family way.[266]

She never mentioned the stresses her husband was under and kept a positive tone in her letters to friends. The boys were ensconced in their school in Geneva and Ridley was managing their arrangements.

Over in Europe, Matthew Ridley noted Morris' appeals for more loans were causing a backlash against America. Both Jay and Ridley cautioned against America throwing open her ports without reciprocal agreements with France and England. Ridley continued,

> They want to deprive us of a free trade to their islands, and the ministers have lately said they were in no hurry, the business required reflection, &c.[267]

American banker in Paris, Ferdinand Grand, wrote that the United States was overdrawn by 413,892.13.9 livres, or roughly $80,000, but he was pleased to learn that a line of credit had been arranged with the Dutch firm of Wilink, van Staphorst and Company. American Loan Office Certificates held in Europe amounted to about $100,000, and Grand was working to cover the interest payments. News finally came that the old bills of exchange drawn in Spain during 1779, which had plagued the Office of Finance since its inception, were in the process of being settled, and Thomas Barclay was collecting some money by selling the *Alliance's* final prize, and the *Duc de Lauzun*.[268]

Franklin wrote from France, noting that some of the letters Morris sent to Europe had landed in England and revealed the depths of the difficulties Morris had in supplying the Army. Such revelations were used as a pretext to delay arrangements on the West Indian trade. Franklin remarked that the Farmers General was being very patient because they were not pressing for either repayment of their loans, or timely interest payments from America on the million livres they had loaned. He described their attitude by saying that

> ...now we are at peace, it might not be inconvenient to us to proceed in discharging the debt.[269]

The Farmers General wanted to be repaid in tobacco at a price that had been set years before, in 1781. Their expectation was based on the loan contract, and the price they agreed was not high enough to make the Virginians happy.[270] Along with the end of June, came the resignation of the American Secretary of Foreign Affairs, thus leaving the Continental Government without an international voice.

Morris was busy, as Agent of Marine, getting tobacco onto the *Alliance* and selling most of the ships in the Navy. The *Hague* was scheduled to be sold, and The *Duc de Lauzun* was under contract to be sold in France. He was contemplating selling the *Bourbon* frigate, which had recently been launched; but looked too expensive to be made fit for sea.[271] The *Alliance* and *General Washington* were in service. Morris had taken office with a two-ship navy, and though there were five by July 22nd, 1783, he was cutting the number back to two. Looking again to the states, Morris sent a circular to the governors in which he mentioned his political adversaries, and the harmful effect they were having. He pointed out that his call for taxes was based on the simple arithmetic that payments had exceeded receipts by over $1,000,000 and it was the responsibility of the states to cover the difference. He argued for cutting expenses and raising revenues as the only way to proceed.

Finally, he thought it was necessary to respond to his critics in the Press. Responding to the anonymous writer, Vox Populi, who wrote in the partisan *Freeman's Journal*,[272] Morris said that the notes he had provided to the soldiers in anticipation of revenue were the subject of "Slanderous Reports" in the press which attempted to undermine his program by claiming he was speculating in those notes. This was a claim he not only denied, he challenged others to prove. None ever did. He pointed out that by discrediting him and his program his political enemies were reducing the value of his notes in the public mind and by doing this they were taking money from deserving soldiers. He wrote,

> The attempt therefore by this slander to injure me, is an injury to those who have received my paper...

He continued that popular efforts to discredit his notes were going to ruin the Public Credit and the result of that would be that

> ...the Government becomes chargeable with flagrant injustice... and in the whole proceeding those are made the victims, who confided in the Faith of the Government.[273]

Old business revisited Morris' office. John Irwin arrived from Fort Pitt and wished to receive his salary and cash for his expenses. Morris requested an accounting of his activities in western Pennsylvania, and Irwin stated the records would fill a wagon and were too bulky to bring over three hundred miles east. Morris rejoined that there had been complaints about fraud at Fort Pitt, and he had to talk to the treasurer.

It seemed everyone had a "good idea." The paymaster found some of the 1782 subsistence notes and wanted to exchange them for cash.[274] There was none for the purpose. Abraham Clark, Congressman of New Jersey, wanted to create new treasury notes that would make war debts transferable to other parties, just as the old Loan Office Certificates had been. Morris replied that all such certificates depreciated in value because there were too many for the market to absorb, and too little faith that the Government would fund them. He continued that this resulted in speculation in the papers, and hording by those who offered little to the original holders; thus, making the original holders mad, and empowered the speculator to sue for their full value, creating the possibility of a "run on the bank." He also said that once the original holders no longer have the certificates, funding them becomes more difficult because it is hard to justify enriching speculators. This reduced the possibility that they will be funded and hurt American creditworthiness. Nearly six months later a Congressional committee reviewed Morris' response, and they decided to ignore his input and instructed him to make the treasury certificates transferable.[275]

North Carolina responded to Morris' latest circular with the continued delay of the installation of a Continental Commissioner to settle their war account with the Congress. The states pressed for the use of state paper in Continental payments, and Morris continued to insist on specie as the means of exchange. New Hampshire wanted Congress to issue new Treasury certificates that could be substituted for Loan Office Certificates or for specie, according to the accepted rate of depreciation. These would then be used to pay the requisitions of the 1780's. Morris objected to New Hampshire's plan for two reasons. He was against paying loan interest with another form of paper (called an indent), and he wanted to get rid of the state controlled Continental Loan Officers. He did not want to see them have any more to do with public money because of what he saw as corrupt practices.[276]

Morris' political adversaries, Howell of Rhode Island and Higginson of Massachusetts, wanted to implement New Hampshire's plan throughout all the states. Congress considered adopting the arrangement so the states could issue indents to loan certificate holders within their states and deduct the value of those indents from the amount they owed the Continental Government as their requisition. Congress adopted this system in April 1784. In effect they handed state officers the ability to pay their requisitions with an invented currency with no basis in value. By 1785, when Morris was well out of office, it became clear that more than a few Loan Officers were issuing certificates according to their own ideas and without concern for actual debts, or their job description. Congress concluded,

> ...without the gift of prophecy...the commissioners of the Treasury will never be able to ascertain what, if any monies, are in the hands of several officers, to control its disposition, or to prevent those abuses in the payment of interest, which, without the greatest vigilance will creep in, to the enormous augmentation of the national debt.[277]

Morris continued selling Continental ships to raise money and cut costs. The sale of the *Bourbon* and its stores, including the sale of masts and spars, moved ahead on August 5th when Morris sent the advertisement to Thomas Read in Connecticut. Around the same time, however, Virginia, in an effort to save their own money, offered two of their state navy ships to Congress for the Continental Navy. Morris declined,

> That altho' is an object highly desirable to establish a respectable Marine, yet the situation of the public treasury renders it not advisable to purchase ships at present...[278]

He learned the *America* had sailed out of New Hampshire waters, under the French flag. He had to decline paying some Connecticut state sailors because the states had not paid the requisition of 1782. He made a similar reply when he was asked about payment to the great general Thadddeus Kosciusko. Morris did, however, suggest that Congress might make an exception for Kosciusko, but he (Morris) had to treat all unpaid military men on the same basis.[279]

A pleasant surprise came when Rhode Island remitted $54,171 to the Continental Treasury. Morris was pleased,

> It gives me great pleasure to find that your state are beginning to recover from their late infatuation. In the good sense of the Eastern states I have always reposed much confidence and I will not be persuaded that they have not just intentions although errors may for a while too fatally intervene.[280]

Morris praised the good efforts of Rhode Island, but in general, with the states focused on themselves.

Morris sought money everywhere he could and tried to make the most of America's best bulk commodity, tobacco. He pressed George Eddy for money from the 1781 Yorktown tobacco agreement. It had not all been paid.[281] The Commissioner to settle the accounts of Virginia had yet to begin his work, but Virginia had supplied $9,585 in tobacco as part of their quota.[282] Morris arranged for Mr. La Caze to buy as much of the public Virginia tobacco as he wanted. La Caze was to have a man on the spot to set the price with Morris' agent in Virginia. Mr. La Caze gave Morris a note to cover the purchase, with the expectation that any unspent amount would be returned. Morris discounted the note at the Bank of North America and withdrew cash. Later, La Caze was attempting to purchase tobacco with notes of uncertain value. Morris asked La Caze to pay for tobacco in notes the bank would accept.

The behavior of the states made the American-Dutch relationship most important, and Adams played a key role there. He wrote Morris that success in Holland lay not in agreements with the Government, but in maintaining American creditworthiness. In his wisdom he hazarded a suggestion to Morris, "But I beg leave to suggest the question, whether an application of Congress to the states would not succeed?"[283] Adams might have better asked his friend Arthur Lee to lend his assistance in an effort which Morris had pursued unrelentingly for years. Adams suggested instead that the individual states should send produce that would be used to support American loans in Holland. This suggestion overlooked the structure of the loans. The Continental Congress had made them, not the individual states.

Morris wrote to Adams on the topics of loans from Holland, the glorious peace, and the feeble efforts of the states. He agreed with Adams that the Confederation needed to be made stronger and added,

> But unfortunately for America the narrow and illiberal prejudices of some have taken such deep root that it must be difficult and may prove impracticable to remove them.[284]

He might well have been alluding to Adams' friend Arthur Lee in the hopes that Adams might have influence with him. Then he forwarded extracts of Adams' letters to Governor Hancock in Boston. He did this to promote the passage of the impost of 1783.

The use of tobacco to pay the interest on the Dutch loan was still in the works. Captain Barry was nearly ready to sail the *Alliance* to Holland with the Virginia Tobacco. In accordance with his usual practice Morris sent a note (this time from the Marine Department) to pay for work done to get the *Alliance* ready for sea. That note was to be turned into cash at the Continental Receiver's office. In addition to this note the cash value of the tobacco was to be credited against the Virginia specie requisition of 1783. He instructed the Virginia tax receiver to accept the tobacco buyer's bill of exchange drawn on the Marine Department and to cash it.

> Mr. Clark's bill for the amount drawn on me as Agent of Marine will be received in the Treasury as a remittance on the account of the taxes of Virginia. I am also to request that he may obtain the cash for such bill as soon as your convenience will admit.[285]

The first portion of the Dutch loan had gone to pay the overdrafts on the French Bank from a 1781 loan. This transfer occurred in July 1783, and was much larger than Morris knew, because of the slow pace of letters crossing the ocean. This transfer meant that less money was available for use in America. Meanwhile, Morris was selling bills of exchange backed by the Holland loan for much needed cash. He remained optimistic that the loan would fill, even though his European counterparts had advised him that money was scarce in Europe. He was willing to gamble, and in April he drew $200,000 using notes payable in 90 days. He thought that would give the Dutch plenty of time to fill the subscription to the loan. In August he sold another 165,000 florins, or about $41,000 worth of bills of exchange, before he stopped for a while. He used some of his available money to pay Greene's bills and to cover the payment to the contractor to Greene's army.[286] In September Morris received news that the subscription was filling well in Holland, and then he wrote to the Dutch that he would draw another $200,000. Congress started to make noises to stop using loans from Europe, but they did not act.

To avoid further interference by Congress, and to make sure there were no overdrafts in unfriendly hands, Morris sold $300,000 from the Dutch loan to several of his business associates, John Ross, Peter Whitesides and Co., and Isaac Hazlehurst. These gentlemen agreed to buy the Dutch bills of exchange under an arrangement that would not require them to pay for 150 days, and if the loan was not fully subscribed by that time, they could back out of the deal and get their money returned. This was a kind of option, and it got rid of the threat of overdrafts and Congressional interference.

While these individuals took financial risks to aid the nation, Morris saw national behavior in terms of its willingness to do justice to individuals. On September 15th one of the three disabled veterans whom Morris supported, John Jordan a native of Bengal, (described as "black") appeared before Congress. Three of Morris' most vocal critics, Higginson, Bland, and Ellery tried to forbid that sailor his pension. President of Congress, Charles Thompson, noted at the time,

> This recommendation was sufficient to excite the opposition of those whose malice seems so inveterate that they would risqué their salvation to ruin the man & trample on every feeling of humanity & violate every law of justice to gratify their resentment.

Morris' critics failed to convince Congress, and this man and two others were allowed pensions for life.[287]

In a separate case, an ex-prisoner of war came to the Office and demanded immediate payment on a long note he held. The Conversation did not proceed much further than that. Morris wrote,

> This gentleman was too full of his own opinion to hear those of any other person and Mr [G.] Morris left him to enjoy them contenting himself with the assurance that we cannot do otherwise.[288]

Another, more familiar individual, sought attention. John Holker had lost some Loan Office Certificates and wanted them replaced; Morris declined to help until their value could be ascertained.[289] A couple of days later Holker wanted money on the account of Daniel Parker & Co., a firm in which Holker had an interest.[290] Morris decided to cash one of Holker's checks at the Office of Finance, or in the terms of the day, to discount a note for him. This was done, and the Office of Finance profited by $556.[291] Holker was in need of funds and was pressing Morris for a settlement of their business dealings. Morris' later request that Congress settle the accounts of the Secret Committee was probably an outgrowth of this meeting.[292]

During this time, when pressures came at him from all sides, Morris heard from an old friend in England with whom he had done business before the war. He wrote back and told him of his life, I

> ...have been of some use in establishing the Independence and Liberty of this country. I have a family that makes me perfectly happy so far as it depends on them, a most worthy woman as my wife and six good children four boys and two daughters ... I have car-

> ried on considerable business during the war by one means or other and with very various success, sometimes I have made immense sums and at others lost them again for the whole was a lottery as we could not get insurance. I can however upon the whole set down perfectly content on the score of property... I have lost during the war not less than 150 sail of vessels first and last in which I was interested but as one or two successful voyages paid for ship and cargo I am upon the whole rather a gainer. At present I fill the most important office in the American Government but am trying to get rid of it because I want ease and indulgence to compensate for a life of labor and bustle.[293]

Morris got back to work and took steps to raise funds where he could. In the first week of August 1783 the Marine Office advertised the *Bourbon* for sale at a public auction. The advertisement ran in a variety of Pennsylvanian, as well as New England papers. The sale was to be held in Middletown Connecticut nearly seven weeks later. Payment was expected in "cash, bank notes or Notes of the Financier."[294] Shortly thereafter he advertised the *Hague* to be sold at public auction in Boston. Acceptable forms of payment were the same.[295] This again became a topic of complaints by his critics who wished to pay with Loan Office Certificates. Morris had consistently refused to convert those Certificates unless directed by Congress, because he was not able to ascertain their hard money value.

While Morris moved ahead with selling ships, he requested Congress to help him in settling the Marine accounts by settling the accounts of the older committees.

> The accounts of the Secret and the Commercial committees of Congress are far from being inconsiderable, either as to their nature or magnitude. They are involved with others, and have extended themselves to different parts of the United States, and to Europe and the West Indies. There are more particularly connected with the Marine Accounts and with any others, but the settlement of them is highly necessary.[296]

Congress did not immediately act on this request.

Some bits of old business never seemed to get finished, and George Eddy was again headed to New York to finally get the Yorktown Tobacco account settled; also in New York, the contractors to the Northern Army, who in 1782 had an argument over some beef, were found liable in court to pay for it, and they intended to sue the Office of Finance for repayment.[297]

Even with the unsettled business of the past, military expenses continued. A paymaster to the 5th Pennsylvania Regiment was robbed of about $7,000 meant as subsistence for the Officers.[298] Morris wrote back to tell him that only Congress could provide relief for his troubles. Captain James Nicholson reported that he had finished the duty of bringing soldiers from the Southern Department to the North by water. Colonel Harmer of the Southern Army insisted that Morris provide his troops with three months' pay, even though General Greene had already supplied that amount. Morris declined the suggestion to pay some soldiers more than others; and held that only Congress could act to break the system he had worked so hard to create.[299]

Morris scrambled to cobble together money to meet current engagements, but long term American financial health would rely on the establishment of new trade arrangements. Keeping Cuba open to American trade was part of that effort, and the question of Oliver Pollock's role there was key. The interim Captain General of Louisiana and Florida in Havana, Josef de Ezpeleta, announced to Morris that he would treat Oliver Pollock with the same respect that Governor Don Bernardo De Galvez would. He followed up by saying that Congress delivered a message through Pollock that they would not pay the $74,087 Pollock had gotten from the Spanish until it was determined if that money was for America or Pollock's personal use. Ezpeleta had to refer that question to Spain for an answer.[300]

Another sticking point came to Morris' attention when the Commissioner of Accounts for Pennsylvania, Benjamin Stelle, requested even more clarification in detail on Morris' instructions. He wanted explicit directions and sent Morris a twenty-one-point questionnaire.[301] Morris provided answers to his questions, but it was clear from his responses that he expected Stelle to do as all the other Commissioners had done and figure it out for himself, using existing and available information.[302] The queries triggered Congressional involvement in the settlement because a copy of the questions had also been sent to Congress. In his answers Morris was careful not to overstep the bounds of his office and said only Congress could decide some of the questions. This process was used as an opening for Congress to become more involved in the contentious issue of the settlement of state debts. David Howell, of Rhode Island, was the person who suggested Stelle for the position. Morris had accepted Stelle as part of his general tendency to include all sorts of people in his administration. Morris' was about to feel the bite of such "bipartisanship."

Howell said Stelle was "exceedingly embarrassed in the execution of his commission for want of more explicit instructions." Howell failed to observe that Stelle was the only Commissioner who had these questions. Howell continued to promote his state-oriented agenda,

> I shall soon move the interesting affair of consolidating the public securities; but expect to meet with every opposition from the advocates for continental measures.[303]

The issue was then joined by the Continental Interests and the Agricultural Interests. There was much arguing about the details: When a fence is destroyed during a battle is it to be paid for by the Government? How do you fix the price? What means are used to pay? What about the use of impressed buildings, livestock? Would there be interest paid for supplies impressed, and at what rate? Are the states still liable for the requisitions, and should they be paid in hard money? These issues were not settled until the administration of Hamilton in Treasury. In the meantime people who needed repayment were at a loss. This swelled the chorus of complaint against Morris' work, and was added to the discontent voiced over the payment of soldiers in notes. As stated earlier, the soldiers adopted the idea that Morris was speculating in his own notes to drive the price down and to cheat them.

Morris observed with no small amount of dismay,

> It becomes impossible to serve a people who convert everything into a ground for calumny.... My desire to relieve the Army has been greatly cooled, from the information that many of them have joined in the reproaches I have incurred for their benefit. And the necessity I feel of quitting (at the earliest possible moment) an Office of incessant labor and anxiety, whose only reward is obloquy, will not permit me to even think of any farther anticipations.[304]

Many other people had to scramble just to survive because of their dealings with the Continental Congress. Among them were the teamsters, who remained unpaid. A number of them had purchased their teams on credit, basing their behavior on their faith in payment from the Government. They watched helplessly as many of their oxen died from the Southern heat and lack of forage. Now the dearth of remittances from the states resulted in no payments to the teamsters. Quartermaster Pickering wrote,

> ... many have been sued and stripped of their farms and others are compelled to fly from their state to escape their creditors.[305]

Morris had no power to stop this because the states had not given the funds.

The teamsters were not the only ones feeling pain. "Dealers in paper" also had their problems. Morris frequently learned of the effects of serious mischief in that sphere that he was trying to extinguish. In one such case, Morris wrote to Governor Benjamin Harrison, after a defrauder was discovered in Virginia,

> ... it may after all be extremely difficult to if not impracticable to trace up frauds to their source. This is one of the many evils which arise from a defective and unmethodical system and the evils of such systems are (I am sorry to say) the reasons why many are desirous of seeing it reestablished.

He regretted that he was not given the support he needed to accomplish his task, because he felt, if he had support, he

> ...could have left my successor the pleasing prospect of future wealth unclouded by any dismal retrospect of past poverty. But, all other things out of the question, there is such a disposition among men to traduce and vilify that no prudent man will risk a fair reputation by holding an office so important as mine.[306]

In the same vein Morris shared his dismay with his agent in Rhode Island,

> I have my fears that the states will turn a deaf ear to all applications. Where all this is to end God knows. But it seems to me that one of the first effects must be to dissolve the Confederation. What will afterwards follow whether a new and better bond or total and absolute anarchy time the greater arbiter of human institutions must determine.[307]

Morris received further reports that a speculative market was developing for the notes he had been sending into the field. Staying true to his analysis stated in the 1781 work *On Public Credit,* Morris maintained that such speculations among individuals cannot have any effect on the policies of a Government that had already promised to redeem those notes as a certain price. He pointed out that by redeeming the notes at the face value it would assist the original holders by suppressing speculation, and to do the opposite would cause dumping of the notes which would make the original holders poor, and increase collection by speculators.[308]

Even with this in the background, Morris was convinced by Pickering and Washington to supply Washington with $10,000 in his notes as a way to finance the effort to take control of the western forts.[309] Daniel Parker won the bid, and made arrangements to supply Washington's new campaign in northern New York State. Ultimately, however, Washington abandoned his effort to take possession of the posts in western New York, due to the early onset of winter.[310] Morris told Quartermaster Pickering to apply the $10,000 sent for that mission to pay for the wood Washington needed.[311]

After much anticipation, the time for the advertised sale of the ships had come. Morris directed Captain Thomas Reed on the sale of the *Bourbon,*

> ...take care to set her up at such price as will prevent her being struck off for any trivial sum and that you endeavor to have her sold for as much as possible.

To underscore the importance of getting as much as possible he reminded Reed that

> ...the situation of the ship and our affairs is such that it might eventually become a new source of loss and if so it would be doubtless be converted to an ample source of calumny.[312]

He told Thomas Russell to keep the price up at the auction of the *Hague* by outbidding others, and if necessary to use government money to bid up the price.[313] In other naval business, the one active ship reported in. On August 20th, 1783, John Barry wrote Morris to inform him that the tobacco for Holland had been loaded and he was pleased to be heading to sea once more.[314]

True to their pattern of following through poorly on their commitments to most individuals, Congress did little to improve the sad state of affairs for those youths from the Delaware tribe. Thomas Killbuck came again to Morris. Morris responded, "one of the Indian youths under care of Congress applies for cloths. I tell him that he must get them through Colonel George Morgan to whose care Congress have entrusted that business."[315]

-|-

With peace fully in force, the states asserted their independence. In Maryland, Daniel of St. Thomas Jennifer, refused to accept Morris notes as payment for tobacco that was to be credited as part of the requisition. This was due to Maryland's newly found intention not to pay their requisition, and instead pay their soldiers directly. The forces of disunion were also at work in Congress as a partisan committee made up of Elbridge Gerry of Massachusetts, Abraham Clark of New Jersey, and Arthur Lee of Virginia decided to conduct a close review of Morris' response to Mr. Stelle. A series of letters went back and forth between Morris' Philadelphia office and Princeton, where Congress had gone. Clark seemed to be attempting to get Morris to put into writing something that might incriminate him. Around the same time Arthur Lee and David Howell asked Morris for an updated report on the foreign debt. Gerry met with Morris in Philadelphia. After that meeting Morris wrote Gerry a complete response detailing why Gerry's proposals would fail. Gerry's proposals included altering the mode for settling accounts, forgetting future collections of the 1781, 1782, and 1783 requisitions; collecting all the debts into one big group and assessing the states according to what was actually spent.[316] Congress eventually agreed with Morris to avoid these suggestions.

Keeping to the theme of state sovereignty, Rhode Islanders tried to shift the blame onto Morris when they complained that the money they sent to pay the army was used to pay for other things and that was why there was no money for the Army. This idea was picked up by Massachusetts, who also had not paid their whole requisition. Small wonder that they were not interested in an accounting, when that would reveal their perfidy. Instead, they wanted to lump everything together.[317] An effort was underway to blame Morris for misappropriating the money and to strip the Office of Finance of authority so it would be abolished or at least become useless in managing the finances. The legislature in Massachusetts issued instructions to their delegates to work for the

> ...abridgement of the powers instructed to the office of Superintendent of Finance" and to be "unrelenting" in their push to have "the office of Finance abolished, and a Board of Treasury, consisting of three persons, annually chosen from different states, with proper powers, instituted instead.[318]

As the Congressmen tried to push Morris out of office, and to ruin his financial program, Morris worked to maintain American creditworthiness with interest payments to the Dutch Bankers. Unfortunately, John Barry was distressed to report that his ship full of tobacco would not make it to Holland. The ship started to leak, and the pumps were inadequate. She started to take on an inch every half minute, and the water had reached some of the tobacco. Barry decided to turn around and head for the Delaware Bay.[319]

Trade with Holland was difficult, but trade with Cuba was even more so. Oliver Pollock presented his commission papers to the acting governor of Cuba. Unfortunately, by the time Pollock arrived, Cuba had closed her port to the Americans, without notice. Pollock's bold gambit to arrive and act as if normal trade would continue was in the jeopardy. The acting governor said Pollock could not be installed as agent because there was no order from the king to accept him.[320]

While new efforts were checked, old business kept ticking along. The troops needed money for wood and rations. Captain John Green was sent to Boston to serve on the board of Court Martial. Daniel Parker was paid for transporting troops from the south. Morris sent the accounts of Silas Deane to Arthur Lee's committee for review, and specifically requested that the documents be well maintained.[321] Morris was informed that the Commissioner to New Jersey who was expected to work on the settlement of that state's debt was not operating the office, and nothing was being done.[322] Over the course of the last year Dudley and his team endeavored to find a suitable location for the mint and set about making the minting machines. Apparently ignoring Morris' suggestion to seek employment elsewhere, Benjamin Dudley brought to Morris "the dies for coining in the American Mint."[323] Progress was so slow on the project, that in July Morris came to doubt Congress' resolve in creating the Mint; and suggested again to Benjamin Dudley that he look to the private sector for employment.[324]

When the coins were finally finished and the first set could be seen, the U.S. abbreviation was prominent, and both Liberty and Justice were on the coins. As the coins awaited Congressional action, Morris was planning the first private trade mission between the U. S. and China. Morris recruited a Dr. Johnson to procure articles for trade in his new private venture using the *Empress of China*. Dr. Johnson was paid $1,000 from a company Mor-

ris was interested in, Trumbull, Marmie, & Co. The doctor then set out to western Pennsylvania to purchase ginseng for shipment to the Far East.[325] In doing this Morris was creating the American ginseng trade.

Private ventures went more quickly than public business, particularly in the Marine Department. After reviewing the condition of the leaking *Alliance*, Morris suggested to the President of Congress on September 1st, that the ship be sold as a cost cutting measure.[326] Morris' suggestion was forwarded to a committee consisting of Arthur Lee, William Ellery of Rhode Island, and Elbridge Gerry of Massachusetts. They reported back that the tobacco be unloaded, the officers and crew be dismissed, and the ship surveyed to determine the cost of repairs.[327] The report was not approved until January of 1784. Three months later, in March 1784, Congress resolved that the *Alliance* must be repaired. Morris responded that the *Alliance* and also the *General Washington* should be sold. A year later, in April 1785, long after Morris had left office and after the *Alliance* had been repaired at great expense, David Howell of Rhode Island moved in Congress that the *Alliance* should be sold as a cost cutting measure. She was sold to a party in Philadelphia, but Morris eventually bought the *Alliance*. He put her to use in his growing China trade business. As luck would have it, she returned to Philadelphia from Canton in 1788 with enough valuable cargo to rescue Morris from financial embarrassment.[328]

An old piece of Marine business resurfaced. In 1777 Gustavus Conyngham had been granted, by the American commissioners in Europe, an appointment as a captain in the Continental Navy sailing out of Dunkirk. His commission was seized by the French, who at that time were pretending to be neutral, and he went back to sea as a privateer. In 1783 Conyngham approached Morris, who told him to petition Congress to have his commission reinstated. Congress referred this back to Morris with the instruction that Conyngham be reinstated if his facts were correct. However, after Morris became involved, the matter ended up going before a committee that included Arthur Lee. Lee had previously exhibited his disdain for the American Commissioners in Europe when he encouraged Captain Landais to take him back to America on the *Alliance*. In a decision that was consistent with his earlier stance Lee denied Conyngham's petition based on his contention that the earlier commission was for temporary use only.[329]

Considering the behavior of certain Congressmen, it was wise for Morris to keep his financial exposure in mind. He wanted to accelerate the collection of his notes, and instructed his receiver, Harwood, to accept his notes "as cash notwithstanding the length of their date."[330] He thanked the

Governor of Connecticut for his assistance in collecting taxes, which he understood was "considered to be an unpopular theme."[331] He instructed his receiver in Rhode Island to sell supplies for cash, and to keep honoring his notes at the hard money value. He continued,

> The effects of this procedure will be to lessen the quantity of paper in circulation, to increase the value of it, to extend the circle of credit and to multiply the advocates for taxation because that every person who deposits with you will from that moment apply only to the taxes for relief.[332]

By that he meant that people who turn their notes in for hard currency will know they receive that money from taxpayers, and so they will encourage the taxation system.

False rumors about Morris' speculation in government paper continued to circulate, particularly in states that were unfriendly to his policies. Morris responded to a question from his tax receiver in Rhode Island about his alleged speculating in Loan Office Certificates,

> You ask whether I incline to purchase any Loan Office Certificate – I do not. If I had ever so much ability and inclination I would not under my present official circumstances.... At least I can answer for myself that I have in no instance bought any of these certificates [from the loan offices] but when people in want have sought relief at my hands in a few instances of peculiar distress I have agreed to take them but it was always on their own terms being much more than the certificates were worth.[333]

Moving at the pace set by a remote Congress in Princeton, Morris told the Quartermaster that Congress had appointed commissioners to settle accounts up to the end of 1781 and the teamsters fell into that category. He was not sanguine about the prospects,

> I confess to you that the people suffer injustice and so do hundreds of others. To the injustice they suffer I am no party, but if by relieving them I become a defaulter to those with whom I have made engagements I shall be chargeable with guilt which is now to be answered for by those who delay in the several states the general measures which can alone afford general relief.[334]

Morris saw he was responsible to pay the notes he signed for the Government, and that the states were not doing their part to come up with the money. He had as much at risk due to inaction on the part of the states as the farmers who lost their farms. Morris understood that Americans would only change in the face of crisis, and they did not see their path of disunity leading there, yet. He wrote to Washington,

> I persuade myself that the only effectual means of getting a good American establishment of any kind is to be so long without it that a sense of the want shall stimulate the states into the means of forming it.[335]

The question of Loan Office Certificates issued before 1782 continued to be unanswered. Morris gave his opinion on the subject,

> That the reducing all Loan Office Certificates to their true value, according to the tables of depreciation is doubtless a desirable object.... That every operation which can have the slightest connection with public credit, ought to be conducted on the principles of equal and reciprocal bargain do that the object be performed with the perfect consent of the party as well as of the Government.

He proposed to solve the question by liquidating all the Loan Office Certificates in specie value and give to the holders new certificates "similar to those which they issue in other cases."[336] Thereby he hoped to have only one kind of government certificate, the same kind used by the central government in the final settlement with farmers, states, merchants, whomsoever. The contrasting proposal was to turn the old Loan Office Certificates in for a kind of state paper issued by the state appointed loan officer.

Morris was planning a trip from his office in Philadelphia to Princeton where Congress sat. George and Martha Washington offered a place for him and Mrs. Morris to stay, "we join very sincerely in offering you a bed at our quarters."[337] Before he went, he enlisted the Commissioners of Accounts to observe the country and provide reports on the nature of the conditions they found. He wrote to them,

> ...you will have occasion to travel into different places and therefore you will have an opportunity to render an accurate account of many particulars...

Morris wanted to create an understanding of the real conditions in America. He wanted to know the moral condition of an area, its general population, mode of life, climates, the arts (both fine and useful), and the buildings. He was curious to know if the buildings would be useful in the event of war. He was also interested in knowing the political condition: if it were aristocratic, or democratic. He wanted to know the distribution of lands, and equality of fortunes in the cities and town. He wanted to know if authority was respected and the character of the magistrates and the police force. He asked for information on the modes of tax collection. The commercial state of the areas was to be ascertained, if there was manufacturing, what the roads were like, and the ports. He wanted information on the role of imports and exports, and the value of lands and money (meaning the price of a loan, or interest rate). This was the first ever inventory of America. Their responses have not been found.[338] Later, Alexander Hamilton conducted a similar survey through his customs agents.[339]

Morris noted, with some satisfaction, that the financial settlements were under way in some states, and expressed hope that the system might finally work,

> The Commissioners in many of the states are also employed and I hope and expect that in a short time they will all be so. But if I should be deceived in this expectation and forced into those apprehensions which affect your minds I must confess that I see no possibility of adopting any effectual system if the present cannot operate in the mode intended.[340]

The long-term work of his office was underway, but Morris still had to inch forward on the various tasks before him. He looked for a way to send tobacco to Holland because transportation on the *Alliance* was impossible. He advertised in the paper and checked with Daniel Clark, his agent in Virginia. He also alerted Clark that Mr. La Caze was expected to contact Clark about buying tobacco. On different business, he received news from Fort Pitt that they were sending $2,726 back to the treasury. It was noted that this was the first money ever to return.[341] He ordered the sale of more government stores to raise cash and met with a delegation of Englishmen who were in Philadelphia to discuss the evacuation of New York, and the payment of debts to Englishmen.[342] George Eddy came back from New York with unsatisfactory documentation and apparently no money from the tobacco sale. Arthur Lee took note of a poorly clad military unit and proposed a resolution, which Congress passed, to have Morris account for all clothing purchased for the troops since Morris took office.

In response, Morris reported to Congress on the subject of the clothing purchases.

> No money has been expended for the purchase of it in Europe, by my order; but since coming into office a part of that which was ordered by Colo. Laurens was procured, and also some clothing by Mr. Barclay and also some expenses have doubtless accrued by the lad-

> ing, unlading, relading of it etc. Congress will easily see that I cannot presume or attempt to render accounts of these expenses, until your commissioner in Europe shall have adjusted them and transmitted to me the copies.... To show the confusions which have happened in this business, I do myself the honor to enclose the copy of the only information hitherto received as to the last parcel of these goods which arrived.... No clothing fit for soldiers (or at least very little if any) except linen arrived here before the Preliminaries of Peace.

He described that most of the cloths arrived after the peace and were sold to generate funds to pay the soldiers.

> Wherefore it was most proper to settle the account with the disbanded soldiers, and allow them the value of the clothing due, and to apply the monies arising from a sale of the materials to absorb a part of the heavy anticipations which were made.[343]

Congress had no funds; and had been kept informed throughout the process. Arthur Lee's allies had spent thousands and thousands on cloths that sat in storage in Europe for months, arrived late and turned out to be useless.

Lee could not let that analysis go without response. After all he had seen one unit that needed uniforms; and was ready to overlook the larger picture that a disbanding army needs pay more than uniforms they won't wear. In his response he did not mention why it took so long for the uniforms to arrive, the failings of his allies, or their commissions as purchasers. Instead, he focused his attention on Morris and his department. Lee wrote about Morris,

> ... he thought it was more proper to sell the clothing than to distribute it to the soldiery. In laying out the public money commissions accrue to his friends, in selling the things so purchased, new commissions arise to the sellers. In this case, it is his clerk Mr. Swanwick who is to have this emolument. In the mean time soldiers have been 15 months without their clothing tho two millions of dollars have been take out of the public coffers for that purpose ... public money is lavished away, the soldiery, defrauded & the public plundered.[344]

Clearly Lee had not lost the flourish typical of old fashioned Country Party rhetoric.

-|-

Europe was far removed from factional disputes and peace brought new developments. September 12th, 1783 John Jay, who was familiar with

Morris' interest in the new, wrote to him from France about, "the invention of globes where with men may literally soar above the clouds."[345] He had witnessed the launching of hot air balloons in Paris. Morris replied,

> Pray cannot they contrive to send passengers with a man to steer the course, so as to make them the means of conveyance for dispatches from one country to another, or must they only be sent for intelligence to the Moon and clouds.

Jay also mentioned with relief that the definitive treaty had been signed, and he expected a definitive treaty of commerce. Morris closed his response with this announcement on the subject of trade,

> I am sending some ships to China in order to encourage others in the adventurous pursuits of commerce and I wish to see a foundation laid for an American Navy.[346]

Morris' training as a merchant made it natural for him to seek the new. That included new markets, and new products. One side of Morris' personality, that was not really put to use in his role as Superintendent, was his interest in new technology. He was the first American to have Merino sheep, and eventually gave them to Jefferson. He also attempted to launch a manned balloon from his back yard. He had a sophisticated icehouse behind his house. His greenhouses were state of the art, with the latest cooling systems. He eventually bought a steam engine company; and had the first iron-rolling mill in America. For this reason, and because he was an investor in many businesses, Morris was approached by people with pet projects. For example, he had a meeting with a Mr. Moorhead who claimed to have a perpetual motion machine. Morris was "convinced that his discoveries are very defective."[347]

Thomas Jefferson and Morris shared this interest in new technology. Jefferson, who disliked copying his own letters, had heard of a machine that would allow for automatic duplication. He asked Morris to write Franklin for "one of those writing machines invented there [France] not long since."[348] Morris wrote to Franklin and arranged the purchase and supplied funds from his account to facilitate it.[349]

Both Robert and Gouverneur Morris were active in the development of new markets and sought trade relations with a variety of countries since the resignation of the Secretary of Foreign Affairs, in June. Ridley wrote from Europe on the topic of trade. He said that the goal of the French was

> ...to shut us out from the West India Islands, unless to carry fish paying a duty, lumber, live stock, cattle, and salted provisions and to make in return taffia, coffee and cotton, but no sugar.[350]

The prospects for trade were not improving anywhere. The French were coming to the conclusion that America would become a maritime power, and a competitor as a producer of flour and salted fish. The Americans tried to convince the French that if America could send cheap food to the French West Indies then the Island economies would be more profitable. The French did not want to hurt the interests of their own farmers, who exported flour to the French West Indies, by allowing Americans to do the same. As time went along the French became less and less open to America's free trade proposals, even though the 1778 Treaty of Amity and Commerce between France and America promised free ports in the French islands. In a series of separate agreements made between 1781 and 1783 the French tobacco importers, the Farmers General, had loaned America a total of six million livres. They were willing to reduce the interest due on the loan, but they wanted to speed up the payment of the principle. Congress refused the offer to reduce the interest, mostly because they could not speed up payment of the principle.[351] The terms of that sole-source repayment contract was drawn up according to Gallic mercantile principals, and appeared, to some, to grant a monopoly.

With the Army disbanded, the pace of work slowed in the Office of Finance, but it did go on. Haym Salomon was selling bills of exchange drawn on the Dutch loan to get money for continuing operations, and to cover Morris' notes. Morris' agent, Daniel Clark, sold Virginia tobacco (collected as tax) to Mr. La Caze and the cash went into the Continental tax coffers. One of the ships, chartered years before by the Secret Committee, *The Aurora,* had been lost due to capture by Algerians,[352] and the account of that had to be settled.[353] Morris told the owner that would have to wait until the Secret Committee accounts were settled.[354] He also mentioned that because he had been on that committee it would not be possible for him to work on it.[355]

Joseph Pennell had been installed to settle the Marine Department accounts but, unfortunately, the records from 1776 were not well kept. The different boards and committees who oversaw the Marine expenses used different systems, and there had been no allowance for depreciation in the Marine supply agreements up to 1780, or in the payments made to sailors. He closed,

> You will be better able to judge the difficulties I labor under in laying a proper foundation for a general settlement in this department when I inform you that the Marine Committee have kept no Books of Accounts during their management of the business and their minutes of money matters are not sufficiently expressive to direct the making of necessary entries.[356]

The result of this lack of methodology was the kind of practice John Brown encountered dealing with the Eastern Naval Board in Boston back in 1782, and the source of conflict. Morris wrote back and told him that while it may be difficult or impossible to find all the vouchers it was the job of the commissioners to get all the available information together, and only Congress could "supply the deficit"; meaning only Congress could determine what to do when the documentation was not complete. He also suggested to Pennell that Mr. Hewes kept the records and those should be "at the treasury or in the office of the Secretary of Congress."[357] The issue of depreciation and the rate of pay for people in the marine division lingered until 1787 and settlement was eventually made on the same basis as the pay for the Army.

On September 15th, 1783, Morris' and Willing's business partner Samuel Inglis died. Shortly after this, Morris took John Swanwick into the partnership in his place. This was the beginning of a new firm called Willing, Morris & Swanwick.[358] Making a clerk into a partner was a favor done to Morris by Willing's father, and now it had been extended to Morris' clerk. This was not the usual way of business for all firms. Often partnerships in a merchant trading house were reserved for family members and social equals, not clerks. Later he wrote Willing and Bingham, that the death of Inglis brought about the breakup of the firm Bingham, Inglis & Gilmor, in which Morris had invested. It was at this juncture that Bingham started to work more closely with the Baring brothers, who had also invested in the earlier firm.[359] The Baring brothers would eventually help Bingham finance the separation of Maine from Massachusetts.

Morris helped Swanwick advance, but other young people in the care of Congress were not so lucky. One of the three Delaware Indians who had been under the dilatory care of a Mr. Morgan, was finished with his studies and wanted to go home. Mr. Morgan estimated it would cost about £30 (Pennsylvania money) to supply him with a horse and traveling supplies. The other two were still in school, but one had gotten a young woman pregnant and was going to marry her. These two planned to return to the Indian Territory after they had married, and the young man finished school. Morris referred the request to Congress. A Congressional committee suggested that it would be best to encourage the three young men to stay together in Philadelphia for another year, and to provide for the young woman. They directed Morris to supply them with the necessary funds.[360] For this need, and others, Morris arranged the sale of more public stores, this time at the office of Mr. Swanwick, and made his notes, bank notes, and cash the accepted media of exchange.[361]

Bowing to pressure generated by the partisan press, the Commissioner for settling the accounts of New Jersey left office with the job unfinished. Morris worked to nominate a new commissioner.[362] He wrote to the Governor, telling him that the reason for resignation would make it difficult to find a suitable candidate who could look after New Jersey's interests in the final settlement of accounts, especially now that peace had arrived.[363]

New Jersey and other states were participating only to a marginal degree, but money was still required. Morris contacted the Dutch syndicate that was compiling the funds for the loan. He notified them that tobacco was being shipped to cover the interest payments, and requested that they accept bills drawn in anticipation of the loan, and if the funds were not there, he, Morris, would ship tobacco to cover any shortfall.[364] He wrote to his banker in France, Mr. Grand, that he expected some new money to be put into the Government's account there. He wrote,

> Mr. Barclay will I suppose have put into your hands from the *Alliance* prizes and the sales of the *Duc de Lauzun* some where about three hundred thousand livres.[365]

It was becoming clear that England, France and Spain were closing their ports to American trade, and putting excessive duties on goods from America, that were not forbidden. The consensus of the Office of Finance was that it was better to make no trade agreements when America was in a weak position, but they did not have the authority to make treaties anyway. Both Robert and Gouverneur Morris thought that British trade restrictions would ultimately cause the American states to form a united front, but it would take time.[366] Looking farther east, Gouverneur saw hope for American trade in the possibility of a war between Russia and the Ottoman Empire. He thought that trade with Russia, via the Black Sea, would open markets for American goods.[367]

Morris wrote to Franklin about trade with Europe,

> Until we can navigate the Mediterranean in safety we cannot trade in our own bottoms with the ports of France and Spain which are on that sea.[368]

He pointed out that it would be necessary to ship American goods in English ships if a merchant wanted to trade on the Mediterranean. The British were familiar with the problem of the Algerian pirates, and they saw those pirates as a way of keeping America out of the Mediterranean altogether. One Member of Parliament quipped, that if Algeria did not exist, they would have had to invent it.

The loss of a Secretary of Foreign Affairs was felt as Congress reverted to its earlier committee system. Congress had the power to undertake political treaties. They had actually done this with France and England, but they were wary of seeming to concentrate power in their own hands by asking to make a single treaty that would cover all the states. Instead, Congress did little more than encourage the states to consider the whole Confederation when they went to make their own arrangements. Some states saw the danger of having other states compete with one another in discordant policies. Pennsylvania, in particular, wanted Congress to take the lead. Various states put out calls for harmony, but each state had its own unique set of exports, and even though there was an effort to harmonize the policies of all the states their different interests ultimately resulted in a hodgepodge of regulations. The merchants petitioned Congress for a long-term national policy, but the farmers and planters were not in agreement. There were more farmers than merchants, and their point of view won the day in the State houses up and down the Atlantic seaboard. States used tariffs to lure trade, to the disadvantage of neighboring states. They even put tariffs on trade from one state to another. As these developments unfolded a number of states were trying to enlarge the powers of Congress to allow that body to have the ability to engage in commercial treaties with foreign powers. Doing this required a change to the Articles of Confederation and a single no vote would undo the whole process.

Amid this uncertainty, Morris continued to increase his private business activities. On October 1st, 1783 he formed a new partnership with John Holker and Benjamin Harrison, Jr., the son of the Virginia Governor. It was called Harrison Junior & Co. Morris and Holker contributed the capital of $8,000, while Harrison was allowed to contribute his share over time. The agreement stated,

> The business of the said House shall be confined to the purchase, importation and sale of European goods, and the said acting partner shall not take a concern or interest in any shipping neither shall he engage in the execution of any commission or orders for

> American produce or on account of any person whatever on whose honor and solidity he is depended for reimbursement without the special consent of the said Robert Morris in writing...[369]

The Virginia based firm was thereby confined to European goods, and this meant that it was not involved in the slave trade.

On October 8th the Quakers offered a report to Congress that recommended the end of the slave trade. The action on this report was slow. On December 18th it was sent to a committee consisting of David Howell, Arthur Lee, and Samuel Osgood. Perhaps the citizens of Pennsylvania thought the report would have support from Lee because he had written against slavery in the 1760's. Three months later the committee rejected the report; and it was never sent to the states for ratification.[370] On January 26, 1785 the Quakers tried again when Nicholas Waln delivered a similar petition. It met with similar results.[371]

Autumn

Peace was in the air, and the business of warfare had to be wound down as the calendar moved towards winter. This included paying old bills and settling old accounts. However, at this key moment, there was still no one in charge of American foreign affairs. As a result, members of the Office of Finance stepped forward because of the role international trade would play in generating the funds needed to pay debts, both foreign and domestic.

The Office of Finance looked to the future, but the old business never seemed to let go. The disagreement about beef payments from the end of 1781 was still grinding along. Comfort Sands had lost a round in court and they applied again to Morris for payment. In New York State, Quartermaster Pickering was paying debts with the remainder of the $10,000 that had been allocated for the Western campaign.[372] From its perch in Princeton, Congress instructed Morris to stop the sale of goods that might be useful for clothing for troops. Morris replied that Congress was making the settlement of accounts more, rather than less complicated, and they were also making it difficult for him to redeem the notes he had outstanding. He long suspected they intended to make note redemption difficult. Nevertheless, he complied and did his best in spite of what he saw as an unnecessarily complicated and expensive method of supply.[373]

More locally, an old partnership was under stress. The Chevalier de La Luzerne wrote Morris that Holker had been asked to settle his account as Agent of Marine to the French navy, and yet Holker seemed to be delaying deliberately. The Chevalier asked Morris to encourage

Holker to clear up the business. He also wrote to persuade Morris to be swift in settling accounts for French soldiers, both living and dead.[374] Holker again came to Morris to settle their mutual accounts and was becoming even more insistent.

Morris wanted to get his old accounts settled too. This required Deane's accounts to be settled. He wrote to Arthur Lee on the topic of Deane's account, that the business could not be settled without also settling the accounts of the Secret and Commercial Committees. He attempted to point Lee in the right direction by outlining the arrangements that ended the effort to get goods to trade with the American Indians. He noted,

> Of the several shipments made some arrived, some were taken [by privateers], some were detained by the enemies naval power. The risques being great, it was thought most advisable to abandon the farther prosecution of the plan, which the parties to the contract, then in this country cheerfully consented to, and it was determined that the proceeds of those shipments which might have arrived should be carried into the general public accounts.[375]

Morris also noted that the money sent to Europe for Deane was insufficient for the project anyway, and the remaining funds that went into the general account should be under settlement by Mr. Barclay in France. Nothing was said on the propriety of assigning Lee to settle the accounts of his most bitter rival, Deane. Clearly, however, Morris averred to Lee's pick, Barclay, for the task.

For his part, Arthur Lee persisted in making endless requests for small pieces of data as he burrowed into Silas Deane's account.[376] During the process, Deane contacted Morris from France and maintained that he was falsely stigmatized. Not surprisingly, Deane felt betrayed by those in whom he had placed his trust. Subsequent revelations prove that his secretary, Dr. Bancroft, was most likely responsible for the publication of the letters that led to Deane's disgrace. Consequently, Dean lived in low and reduced circumstances, as a result of the status he held among his former peers. He wrote,

> I passed near eighteen months in Ghent in narrow cheap lodgings, most of the time without a servant, and dining at a table D'hote or ordinary, saw no one, that I could avoid seeing, and corresponded with scarce a single person out of Flanders, except with Dr. Bancroft at Paris.

He was clearly wounded and longed to reclaim his good name, unfortunately he reached out to the wrong man, Dr. Bancroft. Deane was pursuing French bankers and creditors and getting nowhere. He appealed to Morris to make up a shortfall supposedly due from Mr. Ross. Deane contended that in his private capacity he was an interested party in a certain privateer in which Morris owned an interest, and that Morris owed Deane some money. Deane had to rely on papers kept by Morris' long departed half-brother Thomas, but there was no assurance that all those papers were returned to Morris by the brothers Lee. Deane cooperated with Mr. Barclay in the belief that the settlement would benefit him.[377]

Barclay wrote from France that he and Ridley were hard at work on settling the American accounts in Europe, but the work was going slowly,

> ... if I can by the month of October next, make a tolerable settlement, I shall think myself happy.[378]

He was giving himself a year. There were many confusing elements to America's business in Europe. In one case a supply company had sold goods to outfit the *Alliance*, but this was against Franklin's orders. Franklin had arranged for the French Crown to provide the same supplies, so arrangements had to be made to apply to the French crown to pay for the supplies, but the original supplier had died, and the surviving partner was making the adjustment. In another case the Americans asked to review a set of bills as part of an arbitration, but the creditor who held the records refused to have the account examined. In another case a lawsuit was pending, and so on and so on.[379]

Lee wrote from Congress to ask Morris if he knew of Deane's claim about the private debt between Deane and Morris. Obviously, Morris thought this to be out of bounds for a government inquiry. He replied,

> I take the liberty to suggest that the Superintendent of Finance has no official knowledge of the private concerns of Mr. Robert Morris, and cannot therefore furnish information to the committee.

However, Morris conducted an examination of the supplied documents and reported that some money paid to Robert Morris from a prize taken by a privateer was on private account and not part of the money due the public account so "that sum cannot have been credited or refunded to the United States."[380]

Congress may have been good at investigating its servants, but it still was without a permanent home. They had taken up temporary residence in Princeton, and had decided not to return to Philadelphia, even though some prominent Pennsylvanians tried to convince them to come back. This caused a problem for the diplomats who came to America from Europe. They were left without residences, and also found themselves embarrassed because, at that time, there was no Secretary of Foreign Affairs to whom they could present their credentials. One such individual was the minister from the United Provinces (Holland), Pieter J. van Berckel. Morris arranged a reception for the Dutch ambassador.[381] Morris continued to play a semi-official role in international relations when he entertained various Dutch visitors, one of whom ended up founding the Kingdom of the Netherlands, and others who invested in the Bank of North America.[382]

A homeless Congress was an embarrassment to America, but some were pleased about it. One political faction wanted to remove the Continental Congress from the corrupting nature of the urban centers, their wealth and foreign influences. Arthur Lee thought that Congress had to be far from the corrupting influence of Morris in particular. He wrote, "Mr. Robert Morris' undue and wicked influence depends so much on the residence of Congress, in Philadelphia, the fixing of Congress in any other place will I hope restrain it within due bounds." Some other members of the Southern aristocracy agreed with Lee. David Howell of Rhode Island considered Congress to be better without Morris' influence, as did Stephen Higginson. Several state governments worked to attract Congress, but there was a growing sentiment that Congress should be free from state influences and have its own jurisdiction.[383] This was the genesis of the idea of a federal district. Congress resolved to take a permanent site on the Delaware River near Trenton, but there was still the matter of an interim capital. They decided to move back and forth between the site near Trenton and Annapolis, Maryland.

This shuttling back and forth made Congress appear absurd to foreign diplomats. Francis Hopkinson, a satirist who was a friend of Morris, noted that this would require the diplomats to have two embassies, one in each city, as the Congress moved back and forth. Later he suggested that the whole government city should be put on wheels and pulled up and down the coast to accommodate the plan. In a third article he suggested that Congress build a large horse for its home, and put wheels under it so it could be moved, and place its resolutions in a hole found under the tail. All the while, Congress was having trouble attracting enough members to hold a quorum, and little real business got done.[384]

Washington was in Princeton with Congress and he hoped Morris and his wife would visit. That did not happen because of the pressures on Morris to cover his bills. However, on one occasion Martha Washington had to return to Virginia. On her way she passed through Philadelphia. She stayed with the Morrises for a time and did some shopping for furniture while she was in town.[385]

During this period, while Morris was dealing with Arthur Lee's committee, and observing the wanderings of Congress, he also kept a close eye on America's lifeline, the Dutch loan. He was in touch with the Dutch bankers to let them know that he was continuing to sell bills drawn on that loan, but he would stop if they asked him to. In October, Morris purchased $160,000 worth of the Dutch bills of exchange on his own account and put the money into a bank in England. He drew on those bills of exchange from that bank because the exchange rate was better. Morris wrote to Adams about his plan to buy the bills of exchange in anticipation of the Dutch loan. Congress instructed Morris not to make further loans, but Morris was able to get them to agree not to "meddle" with the current one from Holland.[386] This movement from the Dutch bank to the English bank seemed at the time to be a good way to increase the value of the loan, but it turned out that the Dutch loan filled more slowly than expected and that transaction, among others, caused the fears of over drafting the loan and much difficulty in early 1784.

The Office of Finance maintained its effort to create new trade relations. Gouverneur Morris kept up a lively correspondence with English contacts and the French emissaries in Philadelphia on the topic of trade. He wrote John Jay,

> ... if all governments were to agree that commerce should be as free as air I believe they would then place it on the most advantageous footing for every country and for all mankind.[387]

Morris also wrote to Benjamin Vaughn, Lord Shelbourne's private secretary, to improve American commercial prospects. Vaughn was on a committee to determine British West Indian trade arrangements, but Morris' attempt to encourage Vaughn to invest in America went unanswered.

He did all he could to convince those nations to allow free trade with America, but as a member of the Office of Finance he did not have the authority to act for America. Nevertheless, his thoughts found their way to the French foreign ministry where they were considered, but not embraced. He explained the benefits of free trade policies,

> If Europe wishes us to be her customers, she must enable us to pay for the articles we buy from her. If France wishes us to drink her wines, she must let her Islanders eat our bread. Then they will send her more sugar to buy articles in the North of Europe, which her wines alone will not buy. The planter of hemp in Russia will then pay less for his sugar and get more for his hemp. The French vintner will pay less for his hemp and get more for his wine. The American planter will pay less for his wine and get more for his corn. The West Indian will pay less for his bread and get more from his Estate. Thus the whole circle of wealth and happiness is increased by increasing the different articles of each country, and each separate sovereign draws greater revenue from wealthier subjects. More commodities are raised, more carried, more ships bile [built], more seamen bred.[388]

Adam Smith could not have said it better, and he tried.[389]

Ridley wrote from Europe that Adams was recovering from an illness and Franklin was on a visit to England, so commercial arrangements in Europe awaited the arrival of a new Commission for the Treaty of Commerce. Europe was buzzing with rumors of a coming war between Russia and the Ottoman Empire, and English taxes were so high on manufacturing that exports were dipping due to high prices. He continued to say that America was seen as ludicrous in Europe because of its lack of unanimity. He cautioned,

> America however divided by lines or extent has but one interest, that of the whole; and if not attended to, she will become but the puppet of Europe for Hereditary Kings, Princes and Knaves to amuse themselves with.[390]

Later Ridley mentioned that Holker's financial troubles were causing him to feel a pinch in his pocket because Holker had not paid for goods shipped to America on their joint account.

Morris replied that he was unable to help Ridley because neglect of his own affairs, while in Government service, had "injured and deranged" his finances. He also wrote to Ridley about his sons and mentioned his alarm and disappointment that it took so long to get the boys into a school. He mentioned that his son Will was in College in Pennsylvania, and Charles was soon to follow. These younger sons were fired up to compete with the "French boys" and that would serve to provide a comparison between the two educational systems. On the topic of trade, he thought the commerce with France would diminish, but would continue because he believed reciprocal private interests were the true basis of this activity. He wrote,

> ... it is folly to expect that lasting commerce can be established by authority of government, but the force of national attachment or gratitude or indeed upon any other foundation than reciprocity of interests.

He noted that governments tend to interfere and that was not good because

> ... fools, rogues and madmen have too much to say in the governments of this world.[391]

The subject of future trade relations was on the minds of many. Thomas Paine wrote Morris,

> People keep in the habit of wondering why the definitive Treaty and Treaty of Commerce do not arrive, just as if foreign nations would be so foolish to pay respect to our confederated government when we set the example of paying so little to it ourselves.[392]

Paine also sought another secret payment of $100.

Other individuals contacted Morris. John Paul Jones wrote about his rank. He noted that he had been in the naval service since 1775, and in drawing out his case he noted,

> Was it a proof of madness in the first corps of Sea Officers to have, at so critical a period, launched out on the ocean with only two armed merchant ships, two armed brigantines and one armed sloop, to make war against such a power as Great Britain?[393]

He went on to point out that in the second year of the war men with no battle experience were given superior ranks to his, which galled him. To underscore his early role, he stated

> It was my fortune, as the senior of the first Lieutenants to hoist myself the Flag of America the first time it was displayed.[394]

He reviewed his long career including his stint with the French Navy and his expertise in reading English signals. He also mentioned that two ships he had taken as prizes were returned to the English by the Danes, and he wanted restitution from the Court of Denmark for that insult. Ultimately, Jones wished to command the American Navy, and looked to Morris to assist. Morris knew the finances precluded the development of a useful Navy; but forwarded Jones' message to Congress. The issue of the lost prize money lingered in French and Danish courts and interfered with American Danish relations for over eighty years. Finally, in 1848, Congress decided to assume payment on this claim and paid $165,598 for distribution to the heirs of officers and men of the *Alliance* and *Bon homme Richard.*

In other marine business, Thomas Russell, the Deputy agent of Marine for Massachusetts, bought the *Hague* for himself at auction. Morris wrote,

> Congress ordered the ship to be sold, you have bought her, she is yours...

Morris had given Russell instructions to bid up the ship and so he did to the point that his bid was the highest. A critic of Morris' in Congress, Stephen Higginson, alleged,

> ...that the most scandalous conduct has been practiced in the Marine Department, very large sums have been expended upon the public ships and then they have been urged to sell them. The ship *Hague* has had £3600 paid out upon her, and she completely fitted for sea, before she was put up for sale. She sold for £3100 only, because eight days only was allowed for payment... nearly the same thing has happened as to the *Bourbon*. Mr. Morris' agents purchased both of these ships, Mr. Russell bought the *Hague*, and Mr. D. Parker the *Bourbon*."[395]

Morris had predicted these sales would be an "ample source for calumny"[396] and his enemies did not disappoint him. What Higginson failed to mention was that the *Bourbon* was so rotten that it could not make the return voyage from Europe. The vessel was a total loss,[397] and America got the best end of the sale. A few weeks later Morris discovered that a continental navy ship started in 1776, in Higginson's home state of Massachusetts, was still unfinished, seven years later. He looked to sell what he could.

Selling a few ships would not make the nation rich. It was clear that the future of commerce lay, in the short term, on commodity exports, like tobacco. Unfortunately, the effort Morris made to raise funds by selling Virginia tax tobacco to Mr. La Caze was going badly. Mr. La Caze started to complain that the tobacco was rotten, and that he would not pay for it. Morris replied that Mr. La Caze should find a disinterested third party to evaluate the tobacco before any changes in the financial arrangements would be agreeable. He cautioned his tax receiver, George Webb, "This is the more necessary as negligence on the part of the inspectors may produce baneful effects in the whole commerce of Virginia."[398] Morris refused to bow to the will of Mr. la Caze, who wanted a refund on tobacco that he claimed was spoiled. He maintained that la Caze could not dictate the terms of the sale after the sale, and instead he had to prove his charges.[399] Morris did not seek conflict and wrote to the tax receiver in Virginia to be fair to La Caze in dealing with this dispute.[400]

In other commercial news, Morris got word that a company in Edinburgh, Scotland, was becoming involved with Virginia tobacco and with the French tax authority, the Farmer's General, which had the monopoly on tobacco in France. Morris moved quickly to supply them, even at a loss, to ensure his continued role in that commerce.[401] Morris' efforts were hampered by the severity of the winter. William Constable, with whom Morris had a company called Constable, Rucker & Co., offered the suggestion that they become involved in trade with the American Indians, and offered to bid on a government contract. No contract was made while Morris was in office.[402]

The Farmers General had contacted Morris in 1783 about supplying tobacco to France, but he was too busy and declined. After that, Benjamin Franklin obtained the contract for his grandnephew, Jonathan Williams. Williams left France, in November, to work with William Alexander, who resided in Virginia. Working as William Alexander and Company. they agreed to sell tobacco to the Farmers General at thirty livres per quintile, or five dollars for one hundred twelve pounds. The French Crown expected to recoup its investment in America's future through profits in the tobacco trade. The Farmers General operated as a monopoly in France (what taxing agency doesn't?), and Morris was also aware that in 1778 his brother, Thomas, had arranged the first loan to the Continental Government, based on the understanding that the loan would be repaid in tobacco at no more than 32 livres per quintile after the war. The war was over – and years had passed since that agreement was made, but that contract was still valid, and even though the value of tobacco had changed everyone endeavored to adhere to the earlier agreement.

Private initiatives aside, government expenses continued. Morris sought to stop or slow extending these engagements. He began the process of reducing expenses in the military hospital system.[403] Morris had to encourage Edward Fox to press on in his job of settling the hospital accounts. He reminded him that the task was large and difficult but if left undone, "The precedent once established may operate in on the future as well on the past and millions be squandered hereafter in the hope that investigation be abandoned from the difficulty of pursuit."[404]

In other business, Morris offered to pay the tuition of the "Indian boys," but was unable to send cash. South Carolina wanted Congress to help pay for supplies that state had bought from France and used to support the Continental Army. Morris wrote Congress on their behalf. Samuel Hodgdon related a conversation he had with Morris, "finding him in good humor I took the liberty to tell him I should trouble with two small estimates, in the afternoon, he smiled and said he believed he should never get rid of the damned office."[405] On the plus side, Quartermaster Pickering was able to exchange $3000 worth of Morris notes for specie at the New York office of the Continental Receiver.

Money was coming and going in dribs and drabs, and all the while Morris' long-term strategy to unify the nation's economic system was inching along. The settlement of accounts between Virginia and the United States was under the direction of Commissioner Zephaniah Turner. He was having a problem. He wrote, "I have now before me part of the state account of Virginia against the United States, commencing September 13th 1775 and continued to November 14th 1778 on 324 pages of large post paper wrote in a small and close hand, and am informed that not a voucher can be produced for any of their charges against the Union previous to the month of January 1781.... In short every expense whatever, is claimed as a charge against the United States, except their Civil List." Their total came to $2,674,602 in specie and $2,807,849 in nominal money, and that was just for the time between September 1777 and November 1778. He closed with this concern, "At present I see nothing in the prospect before me but confusion, and a large field for altercation with the rulers of this state which I would willingly avoid if possible."[406]

In response Morris wrote, "As there are no vouchers you will at least have no dispute as to the validity of vouchers." He directed the commissioner to focus on the charges and explanations for them. On the nature of the task he counseled, "But difficulties are always to be distinguished from impossibilities. After endeavoring by your utmost exertions to surmount them you will be able to determine which of them are insurmountable."[407]

Mr. Burrall, who was settling the accounts of the Army purchasing department from the time before Morris' tenure noted that, "I apprehend that neither the commissary general or his deputies ever opened any official books ... the deputies only inserted the gross issues of each assistant, and the commissary general upon the whole distinguished only the amounts issued in the different districts, or posts." He concluded that it would be impossible to detect fraud under this accounting method, and so trying to determine the flow of money before paying the honest parties will only delay justice to them and not clarify the perfidy.[408]

While Virginia was good at presenting the Union with a large bill, they had been less forthcoming in other occasions. Robert Walton provided horses for Lee's Legion during February 1781, and General Greene gave him a note drawn on Virginia as payment. Virginia refused the note because they could not offset its value against the requisition of 1781. Lee's Legion was insulted that they were not just given the horses at the end of the war. Mr. Walton was still unpaid two years later.[409] On the other hand, South Carolina had provided the Southern Division with specific supplies over and above their 1782 requisition; and had a credit for the year 1783.

Considering the uneven cooperation he had received from the states, Morris wrote to his receiver in Rhode Island. He believed that state wanted to see the system of Continental Receivers dismantled. Similarly, he was aware that his appointees to the offices of Commissioner of Accounts for the various states kept failing to do their jobs. Henry Sherbourne had been appointed and received. His salary was set; and he was supposed to start work when on October 15th, he suddenly sent in his letter of resignation. He claimed he was just too busy to do the job properly.[410] A commissioner to settle the accounts of North Carolina was installed, but there was little for him to do. Salomon was selling bills drawn on the Dutch loan, but Morris told him not to extend credit for the sales. In the midst of this uncertainty, one of Morris' secretaries, Samuel Lyon, "being disordered in his senses had shot himself" and was "lamented by those who knew him."[411]

Intermittent revenues, and the lack of a solid source of money for the Continent caused The Bank of North America to deny extending more credit to the Continental Government. Instead, they insisted on a repayment of $100,000 from past loans. Morris repaid that by buying for $106,000 a bill of exchange drawn on the expected Dutch loan, using a twelve month note. (The extra $6000 was to pay the interest.) Thus, he was able to delay payment for a year. If it worked out, the bill of exchange he purchased would be taken to the Dutch bank in a year and be cashed. If the Dutch loan had not filled to the expected extent, then the deal would be undone without any penalties and repayment of the $100,000 would be reconsidered. This was similar to the technique he used when he sold similar bills to Ross and Bingham.[412] He repeated this arrangement in sales of $100,000 each to John Ross and his current business partners, Isaac Hazlehurst and Peter Whitesides.[413] These sales went a long way to allowing Morris to close the books on his administration; a step he held critical to his ability to leave office.

Morris wrote the Dutch bankers that he was surprised and disappointed to learn that the French banker had requested so much money to cover bills in France. He mentioned that Massachusetts had passed the limited impost of 1783, and that while there were some delays in ordering the finances of a confederation that was to be expected. He expressed confidence in the promise of America and proposed that when things were put in order Europeans would buy American securities at 6% and be glad about it.

With his attention turned to Europe, Morris complained to John Jay on November 4th that some in Congress were

> ... continually employed in devising measures to prevent my being able to fulfill my engagements, in hopes of effecting my ruin in case of failure.[414]

Keeping to the theme of partisan hostility, he mentioned John Penn, Grandson of William Penn founder of Pennsylvania when he wrote,

> I had always opposed both in my public and private character those unjust measures which have deprived him of so considerable share of his Patrimony. ... It is a great misfortune to his family that they are of a make so little calculated for the turbulence of the times. They are mild tempered, very open and honest, wish well to mankind and would not injure the most insignificant of Gods creatures. ... I will serve them in any thing that I can.

Morris advised Jay to send Carmichael to Thomas Barclay to settle his European accounts, as the proper channel. In discussing his own proposed resignation, he added,

> ...you must acknowledge that it is folly in the extreme to continue in the drudgery of Office after you see clearly that the public cannot be benefited, your own affairs suffering, your feelings daily wounded and your reputation endangered by the malice and misrepresentation of envious and designing men.... I was urged to continue and forced into that anticipation [risking over $800,000 in his notes]. The army was dispersed and since their departure the men who urged these measures most and who are eternally at war with honour and integrity, have been continually employed in devising measures to prevent my being able to fulfill my engagements, in hopes of effecting my ruin in case of failure ... the faction I allude to is but

> inconsiderable in numbers, although they make themselves of some consequence by their assiduity, you know the Lees &c.

Morris thought he could ignore that faction if the states were helping, but they were not. He did not lose faith in the American people and thought

> ... sooner or later the Good Sense of America will prevail and that our Governments will be entrusted in the hands of men whose principles will lead them to do justice.

He reserved his opinion on the folly of the Congress moving from one city to another and back again because he thought any comment he made would "not preserve the decorum which is due from the Servant to the Sovereign."[415]

Back in Philadelphia, Benjamin Stelle's detailed request for instructions and subsequent reports was continuing to cause problems for Morris. Perhaps Morris would have been well advised not to nominate Mr. Stelle for the position. Fitzsimons thought Stelle was making trouble for Morris and working in league with the rest of the Rhode Island delegation. Stelle's report was forwarded to a Congressional committee consisting of Howell, Arthur Lee and Elbridge Gerry, three of Morris' most vocal critics. The Pennsylvania Assembly took it upon themselves to support Stelle, and in response to complaints made by some rural citizens Pennsylvania re-allocated some of its Continental quota to the payment of local accounts, just as local interests in other states had done.[416] Pennsylvania and New Jersey were also using their tax money to pay interest on the Loan office Certificates instead of paying their Continental requisitions.

In November, Morris complied with a September 10th request coming from Lee's committee in Congress for an account of all the notes issued by Morris, on the credit of the United States. He sent three record books from the Office of Finance to Congress in Princeton. These books were the account books for the $800,000 in notes Morris had sent to pay the troops. While Lee lingered over Morris' account books, his fellow partisan, David Howell, acting as if he longed to control the nation's finances, sought to

> ... countermand the application [for a loan] to the court of France, to suspend payment for collection of the taxes called for," and he wondered "by what authority Mr. M[orris] issued notes.[417]

Howell also fought Morris' program by making it difficult for him to arrange new loans, collect taxes, or even see his account books. For his part, Morris issued a report that showed that out of the $8,000,000 requisition for the year 1783 $6,958,212 was unpaid. In other words, about 13% had been collected from the states. To put it another way Morris had over $1,400,000 in personal risk, and all the states combined had contributed less than $1,042,000 for the year 1783. For his risk and trouble Arthur Lee accused Morris of avarice, so there is little wonder why Morris thought that Lee's faction wanted to ruin him.

Morris continued to look for ways to save the government money, which included shutting the military hospitals, but that required finding a "bettering house" to take those soldiers who needed care. The Directors of Pennsylvania Hospital were not interested in taking on the wounded soldiers. Morris had to convince them otherwise. He wrote the directors

> ...that you shall be paid punctually every three months whiles I continue in Office the sum which shall be agreed on.[418]

A few days later the directors of the Hospital agreed to take the soldiers under contract. Morris was then able to break up the military hospital and move the few soldiers.[419]

He advised General Armand to disband the Legion at Yorktown as a peacetime cost saving measure.[420] Morris contacted the President of Congress in March to tell him that he agreed with General Armand that the foreign officers under Armand's command should be paid. He thought the officers were owed about $30,000, but there was no money in the treasury for this. He was willing to use his own notes, but not happily. He wrote, "there is but too much reason to apprehend consequences of the most alarming nature."[421] This was particularly true since Morris expected to leave office and didn't want the next administration to have anything to do with his credit. He also told him that,

> There was a deficiency of half a million to be provided for by the taxes.... The delay of the states in passing laws for granting revenue to fund our debts has left the above mentioned sum ... totally unprovided for and I cannot see the least probability that their general concurrence will be obtained... [422]

The State of South Carolina began, belatedly, to investigate the operations of Captain Gillon, who had been so quick to use German prisoners of war as his sailors, and who was currently missing somewhere in Europe.

Back in the money hunt, Haym Salomon reported that there was no good market for the bills of exchange from Holland.[423] Shockingly, $5,000 in notes had been stolen from Princeton, but the notes were recovered. It just so happened that they were in a bag and had been thrown into a field, where they were later found and returned by a free black man.

Washington wrote from West Point and congratulated Morris on the soon-to-be-accomplished evacuation of the British from New York. He was planning to reduce the number of troops in his charge to 500,[424] but there were more than soldiers to consider. Mr. Moore worked with the quartermaster's department to get repayment for the damages to his property at West Point, New York. Morris helped Moore get certificates to repay him for the use of his property there, and shortly thereafter Moore's neighbor, a Mr. Metcalfe, requested payment for similar damages. Quartermaster Pickering requested notes and cash for his department. Morris was reluctant to extend more credit, and instead referred the quartermaster's office to the tax receiver in New York where he might collect up to $2,000. With the understanding that there was an end to these appeals by the quartermaster, Morris requested a final estimate, which he would consider funding with a last round of his own notes.[425] In this vein Morris had to turn down Washington's request for money. He wrote,

> ...there is not any money in the treasury.[426]

Morris also talked at length with Daniel Parker and convinced him to keep the Morris notes he had on hand, even after they came due. Meanwhile he collected very little from his tax receivers, and used Virginia tobacco as a tax in an effort to pay for the refitting of the *Alliance*.[427]

-|-

On November 24th, 1783 the definitive treaty arrived in America from France, but true to form, Congress, sitting in Annapolis, could not make a quorum to ratify it. Two weeks later, on December 8th, Morris, John Dickinson, two generals and the Philadelphia First City Troop rode out to Frankford, north of Philadelphia, to greet Washington. Washington was feted and celebrated on his way south to meet Congress.

Floating the Debt in Europe

With the directors' approval, Ross went to the Bank of North America and converted to cash, at a discount, one of the $100,000 notes drawn on the Dutch loan. Morris contacted Mr. Whitesides and Hazlehurst to prepare them to convert their notes too, which were also drawn from the same source.[428] This generated much needed cash, some of which was used to pay the U.S. debt to the Bank. Then Morris used those funds to cover the notes he had given the soldiers.[429] Also in December, but unknown to Morris, Grand, the French banker, drew an additional $200,000 from Holland to cover drafts and interest on the French loans. Morris then drew another $40,000 with notes payable in 120 days. After that he made arrangements to send shipments of American tobacco and rice to the Dutch bankers to pay the interest currently due.

At this point in Europe, the Dutch bankers became alarmed because of the number and size of the bills of exchange sold in America that started to arrive in Holland for settlement. The bankers wanted to delay settlement until the situation was clarified, but the holders of the bills demanded immediate payment. The bankers turned to Franklin for money to cover any overdrafts, expecting Franklin to use American money lodged in French banks. They were willing to accept three-month notes from the French bank via Franklin. Adams and Franklin realized that if the French were not willing to cooperate, disaster loomed large. Franklin managed to work out an arrangement where the French and Dutch would "draw and redraw between France and Holland" until payment could be made.[430]

When the news arrived that Americans had drawn an additional $300,000, the Dutch refused to accept the bills, even though they had not been sent. The bankers began to panic because they were unaware that these bills were the ones bought by Morris' friends who were willing to hold them if there was no money on hand. They summoned Adams. He left London and traveled for over forty days during the winter in order to return to Amsterdam for further discussions. The Dutch bankers were not optimistic that they could close the current loan at the current interest rate. Money was scarce because of economic dislocations in France,[431] which had been caused mostly by their financial support for America, and the loss of their island colonies in the Caribbean. The Dutch expected to change the debt offering to a higher interest rate to attract investors.[432]Just as the Dutch were getting worried, news of the Philadelphia mutiny and the evacuation of Congress from Philadelphia spread to Europe and was having a corrosive effect on America's image. Morris tried to calm the waters when he wrote the Dutch Bankers,

> ...it was a mutiny fomented by some inconsiderate rash men among a number of recruits; it was of consequence without system or any defined object. The removal of Congress from Philadelphia was considered by some as the effect of design in members who wished them to sit at a different place and by others it was attribut-

> ed to a groundless apprehension of personal danger but the fact was that they did not conceive it proper or consistent with their dignity to be in a situation liable to insult.[433]

Franklin wrote from France to tell Morris that the Dutch loan was not large enough, and the French were not willing to make any more loans to the U.S. He also mentioned that Mr. Grand, America's banker in Paris, did not have sufficient funds to cover the bills drawn on that account. Franklin blamed this on the unwillingness of people to tax themselves. He wrote,

> I see in some resolutions of town meetings, a remonstrance against giving Congress a power to take, as they call it, the People's Money, out of their pockets ... they seem to mistake the point. Money justly due from the people is their Creditors' money, and no longer the money of the people, who, if they withhold it, should be compelled to pay by some law.[434]

Morris thought that even after all the bills had been paid, and after Grand's deductions had been made that the Dutch should still have 500,000 gilders on hand.[435] He attempted once again to ship tobacco to Holland to cover the interest on the loan. In the meantime he had to defend America's honor,

> It has always been the common trick of the British and their adherents to assert that America had neither Government, Armies or Resources. To all which I answer that America has established her independence.[436]

Ultimately, however, he was forced to ask the Dutch to accept his purchase of a bill of exchange drawn on the account at whatever rate they thought just. He wrote,

> If the payments fall due before you find relief take such measures to obtain money as shall under a view of all circumstance produce that effect with the least loss to the United States. Of these measures I leave to you the entire disposition and I promise you on the part of the United States to reimburse all losses, interests, costs, and changes which may accrue thereupon.[437]

All of this fretting was due to Congress' recent dithering about loans, and Morris' preemptive action to ensure access to funds if Congress actually decided to harm his system.

The uncertainty generated by the debt problem had a negative impact on efforts to make trade arrangements. Lafayette was in Europe trying to open trade and free ports for America. He made translated extracts from some of Morris' letters, and wrote to Morris,

> Your opinion will have a great weight in the affair, because of the confidence Europeans have in your abilities, and the respect which is paid here to your character.[438]

Morris' reputation would be helpful in reviving private trade, even when the nation's reputation was tarnished. Opening trade with the East was another priority for Morris, as he, Holker, and Parker continued to have a series of meetings on the planned trip of *The Empress of China* to Canton. Other subjects of interest also came under discussion, including Parker's contract to supply the Army, and Holker's money problems. Gouverneur Morris asked the Secretary of Congress to supply Captain John Green, formerly of the U.S. Navy, with a "sea-letter" to facilitate Green's trip to China, on *The Empress of China.*[439]

It seemed that as long as the Office of Finance was opened, deserving people applied for funds. A number of French Canadians, who had been loyal to the American Revolutionary cause, sought payment for their work as soldiers. Baron de Kalb's account was still incomplete, and the treasurer suggested that Congress pass a resolution in his favor if all the documents could not be found.[440] David Sproat had been the British Commissary General for naval prisoners held in New York. He sought repayment for his support for Americans held there, and Morris forwarded his letter to Congress for their consideration with a recommendation that Sproat be repaid. Three months later, Congress resolved to make a settlement, but no further action was taken.[441]

Morris noted in December 1783, that Congress could not reach a quorum and that did not really matter because they could not do much anyway. New Hampshire, Connecticut, New York, New Jersey, South Carolina and Georgia had not sent delegates.[442] His only regret was that a quorum was needed to ratify the official peace treaty.[443] He reflected on the tendency in Rhode Island for that state to be swayed by "a few designing and interested men," and worried that even as Congress is presented as being too powerful,

> ... a fatal blow is leveled at the federal Union. If the pernicious design succeeds (and unless the true Friends of America greatly exert themselves it will succeed) what I would ask is to become of the lesser states?[444]

Morris was already thinking about questions that would be answered under the Constitution, some six years in the future.

In the meantime, Holker kept up the pressure for his personal funds, and sought value from his loan office certificates. Canadian refugees were staying with the Army at West Point and consuming two hundred rations per day. General Knox asked Daniel Parker, as contractor to the army, to put three months rations on hand before the winter came on.[445] New Hampshire pitched in and remitted $3000. Haym Salomon sold bills worth 100,000 florins, and Morris drew $20,000 from the account of the continental tax receiver, Mr. Hall, in South Carolina.

Quartermaster Pickering was still in the field, dealing with dissatisfied farmers who had made contributions to the war effort in 1780, and who had not been reimbursed four years later.[446] All accounts from before Morris' tenure were in suspension awaiting a general settlement and many continued to suffer from the inaction of the states.

The Dutch minister to America, Pieter van Berckel, asked Morris to assist Mr. Charles Dumas who had become impoverished through his service to America. Dumas was a Dutchman who was recruited in 1775 by Franklin, and who operated in Holland in the service of Congress as a contact for the Committee of Secret Correspondence. He was not given an official title, but Congress promised to reward him. Dumas then put all his energies into serving the American cause. He was instrumental in assisting America in arranging early loans from Holland and in helping the Beaumarchais arms deals. As a result, his private business suffered, and once weakened, the Lee brothers pressured him to accede to their wishes. He resisted and that brought upon him

> ...the hatred and sarcasms of the opposite party [the Lee brothers] who did him all imaginable ill-turns, without himself having anything to oppose them but his courage and perseverance ... he has nothing to shelter himself from the insults of his enemies who delight and rejoice to see him wasting away: while America triumphs.

So wrote van Berckel.[447] The partisanship of the Lees was such that they were willing to destroy the friends of America who helped the other faction. Arthur Lee was in the Congress at this time, and there is little to indicate he lifted one finger to support Mr. Dumas.

Morris could not overcome the bias of Lee's Congressional allies from New England, and most particularly those who wished for Morris to include them in each decision he made. Clearly, they remained true to their Parliamentarian roots. These feelings were made clear in Samuel Osgood's letter to John Adams when he wrote,

> The Financier & Secretary for foreign Affairs were admirably well adapted to support, and not only so, but to become the principal Engines of Intrigue. The first mentioned Officer, is a Man of inflexible Perseverance. He Judges well in almost all Money Matters; and mercantile Transactions. He well knows what is necessary to support public Credit. But never thinks it necessary to secure the Confidence of the People, by making Measures palatable to them. A Man destitute of every Kind of theoretic Knowledge; but from extensive mercantile Negociations, he is a good practical Merchant; more than this cannot be said with Justice. He Judges generally for himself; and acts with great Decision. He has many excellent Qualities for a Financier, which however do not comport so well with Republicanism.[448]

There was a growing feeling among his detractors that Morris was becoming too much an executive for their tastes. Washington took his own path.

On December 23rd, 1783 Washington went before the Congress, sitting in Annapolis, and resigned his commission.[449] Washington's resignation went far more smoothly than Morris' because Washington's job was over.

Washington's home state, Virginia, passed the impost of 1783, but nothing more was done until all the states agreed. They also reserved the right to pay their Continental requisition in produce, while at the same time they would not admit the use of Morris notes as payment. The reliance on produce increased the tendency for fraud because of the way commodities were valued. Morris understood the ways of the Agricultural Interests and wrote to his receiver in Virginia,

> On this occasion I feel more for your country [VA] than for the affairs of my own office. Depend on it that you will always be in the hands of rapacious and avaricious dealers until you have virtue enough to compel the exact payment of debts and taxes in coin. The consequence of being in such hands is that your people must continue needy and meet the insults of those who prey upon them. Insults the more mortifying from the sense of having deserved them.[450]

Endnotes

1. Papers of Robert Morris, 7:253
2. Papers of Robert Morris, 7:249n ref Writings of Washington xxv,430-431
3. Papers of Robert Morris, 7:256
4. Papers of Robert Morris, 7:257
5. Papers of Robert Morris, 7:260
6. Papers of Robert Morris, 7:249n
7. *Robert Morris*, 7:330
8. Letters of Delegates to Congress, 18:553-554
9. Papers of Robert Morris, 7:275
10. Papers of Robert Morris, 9:412
11. Papers of Robert Morris, 7:284
12. Papers of Robert Morris, 7:291
13. Papers of Robert Morris, 7:270-1
14. Papers of Robert Morris, 7:29 Papers of Robert Morris, 7:293-4
15. Papers of Robert Morris, 7:298
16. Papers of Robert Morris, 7:303
17. Papers of Robert Morris, 7:304-6
18. Papers of Robert Morris, 7:315
19. Papers of Robert Morris,, 7:331
20. Papers of Robert Morris, 7:315
21. Papers of Robert Morris, 7:327
22. Papers of Robert Morris, 7:337
23. Papers of Robert Morris, 7:343
24. Papers of Robert Morris, 7:342
25. Papers of Robert Morris, 7:345
26. Papers of Robert Morris, 7:346
27. Papers of Robert Morris, 7:355
28. Papers of Robert Morris, 7:359
29. Papers of Robert Morris, 7:356
30. Papers of Robert Morris, 7:364
31. Papers of Robert Morris, 7:368
32. *Robert Morris, Audacious Patriot* pg 98
33. *Power of the Purse*, p. 119
34. Papers of Robert Morris, 7:482
35. Papers of Robert Morris, 7:388
36. Papers of Robert Morris, 7:378
37. Papers of Robert Morris, 7:381-2
38. Papers of Robert Morris, 7:391
39. Papers of Robert Morris, 7:403, 403n
40. Papers of Robert Morris, 7:409
41. Papers of Robert Morris, 7:799
42. Papers of Robert Morris, 7:432
43. Papers of Robert Morris, 7:443
44. Papers of Robert Morris, 7:444n
45. Papers of Robert Morris, 7:446
46. Papers of Robert Morris, 7:446-7
47. Papers of Robert Morris, 7:604
48. Papers of Robert Morris, 7:462
49. Papers of Robert Morris, 7:496
50. Papers of Robert Morris, 7:499n
51. Papers of Robert Morris, 7:735n
52. Papers of Robert Morris, 7:413n
53. Papers of Robert Morris, 7:413n
54. Papers of Robert Morris, 7:415n
55. Papers of Robert Morris, 7:417
56. Papers of Robert Morris, 7:449
57. Papers of Robert Morris, 7:455
58. Papers of Robert Morris, 7:464
59. Papers of Robert Morris, 7:464n
60. Papers of Robert Morris, 7:464n
61. Papers of Robert Morris, 7:473n
62. Papers of Robert Morris, 7:465n
63. Papers of Robert Morris, 7:472n
64. Papers of Robert Morris, 7:476
65. Papers of Robert Morris, 7:538
66. Papers of Robert Morris, 7:468n
67. Papers of Robert Morris, 7:418n
68. Benson J. Lossing, *Pictorial Field Book of the Revolution*, Vol 1, 1850
69. Papers of Robert Morris, 7:420n
70. Papers of Robert Morris, 7:419n
71. Papers of Robert Morris, 7:417
72. Papers of Robert Morris, 7:469n
73. Papers of Robert Morris, 7:633
74. Papers of Robert Morris, 7:502n
75. Papers of Robert Morris, 7:503n
76. Papers of Robert Morris, 7:558
77. Papers of Robert Morris, 7:685
78. Papers of Robert Morris, 7:668
79. Papers of Robert Morris, 7:687
80. Papers of Robert Morris, 7:541-453
81. Power of the Purse, p 221
82. Papers of Robert Morris, 7:560
83. Papers of Robert Morris, 6:462-470
84. *The Great Republic*, pg. 479
85. Papers of Robert Morris, 7:510
86. Papers of Robert Morris, 7:526-8
87. Papers of Robert Morris, 7:594-6
88. Papers of Robert Morris, 7:597
89. Papers of Robert Morris, 7:598
90. Papers of Robert Morris, 7:600

91. Papers of Robert Morris, 7:603
92. Papers of Robert Morris, 7:635
93. Papers of Robert Morris, 7:656
94. Papers of Robert Morris, 7:757
95. Papers of Robert Morris, 7:616
96. Papers of Robert Morris, 7:647
97. Papers of Robert Morris, 7:649
98. Papers of Robert Morris, 7:643
99. Papers of Robert Morris, 7:679
100. Papers of Robert Morris, 7:641
101. Papers of Robert Morris, 7:645
102. Papers of Robert Morris, 7:714, 734
103. Papers of Robert Morris, 7:659
104. Papers of Robert Morris, 7:704
105. Papers of Robert Morris, 7:680
106. Papers of Robert Morris, 7:655
107. Papers of Robert Morris, 7:664
108. Papers of Robert Morris, 7:740
109. Papers of Robert Morris, 7:653
110. Revolutionary Diplomatic Correspondence, 6:368-372
111. Papers of Robert Morris, 7:670
112. Papers of Robert Morris, 7:676
113. Papers of Robert Morris, 7:701-2
114. Papers of Robert Morris, 7:578
115. Papers of Robert Morris, 7:703
116. Power of the Purse, pg. 86-88
117. Papers of Robert Morris, 7:560
118. Papers of Robert Morris, 7:709
119. Papers of Robert Morris, 7:727
120. Papers of Robert Morris, 7:760
121. Papers of Robert Morris, 7:757-8
122. Papers of Robert Morris, 7:720
123. Papers of Robert Morris, 7:725
124. Revolutionary Diplomatic Correspondence, 6:299
125. *Journals of the Continental Congress*, v. 33, pg. 753
126. Papers of Robert Morris, 7:747
127. Papers of Robert Morris, 7:745
128. Papers of Robert Morris, 7:766
129. Letters of Delegates to Congress, 19:767-768
130. Papers of Robert Morris, 8:44
131. Papers of Robert Morris, 7:778
132. Papers of Robert Morris, 7:778
133. Papers of Robert Morris, 7:790
134. Papers of Robert Morris, 7:761-4
135. Papers of Robert Morris, 8:7
136. Papers of Robert Morris, 8:5-6
137. Papers of Robert Morris, 8:90
138. Papers of Robert Morris, 8:10
139. Papers of Robert Morris, 8:11
140. Papers of Robert Morris, 8:21
141. Papers of Robert Morris, 8:41
142. Papers of Robert Morris, 8:19
143. Papers of Robert Morris, 8:11; 8:25
144. Papers of Robert Morris, 8:28
145. Papers of Robert Morris, 8:23
146. Papers of Robert Morris, 8:45
147. Papers of Robert Morris, 8:24
148. Papers of Robert Morris, 8:39
149. Papers of Robert Morris, 8:39
150. Papers of Robert Morris, 8:159
151. Letters of Delegates to Congress, 20:250
152. Letters of Delegates to Congress 20:250
153. Letters of Delegates to Congress, 20:247
154. Papers of Robert Morris, 8:256
155. Papers of Robert Morris, 8:301
156. Papers of Robert Morris, 8:331
157. Papers of Robert Morris, 8:45
158. Papers of Robert Morris, 8:59
159. Papers of Robert Morris, 8:65
160. Papers of Robert Morris, 8:66
161. Papers of Robert Morris, 8:73-4
162. Papers of Robert Morris, 8:72
163. Papers of Robert Morris, 8:74
164. Papers of Robert Morris, 8:80
165. Papers of Robert Morris, 8:399
166. Papers of Robert Morris, 8:84
167. Papers of Robert Morris, 8:89
168. Papers of Robert Morris, 8:92
169. Papers of Robert Morris, 8:91
170. Papers of Robert Morris, 8:93-4
171. Papers of Robert Morris, 8:102
172. Papers of Robert Morris, 8:109
173. Papers of Robert Morris, 8:114
174. Papers of Robert Morris, 8:130
175. Papers of Robert Morris, 8:108
176. Papers of Robert Morris, 8:112-3
177. Papers of Robert Morris, 8:116
178. Papers of Robert Morris, 8:120
179. Papers of Robert Morris, 8:126
180. Papers of Robert Morris, 8:131
181. Papers of Robert Morris, 8:132

182. Papers of Robert Morris, 7:729
183. Papers of Robert Morris, 8:140
184. Papers of Robert Morris, 8:144
185. *Robert Morris and the Holland Land Company*, pg. 38
186. Ver Steeg, pg. 179
187. Papers of Robert Morris, 8:342-343
188. Papers of Robert Morris, 8:157
189. Papers of Robert Morris, 8:436
190. Papers of Robert Morris, 8:168
191. Papers of Robert Morris, 8:145-47
192. Papers of Robert Morris, 8:170
193. Papers of Robert Morris, 8:171
194. Papers of Robert Morris, 8:151
195. Papers of Robert Morris, 8:152
196. Papers of Robert Morris, 8:155
197. Papers of Robert Morris, 8:188
198. Papers of Robert Morris, 8:153
199. Papers of Robert Morris, 8:158
200. Papers of Robert Morris, 8:165
201. Papers of Robert Morris, 8:46-49
202. Papers of Robert Morris, 7:781n
203. Papers of Robert Morris, 8:177
204. Papers of Robert Morris, 8:181
205. Papers of Robert Morris, 8:181
206. Papers of Robert Morris, 8:165
207. Papers of Robert Morris, 8:184
208. Papers of Robert Morris, 8:187
209. Papers of Robert Morris, 8:216
210. Papers of Robert Morris, 8:197
211. Papers of Robert Morris, 8:184-5
212. Papers of Robert Morris, 8:192
213. Papers of Robert Morris, 8:196
214. Papers of Robert Morris, 8:223
215. Papers of Robert Morris, 8:197
216. Papers of Robert Morris, 8:202
217. Papers of Robert Morris, 8:219
218. Papers of Robert Morris, 8:202
219. Kenneth Bowling, "New Light on the Philadelphia Mutiny of 1783: Federal-State Confrontation at the Close of the War for Independence." *Pennsylvania Magazine of History and Biography* VCI, 101, 1977
220. Papers of Robert Morris, 8:203
221. Papers of Robert Morris, 8:202
222. Papers of Robert Morris, 8:204
223. Papers of Robert Morris, 8:206-7
224. Papers of Robert Morris, 8:214
225. Papers of Robert Morris, 8:222
226. Papers of Robert Morris, 8:224
227. Papers of Robert Morris, 8:226
228. Papers of Robert Morris, 8:232
229. Papers of Robert Morris, 8:234
230. Papers of Robert Morris, 8:234
231. Papers of Robert Morris, 8:199
232. Papers of Robert Morris, 8:200
233. Papers of Robert Morris, 8:200
234. Papers of Robert Morris, 8:205
235. Papers of Robert Morris, 8:209
236. Papers of Robert Morris, 8:254
237. Papers of Robert Morris, 8:255
238. Papers of Robert Morris, 8:243
239. Papers of Robert Morris, 8:261
240. Papers of Robert Morris, 8:252
241. Papers of Robert Morris, 8:249
242. Papers of Robert Morris, 8:264-5
243. Papers of Robert Morris, 8:267
244. Papers of Robert Morris 8:263
245. Papers of Robert Morris, 8:265
246. Papers of Robert Morris, 8:265
247. Papers of Robert Morris, 8:271
248. Papers of Robert Morris, 8:273
249. Papers of Robert Morris, 8:275
250. Papers of Robert Morris, 8:277
251. Papers of Robert Morris, 8:279
252. Papers of Robert Morris, 8:281-284
253. Papers of Robert Morris, 8:281
254. Papers of Robert Morris, 8:287
255. Papers of Robert Morris, 8:437
256. Papers of Robert Morris, 8:490
257. Papers of Robert Morris, 8:289
258. Papers of Robert Morris, 8:306-9
259. Papers of Robert Morris, 8:315
260. Papers of Robert Morris, 8:334
261. Papers of Robert Morris, 8:312
262. Papers of Robert Morris, 8:322
263. Papers of Robert Morris, 8:323
264. Papers of Robert Morris, 8:319-20
265. Papers of Robert Morris, 8:342
266. Papers of Robert Morris, 8:343
267. Papers of Robert Morris, 8:313
268. Papers of Robert Morris, 8:316
269. Papers of Robert Morris, 8:345
270. Papers of Robert Morris, 8:347
271. Papers of Robert Morris, 8:325

272. Papers of Robert Morris, 8:236
273. Papers of Robert Morris, 8:350-1
274. Papers of Robert Morris, 8:358
275. Papers of Robert Morris, 8:360
276. Papers of Robert Morris, 8:365
277. Papers of Robert Morris, 8:3676-8
278. Papers of Robert Morris, 8:361
279. Papers of Robert Morris, 8:363-4
280. Papers of Robert Morris, 8:357
281. Papers of Robert Morris, 8:380
282. Papers of Robert Morris, 8:382
283. Papers of Robert Morris, 8:354
284. Papers of Robert Morris, 8:532
285. Papers of Robert Morris, 8:357
286. Papers of Robert Morris, 8:384
287. Papers of Robert Morris, 8:249
288. Papers of Robert Morris, 8:400
289. Papers of Robert Morris, 8:404
290. Papers of Robert Morris, 8:413
291. Papers of Robert Morris, 8:413
292. Papers of Robert Morris, 8:416
293. Papers of Robert Morris, 8:406
294. Papers of Robert Morris, 8:397
295. Papers of Robert Morris, 8:415
296. Papers of Robert Morris, 8:416
297. Papers of Robert Morris, 8:401
298. Papers of Robert Morris, 8:403
299. Papers of Robert Morris, 8:435
300. Papers of Robert Morris, 8:410
301. Papers of Robert Morris, 8:416-7
302. Papers of Robert Morris, 8:418-20
303. Papers of Robert Morris, 8:420
304. Papers of Robert Morris, 8:424-5
305. Papers of Robert Morris, 8:438
306. Papers of Robert Morris, 8:441
307. Papers of Robert Morris, 8:444
308. Papers of Robert Morris, 8:424-5
309. Papers of Robert Morris, 8:434
310. Papers of Robert Morris, 8:467
311. Papers of Robert Morris, 8:489
312. Papers of Robert Morris, 8:442
313. Papers of Robert Morris, 8:442
314. Papers of Robert Morris, 8:445
315. Papers of Robert Morris, 8:449
316. Papers of Robert Morris, 8:452-5
317. Papers of Robert Morris, 8:456
318. Papers of Robert Morris, 8:456-7
319. Papers of Robert Morris, 8:458
320. Papers of Robert Morris, 8:459
321. Papers of Robert Morris, 8:465
322. Papers of Robert Morris, 8:466
323. Papers of Robert Morris, 8:465
324. Papers of Robert Morris, 8:439
325. Papers of Robert Morris, 8:480
326. Papers of Robert Morris, 8:481
327. *Journals of the Continental Congress,* 25:538
328. Papers of Robert Morris, 8:481-2n
329. Papers of Robert Morris, 8:554
330. Papers of Robert Morris, 8:482
331. Papers of Robert Morris, 8:484
332. Papers of Robert Morris, 8:485
333. Papers of Robert Morris, 8:539
334. Papers of Robert Morris, 8:486
335. Papers of Robert Morris, 8:488
336. Papers of Robert Morris, 8:491
337. Papers of Robert Morris, 8:492
338. Papers of Robert Morris, 8:494-6
339. Alexander Hamilton, pg. 139
340. Papers of Robert Morris, 8:497
341. Papers of Robert Morris, 8:500
342. Papers of Robert Morris, 8:502
343. *Journals of the Continental Congress,* 25:575
344. Papers of Robert Morris, 8:511-515
345. Papers of Robert Morris, 8:507
346. Papers of Robert Morris, 8:786
347. Papers of Robert Morris, 8:399
348. Papers of Robert Morris, 8:435
349. Papers of Robert Morris, 8:526
350. Papers of Robert Morris, 8:509
351. Papers of Robert Morris, 8:519-520
352. Papers of Robert Morris, 5:6-7
353. Papers of Robert Morris, 8:517
354. Papers of Robert Morris, 8:526
355. Papers of Robert Morris, 8:538
356. Papers of Robert Morris, 8:522
357. Papers of Robert Morris, 8:528
358. Papers of Robert Morris, 8:518
359. Papers of Robert Morris, 8:755-756
360. Papers of Robert Morris, 8:535-536
361. Papers of Robert Morris, 8:527
362. Papers of Robert Morris, 8:527
363. Papers of Robert Morris, 8:180
364. Papers of Robert Morris, 8:530
365. Papers of Robert Morris, 8:533

366. Papers of Robert Morris, 8:549

367. Papers of Robert Morris, 8:548

368. Revolutionary Diplomatic Correspondence, 6:706-709

369. Papers of Robert Morris, 8:562-563

370. Journals of the Continental Congress, 25:660

371. *Journals of the Continental Congress,* 28:19

372. Papers of Robert Morris, 8:565

373. Papers of Robert Morris, 8:602

374. Papers of Robert Morris, 8:769

375. Papers of Robert Morris, 8:568

376. Papers of Robert Morris, 8:601

377. Papers of Robert Morris, 8:601-613

378. Papers of Robert Morris, 8:660

379. Papers of Robert Morris, 8:660-661

380. Papers of Robert Morris, 8:614

381. Papers of Robert Morris, 8:617

382. Papers of Robert Morris, 8:813

383. Papers of Robert Morris, 8:663

384. Papers of Robert Morris, 8:662-667

385. Papers of Robert Morris, 8:591

386. Papers of Robert Morris, 8:390

387. Papers of Robert Morris, 8:786

388. Papers of Robert Morris, 8:594

389. Wealth of Nations, 509-540

390. Papers of Robert Morris, 8:599-600

391. Papers of Robert Morris, 8:731

392. Papers of Robert Morris, 8:621

393. Papers of Robert Morris, 8:574

394. Papers of Robert Morris, 8:581

395. Papers of Robert Morris, 8:597

396. Papers of Robert Morris, 8:442

397. Papers of Robert Morris, 8:326n

398. Papers of Robert Morris, 8:620

399. Papers of Robert Morris, 8:738

400. Papers of Robert Morris, 8:768

401. Papers of Robert Morris, 8:739-742

402. Papers of Robert Morris, 8:775

403. Papers of Robert Morris, 8:193

404. Papers of Robert Morris, 8:623

405. Papers of Robert Morris, 8:650

406. Papers of Robert Morris, 8:653-654

407. Papers of Robert Morris, 8:710

408. Papers of Robert Morris, 8:713

409. Papers of Robert Morris, 8:654-655

410. Papers of Robert Morris, 8:621

411. Papers of Robert Morris, 8:673

412. Papers of Robert Morris, 8:646

413. Papers of Robert Morris, 8:648

414. Papers of Robert Morris, 8:390

415. Papers of Robert Morris, 8:707-708

416. Papers of Robert Morris, 8:727

417. Papers of Robert Morris, 8:745

418. Papers of Robert Morris, 8:783

419. Papers of Robert Morris, 8:797

420. Papers of Robert Morris, 8:751-752

421. Papers of Robert Morris, 9:186

422. Papers of Robert Morris, 9:192

423. Papers of Robert Morris, 8:765

424. Papers of Robert Morris, 8:770

425. Papers of Robert Morris, 8:773

426. Papers of Robert Morris, 8:784

427. Papers of Robert Morris, 8:795

428. Papers of Robert Morris, 8:797

429. Papers of Robert Morris, 8:390

430. Papers of Robert Morris, 8:392

431. Papers of Robert Morris, 8:759

432. Papers of Robert Morris, 8:835

433. Papers of Robert Morris, 8:808

434. Papers of Robert Morris, 8:840

435. Papers of Robert Morris, 8:852

436. Papers of Robert Morris, 8:850

437. Papers of Robert Morris, 8:853

438. Papers of Robert Morris, 8:843

439. Papers of Robert Morris, 8:847

440. Papers of Robert Morris, 8:801

441. Papers of Robert Morris, 8:805

442. *Journals of the Continental Congress,* 25:837

443. Papers of Robert Morris, 8:811

444. Papers of Robert Morris, 8:817

445. Papers of Robert Morris, 8:823

446. Papers of Robert Morris, 9:19

447. Papers of Robert Morris, 8:829

448. Letters of the delegates to Congress 21:187

449. *Journals of the Continental Congress,* 25:837

450. Papers of Robert Morris, 8:836

X

1784

Winter

On New Year's Day 1784 Morris contacted the merchant company, William Alexander and Company, with the news that he was starting a tobacco shipping firm in Baltimore. It was called Tench Tilghman & Co.[1] Tench Tilghman had been a lawyer and an aide de camp to Washington during the war. Morris informed Alexander and Williams that Tilghman would be operating the company, and Morris retained an ownership interest.

Alexander and Williams were not well funded; and their credit was not as strong as Morris'. They were, however, operating a firm with revenues, and Morris started backing the two of them. By acquiring a one-third interest in the partnership, he became a silent partner in February. He bought into the firm because he trusted Alexander's ability to keep the purchase price of tobacco low. Alexander and Williams operated the company, but they found it difficult, if not impossible, to make a profit at the rate set by the contract with France. The American tobacco growers were used to dealing with merchants who could afford to lose a small amount of money when they sold tobacco in Europe, because those merchants would take the foreign money and buy items, which they would sell at a great profit in America. It was not possible to just take American money to buy the imports because there was only state money and Europeans were reticent to accept such uncertain currency. To make the profit Alexander needed, he bought lower quality cheaper tobacco, and eventually the French declined to deal with him further. After this happened Morris' other companies took over the business.

While Morris worked quietly to rebuild his fortunes, the mind of Congress was on acquiring funds. They waited to hear, patiently, as the impost of 1783 was still under consideration by the states. Rhode Island had become somewhat infamous for stopping the impost of 1781, and their opposition had not died with it. Arthur Lee noted that Rhode Island was "very little disposed" to ratify the new impost. Lee's allies, Howell and Ellery, sought to use their old arguments once again against the new proposal. The other states realized this, and so the new impost was crafted to answer Rhode Island's earlier objections. Nevertheless, they expected Rhode Island to "invent new objections" and attempt to defeat the new measure. Howell did not disappoint and fabricated the argument that the design was for all other states to become "tributaries" to Pennsylvania as money was drawn from the smaller states to be sent overseas.[2]

While all this was going on, Morris met with the War Department. They considered selling, and then decided to retain, the supply of shot and powder kept on the Susquehanna. General Knox, who had risen to the position of Commander in Chief after Washington's retirement, wrote Morris to inform him that he had hired Daniel Parker to supply the troops. He also requested that Morris continue the contracting system for supplying the army.[3] The paymaster, John Pierce, needed seven or eight hundred dollars to pay his troops, and to provide the officers with subsistence money.[4]

In an effort to wind up his role with the army, Washington sent Morris an account of his expenses, and requested that Morris reimburse him for the one hundred dollar payment he had made to each of his aides.[5] In closing the letter he wrote,

> I cannot close this letter without a renewal of those sentiments of friendship and regard which I have always felt and professed for you, nor without those expressions of my sensibility for the many instances of polite attention and civilities which I have received from Mrs. Morris during my late stay in Philada.[6]

Finally he added that Robert and Mary would be welcome to visit the Washington family in Virginia.

Now that the war was over, and the Bank of North America was an undisputed success, there was a growing movement in Pennsylvania to start a new commercial bank, called The Bank of Pennsylvania. Gouverneur Morris believed this effort was largely supported by Quakers, Tories, and those who had been engaged in usury during the war. (During the war there had been a practice of lending private money at 5% per month.) The new bank needed a charter and was the topic of much discussion in the Pennsylvania Assembly.

The politics of the new bank were based on the usual motivators, greed and envy. The shortage of specie, and the resulting decision of the trustees of the Bank of North America to be very selective in the granting of loans gave rise to resentment, mostly among those who were not granted loans for which they had applied. The Bank of North America remained silent in their refusal and did not outline their policies. However, they did not lend to encourage the export of specie, to support private usury, or "flagrant speculation."[7] The disappointed attributed their failure to get a loan to bank favoritism, which was partly true to the degree the bank favored giving loans to people they expected would repay them. The opposition also blamed the political power of Robert Morris, who held a number of bank shares. On a different track, in the beginning of 1784, the state of Pennsylvania started to investigate the creation of a land bank, and the printing of new paper currency. Morris was against new emissions of paper currency and told Thomas Paine as much.[8]

Unfortunately, one piece of private business was not going well. Morris' discussions with Holker had reached the point that they stopped talking and started to communicate by letter. Morris wrote Holker,

> ... it appears that you as Agent of Marine and Council of France are debited in account with the United States for a balance of sixty one thousand and ninety four dollars and seventy eight nineteenths of a dollar.[9]

Holker referred the matter to La Luzerne, the French Minister in Philadelphia. Morris sent his records over to Holker to facilitate a settlement.

Morris was disappointed with the remittances of the states too, and worried about his personal liability. He wrote one receiver,

> Your state I perceive are growing hourly more remiss in their exertions which is very unpleasing reflection to me who have taken such deep engagements for the public service.[10]

The Marine Department got only scant attention, after the ships had sold at auction. However, the course of naval justice continued. In late December, Morris, as Agent of Marine, confirmed the judgment in two separate courts martial.[11] The naval officers who were members of the court martial proceedings requested payment, to meet the expenses they had as a result of staying on shore in a city far from home.[12] Morris contacted the Treasurer who in turn replied that Morris should fix a general rule

> ... ascertaining that allowance shall be made to every Rank of Officers in the Navy, whilst employed on shore.[13]

Morris contacted Congress, but they were slow to approve the payments. Meanwhile Morris made arrangements to place disabled soldiers in hospital.[14]

Morris again observed there was a final peace treaty, which had not been ratified because Congress did not have a quorum to take the vote. Within a week after the arrival, in Annapolis, of the ninth state delegation to Congress, the definitive treaty was ratified. Morris dispatched David S. Franks to carry the treaty, and various letters to Holland.[15] Unfortunately that was only part of the equation. There was no trade agreement yet. The exchange of diplomats between the United States and Britain was delayed by Britain's disinterest in signing a commercial treaty, which in turn discouraged America from sending an ambassador. Protocol demanded that Britain must first receive an ambassador before sending her own abroad, so nothing was done.[16] Gouverneur stayed involved by consulting on the topic of foreign trade, even advising Roger Sherman that it was better to make no deal with the British, than a bad one.[17] So, there was peace without prosperity.

In Europe, the Marquis de Lafayette carried on his campaign to convince France, and other European states, to open their ports to American commerce. His communication with the French minister resulted in the opening of several ports, as he used letters from Gouverneur Morris to good effect. Gouverneur was also in touch with John Jay, who was in France at the time. Gouverneur's messages were a mix of personal thoughts and political insight. He judged that the opposition within America to the formation of a national government was rooted in old habits, and as such was actually a form of conservatism, as defined in the classic sense. He wrote,

> ...the present generation may feel colonial oppositions of opinion, that generation will die away, and give place to a race of Americans.

During this period there was much discussion about the effect of luxury on the newly rich, and the resulting effect on society as a whole. The Morrises were targets of unkind observations on this subject made by those who were unable to indulge themselves in this trend. Gouverneur wrote,

> Luxury is not so bad a thing as it is often supposed to be; and if it were, still we must follow the course of things, and turn to advantage what exists, since we have not the power to annihilate or create. The very definition of luxury is as difficult as the suppression of it, and if I were to declare my serious opinion, it is that there is a lesser proportion of whores and rogues in coaches than out of them.[18]

Gouverneur's tendency to make light of serious subjects made him appear to his enemies to be too clever and more frivolous than he actually was. His friends, however, found him to be disarming, funny, and charming.

Holker vs. Morris

William Bingham was back in Philadelphia from his stint in Martinique. He brought with him one of the first umbrellas found in America. He had used it in the West Indies to keep the sun off, but in Philadelphia it was used more profitably to fend off the rain. He was pleased with the new fortune he made during the war and sent Morris crests for his new carriage. Morris had to explain that he had no crests and the gift was made as a kind of practical joke. He explained,

> ...the mistake was occasioned by an impudent young rascal that pretended to know a great deal more about me and my affairs than he had any pretensions to.[19]

The basis for the "joke" was the idea that Morris had delusions of grandeur that far outstripped his origins, and by supplying him a coat of arms in the new post-colonial city the "young rascal" was making a joke based on those who accused Morris of being too grand for his own good. Morris had to get the coach repainted. Ha ha.

Another, less happy, old associate, John Holker, kept Morris occupied with his never-ending insistence on the subject of his accounts.[20] Morris opened the package of papers that Holker had returned. He wrote,

> I was astonished to find the draughts of my accounts ... were detained and very imperfect copies made out in a French hand writing were substituted, with notes and remarks such as I deemed very impertinent.... I felt myself angry at this kind of treatment.

He went over to Holker's house and demanded the originals and found "these also were scratched, blotted, and remarked on." In a subsequent conversation it became clear that Holker wanted Morris to pay for the depreciation of the currency. Morris proclaimed, "I would never pay one farthing of it." He said it was as "if he had placed fruit in my cellar [and] demanded payment for the rotting of it." That was the beginning of their long and bruising legal struggle.[21]

Holker faced the prospect that the French Minister would return to France before Holkers' account was settled. He worried in a letter to Morris,

> ...the necessity of the case, my reputation, my interest, and fortune are too deeply concerned, not to claim every exertion on your part.[22]

Morris took time away from the Office of Finance to work on the settlement of his accounts with Holker. He left Gouverneur in charge during his absence. Robert lived nearby, so he was not far if needed.[23] Holker was pleased to learn that Morris was working on the accounts, but to complicate matters he asked Morris to express the accounts in an unusual format that would benefit only himself.[24]

Morris was closing other accounts as well. As he looked to end his tenure in office, he tried to get Congress to focus on closing the books of the old Secret Committee as a step to settling the accounts of the Marine committees, and those of various individuals, including himself.[25] He also closed the government's account with his banker in Paris. He did this by instructing Le Couteulx and Co. to transfer the government funds to his private account, so he could draw bills from that account and use the money to pay into the government Treasury. He also arranged to protect John Ross, who also had remitted a bill drawn from the Dutch loan, by appealing to his French bankers to cover the bill, and upon its arrival, to contact him for the funds. He added that he was optimistic that such preventative steps would not be necessary because he expected the Dutch loan to be fully subscribed now the war was over.[26]

Morris attempted to unravel the problem with John Banks, who had unilaterally retained two thousand seven hundred and fifteen dollars sent to General Greene of the Southern Department. He contacted the man who was owed the money, the deputy quartermaster Pettit, and as he described the necessity of recovering the money he wrote,

> Almost every day of my life presents scenes of distress sustained by those whose zeal and confidence have placed their property in the hands of the United States. Many whose claims are settled and finally adjusted, would be in very easy circumstances if the debt were paid; and are in extreme indigence from the withholding of it.

He continued,

> ...every debt rests on equal principles of justice therefore that all have an equal right to payment.[27]

He said he would "do all which I can for your relief" and he worked out a plan to pay Charles Pettit for the ammunition he supplied.[28]

In regard to helping the army, Morris was able to supply them with enough funds to "pay the officers their subsistence in specie at the commencement of every month."[29] He did this by sending notes to be exchanged at the state tax receiver's office for silver. Massachusetts was the only northern state that was able to meet the requirement, and the notes were exchanged there until June when the regiment was discharged from West Point.[30] Morris wrote to Congress on the quartermaster's behalf and asked if there was going to be any money paid to people whose property was damaged during the war, and if there would be a difference between paying people whose property was taken and used by the troops and paying people whose property was destroyed during battle. He wrote, "are charges for buildings, fences, wood, etc damaged or destroyed by continental troops or militia to be allowed."[31] He also asked if damages done by the enemy were to be paid for by Congress. Morris continued to sort out the details of military settlements. He distinguished between expenses coming from his administration, and those that came before, and he determined the cost of the items based on the value at the time they were taken.

Settlements were undertaken everywhere, but the state debt accounting went slowly. The Governor of North Carolina graciously informed Morris that the legislature had not met during the year and so the Continental Comptroller Morris nominated was not installed, and would not be until April, four months in the future. It seemed the state comptroller was ready to settle accounts, but that would not be possible until the Continental Comptroller was at work. Clearly North Carolina was not in a hurry to work with Morris' office.

In another case of delayed justice, a regiment of Canadian refugees who had fought on the American side had petitioned Congress for their pay. Morris supported the idea of supplying them with land in the western territories as a way of rewarding them and taking them off the pensioner list.[32] He thought that if America voluntarily agreed to make this kind of payment to the Canadian refugees, then Canada would look favorably upon the United States. He also considered that a commissioner sent to Canada to settle the accounts would be able to supply useful intelligence to the Congress.[33] Congress did not act for a year and a half, long after Morris left his office.

John Holker was not about to wait for results. He pressed Morris again for an accounting according to his designs. He refused to allow for depreciation of the currency. He bought Continental currency before it was devalued at the rate of 40:1.[34] His insistence on making Morris pay for the depreciation was the chief disagreement between these men. At the same time Holker and Morris were having this difference, they were still partners, in the boldest trading venture to date. Another one of their business associates, Daniel Parker, was in New York getting the *Empress of China* stocked with merchantable items and out to sea. Morris wrote to the captain, John Green, to act in a way that would bring honor to America, and he supplied him with a copy of the Declaration of Independence, various treaties with European powers, and Sea Letters from Congress that Gouverneur Morris had procured.[35]

Gouverneur Morris was manning the Office of Finance while Robert worked on Holker's accounts. During a particularly violent snowstorm he took a moment to write Alexander Hamilton. He told of an event wherein the government of Pennsylvania decided to celebrate the signing of the definitive treaty with England by constructing a temporary "triumphal arch" and producing a fireworks display. This construction was a wood frame affair that was covered in painted canvas. There were lanterns on the inside "with no protection against the flames." The device was designed by Charles Wilson Peale whom G. Morris described as being

> ... one who supported the Revolution by the powers of eloquence, notably displayed at the corners of streets, to such audience as can usually be collected at such places.

The contraption burst into flames, and it was feared that the city might burn with it. G. Morris noted,

> You will perhaps be curious, as I was, to know what put it into their heads.

He opined,

> ... the exhibition would have been perfectly ridiculous, but for the death of one spectator, and the wounds of others.

Next, he took up the topic of the newly proposed bank. He described the various backers, and with typical wit he showed the nature of each spinning on a verbal barb. He described the backers as a collection of Tory sympathizers and usurers, with a few well-meaning dupes thrown in for respectability.[36]

The subject of the proposed new bank kept many of Morris' friends busy. Haym Salomon, a stockholder in the Bank of North America, told Morris that the prospective board members of the proposed bank formed a political alliance to forward their plans,[37] and it was discovered that the President of the Pennsylvania Assembly was a subscriber to the new bank. Morris saw the new bank as being

> ... hurtful to the credit and commerce of the state as well as injurious to the United States.[38]

This was due to that bank's support for new paper money, and its anticipated interference in national funding issues. The Bank of North America petitioned the Assembly in opposition to the incorporation of the new bank. People affiliated with the Office of Finance, G. Morris and James Wilson, also opposed the new bank, and they addressed the Assembly on that topic. Alexander Hamilton, who was busy starting his own bank in New York, offered his opinion on the formation of a new bank in Pennsylvania. He noted that it probably would not be a true evil if it were formed, but the old bank might offer to merge with the new one, even before it was chartered, so both could be well managed by the steady hands of experience.[39]

Myriad tasks passed through Morris' doors. His role as Agent of Pennsylvania created work for him when a Mr. Meredith sought payment for an old bill drawn on the Bank of Pennsylvania back in 1781. Morris directed him to the Treasury for funds.[40] He finally settled the lingering problem of the protested 1779 bills of exchange drawn on John Jay in Spain. He also kept working to appoint settlement commissioners in the various states and tried to keep the spirits of this team high.[41] The task of the state commissioners was daunting. He wrote to William Imlay who was toiling in Massachusetts,

> ...you must agreeably to your appointment do what shall (on the whole) appear just and right. The infinity of circumstances renders it impossible to state any rules to which some objections will not arise and from which some exceptions must not be made.[42]

It is reasonable to consider that Morris had the difficult commissioner of Pennsylvania, Mr. Stelle, in mind when he wrote this to Imlay.

The work of the settlement commissioners was difficult because Morris, and his team, tried to rationalize a system that had been created on an ad hoc basis. The process was somewhat like retrofitting reason onto inspiration, so it was difficult to lay down serious hard and fast rules. As proof of the disorganized state of the supply system, as it existed before Morris' tenure, Morris kept finding and selling unneeded supplies. He discovered that there was a store of supplies left over from a 1776 ship building project, this time in Poughkeepsie, New York. He ordered it sold. A former Connecticut Congressman informed Morris that there were, "considerable quantities military stores and clothing belonging to the United States..." in Connecticut "and not under the care of any person authorized to secure or dispose of them."[43]

The treasurer was also cleaning up old accounts. He told Morris that a Mr. Chaumont, of France, was appointed by United States ministers to ship stores for the public, and he owed the United States 1,645,247 livres, or about $300,000. This was the same Mr. Chaumont who sought payment from America for his work as agent for the French military. The treasurer suggested a settlement be arranged.[44]

The work of the Office of Finance was of little interest to John Holker, who would not be ignored and wrote again for the settlement of his account. Morris wrote Holker that he was trying to assist in the settlement of Holker's account with the United States, and he had contacted the Comptroller. Morris also suggested that Holker contact Mr. Chaumont in France and encourage that man to contact Mr. Barclay who was conducting the settlement of American accounts there. Morris also told Barclay to contact Chaumont as part of the settlement work, to complete the circuit.

The Continental Congress was still operating in Annapolis without a head of foreign affairs, and so the Office of Finance kept in touch with the French Ministers. Mr. Barbé-Marbois wrote to Gouverneur about life in the temporary capital,

> If dinners with thirty people, balls, tea parties, Whist, and snow up to the shaft of the coach are the happiness of life there are not in the universe two mortals happier than M. the Chevalier de la Luzerne and myself.

The courtly language of the diplomat was clearly evident in this letter, but one might imagine he missed the opera, the orchestra, and other amusements, which did not exist in Annapolis at the time. His letter also breathed some life into the shared hope that the impost of 1783 might actually pass all the states.[45]

Robert kept his eye on foreign relations; and told the Dutch bankers that he was pleased to learn they had received the tobacco he had worked so hard to ship. He also mentioned his expectation that the impost of 1783 would pass, to encourage them to believe that they would be repaid.[46] Based on his assumption that the states would ratify the impost, Morris advertised for "Contracts for Foreign Debt Payment"[47], and solicited proposals. The French minister, La Luzerne, was less sanguine than Morris about the prospects of success for these contracts. He refused to state outright that Morris' advertisement was a hollow confidence-building measure, instead he doubted that America would be able to pay even the interest because he saw America as a "flourishing nation and a people living in abundance," but with the poorest government in the universe.[48]

In news from New York, Daniel Parker wrote to tell Morris that the weather had been so severe the *Empress of China* was unable to leave port, but other than that everything was ready for great success in the venture. Part of the cargo of the *Empress* was $2,500 in silver specie. Morris exported this to buy goods in China. To get this silver Morris had previously purchased bills of exchange drawn on the Dutch loan with his own funds and placed the proceeds into Herries bank in England. Then in December he went to the Bank of North America and withdrew silver by discounting a bill drawn on his account in England. Morris did this because he understood that American accounts in Europe were in the black, but that was based on information Barclay supplied back in September.[49] In early February he was pleased to hear that a new loan had been opened, but he was not sure if that was true, however he knew that the tobacco had reached Holland as an interest payment.[50]

Unfortunately, news came on February 9th that one of Morris' bills drawn on the Dutch loan contributed to an overdraft.[51,52] He immediately took steps to fix the problem. He drew on his personal credit to the amount of £300,000 for ninety days from his private banker in France, Le Couteulx and Co., to finance the purchase of seven hundred hogsheads of tobacco that would be sold in Europe. He expected that he could cover the 90-day note by selling the tobacco, and the profit would go to cover the note that was protested for lack of funds in the U.S. loan in Holland.[53]

Rhode Island was as helpful as ever in this effort to protect American solvency. That state was collecting its own taxes and using the funds to pay its own citizens. Foreign debt was not of great interest to them. Just as Howell had falsely claimed that the money from the impost of 1781 was not needed, his ally Ellery claimed that stories of Morris' overdraft were not to be accepted at face value. He considered the whole story to be a ploy; and went on to decry the passage of the new impost by the state of Massachusetts where he claimed it took

> ...the total prostitution of every power and faculty of body, mind & office to carry the point.[54]

Morris was clearly on his own. He estimated that Grand and Barclay held 500,000 livres on America's account between them, and he expected the imminent arrival of five hundred hogsheads of tobacco in Amsterdam, but for the sake of prudence he did not rely on those funds in his calculations. He allowed that there might be a shortfall in the Dutch financing of about 500,000 gilders. He asked Franklin to make sure American bills were not protested in Holland through "circuitous negotiations" so the timing of repayment could be delayed until more tobacco could be shipped, or taxes could be collected. He cautioned Franklin that time was needed because it was February, and all the ports were shut due to ice. The year 1784 was in the midst of what has become known as the "little ice age." The weather was so cold major ports froze solid. New York Harbor, the Delaware River, and the Chesapeake were all frozen over, so the ports of New York, Philadelphia and Baltimore were effectively closed for months at a time. Frozen ports stopped shipping and held up the transport of goods from America. The weather caused much delay and difficulty for Morris as he tried to send bulky cargo on ships to cover financial obligations that were due on certain dates, regardless of the weather.

Morris had not heard from Thomas Barclay, American agent in France, since September 1783 so he wrote to confirm his understanding of the conditions in Europe. He asked the amounts gained from the sale of the prizes the *Alliance* took, and the sale of the ship *Duc de Lauzun.* Morris estimated that Barclay should have 300,000 livres on hand from which expenses and commissions would be paid. To complicate matters, Morris learned that the French had seized some American supplies being kept at Nantes, to offset non-performing loans. Morris told Barclay to contact the American diplomats and get them to protect American public property, because allowing this seizure was an insult to America. He was not pleased to be uninformed on the topics of American finances in France and sent a copy of his letter to Franklin, so Franklin could prod Barclay and keep him informed about the disappointing Dutch loan.[55]

Morris' financial efforts were trapped in the ice. This reinforced the importance of Morris' efforts to convert the country from an economy based on barter and farm goods, to an economy based on money. If Morris had a reliable and well-funded banking system to use in America, he could have sent bills of exchange to Europe instead of hundreds of hogsheads of tobacco. Packet ships were getting through while the much larger cargo ships were not. Unfortunately, the American economy was still not ready. There was no national currency, and state currencies were not stable enough to pass reliably in European banks.

Morris wrote his banker and said he estimated that Americans in Europe had enough public money (in the form of French currency) to cover the overdrafts on the Dutch loan and directed him to get that money into the American account at the bank. He expected Grand to protect America's good name abroad. He wrote,

> On this occasion I confidently rely on your efforts, and I persuade myself that the credit of the United States, so long preserved in Europe, thro doubtful and dangerous events, will not now be suffered to expire for the want of a very little timely aid and attention.[56]

Morris knew that it was Grand who drew down the funds in Holland to pay expenses and interest on the French loan to the point that Morris' bills from America might be protested. He understood that the slow pace of trans-Atlantic communication was the reason that both he and Grand ended up drawing upon the very same funds. Morris coupled this with the disappointing subscription to the Dutch Loan, and while not admitting that he was overly optimistic in his expectations, he offered the same strategy to the Dutch Bankers that he proposed to Franklin. The route of "circuitous negotiations" would delay payments on outstanding bills until the produce could be shipped from America's frozen seaports. He told them of the private sales of 100,000-guilder bills of exchange, and that the individuals who purchased them were pledged not to cash them until it was sure that the bills would not be protested. He mentioned that a measure of his confidence in their operations could be taken from the fact that he purchased a one-million-guilder bill of exchange with his personal funds and was holding it until it could be successfully negotiated in Holland.[57]

On February 13th, 1784 Morris wrote a private letter to Franklin, giving an account of his situation so Franklin could see the financial picture as Morris did. He wrote,

> My present actual engagements are threefold vizt. first general engagements for the public service not satisfied, including therein the notes issued by me which remain in circulation. Secondly, my bills of exchange unpaid. And thirdly, my debts to the national bank.

Morris estimated the first to be "under rather than over one hundred thousand dollars." The second was the one-million-guilder bill of exchange he still held on the Dutch loan, of which he estimated the unpaid portion to be worth about $200,000. The debt he owed to the Bank was of $340,000 due to "discounting notes received for the bills of exchange" at the bank until those bills of exchange were paid in Europe. Morris' total financial exposure at this point was $650,000.[58] He noted that the states had remitted more than $200,000, and that more relief may be expected from the sale of confiscated lands. However, he estimated that considering current expenses to run the government he would be able to reduce his exposure to $400,000 by the next September, and he would need $40,000 per month to pay this off before he could leave the office of finance. His plan was to borrow $100,000 from the Bank of North America and purchase tobacco and rice with cash, credit and bills drawn on himself to double the value and ship $200,000 worth of products. He expected taxes coming in during April would pay for the credit and bills drawn on himself, and the taxes coming in during June would be used to repay his personal loan from the bank. The sale of the products would generate funds in Europe to service the American debt there. In the meantime he expected Franklin to delay payments in Europe by drawing bills payable in 60 or 90 days from a series of banks in France, Holland, and England. A 60-day bill drawn in France would be paid with a 90-day bill from a bank in England, and that would be paid with a 60-day bill drawn from a different French bank. Doing this delayed the final settlement by six to seven months and that bought the time needed for the produce to arrive from America. This was the route of "circuitous negotiations" mentioned earlier.[59] The new loan that covered the overdraft was opened in Holland on February 18th. News of the new loan did not arrive until May.[60]

A few days later, on February 22nd, Washington's birthday, *The Empress of China* left New York harbor, and thus began America's first step in creating the China Trade. The $2,500 that started the flurry of banking activity was just beginning a long and interesting trip. John Holker, who was a co-owner of the *Empress,* continued his campaign to prove Morris owed him money. He thought Morris owed him for his work as an agent, work that caused Morris much political difficulty in 1779. He thought Morris owed him for bills of exchange Morris drew on the account of the French Marine, and for other personal business they had together. Holker was getting more and more heated in his responses as he reacted to Morris' observation on the overwrought style of Holker's previous letters.

Another member of Morris' team, Haym Salomon, saw a future for himself in a city he had left to the British, back in 1776. He asked for letters of recommendation from Morris because Salomon was going to move to New York and pursue a career as a broker and auctioneer. Just at this time, one of Morris' shipping partnerships was suffering. His partner in Baltimore, Jonathan Hudson, was not applying the funds he received according to agreements. Morris tried to keep him focused on the proper course, but Hudson went bankrupt within the next two years.[61] Morris did contact the Farmer's General in France to let them know he was gathering a selection of tobaccos for review and shipment.[62] This was in anticipation of future orders for specific types of tobacco to be shipped under the debt service contracts Morris intended to use to pay off America's obligations to France.

American debt in Holland was on Adams' mind as he made his frigid way from London to Amsterdam through the winter. There he worked with America's creditors to get the city fathers to fill the existing America loan, but they refused. He was able to arrange a second loan, at a higher rate than the first, but he had to ignore Congress' instructions in the process. That last loan was ultimately used to cover the bills held in security by Morris and his friends, thus allowing Morris to retire from office with his obligations met.[63]

Matthew Ridley wrote from England. He had recently lost his son, and his wife, to death by disease, and wrote to Morris about his living son's reaction. He also mentioned the confusion caused by the lack of a trade agreement between the U.S. and England. In a more positive note he said,

> I am informed there is a great possibility of your late Bills [of Exchange] being paid. If they should America will have a great obligation to Mr. Adams.[64]

This happy news would not be confirmed until May.

Money was on the mind of others, as well. Jefferson was a newly elected member of Congress sitting in Annapolis. He wrote Morris with the verve of a freshman in office, wanting to know about the status of the $8,000,000 requisition made in November 1781. He mentioned that this money was greater than the amount needed, and the surplus must be appropriated. This was based on the idea that states had actually paid the requisition, but the facts current at that time showed nothing of the sort. He continued to explore the September 1782 resolution by Congress requisitioning $1,200,000 for the payment of interest. The states were allowed to use money collected for this purpose to pay local holders of Loan Office Certificates, and Jefferson wanted to know if the remainder had been sent to the Treasury. He also wanted to have the list of employees in the Office of Finance for the new budget. Such questions were the result of the distance between Morris in Philadelphia and Congress in Annapolis, the turn-over in Congress, which resulted in the loss of continuity in administration, and of the prevailing sentiment that the states had been working hard to pay for the war. For all of the supposed effort being made by the states, the Treasury was empty and the interest for the foreign loans was barely being met.

Back in the frozen port city of Philadelphia, Morris responded to Congressman Jefferson's letter about finances. He confirmed that the requisitions, if paid, would cover the costs of the war that occurred during his tenure, and he also confirmed that the excesses would be used to pay the debt incurred from 1782 and 1783. This was a time period when foreign debt grew; and the Loan Office Certificates were no longer issued. He pointed out that over eight million dollars was still due from the states, and one million of that eight would pay the "unfunded expenditures" from his time in office. He clarified,

> I mean such part of the public debt as arose in that year and which not having been carried to the account of the public debt but remaining due on my office engagements and anticipations must still be provided for out of requisitions.

Morris was referring to the money he currently had at personal risk, and funds he expected to pay for the continuation of government. He did not expect the states to comply any time soon, and added,

> ...if only one hundred thousand dollars were employed in payment of our funded debt before January next, in addition to the provision for paying the interest, we might then consider the Independence of our Country as firmly established.

He understood that the states were doing something to repay their debts to their own citizens, and he added his difficulties were a result of the construction of his position,

> The idea of an officer dependent only on Congress amenable only to them and consequently obedient only to orders derived from their authority is disagreeable to each state and carries with it the air of restraint. Every such officer finds a weight of public opinion to contend with.[65]

In response to Jefferson's other points, he sent along the civil list for his department and a budget. Morris objected to paying the expenses of the President of Congress without having any control over those expenses. He thought a more economical system would be better and suggested supplying such officers of government with a salary, and allowing them to manage their own expenses from that. He was not angling for another government position, which he made clear when he wrote,

> I speak for my successor or rather for my country. Neither the powers nor the emoluments of the office have sufficient charms to keep me in it one hour after I can quit it...

Morris noted that in the past

> ...there seems to have existed a solicitude how to spend money conveniently and easily but little care how to obtain it speedily and effectually.

He proposed, as he had since 1775, the use of competent executives to look after the public's business.[66]

Spring

On March 1, 1784 Morris began his first debt service contract as a participant in the tobacco trade with the Farmers General. He did this through the firm, Williams and Alexander.[67] Later, in September, when Morris was a month from leaving office, he sought a contract in his own name. At that time, he predicted that too much tobacco was being grown, and that would necessarily drive the price down.[68] In the meantime, he allowed Alexander to participate in the profits, but when Alexander faltered Morris dealt through his Baltimore firm Tench Tilghman and Co. They negotiated a price of 36 livres per quintile, or about six dollars for 112 pounds. The deal was closed by Morris' banking house in Paris, Le Couteulx and Co. Morris arranged to buy tobacco that had been collected as part of the requisition from Virginia, and to ship it to France for resale.[69] The French government controlled the importation and sale of tobacco to maximize its income which would go to pay America's debt, so Morris' contract with the sole taxing agency in France was considered, by his political rivals, to be a monopoly of export of American tobacco to France.[70] Morris heard that people were ready to complain about the Farmers General contract, and he confided with Alexander.

> To whom is it to be addressed, to the Farmers General, they are interested to support it, if to the King he must support the Farmers for they support him. If to the tobacco planters, they will sell to those who want to buy and can pay, it will not do.[71]

He generally understood popular discontent, but in this case, he saw the situation as an agreement to service the national debt, and not an example of regular trade practices.

Morris worked to expand his private ventures, but his work in the Office of Finance was not over. William Smith, who had been one of the negotiators with Daniel Parker to oversee the evacuation of New York, and who also signed the Book of Negroes, wrote Morris, and requested that his account be settled and his expenses paid. On March 10th Morris advanced the group of commissioners over $3,000 and assisted them in their settlement.[72] The comptroller of the treasury was unwilling to pay these commissioners. He claimed that there had been no authorization by Congress to pay their expenses, or for their time. He decided to refer the matter to Congress.[73]

Morris still had to deal with the endless wrangling of the states, as they enacted new barriers to collecting or remitting funds to Congress. Considering their small contributions, he wrote to the paymaster,

> ...the legislatures think they do a great deal in giving the means sufficient to keep us from starving.[74]

Connecticut paid their tax in depreciated state currency, and Morris ordered his receiver to burn it.[75] In Pennsylvania, people in Lancaster County refused to pay taxes, if the money was to be sent to Congress. In Philadelphia, people were ignoring the timed nature of notes from the office of finance and cashing them in immediately upon receipt, thus removing any reason to issue them. Morris wrote to Whipple in New Hampshire,

> I only wish every member of every legislature were as much teased, harassed, and tormented to do what the legislature alone can do as I am to do what I alone can not do.[76]

Among those harassing Morris was John Nicholson, comptroller for the state of Pennsylvania. He contacted Morris about supplies that had been purchased in 1781. It seems that by 1784 many of them had spoiled in storage and Nicholson was seeking to be reimbursed for the original cost of the items. It had been Morris' job as Agent for the state of Pennsylvania to pay for these supplies, but he did not think he was responsible for their status three years later especially since, he said,

> I think every thing of that sort ought long since to have been adjusted.[77]

Morris continued to encourage the tax receivers to arrange the sale of public supplies "which for want of care and attention are wasting away."[78]

Pennsylvania continued to focus on itself, just as John Holker attended to his needs to the exclusion of all else. Holker emerged from his counting house and contacted Morris to make it clear that he refused to consider including any calculations for currency depreciations in his settlement with his former partner. Morris insisted that depreciation be considered. Morris, for his part, was not willing to be financially responsible for currency depreciation that was enacted by Congress, and that was, in any case, far beyond his control. He also lost money as a result of these forces, and ironically he had spent much of his time fighting the kind of paper money that led to this depreciation. In response to Holker's refusal to accept depreciation as a fact of life in the wartime economy, Morris severed ties with him. Morris informed Holker that the only way to settle their disagreement was through the courts.[79] They divided their interests. He contacted Turnbull, Marmie and Co. to find if they wanted to stay with Holker, or Morris. He left the choice to them. Holker kept his interest in Harrison Junior & Co. of Virginia. Morris kept his interest in Turnbull, Marmie & Co.[80]

Morris worked to close his affairs with Holker, but the old business of the Office of Finance was hard to close. Back in 1781 Morris had allowed Comfort Sands & Co. to terminate their contract voluntarily, even though they later denied they wanted to. This denial caused Comfort Sands & Co. to sue the Government, and that suit went forward. The company that had picked up the remainder of that contract to supply the "Moving Army" was Sands, Livingston & Co., a group made up of many of the same people including William Duer, with John Holker as a backer. Sands, Livingston & Co. fell into a dispute over some beef, and they wanted Morris to pay for their extra expenses. Morris thought that would undermine his policy of establishing a system of supplying the army with government contracts. Instead at that time he encouraged Sands, Livingston & Co. to seek justice through the courts. Morris wanted to reach settlements with Comfort Sands & Co and with Sands, Livingston & Co. before he left office. He was not sure he had the power to enter into binding arbitration, but he did not want to leave their fate in the hands of others. In 1784 he offered to send the business to Congress for resolution.[81] Later he requested authority from Congress to send the matter to arbitration.[82]

Financial settlements were on the minds of America's ally as well. The French minister La Luzerne contacted Morris about payment to French officers whose accounts were still open. Morris wrote to Paymaster General Pierce, in support of La Luzerne's effort. Then he replied to La Luzerne that the business was in the hands of the paymaster. Another Frenchman, and friend of America, was still busy overseas. The Marquis de Lafayette was acting in a private capacity as he attempted to broker an arrangement with France for American ships to have access to various French ports.[83] He tried to get import duties removed, or at the very least, applied in a rational manner. At the time, trade duties were largely unpredictable; and this uncertainty resulted in few American ships entering French ports for fear of losing money in the process. Morris forwarded the Marquis' letter to Congress and noted,

> The masterly manner in which the marquis had treated a subject foreign to his former habits and view merits great applause ...[84]

Developing foreign trade stayed on the agenda of the Office of Finance. Gouverneur Morris contacted the Marquis de Chastellux, and Robert contacted the Marquis de Lafayette, to promote the idea of allowing American ships to use a small French island off the east coast of Madagascar, Réunion, as a free port. In France, this had the support of merchant Pierre-Samuel Dupont de Nemours. Another island free port was Ile de France, now known as Mauritius. The King of France allowed American ships to use these ports, but not as a free port. The French saw this as a way to grow the East Indian trade and use American ships in the process. They did not want American ships to carry goods from Europe to East Asia, but they were happy to allow them to carry goods to their islands from America. The effort was uneven during the first years, and did not really become profitable until the wars of the French Revolution, when the idea of free ports became a reality.[85]

The news from the Spanish realm was not good. Oliver Pollock reported from Havana, Cuba, that the port was closed to American vessels. He thought he could be of no service to America in that Port.[86] By closing the port, the Spanish made trade with Americans illegal. This meant that all the cargo Pollock brought for trade was suddenly considered contraband. In his next letter Pollock informed Morris that conditions were deteriorating for all Americans in Havana.

An American captain reported that he had entered Havana to fix his ship after a storm. When he went into the town, Spanish officers entered the ship and abused the crew, struck the flag, and detained the pilot. The Government decided

> ... to apprehend all Americans without distinction ... put them in gaol and afterwards send them away from here.

Pollock wanted to leave Havana if there was to be no treaty.[87] Morris wanted to reopen Havana to American trade. He wrote to Rendón on that topic, and in addition to promoting trade as a general means of creating prosperity, Morris' gambit was to suggest that the proximity of America with Cuba would prove too tempting for smugglers, and he said that it was better to have a well-managed legal trade to provide a force to counter that tendency. Rendón was not in favor of supplying Cuba with products sent on American ships, and so he undermined Morris' efforts.[88]

Overdraft in Holland?

By the end of March 1784 Morris informed Congress on the subject of the potential overdraft of the Dutch loan. It was unknown, at that time, if Adams had succeeded in securing a second loan, and this was not anticipated because Congress had expressed its mind that there should be no new loans. Instead, Congress formed a committee to look into funding options and put Jefferson at its head. Among the ideas that came from this committee was that Congress might seek loans from American banks. They also considered making an emergency appeal to the states for funds. Few Congressmen voted for that. Rhode Island was convinced the bills would not be protested in Holland, and that other richer states should pay in any case.[89] Morris lamented that the lack of cooperation between Rhode Island and his office could be attributed to suspicions about Morris' motives, and prejudice that made it impossible for them to see the poverty of America's government.[90] He wrote on the topic of these curious prejudices to Huntington, a congressman from Connecticut. He said that he would quit as soon as possible so a replacement could be named,

> My successor or successors will perhaps be believed when they describe our situation and at least that voice of party which had hitherto opposed the public service on private principals will be silenced.[91]

For the time being, however, Morris was in office and it was up to him to make ends meet. He continued to make plans for the bills he expected were protested.

> Not being able to sell bills on Holland as fast as the money was wanted and not daring to risk the public money in British hands at that period, I bought up the public bills at the current price and remitted them to my friends Herries & Co., drew in my private capacity on the credit of those remittances and thus by selling bills

> on Holland or England at the choice of the purchaser I raised the sums necessary. But now I receive intelligence that the stoppage of the loan had compelled the commissioners tho very reluctantly to suffer my bills to be noted, (i.e., held for lack of backing).

Morris was unaware that the Dutch bankers had ignored his advice that he had arranged for the private purchase of the original loan, and that some of his friends were still holding the funds until it would fill in Europe. They also ignored Morris' instructions to Franklin and Grand to cover the loans. Instead, they concluded that America's finances were as bad as rumored; and they took the most pessimistic view.[92] They assumed that the French contingent would do nothing; and that all the notes Morris' friends were holding were actually on their way to be cashed. So, when they protested Morris' bill they acted on the basis of rumor and fear instead of fact, but the rumors were credible because of the behavior of the states. The bankers did not honor Morris' note immediately instead they put it on hold and summoned Adams to Amsterdam and petitioned the town council to back the loan. That was refused, so it became necessary to create the new higher cost loan, mentioned before. Morris hoped and expected that a new loan in Holland would save his credit, but he was worried that might not be the case. He noted,

> ...yet my numerous but unprovoked and undeserved enemies will not fail to make the worst of the very evil which their misconduct has brought upon the country and in which I am unexpectedly involved.[93]

With things looking grim in Europe, Morris told George Hall, receiver for South Carolina, that to get money to the Continental Treasury, he would draw $20,000 from the amount he thought Hall had collected.[94] The receiver of taxes for the state of New York, Tillotson, grew tired of the obloquy being heaped on him and resigned in March 1784.[95] Maryland was still remitting nothing on their state quota. Morris wrote,

> The state of finances is almost desperate and unless speedy and effectual measures be taken all hope must soon be discarded.[96]

While Morris endeavored to wrap up old matters, Congress proceeded with plans to ascertain the future of the area known as the Western Lands, and adopted Pickering's proposal to keep this area free of slavery.[97] This area, also called the Northwest Territory, later became the states of Michigan, Illinois, Indiana, Wisconsin, and Ohio. There had been conflicting claims to the lands. Once it was finally stipulated that Virginia had ceded their claims to the land, Congress elected commissioners of Indian Affairs to make arrangements with the hostile and friendly Native Americans who inhabited that vast area. The commissioners were Rogers Clark, Oliver Wolcott, Nathanael Greene, Richard Butler, and Stephen Higginson. Greene and Higginson declined, but Arthur Lee and Benjamin Lincoln stepped forward and became active as Commissioners of Indian Affairs.

With the peace secured and expansion underway, the new post-war Congress worked to develop a financial strategy. Morris tried to stop them from issuing more new paper money. Congress was also considering borrowing from new banks in New York and Boston, and Jefferson wanted Morris' opinion of the nature of the loan. They thought they might support the government through a mortgage taken out on the "western lands."[98]

Morris replied to Jefferson's letter about loans from American banks. He thought that the young banks would not have sufficient capital to support the loans. He pointed out that since the mint had not started operation there was no American currency, and much of the foreign currency was being used to buy imports, so the hard money was being exported and was unavailable. The money that was available was going to be needed to repay existing loans from France and Holland. In any case he did not expect the banks to make loans to the U.S. if there was no expectation of repayment. He closed,

> It is true that the situation of affairs is very disagreeable, but it is better to bear up and struggle hard against present difficulties, than lay the foundation of future evils.[99]

Morris also addressed Jefferson about the use of funds requisitioned from the States to pay expenses from before Morris' tenure. Morris suggested that if Congress used funds from the 1782 requisition to pay the debts from before 1781, then used the remainder to pay the debts from 1782, the practice would be difficult to defend because the amount received was too small and it was raised for a different purpose.[100] Morris was patient with the changing Congress, but the nature of the questions and replies display a lack of administrative continuity on the legislative side, and without institutional memory the same mistakes were likely to be made again and again.

He kept up the regular business within the Office of Finance. He worked to build new international trade relations, and he met with the commercial agent of Saxony on the topic. As usual familiar people kept moving in and out of the scene. George Eddy offered to buy bills of exchange; Morris declined. There were already problems with the funds underlying those bills, and selling more, which might be quickly cashed, would increase the difficulties. Daniel Parker was paid $15,000 on his latest contract to supply the army.[101] Morris paid the crew of the *George Washington*.[102] He also encouraged Congress to accept his advice and sell the *Alliance* and *George Washington*.[103] The supplier of ox teams in Massachusetts sought payment from his home state. The governor of that state wanted the payment to be considered as part of their requisition. The question went to Congress, and Jefferson asked Morris on the point of not having paid the bill before this moment. Was it because of Morris' policy of only paying for expenses he incurred?[104]

Morris reiterated that he refused to be liable for debts from before his administration. He explained that the system from that time was so deficient that the amounts owed were impossible to ascertain with any reliability. The reason for this was largely due to the behavior of some of the people who were involved in the Loan Offices.

> Affairs were so complicated that it was hardly possible to say who was at fault and while every individual officer took care to excuse himself, blame was placed on Congress ... the expense which attends the settlement of the old accounts is the least mischief which had resulted.

He cautioned about the trend in Congress to reestablish these offices, which he saw as dens of corruption,

> ... it is an expensive and pernicious establishment without being attended with a single good effect to compensate the mischief.[105]

He suspected the people who wanted the re-establishment of this system were somehow benefiting from it. Clearly Morris was trying to bring Jefferson up to speed on the issues his office had long considered. At the same time, he wrote the President of the new Congress to reinforce the reasons behind the policies that had guided the Office of Finance for years.

During the course of dealing with the old business, new people occasionally showed up in Morris' office. A Mr. Cazeau was a French Canadian. He claimed to have had a verbal agreement with Benedict Arnold to supply flour to his army. He had made a claim against the United States and Congress agreed to pay. The Treasurer doubted the validity of the claim and hesitated to pay it. He asked Congress to reconsider their instruction to pay. He cautioned against making exemptions for individuals on flimsy evidence,

> The best emotions of the mind by this means become the sources of evil and pity for one operates injustice to many.[106]

Congress eventually decided not to pay Cazeau, who in turn tried to pressure the French Court into forcing America to pay.

By early April, Morris was trying to insure American solvency in Europe. He contacted his French banking house, Le Couteulx and Co. to tell them that tobacco, to be sent as part of the debt service contract, was in Virginia awaiting shipment, but they should expect it to arrive on "a very fine fast ship." He told his banker in France that he expected the new shipment of tobacco to cover £300,000 drawn from the French bank by bills of exchange that Morris' office sold.[107]

He thought the hard winter and resulting lack of shipments from America would have increased the price of tobacco in Europe, and he hoped the Farmers General would be pleased at that.[108] Even so, he thought that tobacco in Virginia was too expensive to purchase for export with hard money, and in any case the bank had stopped cashing notes. This was due to lack of hard money resulting from the closure of Havana to American ships, the failure of America to pay her loans from Europe, and general lack of trade. Morris used state requisition payments to buy the tobacco for this debt service deal, and there may have been some inflation in the price of tobacco due to the rate at which it was credited within the tax system. To deal with the local cash crunch, Morris had his agent accept cash and notes from the tax collector in Maryland and send the cash to Philadelphia, and the notes to buy tobacco "fit for the French market" for export.[109]

Another member of the Office of Finance, Gouverneur Morris, looked to improve his lot by developing some personal business in Europe. He thought the impost of 1783 would be ratified. He attempted to convince William Carmichael to enter into a private arrangement in which the two of them would buy up the discredited American debt in Europe at a discount and hold it until the U.S. Government finally decided to repay it. They did not manage to pull this off.[110] Gouverneur was also in contact with a friend of America living in London,

> Everything I have read from America seems to have been written in the belief that Great Britain can't do without us and that we can bring them to do what we please by scolding.[111]

He thought this to be a poor strategy because England was convinced America could not do without the trade with the West Indies. He concluded,

> It is my opinion that every power in Europe wishes us to be thirteen (or thirty of you please) separate, independent, unconnected states – and they will contribute all their power to make us so.[112]

While Gouverneur attempted to corner the market on American debt in Europe, Robert worked to tie up the loose ends of the Marine Department. The *General Washington* was advertised for sale on April 16th, 1784. Congress resolved to allow payment to be made in loan office certificates and in "other liquidated debts due from the United States."[113] Morris contacted Joshua Barney, former captain of the *General Washington,* and asked him to undertake the management of the sale of that ship.[114]

The Navy was being sold off, and Morris turned his attention to the Army. Comfort Sands & Co. were to be paid $1,102 from the old contract from 1782 for a 2% allowance on flour.[115] Unfortunately, Morris' ability to help other deserving supplicants had still not improved. He could not pay John Sullivan in New Hampshire because that state had paid nothing and there were no public stores there that could be sold for ready money. He wrote to Sullivan,

> To whom must I look for money but to the states? And if they will not grant it from whence is it to be delivered? If they will not grant it for payment of that is due to their own citizens (that is to themselves) for what purposes will they grant it?[116]

The Comptroller was trying to settle the account of the Baron von Steuben, but the lack of documentation frustrated his efforts. The Quartermaster General, Timothy Pickering, was trying to settle the accounts of the "artificers" who served the Army. Their numbers had been reduced in 1781 as a cost saving measure, but the old accounts were still open, and they had not been part of the half-pay furlong procedure of 1783. Pickering suggested they be paid, but there was no money for them.[117] Morris appealed to Congress for a decision.

One of Morris' partners, Peter Whitesides, still held an option on a bill of exchange drawn on the Dutch loan. He approached Morris because he had taken the option as part of Morris' effort to cover Congress' debt to the Bank of North America, but Whitesides' obligation to the bank was due.[118] Morris extended to Whitesides a note similar to the one held by his partner, Isaac Hazlehurst. Then Morris wrote the Dutch bankers to learn the actual fate of the bills he feared were protested. He also informed them that a shipment of rice was on its way from the Carolinas. He had not yet received a letter they had sent two months earlier, which stated that a second loan had been secured and the bills were really not protested.[119]

Such matters did not weigh down Congressman Jefferson. Instead, he was looking to the future when he asked Morris for a copy of his earlier work on coinage. He wrote,

> Finding on my coming to Congress last that the subject had been resumed and had passed through your hands I endeavored to get a sight of your report. Having however been delivered from one committeeman to another till the whole of them had got out of place, the paper is not now found.

He also mentioned that he had an "insurmountable aversion to copying" and requested that his notes on coinage be returned with Morris' reply. Finally, he closed by thanking Mrs. Morris for helping his daughter who was studying in Philadelphia at the time.[120]

Congressman Jefferson drafted a response to Morris' proposal on coinage. Instead of simply demanding the end of Morris' currency plan, Jefferson threw up a series of rhetorical roadblocks, and misrepresented Morris' work. He pretended that it used a coin for the "unit" representing the lowest common denominator, and then declared that the unit was too small. He wrote,

> The price of a loaf of bread 1/20 of a dollar would be 72. units. A pound of butter 1/5 of a dollar 288. units. A horse or bullock of 80. D value would require a notation of 6. figures, to wit 115,200, and the public debt, suppose of 80. millions, would require 12. figures, to wit 115,200,000,000 units. Such a system of money-arithmetic would be entirely unmanageable for the common purposes of society.[121]

Jefferson favored using the Spanish milled dollar as the base unit. At the time of Jefferson's suggestion, accounts were kept in state currencies, and the Spanish dollar had changed in value since it had been used as part of the calculations that led to the theoretical unit found in Morris' proposal. Morris thought that forcing the Spanish Dollar on all the states at that time would cause financial losses due to rounding errors and make it difficult for merchants to convert their state money accounts to the new currency. Morris' currency system allowed merchants to convert the amounts on their books into the proposed currency more accurately, Jefferson's did not take into account the merchants' concerns. He favored the farmer and the status quo,

> The conversion of the merchants account is but a single operation. Once done it is done forever.... The adoption of the Financier's unit may relieve this one operation of the merchant yet it throws the difficulty on the farmer who knows what a dollar is but of the Financier's unit the farmer is ignorant.

Morris favored small units for small business use. Jefferson thought that small units were unmanageable and not needed by the poor or small businessmen.[122] He stated,

> I only go to 1/100 because as yet the people in some states could only be induced to that and in no state have they demanded lower.

After reviewing Jefferson's response, Morris contended that Jefferson's proposed coin was too large for daily use by shopkeepers and the poor,

> ...we must consider that the 1/100th of a dollar is not sufficiently small ... and that when the poor are purchasers or vendors it does not admit of the divisibility necessary for their affairs.

He also disagreed with Jefferson's proposed proportion of gold to silver. Morris was worried that if gold became the basis of the currency then it would be easily exported to England and ultimately substituted with English light gold, which was of less value. Morris favored silver as a way to keep the hard currency in America.[123] However, bowing to the wishes of Congress, Morris changed the configuration to produce larger value coins by changing the value of his proposed coins by a factor of one hundred. What had been 100 units became a one, and what had been a five copper became .05, like a modern nickel. Morris sent along the sample coins he had struck for the purpose of proposal; and asked Jefferson to forward them to the President of Congress. These are now thought to be the Nova Constellatio set.

Morris continued to work towards creating a mint. Progress was not swift. Congress waited until Morris left the Office of Finance, and a Treasury Board was in operation under the guidance of Arthur Lee, before agreeing on the configuration of the currency. Lee's allies, Samuel Osgood and David Howell of Rhode Island managed to get Jefferson's proposals circulated in the press. Nearly a year later, in 1785, Congress chose Jefferson's configuration sighting press reports as evidence of popular support. They set the Spanish milled dollar (at 362 grains of silver) as the basis for the American currency.[124] The Morris' at the Office of Finance suggested in 1783 that the currency use on a coin worth 400 grains of silver, and a 1/100th piece worth 4 grains.[125] The new coin was not minted until 1791. The difference was 38 grains of silver, or about 10% in value, and the cost was eight years of economic uncertainty. After Jefferson's coinage system was adopted the word "Justice," as suggested by the Office of Finance, was removed from the coins and is still missing from American currency, but "Liberty" remains.[126] (Jefferson's Autobiography 1743-1790, see appendix).

While these coinage discussions were underway, in the Spring of 1784, news started to filter into Philadelphia that the new Dutch loan had come through. Daniel Parker told Morris that some of the bills he drew from Holland had been paid.[127] Official notification of the new Dutch loan finally arrived on May 4th. That loan covered the notes that had been posted in December, and it was expected to cover the bills drawn and held by Morris' friends.[128] When the news reached Jefferson, he was chagrined that such high interest had to be paid and considered that it was due to the "business of supplies,"[129] instead of properly associating the high rate with low American creditworthiness. Congress accepted the loan, and forbade Adams from making any more without explicit approval. Morris wrote John Adams and thanked him,

> And now I am about to leave this office let me return to your Excellency my sincere thanks for the assistance which has at different times been derived from the exertion of your industry and talents.[130]

With Morris on the way out, Congress was on the way to reverting to its past practices. Samuel Osgood opined,

> But I hope it will be generally agreed, that if it was necessary to create an omnipotent Financier in 1781, that Necessity does not exist now. I am clearly against the Office in its present Form. And I am not sure any Form will do.[131]

On May 7th Jefferson's "Grand Committee" recommended the re-creation of the Board of Treasury. French Minister La Luzerne was alarmed at the rebirth of this system; and thought it did not bode well for the repayment of America's debt to France. However, Morris stayed at his post until the end of October, and the board did not convene for months after that. Implementation of the Treasury Board recommendation was placed into the hands of Morris' adversaries: David Howell and Eldridge Gerry. Arthur Lee managed to get himself appointed to a position on it. Also on May 7th, Jefferson was appointed minister to Europe. Morris made arrangements for Jefferson's trip to France where Jefferson was to be installed, arranging with Grand, the French banker, to pay Jefferson his salary of $11,000 per year.[132]

In a cost saving move, Morris dismissed the confidential messenger he hired during the war.[133] He also reminded the President of Congress that there was no committee to review the conduct of the Office of Finance, which he had suggested and endorsed two years earlier. Morris maintained his effort to rebuild his private enterprises. On May 10th he formed a partnership with William Constable and Gouverneur Morris. Constable was set to be the operating partner. The offices were to be on what is now Pearl Street on Manhattan Island. John Ricker joined this firm a month later. They intended to provide flour and other goods to the French and Spanish islands, but nothing came of this. Instead, the firm became active in trading in the Far East.[134] Also on this day, there was a demonstration of manned flight in a hot air balloon. It ascended from Morris' garden behind his house on Market St. Morris attempted to raise money for a manned flight enlisting Swanwick as treasurer, but unfortunately the cooker used to heat the air became dislodged and fell from the balloon structure. It crashed through the roof of an outbuilding, and the balloon descended. The later, and more successful flight by Mr. Peter Carnes in Baltimore put an end to the air race.[135]

Morris put aside futuristic ventures and geared up his regular business activities. He arranged with one of his shipping companies to buy wheat or rum for export, and he learned that the Farmers General would still be pleased to deal directly with him. Morris was also doing some business with his daughter Polly's husband Charles Croxall. He had to inform his associate in Baltimore about the conflict with Holker. Morris seemed concerned that Holker might be spreading "wild stories" about their fight.[136]

He also contacted the Farmers General, "I take much pleasure in entering into commercial dealings with you." He recommended a shipment of various tobaccos so the Farmers General would know what was available in America and place their orders accordingly.[137] One of his companies, Peter Whitesides & Co., responded to the government advertisement for a contract to service the debt to France. Morris told the Virginia receiver, Webb, that Whitesides was willing to offer $40,000 "in hand and the remainder as fast as the tobacco should be delivered." They also offered to pay $5 per hundred-weight over and above the standard commission.

These were good terms and won the contract for Whitesides, and away from a New York firm, Nelson, Heron and Co.[138]

Morris' partner in developing the China Trade, Daniel Parker, left the Army supply contract in Duer's hand, and tried to build up a business as a merchant trader. The ship he had purchased at auction, the *Bourbon*, was renamed *Comte d' Artois* before sailing to Europe. Unfortunately for Parker, the ship was not seaworthy and much of the cargo she carried was ruined. Parker could not afford such failure.[139] He was so desperate he pilfered $2,300 from the silver horde on the *Empress of China*. Then he abandoned his partnership in the venture, leaving Holker with a pile of unpaid bills. He went to Amsterdam, where he set himself up as a broker of American securities.[140]

Back in the Office of Finance, Morris was pleased to receive $956 from his receiver in Rhode Island, George Olney. He wrote,

> I am glad to find ... that your state have not totally abandoned the idea of making payments into the public treasury.

Morris also received $837 from Massachusetts.[141] He accepted $10,000 in value from Virginia in the form of public tobacco.[142] This was on the same day the Baron von Steuben wanted to collect the $10,000 that Congress had settled on him. Morris directed him to Massachusetts where Morris thought he could collect the hard money he needed. He contacted Lovell, his receiver in Massachusetts and instructed him to honor Steuben's notes, and to send the remainder to the Treasury. Morris thought $20,000 would come in.[143]

Unexpectedly, Morris learned of a piece of unfinished business from 1777. A Mr. Jett had been asked to use public money to buy tobacco for shipment to Europe as part of a Secret Committee effort. Morris told Mr. Jett to sell the tobacco and send the money to the Treasury.[144] Such belated discoveries demonstrated that settling the accounts of the old Secret Committee would be difficult. After much work Morris had the commissioner of accounts from the Marine Department deliver the papers of the Secret and Commercial Committees to Congress for settlement. The same commissioner informed Morris that agents for the early Marine Boards were not closely managed and

> ... it does not appear by their papers how they accounted individually to the committee, different members having received and paid monies so that it is impossible for me to tell in whose hands the deficiency rests.

Additionally, there was no set commission for prize agents under early Marine Boards. There was also no provision in the law for repayment of any such monies and there was no clear way to determine which funds came from prizes and went back to the states, or which came from Congress and went to the states. It was a mess because there was also no way of knowing what, if anything, was repossessed by the creditors.[145] Morris requested Congress investigate the agents who worked during the period before Morris became Agent of Marine. Congress took no action after Morris left office. Little progress was made in settling the Marine accounts and the lack of settlement in those and the Secret Committee accounts caused Morris difficulties for years. Lack of settlement provided opportunity for demagogues to accuse Morris of being a public defaulter, and this became an issue in 1789 during the argument over the ratification of the Constitution. The committee accounts were finally settled in 1795 eleven years later, long after Morris left public office.[146]

The state of Rhode Island persisted in not even considering the impost of 1783. Many, including Jefferson and Rendón believed they would eventually agree to the measure, and thought that state just wanted to be the last to approve. There was guarded optimism. Morris hoped Nathanael Greene would prevail upon the legislature of his home state, Rhode Island, to pass the impost of 1783. Much attention was focused on the smallest state, and the new impost was modified to suit her concerns.

He cautioned that Rhode Island's lack of hearty cooperation with Congressional requisitions hurt American credit overseas when he wrote,

> ... the translation into the Dutch newspapers of our disputes, quarrels, refusal to grant compliance to the requisitions of Congress &c &c it is said, spread the alarm amongst the capitalists in Holland, and instead of continuing to lend they begun to sell those obligation of Mr. Adams under par.... In this state of things I have been obliged to involve myself in heavy engagements to keep things going and my mind has been far from easy.[147]

Morris and his allies were not pleased to learn that Governor Clinton, of New York, had led that state to reject the impost of 1783 as it was, and instead burdened it with untenable conditions.

In local political news, Pennamite Wars were on again. The Pennsylvania Assembly sent Justice of the Peace Alexander Patterson and a band of Rangers into the Wyoming Valley in Pennsylvania, near modern Wilkes-Barre. The Trenton arbitration of 1782 had been decided in favor of

Pennsylvania. The settlers from Connecticut became worried that the farms they had carved out of the wilderness would be taken from them by the State of Pennsylvania, then under the control of the "Constitutionalists." These fears were well founded. The "Constitutionalists" in the Assembly decided not to honor the settlers' property titles. The Rangers went north from Philadelphia to enforce the will of the Assembly. These settlers did not want to lose title to the land they had settled. Most of the able-bodied men who had tamed the wilderness were dead because of earlier conflicts with the Iroquois. The remaining residents (a.k.a. Yankees) were mostly old men, women and children. They put up a fight under the leadership of John Franklin to protect what they saw as their property. They had paid for it with their blood and argued it was still Connecticut's by grant and charter. Patterson's method of settling the dispute over property titles included the techniques of property seizure and imprisonment without trial. This enflamed the situation. Patterson extended the earlier "Constitutionalist" policies of thuggery and intimidation to new levels as he conducted a form of "ethnic cleansing"

In May 1784 Patterson took it upon himself to remove the settlers from Pennsylvania. The desperate group of dispossessed old men, women and children were driven out of their homes, and those who did not hide in the woods were forced to walk sixty miles through the wilderness to the Pennsylvania border of the Delaware River, without food or supplies. Many died along the way. Public opinion swayed in favor of the settlers. The Assembly dispatched John Armstrong to the area with four hundred members of the militia to arrest Patterson and establish peace. Armstrong, former mutineer and lately Secretary of the Executive Council, made promises of peace and compromise. As soon as the Yankees and Patterson's Rangers were all disarmed, Armstrong rounded up as many settlers as he could and threw forty-six of them into jail, leaving Patterson at large. The Pennsylvania citizens were horrified by this dishonesty and brutality. The states of Vermont and Connecticut sent troops into the area to avenge the injustice. The Assembly then dispatched Timothy Pickering to the area to settle the matter. He arrested Yankee leader Franklin and allowed Connecticut settlers to keep their land titles. Before it was all over, Pickering was captured and held in the woods by the Yankees for three weeks, but he was released when it was clear Pickering would not release their leader, Franklin. Franklin was eventually freed and elected to state office. Two years later, in 1786, Luzerne County was formed; and this helped bring peace to the valley. Ultimately, after proving himself by this brand of diplomacy with the settlers in the Wyoming Valley, John Armstrong rose in favor during the Jefferson Administration, and was made a minister to France and then to Spain.

Summer

Morris guided the tobacco business on public account and sent 200,000 livres to his banker, Le Couteulx, for remittance to Mr. Grand as part of the debt repayment. He also sold public tobacco in America, and sent the money to Europe, via packet ship, because bad weather had stopped the shipment of tobacco during the winter.[148] There was some private time to consider a little rum speculation, and the purchase of claret from France.[149] Also he tried to pay off bills drawn on Willing, Morris & Co. and to close the books on that firm.[150]

-|-

Before he left the office he had held for years, Morris endeavored to put America on a firm financial foundation. His hard money policies and national vision had won America's War of Finance during his term in office, but it seemed that the states had learned little or nothing. Rhode Island seemed immune to reformation. It was still holding out, and not passing the impost. Morris saw this as the work of a few partisans;

> A number of little arts are practiced on this subject for which I have too much contempt to take any notice of them...The accounts of last year have been delayed because I wish to close all my public accounts and quit the painful and envied station which has given some men so much trouble. Their labors have not been quite in vain for they have impeded the public service and embittered the moments spent by me in cares to prevent those evils which were the necessary result of their efforts. Before your towns cry out against further taxation let them first pay what they ought to have paid near two years ago.[151]

Morris tried to use his own exit from office as a means of encouraging Rhode Island to pass the impost. He wrote the governor of that state,

> I hope your Excellency will believe me when I seriously assure you that the greatest advocates for a change cannot more earnestly desire my dismission than I myself do. I hope their sincerity and mine will speedily be put to the trial. They by granting money and I by resigning can best evince that our professions are founded in truth.

Suggestions that Morris sought special benefits from his office still haunted his efforts to convince the states to pay what they had already promised. He continued,

> To me it can produce neither honor nor power nor profit. The advantages I may derive will be in common with all my fellow citizens and I shall share also the burden in common with them.[152]

Morris' political opposites had succeeded in making it appear to many, including Morris, that their objections were based on personalities, but the reality of the situation was that Rhode Island was protecting their slave trading business, and their slave powered rum business. Thus, it can be seen that part of the legacy of slavery is the degradation of Morris' reputation, and this will be true as long as people repeat the claims of the pro-slavery forces: David Howell, Arthur Lee, and Henry Laurens.

As it was in 1784, the tiniest state was the biggest problem to American solvency because of their interest in maintaining the slave economy. On the other hand, Morris was able to congratulate Connecticut on passing the impost,[153] which they did over their general opposition to funding congressional efforts and their particular aversion to the payment of army pensions by Congress. However, they favored the impost because they suffered from being near two states with state import taxes and they wanted to have a unified import strategy among the states.

North Carolina passed the impost. They also agreed to cede their claims to western lands; and passed a poll tax to cover the debt that would not be paid by the impost alone. Unfortunately, they kept the money until all the states agreed to send theirs to Congress.[154]

Progress was slow in Virginia as well. The commissioner to settle the state's account, Turner, had been installed. He had received an accounting without supporting vouchers, about which he had written Morris. However, the state Solicitor General refused to provide any more information because he had a narrow view of what was required, and he thought that he had to provide information only on certain debts authorized by Congress. Naturally, without all the information Turner could not do his job. When Congress instructed the Solicitor General of Virginia to provide all the necessary information, he responded that it was difficult to disentangle all the claims. The process inched ahead over such obstacles.

In the middle of June, Morris received word that South Carolina was ready to remit $34,780. Morris made arrangements to receive this amount into the treasury. The receiver in New Jersey reported that several counties had paid their quotas, but he could not say the same for all the counties in that state.

Pennsylvania had passed the impost, but Morris still had to counsel his home state against the Assembly's efforts to restart the use of land banks and paper currency. He wrote,

> Pennsylvania I hope will have more sense than to adopt a measure equally unwise and unjust ... for I cannot doubt that the hour of emission will be the date of depreciation.[155]

They did issue the new money, but it lost value before the print run was finished. Morris referred to the currency as 'so called money'.[156] In a different but related matter he met with John Nicholson, comptroller of Pennsylvania, on the subject of Morris' activities as Agent of the State of Pennsylvania.[157] Morris maintained that he had increased the value of Pennsylvania's currency to the point that fewer Pennsylvania Pounds were needed to equal the requisitioned amount and adjustments to the state's account should be made on that basis. Nicholson wanted his state to be credited according to the number of Pounds supplied, not their value. That way he would be repaid in high value Pounds for the low value Pounds his state had originally contributed. Discussions continued.

Eventually discussions between Nicholson, of Pennsylvania, and Morris reached an impasse. Morris wanted to close the books on his department. He offered an expedient when he wrote in his own settlement on the account, and this enraged the Pennsylvanians. The state decried his arrogance. To force a settlement that was more beneficial to Pennsylvania the state comptroller, John Nicholson, countered in September 1785, that because Morris had not spent the money as directed he should be personally responsible for the unspent amount of $98,389. Here was a situation where Morris had increased the value of the money with which he was entrusted by 150%, and in return he was basically called a thief. Such was the political climate in Pennsylvania. It was not until 1786 that a final settlement was reached. Using a slightly modified approach to the one Morris took in 1784, Pennsylvania released Morris from his liability and the state of Pennsylvania was able to get slightly greater credit when it finally settled with the Federal Government during the Washington administration.[158]

Morris entered into arbitration with John Holker, and contacted Pieter van Berckel, the Dutch minister, to fight whatever rumors John Holker might be spreading.[159] The arbitration dragged on. Holker had requested vouchers from Morris' records, but then suddenly he experienced difficulties in using them and requested even more records from Morris.[160] Morris learned that Holker was trying to raise a public clamor against him, but the more he tried to do this, the worse Holker looked. Once he realized this, he stopped and redoubled his efforts to settle through the arbitration. Morris came to believe that

> Mr. Holker is very avaricious, he is eager and greedy after wealth and has pushed and grasped after it by so many pursuits and in such various channels that he has gone beyond the length of his tether. He has dissipated his property in so many schemes that he cannot get it together again and it was his keenness in these pursuits that made him more indifferent about the settlement of his accounts than otherwise he would have been.[161]

Morris wrote to John Rucker, who was in Paris, to explain this affair and to inoculate himself against whatever rumors Holker was attempting to spread against him in France.

Matthew Ridley wrote from Europe and tried to put Morris' mind at rest. He said that Holker was not waging a campaign against Morris' reputation in France, and that thoughtful men there waited for the results of the arbitrations. Ridley also wrote that Morris' sons were doing well and were "two of the best children in the world"; welcome news to a fond parent, one can be sure.

Ridley mentioned that Holker's fortunes were on the decline in France. It seemed Holker was out of credit, and this was causing personal harm to Ridley because Ridley was engaged in business with him. The trading house that Morris had surrendered to Holker, Turnbull and Co., was treating Ridley poorly. He wrote,

> The conduct of the house Turnbull & C. is unpardonable. They have exposed me to all the horrors and disgrace of bankruptcy ... they owe me near £4,000 Stg [sterling] for accepted and paid bills.... The difference that I hear has arose between you and Mr. Holker give me great uneasiness.... I wish I had been with you. I am vain enough to think I might have been able to prevent the differences.[162]

The final result of Ridley's arrangement with Holker is unknown, but it might be noted that Holker never returned to Europe.

Gouverneur Morris had his mind on Europe too, and he continued to pursue his idea of privately speculating in American debt certificates there. He expected to work with Daniel Parker, and a former aide to Washington, Ben Walker.[163] Gouverneur also tried to interest Robert Livingston in the debt purchase plans. In his explorations, Gouverneur learned the fate of Benedict Arnold. It seemed that Arnold was riding in his coach in London when an elderly gentleman recognized the coat of arms on that coach. It so happened this elderly gentleman was a family member who settled £1,500 per year on Arnold, or so the story went.[164]

Robert tried mightily to tie up loose ends before he left office, and set in motion the wheels of justice that he felt would otherwise stop in his absence. To that end he moved forward on the settlement with Comfort Sands, & Co. He also arranged for the purchase of medals and commemorative swords for officers. The case of Paymaster General, John Pierce, shows why Morris tried so hard to settle old claims. Pierce found himself in the odd situation of not getting paid at the same rate as his predecessor. His pay rate was not taken up under the Treasury Board which succeeded Morris, but it was finally set seven years later, in 1791, with Hamilton in Treasury and Washington in the Presidency.

Private citizen, George Washington, wrote from Mount Vernon to introduce his nephew to Morris, and to learn if there were any employment opportunities for the young man. He also asked for a little consulting on the topic of icehouse construction. Morris had a very competent icehouse behind his home on Market Street, and Washington's icehouse was not holding the cold as well. Morris had some difficulty in helping Washington's nephew gain a position in a mercantile house, but did manage to arrange an offer of a position in his New York firm, Constable, Rucker & Co. He also responded to Washington's question about the icehouse and described in detail just how his worked and why. He emphasized the importance of gravel on the bottom, suspending a floor for the ice to rest upon, and finally insulating the walls and ceiling with straw.[165]

These domestic concerns were a world away for Thomas Barclay, who was still at work in France trying to settle American accounts. He forwarded the accounting that Silas Deane had constructed and reminded Morris that Deane was very desirous to have his affairs with America put in order. Morris contacted Thomas Barclay and expressed his worry that the final settlement of America's wartime finances in Europe was not going to be finished before he left office. He wrote, "I am going out of office and it gives me much concern that any matter should remain unclosed in which I have been engaged. I hope this will not be the case as I am in the hourly expectation of hearing from you somewhat farther and more satisfactory."[166] Morris was right to be worried. This letter survives only in the hand of his arch-rival, Arthur Lee. Lee took a position on the newly reconstituted Treasury Board that was created after Morris' tenure. Barclay suffered from neglect for a time, however Barclay's attentions were directed elsewhere when, in October 1785, he was asked by Jefferson to negotiate a treaty with the King of Morocco. That treaty was concluded and America's treaty with Morocco is the oldest international treaty still in force in America.

Rhode Island does it Again

News came from Rhode Island that the legislature had voted down the impost of 1783. Many in Congress were astonished; one asked, "What could be done with such a people?" Another congressman said, "the cursed state ought to be erased out of the confederation." Rhode Island's action effectively stopped the nationalization of the debt until after the Constitution was signed. So, just as Morris was poised to leave office, the states reasserted themselves in a move that weakened America in the eyes of the European powers.

Nathaniel Greene wrote about his home state's failure to pass the impost of 1783. He described the arguments of the opposition, Mr. Howell and Mr. Ellery. Greene said,

> Mr. Howel undertook to prove that state would lose four fifths of its revenue collected upon it.... He insisted upon the credit of the United States standing fair in Europe and that the bills noted for protest in Holland was from the scarcity of money from the numerous applications and not from any apprehension of our funds.

This was an attack on Morris' management of the finances, and a complete misrepresentation of the facts, but the argument won the day. Greene continued,

> The truth of the matter is a large majority of the members are incompetent judges of so complicated a question ... the people have much less wickedness than ignorance, but the latter is equally fatal to a just policy.[167]

On the topic of Rhode Island's non-participation Morris wrote,

> Time will show how far their reasonings are good and their intentions honest. Under present views however it would seem as if Rhode Island had not much to expect from the annihilation of Congressional authority.[168]

Nathaniel Greene wrote again, "People here are poor and money difficult to be got on any terms." He went on to ask if he could borrow about $500 to help in his efforts to buy slaves for the plantation he had been granted by the state of South Carolina.[169] Morris wrote to the Dutch Bankers to arrange a personal loan for Nathaniel Greene. The loan was never secured, and Greene eventually died of heat stroke suffered from working the farm himself.[170]

The impost was dead and gone, but Morris did not give up. He wrote to the receiver in Rhode Island that even though the state had voted down the impost, he hoped they might comply with the requisitions agreed to under the existing Articles of Confederation.[171] In other news from up north, Morris learned that the State of New York was considering making their new banks receivers of taxes. Gouverneur cautioned Hamilton about accepting state paper money in his newly formed Bank of New York, and suggested he keep that bank as independent of the state government as possible.[172] Gouverneur did not expect much cooperation between that bank and the Bank of North America in Philadelphia, nor did he expect a mint to be put into operation quickly.

Robert learned that New Hampshire had £25,000 in state money, but not for the use of the United States, meaning they did not want to turn it over to Morris. However, they would accept notes that could be used to draw from those funds in favor of Generals Sullivan, Hazen, and Lincoln for their claims on the treasury.[173] Because of this, Morris was unable to get any funds from the New Hampshire tax receiver, Whipple, for John Langdon, of the Marine Department. Morris directed Langdon to the Massachusetts tax receiver for the money he needed.[174] Whipple had nothing to do under these circumstances and left the office of receiver.

Later, the state of New Hampshire tried to pay their requisition in "old emission" continental money that, back in 1781, had been depreciated at the rate of 40:1. Morris doubted he could comply because he did not think Congress had agreed with this. He wrote, "I do not know of any resolution of Congress which applies to this object." He went on to say,

> I conceive the claim of the state to be just and therefore had I been a member of Congress I should most assuredly have voted for a resolution to establish it.[175]

New Hampshire, Massachusetts and Rhode Island collectively held nearly half of the old "continentals" and they all sought to use them to pay the requisitions. This would have removed them from circulation and increased the value of the remaining half, but that was not to be. It was not until two years later that the Congress allowed such exchanges, and then at the rate of 50:1[176]

The "genius & habbits" of the past was once again in control, and Morris regretted that under the direction of the Grand Committee, Congress was on the path to reestablishing the Loan Offices. He wrote,

> The system of loan offices appeared to me for a long time past to be a very bad one. The present arrangements were taken by Congress without my knowledge and I can only judge of them as you do by the perusal.... I consider this kind of paper as a mere shadow."[177]

He continued,

> ...it is an expensive useless establishment necessarily involving intricacy and confusion that I might perhaps add is founded on principles of disunion. If the national debt be managed on proper principles the loan offices must cease....[178]

Morris expanded on the topic with one of his tax receivers,

> I am well persuaded that the members of the last Congress were desirous to abolish the office of Receiver and to establish that of Loan Officer. Much of this desire may be attributed in some to their dislike of me and in others to the necessity of gratifying particular dispositions in order to accomplish particular purposes. It is a pleasant thing to serve wise and constant masters for such are grateful. The members of Congress are not half so bad as the character they give each other, but I wish you and I very fairly quit of them.[179]

Upon examination of this letter Arthur Lee wrote,

> Mr. Morris does not pay a very high compliment to those members of Congress with whom he associated, and who were probably the calumniators he alludes to.[180]

Morris answered the question from tax receiver Hall on the topic of the re-establishment of the loan offices,

> The arrangement made by the legislature as a temporary expedient until the general plans of the United States shall have taken their due effect.[181]

Morris did not seem to consider the loan office arrangement to be a viable long-term solution to the American financial problems and clearly thought that his system, or some other national system, would be the best way to go.

Morris kept up his effort to install Commissioners to settle the state accounts, and he did so to create a just economic policy that would continue after he left office. He nominated Mr. Montgomery to that position in the state of South Carolina.[182] He contacted the Governor of North Carolina to say he would try to find a commissioner for that state. He differed with North Carolina for denying Congress' intention of making the Commissioner a final judge, and rather treating him as an arbiter. Morris also objected with their unilateral decision to take depreciation against Congress' will. Congress had clearly stated that goods would be judged according to their specie value at the time of requisition.[183]

Morris carried out Congress' wishes to inform the existing Loan Officers that a new certificate could be substituted for the old. He did not like the policy, but he was duty bound to follow their instructions. He commented that it would be a good idea for the newly considered bank of Massachusetts to be the receiver of taxes, but he still did not think well about the intended three-man treasury board.

> Men are more apt to trust one whom they can call to account than three who may not hold themselves accountable, or three and thirty who may appoint those three.... The peace having given our domestic and coffee house politicians a little more leisure they will have time not only to find fault but to find out where the fault lies which tho not always the more easy it is not always the less useful task.[184]

He continued to use his remaining time in office to do what he could to obtain justice for individuals. Abraham Skinner was owed $38,892 for outlays he made when he paid for the care of prisoners of war. Morris sent a letter of credit on the receiver of New York to Skinner. He intended for Skinner to apply to the State of New York for repayment. Skinner was not paid by New York during the tenure of the Treasury Board, and it was not until 1790, six years later, when Hamilton was in Treasury, that Congress finally paid him.[185]

Thomas Killbuck wrote to Morris for help in gaining permission to go back to his home in the Delaware nation,

> Soon if Congress willing, and because please now, and I think I must go home this summer to see our friends, I long to see them, and I have learn my book, and I am in great want of close [clothes] at this time and people dond like to see me because I have no close fite to weare and please to answer.

After a stay of several years under the care of Congress, Thomas Killbuck was an apprentice farmer with marginal reading and writing skills.[186] Morris appealed to Congress to allow Killbuck to return to his people in Ohio. Congress did not act.

A month passed and Morris addressed Congress yet again for relief in the case of the Indian boys in their care.

> This young man was here yesterday, and tells me that his cousin as well as himself are extremely desirous of going back to their own country; and he complains much that he is kept bare both of money and cloths." Morris recommended that Congress, "send both of these youths to their own country with some degree of splendor.[187]

Lack of Congressional action caused Morris to write again to try to help Thomas Killbuck,

> It is a pity this lad should be in such want as he expresses himself to be and therefore I sincerely wish him to be provided with the necessaries fitting to him.[188]

Major Commander Joseph Marbury, of Maryland, wrote to Morris and requested that a Mr. Fowler be repaid for the £926 that Fowler had given the troops in anticipation of being repaid from Continental funds. Fowler now found himself short of funds and was being hounded by creditors. Morris petitioned Congress on Fowler's behalf, but Morris was out of office before action was taken. It went to the Treasury Board and Congress took no action until March 1785. In the meantime the Treasury Board, under Arthur Lee's leadership, summarily dismissed similar petitions. The only reason they took this petition was because Morris had intervened. A settlement was not reached until 18 months after the first steps were taken.[189]

-|-

On July 2nd, 1784, exactly eight years after the Declaration of Independence was passed, Congress resolved to discharge all but fifty-five of the troops garrisoned at West Point. The much dreaded standing army was almost gone. The released troops settled their own accounts on the spot by dividing funds previously supplied via a Morris note that was drawn against taxes collected from the state of Massachusetts. Robert continued to do what he could to promote international trade and wrote letters of introduction for a gentleman from the Court of Saxony. He sent them to the Governors of New York and Massachusetts. Such new arrangements became increasingly important because trade relations with a former ally were deteriorating. The self-inflicted weakness and poverty of America's government was not helping to advance its interests with foreign powers. The Spanish Governor of Louisiana decided to shut the port of New Orleans to American, British, and French ships. This locked American ships out of the Gulf of Mexico. Spain also refused to allow Americans to charter Spanish ships to carry American goods through the port. Around the same time American merchants were no longer allowed to settle their accounts in Havana due to the Spanish embargo there. This was just a prelude of worse things to come for American Counsel Oliver Pollock. By July 7th, 1784, Pollock's attorney had already been detained in New Orleans and was being held as a hostage to force Pollock's hand.[190]

Oliver Pollock was arrested in Havana because of a suit filed in the Spanish city of New Orleans for non-payment of over $84,000 Pollock had borrowed in France for Virginia, and which he expected the Continental government to repay. They had not. Pollock asked Morris to insure those accounts were settled speedily, and to appeal to Congress to get him out of jail. Pollock related that armed soldiers had gone to his house and, with bayonets fixed, seized his carriage and mules, even though that was contrary to local Spanish laws.[191] This kind of treatment of the American Agent did not bode well for Spanish-American relations. Congress considered the fate of Oliver Pollock and decided that it was an affront to find one of its citizens thrown into a Spanish prison in Havana. They said they would take action.

Just as America's southern neighbor was becoming hostile it became clear in the northwest that the British were not evacuating the outposts quickly or voluntarily. The Commissioners of Indian Affairs met in New York in August and recommended that Congress take possession of the British held forts at Detroit and Niagara. Congress looked to assemble a force of seven hundred men to accompany the commissioners and accomplish the task.[192]

Quartermaster Pickering compiled an estimate for the cost. Congress sought funds from Morris as Superintendent of Finance. Morris was reluctant to become involved in building up military supplies in anticipation of a new treaty with the Indians. About this refusal it was said,

> That there are not yet sufficient funds to absolve his existing engagements.... That he cannot comply without involving a longer continuation in office.

Morris asked that no further applications of this kind be made until he could quit.[193]

From his position on the Commission of Indian Affairs, Arthur Lee wrote to John Adams,

> Our treasury is as low & the prospect of raising it by taxes, as unpromising as possible. Either the present Superintendent must continue in with powers calculated solely to convert every thing to the emolument of himself & his creatures; or if a reform is made, he & his immoral assistant [G. Morris] have malignity enough to endeavor to ruin where they can no longer plunder. However there is a plan before Congress for reforming the department, by putting it into Commission & prohibiting the Commissioners from being engaged in trade or commerce: which I hope will take place.[194]

Lee did not propose that the new Commissioners would be forbidden from engaging in the business of owning plantations that could sell goods to supply the effort. Nevertheless, the commissioners continued to make plans. They came back to Morris with a new idea.

Against his better judgment, but in accordance with the wishes of the Commissioners for Indian Affairs, Morris directed supplies be gathered, and he advertised for a military supply contract to service the western posts during negotiations with the Indians. William Duer won the contract to supply the army for this venture.[195] Morris noted that the British had not given up the posts and he wrote,

> To judge on the propriety of holding a treaty under present circumstances does not fall within my province. It is however my duty to mention that the public treasury can ill bear unnecessary expenditures ...[196]

The needed force was slow to assemble. The President of Pennsylvania was not inclined to supply and feed the Continental troops during this venture, even though they had recently had no difficulty dispatching four hundred militia men to the Wyoming valley to attack old men, women and children.

Morris kept in touch with the French to settle the accounts of their officers who fought for America.[197] Discussions between Morris and French minister Barbé-Marbois were not going smoothly. The French minister was most unhappy about the prospects of America repaying the French loans. He had imbibed a negative opinion of Morris during his time in Rhode Island, and that opinion worked against America at this point. Morris attempted to reassure Barbé-Marbois that American funds and efforts to repay France were solid. Barbé-Marbois communicated to the French ministry that Morris' efforts were null, and that the Dutch complained about the expected shipment of the rice and tobacco. One supposes he held Morris responsible for the harsh winter, which was the true cause of the delay, but no further information is available on that. Morris had ordered the shipment in December 1783, but only one shipment was sent directly to the Dutch bankers, due to the weather.

The tobacco was sent to cover the note Morris had expected would be protested by the Dutch. Unfortunately, in the 18th century, communications were too slow to supply Morris with the information he needed in a timely fashion. However, the Dutch notes were ultimately paid because Adams arranged a second loan, and the tobacco was used to pay on Morris' note drawn against the English bank, which would have otherwise drawn down the first Dutch line of credit and subsequently harmed American credit in Europe. Further purchases of tobacco were made difficult because foreign ships were coming to American ports and bidding up the price of the commodity. Morris thought this would quickly result in oversupply in foreign markets; and that would cause a reduction in the price and a bursting of the bubble in tobacco speculation.[198] Barbé-Marbois did not elaborate on this in his discussions with the French ministry. Instead, he noted that Americans were not necessarily inclined to continue shipping produce after Morris left office, and that the balance of trade was so lopsided against America it was unlikely they would have funds to make payments in the foreseeable future.[199] Morris kept working to shore up American credit and wrote the Dutch bankers. He asked them to send some of the money collected in the process of syndicating the new loan, to the American Banker in France, Mr. Grand. Morris expected Grand to use the funds to make a payment of 400,000 livres on the French loan.[200]

In honor of America's great ally, August 25th, 1784, was the day for celebrating the birthday of Louis XVI. A great celebration was held in Philadelphia. Morris took this occasion to announce the successful payment of the interest on the French Loan.[201]

Across the sea, Lafayette continued his private mission to secure free ports for American ships. But, back in America, the French minister Barbé-Marbois wrote Morris to be sure it was understood that the French intended to be repaid both the principal and interest on the loans they had made to the US, most particularly the French backed loan from Holland.[202] Both Morris and Barbé-Marbois understood that Morris was about to leave office, and this communication was a means to inform his successor that France had not forgotten, or forgiven, the debt. Morris responded that he fully intended to pay both the interest and the 10,000,000 livres of principle. He said that he thought the American agents in France would have already paid the interest through the sale of American property and supplies there as long as those supplies had not been seized for non-payment by other parties. Morris hoped to encourage the French to release American property in France, so the King could be repaid.[203]

The French Crown was worried, and so were the men in America who worked hard and risked their fortunes to supply America's needs. On September 1st, Sands, Livingston and Co. entered into arbitration over their disagreement with the Office of Finance. Unfortunately, they were still reluctant to share their records, and this made the process proceed with great difficulty.[204] The settlement was not reached while Morris was in office, which he regretted.[205] The issue was not resolved until 1834, during the Presidency of Andrew Jackson; that is, fifty years after the fact.[206]

Congress had not taken action on the proposed settlement of the original Moving Army Contract between the U.S. and Comfort Sands & Co. Morris determined to move the matter to arbitration so it could be settled before he left office. He did this with uncertain knowledge that it was within his power. He wrote,

> I cannot think of leaving you exposed to the inconvenience of future solicitations for justice and will therefore risk the submission of your demand to arbitration.[207]

He followed that up with a second letter,

> But I must pray you, for your own sakes to consider, that I am desirous of quitting this office and that you may experience difficulties should I leave it while that matter is unsettled.[208]

On September 6th, Comfort Sands & Co. entered into arbitration, but the process was delayed because Comfort Sands & Co. was also not willing to open their books and allow the arbitrator to see the records. The effort stalled until after Morris left office. In 1785 arbitration started up again and two years later they were awarded a total of nearly $40,000. The minority opinion of the arbitration board was the same as Morris'. He stated that the Government was not responsible for money lost through discounting of Morris' notes, and that the discounting was the source of the shortfall. Congress did not act on the arbiter's determination, mostly because of a conviction on their part that Daniel Parker and William Duer were also responsible for the losses, and even though they were not contractors of record they should be held liable anyway, because they were partners in Comfort Sands & Co. Congress also included consideration that there had been later contracts between the Superintendent and Daniel Parker & Co. and they suspected that might have a bearing on the matter, somehow, even though it was not clear exactly how.[209]

Back in November 1782, Daniel Parker had contracted to supply the Army in New York and New Jersey. His company was to supply them, but the first payment of $100,000 was to be delayed for ninety days, but payable with notes of exchange drawn from the French loan. Morris made other advances to Parker to keep the soldiers supplied between the onset of the Newburgh Affair and the furloughs of most of the army. Duer and Parker continued to supply the Army, until it was disbanded in June, at a certain rate that was set by the contract, but not necessarily associated with the size of the army. Any lack of regularity was due to the way the soldiers traded their Morris notes for supplies in Parkers warehouse. These payments became the focus of a dispute and went unsettled because Parker had sailed to Europe in May 1784 in order to avoid his creditors. Parker's partner, Duer, had not benefited from these payments to Parker, and now that Parker had disappeared in Europe, he appealed for payment for the supplies he had delivered. When Duer initially requested payment Morris refused, sighting the overpayment to Parker as a reason. Duer and Parker were backed by a silent partner, John Holker. Holker was pressing Duer for the payment because of Holker's continuing financial difficulties. Morris was later convinced to make the payments to Duer, but he then applied to Holker for repayment for the overpayments to Parker. Holker was still on track to pursue Morris through the legal system. He was sure he would win in arbitration in his private case against Morris, and he requested that the proceedings be made public so all could see the facts.[210]

Morris contacted Holker and requested that he return the overpayment made to Daniel Parker & Co.

> I have delayed until the last moment, making farther application on this disagreeable subject, but some settlement must take place before I leave office which I am about to do.[211]

Holker replied that he needed to discuss the matter with William Duer before making whatever payments were proper. Duer did not believe he or Holker were responsible for Parker's debt, even though Holker had signed a $200,000 bond on the contract. Instead of paying, Holker tried to link Parker's debt to the U.S. with the Sands, Livingston & Co. dispute over the Moving Army Contract; that is the old dispute about the extra beef that they bought at high prices after the failure of the Comfort Sands contract. The case proceeded through the Pennsylvania Supreme Court, but the public's claim against Parker was finally settled through the Treasury Board under a framework that covered a number of contracting disputes, many of which involved the same people: Comfort Sands, Walter Livingston, William Duer, Daniel Parker and of course John Holker, who held an interest in each firm. It might be noted here that both Walter Livingston and William Duer worked as commissioners for the new Treasury Board when the board reached that settlement. In the end, Morris never recovered the money from Holker.[212]

In the early summer of 1784, Morris became more active in his private business and counseled his business partners. He wrote Tench Tilghman that prospects for tobacco sales in Europe were not good because the purchase price was still too high, and the selling price too low. He expected the sale price to rise within the year, so he cautioned Tilghman to support Alexander's efforts to buy as cheaply as possible and thus push the purchase price down so trade would be profitable. He said,

> ... it is the duty of every merchant to aim at this point because it is in the interest of commerce and the interest of the country that it should be so, and if such is the invariable line of your conduct, not only Mr. Alexander but all others will come sooner or later to the conviction of it and of course have no jealousies on that score.[213]

William Alexander had difficulty buying tobacco at a price he could afford, but the Farmers General still demanded a shipment. This put him in a losing situation. Morris made arrangements for Peter Whitesides to purchase tobacco, offered by Virginia as part of the tax system. This allowed Virginia to pay tax in tobacco, and for money to be sent to the treasury. Whitesides then exported the tobacco for sale in Europe. In this way, Virginia's tobacco was used to pay the war debt.

In September, Morris asked Tilghman to put together a shipment of tobacco samples. He ordered 300 to 400 hogsheads of different kinds of tobacco to be sent to France. He wanted the Farmers General to be able to place orders of particular types and grades in the future, and he could not wait for the prices to go down before making this contract. He wrote that he was dispatching Mr. Croxall's ship, in an attempt to include the husband of his first daughter, Polly, in what he hoped would be a good to the business.[214]

Morris' attempt to include Charles Croxall within his trading system did not work out well. Croxall fell into disputes, and Gouverneur Morris suggested that he give up on being a merchant and instead focus on farming. He wrote to Croxall,

> I will consider only two of the obstacles in your way viz the want of coolness and of perspicuity. You yourself complain of the warmth of your own temper urging you into precipitancy of conduct. The natural consequences of such temper and conduct are that persons of cool design must gain fair advantage over you, and that you must often neglect the honest and fair advantages which fortune places within your reach.[215]

-|-

In the middle of September, Quartermaster Pickering delivered a final accounting of what was due to the Quartermaster Corps from the period of 1782 to 1784. It was over $110,000.[216] Morris responded by signing a warrant, but he knew that there was not enough in the treasury to cover it. The warrant was expected to act as a legal commitment to pay the bill, even under the new Treasury Board.[217] He contacted the receivers of Continental taxes in eight states and encouraged them to collect the funds that Pickering required.[218] The record of the various states was in keeping with their past practices. New York paid nothing, but probably made payments within the state. Rhode Island paid about half the amount requested. Delaware paid less than that. New Jersey, Pennsylvania, and the others met their quotas.[219]

Morris was near the end of his tenure as Superintendent when he wrote his personal thoughts to a colleague, George Olney,

> America is indebted to France and to the Subjects of the United Netherlands. This is the debt of the United States, not of individual states, nor of private citizens. The resort of payment therefore is to America collectively, and the application must be to Congress, and the general representative. The duty to pay is absolute; but the means can only be derived thro the states. If the states refuse, have Congress the right to compel? The answer to this question decided whether we be one or thirteen. The consequences are evident. America delays justice, France and Holland have therefore the right to exact it and the means to compulsion are at hand, since they can always seize our ships. If they confine the seizures to the ships of delinquent states, will this be agreeable to such state? If the seizure be general will that other states be content? In all this, Congress you see are out of the question. They have neither the power nor the inclination to do, what some folks call their duty, but which

> can never deserve that name until men are held to the performance of impossibilities.[220]

Before he left office, Morris tried to conclude the business of shipping American goods from Europe, and asked John Ross to deliver materials, valued at over $60,000, that he had not shipped during the war because there was a of lack of vessels to run the blockade. Ross sent a shipload of the goods from France, but they remain unaccounted-for, even to the present day. This quantity of goods was considered part of the Secret Committee settlement finalized in 1795, which found Willing, Morris & Co., which included Ross, in arrears for over $90,000.[221]

As Morris endeavored to close the business in France, he learned what had happened to the supplies that had been seized in Europe. Beaumarchais' agent in Spain, who had operated part of Hortalez & Co. refused to surrender materials, which Americans considered theirs. Morris later discovered that these war materials had been used by Count D'Estaing, and the transfer of the £31,958 worth of supplies should have been accounted for back in 1781. Beaumarchais moved forward with his claims against the United States over the 1777 transaction which supplied the rifles that won the battle of Saratoga. As the case moved forward, Morris asked that the loss of 36,000 livres he suffered over the bad business of the privateer *Audacieux* be considered against Beaumarchais.[222] Silas Deane's accounts were sent to Congress for review, as were the Lees' accounts from their time as commercial agents for America in Spain. The bills of two diplomats, Adams and Laurens, were also sent to treasury for payment. Deane's accounts were scrutinized, while for Arthur Lee, "every kind of evidence was accepted in lieu of vouchers."[223] Morris remarked that he would like to see the final accounting with the American banker in Paris, Mr. Grand, before leaving office. Finally, he wished Barclay well in his dealings with the new Treasury Board.[224]

Morris wrote the American agent in Spain, William Carmichael, with the unhappy news of Pollock's treatment at the hands of the acting governor of Cuba. Morris also wrote to Congress in support of Pollock's claims, and to alleviate his suffering in a Cuban jail. He informed the President of Congress about Lafayette's progress in trade negotiations with France. Six months later, that letter was forwarded to John Jay, who, by then, had become the Secretary of Foreign Affairs.[225] Morris thanked Charles Dumas, unofficial chargé d' affairs for America in Holland, for assisting in finding the funds. He thanked John Paul Jones for his zeal. He thanked Benjamin

Franklin for his support of Morris' tax policies. He outlined the final arrangements for paying salaries in Europe, and for the payment of 400,000 livres on the Dutch loan that had been backed by the French.[226]

Morris thanked his private banker for accepting his bill for 300,000 livres; the one that had become put on hold, but was not protested because Morris was able to ship American products to cover overdrawing on the Dutch loan. He told them to pay the American debt to Mr. Grand using funds gained through the sale of public tobacco. He then directed them to stay in contact with the Board of Treasury when they sent public letters.[227] He contacted the Dutch bankers to alert them that various drafts may be expected, but that the total should not be more than 200,000 gilders. He tried to give them confidence that America would be good for the rest of the money owed and explained why he felt it was necessary to risk overdrawing the loan. He wrote,

> But when a country is at war for political existence and the life and fortune of every citizen dependent on the controversy the stake played for is too great to mind a risk which may involve the loss of two or three hundred thousand gilders when that risk is necessary to save the game.[228]

Even though he had made arrangements for his private French banker to pay 400,000 livres in interest to Grand as American banker for the French loan, he also alerted the Dutch bankers that they may be called upon to honor Grand's request for 100,000 guilders. Ultimately enough was raised in Holland to provide for the interest payments and there was no default.

Morris wrote to the Dutch bankers,

> I shall in a few days leave the Office I now hold and retire to the situation I have long and ardently desired and pursued that of a private citizen in a free country.[229]

On September 30th, Morris wrote the Board of Treasury,

> On this day therefore which completes the third quarter of 1784 I shall terminate my operations.[230]

When he turned in his commission he wrote,

> It gives me great Pleasure to reflect that the Situation of public affairs is more prosperous than when that Commission issued. The Sovereignty and Independence of America are acknowledged...

> may they be firmly established, and effectually secured! This can only be done by a just and vigorous Government. That these states therefore may be soon and long united under such a Government, is my ardent Wish and Constant Prayer.[231]

Morris submitted for publication his accounts as Superintendent of Finance. When he did, he wrote to the citizens,

> The master should know what the servant has done. To the Citizens of the United States of America, therefore, the following pages are most humbly submitted.[232]

That volume was not published or otherwise made public for years, leaving plenty of opportunity for others to question the record.

As it was in 1778, when Morris attempted to retire from Congress and look after his private business affairs, so it was in 1784. Morris' attention was drawn to a number of details after he left the Office of Finance. Among them was publishing an advertisement that he would be personally responsible for all of his outstanding notes at face value, if the notes were not otherwise paid.[233]

Morris' letter and accounts went to a non-existent Board. It was not until ten months later, in July 1785, that the new Board was in place.[234] When Jefferson heard this he wrote to Monroe,

> I am sorry to see a possibility of Arthur Lee's being put into the Treasury. He has no talents for the office and what he has will be employed in rummaging old accounts to involve you in eternal war with Morris and he will in a short time introduce such dissentions into the commission as to break it up.[235]

Lee stayed on the board until it was disbanded in 1789 as a result of the Constitution being enacted. During Lee's tenure the states reverted to their old habits of Loan Office indents, paper currencies, debt payment discrimination, and often not paying non-residents. Ultimately, in 1791, Madison's committee to review the work of the Financier concluded that Morris left a positive balance of $21,986 in favor of the United States.[236]

Out of Office

The arbitration between Morris and Holker dragged on and ended when Holker refused to renew the arbitration bonds in October 1784. That forced the issue back into the Courts. By March 1785, the French minister, Barbé-Marbois, convinced the Pennsylvania Assembly to enact a special law making it possible for Holker to sue Morris on behalf of the King of France. The problem Morris saw in this piece of legislation was that it applied to events that occurred before the law was passed. As such it was an *ex post facto* law, and clearly against the Pennsylvania Constitution, which the "Constitutionalists," who passed it, did not seem to mind.

The Law passed in April 1785, and the local and international reaction was unanimously negative. The "Constitutionalists" began to lose political favor with the citizens of Pennsylvania, and this was only one of many reasons. After much delay the Morris/Holker lawsuit moved into the Supreme Court of Pennsylvania in October 1785. Also in October, Morris' Republicans once again took control of the Pennsylvania Assembly, but only by a small margin. Morris was re-elected to the Assembly on October 11th, 1785. It was from this seat in the Assembly that Morris defended the Bank of North America, was appointed to attend the Annapolis Convention, and the Constitutional Convention two years later. His record ultimately won him a seat in the U.S. Senate.

Four days after his re-election to the Assembly, Morris won his case in court when a jury decided that Morris was answerable only to Holker, and not the King of France. That decision sent the two men back to arbitration and the court set forth the guidelines. Holker agreed to submit to the arbitration by January 1786. The decision was finally handed down in April 1789, that Holker owed Morris £1,570 in Pennsylvania currency. By this time Holker was in utter disgrace in France, and his accounts were never settled with the French Government. He filed two more suits against Morris. In one Morris was awarded £4,700 but the result of the third has not been found.

Contract to service the Debt

In January 1785, Morris contracted with the Farmers General to deliver 60,000 hogsheads of tobacco over a three-year period.[237] Also in 1785, Morris' company, Constable, Rucker and Co. contracted with Congress to service the foreign debt. These two contracts combined to fulfill part of America's obligation to her allies. The trading company bought tobacco in Virginia in much the same manner as Morris had done as Superintendent of Finance, using state tax receipts to offset that state's debt to the Congress. Then, under a sub-contract to Williams and Alexander, Constable, Rucker and Co. shipped the tobacco to the Farmers General, the French tax agency. Profits, minus a small commission, went to pay the interest on the Dutch loan, which, at that point, the French had covered for America.

Virginian tobacco farmers objected because they saw this contract as a monopoly. Morris saw it as a contract to pay the nation's debt to the French tax agency, which just happened to be the sole importer of tobacco into France. He was back into controversy. Never one to bend to the winds of public opinion, and always stay with the terms of a contract, Morris wrote to Horatio Gates on the solution to the current problematic political period,

> Popularity is the reigning idol in the United States, therefore make it popular to promote public Justice and unpopular to oppose it. The work will then be done.[238]

Morris' prediction about the price of tobacco falling came true while he was fulfilling his contract (a.k.a. monopoly), and growers blamed him for the price shift. Virginia tobacco farmers were not pleased to see their profits eroded and complained mightily. Morris' contract with Congress fell under attack from Jefferson, who was in France as the American Ambassador, and also by Lafayette who was a champion of free markets. During 1785 and 1786 Morris used private notes to pay for tobacco instead of transporting silver coins into the fields and markets of Virginia. The Virginia legislature decided to outlaw the use of private notes as currency in circulation. To overcome this, Morris made his notes payable to specific individuals instead of his former practice of making them payable to "bearer."

On the European side of the Atlantic, French merchants thought that Morris and Alexander charged too much for the tobacco, so they too were unhappy. Morris' reputation was suffering at this time due to his long disagreement with John Holker. He got no support from Ambassador Jefferson, who spent his energies decrying the contracts. Morris' position in France was further damaged by his use of American ships to transport the tobacco, and his use of London banks to handle his finances. Under these circumstances the debt service contract was not exactly broken, but Morris' position as a sole source supplier was eliminated. However, Morris' sale price was set by his contract with the Farmers General, at the same time the purchase price of the tobacco rose in the United States when speculators moved in. A low selling price and a high purchase price removed incentives for doing the business.

Once Morris' sole source role ended, a flood of tobacco was sent to France by a variety of merchants; this drove the market price down in France and the resulting low profits discouraged the Crown from relying on imported tobacco as a source of revenue. In France, they turned to domestic tobacco production. This resulted in the increase of taxes within France.[239]

In the summer of 1785, still operating under the debt service contract, Morris' company, Constable, Rucker and Co., bought bills of exchange in America that had been drawn on the Dutch loan. Then they carried the bills to Morris' French banker, Grand, as payment for interest due in 1784. In the third arrangement, signed in December 1785, they tried a different tactic. They accepted payment (to be transmitted to Europe) in the form of silver money, Pennsylvania paper currency, and New York paper currency. They signaled Rucker, who was in England, to pay the loan debts with timed bills of exchange drawn on the American accounts. John Rucker's father, who was a well-established merchant and banker whose interests spanned Europe, was more conservative than his son and he insisted that John refuse to honor these timed bills drawn on an American account based on state currency. John Rucker complied with his father's wishes. The paper currency Morris' group had in hand did not hold its value for the duration of the exchange, so the partners in America tried to undo the deal and return the paper currency at pre-depreciation levels. No one, including the issuing states, was willing to accept depreciated currency any more than Rucker was. It was then observed that the younger Rucker started to behave erratically, and within two years he was dead. Rucker's refusal in 1787 to honor the bills of his partners, put Morris and his company at risk for over $82,000.[240] This signaled a halt to America's effort to repay its debt to France, because Congress just stopped trying until Hamilton came on the job the following year, after the Constitution was signed.

The problem caused by the instability of and depreciation in local paper currencies forced the Morris' shipping partnership into disagreements with the Treasury Board. The Treasury Board, under Arthur Lee, tried to hold Constable, Rucker & Co. liable for over $82,000 in interest payments due the Dutch. Ultimately the partners were able to supply sufficient documentation to ward off much of this claim. A settlement was reached, and the partners paid $16,255 in 1798; just at a time when Morris' financial situation could not have been worse.[241] Morris never really recovered from the financial body blows he received during these debt service contracts, and his efforts to recover drove him to more and more risky financial operations. The idea that Morris finally went bankrupt as a result of financing the Revolution arose from these conditions.

By 1787 the states had taken to issuing new rounds of paper money and using Loan Office indents to pay their own citizens. In the process they often ignored the debts to non-citizens within their state's borders.

Little consideration was paid to foreign debt and requisitions to be paid in specie due to Congress were ignored.[242]

Over in France, Barclay's part of the settlement of the Secret Committee accounts was completed in 1787. Unfortunately for him, Congress had stopped paying him for his services in Europe between the time Morris left office in 1784, and the start of his work for America in Morocco from 1785 to 1786. This placed him in a financial bind, and he was sued in France for nonpayment of debts. He went to prison in Bordeaux for a time over unpaid debts and had to flee Europe to escape similar suits. Barclay left Europe in July 1787 and returned to America with the settlement for the Secret Committee account in hand. The new Treasury Board, under the lead of Arthur Lee, did not accept this work as final, even though Barclay had the authority to make a final settlement. Apparently, to Lee, Barclay was competent to make a treaty with Morocco, but not settle the books of the Secret Committee. Instead, the Board invented a claim that they had the right to review the work. No one questioned the propriety of Arthur Lee dismissing a settlement that covered the work of both Robert Morris and Silas Deane. It was sent back to Congress and completion remained elusive.[243]

After Morris could no longer use tobacco to repay the interest on foreign loans Congress stopped its interest payments in 1785, and further defaulted in 1787. Back in France, the end of America's debt service, economic troubles stemming from their losses in the West Indies, and the unpopular internal taxation of farmers, all caused increased political tension. Over time that led to the convocation of the Estates-General in 1788, which in turn led to a power grab by the Third Estate in 1789, and eventually to the French Revolution.[244*]

Silas Deane spent much of the rest of his life trying to regain his reputation. In 1789, just before boarding a ship to America, Deane died suddenly and unexpectedly. It has been speculated that Deane was headed back to America because he finally had the proof to redeem his name. He was traveling in the company of his secretary, Dr. Edward Bancroft. While it was unknown to Deane at the time, his secretary, who was a British spy, is now suspected of destroying Deane's reputation by sending his letters to the press. The cause of Deane's ultimate demise has not been determined, but it might be noted that Dr. Bancroft, who shared Deane's last days on this earth, had an expertise in poisons.

Arthur Lee ended his term on the Treasury Board in 1789. He took the anti-federalist side during the debate over the Constitution, but still hoped for Presidential appointment from George Washington. After that failed to materialize, he retired to his Virginia plantation, "Lansdowne," where he died in 1792.[245]

Matthew Ridley and his surviving child lived in London after the death of his wife and other child. Then they returned to America in 1786 and moved to Baltimore with his family. In 1787 he married Kitty Livingstone, who had lived with the Morris' in the early 1780's. The new couple had two daughters. Ridley died in 1798, six days before their second daughter was born.

At the end of the war, David S. Franks was rewarded for his patriotic work with a position as American vice-consul at Marseilles. In 1786 he worked with Barclay in the negotiations of the Treaty of Morocco. Nevertheless, he was continually attacked by anti-nationalist partisans in Congress for his earlier association with Benedict Arnold; and was dismissed from service. He came back to America bankrupt and discredited. In 1789, his honor was restored, and Congress granted him 500 acres for his service. Franks died during the yellow fever epidemic in 1793 at the age of 53.

William Bingham served on the board of the Bank of North America and became a founder of Dickinson College. He held a variety of elected offices between 1786 and 1791; and liked to entertain in a large house he had built in Philadelphia. It was modeled after a club in London. He was painted by Gilbert Stuart standing proudly by his sweeping marble stairway. Bingham married Anne Willing, whose busty likeness graced an early American coin. He traveled in England, and after he returned to America, he helped finance the deal that separated Maine from Massachusetts. In 1795, he became a Senator from Pennsylvania when he won the seat Morris vacated. After the death of his wife, he left America to join his daughter in England. He died there in 1804

John Holker never returned to France. His legal troubles were not resolved to his satisfaction, and the subsequent lack of a final settlement with the French Crown resulted in his continued stay in America. He lived in Springburg, Virginia and died in America in 1822.

Oliver Pollock was eventually released from jail in Havana, because of American lobbying efforts, and the return of the Spanish Governor to that island. He then went back to Philadelphia. Later, in 1791, Alexander Hamilton arranged a financial settlement for him, for his work financing Virginia's campaign on their western frontier. This did not free him from his troubles, and in 1803 he landed in debtor's prison, a resting place of many an American Patriot. Ultimately, Pollock left prison and politics. He regained some stature as a private man of business and retired to St. Francisville, part of the Louisiana Territories. He died in 1823.

After Gouverneur Morris left the Office of Finance, he had a varied and complex career. Among his accomplishments: he wrote the final version of the Constitution, he transplanted the idea of an urban grid pattern from Philadelphia to New York, he was an American diplomat in Paris 1792-1794, he married one of the Randolphs of Virginia, served as a Senator from New York from 1800 to 1803, and eventually was Chairman of the Erie Canal Company. He died in 1816.

The Dutch firms that put together the subscription loan to the United States, the Willinks, and the van Staphorst firms, remained active in American trade and became involved in Morris' business activities after the war.[246] They were the original partners of the Holland Land Company to which Morris sold millions of acres of New York State real estate, a 1791 transaction that got Morris out of the debt he had acquired attempting to service the American debt to France.

The US Constitution of 1789 allowed the new Washington administration to have a revenue source that had long been desired by Morris, a tariff collected at the ports. With that, in 1790, Hamilton was able to renegotiate the French loan under lower interest rates. He also refinanced the old Dutch loan and got a new loan from the Dutch to settle the Spanish loans. He was able, mostly, to pay the interest on these loans, and also diplomatic expenses.

Finally, James Swan took on the problem of the huge $2,024,899 debt to France.[247] He had been involved with the Boston Tea Party at the age of nineteen, in 1773, and became a provisioner to the French forces in America during the Revolution. Consequently, they owed him a lot of money after the war. He went to settle his own account with France. Instead, he became their agent, and then bought up the debt in 1795, just as Gouverneur Morris had tried to buy American debt in the 1780's. Thus, the loan was repackaged, and sold at a profit to American investors. In 1796, the US Government counted the debt to France as being repaid.[248] Even so, Congress still paid the state debts, and private investors holding Loan Office Certificates and the descendent instruments.

Like so many patriots, Swan ended up spending time in a debtor's prison, but in France. By remaining incarcerated there for twenty-two years he avoided much of the tumult of the Napoleonic era. He was released from his prison in St. Pelegie, after King Louis Phillipe took the throne in 1830, and forgave all debt. Then Swan, at the age of 76, visited his old friend Lafayette, and died shortly thereafter. [249] Nevertheless, there is now an island named for him. It sits off the coast of Maine, between Jericho Bay and the Gulf of Maine.

Endnotes

1. Papers of Robert Morris, 9:3
2. Papers of Robert Morris, 9:435
3. Papers of Robert Morris, 9:4-5
4. Papers of Robert Morris, 9:7
5. Papers of Robert Morris, 9:8
6. Papers of Robert Morris, 9:8
7. Papers of Robert Morris, 9:639
8. Papers of Robert Morris, 9:9
9. Papers of Robert Morris, 9:11
10. Papers of Robert Morris, 9:11
11. Papers of Robert Morris, 8:838
12. Papers of Robert Morris, 9:30
13. Papers of Robert Morris, 9:28
14. Papers of Robert Morris, 9:13
15. Papers of Robert Morris, 9:54
16. Papers of Robert Morris, 9:75
17. Papers of Robert Morris, 9:25
18. Papers of Robert Morris, 9:17
19. Papers of Robert Morris, 9:40
20. Papers of Robert Morris, 9:21
21. Papers of Robert Morris, 9:411
22. Papers of Robert Morris, 9:29
23. Papers of Robert Morris, 9:30
24. Papers of Robert Morris, 9:38n
25. Papers of Robert Morris, 9:21-22
26. Papers of Robert Morris, 9:24
27. Papers of Robert Morris, 9:31-32
28. Papers of Robert Morris, 9:53
29. Papers of Robert Morris, 9:41
30. Papers of Robert Morris, 9:42n
31. Papers of Robert Morris, 9:49
32. Papers of Robert Morris, 9:54
33. Papers of Robert Morris, 9:61
34. Papers of Robert Morris, 9:55-56
35. Papers of Robert Morris, 9:65-66
36. Papers of Robert Morris, 9:69-70
37. Papers of Robert Morris, 9:97
38. Papers of Robert Morris, 9:97
39. Papers of Robert Morris, 9:129
40. Papers of Robert Morris, 9:89
41. Papers of Robert Morris, 9:84
42. Papers of Robert Morris, 9:88
43. Papers of Robert Morris, 9:86
44. Papers of Robert Morris, 9:88
45. Papers of Robert Morris, 9:80
46. Papers of Robert Morris, 9:94
47. Papers of Robert Morris, 9:95
48. Papers of Robert Morris, 9:96
49. Papers of Robert Morris, 9:102
50. Papers of Robert Morris, 9:94
51. Papers of Robert Morris, 9:104
52. Papers of Robert Morris, 9:99n
53. Papers of Robert Morris, 9:107
54. Papers of Robert Morris, 9:436
55. Papers of Robert Morris, 9:103
56. Papers of Robert Morris, 9:106
57. Papers of Robert Morris, 9:109-110
58. $650,000 in 1784 is about $14,000,000 in terms of modern commodities, but in comparison to the size of the economy the base amount translates to over fifty billion dollars {http://www.measuringworth.com/calculators/uscompare/index.php}
59. Papers of Robert Morris, 114-115
60. Papers of Robert Morris, 9:309
61. Papers of Robert Morris, 9:118-119
62. Papers of Robert Morris, 9:127
63. Papers of Robert Morris, 8:392
64. Papers of Robert Morris, 9:131
65. Papers of Robert Morris, 9:134
66. Papers of Robert Morris, 9:136-137
67. Papers of Robert Morris, 9:150
68. Papers of Robert Morris, 9:201
69. Papers of Robert Morris, 9:162
70. Papers of Robert Morris, 9:152-155
71. Papers of Robert Morris, 9:276
72. Papers of Robert Morris, 9:146
73. Papers of Robert Morris, 9:173
74. Papers of Robert Morris, 9:175
75. Papers of Robert Morris, 9:253
76. Papers of Robert Morris, 9:176-177
77. Papers of Robert Morris, 9:164
78. Papers of Robert Morris, 9:183
79. Papers of Robert Morris, 9:213
80. Papers of Robert Morris, 9:205
81. Papers of Robert Morris, 9:166-167
82. Papers of Robert Morris, 9:239
83. Papers of Robert Morris, 9:177
84. Papers of Robert Morris, 9:259
85. Papers of Robert Morris, 9:336-340
86. Papers of Robert Morris, 8:504
87. Papers of Robert Morris, 9:188-189
88. Papers of Robert Morris, 9:266-275

89. Papers of Robert Morris, 9:311
90. Papers of Robert Morris, 9:198
91. Papers of Robert Morris, 9:206
92. Papers of Robert Morris, 9:308
93. Papers of Robert Morris, 9:199-202
94. Papers of Robert Morris, 9:205
95. Papers of Robert Morris, 9:208
96. Papers of Robert Morris, 9:209
97. *Negro President*, p 21-25
98. Papers of Robert Morris, 9:217-218
99. Papers of Robert Morris, 9:240
100. Papers of Robert Morris, 9:291
101. Papers of Robert Morris, 9:152-155
102. Papers of Robert Morris, 9:256
103. Papers of Robert Morris, 9:227
104. Papers of Robert Morris, 9:245-246
105. Papers of Robert Morris, 9:291
106. Papers of Robert Morris, 9:252
107. Papers of Robert Morris, 9:265
108. Papers of Robert Morris, 9:226
109. Papers of Robert Morris, 9:247-248
110. Papers of Robert Morris, 9:227-229
111. Papers of Robert Morris, 9:233
112. Papers of Robert Morris, 9:233-234
113. Papers of Robert Morris, 9:258
114. Papers of Robert Morris, 9:333
115. Papers of Robert Morris, 9:256; 260
116. Papers of Robert Morris, 9:264
117. Papers of Robert Morris, 9:281-283
118. Papers of Robert Morris, 9:277
119. Papers of Robert Morris, 9:279n
120. Papers of Robert Morris, 9:286
121. *Jefferson's Autobiography* 1743-1790
122. Papers of Robert Morris, 1:304n
123. Papers of Robert Morris, 9:299-301
124. Papers of Thomas Jefferson, 7:194-98, 202
125. Papers of Robert Morris, 9:617
126. "Notes on Coinage Papers" of Robert Morris, 4:28-29
127. Papers of Robert Morris, 9:256
128. Papers of Robert Morris, 9:312
129. Papers of Robert Morris, 9:312
130. Papers of Robert Morris, 9:396
131. Letters of the delegates to Congress 21:326
132. Papers of Robert Morris, 9:362
133. Papers of Robert Morris, 9:319
134. Papers of Robert Morris, 9:325-329
135. Papers of Robert Morris, 9:332
136. Papers of Robert Morris, 9:295-7
137. Papers of Robert Morris, 9:334-335
138. Papers of Robert Morris, 9:365
139. Papers of Robert Morris, 9:465
140. Rappleye, pg. 388
141. Papers of Robert Morris, 9:344-345
142. Papers of Robert Morris, 9:47
143. Papers of Robert Morris, 9:363
144. Papers of Robert Morris, 9:431
145. Papers of Robert Morris, 9:359
146. Papers of Robert Morris, 9:354-355
147. Papers of Robert Morris, 9:349
148. Papers of Robert Morris, 9:370
149. Papers of Robert Morris, 9:367
150. Papers of Robert Morris, 9:367;379
151. Papers of Robert Morris, 9:373
152. Papers of Robert Morris, 9:421-422
153. Papers of Robert Morris, 9:371
154. Papers of Robert Morris, 9:376
155. Papers of Robert Morris, 9:369
156. *Morris' Account*, pg. 72
157. Papers of Robert Morris, 9:382
158. Papers of Robert Morris, 7:31-34
159. Papers of Robert Morris, 9:363; 366
160. Papers of Robert Morris, 9:384
161. Papers of Robert Morris, 9:414-416
162. Papers of Robert Morris, 9:469; 9:520
163. Papers of Robert Morris, 9:387
164. Papers of Robert Morris, 9:388
165. Papers of Robert Morris, 9:394
166. Papers of Robert Morris, 9:397
167. Papers of Robert Morris, 9:440
168. Papers of Robert Morris, 9:475
169. Papers of Robert Morris, 9:426
170. Papers of Robert Morris, 8:824
171. Papers of Robert Morris, 9:462
172. Papers of Robert Morris, 9:4323
173. Papers of Robert Morris, 9:464
174. Papers of Robert Morris, 9:477
175. Papers of Robert Morris, 9:444
176. Papers of Robert Morris, 9:444n
177. Papers of Robert Morris, 9:458
178. Papers of Robert Morris, 9:460
179. Papers of Robert Morris, 9:461
180. Papers of Robert Morris, 9:462n
181. Papers of Robert Morris, 9:516

182. Papers of Robert Morris, 9:467
183. Papers of Robert Morris, 9:474
184. Papers of Robert Morris, 9:492
185. Papers of Robert Morris, 9:546-547
186. Papers of Robert Morris, 9:26
187. Papers of Robert Morris, 9:478
188. Papers of Robert Morris, 9:518
189. Papers of Robert Morris, 9:451-453
190. Papers of Robert Morris, 9:449
191. Papers of Robert Morris, 9:507
192. Papers of Robert Morris, 9:496
193. Papers of Robert Morris, 9:455
194. Papers of Robert Morris, 9:585
195. Papers of Robert Morris, 9:516
196. Papers of Robert Morris, 9:497
197. Papers of Robert Morris, 9:211
198. Papers of Robert Morris, 9:504
199. Papers of Robert Morris, 9:500
200. Papers of Robert Morris, 9:505
201. Papers of Robert Morris, 9:506
202. Papers of Robert Morris, 9:485-486
203. Papers of Robert Morris, 9:491n
204. Papers of Robert Morris, 9:527
205. Papers of Robert Morris, 9:548
206. Papers of Robert Morris, 6:504
207. Papers of Robert Morris, 9:448
208. Papers of Robert Morris, 9:463
209. Papers of Robert Morris, 9:166-168
210. Papers of Robert Morris, 9:515
211. Papers of Robert Morris, 9:543
212. Papers of Robert Morris, 9:481-482
213. Papers of Robert Morris, 9:446-447
214. Papers of Robert Morris, 9:525
215. Papers of Robert Morris, 9:573
216. Papers of Robert Morris, 9:533
217. Papers of Robert Morris, 9:546
218. Papers of Robert Morris, 9:546
219. Papers of Robert Morris, 9:547n
220. Papers of Robert Morris, 9:528
221. Papers of Robert Morris, 9:529
222. Papers of Robert Morris, 9:514
223. Power of the Purse, pg. 197
224. Papers of Robert Morris, 9:535
225. Papers of Robert Morris, 9:538
226. Papers of Robert Morris, 9:542
227. Papers of Robert Morris, 9:544
228. Papers of Robert Morris, 9:550
229. Papers of Robert Morris, 9:572
230. Papers of Robert Morris, 9:548
231. Papers of Robert Morris, 9:xi
232. Papers of Robert Morris, 9:691
233. Papers of Robert Morris, 9:568
234. Papers of Robert Morris, 9:593
235. Letters of Delegates to Congress, 22:328
236. *American State Papers*, 2nd Congress, 1st Session, Miscellaneous, 1:38
237. Contract, New York Public Library, call # S 0825
238. Papers of Robert Morris, 9:578
239. Papers of Robert Morris, 9:152-156
240. Chenow pg. 30
241. Papers of Robert Morris, 9:96 n3
242. *Power of the Purse*, p. 225-227
243. Papers of Robert Morris, 7:174
244.* Many members of the Farmers General ended up being executed during the bloody Reign of Terror in Paris in 1793.
245. "Louis W. Potts," American National Biography Online
246. Papers of Robert Morris, 6:428
247. Office of the Historian, Foreign Service Institute, United States Department of State, https://history.state.gov/milestones/1784-1800/loans
248. *American State Papers*, House of Representatives, 4th Congress, 1st Session, Finance: Volume 1:308
249. Ellen Tyrell, https://blogs.loc.gov/inside_adams/2011/12/who-was-james-swan/, 2011

XI

Epilogue

Morris was the leading executive in America during his tenure as Superintendent of Finance, but he was not the President. He held an office more like that of Prime Minister of Finance for the Continental Congress, but his actions, when compared to those of the former committee system, demonstrated the effectiveness of executive officers in the American system of government. However, in 1784 America was not ready for a President of the United States, or even to be the United States; rather, a Confederation was more suitable to the climate of the day.

Some prominent men of his time resented Morris' executive authority and wished he had been more inclusive and flexible during his tenure as Superintendent. In other words, they wanted to exert their own political influence. Morris, however, realized that these same individuals had nearly lost the war, so he followed a program of his own design. Partisans from New England and the South did not appreciate his presence as an executive because they saw him as an upstart merchant unfit to be a "law giver." Certainly, those with an interest in the slave economy, notably Rhode Island, Virginia, and South Carolina, were busy undermining Morris' efforts as much as they could. The reluctance many had for embracing Morris' policies was caused by their own colonial past, beyond which they could not get. Morris called this the "genius & habbits" of the old thinking. Adams famously wrote that Morris,

> ... does not always vote for what you and I should think proper, it is because he thinks that a large Body of People remains, who are not yet of his Mind.

It is so often the case that a visionary sees the world as others cannot.

When Morris left the Office of Finance, he submitted his official records for publication. He wanted the public to have access to the details of their business. However, the Congress did not publish the record for years. As a result, Morris' tenure was subject to discussion, conjecture, doubt, and mis-characterization as one committee after another delayed reporting on his work. This delay served the purposes of his political enemies. It had a negative impact on his ability to conduct his private business, and to aspire to other positions in public life.

Morris was not giving up by stepping away from center stage; he was reusing an old technique. During the years 1777-1780 Morris' allies withdrew their support from the Pennsylvania Assembly while it was under the control of the radical "Constitutionalists." This allowed the citizens to see that the policies of those "Constitutionalists" were aimed at failure. Similarly, in the mid to late 1780's Morris and the nationalists allowed their political adversaries to try their hands at management of the Confederation. Morris considered the failure of those adversaries to be likely; and sought to make that point clear to the citizens by allowing those adversaries to prove their incompetence. The ensuing years of disharmony, injustice and disorganization convinced the states that a stronger national bond was needed. The Constitution was eventually written and ratified as a result of those realizations. The hard lessons were learned just in time to keep the Great Powers of Europe from making America the playground for their brand of power politics.

Morris Falters

Strictly speaking, Morris did not lose money by financing the Revolution during his tenure of Superintendent. He admitted that, although he had lost one hundred fifty ships, he had just about broken even. He did, however, lose money from two related efforts, and he was never really able to recover his economic footing. The first event was Morris' contract to service America's national debt to France. This contract took the form of tobacco shipments from Virginia to the French taxing authority, the Farmers General. Thomas Jefferson's interference with that trade cost Morris over $30,000.

After the market for tobacco was ruined by interfering Virginians, Morris tried to pay America's debt to France with a variety of state currencies, notes and specie. Unfortunately, his European partner would not accept his bills of exchange, and Morris was unable to get the issuing state to redeem its own paper money at face value. At the same time, he was still liable for its face value in Europe. He was caught in the downdraft of the depreciation of state currencies. This was clearly a losing situation for Morris.

In the years after Morris left office in 1784, many people suffered economically because they were not reimbursed for their financial support of the revolution. Farmers, merchants, artificers, teamsters, seamstresses, loan office certificate holders and others were simply left unpaid for years, or they were paid in depreciated currencies. Payments in depreciated state currencies, and the states subsequent refusal to honor that currency at face value, led to such events as Shay's Rebellion in Massachusetts, and angry protests in rural Pennsylvania that closed the roads. The large states focused on paying their own state's debts; and were not quick to pay Continental Debts. Small states eventually realized that taxing their citizens into poverty just to repay the same citizens for loans was not workable. Congressional authority was at a low point, and on more than one occasion Congress could not even make a quorum.

The Treasury Board learned to regret their support for the re-establishment of the Continental Loan Offices as the abuse of indents grew. Allowing local loan officers to issue debts to pay other debts was, in effect, giving them permission to issue their own currency with no accountability to others. The Treasury Board's letters to recalcitrant state governments began to sound very much like Morris'. People decided to hold onto "their money," as the economy groaned under the weight of the economic hodgepodge of state and foreign currencies, state and continental loan office certificates, and indents. They were willing to overlook that they were holding onto money owed to others who had actually paid for the war. During this period small states began to realize that they needed help from the large states to repay their citizens for loans those citizens made to support the war. This was one of the driving forces behind the ratification of the Constitution.

Morris noted that paying for the war was no longer the problem; rather the real problem was repaying those who had already paid for the war. The political difficulty of doing this was made clear when Morris wrote to Gouverneur Morris that "the contest now is only, whether the whole shall reimburse the few."[1] Morris commented that once the money was returned to its source, the moneyed men would invest it in ways that would benefit all. He contrasted that with the tendency of the lower and middling sorts to spend money buying trinkets and drink. These observations did not make him popular, but soon after the national economic program was put into effect, and the war debt was on the way to being repaid, American banks began making loans that were used to finance planting, shipping, manufacturing, and internal improvements.

Disdain for any Executive

A defining aspect of Morris' tenure as Superintendent of Finance, and one that is familiar to students of the Presidency, was the nature of the highly partisan opposition Morris faced as the first executive in the evolving American system of government. Modern Presidents find such opposition to come on personal, political, and policy grounds. Morris' experience was no different. The force of this opposition was so strong that their message has, to some degree, lingered in the histories and shaped the image of Morris' work.

A prominent member of Morris' opposition was, as we have seen, Arthur Lee. Arthur had not inherited any of his family's 30,000-acre property in Virginia; and was disappointed with his level of success in London. He took up with the Radical Whigs there, and perfected an emotional political style of rhetoric. He blamed others for his problems, while at the same time making himself so difficult to be around that everyone, but his close associates, thought it best to avoid him. His economic envy shifted focus from Ben Franklin, to Silas Deane, and eventually to Morris. While he was excoriating his political foes in public for profiteering, he was amassing a fortune on his own by doing just what he accused others of doing. His activities were not scrutinized because, as an agitator against the middle state merchants, Lee was favored by the elite southern planters and the radicals from New England.

Arthur Lee overlooked no opportunity to attack Morris. When Morris first encountered the arrows of false accusation it was Arthur Lee who loaded the quiver. Some historians, who adopted Lee's view of events, have used these his notes as reliable guides. This has colored the current interpretation of Morris' career among consensus historians. ¬For example, after Morris left office, it was Arthur Lee's treasury board that accepted Jefferson's slightly modified version of Morris' proposal for the currency, and Jefferson got much of the credit for the work of Morris' office.

That was the same Arthur Lee who wrote broadsides against the slave trade while he was in London, but on October 8, 1783, as a congressman, he rejected Quaker petitions for the abolition of the slave trade.12 Arthur Lee did not act alone. His supporters have been called "The Radicals" after the Radical Whigs of old, but it would be better to call them "The Localists" since their common interest was maintaining the sovereignty of their local states. Under the surface, however, one can see Lee's strongest supporters, other than the Adams', were heavily invested in the slave trade, and slave powered economy.

The theme uniting the anti-slavery Adams, with the pro-slavery Lee faction was the belief in their shared "Republican Virtue" along with their idea that they had just won a war against a monarch, and didn't want a new one. After the mainstay of the Federalists, Morris, went to debtor's prison the year after Adams was elected, any alliance between pro-slavery forces and Adams became unnecessary. Jefferson's rising rhetoric casting Morris and Adams as "Monocrats" was a neat political trick that gave Jefferson's faction power. Jefferson used his claims of "Republican Virtue" to good advantage to woo the backcountry farmers, and he performed well as a simple farmer when he entertained diplomats. However, when it comes to actual power, the telling point is that the ultimate beneficiary of Arthur Lee's partisanship was Jefferson who wanted to create a Virginia Dynasty and crush the Federalists, while the Federalists themselves could not wait to leave government, and be free men in a free country.

Recovering Lost Time

Morris saw his exit from the Office of Finance as a welcome event. From that point on he undertook larger and larger projects, as if to make up for opportunities he had lost while in public service. He also rejoined the Pennsylvania Assembly. From this position, he acted to protect minority rights when he was finally able to pass a bill that overturned the religious test laws, which had disenfranchised half the voters of the state since 1776.[2] He worked to restore property rights to those who had been dispossessed by the "Constitutionalists," and to restore the University of Pennsylvania to private hands. He voted to repeal the law forbidding theatrical performances, and, in private, he helped fund the New Chestnut Street Theater. He also worked to keep the Bank of North America alive. Later he was appointed to be a delegate to the constitutional convention. He managed to fill the delegation with allies including the former lawyer for the Office of Finance and abolitionist, James Wilson, the financial supporter of the African Episcopal Methodist Church Thomas Fitzsimmons, and abolitionist Gouverneur Morris. Gouverneur was appointed as a delegate from Pennsylvania, although he was a New Yorker. Morris also hosted Washington for the duration. Together they made a fitting statement, when on the first day of the convention he and Washington arrived in Morris' horse drawn coach. This was noteworthy because both were living in Morris' house, which was less than 1000 feet from Independence Hall, where the convention was being held. While Morris said little during the working sessions of the constitutional convention, he was well known for holding after-hours discussions in his house, as he and his allies mulled over the day's events. Later, as a U.S. Senator, he sent the official letter to Washington that informed his friend George that George had been made President. As a senator, he arranged for Philadelphia to become the capital for ten years and participated in forty-one committees through which he implemented his nationalist vision, enhanced the nation's infrastructure, supported the establishment of the U.S. Navy, and supplied the designs for the first six ships.

Washington had offered Morris the position of Secretary of the Treasury, but Morris proposed Hamilton instead. Morris realized he had become a political lightning rod, and his experience as Superintendent taught him that support in the Congress was key to implementing his program. Morris also knew that his private economic activities would have been limited as a member of the Executive Branch, and he wanted to avoid past controversies while rebuilding his fortune. Hamilton reworked and modified Morris' earlier proposal *On Public Debt,* and the program was put into law with the help of Morris and his allies in Congress. Hamilton also used the state debt information gathered in the settlement process started during Morris' term as Superintendent as the basis for the assumption agreement.

One of the elements Hamilton's program shared with Morris', was the taxation of whiskey. This led to the Whiskey Rebellion, the origins of which can be traced to anti-federalist Virginians in backcountry Pennsylvania. Particularly interesting was the activity of Albert Gallatin, who went from Virginia to western Pennsylvania, and managed to be present at the most vociferous meetings. After it was all over, he excused himself. Jefferson's political operatives demagogued this event, and when Jefferson became President, there was a position for Gallatin in Tom's cabinet.

It is telling that on the state level, the political influence of the backcountry population was not welcomed in Virginia, or the Carolinas. The elite planters in both states maintained their political power even though it was out of proportion to their numbers. For example, in South Carolina the backcountry was represented "by no more than a half-dozen delegates," while the low-country planter elite held the remainder of the one hundred seats in the Legislature.[3] Nevertheless, the remnants of the "Constitutionalists" in the backcountry of Pennsylvania were a useful force for the Old Dominion to exploit and manipulate in reaching their ultimate political goal of unseating the Federalists. When considering their protestations of innocence, one is reminded of the success of the Southern Elite in casting themselves as "simple farmers" in the election of 1800.[4]

Gouverneur Morris noted,

> We should remember that people never act on reason alone. The rich take advantage of their passions and make those the instruments of oppressing them.[5]

The political behavior of the southern ruling class grew out of centuries of experience in exploiting others whom they did not see as equals. Many of the lessons learned by the slaveholders taught them that sly manipulation and a system of rewards were the best ways to bring about compliance. This is one of the real legacies of slavery.

Transforming the Economy

After establishing the governmental system that he had envisioned for years, Morris set out to transform the economy. He and his trading partners developed foreign trade as far as China, India and the Levant. Acting in the role of a venture capitalist, he financed various manufacturing companies to increase domestic production, including a steam engine company, a glass works, and an iron-rolling mill. His trading venture to China yielded more than timely profits. He learned about the Chinese transportation system, which used internal canals that were safe from seaborne attack. He started several canal companies with the goal of making inland connections between great American rivers. If these canals had been completed a generation earlier, they would have been useful in countering the British embargo. He and his associates even launched a hot air balloon from his back yard on 190 High Street. Unfortunately, the pilot had to jump out when the wind blew the basket against a building and the cooker plunged into a roof below. This was a few weeks before a more successful launch in Baltimore, that is now considered the first manned flight in America.

Morris worked to establish peace with the Native Americans, and to populate the frontier through a number of real estate ventures. He speculated in the western Pennsylvania "Depreciation Lands" with former state comptroller John Nicholson. At one point, Morris owned the western half of New York State, and his son Thomas negotiated the sale with the Senecas under the Treaty of the Big Tree. Morris sold the New York property to the Holland Land Company. That company included some of the Dutch investors who had loaned money to the Continental Congress in its days of dire need. This sale helped Morris overcome some of his lingering money problems and convinced him that real estate speculation was profitable. Just as other American merchants made new fortunes servicing the needs of Europe during the French Revolutionary Wars, Morris focused on his new lines of endeavor, leaving the war trade to others. This was mostly because Morris was concentrating on the China Trade, and later was forced to sell off his shipping interests to settle his accounts with the Government. Finally, in 1793, Morris was debt free. 1793 was also the year Morris, as a member of the American Philosophical Society, supported the Michaux Expedition, which was the forerunner of the Lewis and Clark Expedition.

The next year, 1794, he hired Pierre L'Enfant to design and build a new house. The house was enormous by American standards of the day. It was 120 feet by 60 feet.[6] It had two levels of basement and three aboveground floors. The cost exceeded $80,000.[7] Against Morris' wishes, it became subject to large cost overruns because of the ambition of the builder, L'Enfant, and his extravagant use of marble. Soon, however, Morris suffered major losses due to the collapse of the two banking houses, one in London and the other Dublin.[8] These losses were probably from speculation in English canal development, which was just experiencing the painful end of a "bubble" at that time.

Problems Multiply

One of Morris' real estate ventures in Georgia became problematic when the Georgia State legislature assumed ownership of a project of his, in a corrupt move that was the basis for the Yazoo Lands scandal. In the spring of 1794 Morris' Asylum Company was trying to sell land to French nationals fleeing the terrors of war in Europe. To end this exodus, Joseph Fauchet, the French Ambassador to America during the French Reign of Terror, published letters in America and Europe that misrepresented Morris' properties as worthless. Morris was put into the position of refuting Fauchet's charges while the Yazoo controversy was exploding in the newspapers.[9] At the same time, Jay's Treaty was under consideration in the U.S. Government, so Morris had to temper his response.

The final official government action taken on Morris' accounts was the convening of a committee to create the long-delayed settlement for the Willing, Morris & Co. Like other previous investigations, this remarkable process was started after Morris left public office in 1795. The committee ignored the earlier settlement done by Mr. Barclay while Barclay was in France; and they disregarded the vouchers Morris provided.[10] The committee of two charged depreciation in a way Morris thought very unfair.[11] Ultimately, they handed Morris, as the lead in Willing, Morris & Co., a bill for over $93,312.63.[12] Morris apportioned part of that to Ross, and the remainder to Willing, at 50%, and himself at 50%.[13] Morris noted the people appointed to the work were unfamiliar with the accounting methods of merchants. One of the committeemen, Oliver Wolcott Jr., was a banker and a lawyer from northern Connecticut. The other was Nicholas Eveleigh, a planter and officer in the South Carolina 2nd Regiment. Both were honorable men, who had been appointed to the task by Washington, but neither had experience as a merchant. This settlement forced the liquidation of his shipping firm, and effectively cut Morris off from the only steady moneymaking business Morris ever had. He focused on other endeavors.

However, the books of all the other committees where Robert served closed even or with a balance in favor of the Government, meaning Morris was owed money. During the period of debt settlement after the war, there were a total of over 400 accounts in question, and only a quarter of them were ever closed. Among the accounts that were never acted upon was one for $3,500,000, another for $958,000 and a third for $4,000,000 (all in currency).[14] Nevertheless, Morris and his network were held to the closest scrutiny and the most exacting requirements for proof. Curiously, at the same time the rules seemed different for Arthur Lee from whom vouchers were not required, and any kind of evidence was accepted.[15] Arthur received at least one payment of $60,000 under those conditions; after all, he was a Virginia gentleman.

Talleyrand was in America during that period, evading an arrest warrant issued by the revolutionary French Government. In May 1796, he took an unexpected interest in American real estate. This was a change from a position he had taken two years earlier against speculating in American land.[16] Talleyrand contracted to buy 108,875 acres of Morris' property in Pennsylvania for a little over one dollar per acre. He was quite aware that Morris expected to sell this land to relieve his debts.[17] He secured an option on the property, holding the rights and making only a small payment. Shortly thereafter, Talleyrand returned to Europe, where he showed no further interest in the property, particularly in paying for it. Ultimately, Morris reckoned Talleyrand owed him $142,500.[18] Within the year he became the French foreign minister in the administration of Napoleon, which actively favored the American Anti-Federalists. Talleyrand later brought fellow anti-Morris partisan, Joseph Fauchet, into his department. Talleyrand never paid for the property, and before Morris could find a new French buyer the Pennsylvania Assembly passed a law in 1797 forbidding sale of Pennsylvania lands to aliens. This reduced the market, and depressed prices. Morris was able sell some of the property at about fifty cents per acre. He had been expecting to satisfy his "debt" to the U.S. Government with the full payment from Talleyrand, with some left over for other commitments.

Morris carried on and worked to build the nation's capital. At one point his group, which included John Nicholson and James Greenleaf, owned 7,234 lots in Washington, DC.[19] Together they raised a number of buildings that still stand, including the John Law House and Wheat Row. Morris and Nicholson counted on Greenleaf to come through on an important Dutch loan, and with the understanding that it had come through, they purchased over 6,000,000 acres of real estate from Pennsylvania to Georgia. Unfortunately, the critical loans did not arrive, due to a series of events that included Greenleaf disgracing himself in Holland in front of an important financier, and the 1796 declaration of war on Revolutionary France by England and Holland. Money stopped flowing from Europe as that Continent readied itself for the Napoleonic Wars. Greenleaf further proved himself to be an untrustworthy partner by retaining for his personal use some of the funds Morris had supplied to pay the DC Commissioners.[20]

Neither Robert's good friend Gouverneur Morris, nor George Washington could dissuade him from even greater risk. G. Morris saw the omens of disaster while in Europe as ambassador to France, but he was unsuccessful in reining in Robert's projects. Washington tried as well. Responding to Washington's cautions Robert stated: "I can never do things in the small, I must be either a man or a mouse."[21] He firmly believed the promise of America and if he had succeeded, he would be celebrated as the most successful contrarian investor in history. It was not to be. Instead, Morris found himself in court. Hamilton's future killer, the attorney general of New York Aaron Burr, brought on this litigation, and charged Morris with creating a fraudulent mortgage. Morris was sure of his innocence; but lost this legal battle in the partisan anti-federalist courts of Governor Clinton's state through "outlawry." It seems his son had not filed some earlier paperwork in a timely manner.[22] This loss cost him over 200 square miles of land in New York State, which represented a significant portion of his remaining capital.

Economic Stress and a Life on Fire

The American economy was imploding due to stresses in Europe. Over 150 companies in Philadelphia went bankrupt,[23] sending more than fifty businessmen to debtor's prison. This was the period when Morris and Nicholson bought out Greenleaf's part of their three-way partnership. Then they arranged to transfer development rights, and operations of the Washington D.C. holdings, to a group of Philadelphia investors, one of whom was merchant Henry Pratt. Unfortunately, after the deal was signed these investors reneged, and wanted to change the terms. Morris could not comply with these after-the-fact demands because he was fully engaged elsewhere. Execution of the deal by the Philadelphia group fell apart. While Morris was trying to sell the rural lands, deal with their uncertain titles, and pay the taxes on them, the Washington Commissioners looked to him to take on the obligations of the Philadelphia investors. He could not do both. With the failure of the deal in Washington D.C., Morris could not satisfy his many debts, including one particular debt of $10,000. Morris and Nicholson still owed Greenleaf some money for his shares, and in the meantime Greenleaf had gone to debtor's prison. The Greenleaf and Eddy families compelled George Eddy to file suit against Morris.

During that time of economic difficulty, Morris was attempting to settle with a multitude of parties, so it was the unexpected suddenness of the demands in the suit that resulted in Morris' inability to gather the funds in a timely manner. This impatience by Greenleaf, via Eddy, is what landed Morris and Nicholson in debtor's prison.[24]

When Morris first arrived in debtor's prison he did not even have enough money to buy paper. He wrote,

> I feel like an intruder everywhere; sleeping in other people's beds and sitting in other people's rooms. I am writing on other people's paper, with other people's ink, – the pen is my own; that and the clothes I wear are all I can claim as mine here.[25]

Morris and his family struggled to settle with one creditor after another. Morris' living conditions improved as his finances were straightened out. This was because prisoners were expected to pay their own way. He tried to protect his beloved property overlooking the Schuylkill River, "The Hills," from his creditors, by creating a new corporation, but to no avail. When he finally had a desk and paper of his own Morris used his time to work on his papers, and diaries. The effort reportedly filled trunks, little of which survives today.

His son William put aside his boyish amusements and rose to the occasion, as he took on a larger role in the family business. He even stayed in Philadelphia during a yellow fever outbreak. William died from that fever while still in his twenties. Even so, Morris would not curse George Eddy, whom he saw as a pawn. He remained as good spirited as he could and undertook a daily exercise regimen whereby he would walk laps around the prison yard, dropping a pebble to mark each circuit. Privately, he regretted some of his dealings with Nicholson. About him Morris wrote,

> A heavy balance will be found due to me on the accounts depending between this my fellow sufferer and myself, probably upwards of $600,000 specie, when all entries are made that the transactions require.
>
> With the purest Intentions, he unfortunately laid a train that ended as it hath done. I here say he laid the train, because there are living Witnesses that I opposed as soon as I knew it; altho' from Infatuation, Madness, or Weakness, I gave way afterwards.[26]

In dark moments he wept over ever meeting James Greenleaf, for whom he had few kind words. His son, Robert, was his agent in Amsterdam, helping with the finances. Still Morris watched helplessly as his affairs were dealt with in the courts from Pennsylvania to Georgia. Millions of acres flew away into the vortex of litigation. Without any direct influence over events he noted with resignation,

> I have just heard of an estate of mine worth $100,000 being sold for $800 to pay taxes. Such things are done.[27]

Morris' friends could not be of much help while he was in bankruptcy. On several occasions, however, George Washington did visit Morris at the prison and take lunch with him there. Any money Morris' friends might have supplied him would have been swallowed up in the multimillion-dollar maw that was already eating Morris' life's work. His faithful friend, Gouverneur Morris, was able to find an annuity for Robert through a good close reading of the Holland Land Company contract. He successfully had that annuity assigned to Robert's wife. Doing this allowed her to have money without letting the creditors put their hands onto it. Later she and Robert lived on this money as their only pension.

One Man's Disaster is Another's Hey Day

William Cranch looked after and lived in Morris' house "The Hills" until he was forced to vacate. Cranch had been a commissioner in charge of development in D.C. After the sheriff seized the property, it fell into disrepair. That place had been the site of much joy, but mysteriously, it burnt shortly before it was sold. One is reminded of the earlier statement by Benjamin Harrison, when he commented on the British occupation of the same place,

> ... tis but a pitiful kind of revenge to fall on houses and gardens for the offences of their owners, but such have been and ever will be the case with the low minded.[28]

Henry Pratt bought Morris' house and property at a sheriff's sale. Pratt removed the burnt building and built a new party house on the site. It is called Lemon Hill after Morris' greenhouses, which also no longer stand. While in prison, Morris wrote to Pratt's friend, Pennsylvania Governor, Thomas McKean, for a temporary parole for himself and Nicholson, so they could avoid a yellow fever epidemic. The governor refused and Nicholson died of that disease two weeks later.

Jefferson's allies used Morris' economic troubles to discredit Morris and Hamilton's economic programs. Many of Morris' former friends had been investors and lost money with him. Some of them turned against him. For example, John Adam's sister was one of those investors, and John was not pleased about Morris' role in that loss. Another prominent former investor was Richard Henry Lee, who was arrested for debt but was paroled to his county in Virginia. That was a little like house arrest with "going to town" privileges.

Morris' house, so proudly designed and embellished by L'Enfant, went unfinished and was recorded in William Birch views of Philadelphia. The roof was rolled iron, and the walls were brick, faced with marble. The windows were never put in, so when it rained the round sound of summer downpours echoed from the cavernous building and filled Chestnut Street with a baleful rumble. Morris' uncompleted house was characterized as a highly visible symbol of his excesses and was dubbed "Morris' Folly." Morris bemoaned,

> Major L'Enfant was erecting for me a much more magnificent house than I ever intended to have built.[29]

Jefferson, as a student of architecture, was keenly interested in the building, which was the most discussed structure in the colonies.

Morris' unfinished house as drawn by Latrobe (not to scale, rotated for comparison)

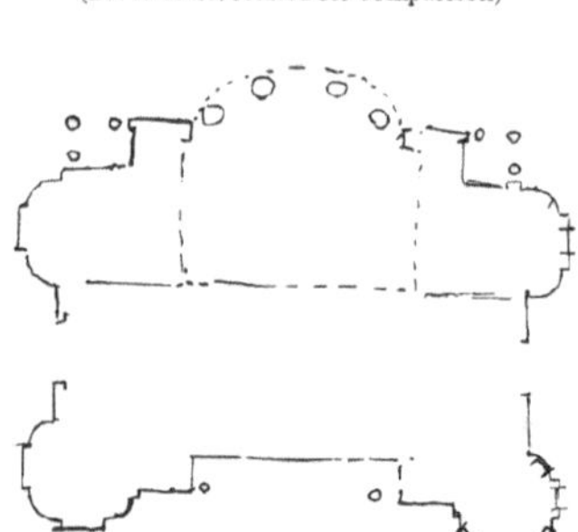

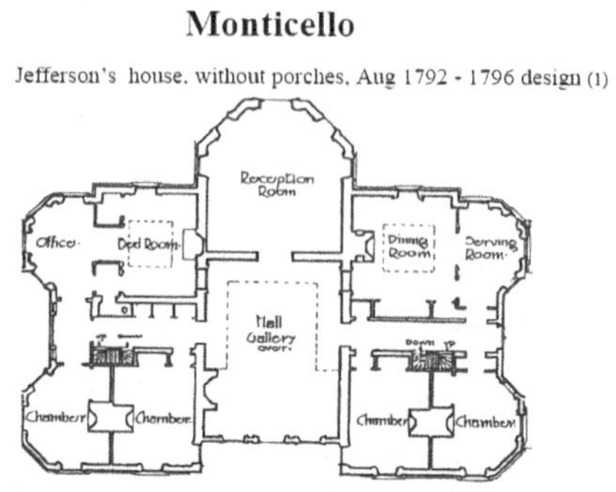

Even though the building was criticized harshly by Jefferson's friend, Henry Latrobe,[30] Latrobe was first in line when the building was finally torn down. He used Morris' house as his quarry for marbles and brick he subsequently used in buildings and monuments. One marble carving from Morris' Folly graces the tomb of the Drayton family, now in the Magnolia Plantation and Gardens, ten miles outside Charleston, South Carolina. William Henry Drayton and Henry Laurens, both from South Carolina, served in the Congress at the same time as Morris. One marble fireplace mantle from the Folly is in Henry Pratt's party house, Lemon Hill, in Fairmount Park. Two others were delivered to the Custis family by Lafayette, during his return tour in the 19th century. The Custis house is now known as Arlington House, which presides over Arlington National Cemetery. Ironically, Robert E. Lee, Arthur Lee's cousin, stood before them on his wedding day when he married into the Custis family.

Trusting in the general population's tendency to find fault in luxury and to focus on local events, the Jeffersonians blamed Morris and Hamilton for the economic downturn in America. Their message pandered to the democratic impulse to tear down anyone who attempted to rise above his station, and generally confused cause and effect. In reality, the downturn was brought on by changes in English trading patterns, coupled with war and upheaval in Europe sinvolving Revolutionary France, and a revolutionary government there that was friendly to the Jeffersonians. It was the condition of the worldwide economy that was Morris' undoing. Recent scholarship shows that Hamilton's new banking system was highly effective at ameliorating the woes, but that was not popularly understood at the time.

With Morris in prison, and the economy seen to be on the rocks, the Federalists were not successful at reminding the voters that they had kept the nation together long enough to win the Revolution, write the Constitution, and secure the peace. Instead, the rhetorical techniques of David Howell and Arthur Lee were recalled and updated for the new election of 1800. In a successful campaign, Jefferson, and to some degree Madison, portrayed the slave holding plutocrats of the South as freedom loving victims of the corrupting influences of the rich "tyrants" in the northern cities. The Jeffersonians made common cause with the yeomen farmers of the North; updating familiar Country Party ideas and substituting the Federalists for the monarchy. They equated city dwellers with sores on the body politic and extolled the virtues and freedom of rural life (freedom that was not shared by 30% of the population of the South, that happened to be born into slavery).[31] By casting themselves as the defenders of Liberty, it was unnecessary to confuse their message with talk of slavery at home. According to the plutocrats of the South, that was a local matter, more about states' rights than anything else, and anyway slave keeping was an unwanted burden, and they still claimed that "our negroes" were better off as slaves. These self-serving excuses acted as a smoke screen. These plutocrats knew a victory for the Old Dominion meant that slavery would not be taxed into oblivion by a Federal Government run by Federalists with an abolitionist bent, like Adams, for example.

The ultimate effect was that Jefferson won the election of 1800, and that began the Virginia Dynasty envisioned by Jefferson and his supporters. He wrote that he would,

> ... sink federalism into an abyss from which there shall be no resurrection.[32]

He and his allies did destroy the Federalists. Jefferson's embargo of 1807 was supposed to reclaim America's Honor in the face of British impressments at sea, but it hurt the Federal Government, which relied on tariffs for revenue. Britain shrugged it off; and looked elsewhere for things to import. However, that embargo did harm the merchant class in the Northeast, which had always been hated by Jefferson's partisans. Many wealthy trading families in the northern states were forced into poverty, and a few old patriots like Tim Pickering started to talk about the secession of New England from Jefferson's United States. At the same time, slavery grew in America's new territories, even though the Northwest Territory was nominally a free area. This was done to enhance the electoral prospects of the Party of Jefferson, because the $3/5^{th}$ rule determined the composition of the Electoral College as well as the House of Representatives. This "slave vote" kept Jefferson's party in power for years.

If one ignores the soaring rhetoric of the Jeffersonians, and looks at the facts, it is clear that the "Revolution of 1800" was actually a great leap backward away from a rapidly modernizing world into a world of racism, sectionalism, isolationism, and slavery. The Jeffersonian reliance on real estate as the basis of wealth naturally gave birth to the idea of Manifest Destiny, which required such policies as the Indian Removal Act.

The End for Morris was Just the Beginning

After the election of 1800, Senator John Marshall, whose brother had married Morris' daughter, managed to get the bankruptcy laws passed. Morris was released in 1801. Totally discredited, and stripped of his very valuable reputation, Robert and his wife lived in a small house in Philadelphia on Ludlow Street near the corner of seventh. It was just around the corner from the Graff House, where Jefferson stayed while he wrote the Declaration of Independence. Morris never regained his prominence even though he tried unsuccessfully to undertake various projects. Jefferson's previous statement that he would make Morris the Secretary of the Navy was never revisited. Morris spent his idle time in the park behind the old state house and was the subject of some derision by wags who found his "old fashioned" clothing amusing. Robert Morris died in obscurity on May 9, 1806, the year after his eldest son died in Europe.

A few months later, Lewis and Clark returned to St. Louis from the Pacific coast, and the opening of the West was to begin in earnest. Morris' vision of the United States, becoming a "great empire" was about to be realized. When the Marquis de Lafayette made his famous tour of America, in 1824. Before visiting the Custis family in Virginia, he made a special point of visiting Mary Morris in Philadelphia. He paid his respects to her and her departed husband during a quiet lunch held in the small home she had shared with Robert. Morris' day had passed, but his work to ensure economic freedom for all Americans was so well established that even today few realize the titanic struggle that was required to get it started, and the price that was paid.

In 1796, Robert's eldest son Robert married Anna Shoemaker, whose father had been a Mayor of Philadelphia, and President of the Pennsylvania Abolition Society. Robert, who had been schooled in Europe, died on that continent, leaving one boy child behind, also named Robert. The signer's second son Thomas, who was also schooled in Europe, lived in Canandaigua, New York. Thomas became a U.S. Representative and later a U.S. Marshall. His third son, Charles, went to the University of Pennsylvania, then to sea. It was rumored that he fought in the Battle of New Orleans, but his story has been lost. His fourth son, William, died from Yellow Fever while he was trying help his father settle the family business and free Robert from debtor's prison. Robert's fifth son Henry lived in Philadelphia and was elected to a minor public office. He died of a heart attack on his way home one day when he was in his 40's. Robert's daughter Hetty married the son of John Nixon, who had read the Declaration of Independence on the steps of Independence Hall. John Nixon went on to become president of the Bank of North America. Robert's daughter Maria married James Marshall, brother to John Marshall. They freed the slaves that populated their city house, and bought property from Lord Fairfax in Warren County, Virginia, called Happy Creek. Their son ran for office as a Whig, on the anti-slavery platform. Their country house is now owned by the Marriott hotel chain.

Sixty years after the "Revolution of 1800" the majority of citizens rejected the rule of the Old Dominion and its descendent group, known to many as "The Party of Slavery." Lincoln, the first Republican president, had not even arrived in Washington before several southern states seceded and took up arms against the Union. After a bloody and wrenching civil war, policies similar to those Morris advocated in the 1780's were put into place in the 1860's. America became a nation based on trade, technology, manufacturing, access to capital, economic freedom, and reciprocal liberty.

PostScript

Robert Morris sought to break up land monopolies and reduce slavery with his tax system. His goal of improving the lot of the yeoman farmer, was equivalent to growing an independent middle class. Today one of America's richest men owns over 240,000 acres of farmland, and other billionaires fill their coffers selling goods made in virtual slave labor camps in China. One is not surprised to learn these oligarchs support the party descended from the Party of Slavery. Morris thought he could restore the finances of America, if only the citizens would not object to working two days to pay a year's worth of national tax. At the time, this was considered to be "too exceptional."[33] Two hundred years later, many Americans work nearly five months a year to make enough money to pay their annual federal tax, and the government is spending itself into endless debt. During his tenure on the Secret Committee, Morris was held personally liable for governmental spending. Imagine how that would work out today, perhaps the U.S. would not be looking forward to trillion-dollar deficits.

During this modern period, The United States government has used taxpayer funds to rescue selected banks, investment houses, insurance companies, manufacturing firms, and labor unions. These large and politically connected groups were deemed to be too big to fail. It was said their demise would create systemic risk that would bring down the nation's economy. If the same policy had been in place in the 1790's Morris would have received a similar "bailout." Such an act would have certainly changed Morris' life, and would have influenced subsequent events. However, given the choice, Adams never pardoned Morris to get him out of jail. Men of that time knew that economic freedom requires a healthy economy where the freedom to succeed is tempered by the freedom to fail. They knew that without economic freedom, there is no freedom at all.

Endnotes

1. *The Life of Gouverneur Morris* 3:17
2. *The Counter-Revolution in Pennsylvania,* p. 180
3. *We the People*, p 373
4. Robin L. Einhorn, *American Taxation, American Slavery*, 2006, p114-115
5. Richard Brookhiser, *What would the Founders Do?* pg. 191
6. The Papers of Benjamin Henry Latrobe, ed Dr Edward C. Carter III series I, *The Virginia Journals of Benjamin Henry Latrobe 1795-1798* pg. 376
7. *Watson's Annals* Chapter 53
8. Claim made by Robert Morris - Robert Morris Letterbook, Library of Congress {**}
9. Chernow, pg. 190
10. Ver Steeg, pg. 24-25; 210 N58; Journals of the Continental Congress, 34:265-266
11. *Morris' Account*, pg. 29
12. Papers of Robert Morris, 9:636
13. *Morris' Account*, pg. 30
14. *Power of the Purse*, pg. 192
15. *Power of the Purse*, pg. 197
16. Chernow pg122 ref Talleyrand to Charles Goring
17. *Pennsylvania History* 36, 152
18. *Morris' Account*, pg. 70
19. Oberholtzer pg. 308-312
20. Oberholtzer p 324
21. *Financier and the Finances of the American Revolution*, 2:269
22. *Account of Robert Morris' property* by Morris, Robert, 1800
23. Chernow, pg. 227
24. Oberholtzer, pg. 346
25. *Robert Morris and the Holland Land Company*, pg. 39
26. *Morris' Account*, pg. 64-65
27. *Robert Morris and the Holland Land Company*, pg. 40
28. *Henkels Catalogue*, pg. 18
29. *Morris' Account*, pg. 11
30. *The Virginia Journals of Benjamin Henry Latrobe*, 2:376-378
31. Einhorn, pg. 113-115
32. Elkins and McKitrick, *The Age of Federalism*, 1993, pg. 754
33. Papers of Robert Morris, 4:318

Appendix

On Coinage

In 1776, Congress created a committee to evaluate the use of the Spanish Milled Dollar, also called the Pillar piece of eight, as the basis for valuing transactions undertaken by Congress. On September 2, 1776 the committee of Congress delivered its report. This effort resulted in a chart of the known currencies from Europe, and their equivalent value in Spanish milled dollars. This way Congress would know how many Dutch Florins would be due, if Congress issued a Bill of Exchange expressed in Dollars, for example. In this chart a English Crown was equivalent to 1.11394 Dollars, and an English shilling was worth .111394 Dollars. This chart also listed the equivalence of minted coins gross weight, and fine silver weight, in terms of troy ounces expressed in pennyweights (DWT) and grains. Some have contended that this was an effort to create a decimal based coinage system for American coinage, however there is no mention of a American coin minted by the Congress, or of the creation of a mint. The simple reading of the document shows it was a chart of equivalence for Congress to use in judging the values of various coins in the war trade, using a common coin with which people were familiar. It particularly stated that financial instruments issued by Congress should be valued in sliver and gold according to the chart, creating a kind of tender law (Journals of the Continental Congress vol 5, pgs 724-28). Thomas Jefferson was on this committee, and they submitted their report the day Jefferson left Congress to return to Virginia and his sickly wife.

Five years after this initial effort, the Superintendent of Finance, Morris, had, since July 1781, been working to establish a mint. He submitted a detailed report to Congress on January 15, 1782. Congress had requested a new chart of equivalencies, and Morris' office took that as an opportunity to propose an American coinage system. Congress let the report languish. On April 26, 1784 Jefferson interested himself in this subject, and wrote to Morris for information about Morris' proposal, which had been set aside.[1]

On the 1st of May 1784 Robert Morris responded to Jefferson.[2]

I have received your favor of the twenty sixth Instant for which I pray you to accept my Thanks. Enclosed you have the Copy of my Letter of the fifteenth of January 1782. to Congress and also Mr. Governeur Morris' Letter to Mr. Helmly of the thirtieth of April 1783. I will add to these such Observations as have occurred on your Notes which agreeably to your Desire are herewith returned.

I agree with you as to your Idea of a Money Unit in the first and second Points but to the third must submit an Alteration. Premising however that in this Letter I shall adopt the Term *Unit* in the Sense in which you have used it viz: as the largest Silver Coin instead of that Sense in which it is applied in my Letter viz. as the lowest fractional Money of Account not represented precisely by any Coin, similar in this Respect to the Portugueze Rea. I think then the third Proposition would stand best in this Way *That its Parts be so correspondent to the present Money of Account as to be of easy Adoption to the People.*

I take it to be a self Evident Proposition that any Coin may be Circulated at a Rate nearly proportioned to it's intrinsic Worth and in that Point of View it is unimportant what the Size or Standard shall be. But the present Object is to go farther and adopt such a Coin as shall become exclusively the circulating Medium and a new Money of Account. It is true that Dollars form our general Circulation but they are not any where the Money of Account. No Merchants Books are kept in Dollars few if any Purchases are made at a Rate specified in Dollars and Parts of Dollars. Let it be supposed then that a Dollar be taken as the *Unit* and divided into an hundred Parts and that a Merchant desirous of adopting the New Coin should balance his Books to open them in it. Let it be a Merchant of Boston and let the first Sum he wants to reduce be £365. this would be expressed thus in the new Coin 1216.662/3. His first Essay therefore would oblige him to combine both Vulgar and decimal fractions. If the same Essay be made on the Books of any other Merchant it would be attended with the same Effect. It is therefore of little Avail that the unit be nearly or even exactly of the Value of known Coins unless it's Parts correspond with the present Money of Account.

In this Letter you will find enclosed my original Letter to Congress of the twenty third of April 1783 together with the Specimens of a Coin there mentioned. These you will be so kind as to deliver to the Secretary of Congress after you have done with them and as the Reasoning on such Subjects is facilitated by a Reference to visible Objects let us take the largest of those Silver Coins as the

Money *Unit* divisible into a thousand Parts each containing 1/4 of a Grain of pure Silver. Here then we have a Piece of Money of convenient Size containing 250 grains of pure Silver, and worth about two thirds of a Dollar viz: 4/2 Virginia Money. The smallest Copper Piece is worth one Farthing Virginia Money and £365. is expressed thus 1752. Suppose we add 6.d.1/4 it will then stand 1752.125. Trials upon other Currencies will shew that all Sums can be brought to agree not only *nearly* but *exactly* to this unless in a very few Cases indeed where 1/15 of the small Copper Piece must be rejected. The Objection you State against this Coin is that the Unit is divided into 1000 Parts whereas you would divide a Unit one third larger into no more than 100 Parts but we must consider that the 1/100 of a Dollar is not sufficiently small to be rejected in any Matter of Accot. and then when the Poor are Purchasers or Venders it does not admit of the Divisibility necessary for their Affairs. The Rea of Portugal is 1/800 of a Dollar and is not found to make any Difficulty in Calculations or Entries but on the contrary to occasion much Convenience. Names are of little Consequence but they are not quite indifferent. Suppose that we call the largest Piece a Dollar the smallest a Shilling and that the Shilling be divisible into an hundred Pence. If a Gold Coin be struck it may be made equal to five Dollars and it's value about that of a Pistole.

This might be called a Pound and would be exactly 20/10 of the Currency of New Hampshire Massachusetts Rhodes Island Connecticut and Virginia. In point of Size I believe that these Pieces of Money would be convenient and I do not think it of small Consequence that the lowest fractional Part be a Quantity of pure Silver equal to an established Weight because in considering foreign Exchanges we can by that Means always bring the Money of Account of foreign Nations to an exact analogy with our own.

On the whole there are but two Points in which we differ the first is as to the Value of the lowest fractional Part of the Money Unit for we agree that it should proceed from thence upwards in a decimal Ratio. The second is as to the Proportion which Gold should bear to Silver. I wish this to be rather too small than too large because I think the Bank Paper may supply the Place of Gold and not of Silver. If therefore we give more for Silver and less for Gold the Gold will be exported and the Silver will stay. To this I add that our direct Means of importing Bullion is Gold from Lisbon and not Silver from the Spanish Territories because the latter will probably continue to be shut against us and we know by Experience that Silver was exported to England in Preference to Gold while our legal Proportion was the same as theirs because theirs being too high Silver always was worth more at Market than the Mint Price. To shew that this continues to be the Case I will observe that the lowest Price Current of Dollars yet received from England is for old Dollars 63/9 and for new Dollars 62/6. per Pound, altho neither of them are so fine as the Sterling Standard which according to Law is worth but 62/. Hence you will see that the *actual* is below the *legal* Proportion and the fixing of the legal Proportion so high is the Cause why all but light Silver is banished from Circulation. If the Piece of five Dollars were made to contain 84 Grains of pure Gold and seven of Alloy this would establish a Proportion of 1. to 14. 37/42 and would be attended with this Advantage that the Piece would weigh exactly three Pennyweight nineteen Grains, without any fractions of a Grain either in the pure [gold or in the] Alloy. The Quantity of Alloy in the Silver is not material to the Value but if it be sufficiently hard all Alloy beyond that Point renders it more liable to Imitation by a baser Composition. Let the Plan be what it may I think it would be advantageous to make the different Pieces of Money consist of Weights represented by a Number of Pennyweights or Grains without Fractions and also to have in each Piece an integral Number of Grains of pure Metal.

I do not think it will be necessary to cause Assays of the different Coins to be made because I have already a Work more perfect in its Kind than any Assays we can have made. It is the Production of a Person employed by the French Court for the Purpose and the only Difficulty in the Application of it consists in the Difference between their Weights and ours. This however is easily surmounted by Approximation. I should suppose that Congress might adopt (before their Adjournment) a Plan for the Coinage and certainly it is an Object which merits immediate Attention. So far from being attached to the Plan which I have held out I am ready to confess that the Subject is not so familiar as I could wish and that I am not for that Reason competent to a decisive Judgment. All which I can pretend to is a general Sketch to be matured by the Wisdom of Congress but I wish that it may meet their speedy Determination.

There is one Point on which you have not said any Thing but which appears to be of Importance viz: how the Expence is to be defrayed. Supposing you to be with me in Opinion that it ought to be by what is called *Coinage* I would hint that the Price to be given for fine Silver or *Mint Price* should be established and if you make a Golden Coin that of Gold also. If the Mint Price of an Ounce of fine Gold be fixed at 28. Dollars this at the Rate of 84. Grains for 5

Dollars would when coined amount to 28.571. being a little more than two per Cent Difference.

I must intreat your Excuse for the Crudeness of this hasty Production which is not so attentively digested as it might have been because I am unwilling to delay it.

Jefferson wrote in his *Autobiography* 1743-1790, on pg 138[3]

They [The Continental Congress] as early as Jan. 7. 1782. had turned their attention to the monies current in the several states, and had directed the Financier, Robert Morris, to report to them a table of rates at which the foreign coins should be received at the treasury. That officer, or rather his assistant, Gouverneur Morris, answered them on the 15th in an able and elaborate statement of the denominations of money current in the several states, and of the comparative value of the foreign coins chiefly in circulation with us.

He went into the consideration of the necessity of establishing a standard of value with us, and of the adoption of a money-Unit. He proposed for the Unit such a fraction of pure silver as would be a common measure of the penny of every state, without leaving a fraction. This common divisor he found to be 1 -- 1440 of a dollar, or 1 -- 1600 of the crown sterling. The value of a dollar was therefore to be expressed by 1440 units, and of a crown by 1600. Each Unit containing a quarter of a grain of fine silver. Congress turning again their attention to this subject the following year, the financier, by a letter of Apr. 30, 1783. further explained and urged the Unit he had proposed; but nothing more was done on it until the ensuing year, when it was again taken up, and referred to a committee of which I was a member. The general views of the financier were sound, and the principle was ingenious on which he proposed to found his Unit. But it was too minute for ordinary use, too laborious for computation either by the head or in figures. The price of a loaf of bread 1/20 of a dollar would be 72. units. A pound of butter 1/5 of a dollar 288. units. A horse or bullock of 80. D value would require a notation of 6. figures, to wit 115,200, and the public debt, suppose of 80. millions, would require 12. figures, to wit 115,200,000,000 units. Such a system of money-arithmetic would be entirely unmanageable for the common purposes of society. I proposed therefore, instead of this, to adopt the Dollar as our Unit of account and payment, and that it's divisions and sub-divisions should be in the decimal ratio. I wrote some Notes on the subject, which I submitted to the consideration of the financier. I received

> his answer and adherence to his general system, only agreeing to take for his Unit 100. of those he first proposed, so that a Dollar should be 14 40/100 and a crown 16. units. I replied to this and printed my notes and reply on a flying sheet, which I put into the hands of the members of Congress for consideration, and the Committee agreed to report on my principle. This was adopted the ensuing year and is the system which now prevails".

It is interesting to note that Jefferson's version of events portrays Robert Morris as the tool of Congress who delegated the work of the coinage system to his assistant. He portrayed Morris' plan in the most confusing way possible by referring to the system in terms of the currency's conversion value, even though Morris stated that the conversion value was not intended to become an actual coin. Then Jefferson went on to express the values of commodities in the conversion unit as if consumers would use that unit whereas actually the conversion unit was meant for merchants as a bookkeeping convenience and the consumer would use the new currency. Jefferson continued and presented the debt in terms of the conversion unit to make it look impossibly small. This was like expressing the national debt in mills for rhetorical effect.

Jefferson also omitted that R. Morris was a champion of a national coinage system and had been working towards one since 1781 (before Congress took up the issue); that Congress passed Morris' Mint proposal in February of the year 1783; and that Morris went to the effort of personally funding a sample currency to encourage Congress, or that Morris had sent those samples to Jefferson for his inspection. Jefferson notes that his ideas were adopted the year after he became involved. The full implementation of the coinage proposal was held up until 1786, after Morris left office, and Arthur Lee had taken over the Board of Treasury. This indicates the delay was due to a factional power struggle wherein the one side made progress impossible until they prevailed.

In the intervening years between 1783 and 1786 the country went through wrenching economic dislocations from an embargo by the British, from the lack of a national currency which spawned state currencies that quickly devalued, by states placing duties on goods from other states, from new trading and fishing patterns set in the peace treaty, from British insistence that payment for old debts be made, and southern insistence they be paid for slaves taken by the British during the war, from the uncertainty that the US could pay its debts to France and Spain, from protests like Shays Rebellion, from destruction at the hands of "Hint Clubs", and so on.

After an evaluation of Jefferson's comments on coinage we see that what Jefferson liked Morris' idea of a decimal currency, but favored larger units than provided in the Morris currency plan. Nominally, the argument was over the value of the base unit in relation to the Spanish Dollar. Morris favored a system that allowed current accounts to be translated into the new national currency. Jefferson seems to have been unconcerned about the effect of his plan on merchants who had current accounts, small traders, small farmers and shopkeepers.

Endnotes

1. *Letters of Delegates to Congress: 21, pg 551*
2. *Jefferson Papers 7:189--92*
3. (1914 ed. G. P. Putnam's sons, New York and London)

LIST OF ILLUSTRATIONS

p. 115: Silas Deane (1738-1789) by Pierre Eugene du Simitiere.

p. 119: Battle of Valcore Island by V. Zveg.

p. 127: Map of Princeton, by John Cadwalader 1776, Library of Congress.

p. 130: Account of Specie Payment from Robert Morris to George Washington, December 31, 1776 George Washington Papers at the Library of Congress, 1741-1799: Series 4. General Correspondence. 1697-1799.

p. 133: Etching of John Hancock (1737 - 1793) after a portrait by Copley

p. 138: "The *Wasp* and the *Frolic*," by Thomas Birch, Courtesy of the Philadelphia Museum of Art

p. 157: "The Birth of Our Nations Flag," by C H Weisgerber

p. 163: "Battle of Germantown at Cliveden," By Schuessele, 1840

p. 164: "Naval Battle Between the *United States* and The *Macedonian*," by Thomas Birch

p. 165: "William Bingham," Etching by A. H. Ritchie, PA Senate Collection

p. 175: "General Horatio Gates," by Charles Wilson Peale 1782

p. 181: "Bernardo De Galvez"

p. 188: "Molly Pitcher," Mary Hays McCauly

p. 207: "Thomas Paine," by Auguste Millière 1876

p. 216: polacre, ship

p. 230: Nathanael Greene (1742 - 1786), by Charles Wilson Peale

p. 260: "General George Washington"

p. 269: "West View of Gibraltar," by John Mace (1782)

p. 270: "James Forten"

p. 272: "Battle of Virginia Capes," 1781 by V. Zveg

p. 274: "Surrender of the English Army commanded by Mylord Comte de Cornwallis to the combined armies of the United States of America and France under the orders of Generals Washington and Rochambeau to YorkTown and Glocester in Virginia," October 19, 1781 by Mondhare. Courtesy of the Architect of the Capital

p. 283: "Gouverneur Morris and Robert Morris" by Charles Willson Peale, Pennsylvania Academy of the Fine Arts, Philadelphia. Bequest of Richard Ashhurst, 1969.20.1.

p. 288: "Bank of North America," 1781, 307 Chestnut St, Phila. PA.

p. 351: "Captain John Barry," by Gilbert Stuart

p. 406: "Independence Hall," 1776

p. 441: "Headquarters at Newburgh," 1783, Benson J. Lossing, *Pictorial Field Book of the Revolution*, Vol 1, 1850

p. 507: "Nova Constellatio" (1000 coin)

p. 617: "An Unfinished House on Chestnut Street" by William Birch.

p. 620: "Morris' floor plan sketch," by H. Latrobe, "Courtesy of the Maryland Historical Society"

p. 620: Monticello floor plan

Bibliography

Ashmead, Henry Graham, *History of Delaware County*, Pennsylvania, L. H. Everts & Co. Philadelphia, PA, 1884.

Baines, Thomas, *Baines History of Liverpool, History of the Commerce and town of Liverpool and of the rise of manufacturing industry in the adjoining counties*. Longman, Brown, Green, and Longmans, London, England,1852.

Baldridge, Edwin R., "Talleyrand's Visit to Pennsylvania, 1794-1976," #36 (April 1969), 145-160 *Pennsylvania History: A Journal of Mid-Atlantic Studies,* Pennsylvania Historical Association, Penn State Press.

Ball, Edward, *Slaves in the Family,* Ballantine Books, New York 1998, 1999.

Banning, Jeremiah, *Banning's Journal A.K.A. Narrative of the Principal Incidents in the Life of Jeremiah Banning,* written by Himself in 1793 formerly in the possession of Mrs. Emily E Banning of Wilmington DE.

Banning, Lance, *The Sacred Fire of Liberty, James Madison and the Founding of the Federal Republic,* Cornell University Press, 1995.

Bernard, Harry, *This Triumvirate of Patriots,* Follett Publishing Company Chicago, IL 60607, 1971.

Beveridge, Albert J., *The Life of John Marshall, Fontiersman, Soldier, Lawmaker 1755-1788* Vol 1-4, Houghton, Mifflin and Company, The Riverside Press, Cambridge, 1919.

Black, Jeremy, *War For America, The Fight of Independence 1775-1783,* Wrens Park Publishing, Gloucestershire, UK, 1991

Bowling, Kenneth R., "New Light on the Philadelphia Mutiny of 1783: Federal-State Confrontation at the Close of the War for Independence." *Pennsylvania Magazine of History and Biography,* 101 (October 1977), pp. 419-450 Historical Society of Pennsylvania.

Brunhouse, Robert L., *The Counter-Revolution in Pennsylvania 1776-1790,* Pennsylvania Historical Commission, Harrisburg, 1942.

Buel, Richard, *In Irons: Britain's Naval Supremacy and the American Revolutionary Economy,* Yale University Press, New Haven and London, 1998.

Caughey, John. "Willing's Expedition Down The Mississippi, 1778," *The Louisiana Historical Quarterly,* January, 1932

Chandler, David Leon, *The Jefferson Conspiracies,* Published by Quill, An imprint of William Morrow and Company Inc. New York, NY 10019 1995

Chernow, Barbra Ann, *Robert Morris, Land Speculator 1790-1801,* Arno Press, A New York Times Company, New York, 1978.

Clark, William Bell, and Morgan, William James, and Crawford, Michael J., *Naval Documents of the American Revolution Vol 1-10* 1774-1775, United States Naval History Division Government Printing Office, Washington, D. C. 1964-1982.

Coughtry, Jay, *The Notorious Triangle: Rhode Island and the African Slave Trade, 1700-1807*, Temple Univ Press, Philadelphia, 1981.

Daughan, George C., *If by Sea*, Basic Books, Member of the Perseus Book Group New York, 2008.

Deane, Silas, *The Deane Papers From 1774-1790* Vols 1-5, New York Historical Society Publication Fund Series New York, NY 1887.

Donnan, Elizabeth ed., *Documents Illustrative of the Slave Trade to America* Vol 2-4, Carnegie Institution of Washington, Washington, DC 1932.

Dudley, William S. and Crawford, Michael J, ed., *The Early Republic and the Sea, Essays on the Naval Maritime History of the Early United States*, Brassey's Inc, 22841 Quicksilver Dr., Dulles, VA 20166.

Einhorn, Robin L., *American Taxation, American Slavery*, University of Chicago Press, 2006 Chicago & London.

Elkins, Stanley and McKitrick, Eric, *The Age of Federalism*, Oxford University Press, NY, 1993.

Ellet, Mrs. E.F., *Queens of American Society*, Porter and Coates, Philadelphia 1873.

Ferguson, E. James, *The Power of the Purse, A History of Public Finance 1776-1790*, The University of North Carolina Press, Chapel Hill 1961.

Ferguson, James E. & Catanzariti, John, eds, *The Papers of Robert Morris, 1781-1784* Vol 1-7, University of Pittsburgh Press 1973.

Fischer, David Hackett, *Albion's Seed, Four British Folkways in America*, Oxford University Press, New York, Oxford UK, 1991.

Fisher, Redwood, "Revolutionary Reminiscences Connected with the Life or Robert Morris, Esq, the Financier," By *The American Whig Review*/Volume 6, Issue 1 July, Wiley and Putnam, etc., New York 1847.

Fiske, John, "John Paul Jones and the Armed Neutrality," *The Atlantic Monthly*. Dec 1887, Volume 60, Issue 362 pg 786-805.

Fiske, John, *The Critical Period of American History*, 4th edition, Houghton, Mifflin and Company, The Riverside Press, Cambridge 1889.

Fiske, John, *The American Revolution, Vols 1& 2*, Houghton, Mifflin and Company, The Riverside Press, Cambridge 1891.

Flexner , James, *The Great Columbian Federal City*, Thomas Publication: American Art Journal Volume: 2 Pages: 30-45, 1970.

Gould, David, *Life of Robert Morris, an eminent merchant*, L.W. Kimball, Boston 1834.

Guttridge, G.H., *The American Correspondence of a Bristol Merchant 1766-1776*, University of California Publications in History, Berkeley, California 1934Vol 22, No 1 pp 1-72 Plate 1.

Hannay,David, *A Short History of the Royal Navy Volume II, 1689-1815*, Methuen & Co.36 Essex St W.C. London, 1909.

Hart, Charles Henry, Robert Morris, *A Sketch, Pennsylvania Magazine of History and Biography*, Historical Society of Pennsylvania 1878.

Henkels, Stan. V. ed., Henkels Catalogue, *The Confidential Correspondence of Robert Morris, Catalogue No. 1183*, Auction Commission Merchant, 1804 Walnut St., Philadelphia. PA, 1917.

Hoffman, Paul ed., *The Lee Family Papers 1742-1795*, University of Virginia Library, Charlottesville VA 1966.

Jefferson, Thomas, and Cappon, Lester J ed., *Letters from Jefferson to Adams 1786, The Adams Jefferson Letters*, The University of North Carolina Press, Chapel Hill and London 1959.

Kaplan, Lawrence S, ed.,*The American Revolution and "A Candid World,"* The Kent State University Press 1977.

Ketchum, Richard M., ed., *The American Heritage Book of The Revolution*, American Heritage Publishing Co., Inc. New York, 1958.

Lee, Richard Henry, *The Life of Arthur Lee; with his political and literary correspondence.* Wells and Lilly, Boston 1829.

Lemaitre, Georges, *Beaumarchais*, Alfred A Knof, NY 1949.

Lewis, Jr. , Lawrence, *A History of the Bank of North America-the First Bank Chartered in the United States, 1781-1881*, J. B. Lippincott & Co, Philadelphia, 1882.

Lincoln, Abraham, "Cooper Institute Address 2/27/1860," *Philadelphia Inquirer*, Nov 3, 1997.

Lossing, B.J., *Pictorial Field Book of the Revolution VII*, Harper Brothers 82 Cliff St, New York NY 1852.

Lossing, Benson .J., *Lives of the Signers of the Declaration of Independence*, 1848, Reprint: Wallbuilders Press.

Maclay, William and Maclay, Edgar Stanton, *Journal of William Maclay United States Senator from Pennsylvania 1789-1791*, D. Appleton and Co. New York, NY 1890.

McCabe, James D. Jr., *The Great Republic*, William Evans & Co. Philadelphia 1871.

McDonald, Forrest, *We The People, The Economic Origins of the Constitution*, Transaction Publishers New Brunswick New Jersey 2002.

Milgrim, Shirley Gorson, *Haym Salomon*, Follett Publishing Company, New York, NY, 1966.

Morris, Richard B., *The Peacemakers, The Great Powers and American Independence*, Harper and Row Publishes, 49 East 33rd St, NY, NY 10016 1965.

Morris, Robert, *The Truth about the Betsy Ross Story*, Wynnehaven Publishing Co, Beach Haven, NJ 08008 1982.

Nuxoll, Elizabeth and Ferguson, E. Jame, "Investigation of Government Corruption During the American Revolution," *U.S. Capital Historical Society Volume 8 no.2*, 1981.

Nuxoll, Elizabeth M., "The Financier as Senator: Robert Morris of Pennsylvania, 1789-1795," Essay within *Neither Separate Nor Equal: Congress in the 1790s* by Kenneth R Bowling; Donald R KennonAthens: Ohio University Press 2000.

Nuxoll, Elizabeth M, "Illegitimacy, Family Status, and Property in the Early Republic; The Morris-Croxall Family of New Jersey," *New Jersey History,* Fall/Winter 1995, New Jersey Historic Society, Highland Park, NJ.

Nuxoll, Elizabeth M, "Robert Morris and the Shaping of the Post-Revolutionary American Economy," unpublished 2001.

Nuxoll, Elizabeth M. & Gallagher, Mary A. Y., eds., *The Papers of Robert Morris, 1781 - 1784 vol 8 & 9,* University of Pittsburgh Press 1996, 1999.

Oberholtzer, Ellis Paxton Ph.D., *Robert Morris: Patriot and Financier,* MacMillian & Company, Ldt, London 1903.

Pamphlet, *Mississippi July 4, 1976, the Mississippi Celebration of the Bicentennial of the American Revolution.* Pub for the Institute of Early American History and Culture at Williamsburg, VA 1976 by the University of North Carolina Press, PO Box 22888 Chapel Hill, NC 27515-2288.

Rappleye,Charles, *Robert Morris, Financier of the American Revolution,* Simon &Schuster 1230 Ave of the Americas, NY NY, 2010 .

Royster, Charles, *The Fabulous History of the Dismal Swamp Company,* Alfred A Knopf, NY 1999.

Rush, Benjamin, *The Autobiography of Benjamin Rush: His "Travels Through Life" Together with His Commonplace Book for 1789-1813.* Princeton Univ. Press, Princeton, NJ 1948.

Rush, Benjamin; L.H. Butterfield, ed., *Letters of Benjamin Rush Vols 1 & 2,* Published for the American Philosophical Society by Princeton University Press 1951.

Russell, Charles Edward, *Haym Salomon and the Revolution,* Cosmopolitan Book Corporation, New York, 1930.

Sandberg, Carl, *Abraham Lincoln,* The Sagamon Edition vol 2, Charles Scribner's & Sons, NY 1940.

Schomberg, Isaac, *Naval Chronology,* Royal Navy, London, 1802.

Shackelton, Robert, *The Book of Philadelphia,* The Penn Publishing Company, Philadelphia, 1918.

Smith, Adam, *The Wealth of Nations, 1776.* Published by Regnery Inc. 1998, An Eagle Publishing Company, One Massachusetts Av, NW.

Smith, Philip Chadwick, *The Empress of China.* Philadelphia Maritime Museum, 1984.

Sparks, Jared, *The Life of Gouverneur Morris with selections from his correspondence and Miscellaneous papers V 1-3,* Published by Gray and Bowen, 1832.

Sparks, Jared, *The Diplomatic Correspondence of the American Revolution Vols 1-12.* N. Hale and Gray & Bowen; G. & C. & H Carvill, NY 1829.

Stinchcombe, William C., *The American Revolution and the French Alliance,* Syracuse University Press, 1969 Syracuse, NY.

Sumner, William Graham, *The Financier and the Finances of the American Revolution Vols 1 & 2*, Dodd, Mead, and Company 1892.

Sumner, William Graham, *Robert Morris*, Dodd, Meade and Co, New York, 1892.

Sumner, William Graham, *Makers of American History: Thomas Jefferson and Robert Morris*, The University Society Inc. New York 1905.

Swiggett, Howard, *The Extraordinary Mr. Morris*, Doubleday & Company, Inc. NY 1952.

Syrett, Harold C., ed. & Cooke, Jacob E. assoc ed., *Papers of Alexander Hamilton Vol XVI* February-July 1794, Columbia University Press, New York & London 1972.

Tise, Larry E., PhD., *The American Counter Revolution, a retreat from Liberty 1783-1800*, Stackpole Books Mechanicsburg, PA 17055 1998.

Ver Steeg, Clarance Lester, *Robert Morris: Revolutionary Financier. With an analysis of his earlier career*, Octagon Press, Ltd., New York 1976.

Wagner, Fredrick, *Robert Morris, Audacious Patriot*, Dodd, Mead, and Company, NYC 1976.

Waln, Robert, Jr., *Biography of the Signers To the Declaration of Independence*, R.W. Pomeroy, Philadelphia 1824.

Warton, Anne Hollingsworth, *Salons Colonial and Republican*, J.B. Lippincott and Co, Philadelphia PA 1900.

Warton, Anne Hollingsworth, *Social Life in the Early Republic*, J.B. Lippincott and Co, Philadelphia PA 1903.

Washington, George edited by Fitzpatrick, John C., *The Diaries of George Washington 1748-1799 V 1-4*, Mt. Vernon's Ladies Association of the Union, Houghton, Mifflin and Company, Boston and New York 1925.

Washington, George,Fitzpatrick, John Clement ed., *The writings of George Washington from the original manuscript sources*, U. S. Govt. Print. Office, 1931 - 1944.

Weigel, George, *An Opportunity to be Lincoln*,The Ethics and Public Policy Center in Washington, D.C. July 5, 2001 .

Wills, Garry, *Negro President*, Houghton Mifflin Co. Boston, New York, 2003.

Wright, Robert E., "Thomas Willing (1731-1821): Philadelphia Financier and Forgotten Founding Father" #63 (October), *Pennsylvania History: A Journal of Mid-Atlantic Studies* ,Pennsylvania Historical Association Penn State Press.

Wright, Robert E., *The First Wall Street, Chestnut Street, Philadelphia, and the Birth of American Finance*, University of Chicago Press, Chicago & London 2005.

Wright, Robert E., *Thomas Willing (1731-1821): Philadelphia Financier and Forgotten Founding Father*, Pennsylvania History (Fall 1996), 525-560. The Pennsylvania Historical Association, Penn State Press.

Wright, Robert E. and Cowen, David J., *An Historiographical Overview of Early U.S. Finance (1784 - 1836): Institutions, Markets, Players and Politics*, National Park Service, INDE 77252, Folder 2.

Yates Snowden, LL. D. editor, *The History of South Carolina* in 5 volumes, The Lewis Publishing CO. Chicago and New York, 1920.

Young, Eleanor, *Forgotten Patriot*, The Macmillian Company, New York 1950.

Index

C

D

E

F

G

H

I

J

K

L

R

X

Y